Governments around the World

GOVERNMENTS AROUND THE WORLD

From Democracies to Theocracies

Fred M. Shelley, Editor

ABC-CLIO™

An Imprint of ABC-CLIO, LLC
Santa Barbara, California • Denver, Colorado

All entries in this book have been written by ABC-CLIO staff. Exceptions include the introductions to the constitutions and charters, which have been written by Fred M. Shelley, and otherwise noted entries.

Library of Congress Cataloging-in-Publication Data

Governments around the world : from democracies to theocracies / Fred M. Shelley, editor.

    pages cm

  Includes bibliographical references and index.

   ISBN 978-1-4408-3812-5 (print : alk. paper) — ISBN 978-1-4408-3813-2 (e-book)

 1. Comparative government.   I. Shelley, Fred M., 1952–

  JF51.G685 2015

  320.3—dc23   2014045310

ISBN: 978-1-4408-3812-5

EISBN: 978-1-4408-3813-2

19 18 17 16 15   1 2 3 4 5

This book is also available on the World Wide Web as an eBook.
Visit www.abc-clio.com for details.

ABC-CLIO, LLC
130 Cremona Drive, P.O. Box 1911
Santa Barbara, California 93116-1911

This book is printed on acid-free paper ∞
Manufactured in the United States of America

CONTENTS

PREFACE

All of the inhabited portions of the earth's surface are divided into countries. The contemporary world contains approximately 200 countries, each of which has control or sovereignty over the territory that it occupies. Each of these countries has a government, which is responsible for functions such as national defense, economic development, the provision of infrastructure such as transportation and communications, and procedures by which disputes are resolved. However, governments in each state operate differently. Each is unique, although countries can be grouped on the basis of similar governance. The theme of this volume is to explore the differences among the structure and operations of the governments of the world.

Governments vary from one another in several ways. Perhaps the most fundamental distinction is between authoritarian and democratic systems of government. In democracies, including the United States, governance rests in the hands of the people and their elected officials. In authoritarian societies, however, governance is concentrated in the hands of only one person, or a small minority of the population, who hold power over the rest of the country's citizens.

Another difference among governments involves the degree to which power is held at the national level as opposed to being divided between national and local authorities. The United States is a federal state. Power is shared officially between the U.S. federal government and the governments of the individual states. This is also the case in Canada, Mexico, Germany, Brazil, India, and other countries. In other countries, all power is held at the national level. Local government, when it exists at all, is merely an instrument of the state, with the purpose of enforcing national policies at a local level.

The structure, operations, functions, and powers of government in most countries are outlined in these countries' constitutions. A constitution specifies the process by which governments are chosen and what they are empowered to do. In the United States and other countries, interpretation of the legality of various laws and policies is based on whether these laws and policies are consistent with the country's constitution. A law declared to be unconstitutional is no longer in effect.

Of course, constitutions are often ignored by governments in power, especially in countries governed by authoritarian regimes. For example, the constitution of Eritrea, which was adopted in 1993, states that democratic elections are to be held at regular intervals. However, no elections have actually been held during the two decades during which the constitution has been in effect.

An important function of government is to guarantee and protect human rights. The constitutions of most countries specify various rights that are held by all citizens and residents of these countries. Human rights take a variety of forms. Some—including the right to vote, the right of free speech, the right to a free press, and the right to assemble peaceably—may be termed political rights. In most countries, rights enumerated in the constitutions include the rights of persons involved in legal and dispute resolution processes. These include the right to a fair trial and the presumption that one accused of a crime is innocent until proven guilty. Many constitutions also include what might be termed social and economic rights. These include the right to health, the right to social security, and the right to education. The United States is unusual among countries of the world in that its constitution does not identify these social and economic rights as fundamental rights.

Most countries belong to one or more international organizations, such as the United Nations, the North Atlantic Treaty Organization, the European Union, and the African Union. Each of these international organizations, and many others, is governed by a constitution or charter. As with constitutions of individual countries, these charters specify the responsibilities of their member countries. They also deal with rights associated with a country's being part of the larger organization. For example, the European Union (EU) guarantees that citizens of all EU countries have the right to travel and move freely among the member nations.

This volume is divided into several sections. The first three chapters deal with governments and governmental processes associated with three major forms of governments: democracies and republics, communist states, and monarchies. Some countries have governments that can be considered transitional among these categories, combining aspects of two or all three of them. Examples are given in Chapter 4. A few countries are run explicitly on the basis of religious principles. These countries, discussed in Chapter 5, are known as theocracies. The governments of some countries do not fit easily into any of the categories listed above. These can be identified as other government types, as covered in Chapter 6.

Chapter 7 deals with some of the world's largest and most important transnational organizations, including the United Nations and the European Union. A major issue associated with governing these organizations is the relationship between the international organizations and their individual members. Throughout the volume, excerpts from constitutions and charters are presented and discussed, providing valuable context underlying the understanding of different types of governance around the world. At-a-glance Facts and Figures tables accompany each country profile as well. Appendix A, "Opposing Viewpoints," deals with five critical questions regarding different geopolitical issues, such as "What will Cuba be like in 2022?" An introduction to the issue is provided, and two scholars have written opposing-viewpoint responses. Appendix B provides a comprehensive listing of every current country in the world and their government types. This volume will provide readers with a better understanding of the major types of government organizations of the world, while also comparing and contrasting specific countries that abide by variations on those systems.

—Fred M. Shelley

Introduction

Governments are institutions via which laws are enacted, public policy decisions are made and enforced, national security is maintained, and disputes are resolved. Each of the world's approximately 200 countries maintains a government that is responsible for carrying out these functions. However, the nature of governance varies widely throughout the world. Governments of various countries differ as to how power is distributed, how decisions affecting the public are made, and the degree to which government controls other social institutions including religion, communications, transportation, education, and the economy.

The purpose of this encyclopedia is to analyze and compare various systems of government used throughout the world today. Governmental types can be divided into several broad categories, and the information about contemporary governments is organized on the basis of these categories. The book also considers the nature of constitutions, or documents that set forth the basic principles of governance within countries. A major function of government is to identify and promote human rights, which are identified and enumerated in most countries' constitutions.

Although the specific nature and operation of government varies greatly among countries, all governments have several common features. Each includes legislative, executive, and judicial functions. The legislative function involves the creation of law and public policy. The executive function is associated with administration of these laws and public policy, while the judicial function involves resolving disputes and interpreting laws.

The differences among these functions are illustrated by the government of the United States. In the United States, Congress is responsible for the enactment of laws. The president and the executive branch administer these laws, while the judiciary is empowered to resolve disputes that may arise under the laws. The U.S. Supreme Court is also charged with evaluating whether laws as passed and enforced are done so in a manner consistent with the U.S. Constitution.

The Constitution includes specific provisions describing relationships among these three branches of government. For example, it specifies procedures by which the president can veto legislation passed by Congress, and the procedure by which a two-thirds majority of Congress can vote to override the president's veto. The constitutions of other countries also describe relationships among different governmental institutions, but these relationships vary from country to country. As an example, the executive and legislative branches of government are separate in the United States but are far more intertwined in the United Kingdom and other countries. The prime minister of the United Kingdom serves simultaneously as a member of Parliament, whereas the president of the United States cannot simultaneously be a member of Congress.

The United States, the United Kingdom, and most other developed countries are democracies, within which governmental power ultimately rests with the people of these countries. In other countries, however, residents have little or no power. Many countries are autocracies, in which power is held by a dictator or a ruling party that includes only a small minority of the population. Dictators generally have executive power. They may or may not hold legislative and judicial power. In some countries, legislatures are nominally separate from the executive but are expected to rubber-stamp the proposals made by the dictator.

Each government also addresses questions of citizenship. Nearly all persons throughout the world are recognized as citizens of one or more countries. Citizenship implies a set of rights and responsibilities associated with formal linkage between individuals and governments. Most countries' constitutions recognize a variety of human rights. Some of these, such as the right to freedom of speech, the right to freedom of religion, and the right to vote, can be considered political rights. Others can be identified as judicial rights. These involve the rights of individuals who have been accused of crimes or violations of the law. Judicial rights also vary among countries but often include the right to a fair trial, freedom from torture or unlawful detention, and the presumption that the accused is innocent until proven guilty.

Other human rights are associated with social and economic activity. Many constitutions include provisions that guarantee to their citizens the rights to education, health care, welfare, and social security. Some, especially in less-developed countries, have clauses in their constitutions that specifically prohibit slavery and forced labor. The United States Constitution is unusual among the world's constitutions in that it does not address these social and economic rights specifically. Under the U.S. Constitution, these are not recognized as fundamental rights, although persons are provided these services in a manner consistent with the Constitution, in practice.

Citizenship also includes responsibility. These responsibilities include the payment of taxes and the responsibility to uphold the law. The constitutions of some countries state specifically that parents are responsible for the care of their children, and that children have the responsibility to care for elderly parents. One of the important functions of government in general is national defense, and some constitutions state specifically that individual citizens have the responsibility to participate in national defense.

In this book, governments of the world are divided into several broad categories, with examples of each type presented and discussed. Entries for each country include discussion of that country's constitution, along with how legislative, executive, and judicial authorities are selected and how these branches of government operate. Each chapter also includes descriptions of the country's geography and economy.

Most countries, except for very small ones, also maintain institutions of subnational or local government. The fifty states that comprise the United States are examples. In some countries, including the United States, the constitutions identify relationships between national and sub-national governments specifically. The Tenth Amendment to the U.S. Constitution states that "The powers not delegated to the United States by the Constitution, nor prohibited by it to the States, are reserved to the States respectively, or to the people," thus specifying the division of powers between the states and the federal government. In many other countries, all power is held at the national level. Local governments are charged with administration of law and public policy, but the people have little or no input into the selection and operation of these local governments.

Most of the world's developed countries are democratic republics. In democratic republics, power rests with the people. Citizens vote for members of the legislature, and in many countries they also vote for the country's president or chief executive. Democratic republics can be divided into two broad categories: presidential republics and parliamentary republics. In presidential republics, such as the United States, the legislative function of government is separated from executive authority. Americans vote for members of the Senate and the House of Representatives and for the president (indirectly, via the Electoral College) at the national level. At the state level, they vote for members of the state legislature and for the governor of their state.

Other countries, including the United Kingdom, are parliamentary republics. In parliamentary republics, the chief executive is also a member of the legislature. In the United Kingdom, voters select members of Parliament. However, the prime minister is selected by Parliament. Usually, the prime minister is the leader of the political party or coalition of parties that holds a majority of seats in Parliament. Thus the prime minister is simultaneously the head of government, a member of Parliament, and the leader of his or her political party. Because the prime minister is the leader of his or her party, many voters base their choice for member of Parliament on the party that is represented by these local candidates.

Some countries are communist states. Communist states controlled large numbers of countries in the middle of the twentieth century, including present-day

Russia, most countries in Eastern Europe, and many countries in Asia, Africa, and Latin America. Today only a few countries, including China, Laos, Vietnam, North Korea, and Cuba, can still be considered communist states. Under communism, power is held by a small oligarchy of persons who hold formal membership in that country's Communist Party. Party members select the country's leaders. The people have the nominal right to vote for legislators, but under Communism the candidates are selected by the Party, and in many cases only one candidate's name would appear on the ballot. Dissent and the formation of political parties opposed to the government are generally prohibited or strongly discouraged, and dissenters have often been persecuted, imprisoned, or exiled.

Communist states are also distinguished from other states in that most communist nations formally ban ownership of property, including means of production. Factories, farms, and other enterprises are formally the responsibility of the state, as opposed to being owned and operated by individual entrepreneurs. Over time, it became recognized that state ownership of means of production was inefficient and largely unsuccessful in distribution of goods and services to the people. Thus, many communist countries have relaxed their restrictions on private ownership of means of production.

Some countries are monarchies. Until the nineteenth century, monarchy was by far the most common form of government in the world. Today, monarchy is still practiced in many of the world's countries, although only a minority of the world's population live in monarchies. Monarchies can be divided into two broad categories: absolute monarchy and constitutional monarchy. In absolute monarchy, the monarch has unconstrained authority over the country's citizens. In effect, an absolute monarch holds dictatorial power. Historically, absolute monarchy was common throughout the world.

Under constitutional monarchy, the powers of the monarch are constrained by the constitution and/or by law. Today, constitutional monarchy is much more common than is absolute monarchy. The world's first constitutional monarchy was the United Kingdom, which became a constitutional monarchy via the signing of the Magna Carta ("Great Charter") by King John in 1215. The Magna Carta specified that political power in England and Wales was to be shared formally between the monarch and the nobility. This power was soon extended to the common people through the establishment of Parliament, including the House of Commons, in the late thirteenth century.

Today, the role of the monarch in most constitutional monarchies is primarily ceremonial. The monarch is the head of state, but in democratic republics that are simultaneously constitutional monarchies, the executive who is elected directly or indirectly by the people is the head of government. In the United Kingdom, for example, the monarch can advise the government or propose legislation, but the government is not obligated to follow the monarch's advice.

Government structures often change over time. For example, some absolute monarchies have evolved into constitutional monarchies. The collapse of the Union of Soviet Socialist Republics and its communist government in 1991 resulted in the creation of fourteen new countries, each of which developed its own system of government. Some—including Estonia, Latvia, and Lithuania—transitioned quickly into democratic republics. Others, including some in Central Asia, became non-communist dictatorships. In Spain, a dictatorship ended with the death of its dictator, Francisco Franco, in 1975. The dictatorship was replaced quickly by a constitutional monarchy that was also a democratic republic, as remains the case at present.

Today, most transitional governments can be found in less-developed countries, especially countries with histories as European colonies. In some cases, dictatorship has alternated with democratic forms of government. Most of Africa's former European colonies, for example, began independence as democracies. However, in many, power was seized by dictators and/or military officers. Some dictators held power for many years, until they died or were overthrown. In other cases, military juntas and government officials held power for a limited time, with new democratic governments elected at least temporarily. Some countries have experienced ongoing transition from democracy to dictatorship and back to dictatorship, over periods as long as several decades.

Religion often plays a role in governance. The constitutions of some countries, such as France and India, specify that these countries are secular states. Other countries identify themselves specifically with particular religions. For example, the constitutions of Libya and Saudi Arabia identify these countries as Islamic states. In these countries, public policy is to be guided specifically by Islamic principles. In a few countries, heads of government are simultaneously religious leaders. In Iran, for example, the leader of the Shi'ite Muslim community has great influence in public policy development, although the formal head of the government is the president, who is elected by popular vote. The Pope of the Roman Catholic Church is also the head of state of Vatican City.

A few countries maintain governments whose structures and activities do not fit easily into the above categories. For example, North Korea is a communist state that has evolved into a dictatorship based on a cult of the leader's personality. Some countries or territories lack full independence. Puerto Rico is a commonwealth that is formally a colony of the United States, and hence its government is subordinate to that of the United States. Palestine claims sovereignty over its territory in western Asia, but its independence is not recognized by the United States and other countries.

Most countries throughout the world are members of international organizations. Nearly all of the world's countries belong to the United Nations, and many also belong to regional organizations such as the European Union, the League of Arab States, and the African Union. Each of these organizations is governed by formal treaties or charters, which specify how common policies are to be developed and how member countries work to coordinate social, economic, and environmental activities. This encyclopedia also includes information about the world's largest and most influential international organizations.

Governance is evolving, and the governmental processes used in each country vary—in some cases, gradually, and in others, abruptly. Historians have documented the rise of democracy over the past century, along with a sharp decline in the number of absolute monarchies and the number of communist states. Some have argued, however, that the number of democracies has reached a saturation point, with more countries beginning to reduce commitment to democracy and increasing the level of authoritarian control. Whether democracy will reach a plateau and begin to decline is anyone's guess, but the only sure thing is the certainty of change itself.

—Fred M. Shelley

CHAPTER 1

DEMOCRACIES AND REPUBLICS

Democracy is a form of governance in which decisions are made via the votes of a country's population. In most democracies, voters elect their leaders according to set laws and principles. A republic is a government in which these elected rulers enact and enforce laws. Although the concept of democracy dates back to ancient Greece, democracy as a form of government in which leaders of a republic are elected by vote of the people did not become widespread throughout the world until the twentieth century. Today, all developed countries and many less-developed countries are democracies. In theory, all citizens are able to participate in the voting process under both direct and representative democracies. However, in practice the franchise has often been restricted by law and/or by custom. For example, in ancient Greece only the elite could participate in the democratic process, while women and slaves were excluded. In the newly independent United States in the late eighteenth and early nineteenth centuries, only white male property owners were eligible to vote. In that sense, these early democracies can be regarded as oligarchies, in which governance is entrusted to only a minority of the population holding elite status. In the United States, the franchise was granted slowly to all adult males and then to women, members of minority groups, and Native Americans. More generally, the history of the twentieth century throughout the world is one of expanding the franchise to previously marginalized populations. Today, universal adult suffrage is the norm in most countries throughout the world.

Democracies and republics can be categorized in several ways. First, they can be divided between presidential republics and parliamentary republics. In presidential republics such as the United States, the president is elected separately from the legislature. The president may or may not belong to the political party that controls a majority of legislative seats. Usually, the president and legislators serve fixed terms whose length is pre-determined. For example, in the United States the president serves a four-year term, members of the Senate serve six-year terms, and members of the House of Representatives serve two-year terms.

In parliamentary systems, the chief executive is simultaneously a member of the legislature. The prime minister of the United Kingdom is simultaneously the chief executive of the country, a member of Parliament, and the formal head of his or her political party. Most democracies in the Western Hemisphere are presidential republics, whereas a majority of democracies in Europe and Asia are parliamentary republics. Some countries, including Russia, can be considered semi-presidential republics. In a semi-presidential republic, the head of state is the president, who is elected separately from the legislature, but the leaders of executive departments are responsible to the legislature and not to the president. Some republics—including the United Kingdom, Canada, and Spain—are also constitutional monarchies. In such countries, the monarch is the head of state, but the president or prime minister is the head of the government.

A further distinction among democracies is the difference between countries with unicameral legislatures and those with bicameral legislatures. In a unicameral legislature, there is only one legislative body, whereas bicameral legislatures contain two houses. Usually, distinctions are made between the two houses. In the United States, for example, legislative power is vested in both the Senate and the House of Representatives. In order to become law, a bill proposing legislation must be enacted by both houses. Members of the Senate and the House of Representatives are elected by popular vote. However, in some countries, members of the upper house of the legislature are appointed rather than elected. In the United Kingdom, for example, most members of the House of Lords are members of the nobility, who are appointed by the monarch, usually upon the advice of the prime minister. However, twenty-six seats in the House of Lords are reserved for high-ranking bishops of the Church of England. Historically, the House of Lords and the popularly elected House of Commons had equal power in the government. Today, however, the power of the House of Lords is circumscribed by law. The House of Lords can review bills passed by the House of Commons but cannot initiate legislation.

Republics can be categorized also as unitary republics or federal republics. In unitary republics, all power is held at the national level. In federal republics, on the other hand, power is shared formally between the national government and local governments. In the United States, the Tenth Amendment to the Constitution specifies that "The powers not delegated to the United States by the Constitution, nor prohibited by it to the States, are reserved to the States respectively, or to the people." Thus the Tenth Amendment specifies the formal division of powers between the federal government and the states, thereby confirming the status of the United States as a federal republic. Generally speaking, smaller countries with more homogeneous populations tend to be unitary republics, whereas larger countries with more diverse populations tend to be federal republics. In addition to the United States, the large and complex countries of Russia, Brazil, Mexico, Germany, Nigeria, and India are federal republics. However, France is a unitary republic despite its large size and heterogeneous population.

Republics can also be differentiated on the basis of the process by which the people select their representatives. In the United States and most other English-speaking countries, territory is divided into districts, and people within each district elect a single representative. In other countries, representative districts are larger, and their voters choose several legislators from their districts. Most countries with single-member districts have only two or three major political parties. For example, Botswana's three largest political parties won a combined 95% of the popular vote in its 2009 legislative elections. However, multi-member districts tend to be associated with more political parties competing for national power. In Taiwan, some legislative districts elect a single representative, whereas others elect more than one representative.

Finally, republics can be categorized on the basis of the relationship between the state and religion. Democracy in the United States is based on the principle of formal separation of church and state. In some constitutional monarchies, a state church continues to be headed by the monarchy but the presence of a state church does not affect the democratic process. Examples are the United Kingdom and the Church of England. In Sweden, a similar relationship between the government and the Evangelical Lutheran Church was established in the sixteenth century, long before Sweden became a democracy. This relationship continued until 2000, when the Evangelical Lutheran Church was disestablished. In other countries, however, religion and the state are intertwined closely. For example, Afghanistan is an Islamic republic whose legal system is governed by the principles of Islam, although the president and members of the national legislature are selected by popular vote. Pakistan and Iran are also Islamic republics.

Differences in the practice of democracy in various countries can be illustrated using specific examples. Canada, for example, is a constitutional monarchy and a parliamentary democracy. The monarch of the United Kingdom is the head of state of Canada. The monarch appoints a governor-general, who is responsible for carrying out the responsibilities of the monarch within Canada. Historically, most governors general were British subjects, but since 1952 the office has been held by native-born Canadians.

The Canadian Parliament consists of two houses: the Senate and the House of Commons. Members of the Senate are appointed, while members of the House of Commons are elected by popular vote. The House of Commons, which currently includes 308 seats, is the dominant branch of the legislature, while the role of the Senate is primarily advisory. As in other parliamentary systems, the prime minister of Canada is the head of the government and is the leader of his or her political party in the House of Commons. The leader of the party that holds the second-largest number of seats in the House of Commons is recognized as the leader of the opposition.

In contrast to Canada, the United States is a presidential republic. The president cannot be a member of Congress and is elected separately from the Senate and the House of Representatives. The Senate includes two members from each state, while membership in the House of Representatives is apportioned among the states on the basis of population. Although the U.S. Constitution does not specify the number of members of the House, this number has been fixed at 435 members since the early twentieth century. Originally, members of the Senate were chosen by state legislatures. However, the Seventeenth Amendment, which was added to the Constitution in 1913, specified that senators, as well as members of the House of Representatives, would be chosen by popular vote.

While Canada and the United States are federal states, France is a unitary state. Like the United States but unlike Canada, France is also a presidential republic. The president of France, who serves as the head of state, is elected by popular vote for a term of five years. The legislature is bicameral and includes the Senate and the National Assembly. Members of the National Assembly are elected by voters, whereas members of the Senate are chosen by a small subset of the electorate including local officials, town councilors, mayors of cities and towns, and members of the National Assembly. Senators serve six-year terms, with half of the members up for reelection every three years.

Canada, the United States, and France have long histories of democracy, whereas democracy has been practiced in Russia only since the collapse of the Soviet Union in 1991. Russia is a semi-presidential republic, in which power is shared by an elected president and the legislature. Russia's president, who serves as the head of state, is elected by popular vote for a four-year term. Russia's bicameral legislature includes the State Duma, or lower house, and the Federation Council, or upper house. Members of the State Duma are selected by popular vote, whereas members of the Federation Council are chosen by groups of local leaders.

Taiwan, formally known as the Republic of China, is a presidential republic with a unicameral legislature. The president and vice president are elected for four-year terms on the same party ticket, as in the United States. The legislature of Taiwan is known as the Legislative Yuan. Currently, 73 of the Legislative Yuan's members are chosen by popular vote from single-member districts, whereas 34 are elected via nationwide balloting. The remaining six seats are reserved for indigenous people. The practice of reserving seats for indigenous populations is followed also in other countries, including India and New Zealand.

Botswana, located in southern Africa, is one of the most successful democracies in sub-Saharan Africa. Botswana has maintained its status as a democracy since becoming independent in 1966. Botswana is a parliamentary republic. Its unicameral legislature, known as the National Assembly, currently includes 61 members, of whom 57 are selected by popular vote. The other four are selected by local chiefs. The president of Botswana, who is both the head of state and the head of government, is selected by the National Assembly. Botswana has become one of the wealthiest countries in Africa, and some observers have attributed Botswana's rapid development to its success in maintaining a stable, multi-party democracy.

—Fred M. Shelley

Further Reading

Robert A. Dahl, *On democracy*. New Haven, CT: Yale University Press, 2000.

John Dunn, *Democracy: A history*. New York: Atlantic Monthly Press, 2006.

Alexander Keyssar, *The right to vote: The contested history of democracy in the United States*. New York: Basic Books, 2009.

Arend Lijphart, *Patterns of democracy: Government forms and performance in thirty-six countries*. New Haven, CT: Yale University Press, 1999.

AFGHANISTAN: Islamic Republic

AFGHANISTAN

Communications	
Facebook Users	
480,000 (estimate) (2013)	
Internet Users	
1,000,000 (2009)	
Internet Users (% of Population)	
5.9% (2013)	
Television	
8 sets per 100 population (2006)	
Land-based Telephones in Use	
135,000 (2012)	
Mobile Telephone Subscribers	
18,000,000 (2012)	
Major Daily Newspapers	
0	
Average Circulation of Daily Newspapers	
Not Available	

Education	
School System	
Afghanistan's school system is still recovering from the effects of the Taliban government, which closed many schools, although schools have steadily reopened since the government's overthrow in 2002. Under the Taliban, schooling officially began at age six, with six years of primary education and six years of secondary education, although in practice educational access was denied to girls and many boys.	
Mandatory Education	
6 years, from ages 6 to 12.	
Average Years Spent in School for Current Students	
9 (2011)	
Average Years Spent in School for Current Students, Male	
11 (2011)	
Average Years Spent in School for Current Students, Female	
7 (2011)	
Primary School–age Children Enrolled in Primary School	
5,767,543 (2012)	
Primary School–age Males Enrolled in Primary School	
3,419,237 (2012)	
Primary School–age Females Enrolled in Primary School	
2,348,306 (2012)	
Secondary School–age Children Enrolled in Secondary School	
2,415,884 (2012)	

Secondary School–age Males Enrolled in Secondary School	**Natural Resources**
1,579,257 (2012)	Natural gas, petroleum, coal, copper, chromite, talc, barites, sulfur, lead, zinc, iron ore, salt, precious and semiprecious stones
Secondary School–age Females Enrolled in Secondary School	**Environment**
836,627 (2012)	**CO2 Emissions**
Students Per Teacher, Primary School	0.2 metric tons per capita (2009)
43.5 (2011)	**Alternative and Nuclear Energy**
Students Per Teacher, Secondary School	Not Available
31.6 (2007)	**Threatened Species**
Enrollment in Tertiary Education	34 (2010)
97,504 (2011)	**Protected Areas**
Enrollment in Tertiary Education, Male	2,359 (estimate) (2010)
73,882 (2011)	**Geography**
Enrollment in Tertiary Education, Female	**Location**
23,662 (2011)	A landlocked country in southwestern Asia, Afghanistan is bounded by Pakistan to the southeast, Iran to the west, China to the northeast, and Turkmenistan, Tajikistan, and Uzbekistan to the north.
Literacy	
32% (2011)	
Energy and Natural Resources	**Time Zone**
Electric Power Generation	9.5 hours ahead of U.S. Eastern Standard
986,100,000 kilowatt hours per year (estimate) (2010)	**Land Borders**
Electric Power Consumption	3,436 miles
2,489,000,000 kilowatt hours per year (estimate) (2010)	**Coastline**
	0 miles
Nuclear Power Plants	**Capital**
0 (2014)	Kabul
Crude Oil Production	**Area**
0 barrels per day (2013)	251,773 sq. miles
Crude Oil Consumption	**Climate**
36,000 barrels per day (2012)	The climate is cold and snowy in the winter, and hot and dry during the summer, with the northeast mountain regions experiencing much cooler weather than the rest of the country. Summer temperatures can reach 120°F in the southwest part of the country, and winter temperatures in the northeastern Hindu Kush Mountains can fall as low as -15°F.
Natural Gas Production	
140,000,000 cubic meters per year (estimate) (2011)	
Natural Gas Consumption	
140,000,000 cubic meters per year (estimate) (2010)	

Land Use	**Industry Products**
13.1% arable land; 5.4% temporary crops; 0.2% permanent crops; 46.0% permanent meadows and pastures; 1.2% forest land; 39.5% other.	Textiles, beverages, oil, soap, natural gas, coal, electric energy, furniture, footwear, fertilizer, cement, handwoven carpets.
Arable Land	**Agriculture Products**
13% (2007)	Wheat, fruit, vegetables, rice, corn, nuts, cotton, wool, karakul pelts, lamb, opium poppy (illicit), cannabis (illicit).
Arable Land Per Capita	
1 acres per person (2007)	
Health	**Unemployment**
Average Life Expectancy	8.6% (2012)
50.5 years (2014)	**Labor Profile**
Average Life Expectancy, Male	agriculture: 78.6% industry: 5.7% services: 15.7% (estimate) (2009)
49.2 years (2014)	
Average Life Expectancy, Female	**Military**
	Total Active Armed Forces
51.9 years (2014)	93,800 (estimate) (2010)
Crude Birth Rate	**Active Armed Forces**
38.6 (estimate) (2015)	0% (2010)
Crude Death Rate	**Annual Military Expenditures**
13.9 (estimate) (2015)	$180,000,000 (2008)
Maternal Mortality	**Military Service**
1,900 per 100,000 live births (2005–2012 projection)	(not available)
Infant Mortality	**National Finances**
71 per 1,000 live births (2012)	**Currency**
Doctors	Afghani
0.2 per 1,000 people (2011)	**Total Government Revenues**
Industry and Labor	$2,333,000,000 (estimate) (2012)
Gross Domestic Product (GDP) - official exchange rate	**Total Government Expenditures**
$23,227,000,000 (estimate) (2015)	$4,122,000,000 (estimate) (2012)
GDP per Capita	**Budget Deficit**
$726 (estimate) (2015)	-8.7 (estimate) (2012)
GDP - Purchasing Power Parity (PPP)	**GDP Contribution by Sector**
$35,358,000,000 (estimate) (2013)	agriculture: 20% industry: 25.6% services: 54.4% note: opium production not included (2011 est.)
GDP (PPP) per Capita	**External Debt**
$1,072 (estimate) (2013)	$1,280,000,000 (estimate) (2011)

Economic Aid Extended	**Exported Goods**
$0 (2011)	Fruits and nuts, wool, cotton, semiprecious and precious gems, carpets, hides and pelts.
Economic Aid Received	
$6,711,000,000 (2011)	
Population	**Total Value of Exports**
Population	$376,000,000 (estimate) (2012)
32,564,342 (estimate) (2015)	**Import Partners**
World Population Rank	United States - 24.9%; Pakistan -22.4%; India - 7.7%; Germany - 5.1%; Russia - 4.3% (2009 estimate)
42 th (2010)	
Population Density	**Export Partners**
118.5 people per square mile (estimate) (2011)	China- 24.4%, United States-16.4%, Pakistan- 23.9%, Tajikistan- 8.9%, Russia -2.9% (2009 est.)
Population Distribution	
23% urban (2011)	
Age Distribution	**Current Account Balance**
0-14: 42.9%	$-743,900,000 (estimate) (2011)
15-64: 54.6%	**Weights and Measures**
65+: 2.4%	The metric system is in use, but traditional weights are also widely used.
(2009)	
Median Age	**Transportation**
18.1 years (estimate) (2014)	**Airports**
Population Growth Rate	52 (2012)
2.3% per year (estimate) (2015)	**Paved Roads**
Net Migration Rate	29.3% (2006)
-1.5 (estimate) (2015)	**Passenger Cars per 1,000 People**
Trade	20 (2010)
Imported Goods	**Number of Trucks, Buses, and Commercial Vehicles**
Wheat, sugar, vegetable oil, tea, cigarettes, petroleum products, transportation equipment, textiles, televisions.	100,000 (2005)
	Railroads
	Not Available
Total Value of Imports	**Ports**
$453,600,000 (estimate) (2009)	Major Inland: 2—Shir Khan, Kheyrabad.

OVERVIEW

Afghanistan is a landlocked country in southwestern Asia. The country's physical layout is dominated by the Hindu Kush Mountains in the northeast and deserts along its western border with Iran. The diversity of the land causes much variety in

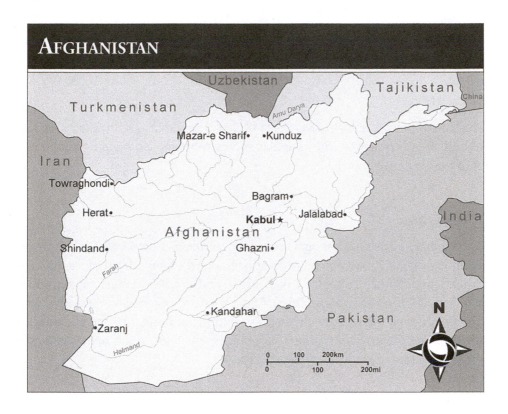

weather around the country: on a single summer day it may be 40°F in the mountains but 120°F in the lowlands. Tajikistan lies to the north of Afghanistan, while Pakistan lies to the east and south. The country's population is estimated to be nearly 32 million. The capital of Afghanistan is Kabul.

GOVERNMENT

Afghanistan gained independence from the United Kingdom on August 19, 1919. The country is a democratic Islamic republic. The current government was established in 2001 after the fall of the fundamentalist Taliban, which had ruled the country since 1996 according to a strict, harshly administered interpretation of Islamic law. Ashraf Ghani was sworn in as the country's president on September 29, 2014. The Republic of Afghanistan is known in the Pashto language as *De Afghanistan Jamhuriat* and in the Dari language as *Jonhuri-ye Afghanestan*. Legislative authority is held by Afghanistan's National Assembly, which convened for the first time in 30 years on December 19, 2005.

Constitution

The most recent Afghan Constitution was signed into law on January 26, 2004. It replaced the 1987 Constitution, although that document was not in force at the time the Taliban took control of Afghanistan in 1996. The 2004 document was finalized by a Grand Council (Loya Jirga) held in December 2003.

Executive

Executive power in Afghanistan is vested in a president—who is head of state and head of government—with several vice presidents and a cabinet making up the rest of the executive branch.

Legislature

Afghanistan's National Assembly convened for the first time in three decades on December 19, 2005. The Assembly comprises a lower house of no more than 250 members, the House of People (Wolesi Jirga), and the 102-member upper house, the House of Elders (Meshrano Jirga). The legislature's members represent a wide variety of Afghan interests, as the membership is not limited to specific political parties and is composed of Islamists, communists, women's rights activists, former Taliban leaders, and warlords, among others.

Judiciary

The 2004 Constitution established a nine-member Supreme Court (Stera Mahkama), whose nine justices are appointed for 10-year terms by the president with approval of the Wolesi Jirga, and subordinate High Courts and Appeals Courts. The constitution requires that no law should be "contrary to Islam"; the state is responsible for creating a prosperous and progressive society based on social justice, protecting human dignity and human rights, creating democracy, and ensuring national unity and equality among all ethnic groups and tribes. In addition, the state must abide by the Charter of the United Nations (1945), international treaties, international conventions signed by Afghanistan, and the Universal Declaration of Human Rights (1948).

Local Government

The nation's 34 provinces are each administered by an appointed governor.

Election Qualifications

All citizens 18 years of age and older are eligible to vote.

POLITICS

Since the Soviet Union invaded in 1979 to support a failing communist government, Afghanistan has been embroiled in decades of conflict and instability. The invasion sparked a guerrilla war that was backed covertly by the United States. International pressure led to the withdrawal of Soviet troops in 1989. They left behind a country devoid of functional infrastructure and a very weak communist government.

Afghanistan became an Islamic republic after Muslim holy warriors (mujahideen) forced the April 1992 resignation of Soviet-installed president Mohammad Najibullah. In 1993, a power struggle began between the ruling coalition's President Burhanuddin Rabbani and Prime Minister Gulbuddin Hekmatyar, resulting in the deaths of thousands of people. However, a new fundamentalist militant group called the Taliban burst upon the scene in February 1995. Taliban fighters ousted the Rabbani government in September 1996 and set up a ruling council in the capital, Kabul. In October 1997, the Taliban proclaimed that the nation would henceforth be called the Islamic Emirate of Afghanistan and would be ruled by a harsh interpretation of Islamic law.

The world's attention turned to Afghanistan in the fall of 2001, after the September 11 terrorist attacks on the United States. Because the Taliban harbored the perpetrators, Osama bin Laden and his Al Qaeda network, the United States and its allies launched a massive assault on the Taliban in October 2001, enabling the opposition Northern Alliance to dislodge the Taliban from most of the country by late 2001.

The country's transition to a broad-based coalition government began under the auspices of the United Nations in December 2001, when four of the country's major ethnic factions signed an agreement to form an interim government scheduled to serve for six months until a permanent government could be elected. In June 2002, the country held its first grand council (Loya Jirga) since the fall of the Taliban to elect a permanent government and arrange elections.

The nation's first-ever direct presidential election was held on October 9, 2004, with more than 15 candidates opposing incumbent president Hamid Karzai. In November 2004, Karzai was declared Afghanistan's first popularly elected president, with 55% of the vote. Afghanistan held its first parliamentary elections on September 17, 2005. A low voter turnout was attributed to various factors, including threats from Taliban insurgents, warlords running as candidates, and voter confusion. The election results, announced in November, showed that a wide variety of lawmakers would serve in the new Afghan legislature, including former Taliban leaders and 68 female legislators. Afghanistan's National Assembly convened for the first time in 30 years on December 19, 2005.

Hamid Karzai, President of Afghanistan, was previously a leader of Afghanistan's United Democratic Front, which worked with U.S. special forces to overthrow the Taliban government in 2001. He was elected President of Afghanistan in 2004 and re-elected in 2009. (Francis Joseph Dean/Francis Dean/Deanpictures/Newscom)

After that historic event, however, Karzai's government increasingly came to be viewed as ineffective and corrupt, while failing to achieve security or create jobs. A resurgent Taliban also stepped up its attacks, especially in southern provinces, triggering the nation's bloodiest fighting in years. Karzai's image was further tarnished as a result of the August 2009 presidential election, after allegations of voter fraud were directed at him and his campaign. September 2010 parliamentary elections were calmer than the 2009 presidential election, but still marred by fraud, intimidation, threats of attacks by the Taliban, and violence. Voter turnout was 36%, and 14 people were killed on election day.

Presidential elections were held again on April 5, 2014. Because of term limits, Karzai was not a candidate. There were attacks by the Taliban in the lead-up to elections, and four were injured by an explosion on election day. Eleven candidates competed in the race, with Abdullah Abdullah of the National Coalition of Afghanistan and Ashraf Ghani, an independent candidate, emerging as the front-runners. A runoff election was held on June 14. The results, however, were delayed because both candidates accused each other of fraud. An audit of all 8 million votes was conducted, and U.S. Secretary of State John Kerry stepped in to broker a power-sharing deal between the two candidates. Finally, in September 2014, the election commission announced Ashraf Ghani president. As part of the deal, Abdullah Abdullah became chief executive officer, a position similar to prime minister. Ghani draws most of his support from the Pashtun population, and Abdullah is supported by the Tajiks and other northern ethnic groups. The arrangement ensures that the groups will be equally represented in Afghanistan's new government, although analysts believe it will be a tenuous coalition.

Political Parties

After the Taliban took control of the country in 1996, all political parties were outlawed. After the Taliban was expelled from power in 2001, Afghanistan's government began addressing the issue of creating political parties. Today, only those parties approved by the Justice Ministry can be officially registered. As of 2012, 84 political parties were registered in Afghanistan.

The National Front of Afghanistan (Jabh-e Melli) was launched in 2011, with the ideals of promoting national unity and democracy. The party supports replacing the current political system with a parliamentary democracy in which the prime minister, instead of the president, is head of government. The National Front was started by former vice president Ahmad Zia Masoud and two anti-Taliban militia leaders, Mohammad Mohaqiq and Abdul Rashid Dostum. The National Front is part of the National Coalition of Afghanistan.

The fundamentalist Islamic Society (Jamiat-i-Islami), which is now active as part of the National Coalition of Afghanistan, draws most of its support from the Uzbek and Tajik ethnic groups.

The most radical of the fundamentalist rebel groups, the Islamic Party (Hezb-i-Islami), was founded by former prime minister Gulbuddin Hekmatyar. Historically the group has been an insurgent movement that fought against the Soviet occupation, as well as the U.S. presence in Afghanistan. Its political arm, which is active and influential in the Afghan government, is thought to have some autonomy from its militant arm.

The Afghan Social Democratic Party (Afghan Mellat) is a nationalist party founded in 1966. The party supports a democratic government, rapid and sustainable economic development for the country, and equal rights for women. The party draws much of its support from ethnic Pashtuns.

The Islamic Unity Party (Hezb-i-Wahdat-i-Islami) is an Iranian-supported rebel coalition that is rooted in the resistance to the Soviet occupation. The party draws support from ethnic Hazaras. Since 2009, the Islamic Unity Party has fragmented into several factions with different leaders.

ECONOMY

Afghanistan's economy has improved since the fall of the Taliban government, but decades of war have wreaked havoc on the country's financial situation. The per-capita gross national product is one of the world's lowest, and Afghanistan is dependent on billions in foreign aid. Despite the nation's valuable natural resources, which include petroleum, natural gas, zinc, iron ore, coal, and copper, there is little infrastructure left to exploit, package, and transport the goods to domestic or international markets. Instead, about 80% of the population is forced to rely on agriculture to make a living, although farming is performed mainly at a subsistence level. Afghanistan imports most of its food staples, such as grain, sugar, and tea. Pakistan and India buy most of Afghanistan's exports, which are typically agricultural in nature, including dried fruits, hides, cotton, and wool. Afghanistan is the world's leading producer of illicit opium, accounting for almost three-quarters of global opium production, with the nation's illegal drug trade growing larger every year.

SOCIETY

Afghans place great importance on ethnic identity, whether their heritage is with settled peoples or those of nomadic origin, like the Hazara and Aimak, whose ancestors arrived centuries ago from the steppes of Asia. The Pashtun make up the largest ethnic group. Many others share their heritage with peoples on the other sides of national borders, as is the case with the Tajiks, Uzbeks, Turkmen, and Balochs. Though there are several thousand Sikhs, Hindus, and Jews in the cities, 99% of the population is Muslim. The majority of Muslims in Afghanistan are Sunni, but a significant minority are Shiite, and conflict between the two groups has contributed to civil wars. The two official languages are Pashto and Dari.

Ethnic Composition

Pashtun – 42%; Tajik – 27%; Hazara – 9%; Uzbek 9%; Aimak – 4%; Turkmen – 3%; Baloch – 2%; other –4%

Language

The official languages are Dari, which is the native language of at least half the population, and is the language of business and government, and Pashto, which is spoken by more than one-third of the people. Turkic is widely spoken as well, mainly by Uzbek and Turkmen people.

Religion

Sunni Muslim – 80%; Shia Muslim – 19%; other – 1%

CONTEMPORARY ISSUES

War/Taliban

Afghanistan has been in almost continuous conflict for decades. Over the past quarter-century, the country's modern troubles began with the Soviet Union's 1979 invasion of Afghanistan. It took 10 years for the nation's mujahideen (Islamic freedom fighters) to drive the Soviets out of the country. This led to a multiyear power struggle that pitted various warlords and Muslim rebel groups against each other, a struggle won by the Taliban, a fierce Islamic militia that took control of the country in 1996 and imposed a harsh fundamentalist government. Because the Taliban had been harboring Al Qaeda, U.S. forces invaded Afghanistan after the September 11, 2001, attacks and helped oust the Taliban by the end of the year. Although a Western-backed government came to power at that time, the country is still not secure. Since 2006, U.S.-led troops have been battling a resurgent Taliban, who have adopted suicide-bombing tactics learned from other Islamic extremists in the Iraq War. Today the Taliban remain a threat in several provinces, particularly in the more remote areas of the country.

A platoon leader with the 82nd Airborne Division's 1st Brigade Combat Team stands by as an Afghan soldier questions a villager about the presence of Taliban in the area in Ghazni province, Afghanistan. U.S. forces cooperated with anti-Taliban fighters to remove Afghanistan's brutal Taliban regime from power in 2001. Since then, American and Afghan soldiers have worked to prevent the re-emergence of the Taliban. (Michael J. MacLeod/ZUMAPRESS/Newscom)

Opium Cultivation

According to recent figures, Afghanistan provides almost all of the world's opium (the main ingredient in heroin and other dangerous drugs), in the form of poppies grown by Afghan farmers. While the U.S. and Afghan governments have attempted to eradicate opium-poppy cultivation—funds from which are allegedly bankrolling the Taliban—observers say the nation's impoverished farmers have no alternative crop to grow, at least none that can earn them enough money to live on. And unless the government offers them some economic alternative, Afghan farmers will continue to grow lucrative opium poppies. One possible solution has been offered by the Senlis Council, a drug-policy think tank, which has proposed a plan that would officially license Afghanistan's opium-poppy crop. Pharmaceutical companies would then process the opium into such medicines as morphine and codeine for use in developing countries that have limited access to these pain-killing drugs.

Poverty

The United Nations Development Programme (UNDP)'s Human Development Index ranks Afghanistan at 175 out of 187 countries worldwide, just one indicator of the country's extreme poverty. The UNDP reports that about 20% of rural Afghan households face a chronic food shortage. Despite some success of the government's back-to-school campaign, more than 40% of all school-age children in Afghanistan today do not attend school. Many poor Afghan children have been forced to quit school to work at jobs or on farms. In addition, due to poor nutrition and health care, resulting from extreme poverty, about 20% of all Afghan children die before the age of five, one-third of which die just after birth.

Environment/Pollution

Because Afghanistan has been at war for so long, little attention has been paid to the degradation of the country's environment, some of which has been caused by agricultural practices not connected to conflict. Afghan wetlands and forest lands have been depleted by hundreds of years of farming and animal grazing, practices that have increased with the growth of the country's population. In addition, much of Afghanistan's wildlife is in jeopardy, with little government effort to prevent hunting or the shrinking of habitat caused by war. Several studies of air pollution in the capital, Kabul, have been conducted in recent years, though the nation currently has no law that specifically addresses the problem and lacks the ability to enforce such environmental regulations.

Excerpt from the Constitution of the Islamic Republic of Afghanistan

The current Constitution of Afghanistan was adopted in 2004. Many of the rights enumerated in the Constitution are subject to the principles of Islam, which is the country's official religion.

The Constitution specifies both political and economic rights. Political rights include the right to vote and the right to a fair trial. It specifically forbids the use of torture and forced confessions in criminal proceedings, and slavery and forced labor are outlawed. The Constitution also grants citizens the right to education and health care, and "the state is obliged to provide free means of preventive health care and medical treatment." Men and women hold equal rights under the law.

As with other Islamic republics, however, Afghanistan's Constitution constrains rights whose exercise can be construed as contrary to the principles of Islam. For example, Afghan citizens are granted the right to form political parties, but these parties' principles and actions must not be "contrary to the principles of sacred religion of Islam." Similarly, the Constitution states that every citizen has the right to free education through college. However, according to Article 45, "The state shall devise and implement a unified educational curriculum based on the provisions of the sacred religion of Islam, national culture, and in accordance with academic principles." Thus the Afghanistan Constitution can be interpreted in terms of efforts to balance Islamic principles with secular human rights as defined in many parts of the world.

Article 22

Any kind of discrimination and privilege between the citizens of Afghanistan are prohibited.

The citizens of Afghanistan—whether man or woman—have equal rights and duties before the law.

Article 23

Life is a gift of God and a natural right of human beings. No one shall be deprived of this right except by the provision of law.

Article 24

Liberty is the natural right of human beings. This right has no limits unless affecting the rights of others or public interests, which are regulated by law.

Liberty and dignity of human beings are inviolable.

The state has the duty to respect and protect the liberty and dignity of human beings.

Article 25

Innocence is the original state.

An accused is considered innocent until convicted by a final decision of an authorized court.

Article 26

Crime is a personal action.

The prosecution, arrest, and detention of an accused and the execution of penalty can not affect another person.

Article 27

No person can be pursued, arrested or detained but in accordance with provisions of law.

No person can be punished but in accordance with the decision of an authorized court and in conformity with the law adopted before the date of offense.

Article 29

Torture of human beings is prohibited.

Punishment contrary to human integrity is prohibited.

Article 30

Any statement, testimony, or confession obtained from an accused or of another person by means of compulsion, are invalid.

Article 31

Every person upon arrest can seek an advocate to defend his rights or to defend his case . . .

The accused upon arrest has the right to be informed of the attributed accusation and to be summoned to the court within the limits determined by law.

In criminal cases, the state shall appoint an advocate for the destitute.

The confidentiality of oral, written or telephonic communications between an advocate and his accused client are immune from invasion.

The duties and authorities of advocates shall be regulated by law.

Article 32

Being in debt does not limit a person's freedom or deprive him of his liberties.

Article 33

The citizens of Afghanistan have the right to elect and be elected.
Law regulates the conditions and means to exercise this right.

Article 34

Freedom of expression is inviolable.

Every Afghan has the right to express his thought through speech, writing, or illustration or other means . . .

Every Afghan has the right to print or publish topics without prior submission to the state . . .

Article 35

The citizens of Afghanistan have the right to form social organizations for the purpose of securing material or spiritual aims in accordance with the provisions of the law.

The citizens of Afghanistan have the right to form political parties . . . provided that:

- The program and charter of the party are not contrary to the principles of sacred religion of Islam, and the provisions and values of this Constitution.
- The organizational structure, and financial sources of the party are made public.
- The party does not have military or paramilitary aims and structures.
- The party should have no affiliation to a foreign political party or sources.

Formation and functioning of a party based on ethnicity, language, Islamic school of thought (mazhab-i fiqhi) and region is not permissible.

A party set up in accordance with provisions of the law shall not be dissolved without lawful reasons and the decision of an authorized court.

Article 36

The citizens of Afghanistan have the right to un-armed demonstrations, for legitimate peaceful purposes.

Article 37

Confidentiality and freedom of correspondence and communication whether in the form of letters or through telephone, telegraph and other means, are immune from invasion.

The state does not have the right to inspect personal correspondence and communication unless authorized by the provisions of law.

Article 38

A person's residence is immune from invasion.

Other than the situations and methods indicated in the law, no one, including the state, are allowed to enter or inspect a private residence without prior permission of the resident or holding a court order.

In case of an evident crime, an official in-charge of the situation can enter or conduct a house search prior to the permission of the court.

The official involved in the situation is required to obtain a subsequent court order for the house search within the period indicated by law.

Article 39

Every Afghan has the right to travel or settle in any part of the country except in the regions forbidden by law.

Article 40

Property is immune from invasion.

Nobody's property shall be confiscated without the provisions of law and the order of an authorized court.

Article 43

Education is the right of all citizens of Afghanistan, which shall be provided up to the level of the B.A., free of charge by the state.

Article 44

The state shall devise and implement effective programs for balancing and promoting of education for women, improving of education of nomads and elimination of illiteracy in the country.

Article 45

The state shall devise and implement a unified educational curriculum based on the provisions of the sacred religion of Islam, national culture, and in accordance with academic principles . . .

Article 47

The state guarantees the rights of authors, inventors, and discoverers, and encourages and supports scientific researches in all areas, and publicizes the effective use of their results in accordance with the law.

Article 48

Work is the right of every Afghan.
Choice of occupation and craft is free within the limits of law.

Article 49

Forced labor is forbidden.
Active participation, in times of war, calamity, and other situations threatening lives and public welfare is one of the primary duties of every Afghan.
Children shall not be subjected to forced labor.

Article 52

The state is obliged to provide free means of preventive health care and medical treatment, and proper health facilities to all citizens of Afghanistan in accordance with the law.
The state encourages and protects the establishment and expansion of private medical services and health centers in accordance with law.

Article 53

The state takes necessary measures for regulating medical services and financial support to descendants of those who were martyred or are missing, to disabled or handicapped, and their active participation and re-integration into society in accordance with the law.
The state guarantees the rights and privileges of pensioners and disabled and handicapped individuals and as well renders necessary assistance to needy elders, women without caretakers, and needy orphans in accordance with the law.

Article 54

Family is a fundamental unit of society and is supported by the state.
The state adopts necessary measures to ensure physical and psychological well being of family, especially of child and mother, upbringing of children, and the elimination of traditions contrary to the principles of sacred religion of Islam.

Source: "Afghanistan Index." International Constitutional Law Project. http://www .servat.unibe.ch/icl/af__indx.html

BOTSWANA: Parliamentary Republic

BOTSWANA

Communications	Primary School–age Children Enrolled in Primary School
Facebook Users	
300,000 (estimate) (2013)	330,775 (2009)
Internet Users	Primary School–age Males Enrolled in Primary School
120,000 (2009)	
Internet Users (% of Population)	169,513 (2009)
15.0% (2013)	Primary School–age Females Enrolled in Primary School
Television	
4 sets per 100 population (2003)	161,262 (2009)
Land-based Telephones in Use	Secondary School–age Children Enrolled in Secondary School
160,500 (2012)	
Mobile Telephone Subscribers	181,741 (estimate) (2008)
3,082,000 (2012)	Secondary School–age Males Enrolled in Secondary School
Major Daily Newspapers	
2 (2004)	88,555 (estimate) (2008)
Average Circulation of Daily Newspapers	Secondary School–age Females Enrolled in Secondary School
75,278 (2004)	93,186 (estimate) (2008)
Education	Students Per Teacher, Primary School
School System	25.4 (2009)
Public schooling in Botswana begins at the age of seven. Students spend seven years in primary school, three years in junior secondary school, and two years in senior secondary education.	Students Per Teacher, Secondary School
	13.9 (2007)
	Enrollment in Tertiary Education
	16,239 (2006)
Mandatory Education	Enrollment in Tertiary Education, Male
7 years, from ages 7 to 14.	7,601 (2006)
Average Years Spent in School for Current Students	Enrollment in Tertiary Education, Female
	8,638 (2006)
12 (estimate) (2006)	Literacy
Average Years Spent in School for Current Students, Male	87% (2012)
12 (estimate) (2006)	Energy and Natural Resources
Average Years Spent in School for Current Students, Female	Electric Power Generation
12 (estimate) (2006)	429,600,000 kilowatt hours per year (estimate) (2010)

Electric Power Consumption	**Capital**
3,118,000,000 kilowatt hours per year (estimate) (2011)	Gaborone
	Area
Nuclear Power Plants	224,607 sq. miles
0 (2014)	**Climate**
Crude Oil Production	Botswana's climate is hot and arid, with desert claiming large sections of the country. The northern and eastern portions of the country receive an average annual rainfall of 18 inches, but rainfall in the west is erratic, with as little as 10 inches falling in some years. Summer temperatures often reach 100°F or higher.
0 barrels per day (2013)	
Crude Oil Consumption	
15,500 barrels per day (2012)	
Natural Gas Production	
0 cubic meters per year (estimate) (2011)	
Natural Gas Consumption	
0 cubic meters per year (estimate) (2010)	**Land Use**
Natural Resources	0.4% arable land; 00.0% permanent crops; 45.2% permanent meadows and pastures; 20.7% forest land; 33.7% other.
Diamonds, copper, nickel, salt, soda ash, potash, coal, iron ore, silver	
Environment	**Arable Land**
CO2 Emissions	0% (2007)
2.2 metric tons per capita (2009)	**Arable Land Per Capita**
Alternative and Nuclear Energy	0 acres per person (2007)
0.0% of total energy use (2010)	**Health**
Threatened Species	**Average Life Expectancy**
18 (2010)	54.1 years (2014)
Protected Areas	**Average Life Expectancy, Male**
179,775 (estimate) (2010)	55.8 years (2014)
Geography	**Average Life Expectancy, Female**
Location	52.3 years (2014)
A landlocked country in southern Africa, Botswana is bordered by Zimbabwe to the northeast, South Africa to the south and southeast, and Namibia to the west and north. A short northern section borders Zambia.	**Crude Birth Rate**
	21.0 (estimate) (2015)
	Crude Death Rate
	13.4 (estimate) (2015)
	Maternal Mortality
Time Zone	100 per 100,000 live births (2005–2012 projection)
7 hours ahead of U.S. Eastern Standard	
Land Borders	**Infant Mortality**
2,494 miles	41 per 1,000 live births (2012)
Coastline	**Doctors**
0 miles	0.3 per 1,000 people (2010)

Industry and Labor		GDP Contribution by Sector	
Gross Domestic Product (GDP) - official exchange rate		agriculture: 2.1% industry: 45% services: 52.9% (2011 est.)	
$16,401,000,000 (estimate) (2015)		**External Debt**	
GDP per Capita		$2,416,000,000 (estimate) (2013)	
$7,704 (estimate) (2015)		**Economic Aid Extended**	
GDP - Purchasing Power Parity (PPP)		$0 (2011)	
$33,388,000,000 (estimate) (2013)		**Economic Aid Received**	
GDP (PPP) per Capita		$126,000,000 (2011)	
$17,596 (estimate) (2013)		**Population**	
Industry Products		**Population**	
Diamonds, copper, nickel, beverages, coal, salt, soda ash, potash, processed meat.		2,182,719 (estimate) (2015)	
Agriculture Products		**World Population Rank**	
Fruit and vegetables, sorghum, pulse, maize, cotton, livestock, dairy products.		142 th (2010)	
		Population Density	
Unemployment		9.2 people per square mile (estimate) (2011)	
17.7% (2012)		**Population Distribution**	
Labor Profile		61% urban (2011)	
Not Available		**Age Distribution**	
Military		0-14: 34.3%	
Total Active Armed Forces		15-64: 61.8%	
9,000 (estimate) (2010)		65+: 3.9%	
Active Armed Forces		(2009)	
1% (2010)		**Median Age**	
Annual Military Expenditures		22.9 years (estimate) (2014)	
$293,000,000 (estimate) (2008)		**Population Growth Rate**	
Military Service		1.2% per year (estimate) (2015)	
Service in Botswana's military is voluntary.		**Net Migration Rate**	
National Finances		4.6 (estimate) (2015)	
Currency		**Trade**	
Pula		**Imported Goods**	
Total Government Revenues		Heavy machinery, transportation equipment, metals, foodstuffs, chemicals, petroleum products, textiles.	
$5,040,000,000 (estimate) (2013)			
Total Government Expenditures		**Total Value of Imports**	
$4,592,000,000 (estimate) (2013)		$4,518,000,000 (2010)	
Budget Deficit		**Exported Goods**	
0.6 (estimate) (2013)		Diamonds, copper, nickel, livestock.	

Total Value of Exports	Paved Roads		
$5,887,000,000 (estimate) (2012)	32.6% (2005)		
Import Partners	**Roads, Unpaved**		
Southern African Customs Union - 74.0%; European Free Trade Association - 17.0%; Zimbabwe - 4.0% (2006)	10,804 (2005)		
	Passenger Cars per 1,000 People		
Export Partners	69 (2009)		
NA	**Number of Trucks, Buses, and Commercial Vehicles**		
Current Account Balance			
$1,375,000,000 (estimate) (2013)	111,000 (2005)		
Weights and Measures	**Railroads**		
The metric system is in use.	552 (2008)		
Transportation			
Airports	**Ports**		
76 (2012)	None.		

OVERVIEW

The landlocked nation of Botswana is located north of South Africa and is bordered on the west by Namibia and on the northeast by Zimbabwe. Much of the country is desert or near-desert (the Kalahari Desert is located in the southwest), but the terrain also includes the swampland of the Okavango Delta in the west as well as a central plateau. Most of the nearly 2.2 million people live in the eastern grasslands, and the capital, Gaborone, is located in the southeast. Because of the country's semiarid climate, drought conditions are frequent; annual rainfall ranges from 10 inches or less in the desert to about 18 inches in the north.

GOVERNMENT

Botswana became an independent parliamentary republic within the British Commonwealth of Nations in 1966. The current president, Lt. Gen. Seretse Khama Ian Khama (the son of the country' founding president, Seretse Khama), inherited the office from former president Festus Mogae on April 1, 2008. Substantial powers, including the appointment of the president, are vested in the National Assembly.

Constitution

Botswana's 1966 Constitution is based on the constitution that was in place when the area was known as Bechuanaland and under British rule. The 1966 Constitution institutes a modified parliamentary form of government, replacing the office of prime minister with a president. The Constitution also includes a bill of human rights.

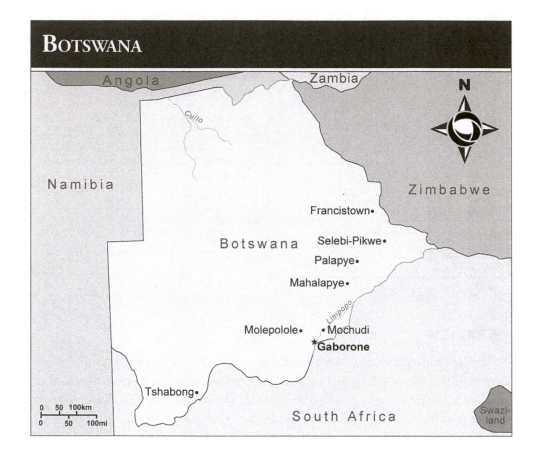

BOTSWANA

Executive

Executive power rests with the president, who also serves as commander in chief of the armed forces. The president is elected by the National Assembly, which functions as an electoral college during national elections, and serves a five-year term concurrent with that of the assembly members. A cabinet consisting of the vice president and 10 other ministers is appointed by the president but is directly answerable to the National Assembly. Legislation approved by the National Assembly may be delayed, but not vetoed, by the president, who also holds the right to dissolve the assembly and call for new elections. In late 1995, the ruling Botswana Democratic Party agreed to limit the presidency to two five-year terms. A constitutional amendment to that effect was approved in 1997.

Legislature

The Parliament is composed of a National Assembly and a House of Chiefs. In the 63-member National Assembly, 57 seats are directly elected by universal adult suffrage. The president and attorney general each hold one seat, and the majority party appoints the remaining four. Assembly members serve five-year terms in single-seat constituencies. The Assembly exercises its legislative powers in conjunction with the 35-member House of Chiefs, which it must consult on matters relating to tribal affairs or constitutional changes. The House of Chiefs consists of the chiefs of the nation's 8 principal tribes, 22 indirectly elected members, and 5 members appointed by the president.

Judiciary

The Court of Appeals is the highest and final court in Botswana. The High Court makes determinations on criminal or civil cases and oversees the Magistrates courts, which hear the majority of criminal and civil cases in Botswana.

Local Government

There are ten rural district councils, four town councils, and two city councils that regulate local affairs. Local executive authority is vested in the district commissioner, appointed by the central government.

Election Qualifications

Botswana has universal suffrage for citizens 18 years of age and older. Citizens living abroad are also entitled to vote.

POLITICS

Under the direction of Seretse Khama, a former chief of the Bamangwanto tribe, Botswana gained independence from Great Britain in 1966 and has been considered a prime example of a stable democracy on the African continent ever since. A popular statesman, Khama ruled for 14 years. Following his death in 1980, his vice president, Ketumile Masire, took over and was reelected in three subsequent elections. In the 1994 elections, the opposition Botswana National Front shook the ruling Botswana Democratic Party (BDP) and captured enough legislative seats to challenge the BDP's 28-year dominance; however, the BDP regained support in 1999 elections, winning 33 of 40 seats in the National Assembly and overcoming earlier popular discontent over the increasing rate of unemployment.

In 1997, addressing a troublesome policy issue of succession in government office, the National Assembly amended the 1966 Constitution to limit the president to two five-year terms. After Masire resigned in March 1998, his vice president, Festus Mogae, took over as head of state. Mogae retained the presidency in October 1999 elections, easily capturing the majority of votes. In October 2004 general elections, Mogae and his ruling Botswana Democratic Party swept the polls, and

Mogae won his second term by a wide margin. The October elections also saw the expansion of the number of popularly elected seats in the National Assembly, from 40 to 57. Mogae stepped down more than a year before the end of his second five-year term, citing the spirit of the 1997 amendments as prohibiting him from serving more than 10 years in office. He was succeeded by his vice president, Seretse Khama Ian Khama, son of Seretse Khama, on April 1, 2008, exactly 10 years since the day he himself inherited the presidency from Masire.

In 2009 legislative elections, the BDP again swept the polls and reinstalled Seretse Khama Ian Khama as president. During his term, Khama has worked to develop agriculture and tourism, and to diversify Botswana's economy. He is well-known as a conservationist and is leading pan-African efforts for sustainable development.

Political Parties

Botswana has maintained a vigorous multiparty system since it first achieved independence in 1966.

The Botswana Democratic Party (BDP—formerly the Bechuanaland Democratic Party) has dominated political affairs since 1965. Founded by the late president Seretse Khama, the center-right party supports parliamentary democracy and maintains close ties with Britain. Seretse Khama Ian Khama is leader of the party.

The Botswana National Front (BNF) is the country's main opposition party. The party, while founded by Dr. Kenneth Koma in 1965 as a pro-communist organization, has since moderated its leftist views. The party draws its support primarily from among the working class.

The Botswana Congress Party (BCP) split from the main opposition BNF party in June 1998 and holds center-left views. Because at the time of the split they took 10 of the BNF's 13 National Assembly seats with them, the BCP was the main opposition party for a short time. However, in the following election in October 1999, the BCP was reduced to a single seat. In 2009 elections, the BCP won four seats to the BNF's six in the National Assembly.

The Botswana People's Party (BPP), which espouses the causes of pan-Africanism and social democracy, was formed in 1960. In 1991, it formed an alliance with the BNF and the Botswana Progressive Union (BPU), called the Botswana People's Progressive Front.

ECONOMY

Once one of the world's poorest nations, Botswana is now among the world's top producers of diamonds, an industry that helped propel economic growth, provided the country with large foreign exchange reserves, and made it one of the wealthiest nations in sub-Saharan Africa. Because of this growth, the poverty rate in Botswana has declined from more than 50% to below 20% since independence. However, these economic gains are being threatened by the nation's staggering rate of AIDS infections. Nearly 40% of the adult population have the virus—among the highest rates in the world—taking many people out of the workforce and contributing to an estimated 17.8% unemployment rate. The nation's economy was also struck by the global recession in 2009, made worse by its near-complete reliance on export revenue from diamonds. The luxury export accounts for more than one-third of Botswana's GDP. The government predicts that the nation's diamond deposits will be exhausted sometime between 2025 and 2030, highlighting the need for economic diversification.

In addition to diamonds, Botswana's natural resources include coal, copper, and nickel. The country's main agricultural industry is cattle production, a mainstay of the economy before the development of the mining industry, and a large section of the population is involved in subsistence agriculture. However, drought and poor soil have affected the agricultural sector, and the country relies on imports for a substantial portion of its food needs. Botswana conducts most of its trade with the four neighboring countries that, along with Botswana, form a tariff-free trade zone called the Southern African Customs Union. Other major trading partners are the European Free Trade Association, the United Kingdom, and Zimbabwe.

SOCIETY

The Setswana word for the most important social grouping is *morafe*, meaning the people who give allegiance to a certain chief. There are eight *morafes* in Botswana: the Bangwato, Bakwena, Bangwaketse, Batawana, Bakgatla, Bamalete, Barolong, and Batlokwa. The chiefs of all eight groups are from the Tswana ethnic group, but the people of the *morafes* include other ethnicities, such as Kalanga, Kgalagadi, Herero, Mbukushu, Subiya, Yei, and Ndebele, all of which are Bantu. Thus, ethnicity and social groups are not the same. Botswana is also home to about 100,000 indigenous tribespeople called the San, many of whom still live a nomadic existence in the Kalahari Desert. Recently, however, the San have been battling the government against a mass forced relocation campaign driving them from their ancient homeland. There are also small minorities of European and Asian descent. English is the official language, but Setswana is the national language. Although Christianity has become familiar to many in Botswana, traditional animist beliefs—the beliefs that animals and inanimate objects such as rocks, rivers, trees, and mountains contain spirits and souls—remain important both as a means of respecting ancestors and for rain-making ceremonies.

Ethnic Composition

Tswana (or Setswana) – 79%; Kalanga – 11%; Basarwa – 3%; other, including Kgalagadi and white – 7%

Language

English is the official language, but Setswana is widely spoken and is considered the national language.

Religion

Christian – 71.6%; Badimo – 6%; other – 1.4%; unspecified – 0.4%; none – 20.6%

CONTEMPORARY ISSUES

HIV/AIDS

The southern African region is the epicenter of the global HIV/AIDS epidemic, and the prevalence of infection in Botswana is the second-highest in the world next to that in nearby Swaziland. In 2012, about one-fourth of Batswana aged 15 to 49 were living with the virus, according to estimates of the Joint United Nations Programme on HIV/AIDS (UNAIDS). In addition, some 53,000 children orphaned by AIDS were registered with the government. Despite the far-reaching impacts of the virus on Botswana's communities, trends since 2001 have been encouraging, as rates of new infections among teenagers and young adults have declined, primarily due to the increased use of condoms. Another positive development in the last few years is a dramatic rise in access to antiretroviral drugs for people in Botswana who are HIV-positive. UNAIDS estimates that some 95% of HIV-positive men and women in the country were receiving antiretroviral therapy by 2012.

One of many signs designed to raise AIDS awareness among the population. The worldwide AIDS epidemic has hit Botswana especially hard. As many as a quarter of Botswana's citizens between 15 and 49 are believed to carry the HIV virus. (Eye Ubiquitous/Newscom)

Illegal Immigration from Zimbabwe

Botswana, often touted as the model of democracy and economic growth in postcolonial Africa, has rapidly transformed since independence from a poor country dependent on money sent home from people working in other countries to a middle-income nation that attracts immigrants from all over Africa. Key to its rapid development was an open migration policy that drew in laborers and skilled professionals to help build its lucrative diamond industry. Recently, however, the economic collapse of Botswana's northeastern neighbor, Zimbabwe, where unemployment has hovered around 80%, led thousands of Zimbabweans to settle in Botswana illegally in search of work. Movement between the two countries is fairly free, and many Zimbabweans cross into the country legally on 90-day visas, citing the purpose of their entry as "Visiting" or "Holiday," and do not leave again when their visas expire. Others enter the country illegally, which makes the exact number of Zimbabweans living in the country difficult to determine, though many estimates are in the hundreds of thousands.

This spike in immigration has led many in Botswana to blame Zimbabweans for woes ranging from a recent upsurge in crime to the economically disastrous spread of foot-and-mouth disease among cattle. Immigrants are often subject to ridicule and are increasingly targeted by anti-immigration vigilantes. Many Zimbabwean-run businesses now exist near the border; however, Zimbabweans typically perform such jobs as cleaning and gardening in the country's shadow economy.

Rights of the San

Botswana came under international scrutiny after human rights groups accused the government of conducting forced evacuations of the country's San minority to gain access to diamond deposits under the traditional San lands of the Central Kalahari Game Reserve. The government denied these claims adamantly, saying that the San were consulted about the relocations and all moved voluntarily. The government also insists that mineral interests did not motivate the relocations, which it says it carried out solely to empower the San by giving them better access to water, schools, and health services.

Many among Botswana's San minority accuse the government of ethnic cleansing and of sanctioning beatings, torture, and the torching of homesteads during the forced evacuation of some 750 people in 2002. In a series of evictions in 1997, 2002, and 2005, a total of approximately 2,500 San were forced out of the reserve. The government set up 63 resettlement camps, where it does provide water and other basic services, but most of these camps' inhabitants live in poverty, completely dependent on government food rations. Most San lived on their traditional lands as hunters and nomadic herders, but in the resettlement camps there is virtually no employment, and alcoholism, crime, and the spread of diseases previously unknown to San communities, including tuberculosis and HIV/AIDS, have grown rampant. Those few San who managed to escape the evictions and continued to live illegally in the Kalahari reserve also faced a crisis, as the government filled many wells in their desert homeland with concrete, cutting off their water supplies.

On December 13, 2006, the San won their four-year legal battle with the government when Botswana's High Court ruled the evictions violated the Sans' constitutional rights. By mid-2007, an estimated 150 to 200 San had returned home; however, the government prevented the return of others, saying that the court ruling applied only to the 229 individuals explicitly named in court documents. The government has also prevented the resettled San from keeping livestock and from installing a new water pump, and in 2014 it also instituted a ban on hunting, in spite of the High Court's ruling that a similar 2002 ban violated the Sans' rights. The vast majority of the evicted San continue to live in resettlement camps.

Excerpt from the Constitution of Botswana

The Constitution of Botswana was drafted initially in 1959, and was revised before Botswana became independent in 1966. It has been in effect ever since.

The constitution establishes what are termed "fundamental rights and freedoms." This section begins by confirming that rights are granted to all Botswanan citizens, regardless of "race, place of origin, political opinions, colour, creed, or sex." These fundamental rights are political rights and include the right to protection under the law, the right to freedom of conscience and freedom of assembly, and the right to privacy.

The right to personal liberty is spelled out in more detail. In effect, murder is prohibited except when executions are carried out in accordance with the due process of law. Nor may a person be detained or "deprived of his personal liberty" absent due process, although the Constitution allows detention in the case of possible spread of an infectious disease, addiction, or vagrancy. This clause is of particular importance because Botswana has one of the highest rates of HIV/AIDS infections in the world. The Constitution also grants freedom of movement, with the caveat that this right can be deprived if its denial is deemed to be in the national interest, including "defence, public safety, public order, public morality or public health." Thus the Constitution of Botswana is more explicit than many others with respect to tradeoffs between individual liberties and national security.

Fundamental rights and freedoms

Whereas every person in Botswana is entitled to the fundamental rights and freedoms of the individual . . . whatever his race, place of origin, political opinions, colour, creed or sex . . . namely

(a) life, liberty, security . . . and the protection of the law;
(b) freedom of conscience, of expression and of assembly and association;
(c) protection for the privacy of his home . . .

Protection of right to life

No person shall be deprived of his life intentionally save in execution of the sentence of a court . . .

Protection of right to personal liberty

No person shall be deprived of his personal liberty save as may be authorized by law in any of the following cases:

in execution of the sentence or order of a court . . .
upon reasonable suspicion of his having committed, or being about to commit, a criminal offence . . .
. . . for his education or welfare during any period ending not later than the date when he attains the age of 18 years;
for the purpose of preventing the spread of an infectious . . . disease;
in the case of a person who is, or is reasonably suspected to be, of unsound mind, addicted to drugs or alcohol, or a vagrant, for the purpose of his care or treatment or the protection of the community;
for the purpose of preventing the unlawful entry of that person into Botswana, or for the purpose of effecting the . . . lawful removal of that person from Botswana.
Any person who is arrested or detained shall be informed as soon as reasonably practicable, in a language that he understands, of the reasons for his arrest or detention.
Any person who is arrested or detained—
. . . shall be brought as soon as is reasonably practicable before a court; and if any person arrested or detained . . . is not tried within a reasonable time, then, without prejudice to any further proceedings that may be brought against him, he shall be released. . .
Any person who is unlawfully arrested or detained . . . shall be entitled to compensation . . .

Protection from slavery and forced labour

No person shall be held in slavery or servitude.
No person shall be required to perform forced labour.

Protection from inhuman treatment

No person shall be subjected to torture or to inhuman or degrading punishment . . .

Protection for privacy of home and other property

... no person shall be subjected to the search of his person or his property [except]:

(a) that is reasonably required in the interests of defence, public safety, public order, public morality, public health, town and country planning, the development and utilization of mineral resources, for the purpose of any census or in order to secure the development or utilization of any property for a purpose beneficial to the community;

(b) that is reasonably required for the purpose of protecting the rights or freedoms of other persons;

Provisions to secure protection of law

If any person is charged with a criminal offence . . . the case shall be afforded a fair hearing within a reasonable time by an independent and impartial court . . .

Every person who is charged with a criminal offence—

(a) shall be presumed to be innocent until he is proved or has pleaded guilty;

(b) shall be informed as soon as reasonably practicable, in a language that he understands and in detail, of the nature of the offence charged;

(c) shall be given adequate time and facilities for the preparation of his defence;

(d) shall be permitted to defend himself before the court in person or, at his own expense, by a legal representative of his own choice;

(e) shall be afforded facilities to examine in person or by his legal representative the witnesses called by the prosecution. . .

(f) shall be permitted to have without payment the assistance of an interpreter if he cannot understand the language used at the court.

No person who shows that he has been tried by a competent court for a criminal offence . . . shall again be tried for that offence.

No person who is tried for a criminal offence shall be compelled to give evidence at the trial.

. . . all proceedings of every court . . . shall be held in public.

Protection of freedom of conscience

. . . no person shall be hindered in the enjoyment of his freedom of conscience . . . the said freedom includes freedom of thought and of religion, freedom to change his religion or belief, and freedom . . . both in public and in private, to manifest and propagate his religion or belief . . .

. . . no person attending any place of education shall be required to receive religious instruction or . . . attend any religious ceremony or observance . . .

No person shall be compelled to take any oath which is contrary to his religion . . .

Protection of freedom of expression

. . . no person shall be hindered in the enjoyment of freedom of expression . . . freedom to hold opinions . . . freedom to receive ideas and information. . . freedom to communicate ideas and information . . . and freedom from interference with his correspondence.

Protection of freedom of assembly and association

. . . no person shall be hindered in the enjoyment of his freedom of assembly and association . . . [exceptions]:

that is reasonably required in the interests of defence, public safety, public order, public morality or public health;

that is reasonably required for the purpose of protecting the rights or freedoms of other persons;

that imposes restrictions upon public officers, employees of local government bodies, or teachers . . .

Protection of freedom of movement

No person shall be deprived of his . . . right to move freely throughout Botswana . . . [With the following exceptions]:

. . . the interests of defence, public safety, public order, public morality or public health . . .

Protection from discrimination

. . . no law shall make any provision that is discriminatory. . .

. . . no person shall be treated in a discriminatory manner by any person acting by virtue of any written law or in the performance of the functions of any public office or any public authority.

Source: "Constitution of Botswana." Website of the Embassy of Botswana. http://www.botswanaembassy.org/files/constitution_of_botswana.pdf

CANADA: Parliamentary Democracy with Constitutional Monarchy

CANADA

Communications	
Facebook Users	
17,800,000 (estimate) (2013)	
Internet Users	
26,960,000 (2009)	
Internet Users (% of Population)	
85.8% (2013)	
Television	
73 (2004)	
Land-based Telephones in Use	
18,010,000 (2012)	
Mobile Telephone Subscribers	
26,263,000 (2012)	
Major Daily Newspapers	
103 (2004)	
Average Circulation of Daily Newspapers	
5,578,000 (2004)	

Education	
School System	
In Canada is governed on a provincial level. The most common system, followed in Alberta, the Northwest Territories, Nunavut, and Prince Edward Island, consists of six years of primary school beginning at age six, followed by six years of secondary school. The Yukon Territory follows a similar system, but divides into seven years of primary school and five years of secondary school. Students in Manitoba, New Brunswick, Newfoundland, Nova Scotia, and Saskatchewan all attend 13 years of school, beginning at the age of five, variously divided into between four and nine years of primary school and between four and Public school nine years of secondary	

school. Ontario students begin primary school at the age of six, attending eight years of primary school and four years of secondary school, while students in Quebec attend six years of primary school and five years of secondary school. The province of British Columbia begins seven years of primary school at the age of seven, followed by five years of secondary school.

Mandatory Education	
Varies by province; most commonly 10 years, from ages 6 to 16.	
Average Years Spent in School for Current Students	
Not Available	
Average Years Spent in School for Current Students, Male	
Not Available	
Average Years Spent in School for Current Students, Female	
Not Available	
Primary School–age Children Enrolled in Primary School	
2,153,778 (2011)	
Primary School–age Males Enrolled in Primary School	
1,103,891 (2011)	
Primary School–age Females Enrolled in Primary School	
1,049,887 (2011)	
Secondary School–age Children Enrolled in Secondary School	
2,583,789 (2011)	
Secondary School–age Males Enrolled in Secondary School	
1,335,814 (2011)	

Secondary School–age Females Enrolled in Secondary School	**Natural Resources**
1,247,975 (2011)	Iron ore, nickel, zinc, copper, gold, lead, rare earth elements, molybdenum, potash, diamonds, silver, fish, timber, wildlife, coal, petroleum, natural gas, hydropower
Students Per Teacher, Primary School	
17.4 (2000)	**Environment**
Students Per Teacher, Secondary School	**CO2 Emissions**
Not Available	15.2 metric tons per capita (2009)
Enrollment in Tertiary Education	**Alternative and Nuclear Energy**
Not Available	22.6% of total energy use (2011)
Enrollment in Tertiary Education, Male	**Threatened Species**
Not Available	77 (2010)
Enrollment in Tertiary Education, Female	**Protected Areas**
Not Available	773,807 (estimate) (2010)
Literacy	**Geography**
99% (2003)	**Location**
Energy and Natural Resources	The second-largest country in the world, Canada stretches across the northern part of North America, excluding Alaska and Greenland. It extends from the Atlantic Ocean to the Pacific, and its southern border with the United States is formed along the upper St. Lawrence Seaway and the Great Lakes, proceeding west along the 49th parallel. It is bordered by the Arctic Ocean to the north and has a northwestern boundary with Alaska.
Electric Power Generation	
618,900,000,000 kilowatt hours per year (estimate) (2011)	
Electric Power Consumption	
549,500,000,000 kilowatt hours per year (2008)	
Electric Power Consumption	
499,900,000,000 kilowatt hours per year (estimate) (2010)	**Time Zone**
Nuclear Power Plants	Same as U.S. Eastern Standard (Ottawa)
19 (2014)	**Land Borders**
Crude Oil Production	5526
4,073,000 barrels per day (2013)	**Coastline**
Crude Oil Consumption	151,492 (includes islands)
2,303,300 barrels per day (2013)	**Capital**
Crude Oil Consumption	Ottawa
Not Available	**Area**
Natural Gas Production	3,844,928 sq. miles
143,100,000,000 cubic meters per year (estimate) (2012)	**Climate**
Natural Gas Consumption	Canada has a climate of extremes, with cold winters (especially inland) and hot summers. Rainfall is light to moderate, and heavy snows occur in the winter, when temperatures are often well below freezing.
82,480,000,000 cubic meters per year (estimate) (2010)	

Land Use	products, wood, metals, minerals, petroleum, natural gas, chemicals, fuels.
5.0% arable land; 0.8% permanent crops; 1.7% permanent meadows and pastures; 34.1% forest land; 58.5% other.	**Agriculture Products**
	Wheat, hay, barley, dairy products, tobacco, maize, cattle, pigs, oilseed, fish.
Arable Land	**Unemployment**
5% (2007)	7.2% (2012)
Arable Land Per Capita	**Labor Profile**
3 acres per person (2007)	agriculture: 2% manufacturing: 13% construction: 6% services: 76% other: 3% (estimate) (2006)
Health	
Average Life Expectancy	**Military**
81.7 years (2014)	**Total Active Armed Forces**
Average Life Expectancy, Male	65,722 (2010)
79.1 years (2014)	**Active Armed Forces**
Average Life Expectancy, Female	0% (2010)
84.4 years (2014)	**Annual Military Expenditures**
Crude Birth Rate	$20,190,000,000 (2009)
10.3 (estimate) (2015)	**Military Service**
Crude Death Rate	Military service is based on a voluntary system.
8.4 (estimate) (2015)	**National Finances**
Maternal Mortality	**Currency**
6 per 100,000 live births (2005–2012 projection)	Canadian dollar
Infant Mortality	**Total Government Revenues**
5 per 1,000 live births (2012)	$687,800,000,000 (estimate) (2013)
Doctors	**Total Government Expenditures**
2.1 per 1,000 people (2010)	$740,800,000,000 (estimate) (2013)
Industry and Labor	**Budget Deficit**
Gross Domestic Product (GDP) - official exchange rate	-2.9 (estimate) (2013)
$1,849,880,000,000 (estimate) (2015)	**GDP Contribution by Sector**
GDP per Capita	agriculture: 1.7% industry: 28.5% services: 69.8% (2012 est.)
$51,594 (estimate) (2015)	**External Debt**
GDP - Purchasing Power Parity (PPP)	$1,331,000,000,000 (estimate) (2012)
$1,534,937,000,000 (estimate) (2013)	**Economic Aid Extended**
GDP (PPP) per Capita	$4,111,190,000 (2011)
$43,594 (estimate) (2013)	**Economic Aid Received**
Industry Products	$0 (2011)
Fur products, fish, transportation equipment, foodstuffs, paper and paper	

Population		Total Value of Exports	
Population		$481,700,000,000 (estimate) (2012)	
35,099,836 (estimate) (2015)		**Import Partners**	
World Population Rank		United States - 51.1%; China - 11.0%; Mexico - 4.6%; Japan - 3.4%;Germany - 2.9% (2009)	
36 th (2010)			
Population Density		**Export Partners**	
8.9 people per square mile (estimate) (2011)		United States - 75.1%; China - 3.7%; United Kingdom - 3.4%; Japan - 2.4%; Mexico - 1.2% (2009)	
Population Distribution			
81% urban (2011)		**Current Account Balance**	
Age Distribution		$-59,500,000,000 (estimate) (2013)	
0-14: 15.9%		**Weights and Measures**	
15-64: 68.6%		The metric system is in use.	
65+: 15.5%		**Transportation**	
(2009)		**Airports**	
Median Age		1,453 (2012)	
41.7 years (estimate) (2014)		**Paved Roads**	
Population Growth Rate		39.9% (2004)	
0.8% per year (estimate) (2015)		**Roads, Unpaved**	
Net Migration Rate		18,517 (2006)	
5.7 (estimate) (2015)		**Roads, Unpaved**	
Trade		389,413 (2008)	
Imported Goods		**Passenger Cars per 1,000 People**	
Motor vehicles and parts, machinery, petroleum, chemicals, telecommunication equipment, computers, fruits, vegetables.		420 (2009)	
		Number of Trucks, Buses, and Commercial Vehicles	
Total Value of Imports		708,000 (2005)	
$320,927,000,000 (2009)		**Railroads**	
Exported Goods		29,011 (2008)	
Motor vehicles and parts, machinery, petroleum, paper and paper products, beverages, wheat, natural gas, precious metals, timber, foodstuffs, coal.		**Ports**	
		Major: 9 (including Vancouver, Montreal, Quebec, St. John's, Goderich, Halifax, Sept Isles).	

OVERVIEW

Canada, on the North American continent, is the world's second-largest country by land area. Comprising ten provinces and three territories, Canada has a population of more than 34 million people, resulting in a much lower population density than its neighbor to the south, the United States. Almost 90% of all Canadians live

CANADA

within 100 miles of the U.S.–Canadian border, which is the longest undefended border in the world. The vast nation has a wide range of terrains and climates. The north has polar and subpolar temperatures. The interior of the nation suffers long and cold winters, while the coastal regions are a little milder. The temperature seldom drops below freezing along the southern part of the country's Pacific coast. Canada's capital is Ottawa.

GOVERNMENT

Canada is a constitutional monarchy that became a self-governing Dominion within the British Empire on July 1, 1867, and became an autonomous member of the Commonwealth of Nations under the British Statute of Westminster of 1931. Because it recognizes the British sovereign as head of state, Canada is a monarchy, although in practice the Canadian Constitution and Canada's Parliament limit the monarch's power. Canada is a confederation with a parliamentary democratic system of government at both the federal and provincial levels. The member provinces exercise a wide range of powers independent of the federal government. The current prime minister of Canada is Stephen Harper.

Constitution

The "living" Canadian Constitution, like that of most of the older constitutional democracies, cannot be found in a single document. It consists of a series of written documents, judicial pronouncements, unwritten customs and usages, and other sources. Of the written documents, by far the most important are the British North America Act (later renamed the Constitution Act)—passed by the British Parliament in 1867—and its amendments, the Constitution Act of 1982, and the Canadian Charter of Rights and Freedoms. Canadian statutes also form an important "written" source of the Constitution (for example, the laws establishing the Supreme Court of Canada and the original Canadian "Bill of Rights").

Judicial interpretation of these statutes has had a profound effect on constitutional practice, notably on the division of powers between the federal government and the provinces. Moreover, the whole Canadian political system is strongly influenced by customs and usages that are not specifically embodied in legislation or judicial decisions. The federal cabinet will resign when it loses the confidence of a majority in the legislature. The governor general will exercise the office's immense powers only with the advice of the cabinet. These are simply customary rules, though, often taken for granted. Many of them have their origin in the British parliamentary tradition. Other usages grew up in Canadian practice—for example, the consultation of the federal prime minister with provincial premiers on important federal issues.

Executive

The British monarch is the titular head of state in Canada, and under the British North America Act (renamed the Constitution Act) is vested with a vast array of executive, legislative, and judicial powers. Royal assent is necessary for all bills to become law. The monarch appoints judges and the officials of the executive branch, and may dissolve the House of Commons and call for new elections. In practice, however, the monarch never exercises these or other powers except according to the advice of the leaders of the elected legislature. This is the central feature of constitutional monarchy in the British and Canadian traditions.

The monarch appoints (on the advice of the cabinet) a governor general who is authorized to exercise most of the Crown's powers in Canada. It is an established convention that the governor general will be a Canadian citizen and that the office will alternate among bilingual Canadians from the English and French communities. The governor general appoints (on the advice of the federal cabinet) a lieutenant governor for each province to represent the sovereign there.

Legislature

The legislative powers of the federal government are vested in the Canadian Parliament, which consists of the monarch, the Senate, and the House of Commons. The role of the monarch and the governor general in the legislative process is now a formality, and "Parliament" is generally understood to refer to the two chambers or even to the House of Commons alone. The members of the Senate (usually a maximum of 112) are apportioned unequally among the 10 provinces and three territories. Quebec and Ontario have the largest delegations, with 24 senators each. Nova Scotia and New Brunswick, the other original members of the federation, have 10 senators each. The other provinces have 6 each, except Prince Edward Island, which has only 4 senators. Direct popular representation in the federal legislature is provided by the 308-member House of Commons.

Judiciary

The Canadian judicial system is essentially a four-tiered structure. At the top of the structure is the Supreme Court of Canada, which hears appeals from both federal and provincial court systems. Below the Supreme Court are federal and provincial courts of appeal, the latter of which function as courts of appeal for the three Canadian territories. The Federal Court, the Tax Court of Canada, and various provincial and territorial superior courts represent the next tier of the judiciary.

The majority of cases that are heard within the Canadian court system come under jurisdiction of the broadest tier of judiciary, the provincial and territorial courts. They are typically divided into divisions with specific concerns, such as small claims, traffic violations, family matters, or criminal cases. All judges within the Canadian court system are members of the legal profession. Lawyers seeking appointments to the bench must apply to committees established to approve appointments, with ultimate power of approval resting with the federal cabinet. Applicants to judgeships above the provincial level must have had at least 10 years' experience practicing law in provincial or territorial courts, and they are appointed by the federal government. Canadian judges are subject to mandatory retirement, usually at the age of 75.

Local Government

Canada comprises 10 provinces and 3 territories. The provinces are Alberta, British Columbia, Manitoba, New Brunswick, Newfoundland, Nova Scotia, Ontario, Prince Edward Island, Quebec, and Saskatchewan. The territories are the Northwest Territories, Yukon, and Nunavut. Each province has its own constitution, but the structure and operation of government, in their broad outlines, are similar to those of the federal government with executive, legislative, and judicial branches. Each province and territory has a popularly elected legislative assembly, with a

Canada's Parliament, which includes the Senate and the House of Commons, meets in the Centre Block of Parliament Hill in Ottawa. Canada is a parliamentary democracy, but it is also a constitutional monarchy in that the monarch of the United Kingdom is recognized formally as Canada's head of state. (Eye Ubiquitous/Newscom)

premier at the helm. Elections occur at least every five years. The establishment and supervision of local governments are the responsibility of the provincial and territorial governments.

The Constitution Act of 1867 outlined the structure and responsibilities of the provincial governments, including the appointment of a lieutenant governor by the governor general of Canada. The territories are under the jurisdiction of the federal government and each has a territorial commissioner that is also appointed by the Canadian government. Both the lieutenant governors and the territorial commissioners serve as heads of state and perform largely ceremonial roles, while leaving the day-to-day government functions to the legislative assemblies and the premiers.

Election Qualifications

Canadian citizens 18 years of age and older are eligible to vote.

POLITICS

The British North America Act of 1867 combined Ontario, Quebec, Nova Scotia, and New Brunswick into the modern state of Canada within the United Kingdom. In 1931, the Statute of Westminster removed legislative control over Canada from the British Parliament and granted it to Canada's Parliament. Power to amend the Canadian Constitution, however, was still with the U.K. The Canada Act of 1982 granted power to amend the Constitution to the Canadian Parliament, and the Constitution Act of 1982 completed the process of national sovereignty.

On the national level, power in Canada has traditionally alternated between the two dominant political parties: the Liberal Party and the Progressive Conservative Party (PCP), which in 2003 merged with the Canadian Alliance to form the Conservative Party of Canada (CPC).

In 2006, the Conservative Party of Canada's Stephen Harper was appointed prime minister, following a Parliamentary vote of no-confidence for his predecessor Paul Martin. Harper formed a minority government and called for elections in 2008 in the hope of achieving a majority for the CPC, but he was unable to accomplish this goal. As head of a minority government from 2006 to 2011, Harper tended to move the party's conservative agenda to the center to be more inclusive and gain support to keep the CPC in power.

A no-confidence vote in March 2011 forced Harper to dissolve Parliament and set Canada's fourth general election in seven years. On May 2, 2011, the CPC won 167 seats, 54% of the total, to give Harper the majority government he had sought. Moreover, the Liberal Party lost more than half its seats to drop to third in representation behind the surging and more socialist New Democratic Party (NDP), which became the official opposition party with 102 seats. Since gaining a majority government, the CPC's platform has focused on lowering taxes, eliminating the deficit by 2015, and strengthening the armed forces. The next elections are to be held no later than October 19, 2015.

Political Parties

The CPC favors lower taxes and smaller, more decentralized, government, though with increased spending on defense and security. More conservative elements of

Stephen Harper, the leader of Canada's Conservative Party, has served as Prime Minister since 2006. In Canada's parliamentary democracy, the Prime Minister is simultaneously the head of government and the leader of his or her political party. (Gao Jing Xinhua News Agency/ Newscom)

the party also speak out strongly on such social issues as opposition to abortion rights and to same-sex marriages.

Founded in 1961, the NDP is a democratic socialist party that favors a planned economy, a wider variety of social welfare programs, and an internationalist (economic and political cooperation) foreign policy.

The Liberal Party favors an expanded social welfare program, cooperation between federal and provincial governments, and a foreign policy cooperative with, but relatively independent of, the United States and other advanced industrial nations.

Bloc Québécois (Québec Bloc) favors sovereignty for Québec within a framework of economic cooperation with Canada. It was formed after the Meech Lake Accord on Québécois sovereignty collapsed in 1990.

The Green Party of Canada was founded in 1983 and, like other green parties, emphasizes environmentalism as well as social justice causes and grassroots democracy. It has struggled to meet the threshold of support needed for federal funding, which it achieved in 2004. In May 2011 elections, the party won its first-ever seat in the House of Commons.

ECONOMY

Although it experienced a sharp decline in economic activity in late 2008, due to the worldwide recession, Canada's economy bounced back quickly and remains one of the world's foremost economic powers. As such, it is a member of the Group of Eight (G8), the world's top industrial nations. Much of its wealth is based on its massive natural resource base, which includes timber, gold, silver, copper, zinc, lead, hydroelectric power, oil, and gas. The Athabasca oil sands in northwest Alberta hold one of the largest oil reserves in the world, and produce 1.5 million barrels a day, a significant portion of Canada's petroleum output. The controversial Keystone XL Pipeline is planned to carry oil from Alberta to refineries in the United States. Three segments of the pipeline are completed, and one segment awaits approval by the United States. The pipeline has the capacity to carry hundreds of thousands of barrels per day. The pipeline is controversial because of the potential damage it could cause to the environment.

Canada is also the world's third-largest producer of natural gas and one of the world's top grain producers. The country's advanced manufacturing sector creates such varied products as motor vehicles and aircraft, paper, chemicals and metals, and electronics. Canada is a member of the North American Free Trade Agreement (NAFTA), along with the United States and Mexico. The nation's 1994 membership in NAFTA sparked a dramatic increase in trade with the United States: 75% of Canada's exports go to the United States. In fact, the United States relies on Canada for most of its foreign energy imports, including oil, gas, and electricity. While the United States accounts for three-quarters of the country's exports, China, the United Kingdom, and Mexico are also major trading partners with Canada.

SOCIETY

The vast majority of Canadians are descendants of immigrants, primarily from Europe, but increasingly from other parts of the world. Only about 4.2% of the population consists of indigenous Indians and Aleuts. Almost 20% of the population is descended from British immigrants, but about 15.5% of the population is of French heritage. Despite the large British-descended population, nearly 40 percent of Canadians are Roman Catholics and only about 5% of the population belongs to the Anglican Church. Many other religions are practiced in Canada, but their total followers are outnumbered by those without any religious affiliation.

Language use is a guide to the Canadian mosaic. Both English and French are official languages. English-speaking groups make up about 60% of the population (though only around 10% in Quebec), while French-speakers comprise almost 85% of Quebec's population, but only 22% of the national total. Five million Canadians are allophones, the term used to describe all people whose native language is not French or English. The vast majority of them live in the large cities, particularly

Toronto, Montreal, and Vancouver. Punjabi, Italian, Spanish, German, Cantonese, Tagalog, and Arabic (in that order) are the principal allophone languages. Although there are more than 50 indigenous languages, those who speak them number less than 1% of the population.

Ethnic Composition

Canadian – 32.2%; English – 19.8%; French – 15.5%; Scottish – 14.4%; Irish – 13.8%; German – 9.8%; Italian – 4.5%; Chinese – 4.5%; North American Indian – 4.2%; other – 50.9% (Some respondents identified more than one ethnic origin.)

Language

French and English are the official languages.

Religion

Catholic – 40.6%; Protestant – 20.3%; Anglican – 8%; Muslim – 3.2%; Hindu – 1.5%; Sikh – 1.4%; Buddhist – 1.1%; Jewish – 1%; other – 0.6%; none – 23.9%

CONTEMPORARY ISSUES

Immigration

Although the Canadian government has in recent years mounted legislation to promote immigration, the current influx of new citizens has not been sufficient to meet the demands for employment. The nation has the world's highest per-capita immigration rate. To offset the effect of Canadians living longer—combined with a declining birth rate—the Canadian government has set a goal of increasing immigration each year by 1% of the current population. The Immigration and Refugee Protection Act (IRPA) went into effect in 2002, with the aim of not only speeding up the processing of applications but also with the intent of attracting "the best and the brightest" to Canada. The IRPA operates on a point system that favors immigrants who speak one or both of the nation's official languages—English or French—as well as university graduates or others who have in-demand professional skills. In 2007, it was reported that the immigration system was backlogged with more than 800,000 applicants, who faced a four-year wait for possible admission.

In 2015, Canada will introduce a new system of immigration called "Express Entry." Under this program, potential immigrants are matched with labor market needs based on their skills. If accepted, candidates' citizenship applications will be processed within six months. The new system is intended to speed up processing time and fill the most-needed positions in the job market, including shortages in the blue-collar sector. Caps on application numbers have been introduced in order to eliminate the processing backlog experienced in previous years.

In addition, Canada has a temporary worker program to attract foreign nationals to Canada without granting them citizenship. This program is intended to fill labor shortages in lower-skilled and short-term industries. The program came under scrutiny first in 2013, when accusations surfaced that some businesses were replacing Canadian workers with the minimum-wage, temporary workers. The government introduced reforms to the program in 2013 and 2014 to improve the system and avoid similar problems in the future.

U.S.–Canadian Relations

The United States and Canada share the longest undefended border in the world, and relations between the two countries have historically been friendly. Following the September 11, 2001, terrorist attacks, U.S. Border Control officials and their Canadian counterparts stepped up their cooperation with each other, sharing intelligence information and office space. Issues involving trade, however, have resulted in disagreements and controversy. The two countries have the largest trade relationship in the world, boosted by the 1989 Canada–U.S. Free Trade Agreement and the North American Free Trade Agreement (NAFTA), enacted in 1994. In 2005, there was a dispute over U.S.-leveraged trade tariffs on Canadian lumber that Canadian authorities and eventually a NAFTA panel found to be in violation of the North American Free Trade Agreement. The provision to "Buy American" in the American Recovery and Reinvestment Act of 2009 also sparked tension between the two countries. Recently, the Keystone XL Pipeline, meant to transport oil from Canada's oil sands to the Gulf of Mexico, has met with divided opinion in the United States and a delayed decision by President Barack Obama on whether or not to allow the pipeline to intersect the midwestern United States.

The two nations have also locked horns on issues involving the Arctic waters of the Northwest Passage, a region over which Canada claims sovereignty. Global warming has increased thawing of ice cover in the Arctic Ocean by about 8% per decade, increasing the capacity of the passage to accept large ships. With the width of the waterway increasing, it has grown more attractive to companies shipping long distances. A typical trip from Europe to Asia through the Panama Canal covers about 12,900 nautical miles, whereas using the Northwest Passage can reduce the distance to some 7,900 nautical miles, saving millions of dollars in shipping costs. Canada contends that the waters represent an internal waterway similar to the Mississippi River in the United States, while the United States maintains that beyond the 12-mile territorial limits surrounding Canada's islands in the Arctic, the passageway is in international waters.

Quebec Sovereignty

The mainly French-speaking people of the province of Quebec believe themselves to be culturally distinct from the rest of the country and have pressed in the recent past for increased autonomy or even secession—although much of the region's population does not want full independence, because it is aware of the economic benefits of remaining linked to the rest of the country. The separatists lost two independence referendums, one decisively in 1980, the other narrowly in 1995. In November 2006, Prime Minister Stephen Harper moved that Quebec be recognized as a "nation within a united Canada," a largely symbolic motion that Parliament approved.

Excerpt from the Canadian Charter of Rights and Freedoms

The Canadian Charter of Rights and Freedoms, adopted in 1982, enumerates the rights of Canada's citizens and permanent residents. Most of the rights enumerated in the Charter were specified previously in the Canadian Bill of Rights, although the Bill of Rights was a law that did not have constitutional status.

The Charter begins with the statement, "Canada is founded upon the principles that recognize the supremacy of God and the rule of law." The charter specifies fundamental rights analogous to those specified in the First Amendment to the U.S. Constitution, including freedom of speech, religion, and assembly.

Most of the other rights specified in the Charter are political rights, as opposed to economic rights. Many of these parallel those specified in the U.S. Constitution, including the right to vote, the right to a fair trial, and the right to equal protection under the law. It also specifies language equality, and all Canadian government documents are now published in both English and French.

Unlike the United States, the provision for equal protection under the law in Canada specifically authorizes affirmative action programs. However, in contrast to some European countries, the Charter does not specify the right to health care, education, or social services. The Canadian judiciary has ruled in several cases that questions of economic rights do not enjoy the constitutional status of political rights as specified in the Charter.

Constitution Act, 1982

Part I

Canadian Charter of Rights and Freedoms

Whereas Canada is founded upon the principles that recognize the supremacy of God and the rule of law:

Guarantee of Rights and Freedoms

The Canadian Charter of Rights and Freedoms guarantees the rights and freedoms set out in it subject only to such reasonable limits prescribed by law as can be demonstrably justified in a free and democratic society.

Fundamental Freedoms

Everyone has the following fundamental freedoms:

(a) freedom of conscience and religion
(b) freedom of thought, belief, opinion and expression, including freedom of the press and other means of communication.
(c) freedom of peaceful assembly; and
(d) freedom of association.

Democratic Rights

Every citizen of Canada has the right to vote in an election of members of the House of Commons or of a legislative assembly and to be qualified for membership therein.

Mobility Rights

Every citizen of Canada has the right to enter, remain in, and leave Canada.
Every citizen of Canada and every person who has the status of a permanent resident of Canada has the right

(a) to move to and take up residence in an province; and
(b) to pursue the gaining of livelyhood in any province.

Legal Rights

Everyone has the right to life, liberty and security of the person and the right not to be deprived thereof except in accordance with the principles of fundamental justice.
Everyone has the right to be secure against unreasonable search or seizure.
Everyone has the right not to be arbitrarily detained or imprisoned.
Everyone has the right on arrest or detention

(a) to be informed promptly of the reason therefor;
(b) to retain and instruct counsel without delay and to be informed of that right; and
(c) to have the validity of the detention determined

by way of habeas corpus and to be released if the detention is not lawful.

Any person charged with an offence has the right

(a) to be informed without unreasonable delay of the specific offence;
(b) to be tried within a reasonable time;
(c) not to be compelled to be a witness in a proceedings against that person in respect of the offence;
(d) to be presumed innocent until proven guilty according to law in a fair and public hearing by an independent and impartial tribunal;
(e) not to be denied reasonable bail without cause;
(f) except in the case of an offence under military law tried before a military tribunal, to the benefit of trial by jury where the maximum punishment for the offence is imprisonment for five years or a more severe punishment;
(g) not to be found guilty on account of any act or omission unless, at the time of the act or omission, it constituted an offence under Canadian or International law or was criminal according to the general principles of law recognized by the community of nations;
(h) if finally acquitted of the offence, not to be tried for it again and, if finally found guilty and punished for the offence, not to be tried or punished for it again; and
(i) if found guilty of the offence and if punishment for the offence has been varied between the time of commission and the time of sentencing, to the benefit of the lesser punishment.

Everyone has the right not to be subjected to any cruel or unusual treatment or punishment.

A witness who testifies in any proceedings has the right not to have any incriminating evidence so given used to incriminate that witness in any other proceedings, except in a prosecution for perjury or for the giving of contradictory evidence.

A party or witness in any proceedings who does not understand or speak the language in which the proceedings are conducted or who is deaf has the right to the assistance of an interpreter.

Equality Rights

Every individual is equal before and under the law and has the right to the equal protection and equal benefit of the law without discrimination based on race, national or ethnic origin, colour, religion, sex, age, or mental or physical disability.

Subsection (1) does not preclude any law, program or activity that has as its object the amelioration of conditions of disadvantaged individuals or groups including those that are disadvantaged because of race, national or ethnic origin, colour, religion, sex, age, or mental or physical disability.

Official Languages of Canada

Everyone has the right to use English or French in any debates or other proceedings of Parliament.

Everyone has the right to use English or French in any debate and other proceeding of the legislature of New Brunswick.

Any member of the public of Canada has the right to communicate with, and to receive available services from, any head or central office of an institution of the Parliament or government of Canada in English or French, and has the same right with respect to any other office of any such institution where

(a) there is significant demand for communications with and services from that office in such language;
or
(b) due to the nature of the office, it is reasonable that communications with and services from that office be available in both English and French.

Citizens of Canada of whom any child has received or is receiving primary or secondary school instruction in English or French in Canada, have the right to have all their children receive primary and secondary school instruction in the same language.

Source: "Constitutional Documents in Canada." University of Ottawa/Constitutional Law. http://www.uottawa.ca/constitutional-law/docs.html.

FRANCE: Republic

FRANCE

Communications	Television
Facebook Users	66 sets per 100 population (2005)
26,000,000 (estimate) (2013)	Land-based Telephones in Use
Internet Users	
45,262,000 (2009)	39,290,000 (2012)
Internet Users (% of Population)	Mobile Telephone Subscribers
81.9% (2013)	62,280,000 (2012)

Major Daily Newspapers	**Secondary School–age Females Enrolled in Secondary School**
103 (2005)	
Average Circulation of Daily Newspapers	2,897,676 (2011)
9,973,422 (2005)	**Students Per Teacher, Primary School**
Education	17.8 (2012)
School System	**Students Per Teacher, Secondary School**
French students begin primary school at the age of six. After five years, they continue to four years of early secondary school, known as college, and then to either a two-year academic program at a lycée or a two-year vocational program at a professional lycée. Students in the vocational track may continue for an additional two years in a professional program.	12.8 (2012)
	Enrollment in Tertiary Education
	2,296,306 (2012)
	Enrollment in Tertiary Education, Male
	1,037,166 (2012)
	Enrollment in Tertiary Education, Female
Mandatory Education	1,259,140 (2012)
10 years, from ages 6 to 16.	**Literacy**
Average Years Spent in School for Current Students	99% (2005)
16 (2012)	**Energy and Natural Resources**
Average Years Spent in School for Current Students, Male	**Electric Power Generation**
16 (2012)	561,200,000,000 kilowatt hours per year (estimate) (2012)
Average Years Spent in School for Current Students, Female	**Electric Power Consumption**
16 (2012)	462,900,000,000 kilowatt hours per year (estimate) (2012)
Primary School–age Children Enrolled in Primary School	**Nuclear Power Plants**
4,155,596 (2012)	58 (2014)
Primary School–age Males Enrolled in Primary School	**Crude Oil Production**
2,126,502 (2012)	70,300 barrels per day (2013)
Primary School–age Females Enrolled in Primary School	**Crude Oil Consumption**
2,029,094 (2012)	217,400 barrels per day (2010)
Secondary School–age Children Enrolled in Secondary School	**Crude Oil Consumption**
5,920,216 (2012)	1,733,000 barrels per day (2013)
Secondary School–age Males Enrolled in Secondary School	**Natural Gas Production**
5,920,216 (2012)	508,000,000 cubic meters per year (estimate) (2012)
	Natural Gas Consumption
	47,990,000,000 cubic meters per year (estimate) (2010)

Natural Resources	Land Use
Coal, iron ore, bauxite, zinc, uranium, antimony, arsenic, potash, feldspar, fluorspar, gypsum, timber, fish	33.7% arable land; 25.7% temporary crops; 2.0% permanent crops; 18.1% permanent meadows and pastures; 28.5% forest land; 17.7% other.
CO2 Emissions	
5.6 metric tons per capita (2009)	**Arable Land**
Alternative and Nuclear Energy	34% (2007)
48.0% of total energy use (2011)	**Arable Land Per Capita**
Threatened Species	1 acres per person (2007)
168 (2010)	**Health**
Protected Areas	**Average Life Expectancy**
106,375 (estimate) (2010)	81.7 years (2014)
Geography	**Average Life Expectancy, Male**
Location	78.6 years (2014)
Located in western Europe, France is bordered by the English Channel to the northwest, Belgium and Luxembourg to the northeast, Germany and Switzerland to the east, Italy to the southeast, the Mediterranean Sea and Spain to the south, and the Atlantic Ocean to the west. The island of Corsica is considered part of metropolitan France, while 10 separate overseas departments and territories also form an integral part of the republic.	**Average Life Expectancy, Female**
	84.9 years (2014)
	Crude Birth Rate
	12.4 (estimate) (2015)
	Crude Death Rate
	9.2 (estimate) (2015)
	Maternal Mortality
	17 per 100,000 live births (2005–2012 projection)
Time Zone	**Infant Mortality**
6 hours ahead of U.S. Eastern Standard	3 per 1,000 live births (2012)
Land Borders	**Doctors**
1,797 miles	3.2 per 1,000 people (2012)
Coastline	**Industry and Labor**
2,130 miles (includes Corsica)	**Gross Domestic Product (GDP) - official exchange rate**
Capital	
Paris	$3,021,356,000,000 (estimate) (2015)
Area	**GDP per Capita**
211,154 sq. miles	$47,030 (estimate) (2015)
Climate	**GDP - Purchasing Power Parity (PPP)**
The climate throughout France is temperate and rainfall is frequent throughout the year. The southern part of the country has warm Mediterranean summers and mild winters. Temperatures in Paris range from 32°F to 75°F.	$2,289,622,000,000 (estimate) (2013)
	GDP (PPP) per Capita
	$35,942 (estimate) (2013)

Industry Products	**Economic Aid Received**
Steel, machinery and equipment, textiles and clothing, chemicals, automobiles, processed food, refined minerals, metals, electronics. There is also a highly developed tourist industry.	$0 (2011)
	Population
	Population
	66,553,766 (estimate) (2015)
Agriculture Products	**World Population Rank**
Wheat, barley, beef, sugar beets, dairy products, cereals, wine grapes, potatoes.	21 st (2010)
Unemployment	**Population Density**
9.9% (2012)	31.2 people per square mile (estimate) (2011)
Labor Profile	**Population Distribution**
agriculture: 3.8% industry: 24.3% services: 71.8% (2005)	85% urban (2011)
Military	**Age Distribution**
Total Active Armed Forces	0-14: 18.6%
352,771 (2010)	15-64: 64.9
Active Armed Forces	65+: 16.5%
1% (2010)	(2009)
Annual Military Expenditures	**Median Age**
$47,800,000,000 (2009)	40.9 years (estimate) (2014)
Military Service	**Population Growth Rate**
Terms of service in the French military are 10 months long but can voluntarily be extended to one to two years.	0.4% per year (estimate) (2015)
	Net Migration Rate
	1.1 (estimate) (2015)
National Finances	**Trade**
Currency	**Imported Goods**
Euro	Machinery, passenger cars, chemicals, mineral fuels and lubricants, textile yarns and fabric, iron and steel, plastic materials, meat and meat products, fruits and vegetables.
Total Government Revenues	
$1,410,000,000,000 (estimate) (2013)	
Total Government Expenditures	
$1,522,000,000,000 (estimate) (2013)	**Total Value of Imports**
Budget Deficit	$559,646,000,000 (2009)
-4.1 (estimate) (2013)	**Exported Goods**
GDP Contribution by Sector	Organic chemicals, cereals, pharmaceuticals, beverages, tobacco, clothing, industrial machinery, office equipment, road vehicles and parts, iron and steel, essential oils and perfume materials.
agriculture: 2% industry: 18.8% services: 79.2% (2012 est.)	
External Debt	
$5,371,000,000,000 (estimate) (2012)	
Economic Aid Extended	**Total Value of Exports**
$8,494,690,000 (2011)	$567,500,000,000 (estimate) (2012)

Import Partners	Paved Roads
Germany - 19.4%; Belgium - 11.6%; Italy - 8.0%; Netherlands - 7.1%; Spain - 6.7% (2009)	100.0% (2010)
	Roads, Unpaved
Export Partners	Not Available
Germany - 15.9%; Italy - 8.2%; Spain - 7.8%; Belgium - 7.4%; United Kingdom - 7.0% (2009)	**Passenger Cars per 1,000 People**
	481 (2010)
Current Account Balance	**Number of Trucks, Buses, and Commercial Vehicles**
$-58,970,000,000 (estimate) (2013)	6,424,000 (2003)
Weights and Measures	**Railroads**
The metric system is in use.	18,152 (2008)
Transportation	**Ports**
Airports	Major: 10—(including Marseille, Le Havre, Dunkerque, Nantes, Rouen, Bordeaux).
473 (2012)	

OVERVIEW

France is one of the world's most advanced industrial nations, and its culture has had an impact all over the world, in large part because of the nation's history as a colonial power. The Western European country still has several overseas possessions, including Corsica, which is considered part of metropolitan France. Metropolitan France has a population of more than 60 million people. Most of the country has mild summers and cool winters, while the Mediterranean coast experiences hotter summers. The French Alps, in the east of the country, are famed for their ski resorts. The nation's capital is Paris, which is considered one of the most beautiful cities in the world and, by many estimates, one of the world's top tourist destinations.

GOVERNMENT

France was first unified as a kingdom by the Merovingian ruler Clovis in 486. As leader of one of two major dynasties in France, Clovis controlled the southern region of modern-day France and Burgundy. The French Republic (République Française) today has a bicameral legislature comprising a Senate and a National Assembly. The president appoints a cabinet and prime minister, responsible for administering the country. The prime minister is accountable to the legislature. The current president of France is François Hollande, and Manuel Valls is the prime minister.

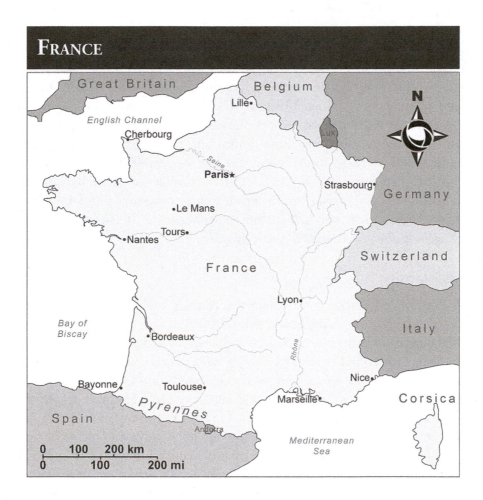

Constitution

The current French Constitution was approved by a national referendum and promulgated in 1958. It was intended to significantly increase the authority of the president within the joint presidential-parliamentary form of government. The Constitution's preamble proclaims the rights of man, national sovereignty, and democratic evolution for the community, consisting of the French republic and its overseas territories. Its 92 articles specify the powers and limitations of the executive, the legislature, and the judicial system.

Executive

Executive power is held by the president, who is popularly elected for a five-year renewable term. The president is the head of state and commander of the armed forces and has the authority to dissolve the National Assembly and arrange for new elections, to call for a national referendum on particular issues, and to assume complete legislative and executive powers during a crisis. The president also possesses a wide range of powers in the realm of foreign affairs and defense, including the right to negotiate and ratify treaties. The power of the president to nominate members of the body that nominates judges and magistrates was reduced by a constitutional amendment adopted in July 1993. The Constitutional Council, which serves as a partial check on the president, must be consulted if emergency powers are invoked. The president appoints a prime minister, who nominates a Council of Ministers (cabinet) that is formally appointed by the president. The prime minister directs the operation of the government, is responsible for national defense, and ensures the execution of the laws. The prime minister and the cabinet are responsible to the National Assembly and are subject to its censure. Ministers are prohibited from holding concurrent seats in the legislature.

Legislature

The bicameral Parliament (Parlement) consists of a Senate (Sénat) and a National Assembly (Assemblée Nationale). The Senate has 348 members, with 328 seats allocated for metropolitan France and overseas departments, 8 seats for the overseas territories, and 12 seats for French nationals abroad. Senators are selected by an electoral college for six-year terms, and one-third of the Senate's membership is renewable every three years. Since 1958, the Sénat has been delegated to a subordinate position, with little power other than the ability to delay legislation under consideration by the Assembly, although the Constitution provides that, in the event of a vacated presidency, the Senate president becomes interim president of the republic until an election takes place. In the 577-seat Assemblée Nationale, 555 deputies serve metropolitan France, and 22 deputies represent overseas departments and territories. Assembly members are popularly elected through a single-member majority system and serve a five-year term subject to dissolution. Specific legislation can be initiated by the assembly in such areas as electoral procedure, the penal code, declaration of war, amnesty, civil rights and liberties, liability to taxation, and the nationalization of industries. The Constitutional Council is a separate 9-member body (with nine-year terms) that ensures the validity of presidential and legislative elections and the regularity of the referendum procedure and also rules on the constitutionality of laws passed by Parlement. The president must consult the Council if he or she invokes emergency powers.

Judiciary

The judicial system is headed by a Court of Cassation, which rules on the interpretation of law and the procedural actions of other courts. The courts of assize (*cours d'assises*) are called upon to hear major criminal cases but have no regular sittings. Subordinate cases are tried by tribunals of first instance (*tribunaux d'instance*), and by tribunals of grand instance (*tribunaux de grande instance*) for more serious offenses. Commercial and correctional tribunals parallel the instance courts, and boards of arbitration settle work disputes. There are specialized tribunals for children under 18 years of age. Appeals from all the tribunals go to the courts of appeal, which also preside over the assize courts.

Local Government

Metropolitan France is divided into 22 regional provinces containing 96 administrative departments, which are headed by locally elected departmental assemblies and regional assemblies. Other units of local government include communes, cantons, and districts. The island of Corsica, which is considered part of metropolitan France, has its own popularly elected legislative assembly.

Overseas Possessions

France has five overseas regions (Guadeloupe, French Guiana, Martinique, Mayotte, and Reunion); five overseas collectivities (French Polynesia, St. Barthélemy, Saint-Martin, St. Pierre and Miquelon, and the Wallis and Futuna Islands); one *sui generis* (unique) collectivity (New Caledonia); one overseas territory (the French Southern and Antarctic Lands); and six uninhabited overseas possessions (Bassas da India, Clipperton Island, Europa Island, Glorioso Islands, Juan de Nova, and Tromelin Island). A General Council and a Regional Council administer the overseas regions, a high commissioner administers the overseas collectivities, and an appointed commissioner administers the territories.

Election Qualifications

All citizens 18 years of age and older have the right to vote.

POLITICS

Following World War II, the French government was challenged with rebuilding a devastated nation. This included nationalizing commerce and industry, developing a welfare state, granting the vote to women, decolonizing Africa and Indochina, and entering into the new European Economic Community (now the European Union).

The mid-1980s saw rising dissatisfaction based on increasing unemployment and racial tensions. The tensions continued through the 1990s, due in large part to the continuing influx and assimilation of Muslim immigrants, legal and illegal, mainly from France's former colonial holdings.

The early 2000s brought a devolution of powers to regional governments, from the highly centralized national government. In 2005, France surprised the

European Union (EU) when French voters rejected the EU's proposed constitution, based on fears that France would lose its sovereignty and that the document would allow an influx of immigrants into the country. Also in 2005, unrest in the Arab and African Muslim community over lack of socioeconomic opportunity resulted in 20 nights of rioting. The government responded by providing more support and jobs to immigrants and their families, but the divisions continue.

In 2012, François Hollande won the presidential campaign based on an agenda to pull France out of the global recession. Hollande failed on his campaign promise to reduce unemployment by the end of 2013 and has raised taxes. In addition, his intervention in a high-profile deportation case of a Roma teen in 2013, contributed to a new low in his approval rating among the French people. In August 2014, Hollande ordered his prime minister, Manuel Valls, to form a new cabinet, after the ministers of economy, culture, and education publicly criticized Hollande's austerity measures. Hollande is France's first Socialist president since François Mitterrand in 1995.

Political Parties

France's political infrastructure is characterized by multiple political parties because of its system of proportional representation.

President Francois Hollande of France. A member of France's Socialist Party, he defeated incumbent Nicolas Sarkozy in 2012 to win a seven-year term as President. (WITT/SIPA/Newscom)

The Union for a Popular Movement (Union pour un Mouvement Populaire—UMP) became an official political party in November 2002. A conservative group with a liberal economic policy, the UMP is the successor to the Rally for the Republic (Rassemblement pour la République—RPR). The RPR was formed in 1976 from the original Gaullist Party and was composed of a variety of groups, united largely by their commitment to French nationalism and the ideals of Charles de Gaulle, World War II hero and founder and first president of the current republic. Its outlook was generally center-right, and it gained support from the middle and upper classes and the rural areas. In June 2002, the RPR formed the Union for the Presidential Majority alliance with the Liberal Democracy, to contest legislative elections, and the party took on its current name shortly after UPM candidate Jacques Chirac (formerly of the RPR) won reelection to the French presidency. The UMP was the ruling party during the one-term 2007–2012 presidency of Nicolas Sarkozy.

The Socialist Party (Parti Socialiste—PS) is committed to achieving moderate socialist and social welfare goals through the democratic process. It advocates the nationalization of key industries and gains its support primarily from labor and trade unions but also has a substantial following among civil servants and the intelligentsia. The Socialist Party rose to become France's ruling party following the victory of François Hollande in the presidential election of May 2012.

The National Front (Front National—FN) is an extreme right-wing group, characterized by many observers as fascist, that stresses an anti-immigration program, rejects all forms of socialism, and advocates popular capitalism. The FN, which draws its support from the urban working class, was led for many years by Jean-Marie Le Pen. It lost its only Parliament seat after the June 2002 legislative election. The party attracted one of its highest vote counts ever in preliminary voting during the run-up to the 2012 presidential election.

The French Communist Party (Parti Communiste Français—PCF) endorses a policy of "socialism in the colors of France," and was deeply influenced by the now-defunct Soviet Communist Party. It opposes the nation's membership in the North Atlantic Treaty Organization (NATO) and the European Union. The PCF is supported by labor and the trade union movement and is a powerful and effective force in local government.

The Union of Democrats and Independents (Union des Démocrates et Indépendants—UDI) and Democratic Movement (Mouvement Démocrate—MoDem) are two centrist parties that formed a coalition in 2014, known as UDI-MoDem.

An ecological party, the Greens (les Verts) is committed to the protection of France's natural resources and environment. The Greens gained only three seats in the National Assembly in 2002. It is presently in an alliance with the PCF.

Smaller French political parties include the liberal Radical Party of the Left (Parti Radical de Gauche—PRG), the socialist Republican and Citizen Movement (Mouvement Républicain et Citoyen—MRC), and the conservative nationalist Movement for France (Mouvement pour la France—MPF) and Rally for France (Rassemblement pour la France—RPF).

ECONOMY

Although France was slower to industrialize than many of its European neighbors, it has advanced rapidly, and in 2014 it had the fifth-largest economy in the world. Large segments of the economy are under state control. The nation is the largest agricultural exporter on the continent, its most significant crops being barley, maize, wheat, and sugar beets. Wine and livestock production are also central to the agricultural economy. The principal products of the industrial sector are processed food, transportation equipment, machinery, and chemical products. There is also a significant luxury goods sector, as well as a growing service sector. Natural resources include bauxite, coal, zinc, fish, and timber. A large proportion of the nation's exports come from the defense industry. Inflation is generally low, but unemployment is relatively high. Living standards are also quite high, with the per-capita gross domestic product hovering at $35,700 in 2013. France conducts the majority of its trade with Germany, Italy, and Belgium. France, along with Germany, has the largest economy in the eurozone. Both countries' economic expansion in 2013 was credited for pulling the eurozone out of a one-and-a-half-year recession.

SOCIETY

Mediterranean, Alpine, and Nordic peoples form the majority of the French population, but in recent decades immigrants from former colonies in Africa and Asia, as well as from other European countries, have made up 6% of the population. Some 80% of the French are Roman Catholic, and the historical influence of the Church has been central to French culture. The country's 4 million Muslims make up the second-largest religious group, with Protestants, Jews, and Buddhists forming smaller groups. French law guarantees freedom of worship, and in recent years the government has worked to reverse the country's long history of anti-Semitism. The French language is jealously guarded by purists who resist the use of such English imports as *le weekend* or *le jogging*. Throughout the nineteenth and well into the twentieth century, French was considered the language of culture by most educated people in Europe and the Americas. It continues to be the only European language known by millions of people in Asia and the Middle East, and is the only language shared by millions of Africans.

Ethnic Composition

The majority of the population is of Celtic and Latin descent, with Teutonic, Slavic, North African, Indochinese, and Basque minorities.

Religion

Roman Catholic – 83%–88%; Muslim – 5%–10%; unaffiliated – 4%; Protestant – 2%; Jewish – 1%

Language

French is the official language. Regional dialects are declining rapidly.

CONTEMPORARY ISSUES

Treatment of Roma

France is home to one of the largest Romani populations in Europe, with estimates of the number of Roma in the country ranging from 300,000 to 500,000. Roma, once known as "gypsies," are an ethnic group who live primarily in Europe. The group, many of whom are nomadic, have been persecuted for generations. According to the European Roma Rights Center, Roma in France suffer widespread discrimination. Although anti-discrimination laws are in place in France, some charge that these laws are rarely enforced in cases of anti-Roma discrimination and repression; unfair treatment of Roma within the French legal system has also been alleged.

Local laws also frequently make it difficult or even impossible for nomadic Roma to halt the vehicles in which they live in or near towns and cities, and designated areas where halting is allowed are often intentionally secluded from the rest of the community, forcing seclusion on Roma who park there. Voting is also somewhat suppressed among Roma, due to local residency requirements that are often difficult for Roma to meet. For example, people living in vehicles with circulation permits, like many Roma, must reside in the same area for three years before they are allowed to vote, while homeless people have to reside in an area only for six months before they can vote. Further, nomadic people considered part of a local population can by law constitute no more than 3% of that population, ensuring that nomads like the Roma have very limited political power.

In August 2010, France attracted international condemnation when it deported some 1,000 Roma who had traveled to France legally under European Union (EU) travel laws, but who had stayed in the country longer than three months without attaining employment, after which time France was free under EU law to deport them. In 2013, the government again came under attack for deporting a record number of Roma (nearly 11,000) and forcibly removing Roma schoolgirl Leonarda

The Romani or Roma people, sometimes referred to derogatorily as "gypsies," are a minority population in France and other European countries. About 500,000 Romani live in France, where many live outside the mainstream of French society in slums or rural villages. (WENNMAN MAGNUS/ZUMA Press/Newscom)

Dibrani, 15, from a school bus to deport her and her family back to Kosovo. The family had made several failed attempts to gain residency. The action was followed by widespread protest; however, in early 2014, a French court upheld the decision to deport the Dibrani family.

Poverty among French Youth

Where once the majority of the poor in France were retirees, there has been a large increase in unemployment among young people since the 1980s. In October 2005, rioting broke out in the low-income neighborhood of Clichy-sous-Bois, outside of Paris, after two impoverished youths were killed and a third injured while fleeing from police. The rioting intensified and spread to other low-income areas, and destruction of property and vehicles was rampant, as a hardline government stance provoked further unrest. The rioters were primarily young, impoverished children of immigrants from North Africa whose parents had struggled in a postindustrial French economy. After almost three weeks of rioting, a government crackdown put an end to the violence, but the underlying poverty and feelings of marginalization remain.

When the French government proposed raising the retirement age in 2010, many French youths were outraged, as delaying retirement directly diminished the number of jobs available to them, making the unemployment problem worse. Many students joined strikes organized by workers' groups, forcing schools to shut down, and violent conflict again erupted between police and younger strikers. In the end, though, the French government did not drop its plans to raise the retirement age; however, in 2012 the new socialist government reversed the decision and dropped the retirement age to 60 instead of 62. The move has been criticized by many financial experts, as it is expected to cost the state billions of euros each year.

The Muslim Community in France

The Islamic community in France is generally better assimilated into French society than Muslims in many other European countries, but there is some conflict between the ardently secular French government and followers of Islam, and this conflict has been on the rise in recent years. In September 2004, a law banning the wearing of overtly religious symbols in public schools came into effect after more than a decade of legislative debate over the wearing of headscarves and hijab veils by Muslim students. Though the ban was mostly tolerated by French Muslims, a number of Muslim students were expelled from schools for failing to observe the new law. This law was deemed unfair by many, since there are far fewer private Muslim schools to which parents can send their children than Catholic or Protestant Christian schools, and many Muslims felt the law was specifically directed at their faith. Despite the protest, in 2010 the French government enacted a formal ban on the wearing of full face scarves in public. The following year, a ban on Muslim street prayers went into effect in the capital, Paris.

France has also seen the exodus of young people to Syria and elsewhere to fight for Islamic extremist groups. Since the Syrian conflict began in 2011, 900 French citizens have left to fight in the war against the Syrian government. In 2014, France's government was pursuing an anti-terrorism bill intended to stop citizens from joining jihadist groups. The majority of French Muslims are of North African origin, largely hailing from the former French colonies of Algeria, Tunisia, and Morocco.

Terrorism

As one of the most visible and powerful nations in the world, the global rise in terrorist activity is concerning to the French. There have been serious threats of terrorist attacks from radical Islamist groups within France since the early 1990s, when French support for the military regime in Algeria earned the ire of Islamist terrorist networks worldwide, and successful attacks were carried out in 1994 and 1995. Recruitment by these networks and their successors has been largely from the impoverished youth of Arab and North African descent who populate many of France's urban slums. The French government has been quite successful in thwarting attacks for the last decade, but a significant threat to the country still exists. The Basque terrorist organization known as Basque Homeland and Liberty (Euskadi ta Askatasuna—ETA) has also been a threat to France, although it primarily operates in Spain and in 2012 announced plans to disband. Many ETA leaders live in the French Basque Country, feeling that the area is safer than in Spain, and a French crackdown on these leaders began in June 2007. Corsican separatist organizations also pose a potential threat, particularly to French politicians and government interests on the island of Corsica itself.

Privatization and Protectionism

Since 2003, the French government has been selling large portions of its state-owned companies to private investors in an attempt to bolster the economy. In 2005, the government sold large percentages of its stake in the utility companies Electricité de France, Gaz de France, and France Télécom (electrical, gas, and television, respectively). The government has ensured that it retains a large enough share of these and similar companies so that it can prevent a complete private takeover, but some other companies were sold entirely. Following the May 2007 election of Nicolas Sarkozy as president, a backlash of economic protectionism was proposed, to prevent foreign control of French industries and protect domestic investment and production. Rising unemployment levels prompted protective action, and the government has blocked the sale of industrially essential French companies to foreign buyers in 2006 and 2007. These and other attempts to promote domestic industries are intended to curb unemployment among unskilled laborers, particularly the immigrant population. France's high unemployment rate (10% in recent years), amid calls by conservative politicians such as then-president Nicolas Sarkozy for deep cuts in spending for the poor and middle class, led directly to Sarkozy's defeat in the May 2012 presidential election by Socialist François Hollande.

Corsican Independence

Since the 1960s, there has been a movement seeking independence for the island of Corsica. Separatist groups there have been engaging in attacks and protests for more than four decades, but the most serious attack occurred in 1998, when the *préfet* (prefect) of Corsica was assassinated. The separatist attacks have been subsiding in the 2000s. In 2014, Corsica's largest militant group, the Corsican National Liberation Front (FLNC) declared they would cease using violence to pursue independence and instead pursue autonomy through politics. And there are others who are pursuing independence by political means rather than violent. In 2010, two pro-independence political parties won a combined 15 seats (out of 51) in the regional assembly.

Excerpt from the Constitution of France

The Constitution of France, establishing France's Fifth Republic, went into effect in 1958. As specified in the Preamble, the Constitution's guarantees of human rights are based on those identified in the Declaration of the Rights of Man and the Citizen, *which was written and put into effect during the French Revolution in 1789. The Constitution identifies France as a democracy and a secular state.*

Consistent with France's self-identification with "liberty, equality, and fraternity," the Preamble pays particular attention to individual liberty. Liberty is guaranteed in that "the exercise of the natural rights of every man has no bounds other than those that ensure to the other members of society the enjoyment of these same rights." It also guarantees the right to vote, the right to property, and the right to freedom of speech. Yet it also calls attention to the need for a "public force," thus authorizing the government to levy taxes upon citizens. In general, the French constitution, unlike many more recently written constitutions, does not deal with rights associated with health care, education, and social securities. Its principles are similar to those of the Constitution of the United States, which was written at approximately the same time and which is also does not identify these services as fundamental rights.

Declaration of the Rights of Man and of the Citizen

Declaration of the Rights of Man and of the Citizen [1789] Adopted by the National Assembly during the French Revolution on August 26, 1789, and reaffirmed by the constitution of 1958.

Preamble

The representatives of the French people, formed into a National Assembly, considering ignorance, forgetfulness or contempt of the rights of man to be the only causes of public misfortunes and the corruption of Governments, have resolved to set forth, in a solemn Declaration, the natural, unalienable and sacred rights of man, to the end that this Declaration, constantly present to all members of the body politic, may remind them unceasingly of their rights and their duties . . .

In consequence whereof, the National Assembly recognizes and declares, in the presence and under the auspices of the Supreme Being, the following Rights of Man and of the Citizen.

Article first—Men are born and remain free and equal in rights. Social distinctions may be based only on considerations of the common good.

Article 2—The aim of every political association is the preservation of the natural and imprescriptible rights of man. These rights are Liberty, Property, Safety and Resistance to Oppression.

Article 3—The source of all sovereignty lies essentially in the Nation. No corporate body, no individual may exercise any authority that does not expressly emanate from it.

Article 4—Liberty consists in being able to do anything that does not harm others: thus, the exercise of the natural rights of every man has no bounds other than those that ensure to the other members of society the enjoyment of these same rights. These bounds may be determined only by Law.

Article 5—The Law has the right to forbid only those actions that are injurious to society. Nothing that is not forbidden by Law may be hindered, and no one may be compelled to do what the Law does not ordain.

Article 6—The Law is the expression of the general will. All citizens have the right to take part, personally or through their representatives, in its making. It must be the same for all, whether it protects or punishes. All citizens, being equal in its eyes, shall be equally eligible to all high offices, public positions and employments, according to their ability, and without other distinction than that of their virtues and talents.

Article 7—No man may be accused, arrested or detained except in the cases determined by the Law, and following the procedure that it has prescribed. Those who solicit, expedite, carry out, or cause to be carried out arbitrary orders must be punished; but any citizen summoned or apprehended by virtue of the Law, must give instant obedience; resistance makes him guilty.

Article 8—The Law must prescribe only the punishments that are strictly and evidently necessary; and no one may be punished except by virtue of a Law drawn up and promulgated before the offense is committed, and legally applied.

Article 9—As every man is presumed innocent until he has been declared guilty, if it should be considered necessary to arrest him, any undue harshness that is not required to secure his person must be severely curbed by Law.

Article 10—No one may be disturbed on account of his opinions, even religious ones, as long as the manifestation of such opinions does not interfere with the established Law and Order.

Article 11—The free communication of ideas and of opinions is one of the most precious rights of man. Any citizen may therefore speak, write and publish freely, except what is tantamount to the abuse of this liberty in the cases determined by Law.

Article 12—To guarantee the Rights of Man and of the Citizen a public force is necessary; this force is therefore established for the benefit of all, and not for the particular use of those to whom it is entrusted.

Article 13—For the maintenance of the public force, and for administrative expenses, a general tax is indispensable; it must be equally distributed among all citizens, in proportion to their ability to pay.

Article 14—All citizens have the right to ascertain, by themselves, or through their representatives, the need for a public tax, to consent to it freely, to watch over its use, and to determine its proportion, basis, collection and duration.

Article 15—Society has the right to ask a public official for an accounting of his administration.

Article 16—Any society in which no provision is made for guaranteeing rights or for the separation of powers, has no Constitution.

Article 17—Since the right to Property is inviolable and sacred, no one may be deprived thereof, unless public necessity, legally ascertained, obviously requires it, and just and prior indemnity has been paid.

French Constitution

Article 3

National sovereignty shall vest in the people, who shall exercise it through their representatives and by means of referendum.

Suffrage may be direct or indirect as provided for by the Constitution. It shall always be universal, equal and secret.

All French citizens of either sex who have reached their majority and are in possession of their civil and political rights may vote as provided for by statute.

Article 4

Political parties and groups shall contribute to the exercise of suffrage. They shall be formed and carry on their activities freely. They shall respect the principles of national sovereignty and democracy.

They shall contribute to the implementation of the principle set out in the second paragraph of article 1 as provided for by statute.

Statutes shall guarantee the expression of diverse opinions and the equitable participation of political parties and groups in the democratic life of the Nation.

Article 66

No one shall be arbitrarily detained.

Article 66-1

No one shall be sentenced to death.

Article 72–3

The Republic shall recognise the overseas populations within the French people in a common ideal of liberty, equality and fraternity.

Source: "Constitution of October 4, 1958." Assemblé Nationale. http://www .assemblee-nationale.fr/english/.

RUSSIA: Federation

RUSSIA

Communications	Primary School—age Children Enrolled in Primary School
Facebook Users	
6,800,000 (estimate) (2013)	5,514,819 (2012)
Internet Users	**Primary School—age Males Enrolled in Primary School**
40,853,000 (2009)	
Internet Users (% of Population)	2,815,598 (2012)
61.4% (2013)	**Primary School—age Females Enrolled in Primary School**
Television	
55 sets per 100 population (2003)	2,699,221 (2012)
Land-based Telephones in Use	**Secondary School—age Children Enrolled in Secondary School**
42,900,000 (2012)	
Mobile Telephone Subscribers	9,165,252 (2012)
261,900,000 (2012)	**Secondary School—age Males Enrolled in Secondary School**
Major Daily Newspapers	
250 (2004)	4,739,735 (2012)
Averwage Circulation of Daily Newspapers	**Secondary School—age Females Enrolled in Secondary School**
13,280,000 (2004)	4,425,517 (2012)
Education	**Students Per Teacher, Primary School**
School System	19.6 (2012)
Russian students begin school at the age of six with four years of primary school. Students then continue to five years of early secondary school before attending two years of academic upper secondary school or four years of vocational training.	**Students Per Teacher, Secondary School**
	8.8 (2012)
	Enrollment in Tertiary Education
	7,983,111 (2012)
	Enrollment in Tertiary Education, Male
Mandatory Education	3,594,654 (2012)
9 years, from ages 6 to 15.	**Enrollment in Tertiary Education, Female**
Average Years Spent in School for Current Students	
15 (2012)	4,388,457 (2012)
Average Years Spent in School for Current Students, Male	**Literacy**
	100% (2010)
14 (2012)	**Energy and Natural Resources**
Average Years Spent in School for Current Students, Female	**Electric Power Generation**
15 (2012)	1,057,000,000,000 kilowatt hours per year (estimate) (2013)

Electric Power Consumption	**Time Zone**
1,038,000,000,000 kilowatt hours per year (estimate) (2012)	8 hours ahead of U.S. Eastern Standard (Moscow)
Nuclear Power Plants	**Land Borders**
33 (2014)	12,514 miles
Crude Oil Production	**Coastline**
10,533,700 barrels per day (2013)	23,398 miles
Crude Oil Consumption	**Capital**
3,195,500 barrels per day (2012)	Moscow
Natural Gas Production	**Area**
669,700,000,000 cubic meters per year (estimate) (2013)	6,592,850 sq. miles
	Climate
Natural Gas Consumption	The climate varies dramatically across the country, with the central regions experiencing a wide range of temperatures and heavy winter snows. The south is more temperate, with average temperatures ranging from 23°F in the winter to 74°F in the summer. Siberia and the north experience very low temperatures in the winter, with short, hot summers, while the eastern part of the country suffers extreme temperatures as well as milder forms of the monsoons typical to other parts of Asia.
45,720,000,000 cubic meters per year (estimate) (2013)	
Natural Resources	
Oil, natural gas, coal, and many strategic minerals, reserves of rare earth elements, timber	
Environment	
CO2 Emissions	
11.1 metric tons per capita (2009)	
Alternative and Nuclear Energy	
8.5% of total energy use (2010)	**Land Use**
Threatened Species	7.4% arable land; 0.1% permanent crops; 5.6% permanent meadows and pastures; 49.4% forest land; 37.5% other.
126 (2010)	
Protected Areas	
1,671,899 (estimate) (2010)	**Arable Land**
Geography	7% (2007)
Location	**Arable Land Per Capita**
Russia extends from northeastern Europe to Asia and is bordered by the Arctic Ocean to the north; Norway, Finland, Latvia, and Estonia to the northwest; Belarus and Ukraine to the west; Georgia, Azerbaijan, Kazakhstan, the Black Sea, the Caspian Sea, China, Mongolia, and North Korea to the south; and the Sea of Japan, the Pacific Ocean, the Barents Sea, and the Okhotsk Sea to the east. The Baltic region of Kaliningrad is separated from the rest of Russia by Belarus and Lithuania.	2 acres per person (2007)
	Health
	Average Life Expectancy
	70.2 years (2014)
	Average Life Expectancy, Male
	64.4 years (2014)
	Average Life Expectancy, Female
	76.3 years (2014)
	Crude Birth Rate
	11.6 (estimate) (2015)

Crude Death Rate	**Annual Military Expenditures**
13.7 (estimate) (2015)	$41,050,000,000 (2009)
Maternal Mortality	**Military Service**
67 per 100,000 live births (2005–2012 projection)	The Russian military uses a selective conscription system, with terms of service lasting from 18 months to two years.
Infant Mortality	
9 per 1,000 live births (2012)	**National Finances**
Doctors	**Currency**
4.3 per 1,000 people (2010)	Russian ruble
Industry and Labor	**Total Government Revenues**
Gross Domestic Product (GDP) - official exchange rate	$439,000,000,000 (estimate) (2013)
	Total Government Expenditures
$2,108,837,000,000 (estimate) (2015)	$450,300,000,000 (estimate) (2013)
GDP per Capita	**Budget Deficit**
$14,769 (estimate) (2015)	-0.5 (estimate) (2013)
GDP - Purchasing Power Parity (PPP)	**GDP Contribution by Sector**
$2,640,737,000,000 (estimate) (2013)	agriculture: 3.9% industry: 36% services: 60.1% (2012 est.)
GDP (PPP) per Capita	**External Debt**
$18,671 (estimate) (2013)	$714,200,000,000 (estimate) (2013)
Industry Products	**Economic Aid Extended**
Coal, oil, natural gas, chemicals, textiles, telecommunications equipment, heavy agricultural and construction vehicles, metals, machinery and transportation equipment, timber. Aerospace and shipbuilding are also major industries.	$240,400,000 (2011)
	Economic Aid Received
	$0 (2011)
	Population
Agriculture Products	**Population**
Grain, potatoes, sugar beets, sunflower seeds, vegetables, cattle, sheep, goats, poultry, milk, eggs, cannabis (illicit), opium (illicit).	142,423,773 (estimate) (2015)
	World Population Rank
	9 th (2009)
Unemployment	**Population Density**
5.5% (2012)	21.0 people per square mile (estimate) (2011)
Labor Profile	
agriculture: 7.9% industry: 27.4% services: 64.7% (2011)	**Population Distribution**
	73% urban (2011)
Military	**Age Distribution**
Total Active Armed Forces	0-14: 15%
1,027,000 (estimate) (2010)	15-64: 71.7%
Active Armed Forces	65+: 13.3%
1% (2010)	(2009)

Median Age	**Current Account Balance**
38.9 years (estimate) (2014)	$74,800,000,000 (estimate) (2012)
Population Growth Rate	**Weights and Measures**
0.0% per year (estimate) (2015)	The metric system is in use.
Net Migration Rate	
1.7 (estimate) (2015)	**Transportation**
Trade	**Airports**
Imported Goods	1,218 (2012)
Machinery, foodstuffs, mineral products, metals, petroleum, natural gas, grain, sugar, chemicals, textiles.	**Paved Roads**
	67.4% (1999)
Total Value of Imports	**Roads, Unpaved**
$160,770,000,000 (2009)	110,614 (2006)
Exported Goods	**Passenger Cars per 1,000 People**
Mineral products, machinery, iron and steel, jewelry, wood and wood products, chemicals, nonferrous metals.	233 (2009)
	Number of Trucks, Buses, and Commercial Vehicles
Total Value of Exports	4,564,300 (2005)
$542,500,000,000 (estimate) (2012)	**Railroads**
Import Partners	54,157 (2006)
China -14.3%; Germany - 13.2%; Ukraine -5.6%; United States - 5.4%; Italy - 4.9% (2009)	**Ports**
Export Partners	Major: 25—including Vladivostok, St. Petersburg, Murmansk, and Kaliningrad; inland—Moscow, Rostov, and Volgograd.
Netherlands - 12.3%; Italy - 7.1%; China - 5.9%; Germany - 4.2%; Poland - 3.8% (2009).	

OVERVIEW

Russia, the world's largest country, covers most of Eastern Europe and all of northern Asia. Along its southern and eastern edges, Russia borders 12 other countries. The Russian territory of Kaliningrad, along the Baltic Sea, is separated from the rest of the country and bordered by Lithuania and Poland. To the north of Russia is the Arctic Ocean, and to the east is the Pacific Ocean. Russia's eastern Pacific coast is only 50 miles away from the U.S. state of Alaska. The Russian climate is marked by extremes, with very cold temperatures in the north and more temperate readings in the south. Because of its northerly location, some parts of Russia experience nearly constant daylight during the summer and little in the winter. Russia is a multiethnic state with a population of about 142.5 million people. Its capital is Moscow.

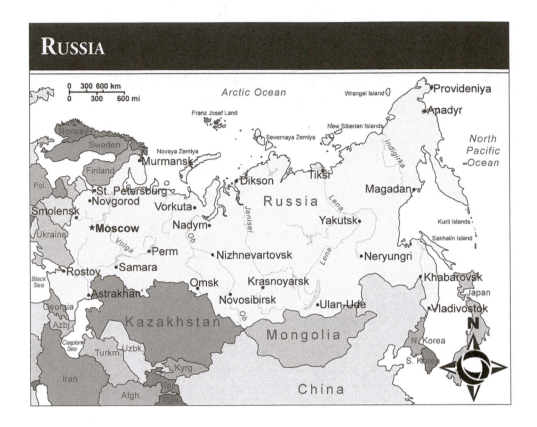

RUSSIA

GOVERNMENT

Russia is a federation of 21 constituent republics established in 1991 and is the successor state of the Soviet Union. The level of political autonomy varies between the federal republics, but recent years have showed a general trend toward greater centralization of authority in the federal government. The country is governed under a multiparty presidential system in which power is shared between the executive, legislative, and judicial branches, which are all independent of one another. The current president is Vladimir Putin, and Dmitry Medvedev is prime minister. Legislative authority resides with the bicameral Federal Assembly.

Constitution

The 1993 Constitution, approved by referendum, provides for a presidential system of government and a bicameral legislature with powers that are substantially reduced. The document also guarantees citizens' civil rights, including the right to private property and universal access to social security, pensions, free health care, and cheap housing. Amendments in 2008 extended the presidential term from four years to six years, extended legislators' terms from four years to five years, and increased parliament's oversight of the government.

Executive

Executive power is vested in the popularly elected president, who may serve no more than two consecutive terms of six years. The president is assisted by a Council of Ministers (cabinet) and a prime minister, who is appointed by the president subject to the approval of the legislature. The president, who serves as head of state and commander in chief of the armed forces, exercises broad executive authority.

Legislature

Legislative authority is vested in the Federal Assembly, which was formed in December 1993. This is a bicameral body consisting of a 450-member lower house (State Duma) and a 166-seat upper house (Federation Council). Within the State Duma, all seats are filled according to proportional representation. Two deputies from each of the federation's administrative regions make up the Federation Council. Legislators in both chambers serve five-year terms.

Judiciary

The Constitutional Court, an independent judiciary, was created in October 1991 to determine the constitutionality of Russia's laws, oversee foreign treaties, and adjudicate territorial disputes. The court's members are nominated by the president and appointed by the Federation Council, which also confirms members of the Supreme Court. In 2001, reforms to the judicial system were implemented, including the introduction of trials by jury and measures to increase the independence of judges.

Local Government

The Russian Federation contains 21 constituent republics; 46 oblasts, or provinces; 9 *krais* (territories); 4 autonomous *okrugs* (districts); the Jewish Autonomous Oblast; and the federal cities of Moscow and St. Petersburg. Each of the federation's 21 republics has its own constitution, president, and legislature, and is autonomous in name if not always in practice. Secessionist violence continues to plague such constituent republics as Chechnya and Ingushetia. The other administrative divisions included in the federation have varying degrees of autonomy. Western governments, including the United States, do not recognize Russia's 2014 annexation of Ukrainian Crimea. Russia has designated Crimea as a republic and its principal city, Sevastopol, as a federal city. These are not included in the numbers above.

Election Qualifications

All citizens 18 years of age and older are eligible to vote.

POLITICS

A former member of the Soviet Communist Party who had been dismissed from the party for advocating radical economic and political reform, Boris Yeltsin rose to power in 1990 as chairperson of Russia's Soviet-era legislature, the Supreme Soviet. Just months ahead of the collapse of the Soviet Union in 1991, Yeltsin was elected to the newly created post of president in the country's first direct presidential elections. Defeating nine challengers, he was reelected to the post in 1996. Throughout his tenure, Yeltsin faced continuous opposition from the legislature, which had been dominated by leftists and hardline members of the Communist Party. A catastrophic financial crisis during 1997–1998 brought additional challenges to the government and seemed to signal an end to the Yeltsin era and a questionable future for Russian capitalism. In a surprise New Year's Eve address in 1999, Yeltsin resigned the presidency, passing the reins to the popular but politically untested prime minister, Vladimir Putin.

On the heels of December 1999 parliamentary elections, in which progovernment parties made an impressive showing, Putin's appointment by Yeltsin

President Vladimir Putin of Russia, who was elected in 2000 and re-elected in 2004. Because the Russian constitution limits the president to two consecutive terms, he was appointed Prime Minister by his successor in 2008 and won the Presidency again in 2012. Putin has been criticized for his authoritarian rule and for Russia's invasion of neighboring Ukraine in 2014. (Alexei Nikolsky/ZUMA Press/Newscom)

uniquely positioned him as a front-runner in the race for president. Although Putin received a smaller majority than had been predicted, he easily defeated his most significant challenger—communist leader Gennady Zyuganov—by more than 20 percentage points. He was inaugurated as president in May 2000. In March 2004, Putin was overwhelmingly reelected president. The results of the election were hardly surprising, as few candidates contested the race, and those who did found access to mass media difficult if not impossible to obtain. European and U.S. poll watchers criticized the slanted media coverage and irregularities at polling stations. Putin continued to be preoccupied with stabilizing the breakaway republic of Chechnya. Following a series of violent attacks on Russian citizens attributed to Chechen extremists, Putin proposed in 2004 to reform the way regional governors would be selected. Other reforms implemented by Putin in 2005, which abolished some benefits for retirees and veterans, were met with protests from thousands of elderly citizens. Putin later made concessions to the protesters and pledged to increase pensions.

Pending the completion of his second term, Putin began grooming two possible successors, Dmitry Medvedev, chair of the giant government-controlled natural gas company Gazprom, and defense minister Sergei Ivanov, appointing both as deputy prime ministers. In the end, Putin announced his endorsement of Medvedev, an ally since Putin's days as deputy mayor of St. Petersburg. Medvedev went on to win the presidency in March 2008 by dramatic margins against his nearest challenger, Zyuganov, who received less than 20% of the vote. Medvedev was inaugurated on May 7, 2008, and immediately nominated Putin to the post of prime minister, a position he had previously held under Yeltsin. Putin was confirmed the following day, making it clear that he had no intention of exiting the political spotlight. In December 2008, despite opposition and questionable constitutionality, Medvedev signed a constitutional amendment that extended the presidential term to six years, effective with the 2012 presidential elections.

Putin was elected president again in a March 2012 election that many independent observers characterized as fraudulent. He immediately appointed Medvedev as his prime minister, causing many pro-democratic opposition groups to cry foul. Putin has shown no sign of relaxing his grip on Russia's government. In early 2014, he came under international pressure to secure the Olympic Games after terrorist bombings threatened to derail the Games in Sochi. Further, recent laws against Russia's homosexual community led many international rights groups to call for a boycott of the Games. Just a few weeks later in March, Putin again raised attention in the West by annexing the Ukrainian region of Crimea, following months of unrest in Ukraine, prompting the European Union and the United States to impose economic sanctions. Tensions increased over the next several months due to Russia's deployment of troops to the Ukrainian border; the downing of a Malaysia Airlines flight by an allegedly Russian-made missile over Ukraine; a number of unannounced and unprecedented Russian military exercises; and more sanctions by Europe and the United States on Russia.

Political Parties

The United Russia party was formed in December 2001 from the merger of Unity (which was formed as a progovernment group to contest December 1999 parliamentary elections and support Vladimir Putin in his campaign for the presidency) and the Fatherland-All Russia alliance (which had been formed just months ahead of December 1999 parliamentary elections).

The Communist Party of the Russian Federation (CPRF) was founded in 1993 as a successor to the Communist Party of the Soviet Union, which was banned in 1991 following a failed coup against the Soviet leadership. The party advocates the restoration of "social justice."

The Liberal Democratic Party of Russia (LDP) is an ultranationalist grouping formed in 1990. The LDP has advocated crime crackdowns and the creation of a Greater Russia by conquest that would include parts of Central Europe, the Middle East, and Asia.

A Just Russia (SR) is a social democratic party formed in 2006 by the merger of three former parties: Rodina, Russian Party of Life, and the Russian Pensioner's Party.

ECONOMY

In 1998, the Russian economy and its currency, the ruble, collapsed. In 2000, however, it rebounded strongly, and government measures successfully controlled inflation. Russia has continued to make regular—and even advance—payments on its national debt, and the government is also credited with balancing the state budget. Oil is one of Russia's most valuable natural resources, and Russia is one of the world's largest exporters of oil. In fact, the economic welfare of the country is largely dependent on the worldwide price of oil. Because of that dependence, the country was hard hit by the global recession in 2008 and 2009. Russia also has immense natural gas, precious metals, and timber supplies, as well as a strong engineering and scientific workforce. The Netherlands is one of Russia's top trading partners, along with China and Germany. Following Russia's military intervention in Ukraine in early 2014, the European Union and the United States imposed sanctions on some high-level Russian individuals as well as some companies, and have threatened to enact additional sanctions if the violence in Ukraine continues. Western analysts believe the sanctions will weaken the Russian economy, while Russian officials have stated the country's economy can weather the storm.

Some of Russia's oil production occurs offshore in the Caspian Sea, where this oil platform is located. Since the breakup of the Soviet Union in 1991, oil has become a mainstay of Russia's economy. As of 2014, Russia was the leading oil producer in the world. (PhotoXpress/ZUMAPRESS/Newscom)

SOCIETY

In modern Russia, the vast majority of the population is ethnic Russian, while Tatars and Ukrainians form the largest minority groups. The Russian language was always favored by the Soviet government and is widely spoken not only among ethnic Russians but also as a second language by many others. Minority populations continue to speak their own languages as well. The Russian Orthodox religion, a form of Christianity, was adopted directly from the Byzantine Empire in 988 CE, and for centuries had a profound effect on Russian art and architecture as well as providing the spiritual foundation of the people. After the 1917 revolution, the Soviet government frowned on religious practice, but many people were able to maintain their beliefs. Since 1991, open religious worship has been an important aspect of nationalist enthusiasm. Followers of Islam are the second most numerous group of believers, behind members of the Orthodox Church.

Ethnic Composition

Russian – 77.7%; Tatar – 3.7%; Ukrainian – 1.4%; Bashkir – 1.1%; Chuvash – 1%; Chechen – 1%; other – 10.2%; unspecified – 3.9%

Language

Russian is the principal and official language, spoken by the vast majority of people, but numerous other languages, including German, Chechen, and Tartar, are also spoken.

Religion

Russian Orthodox – 15%–20%; Muslim – 10%–15%; other Christian – 2%

CONTEMPORARY ISSUES

Declining Influence in Eastern Europe

As Eastern Europe has moved steadily toward greater integration with Western Europe and further from Russia's sphere of influence, Russian relations with many former Soviet republics and satellite states have grown tense and at times explosive.

In November 2013, the president of Ukraine, Viktor Yanukovych, suspended acceptance of a trade agreement between Ukraine and the EU, citing Russia's opposition to an EU–Ukraine trade agreement. In early 2014, after months of unrest, Yanukovych was deposed. The events stirred tension in the Ukrainian region of Crimea, where a majority of the population is Russian. Putin deployed forces to Crimea, which occupied military bases in the Crimean Peninsula and drew condemnation from the United States and the European Union (EU). On March 16, Crimean voters elected to secede from Ukraine and join Russia. The United Nations General Assembly declared the election illegal, and the United States and the EU imposed the toughest sanctions on Russia since the Cold War. Despite that, Putin signed a law on March 21, formally annexing Crimea to Russia. In addition, the deployment of Russian troops to and over the country's border with Ukraine, the West's increasing economic sanctions on Russia, and the July 17 downing of a Malaysia Airlines flight over Ukraine have exacerbated tensions. Ukraine and the United States allege the plane was shot down with a Russian-made missile. Pro-Russian militants and Russia deny any involvement in the tragic incident. In early August, Putin banned imports of agricultural products from those countries that have imposed sanctions against Russia.

Russia's diplomatic ties with Georgia are plagued by the latter's near-endless string of allegations of abuse, ranging from territorial violations to the support of separatist rebels and from ethnic cleansing to espionage. Russia, in turn, resents Georgia's aspirations to join the North Atlantic Treaty Organization (NATO) and the European Union, as well as its increasingly close military relationship with the United States. Ties with Estonia have been equally fraught with problems over that country's treatment of its substantial ethnic Russian minority. The declared independence of Kosovo and the divided pro-West and pro-Russian government factions in Ukraine are two areas where Russia continues to fight to preserve its political influence. Russia's gas resources have also become a leveraging tool in exerting influence in Eastern Europe, as many countries in the region are exclusively dependent on Russia for their gas imports.

The Situation in Chechnya

Since Russia entered the Second Chechen War in 1999, the international media have reported widespread killings and human rights abuses committed by ill-trained and underpaid Russian troops. Following the September 11, 2001, World Trade Center and Pentagon attacks in the United States, Moscow embarked on a public relations offensive, supplying evidence that Islamic fundamentalists connected to terrorist groups in Afghanistan and the Middle East were behind the wave of violence in Chechnya. Rights groups, however, have focused their attention on the conduct of the Russian armed forces, particularly on the use of torture, secret detention facilities, and the disappearance of several thousand Chechens. Some 120 cases have been brought by Chechens to the European Court of Human Rights, and in the landmark case of *Bazorkina v. Russia*, the court ruled for the first time that Russia had violated multiple articles of the European Convention on Human Rights in relation to a single extrajudicial killing. This case may set a precedent for future litigation.

Despite Russian claims that Chechnya is stable, Chechen rebels have continued their campaign of violence against Russian targets, including the downing of a large Russian military helicopter on August 19, 2002, that killed 115 people, and the bloody three-day siege in 2004 of a school in the town of Beslan, in which 330 people—more than half of them children—were massacred. Suicide bomb attacks in Russia, particularly in the Russian North Caucasus, have increased in recent years, and many have been tied to Chechen separatism. Among the most deadly were car bombings in North Ossetia in November 2008 and September 2010; subway bombings in Moscow in February and August 2004 and March 2010; and the 2011 bombing of a Moscow airport that left 36 people dead and injured another 180 people.

Media Freedom

While freedom of the press is guaranteed under the 1993 Constitution, journalism in Russia is a dangerous profession; more than 20 journalists were murdered during Vladimir Putin's first presidential term, and the killings continued during Dmitry Medvedev's tenure and into Putin's second term. Some experts put the death toll of journalists at higher than 300 people killed since 1993. Perhaps the most high-profile of these killings was the murder of world-renowned *Novaya*

Gazeta reporter Anna Politkovskaya, who was shot to death on October 7, 2006, while writing an exposé on Russian-backed Chechen prime minister Ramzan Kadyrov's links to serial kidnappings and torture. Media diversity is also compromised by the indirect government control of some of the country's principal news sources, particularly *Kommersant* and *Izvestia*, both owned by a media subsidiary of the government-controlled natural gas company Gazprom. The government also owns wholly or partially many national television and radio stations. Furthermore, journalists have been threatened with investigations and criminal charges, and some have been brought to trial and convicted for reporting on such politically sensitive issues as corruption, human rights abuses, and organized crime. Concern over media freedom intensified in late 2013 after the Kremlin announced a restructuring of state-owned RIA Novosti—the station known for the least-biased news coverage.

Population Decline

Russia's population has been decreasing steadily for several years. At about 142 million people in 2014, the population could fall by as much as 25 million in the next 15 years. Russia, which dropped from the world's seventh most populated nation to the tenth during 2002 to 2014, has had a higher death rate than birth rate since 1992, a situation unlikely to change and which could prove to be disastrous for the country. The rate of population decline has been around 0.5% each year.

Many Russian women have not been able to afford to get married until later in life or have postponed or canceled plans to have children. In the decade following the collapse of communism in 1991, the birth rate was cut in half. High-risk lifestyles contribute a great deal to Russia's high death rate. It is estimated, for example, that one-third of Russians are addicted to nicotine, which can cause cancer and cardiovascular disease. Even children smoke openly. Alcoholism is also a widespread affliction, affecting approximately 30% of men and 15% of women.

Kurile Islands Dispute

Since the Soviet Union took control of the Kurile Islands immediately after World War II, Japan has disputed Moscow's claims that the Yalta Conference provided it with exclusive administrative rights over the entire archipelago. Tokyo continues to insist that the historically Japanese South Kuriles—specifically, the four islands closest to the Japanese island of Hokkaido—remain its "northern territories." Over the last decade, tensions have continued to escalate, with both sides refusing to compromise and Russia becoming increasingly aggressive in the region. In November 2005, immediately before a diplomatic visit by Putin, a Russian Orthodox church was hastily erected on the Kurile island of Suisho in a location readily visible from Hokkaido. Many Japanese interpreted the prominently placed building as a direct provocation by the Russian government, as the island remains uninhabited and the church will clearly not be used as a religious facility.

Most contentious of all is Russia's refusal to respect the fishing rights of the Japanese, who argue that the surrounding waters fall exclusively within their own economic zone. In 2001, the Japanese government vehemently protested the issuing of permits to a number of South Korean boats to fish in what Japan considers its own waters. South Korea eventually agreed not to fish in the waters after Japan threatened to deny South Korea access to other Japanese fisheries. Since 1994, Russian authorities have detained more than 200 Japanese fishermen in the waters surrounding the four highly contentious islands. Russia and Japan issued a joint statement declaring a commitment to resolving the matter in 2013. In February 2014, meetings were held between Putin and Japanese prime minister Shinzo Abe in Moscow, but no resolution emerged.

Excerpt from the Constitution of the Russian Federation

The current constitution of the Russian Federation was drafted at a constitutional convention in 1993. It was approved by a majority of Russia's voters on December 12, 1993, and went into effect on December 25. The Constitution replaced the Soviet-era constitution that had been in effect throughout the Union of Soviet Socialist Republics (USSR), including Russia, since 1978.

The current Russian constitution contains numerous clauses that dissociate Russia from the USSR. For example, it identifies Russia as a multiparty democracy that respects "ideological diversity," in contrast to the government of the USSR that was controlled by the Communist Party and demanded adherence to the principles of Marxism and Leninism. The Constitution guarantees what are regarded as fundamental human rights and forbids discrimination on the basis of gender, race, religion, language, or nationality. It specifies that "All forms of limitations of human rights on social, racial, national, linguistic or religious grounds shall be banned." Again, this clause stands in contrast to the Soviet policy of Russification, by which national minorities were to be absorbed into the Russian-dominated culture of the Soviet Union.

The Constitution guarantees various political and legal rights, such as the right of free speech and the right to trial by jury. It also specifies that Russia is to be a secular state, but that freedom of religion is to be respected. In addition, the Constitution makes specific reference to various other rights unrelated directly to the political process. These include the right to education, the right to social security, and the "right to a home." However, it specifies obligations of Russian citizens, including the obligation of "able-bodied" adults to take care of disabled parents and the expectation that "Defence of the Fatherland shall be a duty and obligation."

Article 6

Citizenship of the Russian Federation shall be . . . equal, irrespective of the grounds of acquisition.

A citizen of the Russian Federation may not be deprived of his or her citizenship . . .

Article 7

The Russian Federation . . . is aimed at creating conditions for a worthy life and the unhindered development of man.

In the Russian Federation the labour and health of people shall be protected, guaranteed minimum wages and salaries shall be established, state support ensured for the family, maternity, paternity and childhood, for disabled persons and the elderly, a system of social services developed, state pensions, allowances and other social security guarantees shall be established.

Article 13

. . . ideological diversity shall be recognised.

No state or obligatory ideology may be established as one.

. . . political diversity and the multi-party system shall be recognised.

Public associations shall be equal before the law.

The creation and activities of public associations whose aims and actions are aimed at a forced change of the fundamental principles of the constitutional system and at violating the integrity of the Russian Federation . . . shall be prohibited.

Article 14

The Russian Federation is a secular state. No state or obligatory religion may be established.

Article 17

Fundamental human rights and freedoms are inalienable . . .

The exercise of the rights and freedoms of man and citizen shall not violate the rights and freedoms of other people.

Article 19

All people shall be equal before the law and courts.

The State shall guarantee the equality of rights and freedoms of man and citizen, regardless of sex, race, nationality, language, origin, property and official status, place of residence, religion, convictions, membership of public associations, and also of other circumstances. All forms of limitations of human rights on social, racial, national, linguistic or religious grounds shall be banned.

Men and women shall enjoy equal rights and freedoms . . .

Article 20

Everyone shall have the right to life.

Capital punishment until its complete abolition may be . . . only as a penalty for especially grave crimes against life, and the accused shall be granted the right to have his case examined by a jury.

Article 21

Human dignity shall be protected by the State.

No one shall be subject to torture, violence or other cruel or humiliating treatment or punishment. No one may be subject to medical, scientific and other experiments without voluntary consent.

Article 22

Arrest, detention and remanding in custody shall be allowed only by court decision. Without the court's decision a person may not be detained . . . more than 48 hours.

Article 23

Everyone shall have the right to the inviolability of private life, personal and family secrets . . .

Everyone shall have the right to privacy of correspondence . . .

Limitations of this right shall be allowed only by court decision.

Article 24

The collection, keeping, use and dissemination of information about the private life of a person shall not be allowed without his or her consent.

Article 25

No one shall have the right to enter a home against the will of those living there, except for the cases established by a federal law or by court decision.

Article 26

Everyone shall have the right to determine and indicate his nationality.
Everyone shall have the right to use his or her native language

Article 27

Everyone who legally stays in the territory of the Russian Federation shall have the right to free travel . . .
Everyone may freely leave the Russian Federation . . .

Article 28

Everyone shall be guaranteed the freedom of conscience, the freedom of religion, including the right to profess . . . any religion or . . . no religion

Article 29

Everyone shall be guaranteed the freedom of ideas and speech.
Propaganda or agitation instigating social, racial, national or religious hatred and strife shall not be allowed. The propaganda of social, racial, national, religious or linguistic supremacy shall be banned.
The freedom of mass communication shall be guaranteed. Censorship shall be banned.

Article 30

Everyone shall have the right to association, including the right to create trade unions . . . The freedom of activity of public association shall be guaranteed.

Article 31

Citizens of the Russian Federation shall have the right to assemble peacefully, without weapons . . .
Citizens recognised by court as legally unfit, as well as citizens kept in places of confinement under a court sentence, shall be deprived of the right to elect and be elected.

Article 33

Citizens of the Russian Federation shall have the right to address personally, as well as to submit individual and collective appeals to state bodies and local self-government bodies.

Article 38

Maternity and childhood, and the family shall be protected by the State.

Care for children and their upbringing shall be equally the right and obligation of parents.

Able-bodied children over 18 years of age shall take care of disabled parents.

Article 39

Everyone shall be guaranteed social security . . . in old age, in case of illness, disability, loss of the bread-winner, for bringing up children . . .

Article 40

Everyone shall have the right to a home.

People on low-incomes and other persons . . . in need of a home shall receive it gratis or for reasonable payment from the state,

. . . federal programmes for protecting and improving the health of the population shall be financed by the State . . .

Article 43

Everyone shall have the right to education.

Article 46

Everyone shall be guaranteed judicial protection of his rights and freedoms.

Everyone shall have the right to appeal . . . to international bodies for the protection of human rights . . . if all the existing internal state means of legal protection have been exhausted.

Article 47

A person accused of committing a crime shall have the right to the examination of his case by a jury court . . .

Article 48

Everyone shall be guaranteed the right to qualified legal assistance.

Article 49

Everyone accused of a crime shall be considered innocent until his guilt is proved . . .

Article 49

The accused shall not be obliged to prove his innocence.

Article 50

No one may be convicted twice for one and the same crime.

In administering justice it shall not be allowed to use evidence received by violating federal law.

Everyone convicted of a crime shall have the right to appeal

Article 51

No one shall be obliged to give evidence incriminating themselves . . .

Article 59

Defence of the Fatherland shall be a duty and obligation . . .

A citizen . . . shall have the right to replace military service by alternative civilian service if his convictions or religious belief prohibit military service . . .

Article 63

The Russian Federation shall grant political asylum to foreign nationals and stateless Persons . . .

. . . It shall not be allowed to extradite to other States those people who are persecuted for political convictions . . .

Source: "The Constitution of the Russian Federation." Legislation Online. http://www.legislationline.org/documents/section/constitutions

TAIWAN: Multiparty Democracy

TAIWAN

Communications	Primary School—age Females Enrolled in Primary School
Facebook Users	
13,800,000 (estimate) (2013)	Not Available
Internet Users	Secondary School—age Children Enrolled in Secondary School
16,147,000 (2009)	Not Available
Internet Users (% of Population)	Secondary School—age Males Enrolled in Secondary School
66.1% (2008)	
Television	Not Available
43 sets per 100 population (2006)	Secondary School—age Females Enrolled in Secondary School
Land-based Telephones in Use	
15,998,000 (2012)	Not Available
Mobile Telephone Subscribers	Students Per Teacher, Primary School
29,455,000 (2012)	Not Available
Education	Students Per Teacher, Secondary School
School System	Not Available
Taiwanese students begin school at the age of six. Primary school lasts for six years and is followed by three years of early secondary school. Upper secondary school lasts for another three years and follows an academic or vocational program.	Enrollment in Tertiary Education
	Not Available
	Enrollment in Tertiary Education, Male
	Not Available
	Enrollment in Tertiary Education, Female
Mandatory Education	Not Available
9 years, from ages 6 to 15.	Literacy
Average Years Spent in School for Current Students	96% (2003)
	Energy and Natural Resources
Not Available	Electric Power Generation
Average Years Spent in School for Current Students, Male	252,200,000,000 kilowatt hours per year (estimate) (2011)
Not Available	Electric Power Consumption
Primary School—age Children Enrolled in Primary School	242,200,000,000 kilowatt hours per year (estimate) (2011)
Not Available	Nuclear Power Plants
Primary School—age Males Enrolled in Primary School	6 (2014)
	Crude Oil Production
Not Available	21,700 barrels per day (2013)

Crude Oil Consumption	**Area**
1,079,900 barrels per day (2012)	13,900 sq. miles
Natural Gas Production	**Climate**
330,200,000 cubic meters per year (estimate) (2011)	Taiwan has rainy summers and mild winters, with temperatures averaging about 79°F in the summer and about 59°F in the winter. The average annual rainfall is 101 inches.
Natural Gas Consumption	
16,370,000,000 cubic meters per year (estimate) (2011)	
Natural Resources	**Land Use**
Coal, marble, natural gas, limestone, aesbestos	(not available)
	Arable Land
Environment	Not Available
CO2 Emissions	**Arable Land Per Capita**
Not Available	Not Available
Alternative and Nuclear Energy	**Health**
Not Available	**Average Life Expectancy**
Threatened Species	79.8 years (2014)
Not Available	**Average Life Expectancy, Male**
Protected Areas	76.7 years (2014)
Not Available	**Average Life Expectancy, Female**
Geography	83.2 years (2014)
Location	**Crude Birth Rate**
Taiwan comprises one large island and several much smaller islands located about 90 miles off the southeast coast of mainland China. The largest island is called Taiwan (or Formosa) and has a northern coast on the East China Sea, an eastern coast on the Pacific Ocean, and southern and southwestern coasts on the South China Sea. Taiwan is separated from China by the Taiwan Strait on its western coast.	8.5 (estimate) (2015)
	Crude Death Rate
	7.1 (estimate) (2015)
	Maternal Mortality
	0 per 100,000 live births (2005—2012 projection)
	Infant Mortality
	Not Available
Time Zone	**Doctors**
13 hours ahead of U.S. Eastern Standard	Not Available
Land Borders	**Industry and Labor**
0 miles	**Gross Domestic Product (GDP) - official exchange rate**
Coastline	
900 miles	$534,217,000,000 (estimate) (2015)
Capital	**GDP per Capita**
Taipei	$22,743 (estimate) (2015)

GDP - Purchasing Power Parity (PPP)	**GDP Contribution by Sector**
$945,479,000,000 (estimate) (2013)	agriculture: 2% industry: 29.8% services: 68.2% (2012 est.)
GDP (PPP) per Capita	**External Debt**
$40,393 (estimate) (2013)	$146,800,000,000 (estimate) (2013)
Industry Products	**Economic Aid Extended**
Cigarettes, cement, autmobiles, diesel oil, electronics, ships, textiles, clothing, chemicals, processed food, refined sugar, plywood, paper.	$331,840,000 (2011)
	Economic Aid Received
	$0 (2011)
Agriculture Products	**Population**
Sugarcane, vegetables, soybeans, rice, wheat, citrus fruit, tea, maize, sweet potatoes, fowl, pigs, eggs, cows' and cows' milk.	**Population**
	23,415,126 (estimate) (2015)
	World Population Rank
Unemployment	49 th (2009)
Not Available	**Population Density**
Labor Profile	1,659.8 people per square mile (estimate) (2011)
agriculture: 5% industry: 36.2% services: 58.8% (estimate) (2012)	**Population Distribution**
Military	Not Available
Total Active Armed Forces	**Age Distribution**
290,000 (estimate) (2010)	0-14: 16.2%
Active Armed Forces	15-64: 73%
1% (2010)	65+: 10.8%
Annual Military Expenditures	(2009)
$9,780,000,000 (2009)	**Median Age**
Military Service	39.2 years (estimate) (2014)
The Taiwanese military uses a selective conscription system, with terms of service lasting 20 months.	**Population Growth Rate**
	0.2% per year (estimate) (2015)
	Net Migration Rate
National Finances	0.9 (estimate) (2015)
Currency	**Trade**
New Taiwan dollar	**Imported Goods**
Total Government Revenues	Electrical equipment, petroleum, motor vehicles, gold, data processing machines and equipment, telecommunication equipment, foodstuffs, iron, steel, copper, chemicals.
$78,240,000,000 (estimate) (2013)	
Total Government Expenditures	
$90,380,000,000 (estimate) (2013)	
Budget Deficit	**Total Value of Imports**
-2.5 (estimate) (2013)	$251,400,000,000 (2010)

Exported Goods	Weights and Measures		
Office machines, transmission and electronic equipment, telecommunication equipment, artificial resins and plastics, textiles, footwear, foodstuffs, wood.	The metric system is used, but some traditional Chinese weights and measures are also widely employed.		
Total Value of Exports	**Transportation**		
	Airports		
$288,200,000,000 (estimate) (2012)	40 (2012)		
Import Partners	**Paved Roads**		
	Not Available		
Japan - 20.7%; China - 14.2%; United States - 10.0%; South Korea - 6.4%; Saudi Arabia - 4.7% (2010 estimate)	**Roads, Unpaved**		
	271 (2008)		
Export Partners	**Passenger Cars per 1,000 People**		
	Not Available		
China - 41.9%; United States - 11.5%; Japan - 6.6%; Singapore - 4.4% (2010)	**Railroads**		
	983 (2008)		
Current Account Balance	**Ports**		
$56,660,000,000 (estimate) (2013)	Major: 6—Anping, Kao-hsiung, Chi-lung, Hua-lien, Su-ao, T'ai-chung.		

OVERVIEW

Taiwan is an East Asian island nation (which China has long considered a break-away province), located just 80 miles off the Chinese mainland's southeast coast. Formally known as the Republic of China, Taiwan was established in 1949 when Chiang Kai-shek and his fellow Nationalist Party members fled to the island (which the Portuguese had named Formosa) to escape Mao Zedong's communist forces, who had triumphed in China's civil war. Taiwan's warm, tropical climate is marked by frequent cloudiness and southwest monsoons from June to August, although its high summer temperatures extend from April to November. More than 23 million people live in Taiwan. The country's capital and largest city is Taipei, located in northern Taiwan.

GOVERNMENT

Taiwan does not have official recognition as an independent nation. Powerful opposition from the communist government of the People's Republic of China, which considers Taiwan to be a renegade province, has made true independence for Taiwan unlikely. Despite this, Taiwan, officially called the Republic of China, is an operating republic with de facto jurisdiction over its island territory. From 1949

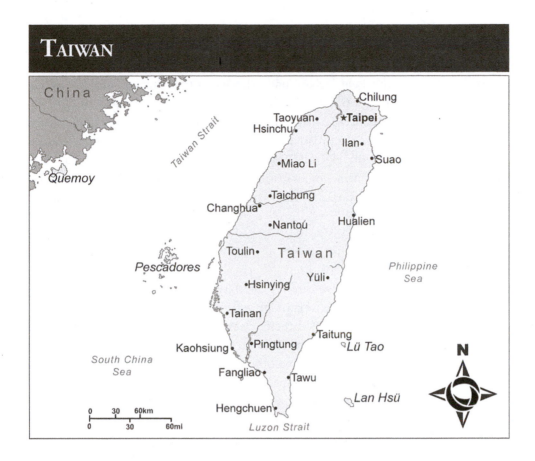

to 1987, Taiwan operated as an authoritarian regime based on martial law and ruled by Nationalist Party (Kuomintang) refugees from mainland China. In 1987, the government began allowing opposition political parties, and by the early 1990s it began submitting itself to democratic elections, effectively transforming into a multiparty parliamentary democracy. The current president is Ma Ying-jeou.

Constitution

The present Taiwanese Constitution is based on the Nationalist Constitution promulgated in Nanjing, China, on January 1, 1947. It provides for a system of five *yuans* (branches or governing bodies) headed by a directly elected Legislative Yuan. The five-power system also consists of the Executive, Judicial, Examination, and Control *yuans*.

Executive

The president serves as supreme head of state and since 1996 has been elected directly. Previously, he or she was elected to a renewable six-year term by the legislature. The president's functions include initiating legislation, commanding military forces, representing the nation in foreign relations, and declaring war and peace. A July 1997 constitutional amendment gave the president a new power to dissolve the Legislative Yuan. The Executive Yuan is headed by the prime minister, who is appointed by the president with the consent of the Legislative Yuan. The Executive Yuan is the nation's highest administrative organ and includes a Cabinet, 14 ministries, and 15 additional councils, agencies, and organizations. The locally elected 29-member Control Yuan has the power to impeach the Executive Yuan or investigate its operations, as well as those of the ministries. The Examination Yuan supervises examinations for entry into public office.

Legislature

The 113-member Legislative Yuan is the nation's highest legislative authority and has the power to change government policy whenever necessary. The Legislative Yuan has 113 members: 73 directly elected members, 34 members elected according to a supplementary member system, and six members elected from aboriginal constituencies. Previously dominated by elderly deputies dating back to mainland China's 1947 elections, in December 1992 the entire Legislative Yuan was opened to elections within Taiwan for the first time ever. A July 1997 constitutional amendment gave the Legislative Yuan the power to impeach the president with a three-fifths vote. Other 1997 amendments stripped the body's right to veto the president's choice of prime minister and granted the president a new power to dissolve the lawmaking body. In 2000, the National Assembly, formerly empowered to amend the Constitution and vote on amendments proposed by the Legislative Yuan, was dissolved and its responsibilities transferred to the Legislative Yuan.

Judiciary

The Judicial Yuan is headed by its own president, who presides over a council of 15 grand justices appointed by the national president to nine-year terms. The Judicial Yuan has jurisdiction over the high courts and district courts and is also responsible for constitutional interpretation. The Supreme Court, which exists within the Judicial Yuan, is the highest court of appeal for civil and criminal cases.

Local Government

Taiwan comprises two provinces and two special municipalities: Fuchien (20 offshore islands), Kao-hsiung, Taipei (the capital), and Taiwan. This latter region, the largest, is Taiwan proper, which is divided into five municipalities and 14 counties. Under a 1997 constitutional reform package, the provincial government system was effectively dismantled. Elections for Taiwan's provincial assembly and governors were suspended upon the completion of the incumbents' terms in 1998. Previously elected provincial offices that have not been eliminated are now filled by central government appointees.

Election Qualifications

All citizens 20 years of age and older may vote.

POLITICS

Taiwan became a province of China in 1945. In 1949, Chiang Kai-shek's ruling Nationalist Party (known locally as the Kuomintang) was driven from mainland China—now called the People's Republic of China (PRC)—by the victorious Chinese Communist Party and established itself in Taiwan as what Chiang claimed was the rightful Chinese government in opposition to the communist PRC. In 1971, Taiwan was plunged into diplomatic isolation when the United Nations replaced Taiwan with the PRC as China's official representative. Martial law was lifted and political parties were legalized in Taiwan in 1987, and in April 1991 Kuomintang president Li Teng-hui declared an end to Taiwan's civil war with the PRC and 43 years of emergency rule. In December 1991, following massive prodemocracy demonstrations, Taiwan held its first legislative elections since 1949. Taiwan's first-ever democratic presidential vote took place on March 23, 1996, with Li winning 54% of the vote.

Two parties today dominate Taiwanese politics: the Democratic Progressive Party (Min-chu Chin-pu Tang—DPP), which won March 2000 presidential elections and supports an independent Taiwan; and the Kuomintang, which supports eventual reunification with the PRC. In July 1999, Li set off a row with Beijing by making statements that China must deal with Taiwan on a nation-to-nation basis. Relations with China were further strained following the election of proindependence DPP presidential candidate Chen Shui-bian in March 2000. Chen's victory over Kuomintang candidate Lien Chan marked the end of the Kuomintang's 51 years of continuous rule. Some observers believe that December 2001 parliamentary elections were an even bigger victory for the DPP, because the DPP gained a majority in the Legislative Yuan (parliament), outpolling the Kuomintang for the first time in history. Thus, the Kuomintang's ability to counteract Chen's legislative agenda had been stifled, as the DPP gained control of a second branch of Taiwan's government.

President Ma Ying-jeou of the Republic of China, which includes the island of Taiwan and small nearby islands. He was elected to a four-year term in 2008 and re-elected in 2012. (Kyodo/Newscom)

The Kuomintang's frustrations came to a boil as a result of the March 20, 2004, presidential election, during which Chen and Vice President Annette Lu were reelected by a razor-thin margin only one day after both were slightly wounded in a failed assassination attempt. Chen agreed to the Kuomintang's demand for an electoral recount, a process that lasted until May 2004, with Chen declared the winner. In 2006, Chen became tainted by an insider-trading scandal. And although the political opposition attempted to oust Chen through a parliamentary vote—something that had never been attempted before in Taiwan—the move failed to gain a majority vote on June 27. In March 2008, former Kuomintang head Ma Ying-jeou, who had resigned as leader of the party in February 2007 after being indicted on corruption charges, won the presidential election, ending the DPP's ruling-party status and handing power back to the Kuomintang after eight years as the opposition party. During his first term, Ma Ying-jeou pursued diplomacy with China that resulted in direct flights, mail service, and eased investment restrictions between China and Taiwan. Ma Ying-jeou was reelected in 2012 and has continued during this term to improve relations with China, resulting in a tenfold increase in Chinese tourists visiting Taiwan, as well as a $160 billion per year trade relationship between China and Taiwan.

In February 2014, China and Taiwan held formal high-level talks—the first since 1949. No formal agreements were made and no agenda was released, but analysts believe the talks included the topics of freedom of the press, economic cooperation, and the establishment of diplomats in each other's territories.

Political Parties

After the termination of martial law in 1987, the formation of political parties was legalized for the first time in Taiwan.

Founded in 1894 in China, the Kuomintang was Taiwan's ruling party for more than 50 years, until its defeat in March 2000 presidential elections. The Kuomintang was Taiwan's dominant political force partly because it was the only legal party until 1987. The Kuomintang promotes constitutional government and a free-market economy. Although the Kuomintang supports eventual reunification with China after the mainland adopts democracy, President Li Teng-hui set off a controversy with Beijing in July 1999 by making statements that China must deal with Taiwan on a nation-to-nation basis. The Kuomintang continued its decline in December 2001 parliamentary elections, when it lost control of the Legislative Yuan to a new Democratic Progressive Party (DPP) majority. The Kuomintang then narrowly lost the 2004 presidential election. However, the Kuomintang rose once again to power with Ma Ying-jeou's victory in the March 2008 presidential election.

With its victory over the Kuomintang in the March 2000 presidential election, the Democratic Progressive Party (DPP) became the first opposition party to take power in Taiwan. The party also narrowly won the 2004 presidential election. The DPP was formed in 1986 by a group of dissidents despite a ban on the organization of new parties. The DPP initially favored total independence from the Chinese mainland. However, in 1999, the DPP renounced its conviction that Taiwan should eventually declare independence from China, reasoning that the nation is already a sovereign entity.

The People First Party (PFP) was founded in 2000 by former Kuomintang heavyweight James Soong, a popular former provincial governor of Taiwan, after he narrowly lost the 2000 presidential election, which he contested as a third-party candidate. The PFP supports unification with China.

The Taiwan Solidarity Union (TSU) was founded in 2000 by supporters of former President Li Teng-hui. Originally taking the stance of Taiwan as a sovereign state, the party has more recently sidelined the independence issue to focus on middle- and lower-class issues.

The Non-Partisan Solidarity Union (NPSU) was established in 2004 by former interior minister Chang Po-ya. The NPSU is a centrist party promoting a "middle way." It takes no stance on Taiwan's political status.

ECONOMY

Taiwan's dynamic capitalist economy is based on manufacturing, mostly of textiles, high-technology goods, petrochemicals, and machinery. Taiwan is a creditor economy, possessing huge cash reserves that have enabled it to invest in Southeast

Asia's economies, and its workforce is well educated. Other than its abundant supplies of fish, Taiwan lacks significant natural resources and must import all its fuel oil from Kuwait and Saudi Arabia. In addition, the country has one of the world's highest proportions of nuclear-generated energy. The United States, Japan, and China are the nation's main trading partners, although Taiwan's relationship with the United States has been problematic since 1972, when the U.S. government under President Richard Nixon recognized China as the ruler of both Taiwan and the mainland. Taiwan has had stronger allies in subsequent U.S. presidents who have committed to normal trade relations and the sale of defensive military equipment to the island state. During the early twenty-first century, Taiwan has been spearheading a drive to relax cross-strait trade and investment restrictions with mainland China. In 2010, Taiwan and China signed the Economic Cooperation Framework Agreement, a preferential trade accord, and in 2012, a currency settlement between the two countries paved the way for an efficient and cheaper currency exchange process. Twenty-seven percent of Taiwan's total exports go to mainland China, while China provides 16% of Taiwan's imports, second only to Japan.

SOCIETY

Taiwanese aborigines make up as much as 2% of the population, and the rest is descended from Chinese immigrants, most of whom arrived from the provinces of Fukien and Kwangtung before 1945. Important distinctions between the mainlanders who came after 1945 and the Taiwanese have faded as the latter group has gained access to positions in government and industry. The official language is Mandarin Chinese, though the Hakka and Min dialects (Taiwanese) are also spoken. Many older residents can still speak Japanese, a remnant of the 50 years, between 1895 and 1945, when Taiwan was ruled by Japan. The Taiwanese have continued the traditional polytheistic approach of China, blending Taoism, Buddhism, ancestral worship, and reverence for such local deities as Matsu, believed to protect seafarers.

Ethnic Composition

Taiwanese – 84%; mainland Chinese – 14%; aborigine – 2%

Language

Mandarin Chinese is the official language. Taiwanese (Min) and the Hakka dialects are also spoken.

Religion

Buddhism, Confucianism, and Taoism – 93.0%; Christian – 4.5%; other – 2.5%

CONTEMPORARY ISSUES

Relations with China

The contentious relations between the island of Taiwan and the mainland People's Republic of China began during the Chinese civil wars before and after World War II, which pitted the Nationalist Party (Kuomintang) government of Chiang Kai-shek against communist rebels led by Mao Zedong. In 1949, on the verge of the communists' victory, the Nationalists retreated to Taiwan, where Chiang established a military dictatorship that, after many years, has evolved into a multiparty democracy. However, the Nationalist Party retained power in Taiwan until the 2000 election of President Chen Shui-bian. Chen was succeeded as president by the Nationalist Party's Ma Ying-jeou in March 2008.

Today, Taiwan claims that it is an independent nation that should be recognized as such by the world community. However, China insists that Taiwan is a rogue province that still belongs to China and thus deserves no such recognition. Many foreign nations have taken China's side, while some have sided with Taiwan. In 1971, the United Nations went so far as to expel Taiwan from the world body and replace it with China. Although there has been a minor thawing of relations in recent years, the dispute has left both countries on edge, with preparations reportedly made for a Chinese invasion of Taiwan amid competing plans for Taiwan to oppose such an invasion—possibly supported by the U.S. military.

Death Penalty/Human Rights

Amnesty International has reported that Taiwan continues to use the death penalty for a wide range of crimes, some of them less egregious than murder. Proposed legislation "to counter terror activities" has been under discussion in the Legislative Yuan for several years; if passed, it would introduce additional crimes, including attempted crimes, for which the death penalty could be imposed.

Although Taiwan is a modern multiparty democracy with a fair human rights record, Human Rights Watch has reported instances in Taiwan of police abusing persons in custody, military hazing, discrimination and violence against women, child abuse and prostitution, and human trafficking. The U.S. State Department has also reported cases of labor exploitation of migrant and domestic workers.

Political Corruption

According to the Global Policy Forum, political corruption in Taiwan can be traced to the intersection of local political and financial interests, called factions, and to the fact that political power often goes to the highest bidder. This power can then be used to enrich those who contributed funds to the "purchase." Before the rise of democracy during the 1990s, vote-buying was considered legitimate.

In recent years, corruption scandals—such as those involving vote-buying, at national and local levels—have shaken Taiwan, with some of these cases implicating the country's top leaders. By mid-2013, 573 officials had been indicted on corruption charges, ranging from bribery and money laundering to forgery and embezzlement.

Excerpt from the Constitution of Taiwan

The constitution of Taiwan, which is known formally as the Constitution of the Republic of China, was drafted in 1946 and went into effect in 1947, when the Republic of China or "Nationalist China" maintained control of portions of the Chinese mainland. The Communists seized control over all of mainland China in 1949. Thus the Constitution of the Republic has de facto authority only over Taiwan and several smaller, nearby islands, although Taiwan continues to claim sovereignty over what is now the People's Republic of China.

The Constitution of the Republic guarantees freedom and equality under the law, including freedom from discrimination on the basis of ethnicity. It establishes basic political rights as fundamental, including the rights to free speech, freedom of religion, freedom of the press, and the right to vote. Education is a fundamental right, and the Constitution of the Republic calls for free public education for children between the ages of six and twelve years. The Constitution of the Republic also identifies social welfare, health, and sanitation as fundamental rights. However, all of these rights can be overridden in situations "such as may be necessary to prevent infringement upon the freedoms of others, to avert an imminent danger, to maintain social order, or to promote public welfare." It also identifies military service as a duty to the State.

Preamble

The National Constituent Assembly of the Republic of China, by virtue of the mandate received from the whole body of citizens, in accordance with the teachings bequeathed by Dr. Sun Yat-sen in founding the Republic of China, and in order to consolidate the authority of the State, safeguard the rights of the people, ensure social tranquility, and promote the welfare of the people, do hereby adopt this Constitution to be promulgated throughout the land for faithful and perpetual observance by all.

Article 1

The Republic of China, founded on the Three Principles of the People, shall be a democratic republic of the People, to be governed by the people, and for the people.

Article 5

There shall be complete equality among the various ethnic groups in the Republic of China.

Article 8

1. Personal freedom shall be guaranteed to the people. Except in case of flagrante delicto, which shall be separately prescribed by law, no person shall be arrested or detained other than by a judicial or police organ in accordance with the procedure prescribed by law. No person shall be tried or punished other than by a court of law in accordance with the procedure prescribed by law.
2. When a person is arrested or detained on suspicion of having committed a crime, the organ making the arrest or detention shall inform him and any relative or friend designated by him in writing of the grounds for his arrest or detention, and shall turn him over to a competent court for trial not later than twenty-four hours after his arrest.
4. When a person is unlawfully arrested or detained by any organ, he or any other person may petition the court to make an investigation. The court shall not reject such a petition and shall, within twenty-four hours, investigate the action taken by the organ concerned and deal with the matter in accordance with law.

Article 9

With the exception of persons on active military duty nobody shall be subject to trial by a military tribunal.

Article 10

The people shall have freedom of residence and of change of residence.

Article 11

The people shall have freedom of speech, teaching, writing, and publication.

Article 12

The people shall have freedom of privacy of correspondence.

Article 13

The people shall have freedom of religious belief.

Article 14

The people shall have freedom of assembly and of association.

Article 15

The right to existence, the right to work, and the right to own property shall be guaranteed to the people.

Article 17

The people shall have the right of election, recall, initiative, and referendum.

Article 18

The people shall have the right to take public examinations and hold public offices.

Article 20

The people shall have the duty to perform military service in accordance with law.

Article 21

The people shall have the right and the duty to receive elementary education.

Article 22

All other freedoms and rights of the people that are not detrimental to social order or public welfare shall be guaranteed under the Constitution.

Article 23

All the freedoms and rights enumerated in the preceding articles shall not be restricted by law except such as may be necessary to prevent infringement upon the freedoms of others, to avert an imminent danger, to maintain social order, or to promote public welfare.

Section 4: Social Security

Article 152

The State shall provide suitable opportunities for work to those persons who are able to work.

Article 153

1. The State shall enact laws and carry out policies for the protection of laborers and farmers in order to improve their livelihood and develop their productive skills.
2. Special protection shall be provided for women and children engaging in manual labor, in accordance with their age and physical condition.

Article 155

The State shall establish a system of social insurance to promote social welfare. To the aged and the physically disabled who are unable to make a living, and to victims of extraordinary calamities, the State shall provide appropriate assistance and relief.

Article 156

The State, in order to consolidate the foundation of national existence and development, shall protect motherhood and carry out a policy for the promotion of the welfare of women and children.

Article 157

The State, in order to improve national health, shall establish extensive services for sanitation and health protection, and a system of public medical care.

Article 158

Education and culture shall aim at the development, among the citizens, of the national spirit, the spirit of self-government, of national morality, a healthy physical condition, scientific knowledge and the ability to earn a living.

Article 159

All citizens shall have an equal opportunity to receive education.

Article 160

1. All children of school age from six to twelve years shall receive free elementary education. Those from poor families shall be supplied with books by the Government.
2. All citizens above school age who have not received elementary education shall receive supplementary education free of charge and shall also be supplied with books by the government.

Article 161

The national, provincial and local governments shall provide a large number of scholarships to assist students of good scholastic standing and exemplary conduct who lack the means to continue their school education.

Article 162

All public and private educational and cultural institutions in the country shall, in accordance with the law, be subject to State supervision.

Article 165

The State shall safeguard the livelihood of those who work in the fields of education, science and art, and shall, in accordance with the development of the national economy, increase their remuneration from time to time.

Article 166

The State shall encourage scientific discoveries and inventions and shall protect ancient sites and monuments of historical, cultural, or artistic value.

Source: "Taiwan's Constitution of 1947 with Amendments Through 2005." Constitute Project. https://www.constituteproject.org/constitution/Taiwan_2005.pdf

UNITED STATES: Federal Republic

UNITED STATES

Communications	Land-based Telephones in Use
Facebook Users	139,000,000 (2012)
154,000,000 (estimate) (2013)	Mobile Telephone Subscribers
Internet Users	310,000,000 (2012)
245,000,000 (2009)	Major Daily Newspapers
Internet Users (% of Population)	1,486 (2008)
84.2% (2013)	Average Circulation of Daily Newspapers
Television	
88 sets per 100 population (2002)	57,347,000 (2004)

Education	
School System	
Educational systems in the United States vary by state, but most states begin mandatory formal education at the age of six, with an optional but increasingly popular year of kindergarten starting at the age of five. Primary education occurs in elementary schools and generally lasts for either five or six years. Secondary education usually lasts for either six or seven years, depending on the primary school system in place, and is usually divided into two phases, the first lasting for three years and the second for three or four years.	
Mandatory Education	
Varies by state; most commonly 10 years, from ages 6 to 16.	
Average Years Spent in School for Current Students	
16 (2012)	
Average Years Spent in School for Current Students, Male	
16 (2012)	
Average Years Spent in School for Current Students, Female	
17 (2012)	
Primary School–age Children Enrolled in Primary School	
24,381,923 (2012)	
Primary School–age Males Enrolled in Primary School	
12,546,521 (2012)	
Primary School–age Females Enrolled in Primary School	
11,835,402 (2012)	
Secondary School–age Children Enrolled in Secondary School	
24,122,437 (2012)	
Secondary School–age Males Enrolled in Secondary School	
12,323,549 (2012)	

Secondary School–age Females Enrolled in Secondary School	
11,798,888 (2012)	
Students Per Teacher, Primary School	
14.4 (2012)	
Students Per Teacher, Secondary School	
14.7 (2012)	
Enrollment in Tertiary Education	
20,994,113 (2012)	
Enrollment in Tertiary Education, Male	
9,026,499 (2012)	
Enrollment in Tertiary Education, Female	
11,967,614 (2012)	
Literacy	
99% (2003)	
Energy and Natural Resources	
Electric Power Generation	
4,099,000,000,000 kilowatt hours per year (estimate) (2011)	
Electric Power Consumption	
3,886,000,000,000 kilowatt hours per year (estimate) (2010)	
Nuclear Power Plants	
100 (2014)	
Crude Oil Production	
12,304,500 barrels per day (2013)	
Crude Oil Consumption	
18,886,800 barrels per day (2013)	
Natural Gas Production	
681,400,000,000 cubic meters per year (estimate) (2012)	
Natural Gas Consumption	
689,900,000,000 cubic meters per year (estimate) (2011)	
Natural Resources	
Coal (largest reserves in world), copper, lead, molybdenum, phosphates, rare earth elements, uranium, bauxite, gold, iron, mercury, nickel, potash, silver, tungsten, zinc, petroleum, natural gas, timber	

Environment	Arable Land
CO2 Emissions	19% (2007)
17.3 metric tons per capita (2009)	**Arable Land Per Capita**
Alternative and Nuclear Energy	1 acres per person (2007)
12.0% of total energy use (2011)	Health
Threatened Species	**Average Life Expectancy**
1,152 (2010)	79.6 years (2014)
Protected Areas	**Average Life Expectancy, Male**
1,385,157 (estimate) (2010)	77.1 years (2014)
Geography	**Average Life Expectancy, Female**
Location	81.9 years (2014)
Occupying a major portion of the North American continent, the United States is bounded by Canada to the north, the Atlantic Ocean to the east, the Caribbean Sea and Mexico to the south, and the Pacific Ocean to the west. The noncontiguous states of Alaska and Hawaii lie to the northwest of Canada and in the central Pacific Ocean, respectively.	**Crude Birth Rate**
	13.4 (estimate) (2015)
	Crude Death Rate
	8.2 (estimate) (2015)
	Maternal Mortality
	17 per 100,000 live births (2005–2012 projection)
	Infant Mortality
Time Zone	6 per 1,000 live births (2012)
(Note: The continental United States covers four time zones.)	**Doctors**
	2.5 per 1,000 people (2011)
Land Borders	Industry and Labor
7,611 miles	**Gross Domestic Product (GDP) - official exchange rate**
Coastline	
12,381 miles	$18,365,805,000,000 (estimate) (2015)
Capital	**GDP per Capita**
Washington, D.C.	$57,158 (estimate) (2015)
Area	**GDP - Purchasing Power Parity (PPP)**
3,617,827 sq. miles	$16,237,746,000,000 (estimate) (2013)
Climate	**GDP (PPP) per Capita**
The climate varies substantially, with average annual temperatures ranging from 77°F in Florida to 10°F in Alaska. The average annual rainfall is 29 inches, with Alabama receiving 65 inches and Arizona seven inches of rain each year.	$51,248 (estimate) (2013)
	Industry Products
	Electronic equipment, transportation equipment, machinery, telecommunications, books and magazines, metals, chemicals, rubber, plastics, foodstuffs and beverages.
Land Use	**Agriculture Products**
18.6% arable land; 0.3% permanent crops; 26.0% permanent meadows and pastures; 33.1% forest land; 22.06% other.	Grains, rice, feed crops, oil-bearing crops, dairy products, livestock, fruit, vegetables.

Unemployment	**World Population Rank**
8.1% (2012)	3 rd (2009)
Labor Profile	**Population Density**
Farming, forestry, and fishing: 0.7% manufacturing, extraction, transportation, and crafts: 20.3% managerial, professional, and technical: 37.3% sales and office: 24.2% other services: 17.6% (2009)	87.8 people per square mile (estimate) (2011)
	Population Distribution
	82% urban (2011)
Military	**Age Distribution**
Total Active Armed Forces	0-14: 20.1%
1,580,255 (2010)	15-64: 66.9%
Active Armed Forces	65+: 13%
1% (2010)	(2009)
Annual Military Expenditures	Median Age
$693,600,000,000 (2009)	37.6 years (estimate) (2014)
Military Service	**Population Growth Rate**
The United States has voluntary military service.	0.8% per year (estimate) (2015)
	Net Migration Rate
National Finances	2.5 (estimate) (2015)
Currency	**Trade**
U.S. dollar	**Imported Goods**
Total Government Revenues	Mineral fuels and lubricants, machinery, transportation equipment, food and live animals, chemicals, clothing.
$2,849,000,000,000 (estimate) (2013)	
Total Government Expenditures	**Total Value of Imports**
$3,517,000,000,000 (estimate) (2013)	$1,604,000,000 (2009)
Budget Deficit	**Exported Goods**
-4.0 (estimate) (2013)	Machinery, transportation equipment, cereals, mineral fuels and lubricants, chemicals, crude materials, aircraft, scientific and telecommunications equipment.
GDP Contribution by Sector	
agriculture: 1.1% industry: 19.2% services: 79.7% (2012 est.)	
External Debt	**Total Value of Exports**
$15,680,000,000,000 (estimate) (2012)	$1,612,000,000,000 (estimate) (2012)
Economic Aid Extended	**Import Partners**
$27,075,960,000 (2011)	China - 19.5%; Canada - 14.2%; Mexico - 11.1%; Japan - 6.1%; Germany - 4.5% (2009)
Economic Aid Received	
$0 (2011)	**Export Partners**
Population	Canada - 19.4%; Mexico - 12.2%; China - 8.6%; Japan - 4.8%; United Kingdom - 4.3% (2009).
Population	
321,362,789 (estimate) (2015)	

Current Account Balance	Passenger Cars per 1,000 People
$-360,700,000,000 (estimate) (2013)	423 (2010)
Weights and Measures	**Number of Trucks, Buses, and Commercial Vehicles**
The imperial system is in use, with some exceptions.	
	8,688,600 (2003)
Transportation	**Railroads**
Airports	
	140,695 (2007)
15,079 (2010)	
	Ports
Paved Roads	
100.0% (2010)	Major: 28 (including New York, Houston, Boston, Philadelphia, Baltimore, San Francisco, Los Angeles, New Orleans, Seattle).
Roads, Unpaved	
1,401,791 (2007)	

OVERVIEW

The United States was founded in 1776 by immigrants seeking to free themselves of the colonial influence of the British monarch. Most of the country is located on the southern portion of the North American continent, although there

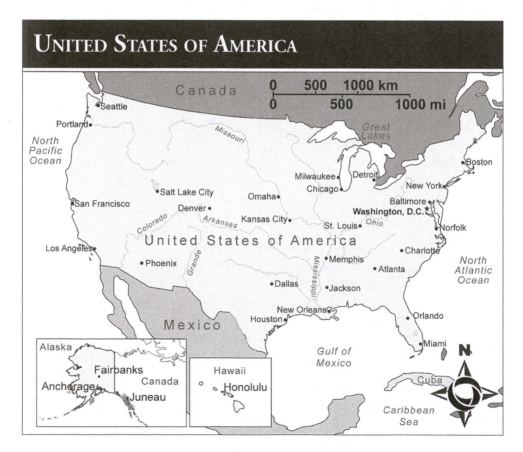

are two outlying states. The United States encompasses a wide variation of terrain and climate, from mountains to plains and subarctic to desert and tropical. More than 318 million people live in the United States. The capital of the United States is Washington, DC.

GOVERNMENT

The United States is a federal republic that declared independence from Great Britain in 1776. The United States of America has a bicameral Congress (composed of the U.S. Senate and the U.S. House of Representatives) and a long-running tradition of democratic multiparty elections. Most of the political powers of government are exercised by the 50 states. At both the federal and state levels, power is shared by the executive, legislative, and judicial branches, which have separate but overlapping powers that act as a system of checks and balances. The president serves as the head of state and head of government. The current president is Barack Obama.

Constitution

The U.S. Constitution took effect in July 1788 and was formally adopted on March 4, 1789. It provides for the establishment of separate but partially interrelated executive, legislative, and judicial branches. The first 10 amendments, collectively known as the Bill of Rights, were ratified by the requisite number of states on December 15, 1791, and took effect on March 1, 1792. They guarantee such basic civil rights as freedom of religion, the prohibition of unreasonable searches and seizures, and the right to keep and bear arms. The Constitution outlines various methods by which it may be amended and such amendments ratified, although only 27 amendments have been added since its inception (including the 10 in the Bill of Rights and two pertaining to the 1919–1933 prohibition against the sale and production of alcohol). The Constitution also provides for the admission of new states.

Executive

Executive power is vested in a president, who may be elected to a maximum of two four-year terms. The president is responsible for the nation's foreign affairs and is also commander in chief of the military. He or she is elected through an electoral college system in which each state is assigned one voter for each representative or senator in Congress. In most states, the candidate who gets the most popular vote in that state is granted all of its electoral college votes, and the candidate receiving the most electoral college votes overall is declared the winner. The vice president is elected on the same ticket as the president and succeeds the president if he or she dies or leaves office. The vice president also serves as president of the Senate and casts deciding votes when necessary. The president is responsible for the execution of federal laws and is aided in this by a cabinet and a massive federal bureaucracy. Cabinet appointments are subject to approval by the Senate. As the position has evolved over the nation's history, the presidency has taken on increased responsibility for policy-making and declaring war, although the latter is formally within the Congress' domain.

Legislature

The United States has a bicameral Congress comprising the Senate and the House of Representatives, which have equal but partially different powers. The 100-member Senate was created to give equal representation to all the states. Each state has two senators elected by popular vote in statewide constituencies, who serve overlapping six-year terms, with one-third of the seats in the chamber coming up for election every two years. Senators must be at least 30 years old. The Senate's particular responsibilities include confirming major presidential appointments and judging the impeachment of public officials. The 435-member House of Representatives was created to give equal representation to all individuals; the number of seats allocated to a state is based on its population. Representatives are elected directly and serve two-year terms. They must be at least 25 years old. The powers of the House of Representatives include the initiation of all appropriation and tax bills (both houses may initiate bills on any other subject) and the initiation of impeachment proceedings against public officials. All statutes must be approved by both houses but cannot pass into law without presidential approval. However, a presidential veto can be overridden by a two-thirds vote of the members of each house. A system of specialized committees conducts most of the business of Congress, with floor votes often based on the committees' recommendations.

Judiciary

The Constitution created one high court, the Supreme Court, and granted Congress the power to create any other federal courts considered necessary. The Supreme Court, which now has nine justices, is responsible for determining the constitutionality of federal laws and executive acts. All federal judges are appointed for life. Supreme Court justices are nominated by the president and are subject to Senate confirmation.

Local Government

The United States includes 50 constituent states and the District of Columbia. Each state has a high degree of self-government but is barred from participating in such areas as defense, foreign affairs, currency and mail, and internal security. Each state has its own constitution and government, which generally reflect the federal system, with a governor, a bicameral legislature (with the exception of Nebraska), and a state court system. Much of the legislation concerning the District of Columbia is determined by the U.S. Congress, and the District has a delegate who may vote on all aspects of legislation except its final passage.

Overseas Possessions

The United States has several dependencies. They include the self-governing incorporated commonwealths of Puerto Rico and the Northern Mariana Islands—both of which have complete political union with the United States—and the unincorporated or external territories of American Samoa, Guam, and the U.S. Virgin Islands, which have a degree of self-government but rely on the United States for aid and defense. For many years, the Marshall Islands, Micronesia, and Palau were associated states of the United States, but they are now independent nations. They each have a compact of free association with the United States, granting them military protection and economic aid. The Marshall Islands achieved independence in 1979, Micronesia became a sovereign country in 1979, and Palau gained full independence in 1994. Puerto Rico, American Samoa, Guam, and the Virgin Islands each send delegates to the U.S. House of Representatives, although the delegates' powers are limited.

Election Qualifications

All citizens 18 years of age and over are eligible to vote.

POLITICS

From 1932, with the first administration of President Franklin D. Roosevelt and the advent of increased government economic and social intervention, the Democratic Party dominated Congress for decades, controlling the House of Representatives for all but 4 of the next 62 years, and the Senate for all but 10 years in that span, even as the Republican Party often dominated the presidency. Since 1994, however, the congressional power balance has shifted more frequently.

The first major dent came in 1980 congressional balloting, when the Republican Party brought an end to the Democratic Party's 28-year hold on the Senate behind the first of Ronald Reagan's two landslide presidential elections. The Democrats regained control of the Senate in 1986. Two years later, Republican Party member George H. W. Bush became the first sitting vice president to win the presidency in more than 150 years, but Democratic Party member Bill Clinton defeated Bush in the 1992 presidential polls, partly due to third-party candidate Ross Perot's splitting of the conservative vote.

The 1994 mid-term legislative elections were disastrous for the Democrats, as the party lost control of the House of Representatives and the Senate for the first time since 1954 and 1986, respectively. Republicans were helped by a large number of Democratic legislators leaving office, leaving open seats, which are generally easier to win than those held by incumbents. Some analysts also stated that voters reacted to what they perceived as an overly ambitious liberal agenda by the Clinton administration. After 1994, President Clinton pursued more centrist policies, and he was reelected in 1996, defeating Republican candidate Bob Dole.

The results of the 2000 presidential election were extremely close and marked by controversy, as the electoral vote hung in the balance until the vote count in Florida could be determined. In December 2000, the U.S. Supreme Court ruled out further recounts, giving the presidency to Republican George W. Bush, who won the presidency despite earning fewer popular votes nationally than his opponent, Al Gore. In 2002, Republicans regained the Senate and increased their majority in the House of Representatives in mid-term elections seen as a public endorsement of President Bush in the wake of the September 11, 2001, terrorist attacks. In November 2004 elections, President Bush was reelected and the Republicans gained still more seats in the House and in the Senate.

In 2006, with dissatisfaction over the Iraq War considered a contributing factor, the Democratic Party gained seats in both the Senate and the House of Representatives, giving them control of both houses of Congress for the first time since 1994. Democrats increased their congressional majorities in 2008 as the nation elected its first African American president, Democratic Party member Barack Obama. In 2010 mid-term elections, however, Republicans once again took control of the House of Representatives with a swing of 63 seats, the largest single-party gain since 1948, and gained 6 seats in the Senate, narrowing the Democratic majority. While a president's party normally loses congressional seats in mid-term elections, the large Republican gains were attributed to dissatisfaction with an economy still struggling from the economic recession of 2008–2009. Also, similar to 1994, many conservative activists maintained that a Democratic president had set too liberal an agenda; this sentiment was amplified by the rise of often well-funded "tea parties" in many areas of the country, which promoted conservative candidates.

Obama won reelection in November 2012, defeating Republican candidate Mitt Romney, a former governor of Massachusetts. In addition, Democrats gained 8 seats in the House of Representatives—not enough to reverse the Republican majority—and 2 seats in the Senate, where they held a 53–45 advantage over Republicans, with 2 Independents. In 2014, however, the Republicans regained control of the Senate.

President Barack Obama giving an address from the White House in Washington, D.C. The United States is a presidential republic, in which the executive and legislative branches of government are separated formally. (DOUG MILLS/UPI/Newscom)

Political Parties

The United States is a multiparty system in which two parties, the Republican Party and the Democratic Party, dominate, in large part by co-opting many of the values of fringe groups. Very few candidates for high office succeed if they are not affiliated with either of these parties, although in 1992, independent presidential candidate Ross Perot succeeded in garnering 19% of the popular vote. U.S. political parties have national organizations, but their membership is very informal in comparison to political parties in other countries.

The Democratic Party, which was originally known as the Republican Party and later as the Democratic Republican Party, is generally a center-left party, though elements of the party span the political spectrum from far left to center-right. The party, which has its roots in the revolutionary era, has traditionally drawn its support from blacks, Jews, the working class, urban dwellers, liberals, and conservative Southerners, but its complexion has changed since the end of the 1970s. Women, the middle class, and homosexuals have become key voting blocs since the November 1992 presidential and congressional elections, and the South has gone rapidly Republican. The Democratic Party has traditionally held power in Congress, but only three Democratic presidents have been elected since 1968, the most recent being current president Barack Obama. The party in general supports a basic social safety net and robust government regulation of the economy.

The conservative Republican Party originally grew out of the antislavery movement of the mid-nineteenth century. The party is to the right of center in its political orientation, but its membership ranges from the extreme right to more centrist elements. It was the nation's dominant party from the 1860s until the 1932 election. It culls most of its support from small-town and rural voters, business people, and voters in the South (which was, until fairly recently, a Democratic stronghold). The party opposes high taxes and government expenditure on welfare programs and regulation of business, while supporting a strong defense program and extensive government intervention in such areas as religion, marriage, and abortion.

Third parties have had limited success in the American political system, although the loose United We Stand America grouping and the Reform Party that supported Ross Perot in the 1992 and 1996 presidential elections, respectively, had some measure of success. Other third parties that have received some support in presidential elections include the leftist Green Party, which advocates environmentalist and pacifist positions; the Libertarian Party, which advocates for the minimization or complete termination of government intervention in the social and economic spheres, and supports fully laissez-faire economics; and the Peace and Freedom Party, a mostly middle-class group that advocates revolutionary change in the direction of socialist and feminist policies.

ECONOMY

The United States has an extremely diverse capitalist economy. Industry—including manufacturing, mining, construction, and utilities—contributes to nearly 20% of gross domestic product (GDP) and includes transportation equipment, food and chemical products, and a wide range of other materials. The nation is home to many of the world's largest multinational companies and is a major center of computer software production. The agricultural sector is also diverse but only contributes about 1% to GDP. The United States has an enormous resource base, including petroleum, coal, copper, iron, mercury, nickel, zinc, gold, and silver. During the first decade of the twentieth century, growth slowed, and unemployment and business failures increased. By the end of the decade, the wars in Iraq and Afghanistan had cost nearly $1 trillion, according to the Congressional Research Service. Federal deficits were also exacerbated by spending programs in response to a severe economic downturn in the fall of 2008, triggered by an ongoing lending crisis that led to the collapse of several large financial institutions. Massive spending plans were introduced in 2008 and 2009 to bolster financial markets and help speed economic recovery. The country's annual average unemployment rate hit 9.6% in 2010, the highest level since 1982. It was not until 2014 that job growth and unemployment rates recovered to pre-recession levels. Despite the slow recovery, the United States remains the world's primary economic power and one of the most affluent of the major industrial nations. Its major trading partners are Canada, Mexico, and Japan, and the country continues to increase its trade with China.

SOCIETY

The United States, known as a nation of immigrants, is a multiethnic country with a rapidly changing demographic. Because the nation has long been and continues to be a highly desirable destination for immigrants, issues surrounding identity in the country are complex. Whites, who largely trace their ancestry back to Europe, are the largest ethnic group, while the Latino population is the most rapidly growing ethnic group in the country.

Diversity has always been present in religious worship, and the U.S. government cannot officially endorse one faith above any other. All of the major Judeo-Christian religions, including Protestantism, Roman Catholicism, Orthodox Christianities, and Judaism, are well-represented but often develop new ideas and practices in the United States. During the nineteenth century, several new sects, including the Church of Jesus Christ of Latter-Day Saints (Mormons), the Seventh-Day Adventist Church, Jehovah's Witnesses, and Christian Scientists, originated here. Increasing numbers of Americans are also practitioners of Islam and Buddhism. English is the nation's dominant language, and many states have passed laws to reinforce that. Yet people of different ethnicities, especially first-generation immigrants, speak their native languages and flavor the English spoken from region to region with many foreign words.

Ethnic Composition

White – 63.7%; Hispanic or Latino – 16.3%; African American – 12.2%; Asian – 4.8%; American Indian and Alaska native – 0.9%; native Hawaiian and other Pacific islander – 0.2%; two or more races – 2.9%

Religion

Protestant – 51.3%; Roman Catholic – 23.9%; unaffiliated – 12.1%; other or unspecified – 2.5%; Mormon – 1.7%; other Christian – 1.6%; Jewish – 1.7%; Buddhist – 0.7%; Muslim – 0.6%

Language

English is the predominant language, but a substantial minority speaks Spanish.

CONTEMPORARY ISSUES

War in Afghanistan

After the World Trade Center and Pentagon attacks of September 11, 2001, most U.S. citizens supported the invasion of Afghanistan, on intelligence that the Taliban government there was providing support and a base for Osama bin Laden and his Al Qaeda network, believed to be responsible for the attacks. In formulating a War on Terror, the George W. Bush administration decided that nations found to be harboring terrorist organizations were fair game for intervention. U.S. and British forces launched the invasion of Afghanistan on October 7, 2001, and within weeks the Taliban government was routed, with most of the leadership fleeing to Pakistan. Bin Laden, however, eluded capture and was believed to be hiding with Al Qaeda operatives in rugged mountainous areas along the Afghanistan–Pakistan border. U.S. and allied forces remained to help build a democratic republic in Afghanistan. Bin Laden was finally killed by a team of U.S. Navy SEALs, in a hideout in Pakistan on May 2, 2011, nearly a decade after the war began. Withdrawal of most U.S. troops, as well as those of NATO allies, is expected by the end of 2014; in May 2014, President Obama announced intentions to leave 9,800 soldiers in the country for another full year once withdrawal occurred in December 2014. As of June 2014, the war in Afghanistan had resulted in 2,182 U.S. combat deaths. Hamid Karzai, president of Afghanistan since December 2001, leads a functioning government, but ongoing Taliban insurgent operations remain a constant threat.

The combined cost of the war in Afghanistan and the 2002–2011 war in Iraq is an ongoing issue for the U.S. economy, especially in light of a slow recovery from the Great Recession of 2007–2009. The wars are estimated to have cost more than $1.5 trillion in direct military spending; however, the accumulated effects of the wars, including the ongoing care of wounded veterans, is expected to eventually cost the United States between $4 trillion and $6 trillion, according to a study by Harvard University.

Immigration

One of the most emotionally charged issues in the United States centers on the subject of illegal immigration. It is estimated that some 12 million workers from Mexico are currently in the country without documentation. Recent discussions in the U.S. Congress have focused on whether to grant these workers amnesty and allow them to remain or to deport them to Mexico and require them to apply for immigration through established procedures. Many observers insist that they should be deported, but even those opposed to their presence in the United

States admit that the removal of such a large group of people would be costly and impractical.

The United States is primarily a nation of immigrants, and at various times in the country's history, immigration has been encouraged to address labor shortages, as was the case during World War I. At other times, such as during the Great Depression, immigrants were made economic scapegoats and faced deportation. The Immigration Reform and Control Act of 1986 was an attempt to penalize employers who employed illegal immigrants while granting amnesty to undocumented workers who could prove continuous residency since 1982. In the early twenty-first century, the nation faced the reality that despite their illegal status, many Mexican immigrants—who often are employed as unskilled labor—contribute to the economy by allowing some businesses to profit by paying lower wages than would be demanded by U.S. citizens. Throughout 2014, national attention was focused on the issue of how to deal with tens of thousands of children and teenagers who streamed illegally across the border, seeking refuge after fleeing poverty, gangs, and rampant crime in their Central American homelands.

Affordable Health Care for America

In March 2010, President Obama signed the Affordable Care Act into law. The sweeping health care legislation constituted the most comprehensive federal health care reform since the mid-1900s, barring insurance companies from dropping coverage due to illness, allowing children to remain on parental health plans until the age of 26, expanding Medicare coverage, and creating a new private insurance exchange (called the Marketplace) to help provide medical coverage for millions of uninsured citizens, among other changes.

At the time the law was created, around 45 million Americans did not have health insurance. Yet, the health care act has sparked great controversy. Private interest groups and citizens, along with more than 24 states, filed legal challenges, and in 2011 the U.S. Court of Appeals in Washington, DC ruled parts of the legislation unconstitutional. A main argument against the law included questions over the right of the federal government to charge U.S. residents an income tax penalty if they did not have minimum essential healthcare coverage; this was viewed as an attempt to force or coerce individuals to purchase health insurance and a violation of constitutional freedoms. In June 2012, the Supreme Court ruled in favor of the law, stating that the individual mandate can be upheld under the Congressional taxation clause in the Constitution.

Some of the provisions of the massive law did not take effect until 2015; however, by 2014, when the individual mandate went into effect, the percent of uninsured Americans had already dropped to the lowest recorded level since 2008.

Excerpt from the Constitution of the United States of America

The Constitution of the United States of America was written during the Constitutional Convention, which was held in Philadelphia in 1787. The document specified that the Constitution would take effect after being ratified by at least nine of the Thirteen Colonies that had recently become independent from the United Kingdom. In part to overcome opposition among many residents of the Thirteen Colonies, the first ten amendments to the Constitution were added in 1791. These ten amendments are known as the Bill of Rights.

The Bill of Rights established as fundamental several political rights that are contained in most of the world's constitutions today. These include freedom of speech, freedom of religion, freedom of assembly, and freedom of the press. It also guarantees the right of the accused to a "speedy and public" trial by jury.

At the time that the Constitution was written, slavery was permitted and practiced in many states, and thus there were no provisions for legal equality among residents of the United States. The concept of equality under the law was established within the Constitution by the enactment of the Thirteenth and Fourteenth Amendments in 1865 and 1868, respectively. These amendments banned slavery and called for "equal protection of the law." The Fifteenth Amendment guaranteed all male citizens the right to vote, and later amendments guaranteed women the right to vote and eliminated poll taxes. However, unlike most of the world's more recently adopted constitutions, the U.S. Constitution does not regard education, welfare, health care, and other social rights as fundamental rights.

We the People of the United States, in Order to form a more perfect Union, establish Justice, insure domestic Tranquility, provide for the common defence, promote the general Welfare, and secure the Blessings of Liberty to ourselves and our Posterity, do ordain and establish this Constitution for the United States of America.

The U.S. Bill of Rights

These amendments were ratified December 15, 1791, and form what is known as the "Bill of Rights."

Amendment I

Congress shall make no law respecting an establishment of religion, or prohibiting the free exercise thereof; or abridging the freedom of speech, or of the press; or the right of the people peaceably to assemble, and to petition the Government for a redress of grievances.

Amendment II

A well regulated Militia, being necessary to the security of a free State, the right of the people to keep and bear Arms, shall not be infringed.

Amendment III

No Soldier shall, in time of peace be quartered in any house, without the consent of the Owner, nor in time of war, but in a manner to be prescribed by law.

Amendment IV

The right of the people to be secure in their persons, houses, papers, and effects, against unreasonable searches and seizures, shall not be violated, and no Warrants shall issue, but upon probable cause, supported by Oath or affirmation, and particularly describing the place to be searched, and the persons or things to be seized.

Amendment V

No person shall be held to answer for a capital, or otherwise infamous crime, unless on a presentment or indictment of a Grand Jury, except in cases arising in the land or naval forces, or in the Militia, when in actual service in time of War or public danger; nor shall any person be subject for the same offence to be twice put in jeopardy of life or limb; nor shall be compelled in any criminal case to be a witness against himself, nor be deprived of life, liberty, or property, without due process of law; nor shall private property be taken for public use, without just compensation.

Amendment VI

In all criminal prosecutions, the accused shall enjoy the right to a speedy and public trial, by an impartial jury of the State and district wherein the crime shall have been committed, which district shall have been previously ascertained by law, and to be informed of the nature and cause of the accusation; to be confronted with the witnesses against him; to have compulsory process for obtaining witnesses in his favor, and to have the Assistance of Counsel for his defence

Amendment VIII

Excessive bail shall not be required, nor excessive fines imposed, nor cruel and unusual punishments inflicted.

Additional amendments

Amendment XIII

Passed by Congress January 31, 1865. Ratified December 6, 1865.

Section 1

Neither slavery nor involuntary servitude, except as a punishment for crime whereof the party shall have been duly convicted, shall exist within the United States, or any place subject to their jurisdiction.

Amendment XIV

Passed by Congress June 13, 1866. Ratified July 9, 1868.

Section 1

All persons born or naturalized in the United States, and subject to the jurisdiction thereof, are citizens of the United States and of the State wherein they reside. No State shall make or enforce any law which shall abridge the privileges or immunities of citizens of the United States; nor shall any State deprive any person of life, liberty, or property, without due process of law; nor deny to any person within its jurisdiction the equal protection of the laws.

Amendment XV

Passed by Congress February 26, 1869. Ratified February 3, 1870.

Section 1

The right of citizens of the United States to vote shall not be denied or abridged by the United States or by any State on account of race, color, or previous condition of servitude.

Amendment XIX

Passed by Congress June 4, 1919. Ratified August 18, 1920.
The right of citizens of the United States to vote shall not be denied or abridged by the United States or by any State on account of sex.

Amendment XXIV

Passed by Congress August 27, 1962. Ratified January 23, 1964.

Section 1

The right of citizens of the United States to vote in any primary or other election for President or Vice President, for electors for President or Vice President, or for Senator or Representative in Congress, shall not be denied or abridged by the United States or any State by reason of failure to pay any poll tax or other tax.

Amendment XXVI

Passed by Congress March 23, 1971. Ratified July 1, 1971.

Section 1

The right of citizens of the United States, who are eighteen years of age or older, to vote shall not be denied or abridged by the United States or by any State on account of age.

Source: "Constitution of the United States." The National Archives. http://www .archives.gov/exhibits/charters/constitution_transcript.html.

CHAPTER 2

COMMUNIST STATES

A communist state is a country that is characterized by one-party rule by a Communist party, whose political activities are guided by Marxist-Leninist principles. In principle, Communist states regard themselves as "dictatorships of the proletariat" with the Communist party guiding and acting in the interests of the entire population. In practice, however, one-party rule in Communist states has tended to enhance the power of Party members, who form a state's elite, at the expense of the majority of the population. Over the course of the twentieth century, numerous countries in Eastern Europe, Asia, and Africa were ruled by Communist governments. As of 2014, however, only five countries can be regarded as Communist states: China, Cuba, Laos, North Korea, and Vietnam.

The concepts underlying Communist ideology are derived from the ideas of Karl Marx (1818–1883), who regarded history as an ongoing struggle between capital and labor. By controlling the means of production, capitalists could control and oppress labor, enhancing wealth at the expense of an increasingly impoverished working class. Marx also regarded the state as an instrument by which capital could increase its control over the working class.

Vladimir Lenin (1870–1924) formulated the concept of the Communist state. Lenin developed the idea that a Communist state, as opposed to the state under capitalism, would be a "dictatorship of the proletariat," which would be led by persons who were fully aware of Marx's theories and who would lead a class struggle that would lead eventually to the overthrow of capitalism as an economic system. Party leaders would manage production and distribution of goods, services, and infrastructure in the interests of the working class. The head of state was also the leader of that country's Communist Party.

However, the first country in which a Communist-oriented government came into power was Russia, where the Bolshevik Communist Party seized power after the Russian Revolution during and after World War I. Lenin became the head of the Communist Party of what would become the Soviet Union and remained the Soviet Union's head of state until he died in 1924. After Lenin's death, Joseph Stalin (1878–1953) succeeded to the leadership of the Soviet Communist Party. Stalin supported the concept of "socialism in one country," by which the Soviet leadership would focus on the development of the Soviet Union itself as a Communist state.

Although Stalin's "socialism within one country" policy dominated the Soviet Union during and after the late 1920s, after World War II Communism spread to other parts of the world. The Soviet Union emerged as a global power after the war, and it supported efforts throughout Eastern Europe to install Communist governments. By the late 1940s, Communist governments had taken power in Poland, Czechoslovakia, Hungary, Bulgaria, Romania, Yugoslavia, Romania, and East Germany. These developments led Sir Winston Churchill to coin the term "Iron Curtain" to describe the ideological divide between Eastern and Western Europe. The Cold War began and continued until the Communist governments of Eastern Europe and the Soviet Union collapsed in the late 1980s and early 1990s. During the Cold War, the Soviets and the Chinese government supported efforts to install Communist governments throughout Asia, Africa, and Latin America. Notably, the Soviets supported the eventually successful efforts of the Chinese Communist Party, led by Mao Zedong (1893–1976), to seize power in China. The Communist Party has remained in control of China's government since 1949.

Communist states collectivized production and have relied on centralized planning in order to manage their economies. Planning was undertaken by members of the Communist Party along with bureaucrats and technical experts employed by the parties. Many of these efforts were unsuccessful, with sometimes disastrous results. For example, in 1958 Mao initiated a program known as the Great Leap Forward. The intent of the Great Leap Forward was to promote rapid industrialization of rural China, including the collectivization of agricultural production. Farmers were forced to abandon private production and work on collective farms, and those who dissented were punished. Others were forced to work in rural industries, leaving a shortage of agricultural workers. Unrealistic production quotas were imposed but could not be met because of ineffective management as well as poor weather. This policy failure led to the Great Chinese Famine, during which between 20 and 40 million people died. For the only time since the Communists took control of China in 1949, the Chinese economy shrunk between 1959 and 1962.

Each Communist state is ruled by its Communist party. In theory, Communist parties were to act on behalf of the interests of the working class, providing the leadership needed for transformation from capitalism to socialism. However, Communist party leaders soon became the elites of their societies. Many were criticized for enriching themselves at the expense of the majority of the people, many of whom suffered from a shortage of consumer goods and the impacts of poor and ineffective planning. Although leaders of Communist states are in theory elected, in practice the candidates are selected by party officials, and opposition is not allowed. Thus Communist states, in effect, are dictatorships.

The world's five remaining Communist states differ considerably as to the interpretation of Communist governance and as to the functions and operations of their governments. Historically, centralization of means of production was a centerpiece of government management in Communist states. Private property, including industries and farms, was confiscated and then managed by government officials. However, many Communist states experienced considerable economic stagnation, which in many cases was associated with bureaucratic inefficiency, ineffective central planning, lack of incentives to innovate, and corruption. Recognizing the impacts of economic stagnation on their countries, some Communist leaders began to retreat from the idea of universal collective production and centralized planning. Instead, some began to permit and even to encourage private enterprise. For example, after Mao's death in 1976 his successors in China allowed limited private enterprise. Private enterprise in China has intensified and has contributed to China's rapid rise as a major economic power. However, China's Communist Party continues to be in firm control of the government, with dissent suppressed and dissidents subject to punishment. The Chinese example illustrates that whether capitalist production and Communist governance can continue to coexist remains an open question.

Other Communist states have approached the question of economic development within the Communist model in different ways. Vietnam has generally followed China's lead. As in China, the Vietnamese Communist Party maintains full control of the government. Public officials are Party members, and only persons whose candidacies are approved by the Party can run for public office. However, Vietnam has also allowed more and more private enterprise, and its economy has expanded considerably in recent years.

The three remaining Communist states—Laos, Cuba, and North Korea—are much smaller states with correspondingly smaller economies. Laos is the smallest of these states, with a population estimated at 6.5 million. The government of Laos is controlled by the Lao People's Revolutionary Party, whose leader is the head of state. The Prime Minister, who is the head of the government, is also a senior Communist official. Given its location adjacent to China and Vietnam, and given its small size, Laos' economy is tied considerably to those of its neighbors, although the majority of Laotians remain self-sufficient subsistence farmers. Tourism has burgeoned in China, Vietnam, and Laos, generating substantial amounts of foreign capital, which is invested in the production process. However, tourism remains under strict control of the governments of these three states, and for the most part the activities and movements of foreign tourists are limited strictly.

While the growth of Communism and the organization of Communist governments in Vietnam and Laos have been influence heavily by neighboring China, the situation in Cuba is much different. In 1959, rebels under the leadership of Fidel Castro (1926–) ousted Cuba's corrupt government and seized power. After taking over Cuba's government, Castro legalized the Communist Party and established strong ties with the Soviet Union. Castro's government was organized along Soviet lines, and these procedures continue today, more than two decades after the collapse of Soviet Communism. The Communist Party is Cuba's only legal political party, and only one candidate who has been endorsed by the Party is permitted to run for each legislative seat. Today, Castro remains the head of state although given his advanced age and uncertain health he has relinquished most of his power.

North Korea also professes to be a Communist state that is organized along the lines established by Lenin in the Soviet Union and Mao in China. However, in practice North Korea can be regarded as an autocracy, with power in the hands of the Communist Party's leader, who functions as a dictator. Kim Il Sung (1912–1994) served as the First Secretary of the Communist Party beginning in 1948, when Communists supported by the Soviet Union seized control of the government. He remained in full control until his death, after which his son Kim Jong Il (1941–2011) took over. After Kim Jong Il died, his son Kim Jong Un (1983–) became North Korea's ruler. Thus members of the same family have held dictatorial powers in North Korea for more than six decades. A cult of personality has been developed around the Kim family. Despite North Korea's poverty and very weak economy, Kim Jong Un's wealth has been estimated at as much as $5 billion U.S. dollars.

—Fred M. Shelley

Further Reading

Anne Applebaum, *Iron Curtain: The crushing of Eastern Europe, 1944–1956*. New York: Knopf Doubleday, 2013.

Richard Pipes, *Communism: A history*. New York: Modern Library Chronicles, 2003.

David Priestland, *The red flag: A history of communism*. New York: Grove Press, 2009.

CHINA: Communist State

CHINA

Communications	Land-based Telephones in Use
Facebook Users	278,860,000 (2012)
560,000 (estimate) (2013)	Mobile Telephone Subscribers
Internet Users	1,100,000,000 (2012)
389,000,000 (2009)	Major Daily Newspapers
Internet Users (% of Population)	1,021 (2004)
45.8% (2013)	Average Circulation of Daily Newspapers
Television	
38 sets per 100 population (2006)	96,762,558 (2004)

Education	Enrollment in Tertiary Education, Male
School System	15,969,145 (2012)
Chinese students begin school at the age of six. After six years of primary school, they continue to three years of early secondary education and three years of upper secondary education.	**Enrollment in Tertiary Education, Female**
	16,416,816 (2012)
	Literacy
	95% (2010)
Mandatory Education	**Energy and Natural Resources**
9 years, from ages 6 to 15.	**Electric Power Generation**
Average Years Spent in School for Current Students	5,398,000,000,000 kilowatt hours per year (estimate) (2013)
13 (2012)	**Electric Power Consumption**
Average Years Spent in School for Current Students, Male	5,322,000,000,000 kilowatt hours per year (estimate) (2013)
13 (2012)	**Nuclear Power Plants**
Average Years Spent in School for Current Students, Female	21 (2014)
	Crude Oil Production
13 (estimate) (2012)	4,459,400 barrels per day (2013)
Primary School–age Children Enrolled in Primary School	**Crude Oil Consumption**
	10,276,800 barrels per day (2012)
99,540,477 (2012)	**Natural Gas Production**
Primary School–age Males Enrolled in Primary School	117,100,000,000 cubic meters per year (estimate) (2013)
98,814,166 (2012)	**Natural Gas Consumption**
Primary School–age Females Enrolled in Primary School	150,000,000,000 cubic meters per year (estimate) (2013)
726,311 (2012)	**Natural Resources**
Secondary School–age Children Enrolled in Secondary School	Coal, iron ore, petroleum, natural gas, mercury, tin, tungsten, antimony, manganese, molybdenum, vanadium, magnetite, aluminum, lead, zinc, rare earth elements, uranium, hydropower potential (world's largest)
95,004,209 (2012)	
Secondary School–age Males Enrolled in Secondary School	
50,174,443 (2012)	
Secondary School–age Females Enrolled in Secondary School	**Environment**
	CO2 Emissions
44,829,766 (2012)	5.8 metric tons per capita (2009)
Students Per Teacher, Primary School	**Alternative and Nuclear Energy**
18.2 (2012)	4.0% of total energy use (2010)
Students Per Teacher, Secondary School	**Threatened Species**
14.5 (2012)	917 (2010)
Enrollment in Tertiary Education	**Protected Areas**
32,385,961 (2012)	1,562,718 (estimate) (2010)

Geography	Average Life Expectancy, Male
Location	73.1 years (2014)
Covering a large part of eastern Asia, China is bordered by Mongolia and Russia to the north; Vietnam, Laos, Thailand, Myanmar, Bhutan, Nepal, and India to the south; Pakistan and Afghanistan to the west; and Tajikistan, Kyrgyzstan, and Kazakhstan to the northwest. China borders the Democratic People's Republic of Korea to the northeast and has a long Pacific coastline.	**Average Life Expectancy, Female**
	77.4 years (2014)
	Crude Birth Rate
	12.1 (estimate) (2015)
	Crude Death Rate
	7.6 (estimate) (2015)
	Maternal Mortality
	56 per 100,000 live births (2005–2012 projection)
Time Zone	**Infant Mortality**
13 hours ahead of U.S. Eastern Standard	12 per 1,000 live births (2012)
Land Borders	**Doctors**
13,760 miles	1.9 per 1,000 people (2012)
Coastline	**Industry and Labor**
9,010 miles	**Gross Domestic Product (GDP) - official exchange rate**
Capital	
Beijing	$10,940,337,000,000 (estimate) (2015)
Area	**GDP per Capita**
3,695,500 sq. miles	$7,961 (estimate) (2015)
Climate	**GDP - Purchasing Power Parity (PPP)**
China's climate varies widely across its diverse geographical regions, ranging from subtropical in the far south to cold and rainy in the east. While the average annual temperature in the north is below 50°F, the northwestern regions are characterized by hot, arid weather.	$13,623,255,000,000 (estimate) (2013)
	GDP (PPP) per Capita
	$10,011 (estimate) (2013)
	Industry Products
	Textiles, iron, coal, cement, machinery, steel, fertilizer, processed foods, wood, armaments, petroleum, automobiles, consumer electronics.
Land Use	
15.1% arable land; 1.3% permanent crops; 42.9% permanent meadows and pastures; 22.0% forest land; 18.7% other.	**Agriculture Products**
	Rice, vegetables, sweet potatoes, sorghum, maize, wheat, peanuts, sugarcane, potatoes, pigs, sheep, cattle, soy beans, cotton, opium (illicit).
Arable Land	
15% (2007)	
Arable Land Per Capita	**Unemployment**
0 acres per person (2007)	4.5% (2012)
Health	**Labor Profile**
Average Life Expectancy	agriculture: 34.8% industry: 29.5% services: 35.7% (estimate) (2011)
75.2 years (2014)	

Military	Age Distribution
Total Active Armed Forces	0-14: 17.9%
2,285,000 (estimate) (2010)	15-64: 73.4%
Active Armed Forces	65+: 8.6%
0% (2010)	-2009
Annual Military Expenditures	**Median Age**
$70,300,000,000 (2009)	36.7 years (estimate) (2014)
Military Service	**Population Growth Rate**
Service in China's military is by selective conscription, with two-year terms.	0.4% per year (estimate) (2015)
	Net Migration Rate
National Finances	-0.3 (estimate) (2015)
Currency	Trade
Yuan	**Imported Goods**
Total Government Revenues	Machinery and transportation equipment, petroleum and petroleum products, telecommunications equipment, plastics, chemicals, fertilizer, steel, iron, foodstuffs.
$2,118,000,000,000 (estimate) (2013)	
Total Government Expenditures	
$2,292,000,000,000 (estimate) (2013)	**Total Value of Imports**
Budget Deficit	$353,300,800,000 (2009)
-2.1 (estimate) (2013)	**Exported Goods**
GDP Contribution by Sector	Clothing, footwear, fabric, machinery and transportation equipment, chemicals, petroleum and petroleum products, fertilizer, minerals, toys, textiles.
agriculture: 10.1% industry: 45.3% services: 44.6% (2012 est.)	
External Debt	
$863,200,000,000 (estimate) (2013)	**Total Value of Exports**
Economic Aid Extended	$2,021,000,000,000 (estimate) (2012)
$0 (2011)	**Import Partners**
Economic Aid Received	Japan - 4.1%; Taiwan - 3.1%; South Korea - 2.9%; United States -2.7%; Germany -1.8% (2009)
$-796,000,000 (2011)	
Population	**Export Partners**
Population	United States - 8.0%; Japan - 3.5%; Germany - 1.9%; South Korea - 1.8%; Netherlands -1.3% (2009)
1,361,512,535 (estimate) (2015)	
World Population Rank	
1 st (2010)	**Current Account Balance**
Population Density	$182,800,000,000 (estimate) (2013)
363.8 people per square mile (estimate) (2011)	**Weights and Measures**
Population Distribution	The metric system is in force, although traditional Chinese measurement units are also widely used.
47% urban (2011)	

Transportation	Number of Trucks, Buses, and Commercial Vehicles
Airports	
497 (2012)	9,555,500 (2005)
Paved Roads	Railroads
53.5% (2008)	48,364 (2008)
Roads, Unpaved	Ports
Not Available	Major: 12 (including Dalian, Qinhuangdao, Tianjin, Qingdao, Shanghai, Huangpu, Yantai, and Ningbo).
Passenger Cars per 1,000 People	
44 (2010)	

OVERVIEW

The world's most populous country and one of the largest in area, China spans much of East Asia. Two-thirds of China's enormous population of more than 1.3 billion live in the lowlands of the nation's east. The capital of the country is Beijing, located in northeast China. Because of its great size, China comprises two

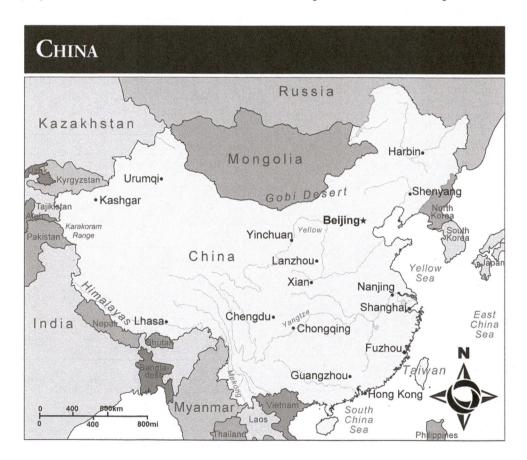

distinct climatic zones: the north and west are semidesert or desert, and are subject to extreme temperature variations; while the south and southeast are warmer and more humid, and receive rainfall all year. However, monsoons in summer bring rain to most of the country. Extreme weather such as droughts and floods are common.

GOVERNMENT

Mainland China was unified under the Qin Dynasty in 221 B.C.E. The People's Republic of China today is a communist state that was established on October 1, 1949, with Mao Zedong at its head. Effective political power rests with the Chinese Communist Party (CCP). China's current president and general secretary of the CCP is Xi Jinping, and the premier is Li Keqiang. The premier chairs the State Council (cabinet), while the president is the head of state. The highest organ of state power is the National People's Congress, although China's legislature follows the will of the ruling CCP. In Mandarin (the Chinese dialect that serves as the nation's principal language), the People's Republic of China is known as *Zhonghua Renmin Gongheguo*.

Constitution

The Chinese Constitution was adopted by the National People's Congress (NPC) on December 4, 1982. It was amended in 1988, 1993, 1999, and 2004, and stipulates that "the People's Republic of China is a socialist state under the people's democratic dictatorship led by the working class and based on the alliance of workers and peasants." It recognizes the CCP as the core leadership of the People's Republic and restores the largely ceremonial post of president as head of state. It abolishes the right to strike and excludes freedom of speech. The Constitution guarantees minority rights and equal pay for equal work, and requires family planning and the payment of taxes.

Executive

Executive power is vested in the State Council, which is headed by the premier and appointed by and accountable to the National People's Congress. The term of the State Council runs concurrent with that of the NPC. The council is composed of the premier (State Council chairperson), vice premiers, state councilors, government ministers, auditor general, and the secretary general, all of whom are responsible to the NPC. The premier presides over the State Council and administers all national policies, with the assistance of the vice premiers and state councilors. Ministers are responsible for matters related to their respective offices. Assisted by the vice president, the president nominates the premier, receives foreign diplomats, appoints representatives abroad, ratifies treaties, announces states of emergency and states of war, and issues pardons and military orders.

Legislature

The National People's Congress is the highest organ of state power and operates in accordance with the will of the CCP. Led by an elected Standing Committee, congressional deputies serve five-year terms and meet once a year. Deputies are elected indirectly by provincial people's congresses, autonomous regions, central government municipalities, and the People's Liberation Army. The NPC has the power to amend the constitution, make laws, elect and recall the president and vice president, appoint and remove the State Council, and approve national economic policies. Between annual congressional sessions, legislative power is exercised by the Standing Committee.

Judiciary

The Supreme People's Court is elected by and responsible to the National People's Congress. It is the highest judicial body and oversees a hierarchy of civil, economic, and administrative lower people's courts. Headed by an independent Supreme People's Procuratorate, a parallel system of courts ensures the observance of law and the prosecution of criminal cases. In addition, the Supreme People's Court supervises corresponding lower procuratorate courts at various regional and local levels.

Local Government

China is divided into twenty-two provinces (excluding Taiwan), five autonomous regions (including Tibet), two Special Administrative Regions (Hong Kong and Macau), and four centrally governed municipal districts. Regional and local administrative authority is vested in provincial and municipal people's congresses indirectly elected to five-year terms; prefecture, city, and county congresses elected to three-year terms; and town congresses elected to two-year terms.

Election Qualifications

All citizens 18 years of age and older are eligible to vote.

POLITICS

China is a communist state in which the Chinese Communist Party (CCP) holds all power. CCP leader Mao Zedong announced the establishment of the People's Republic of China on October 1, 1949, following a civil war in which Chinese communist forces ousted the Nationalist Party (Kuomintang) government of Chiang Kai-shek, which fled to the nearby island of Taiwan. In the 1950s and 1960s, China undertook a massive economic and social reconstruction under Mao.

After Mao's death in 1976, CCP Politburo leader Deng Xiaoping renounced mass political movements and introduced a pragmatic program of socialist economic reform policies, although he staunchly opposed any political reform. Since the economic reforms were instituted, China's gross domestic product has grown on average 10% every year. However, the new prosperity under Deng was tarnished by unchecked corruption, inflation, and industrial pollution. CCP secretary general Jiang Zemin became the most powerful man in China in 1993, when he was elected both president and Central Military Commission chairperson. Upon taking office in 1998, then-premier Zhu Rongji spearheaded the government's efforts to turn ailing state-owned enterprises into profitable stockholding companies, restructure the debt-ridden banking system, halve the government's bureaucracy, and privatize the housing market. At the end of the twentieth century, China's government began a widespread crackdown on corruption, and continues to execute officials found guilty of graft, theft, or other financial improprieties.

In 2003, the National People's Congress officially handed power to a younger generation of leaders, who had been handpicked by their predecessors to take over the reins of government. At the head of China's "fourth generation" of government leaders were Hu Jintao, president of China, and Wen Jiabao, the premier. With Jiang Zemin's retirement as head of China's military in September 2004, China completed the first orderly transfer of power since the communist takeover in 1949, as Hu assumed the role of unchallenged leader of the nation. During his decade in office, Hu maintained political control, resumed state control over some economic sectors, and encouraged foreign investment.

China had become a solid world power by the time Xi Jinping succeeded Hu Jintao in 2013. Together with Premier Li Keqiang, Hu has continued to pursue economic reforms, strong foreign investment, and limited political rights. Although China's economic progress has been considerable (especially in manufacturing), the country still faces the difficult task of maintaining free-market capitalism within a communist dictatorship, while repressing human rights and free speech in a borderless, Internet-connected world.

Political Parties

The Chinese Communist Party (Zhongguo Gongchan Dang) wields complete political control over the nation, although eight small minority parties are permitted to function under the communist banner. Leaders of some of these parties hold high government offices.

The CCP was formalized in 1975 after a period of instability caused by the Maoist Cultural Revolution, launched in 1966. The supreme CCP authority, the National Party Congress, elects a Central Committee, which in turn elects the Politburo and the Secretariat, the party's administrative organ. The Politburo's ruling Standing

Xi Jinping, President of the People's Republic of China and General Secretary of China's Communist Party. He became General Secretary in 2012 and President in 2013. (SK Hon/ EyePress News)

Committee supersedes the Secretariat and forms the nation's effective body of leaders.

Minority parties include the Revolutionary Committee of the Kuomintang, the China Democratic League, the China Democratic National Construction Association, the China Association for Promoting Democracy, the Chinese Peasants' and Workers' Democratic Party, China Zhi Gong Dang, Jiusan Society, and the Taiwan Democratic Self-Government League.

ECONOMY

Under economic reforms, China has gradually moved from a centrally planned economy to a market-oriented system and is currently the largest exporter in the world. Unfamiliar with the workings of such a system, however, the government has halted growth a number of times to rescue the economy from the instability of hot and cold cycles. Despite the nation's impressive economic development during the past two decades, reforming the state sector remains a major hurdle. In the late twentieth century, the government announced plans to merge, sell, or close the vast majority of the state-owned sector and called for increased "public ownership," a euphemism for privatization. However, in recent years, the Chinese government has expressed interest in renewing state ownership in sectors crucial to the security of China's economy, in order to foster growth in those areas.

Despite China's economic improvements, the country remains a developing economy. Nearly 99 million people are living below the poverty line in China. A number of factors pose challenges to China's continued prosperity: a high economic disparity between wealthy city-dwellers and poor farmers; corruption among government officials, both national and local; environmental damage caused by unregulated development; and an increased elderly population due to improved life expectancy, the post-World War II baby boom, and the country's one-child policy.

In the early twenty-first century, Chinese companies have made bold and unprecedented moves to take over U.S. corporations. In 2013, Chinese companies spent $14 billion acquiring U.S. firms or opening U.S. branches of Chinese-owned businesses. Relations between the two countries soured in May of 2014 when the U.S. Department of Justice indicted five Chinese military officers for hacking into six major U.S. corporations and stealing industrial secrets. Chinese foreign ministry spokesperson called the charges "fabricated" and announced that China would suspend its involvement in a joint cyber security work group that was established between the two countries in 2013.

China's main exports include electronics and data processing equipment, clothing, mobile phones, and textiles. The United States is one of China's largest export partners. South Korea is China's largest import partner.

SOCIETY

China has always been home to many peoples, but the Han, who make up over 90% of the population today, are often thought of as the most "Chinese" because their dynasty was the first to systematize imperial government, and their written characters (*hansi* or *Kanji* in Japan) have influenced writing throughout East Asia. Mandarin Chinese is the country's official language, but even among the Han other dialects are spoken. Most of China's national minorities also speak their own languages. Special consideration for such minority nationalities as the Zhuang, Hui, and Uighur has been shown through their exemption from population control programs. For most of the period since 1949 the government has been intolerant of religion, especially Christianity, though it has been more patient with the practice of Islam by national minorities. In recent years, religious practice has become more open, although regulated strictly. However, organized religions are less important to today's Chinese than the folk beliefs that combine Buddhism, Taoism, ancestral worship, and animism.

Ethnic Composition

Han Chinese – 91.9%; other (including Zhuang, Manchu, Hui, Uighur, Miao, Tibetan, Mongol, Korean, Yi, and Buyi) – 8.1%

Language

Mandarin Chinese is the nation's principal language. The Yue (Cantonese), Wu (Shanghainese), Minbei (Fuzhou), Minnan (Hokkien-Taiwanese), Xiang, Gan, and Hakka dialects are spoken locally. The Tibetan, Mongol, and Uighur minorities also speak their own distinct languages.

Religion

China is officially atheist; consequently 52.2% of its residents report no religious affiliation. Of those who do follow a religion, affiliation is: folk religion– 21.9%; Buddhist –18.2%; Christian –5.1%; Muslim – 1.8%; Hindu – less than 1%; Jewish – less than 1%; other (including Daoist) – 0.7%

CONTEMPORARY ISSUES

Environment/Pollution

In recent years, China's economy has grown at one of the fastest rates in the world, but at great cost to the nation's environment. China's environmental degradation can be measured not just by extremely high levels of air and water pollution, but also by public health costs and worker absenteeism. China's air pollution is widespread: smokestacks billow black vapor from antiquated factories, many Chinese still use coal to heat their houses, and a sharp increase in car ownership has choked the nation's roads with exhaust fumes. China also continues to build about two new fossil-fuel power stations every week, leading to the country's status as one of the world's biggest emitters of greenhouse gases.

In addition, China's waterways have been polluted by industrial waste and sewage, which has increased the incidence of waterborne diseases throughout the country. In northern China, encroaching deserts are prompting residents to migrate to overburdened cities. China's rapid industrialization has been accomplished with virtually no concern for its environmental impact, a fact that government leaders are only now beginning to address.

Overpopulation

China is the world's most populous nation, with more than 1.3 billion people. The country's population exploded after the communist takeover in 1949, as people

Residents of Beijing wearing face masks to mitigate the impacts of unhealthy smog. China's Communist government has promoted rapid industrialization and economic development, but China's emphasis on economic growth has resulted in large-scale environmental degradation including air pollution. (CHINE NOUVELLE/SIPA/Newscom)

were encouraged to have more and more children. That all changed during the 1970s, as government leaders realized that the skyrocketing birth rate was causing numerous economic and social problems for China. Thus, in 1979, the government imposed the one-child policy, which encouraged (some say forced) couples to have no more than one child. After the imposition of the policy, China's birth rate fell from 5.83 children per couple in the early 1970s to 2.1 children in 1990. The current figure is about 1.6 children per couple. Still, in 2007, China's top family-planning official warned of an increase in China's population due to a widening of the wealth gap and early marriages in the country's rural areas. By the end of 2011, more people were living in China's cities than in rural areas, a first in the nation's history, which has placed tremendous pressure on the country's resources and exacerbated its already troublesome pollution problem.

Corruption

Corruption has become pervasive throughout China, cultivated in the soil of a booming economy and rampant materialism. In 2005, then-President Hu Jintao told Chinese Communist Party officials that corruption is the main factor threatening the party's ability to stay in power. He called for new rules that would fight corruption by promoting education, institutional accountability, and civil monitoring. Government leaders are fully aware that the vast gap between China's rich and poor, exacerbated by corruption and abuse of power on the part of officials, will lead to widespread social and political dissatisfaction and instability. In recent years, China has seen an increasing number of protests by peasants, with several sparked by revelations that local officials had stolen public funds that were supposed to be used for compensating poor farmers for land the government seized for development projects. There has also been an increase in so-called "naked officials" who send family members overseas to administer private financial accounts largely consisting of public funds diverted from China, and often flee the country themselves.

In addition, China's food and drug exports have come under fire around the world for their inclusion of toxic substances. In 2007, a Beijing court convicted China's former top drug regulator, Zheng Xiaoyu, of taking bribes worth more than $830,000 when he was director of the State Food and Drug Administration. Zheng received the penalty that has become standard in China's most egregious corruption cases: he was executed. Such harsh sentences are supposed to set examples for Chinese citizens considering corrupt practices, though the problem persists at all levels of Chinese society.

Human Rights/Censorship

Although much of China has transitioned to a capitalist-style economy, the country is still a communist dictatorship. The Chinese government regularly jails citizens for exercising any form of freedom of association, religion, and expression, among other human rights. Overt criticism of Chinese Communist Party officials is not allowed, and the country's judicial system is controlled by party officials. According to a 2014 Human Rights Watch report, China has engaged in violent crackdowns on protesters, petitioners, and rights activists across the country since at least 2007. One of the most severe crackdowns on activists occurred in 2013, when more than 50 individuals were criminally detained in the nine months between February and October. China has been cited for discrimination against women, disabled persons, and religious minorities. And arbitrary arrest and detention remain serious problems. According to several international reports, some 160,000 people were serving sentences in China's "reeducation" camps at the beginning of 2013; however, that number began declining in November after the government announced intentions to abolish labor camps in the near future.

Also, China has arrested and forcibly repatriated hundreds of North Koreans who had escaped to China to live in secret, only to be returned to a country whose human rights record is even worse than that of China. In addition, China's 1950 seizure of Tibet has led to continuous charges of brutality and other abuses against Tibetans, who are immediately imprisoned if they protest their treatment. Although China has censored news media since the founding of the People's Republic in 1949, during the twenty-first century, Chinese officials are facing their greatest threat to suppression of free thought and expression: the Internet. In recent years, China has announced new rules aimed at tightening control over news and other items posted on the Internet, and threatening severe punishment for those who do not comply.

Excerpt from the Constitution of the People's Republic of China

The Constitution of the People's Republic of China was adopted in 1982, with subsequent revisions. The 1982 Constitution superseded three previous constitutions that had been adopted since the People's Republic was founded in 1949.

The Preamble to the present Chinese constitution makes specific reference to China's history as a unified state. It also identifies the People's Republic as a socialist state under which the "socialist transformation of the private ownership [of property]" meant that "the lives of the people improved considerably." The Preamble also identifies China as a country whose mission is to support "oppressed" and developing nations in their "just struggle" against capitalism. The Constitution specifies that all land and natural resources belong to the state, as representatives of the people.

The Constitution specifies political rights that are associated with many constitutions throughout the world, including the rights to freedom of speech, freedom of the press, and freedom of assembly. However, in practice these rights are not enforced. Press freedom is restricted severely, and the atheistic Chinese state places significant restrictions on the practice of religion. The Constitution also identifies numerous economic rights, including the right to education and "the right to material assistance from the state and society when they are old, ill, or disabled."

The Chinese constitution also addresses family relationships, including the statement that people "have the duty to support and assist their parents." These clauses are significant in light of China's controversial family-planning programs, but they can also be linked to the Confucian tradition that dates back more than two thousand years.

China is a country with one of the longest histories in the world. The people of all ethnic groups in China have jointly created a culture of grandeur and have a glorious revolutionary tradition.

Great and earthshaking historical changes took place in China in the 20th century.

The Revolution of 1911, led by Dr. Sun Yat-sen . . . gave birth to the Republic of China. But the historic mission . . . to overthrow imperialism and feudalism remained unaccomplished.

. . . the Chinese people of all ethnic groups led by the Communist Party of China with Chairman Mao Zedong as its leader ultimately, in 1949, overthrew the rule of imperialism, feudalism and bureaucrat-capitalism, won the great victory . . . and founded the People's Republic of China. Since then the Chinese people have taken control of state power and become masters of the country.

After . . . the socialist transformation of the private ownership . . . was completed, the system of exploitation of man by man abolished and the socialist system established . . . the life of the people improved considerably.

. . . the successes in [China's] socialist cause have been achieved by the Chinese people of all ethnic groups . . . by upholding truth, correcting errors and surmounting numerous difficulties and hardships. China will be in the primary stage of socialism for a long time to come.

The exploiting classes as a class have been abolished . . . However, class struggle will continue . . . The Chinese people must fight against those forces and elements . . . that are hostile to China's socialist system . . .

China consistently . . . works to strengthen unity with the people of other countries, supports the oppressed nations and the developing countries in their just struggle . . . and strives to safeguard world peace . . .

Article 2

All power in the People's Republic of China belongs to the people.

Article 4

All ethnic groups . . . are equal.

Article 7

The state-owned economy, that is, the socialist economy with ownership by the whole people, is the leading force in the national economy.

Article 9

All mineral resources, waters, forests, mountains, grasslands, unreclaimed land, beaches and other natural resources are owned by the state, that is, by the whole people . . .

Article 10

Land in the cities is owned by the state.

Article 14

The state continuously raises labor productivity, improves economic results and develops the productive forces by enhancing the enthusiasm of the working people . . . and improving the organization of work.

The state properly apportions accumulation and consumption, concerns itself with the interests of the collective and the individual and . . . improves the material and cultural life of the people.

Article 19

The state establishes and administers schools . . . universalizes compulsory primary education and promotes secondary, vocational and higher education as well as pre-school education.

Article 25

The state promotes family planning so that population growth may fit the plans for economic and social development.

Article 33

All persons holding the nationality of the People's Republic of China are citizens . . . All citizens . . . are equal before the law.

The state respects and guarantees human rights.

Every citizen is entitled to the rights and at the same time must perform the duties prescribed by the Constitution.

Article 34

All citizens . . . who have reached age 18 have the right to vote and stand for election, regardless of ethnic status, race, sex, occupation, family background, religious belief, education, property status or length of residence, except persons deprived of political rights according to law.

Article 35

Citizens . . . enjoy freedom of speech, of the press, of assembly, of association, of procession and of demonstration.

Article 36

Citizens . . . enjoy freedom of religious belief.

No state organ, public organization or individual may compel citizens to believe in, or not to believe in, any religion . . . No one may make use of religion to engage in activities that disrupt public order, impair the health of citizens or interfere with the educational system of the state.

Article 37

Freedom of the person of citizens of the People's Republic of China is inviolable. No citizen may be arrested except with . . . decision of a people's procuratorate . . . or a people's court, and arrests must be made by a public security organ.

Unlawful detention . . . is prohibited, and unlawful search of the person of citizens is prohibited.

Article 38

Insult, libel, false accusation . . . is prohibited.

Article 39

Unlawful search of, or intrusion into, a citizen's residence is prohibited.

Article 40

Freedom and privacy of correspondence . . . are protected by law. No organization or individual may . . . infringe upon citizens' freedom and privacy of correspondence, except in cases where, to meet the needs of state security or of criminal investigation, public security or procuratorial organs are permitted to censor correspondence . . .

Article 41

Citizens . . . have the right to criticize and make suggestions regarding any state organ or functionary . . . but fabrication or distortion of facts for purposes of libel or false incrimination is prohibited.

. . . No one may suppress such complaints, charges and exposures or retaliate against the citizens making them.

Article 42

Citizens . . . have the right as well as the duty to work.

. . . the state creates conditions for employment, enhances occupational safety and health, improves working conditions . . .

Work is a matter of honor for every citizen who is able to work. All working people . . . should approach their work as the masters of the country that they are. The state . . . commends and rewards advanced workers.

Article 43

Working people . . . have the right to rest.

The state expands facilities for the rest and recuperation of the working people and prescribes working hours and vacations . . .

Article 44

The state applies the system of retirement for workers . . . the livelihood of retired personnel is ensured by the state and society.

Article 45

Citizens . . . have the right to material assistance from the state and society when they are old, ill or disabled.

The state and society ensure the livelihood of disabled members of the armed forces, provide pensions to the families of martyrs and give preferential treatment to the families of military personnel.

The state and society help make arrangements for the work, livelihood and education of the blind, deaf-mute and other handicapped citizens.

Article 46

Citizens . . . have the duty as well as the right to receive education.

The state promotes the all-round development of children and young people, morally, intellectually and physically.

Article 47

Citizens . . . have the freedom to engage in scientific research, literary and artistic creation and other cultural pursuits.

Article 48

Women . . . enjoy equal rights with men in all spheres of life, in political, economic, cultural, social and family life.

The state protects the rights and interests of women, applies the principle of equal pay for equal work . . . and trains and selects cadres from among women.

Article 49

Marriage, the family and mother and child are protected by the state.

Both husband and wife have the duty to practice family planning.

Parents have the duty to rear and educate their children . . . and children who have come of age have the duty to support and assist their parents.

Maltreatment of old people, women and children is prohibited.

Source: "Constitution." The Central People's Government of The People's Republic of China. http://english.gov.cn/2005-08/05/content_20813.htm.

NORTH KOREA: Communist State with Dictator Leader

NORTH KOREA

Communications		Primary School–age Males Enrolled in Primary School	
Facebook Users			
Not Available		Not Available	
Internet Users (% of Population)		Primary School–age Females Enrolled in Primary School	
Not Available			
Television		Not Available	
17 sets per 100 population (2003)		Secondary School–age Children Enrolled in Secondary School	
Land-based Telephones in Use			
1,180,000 (2011)		Not Available	
Mobile Telephone Subscribers		Secondary School–age Males Enrolled in Secondary School	
1,700,000 (2012)		Not Available	
Major Daily Newspapers		Secondary School–age Females Enrolled in Secondary School	
15 (2004)			
Average Circulation of Daily Newspapers		Not Available	
Not Available		Students Per Teacher, Primary School	
Education		Not Available	
School System		Students Per Teacher, Secondary School	
North Korean students begin their education at the age of five with one year of pre-primary education. Primary school lasts for four years, followed by six years of secondary school.		Not Available	
		Enrollment in Tertiary Education	
		Not Available	
Mandatory Education		Enrollment in Tertiary Education, Male	
11 years, from ages 5 to 16.		Not Available	
Average Years Spent in School for Current Students		Enrollment in Tertiary Education, Female	
Not Available		Not Available	
Average Years Spent in School for Current Students, Male		Literacy	
		100% (2008)	
Not Available		Energy and Natural Resources	
Average Years Spent in School for Current Students, Female		Electric Power Generation	
		21,040,000,000 kilowatt hours per year (estimate) (2010)	
Not Available			
Primary School–age Children Enrolled in Primary School		Electric Power Consumption	
		17,620,000,000 kilowatt hours per year (estimate) (2010)	
Not Available			

Nuclear Power Plants	**Climate**
0 (2014)	North Korea's climate is hot and humid during the summer and cold and dry in the winter. Temperatures range from 21°F to 77°F. Rainfall is concentrated in the summer months, with June and July usually being the wettest.
Crude Oil Production	
100 barrels per day (2013)	
Crude Oil Consumption	
15,000 barrels per day (2012)	**Land Use**
Natural Gas Production	23.3% arable land; 1.7% permanent crops; 0.4% permanent meadows and pastures; 49.3% forest land; 25.4% other.
0 cubic meters per year (estimate) (2011)	
Natural Gas Consumption	
1 cubic meters per year (estimate) (2011)	**Arable Land**
Natural Resources	23% (2007)
Coal, lead, tungsten, zinc, graphite, magnesite, iron ore, copper, gold, pyrites, salt, fluorspar, hydropower	**Arable Land Per Capita**
	0 acres per person (2007)
	Health
Environment	**Average Life Expectancy**
CO2 Emissions	69.8 years (2014)
3.1 metric tons per capita (2009)	**Average Life Expectancy, Male**
Alternative and Nuclear Energy	66.0 years (2014)
6.2% of total energy use (2010)	**Average Life Expectancy, Female**
Threatened Species	73.9 years (2014)
52 (2010)	**Crude Birth Rate**
Protected Areas	14.5 (estimate) (2015)
2,991 (estimate) (2010)	**Crude Death Rate**
Geography	9.2 (estimate) (2015)
Location	**Maternal Mortality**
North Korea is located on the Korean peninsula in Northeast Asia. It is bounded by China to the north and the Republic of Korea (South Korea) to the south.	67 per 100,000 live births (2005–2012 projection)
	Infant Mortality
	Not Available
Time Zone	**Doctors**
14 hours ahead of U.S. Eastern Standard	3.3 per 1,000 people (2003)
Land Borders	**Industry and Labor**
1,040 miles	**Gross Domestic Product (GDP) - official exchange rate**
Coastline	
1,550 miles	Not Available
Capital	**GDP per Capita**
Pyongyang	Not Available
Area	**GDP - Purchasing Power Parity (PPP)**
47,399 sq. miles	Not Available

GDP (PPP) per Capita	**GDP Contribution by Sector**
Not Available	agriculture: 23.3% industry: 42.9% services: 33.8% (2012 est.)
Industry Products	**External Debt**
Cement, iron and steel, fuels, fertilizer, machines, electricity, chemicals, minerals, metals, textiles, processed food, military equipment.	$3,000,000,000 (estimate) (2012)
	Economic Aid Extended
	$0 (2011)
Agriculture Products	**Economic Aid Received**
Rice, corn, potatoes, cotton, soybeans, pulses, tobacco, cattle, pigs, eggs.	$118,000,000 (2011)
Unemployment	**Population**
4.6% (2012)	**Population**
Labor Profile	24,983,205 (estimate) (2015)
agriculture: 35% industry and services: 65% (estimate) (2008)	**World Population Rank**
Military	50 th (2009)
Total Active Armed Forces	**Population Density**
1,106,000 (estimate) (2010)	516.0 people per square mile (estimate) (2011)
Active Armed Forces	**Population Distribution**
5% (2010)	60% urban (2011)
Annual Military Expenditures	**Age Distribution**
$2,300,000,000 (2006)	0-14: 20.9%
Military Service	15-64: 69.4%
North Korea's military utilizes a conscription system, with terms lasting five to eight years for the army; five to 10 years for the navy; and three to four years for the air force. These terms are followed by mandatory part-time service in the Pacification Corps until age 40 and then in the Worker/Peasant Red Guard to age 60.	65+: 9.6%
	(2009)
	Median Age
	33.4 years (estimate) (2014)
	Population Growth Rate
	0.5% per year (estimate) (2015)
	Net Migration Rate
	0.0 (estimate) (2015)
National Finances	**Trade**
Currency	**Imported Goods**
North Korean won	Petroleum, machinery and equipment, coal, grain, sugar, soybean oil, rubber.
Total Government Revenues	**Total Value of Imports**
$3,200,000,000 (estimate) (2007)	$5,051,400,000 (estimate) (2009)
Total Government Expenditures	**Exported Goods**
$3,300,000,000 (estimate) (2007)	Minerals, manufactures, metallurgical products, silk, tobacco.
Budget Deficit	
-0.4 (estimate) (2007)	

Total Value of Exports	Transportation		
$4,707,000,000 (estimate) (2012)	**Airports**		
Import Partners	81 (2012)		
China - 41.7%; Algeria - 31.9%; Fiji - 6.9%; Congo - 2.7%; South Africa - 2.1% (2009 estimate)	**Paved Roads**		
	2.8% (2006)		
	Roads, Unpaved		
Export Partners	15,429 (2006)		
China - 45.8%; Brazil - 6.3%; Lebanon - 5.1%; Saudi Arabia -4.0%; Dominican Republic - 3.9% (2009 estimate).	**Passenger Cars per 1,000 People**		
	Not Available		
	Railroads		
Current Account Balance	3,253 (2006)		
Not Available	**Ports**		
Weights and Measures	Major: 12—including Ch'ongjin, Hungnam, Namp'o, Najin, and Wonsan.		
The metric system is in use.			

OVERVIEW

Occupying the northern portion of East Asia's Korean Peninsula, North Korea lies between China to the north and South Korea to the south. The nation's western beaches overlook the Yellow Sea, and the Sea of Japan extends from the country's eastern shores. North and South Korea are separated on the peninsula by the 38th parallel (a reference to latitude). North Korea has a typical "continental climate"— freezing, snowy winters and warm, rainy summers. North Koreans are ethnically homogeneous, but the population is divided by the country's rigid communist government into three "estate" groups: loyal, hostile, and wavering. North Koreans must be loyal to the ruling Korean Workers' Party (KWP) in order to advance in society, and the percentage of the population deemed "hostile" (such as the children of former feudal landlords, Christians, and relatives of defectors) have virtually no rights. About 60% of North Korea's more than 24 million people live in urban areas. The country's capital is Pyongyang.

GOVERNMENT

North Korea, officially called the Democratic People's Republic of Korea, is a communist state governed by a highly centralized regime in the form of a dictatorship. North Korea gained independence from Japan at the end of World War II on August 15, 1945. The country is headed by the chairman of the National Defense Commission (NDC), who in theory is elected by the Supreme People's Assembly (the national parliament). In reality, the Supreme People's Assembly acts on the direction of the supreme leader, rubber-stamping his choices for government

NORTH KOREA

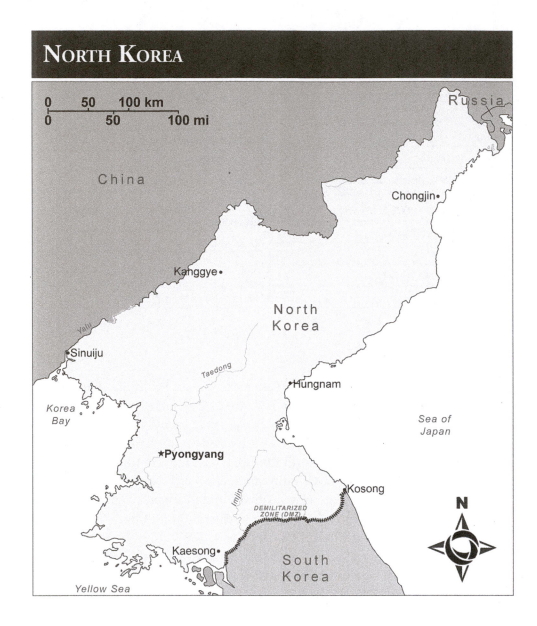

administrators. North Korea was shaken by the sudden death in December 2011 of its supreme leader—NDC chair and Korean Workers' Party secretary general Kim Jong Il, who before his death had arranged for his youngest son, Kim Jong Un, to succeed him. After the death of the country's "Dear Leader," the Korean Workers' Party named Kim Jong Un as his father's "Great Successor."

Constitution

The North Korean Constitution supports the tenets of the KWP and emphasizes the pervasive concept of *juche*, the principle of national self-reliance. The document declares North Korea to be an independent socialist state, advocates the reunification of North and South Korea by peaceful means, and permits private ownership and business incentives. Amendments to the constitution enacted in 1992 eliminated all references to Marxism and Leninism. A 1998 amendment eliminated the post of president, declaring the nation's founder, Kim Il Sung, as "eternal president," and established the chair of the NDC as the highest position in the state. In 2012, an additional amendment declared North Korea to be a nuclear-armed state. Authority to amend the Constitution rests with the Supreme People's Assembly.

Executive

Since September 1998, when a constitutional amendment abolished the presidency, executive authority has been vested in the NDC chairperson. The amendment also replaced the former State Administration Council with a cabinet and established a parliamentary presidium with a chairperson who took over the protocol functions of the presidency. The NDC chair nominates the prime minister and presides over the 22-member Central People's Committee, the cabinet, and the KWP Politburo. Both the Central People's Committee and the cabinet are accountable to the Supreme People's Assembly. Elections for the chairperson are held every four years. These elections are just a formality, as the chairperson typically runs unopposed.

Legislature

The unicameral Supreme People's Assembly (Ch'oego Inmin Hoeui) is North Korea's parliament and is the highest organ of state power. The assembly's 687 members are directly elected every five years from a list prepared by the KWP leadership. The assembly appoints the prime minister and elects the head of state, as well as members of the Central People's Committee and central Standing Committee members. The Supreme People's Assembly also determines state policy, approves the budget, and decides on matters of war and peace. Between sessions, the 15-member Standing Committee assumes legislative authority.

Judiciary

Judicial authority is vested in an independent Central Court, which oversees the Local Court, the People's Court, and the Special Court. All judicial officials are elected by the Supreme People's Assembly to five-year terms.

Local Government

North Korea has nine provinces and two special cities. Each is governed by a directly elected local People's Assembly under the guidance of central state authority.

Election Qualifications

All citizens 17 years of age and older are eligible to vote.

POLITICS

The nation of North Korea was part of the independent monarchy of Korea before being annexed by Japan in 1910. Following Japan's surrender at the end of World War II, Korea was divided into separate occupation zones, with the Soviet Union controlling the North and the United States occupying the South. The communist northern zone was given its present name in September 1948 by the newly established Supreme People's Assembly, headed by Korean Workers' Party leader Kim Il Sung, whose 1950 invasion of South Korea instigated the four-year Korean War. Since the Korean War ended in 1953 without a formal peace treaty, North Korea has been preoccupied with its relations with South Korea, which have been strained over the volatile issues of mutual reduction of armed forces and reunification.

In 1998, more than four years after the death of President Kim Il Sung, the Supreme People's Assembly abolished the presidency and revised the socialist Constitution (1972) to make the NDC chairman the highest position of state. The body then reelected de-facto leader Kim Jong Il as chief of the NDC, completing the world's first communist dynastic succession. The country's long isolation began to thaw in June 2000 with Kim Jong Il's historic summit meeting with South Korean President Kim Dae Jung, the first time the countries' top leaders had met since the Korean Peninsula was divided in 1945. At that point, Kim Dae Jung accelerated his "sunshine policy" of reconciliation with the North, supported by then-U.S. president Bill Clinton. However, those efforts suffered a setback in 2001 with the inauguration of President George W. Bush, whose rhetoric, exemplified by his labeling of North Korea as one member of a modern "axis of evil," caused tension throughout the Korean Peninsula, from which it has yet to recover.

In September 2010, Kim left no doubts as to who he wanted to succeed him, as he promoted Kim Jong Un—the youngest of his three sons—and his sister, Kim Kyong Hui, to the rank of four-star generals in the People's Army, moves considered crucial to North Korean succession. The promotions were announced just before a rare meeting of the ruling KWP, which had not met for 30 years, and was a sign of the growing influence of Kim Jong Il's *songun* policy—in which the military is the top priority of every political decision. The end for Kim came suddenly on December 17, 2011, when he died of a heart attack at the age of 70. Within two weeks of the elder Kim's death, Kim Jong Un was named supreme commander of the Korean People's Army and was declared to be the "Great Successor" to his father's legacy and "Supreme Leader" by government officials and the state-run media.

Kim Jung Un, whose official title is First Secretary of the Workers' Party, is the de facto leader of North Korea, having succeeded his father Kim Jong Il and grandfather Kim Il Sung in that position. Since taking power following the death of his father, Kim Jong Un has pursued a sometimes bizarre course of action based on a cult of personality. (CHINE NOUVELLE/SIPA/Newscom)

North Korea's antagonistic policies toward South Korea and the United States have remained unchanged under Kim Jong Un. In December 2013, Kim Jong Un had his uncle and top official, Jang Song Thaek, executed on treason charges. Observers believe the execution was meant to strengthen Kim's power, but revealed that his control may be weaker than previously thought.

Political Parties

With the exception of one opposition party in exile, the republic's nine political parties fall under an umbrella organization called the Democratic Front for the Reunification of the Fatherland, which was established in 1946 and seeks to reunify North Korea and South Korea along communist lines. Some of its component parties are as follows:

Founded in 1949, the Korean Workers' Party (KWP) dominates the political process. It is organized along traditional Leninist lines under the effective leadership of the politburo. The KWP parallels and controls the republic's political, social, and economic structure at all levels, though in recent years the balance of power has shifted to the military.

The Chondoist Chongu Party, founded in 1946, supports KWP policies and advocates the guiding principle of *innaechon*, the goal of creating "heaven on earth."

Founded in 1945, the Socialist Democratic Party supports the establishment of a democratic socialist society within the guidelines of the KWP.

ECONOMY

North Korea's socialist economy is closed to most of the world and remains fragile because of the leadership's insistence that military spending remain high despite widespread hunger and shrinking funds. The breakdown of trade with the countries of the former Soviet Union confronted North Korea with difficult economic choices. Government officials have taken a few small steps toward economic openness, including the establishment of special economic zones that will utilize foreign investment and specialize in consumer product exports and the legalization of some private farming. Despite these limited moves, North Korea's leadership appears determined to maintain tight political and ideological control.

Malnourishment is widespread in North Korea. The country has struggled for decades to feed its population because of systemic failure, the loss of Soviet aid, and weather-related crop failures. The United Nations reported in 2013 that 2.8 million North Koreans were in need of food aid. Historically, economic aid from western countries has been tied to demands that North Korea cease its nuclear ambitions and therefore, like North Korea's nuclear program, aid has been intermittent. North Korea's economic development remains uncertain in view of international tension over the country's nuclear weapons program and questions about the stability of Kim Jong Un's leadership. North Korea has rich stores of minerals that it exports mainly to China and South Korea. China and South Korea are also the largest suppliers of North Korea's imports, which include petroleum, machinery, grain, and textiles.

SOCIETY

Korea is ethnically homogeneous. Small communities of ethnic Chinese and a few ethnic Japanese reside in North Korea. The language is Korean, and the writing system, based on a 24-letter alphabet, is called *Choson Muntcha*. The written language is different from that of South Korea in that since the Communist state was established in North Korea in 1948, Chinese characters have deliberately been removed. North Koreans, according to their constitution, "have religious liberty and the freedom to oppose religion." Many churches and Buddhist temples were confiscated after World War II, and what little religious activity there is remains under state control. The government favors Chondogyo, a nineteenth-century religion that developed out of the Eastern Learning Movement, for nationalistic purposes, and uses Christianity to make contact with Christians in South Korea and other countries. The principal ideological basis since the late 1940s has been the cult of the leader Kim Il Sung, then, after his death, of his son, Kim Jong Il. Since Kim Jong Il's death in 2011, his son, Kim Jong Un, has become the leader and the focus of national reverence.

Ethnic Composition

Korean – 100%

Language

Korean is the official language.

Religion

Religious activities are largely forbidden by the government; government-sponsored religious groups exist to provide the illusion of religious freedom.

CONTEMPORARY ISSUES

Tension with South Korea

Since the end of the Korean War, North Korea and South Korea have technically remained in a state of war, albeit with a cease-fire agreement. The two countries are currently separated by the Korean Demilitarized Zone (DMZ), a buffer zone established near the 38th parallel (which served as the border between the Koreas prior to the outbreak of the Korean War). While relations were generally tense throughout the entirety of the Cold War era, the two countries began taking steps toward more harmonious coexistence in the 1990s and 2000s. During the 1990s, the North Korean economy was devastated by the effects of poor long-term planning, excessive siphoning of resources to the military, and a series of natural disasters; on the other side of the DMZ, however, the economy of South Korea, one of the newly developed "Asian Tigers," was booming. After Kim Dae Jung took office as president of South Korea in 1998, a new era of peaceful relations began as Kim pursued the "Sunshine Policy" of peaceful direct engagement with North Korea. The South offered economic aid to the North, and joint economic ventures were initiated, including those at the Kaesong Industrial Park near the DMZ in North Korea, where large South Korean companies built plants and employed North Korean workers.

These peaceful overtures came to an abrupt end in 2010, however, following the sinking of the South Korean warship ROKS *Cheonan* in March. The cause of the sinking was initially unclear, but in May the South Korean government officially determined that a North Korean torpedo attack was to blame. Following the announcement of this determination, North Korea immediately suspended diplomatic and economic relations with the South and put the large North Korean military on alert. South Korea resumed propaganda broadcasts that had been suspended during the Sunshine era, and vowed to take the issue to the United Nations (UN) Security Council. In 2013, the UN tightened sanctions against North Korea for conducting nuclear testing, and international spokespeople have since voiced concerns over the nation's use of military exercises as provocation against South Korea.

Human Rights

North Korea is a secretive, rigidly controlled communist dictatorship, and as such it rules its citizens with an iron hand. One of the results of this type of government is the lack of human rights in North Korea. The United Nations (UN) General Assembly has adopted a resolution expressing serious concerns about North Korea's "systematic, widespread and grave violations of human rights," which followed numerous resolutions on the subject by the UN Commission on Human Rights. According to Human Rights Watch, North Korea does not allow freedom of information, association, movement, or religion. The government has banned all political dissent and opposition, labor activism, and personal independence. In addition, North Koreans have been subjected to arbitrary arrests, torture, lack of due process and fair trials, and public executions. Also, the punishment of entire families for "political crimes" remains the norm. North Korea continues to block access by international human rights organizations.

Lack of Food

The government's policy changes in recent years have jeopardized access to food for the most vulnerable North Koreans. In 2005, the government banned the buying and selling of grain by individual farmers and announced that only the state can distribute grain. Aid groups estimate that up to 2 million people have died since the 1990s because of food shortages caused by floods and economic mismanagement.

The UN's World Food Programme has reported that North Korea currently faces a shortage of about 207,000 tons of food. This shortage is especially troublesome for children, pregnant or nursing women, and the elderly. North Korea has a long history of first feeding the elite strata of society—including high-ranking military, police, intelligence, and other officials—and then offering smaller rations (often less than the minimum daily requirement) to the general population.

Escapees/Abductees

Tens of thousands of North Koreans have fled the country to escape hunger and political repression, and most are believed to be hiding in China. However, leaving

North Korea without government permission is considered an act of treason pun-ishable by harsh penalties. Thus, those North Koreans who return from China often face abuse and imprisonment.

According to figures reported by the Korea Institute for National Unification (based in South Korea), some 3,790 South Koreans were kidnapped and taken to North Korea between 1953 and 1995—of whom 485 remain imprisoned there. Some of these abductees have been exploited in propaganda broadcasts to South Korea, while others have been forced to train North Korean intelligence agents. North Korea has repeatedly rejected requests from families of abductees to confirm their relatives' existence, return them, or send their bodies back to South Korea. In addition to its South Korean hostages, the North Korean government has also taken several Americans hostage in recent years. Two journalists were imprisoned for several months in 2009 for having entered the country illegally, and Korean-American missionary Kenneth Bae was sentenced to 15 years in prison in 2013 for committing "hostile acts" against the government. He remains the longest-serving U.S. prisoner in North Korea. In June 2014, North Korean authorities announced they had detained yet another U.S. visitor.

Nuclear Ambitions

North Korea's relations with the United States deteriorated during the early twenty-first century, when the Pyongyang government acknowledged that it has maintained a secret nuclear weapons program in violation of an agreement signed with President Bill Clinton's administration. This announcement was quickly fol-lowed by North Korea's withdrawal from the Nuclear Nonproliferation Treaty. Since then, tensions between North Korea and the West have vacillated with the communist nation's history of threats, rhetoric, and brinkmanship.

In 2012, North Korea instigated an international crisis by launching a rocket, which it claimed put a satellite into orbit. Unanimous condemnation by the United Nations followed the launch, which elicited a series of action from North Korea including an underground nuclear test; cutting a military hotline between North and South Korea; threatening the United States with a pre-emptive nuclear strike and deploying mid-range missiles to its east coast; announcing the re-opening of Yongbyon nuclear reactor; and blocking South and North Korean workers from entering the Kaesong industrial park on the border of North and South Korea. In return, the United States flew nuclear-capable B-52 and B-2 bombers over the Korean peninsula, and both the United States and Japan deployed defensive anti-missile batteries to their territories in the region.

In addition, North Korea's longtime ally China warned North Korea that its actions were unacceptable. In April, Chinese foreign minister Wang Yi stated, "We oppose provocative words and actions from any party in the region and do not allow trouble-making on China's doorstep." One day later, China's leader Xi Jinping reiterated that no nation "should be allowed to throw a region and even the whole world into chaos for selfish gain." Tensions finally eased in May 2012, when North Korea withdrew the missiles aimed at the United States Today, North Korea's relationship with the United States and the rest of the international community remains tense, with the government's intractability on the nuclear issue still a major obstacle to diplomatic progress.

Excerpt from the Socialist Constitution of the Democratic People's Republic of Korea

The constitution of North Korea, known formally as the Socialist Constitution of the Democratic People's Republic of Korea, was written originally in 1948. Since then, it has been revised on several occasions, most recently in 2012.

North Korea is a Communist dictatorship whose legitimacy is linked closely to a cult of personality. The constitution identifies North Korea's first dictator, Kim Il-Sung, as the founding father of the country. The Preamble states that "The great leader Comrade Kim Il Sung is the sun of the nation and the lodestar of the fatherland's reunification." Later revisions recognize Kim's son, Kim Jong Il. After Kim Jong Il died in 2012, power passed to his son, Kim Jong-un. The Constitution identifies itself with the ideology of jeche, *or self-reliance, and credits Kim Il-Sung with the development of this ideology.*

The Constitution identifies North Korea as a "revolutionary" state. It includes guarantees of political rights such as the right to vote, freedom of religion, and freedom of speech. However, these rights are not recognized in practice, as the government is controlled by Kim Jong-un's Workers' Party of Korea and free elections have never been held. Guarantees of the right to education and health care are also identified but not enacted. North Korea is one of the world's most militarized states, and the diversion of resources to the armed forces has had severe effects on North Korea's standard of living. North Korea claims sovereignty over South Korea, and the Constitution makes numerous references to "the Korean people" to include residents of both countries.

Preamble

The Democratic People's Republic of Korea is a Juche*-based socialist fatherland that embodies the idea and leadership of the great leader Comrade Kim Il Sung.

The great leader Comrade Kim Il Sung is the founder of the DPRK and the father of socialist Korea.

Comrade Kim Il Sung, regarding the idea of "Serving the people as heaven" as his motto, was always with the people, devoted his whole life to them, took care of and led the people with his noble politics of benevolence, and thus turned the whole society into one big, single-heartedly united family.

The great leader Comrade Kim Il Sung is the sun of the nation and the lodestar of the fatherland's reunification.

Comrade Kim Il Sung founded the immortal Juche idea, organized and guided an anti-Japanese revolutionary struggle under its banner, created revolutionary tradition, attained the historical cause of the national liberation, and founded the DPRK, built up a solid basis of construction of a sovereign and independent state in the fields of politics, economy, culture, and military.

Comrade Kim Il Sung put forward an independent revolutionary line, wisely guided the social revolution and construction at various levels, strengthened and developed the Republic into a people-centered socialist country and a socialist state of independence, self-sustenance, and self-defense.

CHAPTER 1. POLITICS

Article 1

The DPRK is an independent socialist state representing the interests of all the Korean people.

Article 2

The DPRK is a revolutionary state, which has inherited the brilliant traditions established in the glorious revolutionary struggle against the imperialist aggressors to achieve the fatherland's liberation and the freedom and happiness of the people.

CHAPTER 5. FUNDAMENTAL RIGHTS AND DUTIES OF CITIZENS

Article 63

In the DPRK, the rights and responsibilities of citizens are based on the collectivist principle of "One for all, all for one."

Article 64

The state shall substantially guarantee all citizens genuine democratic rights and freedom, and happy material and cultural lives. In the DPRK, the rights and freedom of citizens shall be further expanded with the consolidation and development of the socialist system.

Article 65

Citizens shall have equal rights in all spheres of the state and social life.

Article 66

All citizens who have reached the age of 17 shall have the right to vote and the right to be elected, irrespective of sex, race, occupation, length of residence, property and intellectual level, party affiliation, political view, or religious belief. Citizens serving in the armed forces shall also have the right to vote and the right to be elected. Persons who have been disenfranchised by a court decision and persons who are insane shall not have the right to vote or the right to be elected.

Article 67

Citizens shall have freedom of speech, press, assembly, demonstration, and association. The state shall guarantee conditions for the free activities of democratic political parties and social organizations.

Article 68

Citizens shall have freedom of religion. This right shall be guaranteed by permitting the construction of religious buildings and the holding of religious ceremonies. Religion shall not be used in bringing in outside forces or in harming the state and social order.

Article 69

Citizens may make appeals and file petitions. The state shall fairly deliberate and deal with appeals and petitions as prescribed by law.

Article 70

Citizens shall have the right to labor. All citizens who are able to work shall choose occupations according to their wishes and talents, and shall be guaranteed secure jobs and working conditions. Citizens shall work according to their abilities and shall be paid in accordance with the quantity and quality of their work.

Article 71

Citizens shall have the right to rest. This right shall be guaranteed by the establishment of working hours, legal holidays, paid leave, rest and recuperation at state expense, and by a variety of continuously increasing cultural facilities.

Article 72

Citizens shall have the right to receive free medical care, and persons who are no longer able to work due to old age, illness, or physical disability, and the old and children who do not have caretakers, shall have the right to receive material assistance. This right shall be guaranteed by free medical care, continuously expanding medical facilities that include hospitals and sanitariums, and the state social insurance and the social security system.

Article 73

Citizens shall have the right to receive education. This right shall be guaranteed by an advanced educational system and the state's people-oriented educational measures.

Article 74

Citizens shall have freedom to engage in scientific, literary, and artistic activities. The state shall grant benefits to inventors and creators. Copyrights, patents to inventions, and other patent rights shall be protected by law.

Article 75

Citizens shall have freedom of residence and travel.

Article 76

Revolutionary fighters, families of revolutionary and patriotic martyrs, families of servicepersons of the People's Army, and disabled soldiers shall receive special protection from the state and society.

Article 77

Women shall be entitled to the same social status and rights as men. The state shall provide special protection to mothers and children by guaranteeing maternity leave before and after childbirth, reducing working hours for mothers with many children, and expanding the network of maternity hospitals, nurseries, and kindergartens, and by implementing other measures. The state shall provide every possible condition for women to participate in society.

Article 78

Marriage and family shall be protected by the state. The state shall take deep interest in consolidating the family, the basic unit of social life.

Article 79

Citizens shall be guaranteed inviolability of the person and the home and privacy of correspondence. Citizens cannot be detained or arrested and their homes cannot be searched without legal grounds.

Article 80

The DPRK shall protect people of other countries who defected while struggling for peace and democracy, for national independence and socialism, and for freedom of scientific and cultural activities.

Article 81

Citizens shall firmly safeguard the political and ideological unity and cohesion of the people. Citizens shall value their organization and collective and highly demonstrate the trait of dedicating themselves to work for the society and the people.

Article 85

Citizens shall always heighten their revolutionary vigilance and struggle by dedicating themselves to the security of the state.

Article 86

Defending the fatherland is the supreme duty and honor of citizens. Citizens shall defend the fatherland and serve in the armed forces as prescribed by law.

Juche is used in North Korea to signify that the masses are masters of the country's development.

Source: "Democratic People's Republic of Korea's Socialist Constitution." North Korean government. http://www1.korea-np.co.jp/pk/061st_issue/98091708.htm.

CHAPTER 3

MONARCHIES

Monarchy is one of the world's oldest forms of governance, and was the predominant form of governance throughout the world from ancient times until the late nineteenth century. Under monarchy, power is concentrated in the hands of a single ruler or monarch. However, monarchies vary on the basis of several factors. These include the degree to which political power is concentrated in the hands of the monarch, the process by which monarchs are selected, relationships between the monarch and the predominant religion of the state, and other rules and policies regarding the powers and rights of the monarch.

The two basic forms of monarchy are absolute monarchy and constitutional monarchy. Under absolute monarchy, the power of the monarch or sovereign ruler is unlimited and unconstrained. The monarch has the authority to create and enforce laws and policies and can impose taxes on the state's population. The monarch's authority to create laws and impose taxes unilaterally is known as rule by decree. Under constitutional monarchy, the monarch's authority is limited and power is shared formally by the monarch and other institutions including elected governments.

In ancient and medieval times, most monarchs were absolute monarchs. In European society, the concept of constitutional monarchy arose in 1215, when King John of England signed the Magna Carta, or "Great Charter." Under the terms of the Magna Carta, John agreed to a formal arrangement by which power was to be shared between the monarchy and the English nobility. Thus the right of the king to rule by decree was limited by this agreement. Later in the thirteenth century, this power-sharing arrangement was extended to the common people. This extension resulted in the creation of Parliament, whose two houses are the House of Lords, representing the nobility, and the House of Commons, representing the rest of the population. This structure of governance remains in place in the United Kingdom today.

An absolute monarch is simultaneously the head of state and the head of government. In most constitutional monarchies the sovereign is the head of state but not the head of government. For example, as of 2014 Queen Elizabeth II, as a constitutional monarch, is the head of the state of the United Kingdom. However, the head of government is the Prime Minister, who is an elected Member of Parliament. In many constitutional monarchies, including the United Kingdom, the role of the constitutional monarch is largely ceremonial. The monarch can and sometime does advise the head of government on public policy issues but does not have the authority to initiate efforts to enact policies consistent with his or her views on these issues.

Past and present monarchies vary on the basis of how monarchs are selected. Usually, a monarch retains his or her sovereignty for life, until he or she dies or abdicates. Many monarchies have procedures to determine the succession in the event of the death or abdication of the ruler. In the Western world, succession is determined by an established set of procedures. In the United Kingdom, for example, the oldest child of the monarch is the heir apparent to the throne. However, in other monarchies, the current monarch designates an heir who may or may not be the oldest son of the current ruler. For example, the King of Saudi Arabia designates a relative as the heir apparent, but there are no rules by which he must choose his heir apparent. Under dynastic succession procedures, the identity of the heir to the throne was known in advance.

Often, dynastic succession procedures privilege males over females, with a woman becoming the monarch only in the absence of eligible male heirs. Such was the case in the United Kingdom before 2011, when succession policies were changed such that the oldest child of the sovereign, regardless of sex, becomes heir apparent if he or she was born after 2011. In fact, some monarchies recognized succession only through the male line; that is, the daughter of a monarch and that daughter's sons or grandsons would be ineligible to succeed to the throne. However, in other states a new monarch was elected when the throne became vacant. For example, during the seventeenth and eighteenth century the King of the Polish-Lithuanian Commonwealth (who was known formally as the King of Poland and Grand Prince of Lithuania) was elected by an assembly of the Polish nobility.

At various times, monarchs are unable to rule for various reasons. The monarch chosen via the rules of dynastic succession may be a child. Other monarchs become incapacitated as a result of illness or advanced age. In such cases, a regent is selected to rule in the name of the monarch. The regent is expected to relinquish power upon the death of an incapacitated monarch, or when a child monarch comes of age.

Although policies involving succession and regency have generally been intended to reduce the possibility of conflict and to increase the power of the monarch in power, conflicts over control of a monarch have occurred very frequently over the course of history. Such contests over the assumption of power have often resulted in civil or international wars. In some cases, conflicts have arisen after two or more potential heirs of a monarch claim the right of succession simultaneously. The Wars of the Roses, which began in Britain in the fifteenth century, illustrates these conflicts. After King Henry V died in 1422, two branches of the ruling Plantagenet family claimed the throne. A civil war broke out between these two branches, the House of Lancaster and the House of York. The war continued sporadically until 1485 when King Henry VII, who was a member of the House of Lancaster but married the daughter of the Yorkist King Edward IV, was crowned. Thus the two rival factions were united, and the Wars of the Roses ended.

By no means have disputes over succession been limited to conflicts within individual monarchies. Often, these disputes result in international conflicts, sometimes including many countries and lasting for many years. For example, the War of the Spanish Succession began in 1701 upon the death of King Charles II of Spain in late 1700. Charles left no heirs, and the Spanish throne was claimed by the royal families of France and Austria. Members of both royal families were related closely to Charles' ancestors. The war involved not only France, Austria, and Spain but other European monarchies and their overseas colonies, lasted for thirteen years, and resulted in thousands of casualties across Europe. It was settled finally in 1714, when France and Austria signed a peace treaty. However, Spain did not end its conflict with Austria formally by treaty until 1720.

Throughout history, many monarchs have maintained only tenuous control over states that they rule. Although conflict has been especially likely when monarchies are ruled by regents or weak sovereigns, on numerous occasions monarchs have had to fight to maintain their control over their states. Potential monarchs sometimes tried to overthrow the sovereigns in power and seize power for themselves. In other cases, monarchies are threatened by foreign monarchs whose rulers may be intent on increasing their own power and influence. Especially in the twentieth century, monarchies have been overthrown and replaced by other forms of government. For example, the last king of Egypt, Farouk, was overthrown in a coup d'etat in 1952. Power was seized by military leaders who eliminated the monarchy, and Farouk and his family were exiled.

Monarchy has often been intertwined with religion. Historically, many monarchs have legitimized their power by claiming that their right to rule had been granted to them and their successors by deities. For example, Chinese emperors claimed the Mandate of Heaven, implying that deities granted them the right to rule. However, the Mandate of Heaven implied that the ruler had the responsibility to reign fairly and justly. In some cases, monarchs have claimed direct descent from deities.

In the Western tradition, some monarchs have claimed what has been called the divine right of kings. The divine right of kings implies that the monarch's right to rule is provided by God, and therefore that the sovereign is answerable only to the divinity as opposed to any earthly authority. The concept of the divine right of kings is associated with absolute monarchy, in that constitutional monarchy implies formal sharing of power with nobilities or other institutions. Although the divine right of kings as a concept has faded into history, some countries still require that their monarchs belong to state religions. For example, the king or queen of England is required to belong to the Church of England and is considered to be the Supreme

Governor of the Church. Members of the royal family who convert to Roman Catholicism or who marry Roman Catholics become ineligible to succeed to the British throne. Similarly, the king of Spain must be a Roman Catholic, whereas the king of Saudi Arabia must be a Muslim, and the king of Bhutan must be a Buddhist. In each case, the religion of the monarchy is that country's state religion. Historically, the populations of some states have been required to practice the religion of the monarchy, and those practicing other religions have in some cases been subject to persecution.

Although monarchy was the dominant form of government throughout the world prior to the nineteenth and early twentieth centuries, today only a minority of countries are monarchies. Only a few of the world's remaining monarchies are absolute monarchies; most of the remaining monarchies in the world today are constitutional monarchies. Saudi Arabia remains an absolute monarchy, while the United Kingdom and Spain are constitutional monarchies. Bhutan's monarchy has been historically an absolute monarchy, but began transitioning to its present status as a constitutional monarchy during the 1950s. Whether these constitutional monarchies should continue, especially when the monarchy is ceremonial and has no role in governance, has been a controversial issue in many of these countries.

—Fred M. Shelley

Further Reading

John Cannon and Ralph Griffiths, *The Oxford illustrated history of the British monarchy.* London: Oxford University Press, 1988.

Derek McKay, *The rise of the great powers, 1648–1815.* New York: Longman, 1983.

Ralph Turner, *Magna Carta.* London: Routledge, 2003.

BHUTAN: Constitutional Monarchy

BHUTAN

Communications	Land-based Telephones in Use
Facebook Users	27,000 (2012)
92,000 (estimate) (2013)	Mobile Telephone Subscribers
Internet Users	560,000 (2012)
50,000 (2009)	Major Daily Newspapers
Internet Users (% of Population)	Not Available
29.9% (2013)	Average Circulation of Daily Newspapers
Television	
3 sets per 100 Population (2004)	Not Available

Education	Students Per Teacher, Secondary School
School System	19.9 (2012)
Students in Bhutan begin schooling at the age of six. After one year in a preparatory class, they attend six years of primary school, then continue to two years of early secondary education. Students then may choose between three years of education at a technical center or four years of high school, which is split into two years of general studies and two years of pre-university studies.	Enrollment in Tertiary Education
	7,400 (2012)
	Enrollment in Tertiary Education, Male
	4,440 (2012)
	Enrollment in Tertiary Education, Female
	2,960 (2012)
	Literacy
Mandatory Education	53% (2005)
12 years, from ages 6 to 18.	Energy and Natural Resources
Average Years Spent in School for Current Students	Electric Power Generation
13 (2012)	7,230,000,000 kilowatt hours per year (estimate) (2010)
Average Years Spent in School for Current Students, Male	Electric Power Consumption
13 (2012)	1,680,000,000 kilowatt hours per year (estimate) (2010)
Average Years Spent in School for Current Students, Female	Nuclear Power Plants
13 (2012)	0 (2014)
Primary School–age Children Enrolled in Primary School	Crude Oil Production
	0 barrels per day (2013)
110,575 (2012)	Crude Oil Consumption
Primary School–age Males Enrolled in Primary School	1,700 barrels per day (2012)
	Natural Gas Production
55,624 (2012)	0 cubic meters per year (estimate) (2011)
Primary School–age Females Enrolled in Primary School	Natural Gas Consumption
	0 cubic meters per year (estimate) (2010)
54,951 (2012)	Natural Resources
Secondary School–age Children Enrolled in Secondary School	Timber, calcium carbide, gypsum, hydropower
66,072 (2012)	Environment
Secondary School–age Males Enrolled in Secondary School	CO_2 Emissions
32,565 (2012)	0.6 metric tons per capita (2009)
Secondary School–age Females Enrolled in Secondary School	Alternative and Nuclear Energy
	Not Available
33,507 (2012)	Threatened Species
Students Per Teacher, Primary School	59 (2010)
	Protected Areas
24.0 (2012)	11,320 (estimate) (2010)

Geography	Crude Death Rate
Location	6.7 (estimate) (2015)
A landlocked country in Asia's Himalaya Mountains, Bhutan is bordered by India to the south and China to the north.	**Maternal Mortality**
Time Zone	420 per 100,000 live births (2005–2012 projection)
10.5 hours ahead of U.S. Eastern Standard	**Infant Mortality**
Land Borders	36 per 1,000 live births (2012)
668 miles	**Doctors**
Coastline	0.3 per 1,000 people (2012)
0 miles	**Industry and Labor**
Capital	**Gross Domestic Product (GDP) - official exchange rate**
Thimphu	$2,115,000,000 (estimate) (2015)
Area	**GDP per Capita**
17,954 sq. miles	$2,827 (estimate) (2015)
Climate	**GDP - Purchasing Power Parity (PPP)**
The mountainous northern part of Bhutan is cold, while the valleys in the center of the country are more temperate and the heavily forested south is semitropical. Rainfall averages between 60 and 120 inches per year; monthly temperatures average 62°F in July and 40°F in January.	$5,354,000,000 (estimate) (2013)
	GDP (PPP) per Capita
	$7,188 (estimate) (2013)
	Industry Products
	Cement, minerals, wood products, processed fruits, textiles, distilled beverages.
Land Use	**Agriculture Products**
3.3% arable land; 0.7% permanent crops; 10.6% permanent meadows and pastures; 83.8% forest land; 1.6% other.	Citrus fruit, rice, corn, potatoes, roots and tubers, cattle, dairy products.
	Unemployment
Arable Land	2.1% (2012)
3% (2007)	**Labor Profile**
Arable Land Per Capita	agriculture: 43.7% industry: 39.1% services: 17.2% (estimate) (2004)
0 acres per person (2007)	
Health	**Military**
Average Life Expectancy	**Total Active Armed Forces**
69.0 years (2014)	6,000 (estimate) (2004)
Average Life Expectancy, Male	**Active Armed Forces**
68.1 years (2014)	0% (2004)
Average Life Expectancy, Female	**Annual Military Expenditures**
70.0 years (2014)	$22,000,000 (2003)
Crude Birth Rate	**Military Service**
17.8 (estimate) (2015)	(not available)

National Finances	Net Migration Rate
Currency	0.0 (estimate) (2015)
Ngultrum	**Trade**
Total Government Revenues	**Imported Goods**
$588,200,000 (estimate) (2013)	Aircraft, fuels, lubricants, machinery, grain, transportation equipment, textiles.
Total Government Expenditures	
$639,500,000 (estimate) (2013)	
Budget Deficit	**Total Value of Imports**
-2.4 (estimate) (2013)	$533,000,000 (2008)
GDP Contribution by Sector	**Exported Goods**
agriculture: 16.7% industry: 45.4% services: 37.9% (2011 est.)	Cement, cardamon, gypsum, timber, fruits, spices, hand-made crafts, electricity, jewels.
External Debt	**Total Value of Exports**
$1,275,000,000 (estimate) (2011)	$725,200,000 (estimate) (2012)
Economic Aid Extended	**Import Partners**
$0 (2011)	India - 63.0%; Japan - 12.3%; China - 5.1% (2008)
Economic Aid Received	
$144,000,000 (2011)	**Export Partners**
Population	India - 86.3%; Bangladesh - 8.1%; Italy - 1.5% (2008)
Population	
741,919 (estimate) (2015)	**Current Account Balance**
World Population Rank	$401,500,000 (estimate) (2013)
161 th (2010)	**Weights and Measures**
Population Density	The metric system is in use.
39.5 people per square mile (estimate) (2011)	**Transportation**
	Airports
Population Distribution	2 (2012)
35% urban (2011)	**Paved Roads**
Age Distribution	40.4% (2010)
0-14: 29.5%	**Roads, Unpaved**
15-64: 64.8%	1,901 (2003)
65+: 5.6%	**Passenger Cars per 1,000 People**
(2009)	46 (2009)
Median Age	**Railroads**
26.2 years (estimate) (2014)	Not Available
Population Growth Rate	**Ports**
1.1% per year (estimate) (2015)	None.

OVERVIEW

Bhutan is an ancient kingdom nestled in the Himalaya Mountains of South Asia. It is surrounded by India on three sides and Tibet (now part of China) to the north. Dramatic changes in elevation throughout the country have produced a diverse climate, varying from temperate in the central mountain valleys (with temperatures ranging only from 40°F in January to 62°F in July) to the extremely hot Duars Plain to the extremely cold northern mountains. Rainfall can measure as much as 120 inches per year. The country's terrain is dominated by the Himalayas in the north but is densely forested in the south, which helped keep Bhutan isolated from the rest of the world for centuries. In recent years, however, Bhutan has begun to welcome the outside world. In the 1970s, the country began accepting small numbers of visitors; in 1999 it lifted its ban on television and, more recently, even embraced the Internet. Still, Bhutan continues to jealously guard its traditions, historic culture, and Buddhist religion. An influx of mainly Hindu Nepalis, despite a 1959 law banning their immigration, is a source of tension within the otherwise peaceful kingdom of 750,000. Bhutan's capital is Thimphu.

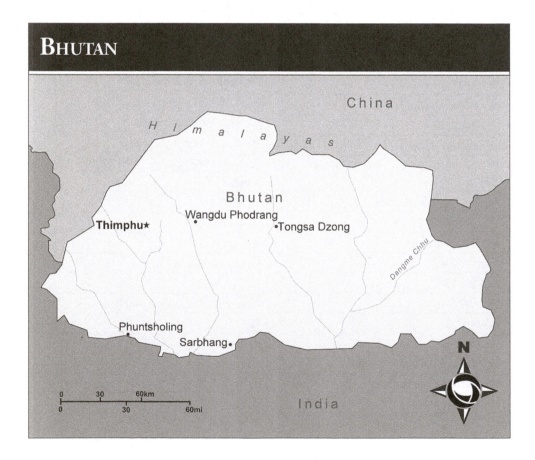

GOVERNMENT

Bhutan has never been colonized. Its hereditary monarchy was established in 1907 with the election of Gongsar Ugyen Wangchuck as the nation's first king. Bhutan operates under a modified form of constitutional monarchy, and today is the world's only independent Buddhist monarchy. In recent years, the country's monarchs have been moving the nation toward democracy, and Bhutan has never been colonized. Its hereditary monarch was established in 1907 with the election of Gongsar Ugyen Wangchuck as the nation's first king. The current king is Jigme Khesar Namgyel Wangchuck, who succeeded his father, Jigme Singye Wang-chuck, in 2006. Bhutan's prime minister is Tshering Tobgay. Legislative authority rests with the National Assembly (Tshogdu) and the National Council (Gyelyong Tshogde). In the native Dzongkha language, the Kingdom of Bhutan is known as Druk-yul.

Constitution

While he was still king, Jigme Singye Wangchuck commissioned the writing of a constitution. In 2005 a draft of that proposed document was distributed to Bhutanese citizens, with a request for their views on it. The 34-article constitution outlines the role of the monarchy, clergy, and duties of the Bhutanese people. In 2008, the same year Bhutan held its landmark democratic elections, the constitution was ratified.

Executive

The head of state is a monarch of the Wangchuck dynasty. The king is assisted by the Council of Ministers (Lhengye Shungtsog), the nine-member Royal Advisory Council, (Lodoi Tsokde) and the Head Abbot (Je Khempo) of Bhutan's Buddhist monks. The king chooses the members of the Council of Ministers after consulting with the prime minister. The prime minister is the head of the government. In June 1998, the king passed his power to name the cabinet to the legislature.

Legislature

As part of the country's move toward representative democracy, in March 2008, Bhutan held parliamentary elections for the first time in its history. The bicameral parliament, (Chi Tshog), consists of the 25-member, non-partisan National Council (Gyelyong Tshogde). Twenty of the members are chosen by the country's 20 administrative districts; the other five are appointed by the king. The 47 members of the lower house, or National Assembly (Tshogdu), are elected directly.

Judiciary

The Supreme Court consists of five justices and has authority over constitutional matters. A High Court hears appeals from lower courts; each region contains a District or Dzongkhag Court; and within districts are subdistrict or Dungkhag Courts.

Local Government

The country is divided into 20 administrative districts (*dzonghags*), each governed by an appointed district officer (*dzongda*), who supervises administrative and security matters, and an appointed magistrate (*thrimpon*), who heads judicial affairs. The country is further divided into groupings of villages (*gewogs*). Members of village-development committees (*gewog yargye tshopas*) are directly elected by villagers.

Election Qualifications

All citizens age 18 and older are eligible to vote.

POLITICS

In 1910, King Ugyen and the British signed the Treaty of Punakha, which provided that Bhutan would allow Britain to advise on external affairs in exchange for monetary subsidies and noninterference in internal affairs. In 1949, after India gained independence from Britain, Bhutan signed the Indo-Bhutan Treaty, which has similar provisions.

Politics in Bhutan has been virtually nonexistent throughout most of its history because the government was traditionally autocratic until the 1950s, when King Jigme Dorji Wangchuk began the gradual transformation of the government to share administrative responsibility. The current king, Jigme Khesar Namgyel Wangchuck (Bhutan's monarch is traditionally referred to as the "Dragon King"), represents the fifth generation of the Wangchuck dynasty.

Bhutan's physical remoteness has generally allowed it to avoid Asia's numerous conflicts. During the early twenty-first century, however, Bhutan was drawn into India's battle with separatist guerrillas who began attacking targets in the northeastern Indian state of Assam near the Bhutan–India border and would then escape back to their camps in Bhutan. Assam's provincial government continues to demand that India fence off its border with Bhutan to prevent such attacks. The Bhutanese government has warned the Indian separatists to vacate their camps located within Bhutan's borders or face military action.

King Jigme Khesar Namgyei Wangchuck of Bhutan. He became King in 2006 upon the abdication of his father, King Jigme Singye Wangchuck. Jigme Singye Wangchuck oversaw Bhutan's transition from an absolute monarchy to a constitutional monarchy. (Kim Kyung-Hoon-Pool/ZUMAPRESS/Newscom)

In December 2005, King Jigme Singye Wangchuck announced that he would abdicate in favor of his son, Crown Prince Jigme Khesar Namgyel Wangchuck, when the nation held its first national elections in 2008. However, the king surprised the country when he handed power to his son in December 2006. Shortly thereafter, in a speech to 40,000 supporters dressed in traditional Bhutanese robes, the new king promised to maintain his father's legacy of transforming the kingdom into a parliamentary democracy.

The 2008 constitution set the framework for Bhutan's new bicameral parliament, consisting of an upper (National Council) and lower house (National Assembly). Nearly 80% of the population turned out for the 2008 National Assembly elections. The Bhutan Peace and Prosperity Party (Druk Phuensum Tshogpa or DPT) swept the contest, winning 45 out of 47 seats. Jigme Thinley, DPT president, became prime minister. In April 2013, Bhutan held elections for the 25-seat National Council, a largely ceremonial body. National Council members are not associated with political parties and run as independents. In the July 2013 elections for the lower house, the opposition People's Democratic Party claimed the majority, winning 32 seats, while the incumbent majority party, Druk Phuensum Tshogpa, scored only 15 seats.

Political Parties

The Bhutan Peace and Prosperity Party (Druk Phuensum Tshogpa—DPT) was the first ruling party in Bhutan's National Assembly. The DPT swept the nation's first democratic elections in 2008, winning 45 of 47 seats. However, the party lost its majority status in the 2013 elections, which were dominated by the rival People's Democratic Party. The DPT's slogan is "growth with equity and justice," and it supports economic self-reliance, social harmony, environmental integrity, and political justice. The Party believes that solidifying Bhutan's budding democracy is part of its responsibility.

The People's Democratic Party (PDP) became the majority party with the 2013 elections, gaining 32 seats in the National Assembly. The PDP supports equitable socio-economic growth, maintaining a pristine environment, promoting social and family values, improving health and education services, as well as the right of everyone to "live a happy and meaningful life." The PDP has been critical of the DPT's socio-economic policies.

Bhutan Kuen-Ngyam Party (BKP) is a new party that participated in the 2013 Assembly elections but did not win a substantial number of seats. The BKP's motto is "service before self," and it advocates equal opportunities, employment, economic growth, and distribution of wealth, and is dedicated to the democratic process.

Druk Chirwang Tshogpa (DCT) also participated in the 2013 Assembly elections. The DCT platform focuses on the rights of women and the marginalized. DCT also supports a strong sovereignty, transparent and accountable government, and inclusive and sustainable growth and development. Its motto is "unity, prosperity, and happiness."

Druk Nyamrup Tshogpa (DNT) is another new party that participated in the 2013 Assembly elections. The DNT promotes social democracy based on freedom, justice, and solidarity. DNT bills itself as a "people-centric party" that supports creating an environment in which all are enabled to pursue individual opportunity.

The Bhutan People's Party (BPP), formed in 1990, works in exile in Nepal and advocates for ethnic Nepalese living in Bhutan, known as Lhotshampas. The Lhotshampas were stripped of their Bhutanese citizenship in the 1970s and thus are neither allowed to vote in Bhutan's elections nor run for office. The BPP seeks freedom regarding religion, press, and speech as well as equal rights for all races.

ECONOMY

Despite having one of the world's smallest and least-developed economies, Bhutan's gross domestic product has nearly quadrupled since the 1980s. Most of the country's people own their own animals and plots of land, and grow enough food to feed their families. The Bhutanese government has made progress in improving social welfare, providing free health facilities to more than 90% of the population.

Beginning in the early twenty-first century, Bhutanese citizens were required to pay personal income taxes for the first time.

Bhutan uses a market economy system but carefully controls contacts with the outside world. Possessing very few natural resources other than the nation's dense forests, Bhutan's energy comes mainly from hydroelectric power. And while preserving forests is a major objective, one of Bhutan's top exports to India—its main trading partner—is timber. Three economic sectors—food processing, wood products, and cement—comprise most of Bhutan's industrial base. Almost all of the country's manufacturing is in the south, near the Indian border. In the north, the breathtaking mountain scenery, along with its carefully guarded ancient culture, have made it a desirable destination for tourists. But Bhutan's leaders, trying to balance the need for economic growth, which tourism would bring, with the desire to preserve both the country's natural beauty and its culture, restrict tourists to just over 111,000 a year. Still, interacting with the world beyond its borders has brought opportunities to Bhutan. In 2014, the Bhutan News Service announced a partnership with Japanese auto giant Nissan that would provide a fleet of electric cars to the Bhutanese. Also in 2014, Bhutan announced plans to build four hydroelectric power plants with India in the next few years. Finally, the country announced in December 2013 the opening of Bhutan's very first ice cream-production plant.

SOCIETY

In Bhutan the Buddhist faith permeates all aspects of secular life. Mahayana Buddhism is the official religion of the country, and to ensure its future importance one son from every family is encouraged to attend monastic school. The people of Bhutan are called Drukpa, but there are three ethnic groups within this category. The Sharchops are the oldest inhabitants and reside primarily in the east. The Ngalops came from the Tibetan plateau and were the original importers of Buddhism. The Lhotshampas came from Nepal in the early twentieth century and live in the southern plains. The national language is Dzongkha, but dialects differ enough to make it difficult for people from one region to understand those from another. English is also taught in the schools.

Ethnic Composition

Ngalop – 50%; ethnic Nepalese – 35% (includes Lhotshampas); indigenous groups – 15%

Language

The official language is Dzongkha, although other Tibetan as well as Nepalese dialects are spoken.

A Buddhist monk at the Trongsa Dzong Monastery. About 70 percent of Bhutan's people are Buddhists. (Alec Conway Tips Rf/ZUMA Press/Newscom)

Religion

Lamaistic Buddhism – 75.3%; Indian- and Nepalese-influenced Hinduism – 22.1%; other – 2.6%

CONTEMPORARY ISSUES

Transition to Democracy

Until recently, Bhutan had been ruled by an absolute, hereditary monarchy for more than 100 years. However, the country has virtually completed its transition to a constitutional monarchy, with parliamentary elections held in December 2007 and March 2008, and again in July 2013. And unlike most of the world's prodemocracy movements, Bhutan moved toward free elections not because of a popular sentiment, but because of the efforts of the monarchs themselves. Bhutan's former king Jigme Singye Wangchuck began the process by disseminating a draft constitution to Bhutan's people and then, in December 2006, handing over the throne to his son, Oxford-educated Jigme Khesar Namgyel Wangchuck.

Because the Bhutanese people were prodded toward democracy by their monarch (some Bhutanese still fear life without the king's rule), the political issues facing the country today involve how difficult it will be for the Bhutanese to transition to a more open, representative government. One problem is that Bhutan has little experience with political parties: the monarchy had never allowed the organization of parties before March 2007. After the 2008 elections, two major parties emerged: the People's Democratic Party and the Bhutan Prosperity Party. Despite high participation in the elections, it is unclear whether Bhutan's citizens will adapt to a parliamentary democracy or whether the country will fall back into dependence on royal rule. It is also unknown whether the nation's new democratic government will embrace all of Bhutan's citizens, or whether it will exclude non-Bhutanese ethnic groups.

Discrimination Against Ethnic Nepalis

Multiple coordinated bombings in Bhutan's capital, Thimpu, on January 20, 2008, marred the image of the country as a serene Buddhist paradise. A previously unknown group, the United Revolutionary Front of Bhutan, claimed responsibility, saying that the change to a new form of government will not benefit all of the country's citizens. Authorities interpreted this to mean that the blasts were designed to highlight the plight of Bhutan's ethnic Nepalis.

During the 1980s, the monarchy and the privileged class began viewing the growing ethnic Nepali population as a threat to native Bhutanese culture. As a result, the government imposed discriminatory laws against Nepalis that stripped them of citizenship. During the early 1990s, Nepalis began to suffer harassment in advance of a more serious measure: expulsion from the country. Soldiers forced Nepalis to renounce their homeland and sign away the rights to their homes. They then expelled the families from Bhutan. For almost two decades, at least 120,000 stateless Bhutanese Nepalis lived in refugee camps in Nepal; the United Nations High Commissioner for Refugees began a resettlement program in 2007 that has since resettled some 90,000 refugees in eight countries around the world. In all these years, Bhutan's government has not allowed any refugees to return. It remains to be seen whether the new government can be truly democratic if it continues the exclusionist policies of the monarchy.

Alleviation of Poverty/Community Forestry

Although Bhutan was one of the world's poorest countries until the 1980s, it has made significant economic progress in recent years. Still, most of its citizens work as subsistence farmers, and many of them are landless sharecroppers who earn less than $1 a day. Because much of Bhutan's countryside is forested (70% of which is protected), the government has initiated a "community forestry" poverty-reduction program. The program allows rural Bhutanese to sell excess timber and other forest products for their own profit. In addition, community forestry makes more wood available for rural participants' own consumption. The government has now approved some 200 community forests, and more than 9,700 rural households are involved in the program.

Border Issues with China and India

Because Bhutan is located between the much larger powers and acts as a buffer between South Asia and East Asia, border issues with China and India have long plagued the nation. In 2007, Bhutan and India updated their Perpetual Peace and Freedom Agreement (originally signed in 1949), mandating greater Bhutanese control of border areas. The revised agreement also will allow Bhutan more freedom to pursue military purchases and foreign policy initiatives. In recent years, an ongoing problem for the two countries has involved Indian rebels escaping over the border and establishing hideouts in Bhutan. Under Indian pressure, Bhutan launched a military campaign to flush out Indian militants operating within Bhutan, though the problem remains.

Because Bhutan touches China's disputed Tibet region, that border area has also been a source of friction. Bhutan and China have long disputed their common border, which follows such geographic features as the watershed of the Chumbi Valley in the northwest and the crest of the Himalayas in the north. Tensions between Bhutan and China increased with China's 1950 invasion of Tibet. The territory seized by China's People's Liberation Army included eight western Tibetan enclaves that had been administered by Bhutan since the seventeenth century. A related issue emerged over the flight of thousands of Tibetan refugees to Bhutan. Tensions have mounted with each of the Chinese crackdowns on Tibetan uprisings from the 1950s to the present. Since 1984, the two nations have held a series of meetings between their foreign ministers to discuss border issues in an attempt to smooth relations; the twenty-first round of talks was held in August 2013 and ended inconclusively. In 1998, the two countries signed the Agreement to Maintain Peace and Tranquility on the Bhutan–China Border, which is the only such agreement ever signed by Bhutan and China.

Excerpt from the Constitution of Bhutan

The Constitution of Bhutan was adopted in 2008 after several years of planning and deliberation. It was the first written constitution of Bhutan, which for most of its history had been an absolute monarchy. However, the Constitution specifies that Bhutan would be a democratic constitutional monarchy, although the king, as the head of state, is invested with numerous royal prerogatives. The basic philosophy of the Constitution is that governance in Bhutan is to "enable the true and sustainable development of a good and compassionate society rooted in Buddhist ethos and universal human values."

The Constitution enumerates both political and economic rights. Many of the fundamental rights granted to Bhutan's citizens via its Constitution are analogous to political rights specified in the U.S. Constitution, including the rights of free speech, freedom of religion, and equality before the law. However, the State may impose "reasonable restrictions" on the exercise of these rights when such are deemed necessary because of national security or when the exercise of these rights affects others.

The Constitution also specifies numerous economic rights, some of which are based on Bhutan's philosophy of promoting "Gross National Happiness." For example, the Constitution calls for "fair and reasonable remuneration" for work and specifies that the State should promote equality of wealth. The right to education and the right to health care are also stated in the Constitution. It also calls specifically for protections for women and children. In a region of the world in which sex trafficking is relatively commonplace, the Constitution specifies that the State has the responsibility "to take appropriate measures to ensure that children are protected against all forms of discrimination and exploitation including trafficking, prostitution, abuse, violence, degrading treatment and economic exploitation."

Fundamental Rights

All persons shall have the right to life, liberty and security of person and shall not be deprived of such rights except in accordance with the due process of law.

A Bhutanese citizen shall have the right to freedom of speech, opinion and expression.

A Bhutanese citizen shall have the right to information.

A Bhutanese citizen shall have the right to freedom of thought, conscience and religion. No person shall be compelled to belong to another faith by means of coercion or inducement.

There shall be freedom of the press, radio and television and other forms of dissemination of information, including electronic.

A Bhutanese citizen shall have the right to vote.

A Bhutanese citizen shall have the right to freedom of movement and residence within Bhutan.

A Bhutanese citizen shall have the right to equal access and opportunity to join the Public Service.

A Bhutanese citizen shall have the right to own property, but shall not have the right to sell or transfer land or any immovable property to a person who is not a citizen of Bhutan, except in keeping with laws enacted by Parliament.

A Bhutanese citizen shall have the right to practice any lawful trade, profession or vocation.

A Bhutanese citizen shall have the right to equal pay for work of equal value.

A Bhutanese citizen shall have the right to freedom of peaceful assembly and freedom of association, other than membership of associations that are harmful to the peace and unity of the country, and shall have the right not to be compelled to belong to any association.

Every person in Bhutan shall have the right to material interests resulting from any scientific, literary or artistic production of which he or she is the author or creator.

A person shall not be deprived of property by acquisition or requisition, except for public purpose and on payment of fair compensation in accordance with the provisions of the law.

All persons are equal before the law and are entitled to equal and effective protection of the law and shall not be discriminated against on the grounds of race, sex, language, religion, politics or other status.

A person charged with a penal offence has the right to be presumed innocent until proven guilty in accordance with the law.

A person shall not be subjected to torture or to cruel, inhuman or degrading treatment or punishment.

A person shall not be subjected to capital punishment.

A person shall not be subjected to arbitrary or unlawful interference with his or her privacy, family, home or correspondence nor to unlawful attacks on the person's honour and reputation.

A person shall not be subjected to arbitrary arrest or detention.

A person shall have the right to consult and be represented by a Bhutanese Jabmi of his or her choice.

. . . nothing in this Article shall prevent the State from subjecting reasonable restriction by law, when it concerns:

(a) The interests of the sovereignty, security, unity and integrity of Bhutan;
(b) The interests of peace, stability and well-being of the nation;
(c) The interests of friendly relations with foreign States;
(d) Incitement to an offence on the grounds of race, sex, language, religion or region;
(e) The disclosure of information received in regard to the affairs of the State or in discharge of official duties; or
(f) The rights and freedom of others.

23. All persons in Bhutan shall have the right to initiate appropriate proceedings in the Supreme Court or High Court for the enforcement of the rights conferred by this Article . . .

Principles of State Policy

The State shall endeavour to apply the Principles of State Policy set out in this Article to ensure a good quality of life for the people of Bhutan . . .

The State shall strive to promote those conditions that will enable the pursuit of Gross National Happiness.

The State shall endeavour to create a civil society free of oppression, discrimination and violence, based on the rule of law, protection of human rights and dignity, and to ensure the fundamental rights and freedoms of the people.

The State shall endeavour to protect the telephonic, electronic, postal or other communications of all persons in Bhutan from unlawful interception or interruption.

The State shall endeavour to provide justice through a fair, transparent and expeditious process.

The State shall endeavour to provide legal aid to secure justice, which shall not be denied to any person by reason of economic or other disabilities.

The State shall endeavour to develop and execute policies to minimize inequalities of income, concentration of wealth. . .

The State shall endeavour to ensure the right to work, vocational guidance and training and just and favourable conditions of work.

The State shall endeavour to ensure the right to rest and leisure, including reasonable limitation of working hours and periodic holidays with pay.

The State shall endeavour to ensure the right to fair and reasonable remuneration for one's work.

The State shall endeavour to provide education for the purpose of improving and increasing knowledge, values and skills of the entire population with education being directed towards the full development of the human personality.

The State shall provide free education to all children of school going age up to tenth standard and ensure that technical and professional education is made generally available and that higher education is equally accessible to all on the basis of merit.

17. The State shall endeavour to take appropriate measures to eliminate all forms of discrimination and exploitation against women including trafficking, prostitution, abuse, violence, harassment and intimidation at work in both public and private spheres.

18. The State shall endeavour to take appropriate measures to ensure that children are protected against all forms of discrimination and exploitation including trafficking, prostitution, abuse, violence, degrading treatment and economic exploitation.

19. The State shall endeavour to promote those conditions that are conducive to co-operation in community life and the integrity of the extended family structure.

20. The State shall strive to create conditions that will enable the true and sustainable development of a good and compassionate society rooted in Buddhist ethos and universal human values.

21. The State shall provide free access to basic public health services in both modern and traditional medicines.

22. The State shall endeavour to provide security in the event of sickness and disability or lack of adequate means of livelihood for reasons beyond one's control.

Source: "Bhutan Constitution." United Nations Office on Drugs and Crime. track. unodc.org/LegalLibrary/LegalResources/Bhutan/Laws/Bhutan%20Constitution.pdf

SAUDI ARABIA: Absolute Monarchy

SAUDI ARABIA

Communications	
Facebook Users	secondary education, followed by three years of either academic or technical upper secondary education.
6,000,000 (estimate) (2013)	**Mandatory Education**
Internet Users	(not available)
9,774,000 (2009)	**Average Years Spent in School for Current Students**
Internet Users (% of Population)	
60.5% (2013)	16 (estimate) (2012)
Television	**Average Years Spent in School for Current Students, Male**
27 sets per 100 Population (2004)	
Land-based Telephones in Use	15 (estimate) (2012)
4,800,000 (2012)	**Average Years Spent in School for Current Students, Female**
Mobile Telephone Subscribers	
53,000,000 (2012)	16 (estimate) (2012)
Major Daily Newspapers	**Primary School–age Children Enrolled in Primary School**
12 (2004)	
Average Circulation of Daily Newspapers	3,583,488 (2013)
Not Available	**Primary School–age Males Enrolled in Primary School**
Education	
School System	1,851,440 (2013)
Primary education in Saudi Arabia begins at the age of six and lasts for six years. Students then attend three years of early	**Primary School–age Females Enrolled in Primary School**
	1,723,048 (2013)

Secondary School–age Children Enrolled in Secondary School	**Natural Resources**
	Petroleum, natural gas, iron ore, gold, copper
3,214,012 (estimate) (2013)	
Secondary School–age Males Enrolled in Secondary School	**Environment**
	CO2 Emissions
1,737,135 (estimate) (2013)	16.1 metric tons per capita (2009)
Secondary School–age Females Enrolled in Secondary School	**Alternative and Nuclear Energy**
	0.0% of total energy use (2010)
1,476,877 (estimate) (2013)	**Threatened Species**
Students Per Teacher, Primary School	103 (2010)
10.4 (estimate) (2012)	**Protected Areas**
Students Per Teacher, Secondary School	607,879 (estimate) (2010)
11.3 (2012)	**Geography**
Enrollment in Tertiary Education	**Location**
1,206,007 (2012)	Occupying most of the Arabian peninsula in southwestern Asia, Saudi Arabia is bordered by Iraq, Jordan, and Kuwait to the north, Yemen to the south, Oman to the southeast, and the United Arab Emirates and Qatar to the east. It has a long western coastline on the Red Sea facing Egypt, Sudan, and Ethiopia, and a shorter coastline on the Persian Gulf facing Iran.
Enrollment in Tertiary Education, Male	
611,861 (2012)	
Enrollment in Tertiary Education, Female	
594,146 (2012)	
Literacy	
94% (2013)	
Energy and Natural Resources	**Time Zone**
Electric Power Generation	8 hours ahead of U.S. Eastern Standard
239,200,000,000 kilowatt hours per year (estimate) (2011)	**Land Borders**
	2,744 miles
Electric Power Consumption	**Coastline**
190,900,000,000 kilowatt hours per year (estimate) (2010)	1,640 miles
Nuclear Power Plants	**Capital**
0 (2014)	Riyadh
Crude Oil Production	**Area**
11,591,900 barrels per day (2013)	864,869 sq. miles
Crude Oil Consumption	**Climate**
2,861,000 barrels per day (2012)	While most of the country is arid desert, the coastal regions have high humidity with temperatures between 100°F and 120°F in the summer. Temperatures in the interior reach up to 129°F and some areas go without rainfall for several years. With the exception of mountainous regions, winters are mild.
Natural Gas Production	
103,200,000,000 cubic meters per year (estimate) (2012)	
Natural Gas Consumption	
99,230,000,000 cubic meters per year (estimate) (2011)	

Land Use	Agriculture Products
1.6% arable land; 0.1% permanent crops; 79.1% permanent meadows and pastures; 1.3% forest land; 18.0% other.	Wheat, dates, tomatoes, barley, watermelons, vegetables, sheep, goats, poultry.
Arable Land	**Unemployment**
2% (2007)	5.6% (2012)
Arable Land Per Capita	**Labor Profile**
0 acres per person (2007)	agriculture: 6.7% industry: 21.4% services: 71.9% (estimate) (2005)
Health	
Average Life Expectancy	**Military**
74.8 years (2014)	**Total Active Armed Forces**
Average Life Expectancy, Male	233,500 (estimate) (2010)
72.8 years (2014)	**Active Armed Forces**
Average Life Expectancy, Female	1% (2010)
76.9 years (2014)	**Annual Military Expenditures**
Crude Birth Rate	$41,200,000,000 (2009)
18.5 (estimate) (2015)	**Military Service**
Crude Death Rate	Service in the Saudi armed forces is voluntary.
3.3 (estimate) (2015)	**National Finances**
Maternal Mortality	**Currency**
23 per 100,000 live births (2005–2012 projection)	Saudi riyal
Infant Mortality	**Total Government Revenues**
7 per 1,000 live births (2012)	$302,600,000,000 (estimate) (2013)
Doctors	**Total Government Expenditures**
0.9 per 1,000 people (2010)	$258,400,000,000 (estimate) (2013)
Industry and Labor	**Budget Deficit**
Gross Domestic Product (GDP) - official exchange rate	6.2 (estimate) (2013)
	GDP Contribution by Sector
$790,905,000,000 (estimate) (2015)	agriculture: 1.9% industry: 64.8% services: 33.3% (2012 est.)
GDP per Capita	**External Debt**
$25,320 (estimate) (2015)	$149,400,000,000 (estimate) (2013)
GDP - Purchasing Power Parity (PPP)	**Economic Aid Extended**
$962,132,000,000 (estimate) (2013)	$4,773,290,000 (2011)
GDP (PPP) per Capita	**Economic Aid Received**
$32,469 (estimate) (2013)	$0 (2011)
Industry Products	**Population**
Petroleum products, refined petroleum, petrochemicals, fertilizers, cement, crude steel, plastic products.	**Population**
	27,752,316 (estimate) (2015)

World Population Rank	Import Partners
42 nd (2009)	United States - 12.8%; China - 11.3%; Germany - 8.0%; Japan - 6.4%; United Kingdom - 4.9% (2009 estimate)
Population Density	
30.2 people per square mile (estimate) (2011)	**Export Partners**
Population Distribution	United States - 17.1%; Iraq - 17.0%; India - 13.5%; Saudi Arabia - 10.5%; Syrian Arab Republic - 4.2% (2009).
82% urban (2011)	
Age Distribution	**Export Partners**
0-14: 38%	Japan - 15.4%; China - 12.7%; United States - 12.3%; South Korea -10.4%; India - 7.7% (2009 estimate).
15-64: 59.5%	
65+: 2.5%	**Current Account Balance**
(2009)	$132,200,000,000 (estimate) (2013)
Median Age	**Weights and Measures**
26.4 years (estimate) (2014)	The metric system is in use.
Population Growth Rate	**Transportation**
1.5% per year (estimate) (2015)	**Airports**
Net Migration Rate	216 (2012)
-0.6 (estimate) (2015)	**Paved Roads**
Trade	21.5% (2005)
Imported Goods	**Roads, Unpaved**
Transportation equipment, machinery, base metals, textiles, chemical products, vegetable products, pearls and precious stones, live animals, scientific instruments, foodstuffs.	108,021 (2006)
	Passenger Cars per 1,000 People
	139 (2005)
Total Value of Imports	**Number of Trucks, Buses, and Commercial Vehicles**
$92,742,000,000 (estimate) (2009)	Not Available
Exported Goods	**Railroads**
Crude and refined petroleum products, chemicals, resins, plastics, rubber.	865 (2008)
	Ports
Total Value of Exports	Major: 11 (including Jiddah, Jizan, Ad Dammam, Ras Tanura, Al Jubayl, Yanbu al Bahr, Duba).
$381,500,000,000 (estimate) (2012)	

OVERVIEW

Saudi Arabia, which is geographically, politically, and economically the dominant nation in the Arabian Peninsula/Persian Gulf region, lies between the Gulf and the Red Sea, bordering on Iraq, Jordan, Kuwait, Oman, Qatar, the United Arab Emirates, and Yemen (with which a large portion of the boundary is defined only approximately). The landscape of Saudi Arabia is a mix of narrow coastal plains, mountains, and enormous sandy deserts dotted with densely populated oases. There are no rivers or permanent bodies of water and scant arable land, although there is significant grazing land in the north that is utilized by nomadic herders. Saudi Arabia has a dry, desert climate, characterized by brutally hot summer days and freezing winter nights. Annual rainfall is low and unpredictable, sometimes falling all at once from one massive storm; some areas do not receive any rain for years at a time. Sand and dust storms are frequent throughout the country. The national language is Arabic. The population of almost 27.3 million people includes more than 6 million foreign workers. The capital of Saudi Arabia is Riyadh.

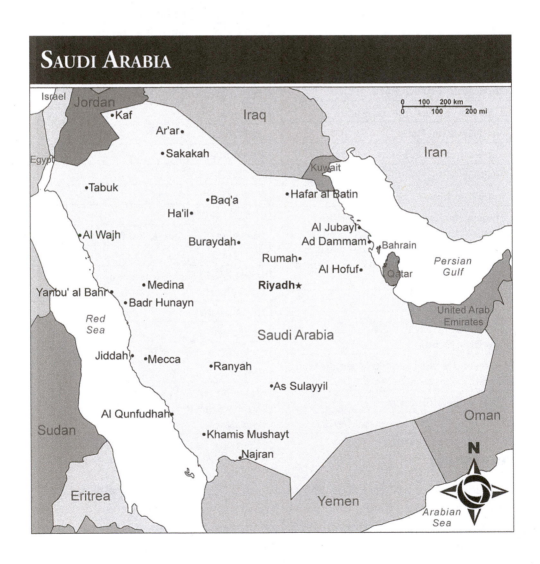

SAUDI ARABIA

GOVERNMENT

The Kingdom of Saudi Arabia is a monarchy headed by a king, and political power rests predominantly with the royal family. King Abd al-Aziz ibn Saud united the regions of Nedj and Hejaz on September 23, 1932, to create Saudi Arabia, reestablishing the power his family had possessed in the eighteenth and nineteenth centuries. Appointed government ministers rule according to the sacred tenets of sharia (Islamic law), and legislation is enacted by royal decree. The concept of separation of religion and state is not accepted by the Saudi government or by many of its citizens. Abdullah ibn Abd al-Aziz al-Saud became king in 2005. Abdullah died in 2015 and was succeeded by his half-brother, Salman ibn Abd al-Aziz al-Saud.

Constitution

In 1980, the ruling monarchy appointed an executive committee to draft a 200-article basic "system of rule" based on sharia. On March 1, 1992, the king established by decree a formal written Saudi Arabian Constitution and Bill of Rights as part of a series of political reforms to decentralize political power and allow greater provincial autonomy.

Bank notes showing the portrait of King Abdullah bin Abdulaziz Al Saud, who ruled Saudi Arabia from 2005 until his death. The Saud family has ruled Saudi Arabia, one of the world's last absolute monarchies, since 1902. (Tim Brakemeier/dpa/picture-alliance/Newscom)

Executive

All political power in Saudi Arabia is ultimately vested in the king, who serves as head of state, head of government, and supreme religious leader. The king also holds the post of prime minister and appoints and leads a Council of Ministers (cabinet), which includes many royal family members who advise him on matters of legislative and executive policy. Under an August 1993 decree, the king limited the terms of office for cabinet ministers to four years, with the possibility of a two-year extension. (Ministers previously served unlimited terms.) Cabinet decisions are reached by majority vote subject to royal sanction. The king also consults with lower advisory councils, whose members are nominated or approved by him. The nation's two most powerful advisory councils are the Ulemas Council, a highly conservative group of Muslim theologians; and the Supreme Council of Islamic Affairs, which was created in October 1994 to dilute the powers of the *ulemas* and oversee policies on education, foreign policy, and the economy.

Legislature

Saudi legislation is passed by royal decree, though the right to petition the king directly is a well-established tradition. The country has no independent legislature, although a 60-member Consultative Council (Majlis al-Shura) was approved by decree in March 1992 as a branch of the executive government. The Council was later enlarged to 150 members. On August 20, 1993, the king appointed 60 members of the Council from among thousands of prominent Saudi citizens bearing no relation to the ruling Saud family. The quasi-legislative body, first sworn in on December 28, 1993, is empowered to debate issues presented for discussion by the king and reach decisions by majority vote. The Consultative Council submits decisions to the king for adjudication if there is disagreement among Council members, who serve four-year terms and do not hold public sessions. The body is led by a speaker selected by the king. In 2011 King Abdullah decreed that women could serve as full members. Previously, they were only allowed to participate as nonvoting members.

Judiciary

The country's independent judiciary is headed by a High Court that reviews criminal cases and passes sentences of death, cutting, and stoning for criminal offenses. Judges are recommended by the Supreme Judiciary Council, consisting of 10 high-level judicial heads, and appointed by royal decree. There is a Court of Appeals and specialized courts that hear criminal, labor, personal, general, and commercial suits. The king is the highest judicial authority and has the power to pardon.

Local Government

Saudi Arabia has 13 administrative emirates (provinces) that are governed by municipal councils presided over by a governor and a deputy governor. Half of the council members are elected, and half are appointed. A royal decree in 1994 further divided the emirates into 103 governorates. The municipal councils are the only government body with elected members and do not hold strong influence in Saudi government.

Election Qualifications

All men 21 years of age and older may vote in municipal council elections. In 2011, King Abdullah announced that women will be able to vote in the 2015 elections.

POLITICS

After his ascension to the throne in 1982, former Saudi king Saud Fahd faced pressure from liberals calling for the modernization of Saudi Arabia's political system as well as pressure from Islamic fundamentalists seeking an even stricter implementation of sharia. Responding partially to both groups, Fahd enacted the country's first written rules of governance in 1992, establishing the legislative Consultative Council, and also created a Supreme Council on Islamic Affairs in 1994, which was viewed as a measure to counteract the growing popularity of Islamic fundamentalism.

In 1995, Fahd conducted a sweeping government shakeup in which many top positions—including finance, industry, and petroleum—changed hands, with younger, reform-minded technocrats replacing many veteran ministers. More than half of the country's senior civil servants were also replaced at that time. Although the royal family retained the top government spots, the reorganization was the first significant government change in 20 years and was seen as an attempt by Fahd to combat the perceived threat of growing fundamentalist zealotry.

After suffering an apparent stroke in 1995, Fahd officially transferred authority for national affairs to his half-brother, Crown Prince Abdullah, in January 1996. Although the king resumed official authority again a month later, Abdullah acted as de-facto head of government for much of the time until Fahd's death in August 2005, when the crown prince became Saudi Arabia's new monarch. In 2005, King Abdullah ordered that the Saudi judiciary be revamped to meet higher judicial standards that affirm the judiciary's independence and impartiality. The same year, the country's first local elections were held. Men were allowed to vote and stand for election to fill the seats of half of each of the country's municipal councils. The municipal councils are the only level of government in which some members are elected. In 2011, King Abdullah announced that women would be able to stand for office and vote in the 2015 elections.

Political Parties

There are no political parties in Saudi Arabia.

ECONOMY

Although crude oil has been extracted from Saudi Arabia's vast deserts since the 1930s, it was not until the increase in world prices following the 1973 Arab boycott of the United States and other Western nations that the kingdom saw its revenues rise exponentially. Since then the Saud family has invested heavily in the country's infrastructure, creating university and health care systems that are among the best in the world. The largest oil producer and exporter in the world, Saudi Arabia possesses nearly one-fifth of the planet's proven reserves. Oil accounts for 80% of government revenues and 90% of the nation's exports; consequently, major trading partners, including the United States, Japan, and China, are led by heavy petroleum consumers. Fully 95% of all oil is produced for the state-owned Aramco corporation. A leading member of the Organization of Petroleum Exporting Countries, Saudi Arabia is both blessed and cursed by such an enormous supply of "black gold" and has pressed for production quotas designed to stabilize world prices. The government has also been encouraging growth in the private sector in order to diversify the economy.

SOCIETY

The traditional divisions between and among the Arabs (*al-hadar*) and the Bedouins (*al-badiyah*) has been muted in recent decades. While the majority of residents are Arabs or Bedouins, perhaps a quarter of the population consists of temporary immigrant workers from Asia and around the Arab world. Arabic is the official language. Saudi Arabia is the birthplace of Islam—which is the official religion—and home to two of the religion's holiest shrines, in Mecca and Medina. Saudi Islam is more conservative than the Islam practiced in other countries. Most of the population is Sunni Muslim, with a small minority adhering to the Shiite sect. Most forms of religious expression inconsistent with the government-sanctioned interpretation of Sunni Islam are restricted. Although the large immigrant community includes other faiths, non-Muslims are not allowed to become citizens.

Ethnic Composition

Arab – 90%; Afro-Asian – 10%

Language

Arabic is the official language.

Religion

Sunni Muslim – 85%–90%; Shiite Muslim – 10%–15%

CONTEMPORARY ISSUES

Restrictions on women

Saudi Arabia adheres to a strict interpretation of sharia law, which severely limits the rights of women. Women are required to wear a full *abaya*, which covers the whole body with the exception of a small window for the eyes. Women make up a mere 5% of the Saudi workforce and are limited in the types of jobs allowed to them, primarily working in all-female environments. Until 2015, voting in local elections was reserved for men only. Women are denied the right to testify in court proceedings due to the belief that women are more swayed by their emotions and incapable of understanding public life, which is to be dominated by men. Women are to be accompanied by a male relative when leaving the home and are not allowed to drive. On several occasions various political leaders have supported bills that would allow for more employment opportunities; however, these measures have been consistently rejected by the Saudi cabinet.

Human rights

Although Saudi law officially allows for the private practice of religions other than Sunni Islam, as well as Shiite Islam, practitioners of these faiths are often punished due to the ambiguity of what constitutes "private worship." Sharia law is applied to Muslim and non-Muslim citizens alike, and Saudi Arabia's conservative interpretation of the law allows for public floggings, amputations, and stonings for crimes of varying degrees, including blasphemy, adultery, and homosexuality, which is illegal in Saudi Arabia. There are a number of political prisoners in the country who are subject to torture. Many accuse Saudi Arabia of using the global "war on terror," which it supports, to justify the arrest or killing of numerous critics of the state.

Saudi Arabia houses some 9 million migrant workers, many of whom enter the country under its migrant worker sponsorship system. Called the *kafala* system, the employer-sponsored program has been criticized by Human Rights Watch and other international organizations for promoting labor exploitation and slavery-like conditions as it gives too much power to employers who may violate Saudi law by confiscating passports, withholding wages, or depriving employees of food, among other activities. In 2012, the Saudi government proposed abolishing this system but later decided to keep it in place without making any permanent changes to residency or migrant worker laws. In mid-2013, authorities began massive raids across the country to find and detain any migrant workers who were no longer working for their sponsorship employers; any workers found in violation of the *kafala* system were given until November to find a new employer to sponsor them or risk deportation.

Relations with the United States

Although staunch allies, Saudi Arabia and the United States have had a fair share of disagreement. After the September 11, 2001, terrorist attacks on U.S. soil, in which 15 of the 19 hijackers were Saudi nationals, the Arab nation voiced its complete support of the U.S. war on terrorism; however, the United States expressed frustration over the Saudi government's refusal to allow access to the families or records of the hijackers. In a 2004 report issued by the 9/11 Commission, Saudi Arabia was described as "a problematic ally in combating Islamic extremism." Although used as a base for U.S. military operations during the Persian Gulf War, Saudi Arabia has been increasingly hesitant to host U.S. troops, and the U.S. military has removed most troops from Saudi soil in favor of neighboring Qatar. Saudi Arabia opposed the U.S.-led invasion of Iraq in 2003, partially due to the Arab country's fear of a Shiite revival in the region, which it feels would be a threat to its Sunni regime. The rift between the countries continued to grow as a result of tensions over the Arab Spring uprisings in 2011 and the Saudi government's disappointment in the lack of active U.S. involvement in the Syrian civil war.

Relations with Israel

Saudi Arabia does not officially recognize Israel and believes that Israel should withdraw from all occupied territories and relinquish control of Jerusalem to Palestinian nationals. Saudi Arabia did not support the Camp David peace accords between Egypt and Israel in 1978 and broke diplomatic ties with Egypt as a result of the accords, but the two Arab countries later reconciled. Although Saudi Arabia does not have any diplomatic or trade relations with Israel, it claims support for U.S.-backed Israeli–Palestinian peace negotiations, even proposing its own peace initiative in 2002. More recently, Israel and Saudi Arabia have come together in their concerns over the continued nuclear program in Iran.

Excerpt from the Constitution of the Kingdom of Saudi Arabia

Saudi Arabia is governed under the terms of its Basic Law, which includes aspects of governance and human rights that are analogous to those contained in the formal constitutions of other countries. The Basic Law was adopted by proclamation of Saudi Arabia's King Fahd in 1992. The Saudi state does not regard the Basic Law as a constitution because "Its constitution is Almighty God's Book, The Holy Qur'an, and the Sunna (Traditions) of the Prophet [Muhammad]." Thus the Basic Law identifies Saudi Arabia as an Islamic state. It regards the family as the fundamental building block of Saudi society and, in doing so, establishes the state's responsibility to "promote family bonds and Arab-Islamic values."

That Saudi Arabia is an Islamic state is reinforced throughout the Basic Law. The Basic Law specifies that "Saudi society is based on full adherence to God's guidance. Members of this society shall cooperate amongst themselves in charity, piety and cohesion." The right to education is guaranteed, although one of the specified goals of education is to "implant the Islamic Creed in the hearts of all youths." The Basic Law also identifies the rights to public health, social security, and assistance to the disabled along with the responsibility to "enact laws to protect the worker and the employer."

CHAPTER ONE

GENERAL PRINCIPLES

Article 1

The Kingdom of Saudi Arabia is a sovereign Arab Islamic State. Its religion is Islam. Its constitution is Almighty God's Book, The Holy Qur'an, and the Sunna (Traditions) of the Prophet (PBUH). Arabic is the language of the Kingdom. The City of Riyadh is the capital.

CHAPTER THREE

THE VALUES OF SAUDI SOCIETY

Article 9

The family is the nucleus of Saudi Society. Members of the family shall be raised in the Islamic Creed, which demands allegiance and obedience to God, to His Prophet and to the rulers, respect for and obedience to the laws, and love for and pride in the homeland and its glorious history.

Article 10

The State shall aspire to promote family bonds and Arab-Islamic values. It shall take care of all individuals and provide the right conditions for the growth of their talents and skills.

Article 11

Saudi society is based on full adherence to God's guidance. Members of this society shall cooperate amongst themselves in charity, piety and cohesion.

Article 12

Consolidation of the national unity is a duty. The State shall forbid all activities that may lead to division, disorder and partition.

Article 13

The aim of education is to implant the Islamic Creed in the hearts of all youths, to help them acquire knowledge and skills, to qualify them to become useful members of their society, to love their homeland and take pride in its history.

Article 26

The State shall protect human rights in accordance with the Sharia.

Article 27

The State shall guarantee the rights of the citizens and their families in cases of emergency, illness, disability and old age. The State shall support the Social Insurance Law and encourage organizations and individuals to participate in philanthropic activities.

Article 28

The State shall facilitate job opportunities for every able person, and enact laws to protect the worker and the employer.

Article 29

The State shall patronize sciences, letters and culture. It shall encourage scientific research, protect the Islamic and Arab heritage, and contribute towards Arab, Islamic and human civilization.

Article 30

The State shall provide public education and commit itself to the eradication of illiteracy.

Article 31

The State shall look after public health and provide health care for every citizen.

Article 36

The State shall provide security for all citizens and residents on its territories. No-one may be confined, arrested or imprisoned without reference to the Law.

Article 37

Dwellings are inviolate. Access is prohibited without their owners' permission. No search may be made except in cases specified by the Law.

Article 38

No-one shall be punished for another's crimes. No conviction or penalty shall be inflicted without reference to the Sharia or the provisions of the Law. Punishment shall not be imposed ex post facto.

Article 39

Mass media and all other vehicles of expression shall employ civil and polite language, contribute towards the education of the nation and strengthen unity. It is prohibited to commit acts leading to disorder and division, affecting the security of the state and its public relations, or undermining human dignity and rights. Details shall be specified in the Law.

Article 40

The privacy of telegraphic and postal communications, and telephone and other means of communication, shall be inviolate. There shall be no confiscation, delay, surveillance or eavesdropping, except in cases provided by the Law.

Article 41

Residents in the Kingdom of Saudi Arabia shall abide by its laws, observe the values of the Saudi community and respect Saudi traditions and feelings.

Source: "The Basic Law of Governance." Royal Embassy of Saudi Arabia. http://www.saudiembassy.net/about/country-information/laws/The_Basic_Law_Of_Governance.aspx

SPAIN: Parliamentary Monarchy

SPAIN

Communications	Primary School–age Children Enrolled in Primary School
Facebook Users	
17,000,000 (estimate) (2013)	2,816,584 (2012)
Internet Users	**Primary School–age Males Enrolled in Primary School**
28,119,000 (2009)	1,452,603 (2012)
Internet Users (% of Population)	**Primary School–age Females Enrolled in Primary School**
71.6% (2013)	
Television	1,363,981 (2012)
55 sets per 100 Population (2004)	**Secondary School–age Children Enrolled in Secondary School**
Land-based Telephones in Use	
19,220,000 (2012)	3,296,129 (2012)
Mobile Telephone Subscribers	**Secondary School–age Males Enrolled in Secondary School**
50,663,000 (2012)	1,686,545 (2012)
Major Daily Newspapers	**Secondary School–age Females Enrolled in Secondary School**
151 (2004)	
Average Circulation of Daily Newspapers	1,609,584 (2012)
6,183,000 (2004)	**Students Per Teacher, Primary School**
Education	12.6 (2012)
School System	**Students Per Teacher, Secondary School**
Spanish students begin their primary education at the age of six. After six years, they continue to four years of early secondary education, followed by two years of academic or technical upper secondary school.	11.4 (2012)
	Enrollment in Tertiary Education
	1,965,829 (estimate) (2012)
	Enrollment in Tertiary Education, Male
Mandatory Education	911,887 (estimate) (2012)
10 years, from ages 6 to 16.	**Enrollment in Tertiary Education, Female**
Average Years Spent in School for Current Students	
17 (estimate) (2012)	1,053,942 (estimate) (2012)
Average Years Spent in School for Current Students, Male	**Literacy**
	98% (2012)
17 (estimate) (2012)	**Energy and Natural Resources**
Average Years Spent in School for Current Students, Female	**Electric Power Generation**
18 (2012)	276,800,000,000 kilowatt hours per year (estimate) (2011)

Electric Power Consumption	**Time Zone**
249,700,000,000 kilowatt hours per year (estimate) (2011)	6 hours ahead of U.S. Eastern Standard
	Land Borders
Nuclear Power Plants	1,183 miles
7 (2014)	**Coastline**
Crude Oil Production	3,084 miles
33,600 barrels per day (2013)	**Capital**
Crude Oil Consumption	Madrid
1,204,100 barrels per day (2013)	**Area**
Natural Gas Production	194,834 sq. miles
61,000,000 cubic meters per year (estimate) (2012)	**Climate**
Natural Gas Consumption	Less temperate than most areas of western Europe, Spain has hot summers in most regions, with temperatures averaging about 95°F. The mountainous areas of the interior have cold winters.
35,820,000,000 cubic meters per year (estimate) (2010)	
Natural Resources	**Land Use**
Coal, lignite, iron ore, copper, lead, zinc, uranium, tungsten, mercury, pyrites, magnesite, fluorspar, gypsum, sepiolite, kaolin, potash, hydropower, arable land	25.5% arable land; 9.7% permanent crops; 22.2% permanent meadows and pastures; 37.1% forest land; 5.5% other.
Environment	**Arable Land**
CO2 Emissions	26% (2007)
6.3 metric tons per capita (2009)	**Arable Land Per Capita**
Alternative and Nuclear Energy	1 acres per person (2007)
17.7% of total energy use (2011)	**Health**
Threatened Species	**Average Life Expectancy**
240 (2010)	81.5 years (2014)
Protected Areas	**Average Life Expectancy, Male**
47,661 (estimate) (2010)	78.5 years (2014)
Geography	**Average Life Expectancy, Female**
Location	84.7 years (2014)
Spain occupies 80% of the Iberian Peninsula in southwestern Europe. It is bordered by France to the north and Portugal to the west, and has coastlines on the Bay of Biscay to the north, the Atlantic Ocean to the west and southwest, and the Mediterranean Sea to the southeast. The nation also encompasses the Canary Isles, situated in the Atlantic Ocean, the Balearic Islands, located in the Mediterranean Sea, and some enclaves within Morocco.	**Crude Birth Rate**
	9.6 (estimate) (2015)
	Crude Death Rate
	9.0 (estimate) (2015)
	Maternal Mortality
	92 per 100,000 live births (2005–2012 projection)
	Infant Mortality
	4 per 1,000 live births (2012)

Doctors	**Total Government Revenues**
3.7 per 1,000 people (2012)	$505,100,000,000 (estimate) (2013)
Industry and Labor	**Total Government Expenditures**
Gross Domestic Product (GDP) - official exchange rate	$597,300,000,000 (estimate) (2013)
	Budget Deficit
$1,466,357,000,000 (estimate) (2015)	-6.8 (estimate) (2013)
GDP per Capita	**GDP Contribution by Sector**
$31,601 (estimate) (2015)	agriculture: 3.3% industry: 26.4% services: 70.3% (2012 est.)
GDP - Purchasing Power Parity (PPP)	
$1,411,493,000,000 (estimate) (2013)	**External Debt**
GDP (PPP) per Capita	$2,278,000,000,000 (estimate) (2012)
$30,620 (estimate) (2013)	**Economic Aid Extended**
Industry Products	$2,281,710,000 (2011)
Wine, cement, iron, steel, sulfuric and nitric acids, automobiles, metals, chemicals, machine tools, textiles, clothing and footwear, food and beverages. Shipbuilding and tourism are also major industries.	**Economic Aid Received**
	$0 (2011)
	Population
	Population
	48,146,134 (estimate) (2015)
Agriculture Products	**World Population Rank**
Wine grapes, olives, vegetables, sugar beets, citrus fruit, potatoes, barley, wheat, poultry, sheep, pigs, cows' milk and other dairy products, fish.	32 nd (2009)
	Population Density
	240.0 people per square mile (estimate) (2011)
Unemployment	**Population Distribution**
25.2% (2012)	77% urban (2011)
Labor Profile	**Age Distribution**
agriculture: 4.2% industry: 24% services: 71.7% (estimate) (2009)	0-14: 14.5%
	15-64: 67.1%
Military	65+: 18.4%
Total Active Armed Forces	(2009)
128,013 (2010)	**Median Age**
Active Armed Forces	41.6 years (estimate) (2014)
0% (2010)	**Population Growth Rate**
Annual Military Expenditures	0.9% per year (estimate) (2015)
$11,700,000,000 (2009)	**Net Migration Rate**
Military Service	8.3 (estimate) (2015)
Service in the Spanish military is voluntary.	**Trade**
National Finances	**Imported Goods**
Currency	Machinery and transportation equipment, electrical equipment, textiles, plastics,
Euro	

chemicals, rubber, wood and wood products, base metals, fish, mineral fuels and products, cinematographic equipment.	**Weights and Measures**
	The metric system is in use.
Total Value of Imports	**Transportation**
$287,775,000,000 (2009)	**Airports**
Exported Goods	152 (2012)
Machinery, motor vehicles, base metals, chemicals, vegetable products, alcoholic beverages, textiles, footwear and accessories.	**Paved Roads**
	99.0% (2003)
	Roads, Unpaved
Total Value of Exports	0 (2006)
$303,800,000,000 (estimate) (2012)	**Passenger Cars per 1,000 People**
Import Partners	481 (2010)
Germany - 15.0%; France - 12.8%; Italy - 7.2%; China - 5.9%; Netherlands - 5.2% (2009)	**Number of Trucks, Buses, and Commercial Vehicles**
	4,908,000 (2005)
Export Partners	**Railroads**
France - 19.3%; Germany - 11.1%; Portugal - 9.2%; Italy - 8.2%; United Kingdom - 6.2% (2009).	9,500 (2008)
	Ports
Current Account Balance	Major: 19 (including Barcelona, Bilbao, Santa Cruz de Tenerife, Cartegena, Las Palmas, Cadiz, Valencia.
$2,100,000,000 (estimate) (2013)	

OVERVIEW

Located in Western Europe, Spain is one of the continent's top tourist attractions because of its spectacular and historic cities, beautiful resort destinations, and extensive network of national parks. The nation is dominated geographically by a central plateau that is surrounded by hilly regions. The Pyrenees, in the north, are the principal mountain range. The nation's climate is temperate, with hot summers in most areas and cold winters in the mountainous regions. Spain has an ethnically diverse population of about 43 million people. Its capital is Madrid.

GOVERNMENT

The unification and liberation of present-day Spain was complete in 1492 upon the expulsion of the Muslim Moors. Spain (España) today is a constitutional monarchy with a parliamentary system whose power is centered in the bicameral General Courts (Cortes Generales). The hereditary monarch is the head of state, and the prime minister is the head of government. The cabinet, led by the prime minister, is the state's highest executive institution. The head of state is King Felipe VI, and the current prime minister is Mariano Rajoy.

Constitution

The present Spanish Constitution, enacted on December 29, 1978, declares Spain to be a hereditary monarchy and a democratic state. It guarantees the autonomy of all nationalities and regions, but asserts the "indissoluble unity" of the nation. The Constitution is the nation's seventh since 1812 and was amended in 1992 and 2011.

Executive

The monarch, who serves as head of state, appoints the prime minister on the advice of the General Courts (Cortes Generales). The monarch approves all legislation, commands the military, and represents the state in international matters. Ascent follows the male line unless the royal family yields no sons, in which case ascent follows the female line. The powers of the monarch are mostly nominal and depend on the advice of the legislature, to which the government is also responsible. Most executive functions are carried out by the prime minister, who is supported by a Council of Ministers (cabinet). The monarch appoints the cabinet on the prime minister's advice. A 23-member Council of State serves as the supreme consultative body to the prime minister.

Legislature

Supreme legislative power is vested in the bicameral Cortes Generales, whose members serve four-year terms. The influential lower Congress of Deputies (Congreso de los Diputados) has 350 members elected from provincial constituencies, with seats allocated based on proportional representation. The less powerful upper Senate (Senado) consists currently of 265 representatives: 208 are directly elected by territorial representation, and 57 are appointed by regional legislatures. The legislature convenes publicly twice a year for four to five months, and a 21-member standing committee oversees legislative affairs during periods of recess or elections. Measures are passed in both houses by a simple majority with all members present. Either house may initiate legislation. The Congress of Deputies takes precedence if an agreement cannot be reached between both houses. The prime minister is empowered to dissolve the Cortes Generales and order an election.

Judiciary

The highest courts in Spain are the Supreme Court or Tribunal Supremo and the Constitutional Court or Tribunal Constitucional de España. Supreme Court judges are proposed by the General Council of Judicial Power—a 20-member

The Convent of the Salesas Reales in Madrid, where the Supreme Court of Spain is located. As with other democracies throughout the world, Spain's government consists of legislative, executive, and judicial branches. (Jose Caballero Digital Press Photos/Newscom)

council made up of presidential appointees, lawyers, and jurists—and appointed by the monarch. The monarch is chair of the General Council. The monarch appoints Constitutional Court judges, who serve for nine-year terms. The autonomous communities' superior courts of justice represent local governments and are subordinate only to the Supreme Court.

Local Government

The Constitution grants political autonomy to provincial, regional, and municipal governments, including the right to decide governmental structures and practice different cultural traditions, but local policies must conform to constitutional law. There are 50 provinces, each headed by a civil governor and guided by a popularly elected governing council. There are 17 autonomous regions that, every four years, elect their own legislative assemblies, which then elect regional presidents from among their members. Autonomous regions are designed to support the interests of the country's many ethnic and linguistic minorities, most notably the Basques of the northwest and the Catalans of the northeast.

Election Qualifications

All citizens 18 years of age and older are eligible to vote.

POLITICS

Spain was governed from 1939 to 1975 by fascist dictator Gen. Francisco Franco, whose nationalist forces won the nation's 1936–1939 civil war. After Franco's death in 1975, the monarchy (abolished in 1931) was reinstated, and King Juan Carlos de Bourbon ascended to power. The king introduced a program of rapid democratization, including the establishment of an elected bicameral legislature in 1976 and a new Spanish Constitution, approved by national referendum, in 1978.

Since the establishment of the legislature in 1976, government control has been held, alternately, by conservative and socialist administrations. Government corruption scandals, terrorist events, and economic troubles have signaled the end of one administration and the beginning of a new one over the years. For example, conservative prime minister Jose Maria Aznar's Popular Party (Partido Popular—PP) lost power in 2004, just days after a massive March 11, 2004, terrorist attack on trains in the capital, Madrid. Aznar's support of the Iraq War and his initial claim that the separatist group Basque Homeland and Liberty (Euskadi ta Azkatasuna—ETA) was responsible for the attack—rather than Al Qaeda, as was later determined—led to his election loss. The leftist Spanish Socialist Workers' Party (Partido Socialista Obrero Español—PSOE) won the election with 42.6% of the vote, and José Luis Rodríguez Zapatero became prime minister one month after the train bombing.

Zapatero's party won legislative elections again in 2008, leading to another term for Zapatero. In November 2011, however, elections were held in the midst of Spain's financial crisis, the euro crisis, and the continuing global economic downturn. Because of this, the PP was voted back into power, paving the way for the conservative party's leader Mariano Rajoy to become Spain's prime minister in December. During his term, Rajoy has introduced a series of tough austerity measures to counter the financial crisis. These measures have led to labor strikes, protests, and even threats of secession by the region of Catalonia. In 2014 however, Spain's economy was making some very modest gains. If the economy continues its turnaround, Rajoy's Popular Party may be able to hold onto the majority in the country's next legislative elections, which are scheduled for December 2015. In June 2014, King Juan Carlos abdicated the throne, and his son Felipe VI took power. Juan Carlos's abdication reignited for many the debate over the relevance of the monarchy as Spain struggles to emerge from economic crisis.

Political Parties

Restrictions on political activity were lifted in 1976, and the 1978 Constitution later endorsed freedom for all political parties.

Founded in 1879, the leftist Spanish Socialist Workers' Party (Partido Socialista Obrero Español—PSOE) has moved away from its traditional commitment to Marxism and toward a more social democratic orientation.

Founded in 1976, the center-right PP was known as the Popular Alliance (Alianza Popular) until 1989. The PP presents itself as a moderate Christian democratic alternative to the PSOE but in recent years had become known for its crackdown on Basque separatist terrorism and support for U.S. policies on international terrorism. The Liberal Party (Partido Liberal—PL) briefly joined the PP prior to the 1989 elections but has retained a separate registration outside the legislature.

In 1986, several left-wing parties joined with a number of independents and smaller ecological and pacifist groups to form the United Left (Izquierda Unida—IU). The alliance includes the Progressive Federation, the Carlist Party, the Humanist Party, the Republican Left, and the Unitarian Candidature of Workers.

The center-left Convergence and Union (Convergencia i Unio—CiU) was formed in 1979 as an electoral coalition of two Catalan parties, the nationalist

Spain's King Felipe VI and Labour Minister Fatima Banez attending a foreign trade summit in Madrid in 2014. Spain is a constitutional monarchy and a parliamentary democracy. Its current government was established in 1975, after the death of long-time dictator Francisco Franco. King Felipe VI assumed the throne in 2014 following the abdication of his father, King Juan Carlos I. (Sergio Barrenechea/EFE/Newscom)

Democratic Convergence of Catalonia (Convergencia Democratica de Catalunya) and the Democratic Union of Catalonia (Unio Democratica de Catalunya). After the June legislative 1993 elections it became an ally of the PSOE.

Other parties representing Spain's Catalan region include the Initiative for Catalonia Greens (Iniciativa per Catalunya Verds—ICV) and the socialist Republican Left of Catalonia (Esquerra Republicana de Catalunya—ERC), which supports Catalonia's independence from Spain.

The Basque Nationalist Party (Partido Nacionalista Vasco—PNV) is the Basque region's ruling party. A moderate grouping, it lobbies for increased autonomy with separate police and administrative forces.

The political party Basque Solidarity (Euzko Alkastasuna—EA) is a social democratic group that supports the creation of a separate Basque nation independent of Spain.

The now-outlawed United People (Herri Batasuna—HB) was created in 1978 as an alliance of several Basque extremist groups and was the political wing of the terrorist group Basque Homeland and Liberty (Euskadi ta Askatasuna—ETA). In 1984, the Supreme Tribunal overturned an Interior Ministry demand to outlaw HB for its links to ETA. However, in 2003 the Supreme Tribunal reversed its earlier decision after determining that HB and its sister party, Batasuna, were identical to the ETA. Spain's Constitutional Court upheld the decision banning the two parties in January 2004.

Some other parties representing regional interests in the Cortes Generales include the liberal, five-party Canarian Coalition (Coalicion Canaria—CC); the Valencian Left (Esquerra Valenciana—EV); the socialist Galician Nationalist Bloc (Blogue Nacionalista Galego—BNG); the Aragonese Council (Chunta Aragonesista—CHA); the Andalucista Party (Partido Andalucista—PA); and the separtist Navarra Yes (Nafrroa Bai—Na-Bai).

ECONOMY

Tourism is at the heart of the Spanish economy; however, visitor rates have declined in recent years due to competition posed by cheaper areas. Labor costs are low, but living standards, while not as high as in many other parts of Europe, are still comfortable. The industrial sector focuses largely on automobile manufacturing, shipbuilding, steel, shoes, textiles, and chemicals. The top agricultural products include citrus fruit, wine, olives, grain, vegetables, and livestock. The nation supplies nearly all its own food needs. Spain has reserves of coal, lignite, uranium, mercury, iron ore, gypsum, and several other minerals, but is forced to import most of its energy resources. The nation's top trading partners are France, Italy, and Germany.

As with most of Europe, the current economic crisis has badly hurt Spain, which led to the 2011 election of a conservative government. Unemployment rates have skyrocketed. In fact, the country has one of the worst jobless rates in the European Union: in 2007, the unemployment rate was 8%, but by 2013 it was higher than 26%. The government introduced austerity measures such as cutting rail routes as well as public assistance funds, and raising taxes to address growing public debt, which is predicted to exceed 100% of the country's GDP in 2015. The economy began to show signs of a slow turnaround in 2014.

SOCIETY

Spain's population is a mix of the indigenous Iberian population and various peoples that have invaded the country over the centuries. The dominant cultural and linguistic groups include Andalusians, Castilians, Catalans, Galicians, and Basques, who appear to be ethnically and linguistically distinct. Castilian Spanish is the language that is most commonly used (and indeed spoken throughout the world). The Moorish influence is evident in this language, which has borrowed more words from Arabic than from any other language except Latin. Almost the entire population identifies as Roman Catholic, but the influence of the Church has declined in recent years, most evident in the legalization of same-sex marriages in June 2005. A significant minority practices Islam, and rising immigration rates have resulted in a growing number of Muslims in the country.

Ethnic Composition

Spain is composed of Mediterranean and Nordic peoples.

Language

Castilian Spanish is the principal language. Catalan is spoken widely in the northeast, and Basque and Galician are predominant in the northwest.

Religion

Roman Catholic – 94%; other – 6%

CONTEMPORARY ISSUES

Basque Separatism

Under the Spanish Constitution (1978), regions and nationalities are allowed largely autonomous self-government. One of the most distinct nationalities in the country is that of the Basque, a proud and ancient people who have lived in the land around the western Pyrenees Mountains for thousands of years. The Basque Country was among the first areas in Spain to be granted autonomy, but the autonomous region does not include all of the traditional Basque lands in Spain. Navarre, another largely Basque area, is also an autonomous community within Spain. Both of these autonomous regions have their own parliament and executive, enlist their own police forces, and collect taxes independent of the larger Spanish government. Still, many Basque people hope that their historical lands stretching from northern Spain into southwestern France will be allowed complete independence.

A Basque nationalist movement began in the late nineteenth century but was suppressed by Francisco Franco during his dictatorial regime from the late 1930s until the middle of the 1970s. In 1959, a group of extreme Basque nationalists created the organization called Basque Homeland and Liberty (Euskadi ta Azkatasuna—ETA) in order to secure independence for the Basque people. The group quickly became a terrorist organization, using bombings and kidnappings to bring attention to their cause. Spanish and French operations against ETA have led to the capture of several important members of the separatist group, including political and military leader Francisco Javier López Peña, who was apprehended in southern France in May 2008, and major cell leader Arkaitz Goikoetxea, who was captured two months later. In all, police have arrested more than 300 known or suspected ETA members and broken up its most active cell. In 2011, ETA declared a "definitive end to armed activity," and in early 2014 the organization said it would hand over its weapons; however, the action has not yet occurred, as the Spanish government has stated it is unwilling to negotiate for terms and is holding out for a full declaration of defeat.

Islamist Terrorism

The involvement of Spanish troops in the U.S.-led Iraq War made Spain a prime focus of Islamic terrorist groups looking to undermine international support for the already-unpopular war. In March 2004, a series of attacks on commuter trains in the capital city of Madrid killed 191 people and wounded more than 2,000. These attacks were initially thought to be the work of ETA but were later determined to have been planned and undertaken by Islamic extremists seeking to mimic the methods of the international terrorist organization Al Qaeda. Since that time, Islamic militants have been watched carefully, and a major intelligence effort has been undertaken to prevent further terrorist attacks by Islamist groups. Because of the close proximity of Morocco and Algeria, countries where Islamic extremism is on the rise, Spanish authorities keep a close eye on who is entering the country. Al Qaeda cells are strongly suspected to be active in Spain, even if they were not responsible for the March 2004 bombings, and Al Qaeda operatives in Spain are known to have had a significant role in planning the September 11, 2001, World Trade Center and Pentagon attacks in the United States. Additionally, Spain has become a recruiting ground for militants fighting in Iraq and North Africa, and Spanish police have arrested numerous people suspected of recruiting for such causes.

Spanish North Africa

Spain currently controls two small enclaves on the North African coast—Ceuta, on the Moroccan tip of the Strait of Gibraltar, and Melilla, further east on the Moroccan coastline—and the Canary Islands, located off the coast of Morocco. Spain conquered Melilla in 1497, while Portugal took Ceuta in 1415, but it became a Spanish possession in 1640. Today, Ceuta and Melilla are integral parts of the Spanish state, and their populations are overwhelmingly Spanish, but Morocco claims the cities as part of its sovereign territory. Spain has refused to entertain the idea of transferring possession of the cities to Morocco, and the standard of living in Ceuta and Melilla is significantly higher than in neighboring Moroccan cities. Since both places constitute actual borders between Morocco and Spain, they are guarded and serve as Spanish entry points that are frequently used by North African migrants looking to establish themselves in Europe. The Canary Islands are also an attractive destination for migrants, who make the dangerous sea crossing from points as far south along the West African coast as Guinea.

Gibraltar

At the far southern tip of the Spanish mainland, the tiny peninsula of Gibraltar juts into the Mediterranean Sea. A strategic position overlooking the Atlantic entrance into the Mediterranean, this peninsula has been under British control since it was captured from Spain in 1704 during the War of the Spanish Succession; the peninsula was formally ceded to the United Kingdom in the 1713 Treaty of Utrecht. Today, Spain declares that the peninsula should revert to Spanish control, while the United Kingdom refuses to consider such a reversion because it has important military facilities in Gibraltar. In 2002, the two countries agreed in principle to a power-sharing arrangement, but a mandatory referendum of Gibraltar's residents overturned the agreement. In 2006, a landmark agreement that eased border restrictions was put into place, and residents voted to adopt a new constitution, temporarily reaffirming their right to home rule. Spain and the United Kingdom continue to discuss possible options, and the European Union has pushed both sides to resolve the issue, but tensions have increased in recent years due to such issues as border delays and fishing rights.

Drugs and Smuggling

Spain is currently the largest consumer of cocaine in Europe, and its young adult population is among the largest market for marijuana. Spanish drug laws are mainly geared toward harm reduction, not the elimination of drugs, and it is not illegal to use or grow cannabis so long as it consumed privately and is not distributed or sold. The transport of drugs, however, is highly illegal, and Spanish authorities have worked hard to crack down on the drug trade. Smuggling from Morocco is common, through such means as yachts, small ships, cars, and even makeshift submarines. The southern Andalusia region, just across a narrow stretch of the Mediterranean Sea from Morocco, lies along a key route for the smuggling of illegal drugs, and many arrests have taken place there. Once the drugs have arrived in Spain, they are transported around Europe, particularly to the United Kingdom and France. While authorities have cracked down on smuggling efforts, Spain is still a major thoroughfare for drugs.

Continued Effects of Economic Recession

The fourth-largest economy in the eurozone, Spain has slowly been rebounding from a massive recession that began in 2008. The economic crisis has contributed to record unemployment, leaving some 5.9 million people without jobs. Although unemployment rates fell between 2013 and 2014, migrant workers suffer from a nearly 37% unemployment rate, and youth unemployment hovers around 55%. The lack of work has led to the exodus of around 40,000 Spanish nationals, many of whom are young adults. It has also left nearly 690,000 households without an income of any kind. The bleak financial picture is creating a major boom in the black market—government reports show that the shadow economy was estimated to equal about 25% of the gross domestic product in 2012 and is continuing to grow.

Excerpt from the Constitution of Spain

The Constitution of Spain went into effect in 1978. In 1975, Spain's dictator Francisco Franco died, and the country transitioned to its current constitutional monarchy. The Cortes Generales, or legislature, appointed a constitutional commission that drafted the Constitution, which was subsequently approved by the Cortes Generales and by public referendum.

The Constitution specifies that human rights "are the foundations of political order and social peace." This clause reinforces the Preamble, which includes the statement that the responsibility of the Spanish state is to "Protect all Spaniards and all the peoples of Spain in the exercise of human rights, their cultures and traditions, languages and institutions.

The Constitution recognizes fundamental political rights, including the right of free speech and the right to artistic expression, academic freedom, and literary expression. Censorship is banned, and Spanish citizens are guaranteed the right to vote, rights to freedom of association and assembly, and the right to a fair trial under the law. The Constitution also provides a specific guarantee of the right to education, specifying that elementary education is to be "compulsory and free." In addition, it states that Spaniards have the right to health care, social and health care, with specific reference to care for elderly and disabled persons. Thus Spain's constitution is very much consistent with the constitutions of other Western European countries with respect to human rights concerns.

Fundamental rights and duties

The human dignity, the inviolable and inherent rights, the free development of the personality, the respect for the law and for the rights of others, are the foundations of political order and social peace.

Article 14

Spaniards are equal before the law and may not in any way be discriminated against on account of birth, race, sex, religion, opinion or any other personal or social condition or circumstance.

Article 15

Everyone has the right to life and to physical and moral integrity, and may under no circumstances be subjected to torture or to inhuman or degrading punishment or treatment. The death penalty is hereby abolished, except as provided by military criminal law in times of war.

Article 17

Every person has a right to freedom and security. No one may be deprived of his or her freedom except in accordance with the provisions of this article . . .

Preventive detention may last no longer than the time strictly required in order to carry out the necessary investigations aimed at establishing the facts . . . the person arrested must be set free or handed over to the judicial authorities within a maximum period of seventy-two hours.

Any person arrested must be informed immediately, and in a manner understandable to him or her, of his or her rights and of the grounds for his or her arrest, and may not be compelled to make a statement.

The arrested person shall be guaranteed the assistance of a lawyer . . .

A *habeas corpus* procedure shall . . . ensure the immediate handing over to the judicial authorities of any person arrested illegally.

Article 18

The right to honour, to personal and family privacy and to the own image is guaranteed.

No entry or search may be made without the consent of the occupant or a legal warrant, except in cases of *flagrante delicto.*

Secrecy of communications is guaranteed . . . except in the event of a court order to the contrary.

The law shall limit the use of data processing in order to guarantee the honour and personal and family privacy of citizens and the full exercise of their rights.

Article 19

Spaniards have the right to choose their place of residence freely, and to move about freely within the national territory.

Article 20

The following rights are recognised and protected:

a) the right to freely express and disseminate thoughts, ideas and opinions . . . ;

b) the right to literary, artistic, scientific and technical production and creation;
c) the right to academic freedom;
d) the right to freely communicate or receive accurate information by any means of dissemination whatsoever.

The exercise of these rights may not be restricted by any form of prior censorship.

The law shall regulate the organisation and parliamentary control of the social communications media under the control of the State . . . and shall guarantee access to such media to the main social and political groups . . .

The confiscation of . . . information media may only be carried out by means of a court order.

Article 21

The right to peaceful unarmed assembly is recognised. The exercise of this right shall not require prior authorisation.

In the event of meetings in public places and of demonstrations, prior notification shall be given to the authorities, who may ban them only when there are well founded grounds to expect a breach of public order, involving danger to persons or property.

Article 22

The right of association is recognised.

Associations which pursue ends or use means classified as criminal offences are illegal.

Associations . . . must be recorded in a register for the sole purpose of public knowledge.

Secret and paramilitary associations are prohibited.

Article 23

Citizens have the right to participate in public affairs, directly or through representatives freely elected in periodic elections . . .

Article 24

. . . all persons have the right of access to . . . the defence and assistance of a lawyer; to be informed of the charges brought against them; to a public trial without undue delays and with full guarantees; to the use of evidence appropriate to their defence; to not make self-incriminating statements . . . and to be presumed innocent.

Article 25

No one may be convicted or sentenced for any act or omission which at the time it was committed did not constitute a felony or offence . . .

Punishments entailing imprisonment . . . shall be aimed at rehabilitation and social reintegration and may not consist of forced labour. The person sentenced to prison shall enjoy . . . fundamental rights . . . except those expressly limited by the terms of the sentence . . . he shall be entitled to paid employment and . . . Social Security benefits . . .

Article 27

Everyone has the right to education.

The public authorities guarantee the right of parents to ensure that their children receive religious and moral instruction that is in accordance with their own convictions.

Elementary education is compulsory and free.

The right of individuals and legal entities to set up educational centres is recognised provided they respect Constitutional principles.

The public authorities shall inspect and standardise the educational system to guarantee compliance with the law.

The public authorities shall give aid to teaching establishments which meet the requirements . . . [of] law.

The autonomy of Universities is recognized . . .

Article 39

The public authorities shall ensure the social, economic and legal protection of the family.

The public authorities likewise shall ensure full protection of children, who are equal before the law . . . The law shall provide for the investigation of paternity.

Parents must provide their children . . . with assistance of every kind while they are still under age . . .

Article 40

The public authorities shall promote favourable conditions for social and economic progress and for a more equitable distribution of . . . income . . .

They shall . . . carry out a policy directed towards full employment.

. . . the public authorities shall . . . guarantee vocational training and retraining; . . . ensure workplace safety and hygiene and . . . adequate rest by means of a limited working day, periodic paid holidays . . .

Article 41

The public authorities shall maintain a public Social Security system . . . which will guarantee adequate . . . benefits in situations of hardship, especially . . . unemployment.

Article 43

The right to health protection is recognised.
The public authorities shall promote health education, physical education and sports. Likewise, they shall encourage the proper use of leisure time.

Article 49

The public authorities shall carry out a policy of preventive care, treatment, rehabilitation and integration of the physically, sensorially and mentally handicapped who shall be given the specialised care that they require . . .

Article 50

The public authorities shall guarantee . . . sufficient financial means for senior citizens.

Source: "Constitution of the Kingdom of Spain." Legislation Online. http://www.legislationline.org/documents/section/constitutions

UNITED KINGDOM: Constitutional Monarchy, Commonwealth Realm

UNITED KINGDOM

Communications	Television
Facebook Users	110 sets per 100 Population (2003)
30,000,000 (estimate) (2013)	**Land-based Telephones in Use**
Internet Users	33,010,000 (2012)
51,444,000 (2009)	
Internet Users (% of Population)	**Mobile Telephone Subscribers**
89.8% (2013)	82,109,000 (2012)

Major Daily Newspapers	**Secondary School–age Females Enrolled in Secondary School**
109 (2004)	2,368,182 (2012)
Average Circulation of Daily Newspapers	**Students Per Teacher, Primary School**
17,375,000 (2004)	18.3 (2012)
Education	**Students Per Teacher, Secondary School**
School System	14.3 (estimate) (2008)
Schooling in the United Kingdom begins at the age of five. Students attend either two years of infant school and four years of primary school or a combined six-year program. Students then continue for five years of academic, technical, or vocational secondary education, and may then follow an optional two-year course known as sixth form.	**Enrollment in Tertiary Education**
	2,495,779 (2012)
	Enrollment in Tertiary Education, Male
	1,091,379 (2012)
	Enrollment in Tertiary Education, Female
	1,404,400 (2012)
	Literacy
Mandatory Education	99% (2005)
11 years, from ages 5 to 16.	**Energy and Natural Resources**
Average Years Spent in School for Current Students	**Electric Power Generation**
16 (2012)	365,700,000,000 kilowatt hours per year (estimate) (2013)
Average Years Spent in School for Current Students, Male	**Electric Power Consumption**
16 (2012)	323,300,000,000 kilowatt hours per year (estimate) (2013)
Average Years Spent in School for Current Students, Female	**Nuclear Power Plants**
17 (2012)	16 (2014)
Primary School–age Children Enrolled in Primary School	**Crude Oil Production**
	916,300 barrels per day (2013)
4,523,583 (2012)	**Crude Oil Consumption**
Primary School–age Males Enrolled in Primary School	1,512,700 barrels per day (2013)
	Natural Gas Production
2,315,677 (2012)	38,480,000,000 cubic meters per year (estimate) (2013)
Primary School–age Females Enrolled in Primary School	**Natural Gas Consumption**
2,207,906 (2012)	51,630,000,000 cubic meters per year (estimate) (2013)
Secondary School–age Children Enrolled in Secondary School	**Natural Resources**
4,849,275 (2012)	Coal, petroleum, natural gas, iron ore, lead, zinc, gold, tin, limestone, salt, clay, chalk, gypsum, potash, silica sand, slate, arable land
Secondary School–age Males Enrolled in Secondary School	
2,481,093 (2012)	

Environment	Arable Land Per Capita
CO2 Emissions	0 acres per person (2007)
7.7 metric tons per capita (2009)	Health
Alternative and Nuclear Energy	**Average Life Expectancy**
10.5% of total energy use (2011)	80.4 years (2014)
Threatened Species	**Average Life Expectancy, Male**
73 (2010)	78.3 years (2014)
Protected Areas	**Average Life Expectancy, Female**
74,259 (estimate) (2010)	82.7 years (2014)
Geography	**Crude Birth Rate**
Location	12.2 (estimate) (2015)
England, Scotland, and Wales, which make up Great Britain, are located on an island off the northwest coast of Europe. Northern Ireland borders the Republic of Ireland on an island to the west of Great Britain. England, Scotland, Wales, and Northern Ireland form the United Kingdom.	**Crude Death Rate**
	9.4 (estimate) (2015)
	Maternal Mortality
	13 per 100,000 live births (2005–2012 projection)
	Infant Mortality
	4 per 1,000 live births (2012)
Time Zone	**Doctors**
5 hours ahead of U.S. Eastern Standard	2.8 per 1,000 people (2012)
Land Borders	Industry and Labor
5 hours ahead of U.S. Eastern Standard	**Gross Domestic Product (GDP) - official exchange rate**
Coastline	$2,992,148,000,000 (estimate) (2015)
7,723 miles	**GDP per Capita**
Capital	$46,077 (estimate) (2015)
London	**GDP - Purchasing Power Parity (PPP)**
Area	$2,391,042,000,000 (estimate) (2013)
99,055 sq. miles	**GDP (PPP) per Capita**
Climate	$37,502 (estimate) (2013)
Although generally temperate, the climate can vary radically. Average temperatures range from 41°F in the winter to 59°F in the summer. Average annual rainfall is 35-40 inches.	**Industry Products**
	Machinery and transportation equipment, beer, aluminum and tin, chemicals, metals, processed food, textiles, clothing, aircraft, coal, petroleum. Shipbuilding is also a major industry.
Land Use	**Agriculture Products**
25.2% arable land; 19.6% temporary crops; 0.2% permanent crops; 47.6% permanent meadows and pastures; 11.8% forest land; 15.2% other.	Wheat, barley, sugar beets, potatoes, livestock, dairy products, fish.
Arable Land	**Unemployment**
19% (2007)	7.9% (2012)

Labor Profile	Population Distribution
agriculture: 1.4% industry: 18.2% services: 80.4% (estimate) (2006)	80% urban (2011)
Military	**Age Distribution**
Total Active Armed Forces	0-14: 16.5%
175,690 (2010)	15-64: 67.1%
Active Armed Forces	65+: 16.4%
0% (2010)	(2009)
Annual Military Expenditures	**Median Age**
$62,400,000,000 (2009)	40.4 years (estimate) (2014)
Military Service	**Population Growth Rate**
Service in the British military is voluntary.	0.5% per year (estimate) (2015)
National Finances	**Net Migration Rate**
Currency	2.5 (estimate) (2015)
British pound	**Trade**
Total Government Revenues	**Imported Goods**
$1,023,000,000,000 (estimate) (2013)	Petroleum and petroleum products, office machinery and data-processing equipment, motor vehicles, electrical machinery, paper and paper products, textiles, clothing, mineral manufactures, chemicals, foodstuffs, fruits, vegetables.
Total Government Expenditures	
$1,112,000,000,000 (estimate) (2013)	
Budget Deficit	
-3.6 (estimate) (2013)	
GDP Contribution by Sector	**Total Value of Imports**
agriculture: 0.7% industry: 21% services: 78.3% (2012 est.)	$482,108,000,000 (2009)
	Exported Goods
External Debt	Petroleum and petroleum products, machinery and transportation equipment, fuels, organic chemicals, iron and steel, beverages, nonmetallic minerals.
$9,577,000,000,000 (estimate) (2013)	
Economic Aid Extended	
$8,473,540,000 (2011)	**Total Value of Exports**
Economic Aid Received	$481,000,000,000 (estimate) (2012)
$0 (2011)	**Import Partners**
Population	Germany - 12.9%; United States - 9.7%; China - 9.5%; Netherlands - 7.0%; France - 6.6% (2009)
Population	
64,088,222 (estimate) (2015)	**Export Partners**
World Population Rank	United States - 14.7%; Germany - 11.1%; France - 8.0%; Netherlands - 7.8%; Ireland - 6.9% (2009)
22 nd (2010)	
Population Density	**Current Account Balance**
637.9 people per square mile (estimate) (2011)	$-93,600,000,000 (estimate) (2013)

Weights and Measures	Passenger Cars per 1,000 People
The metric system has now replaced the imperial system, although some exceptions are made for such traditional items as pints of beer.	457 (2010)
	Number of Trucks, Buses, and Commercial Vehicles
Transportation	4,053,000 (2005)
Airports	**Railroads**
462 (2012)	10,224 (2008)
Paved Roads	**Ports**
100.0% (2010)	Major: 14 (including London, Liverpool, Glasgow, Southampton, Cardiff, Belfast, Manchester).
Roads, Unpaved	
247,533 (2006)	

OVERVIEW

The United Kingdom of Great Britain and Northern Ireland lies off the coast of Western Europe. It consists of England, Scotland, and Wales, on the island of Great Britain, and Northern Ireland on the island of Ireland. The United Kingdom has a reputation for wet weather, and rain is possible at any time. The nation has a fairly temperate climate, although the mountains of northern Great Britain experience harsher temperatures. The United Kingdom has a population of around 64 million. The nation's capital is London.

GOVERNMENT

The United Kingdom of Great Britain and Northern Ireland was established in 1927 after the island of Ireland was divided into the Republic of Ireland and Northern Ireland. The UK is the direct political successor to the earlier united kingdoms of England and Scotland, the United Kingdom of Great Britain, established in 1707, and the United Kingdom of Great Britain and Ireland, which replaced the previous United Kingdom in 1801. A constitutional monarchy with a democratic parliamentary system of government, the United Kingdom includes England, Wales, Scotland, and Northern Ireland. The hereditary monarch is head of state, though the monarch has mostly symbolic power. Executive authority is held by the cabinet, which is led by the prime minister. The cabinet is responsible to the House of Commons in Parliament. The current monarch is Queen Elizabeth II, and the current prime minister is David Cameron.

Constitution

The United Kingdom does not have a written constitution. Its laws are based on statute, common law, and tradition. Changes can be made through acts of

UNITED KINGDOM

Parliament, through the acceptance of new usage, or through judicial decision. The Magna Carta, signed in 1215, began the process in which the law exists on its own, independent of the sovereign and Parliament. The Bill of Rights of 1689 ended a long-standing rivalry between Parliament and the Crown, while the 1832 Reform

Queen Elizabeth II, who became Queen in 1952 following the death of her father, King George VI. The United Kingdom is a constitutional monarchy, and the Queen's powers are largely ceremonial. (Danny Lawson/ZUMA Press/Newscom)

Bill dramatically broadened the basis of representative government. The Human Rights Act of 1998 enforces the rights and freedoms given under the European Convention on Human Rights to citizens. The Constitutional Reform and Governance Act 2010, the Parliamentary Voting System and Constituencies Act 2011, and the Fixed-term Parliaments Act 2011 place some regulations on civil servants and parliamentary processes, such as elections.

Executive

Executive power rests nominally with the sovereign, who serves as head of state and has numerous formal functions, including assent to laws and cabinet appointments. Effective power belongs to the cabinet, members of which traditionally come from the House of Commons. After a Parliamentary election, the sovereign formally appoints a prime minister, who typically is a member of the House of Commons and a leader of the party that won a majority of seats. The prime minister remains a member of Parliament, is head of the cabinet, and meets weekly with the monarch. As leader of the majority party in the House of Commons, the prime minister relies on that party's support. The cabinet is responsible to the House of Commons. The cabinet has largely taken over the duties of the Privy Council, a body of more than 300 members who traditionally advised the monarch. Cabinet members include heads of government departments.

Legislature

The bicameral Parliament consists of the lower house (House of Commons) and the upper house (House of Lords). Each Parliament can serve up to five years, although the prime minister may dissolve parliament at any time and call for elections if he or she wants to consolidate power or if Parliament has no confidence in the prime minister's government. The public elects 650 members of Parliament (MPs) to represent them in the House of Commons. MPs consider and propose new laws, scrutinize government policies, and oversee the nation's finances.

The House of Lords' 780 members share the task of making laws and questioning the government, but they are not elected. There are three ways to become a member of the House of Lords. The most common way currently is to be appointed by the queen, with the advice of the prime minister; appointments are for life, and those members are called life peers. Currently, 700 active members of the House of Lords are life peers. Second, 26 Church of England clergy members sit in the House of Lords. Upon the retirement of a bishop, membership is passed on to the next most senior bishop. For centuries, many in the House of Lords gained membership by inheriting it. A 1999 law ended the right of most hereditary peers to sit and vote in the House, and very few of them remain as voting members.

The House of Commons originates most legislation, often based on cabinet recommendations. After three discussion stages, a bill is passed to the House of Lords, which may suggest amendments but cannot prevent the bill from becoming law. A bill becomes law if it is approved by a majority in the House of Commons and House of Lords, and agreed to formally by the reigning monarch.

Judiciary

The judicial system centers on a Supreme Court, which was established by the Constitutional Reform Act 2005. This court replaced the House of Lords as the highest court of appeal, and its jurisdiction includes Scotland, Northern Ireland, and Wales. Subordinate courts are separated into the Courts of England and Wales, Courts of Scotland, and the Courts of Northern Ireland. Lower courts include magistrates' courts, county courts, and crown courts. The crown courts try the more serious criminal cases that require a jury. Scotland has its own supreme criminal court called the High Court of Justiciary.

Local Government

England is divided into 27 two-tier counties and 56 unitary authorities, which are subdivided into smaller governmental units. In addition, London consists of 32 boroughs. Wales is divided into 22 unitary authorities. Scotland is divided into 32 council areas. Northern Ireland comprises 13 borough councils, 11 district council areas, one city and district council, and one city council. Elected councils exist at each government level.

Overseas Possessions

Of the 16 political entities associated with the United Kingdom, 3 are Crown Dependencies, 12 are internally independent colonies, and 2 are virtually uninhabited territories. The Crown Dependencies include the Isle of Man and the Channel Islands. Among the colonies are Anguilla, Bermuda, the British Indian Ocean Territory, the British Virgin Islands, the Cayman Islands, the Falkland Islands (also claimed by Argentina), Gibraltar, Montserrat, the Pitcairn Islands, St. Helena and its dependencies, and the Turks and Caicos Islands. The uninhabited territories are the British Antarctic Territory, the island of South Georgia, and the South Sandwich Islands.

Election Qualifications

All citizens 18 years of age and older are entitled to vote.

POLITICS

The prime minister is the head of government in the United Kingdom and leads the majority party in the House of Commons. During the late 1990s, some governing power was handed over to Northern Ireland, Scotland, and Wales. The Northern Ireland Assembly, Scottish Parliament, and Welsh Assembly were established and given authority over most domestic matters. The Northern Ireland Assembly was suspended in 2002, due to the volatile political situation in the region. Power was restored to the Assembly in 2007.

Since the early twentieth century, the United Kingdom's government has been dominated by the Conservative and Labour parties. Tony Blair, leader of the Labour Party and prime minister of the UK from 1997 to 2007, oversaw the process of handing over increased authority to the Scottish and Welsh governments, as well as granting some power to Northern Ireland's government. Blair also backed the U.S.-led Iraq War in 2003, an action that became extremely unpopular with his country's voters. Following the July 7, 2005, suicide bombings in London, Blair's government presented a series of sweeping antiterrorism initiatives to Parliament, including a law to criminalize the glorification of terrorism and measures to grant the nation's police forces power to detain suspected terrorists for longer periods of time before charging them with a crime. Due to a number of personal and political scandals within his cabinet and staff, as well as the public's disapproval of the UK's involvement in Iraq, Blair stepped down as Labour leader and prime minister in 2007.

David Cameron, Prime Minister of the United Kingdom and head of state, is also a Member of Parliament and the leader of his Conservative Party. Cameron became Prime Minister in 2010. (Daniel Leal-Olivas/ZUMA Press/Newscom)

Gordon Brown, already a top government official, replaced Blair as prime minister and Labour Party leader. Brown oversaw the end to British involvement in Iraq, which was completed in 2009. As the economy took a downward turn in early 2008, however, Labour's popularity continued to slip, and the Conservative Party dominated local elections that were widely considered a referendum on Brown and his government.

In the 2010 elections, the unpopular Labour Party lost 91 seats in Parliament while the Conservatives gained 98 seats. The Conservative gains were not enough, however, to earn them a majority, and the result was that no party won an ouright majority. The Conservatives formed a governing coalition with the third-place Liberal Democratic Party, and Conservative Party leader David Cameron became the country's youngest prime minister in almost 200 years.

Faced with a country still feeling the effects of the 2008 global recession, Cameron has focused on reducing the budget deficit by cutting government spending. He has responded to growing discontent with membership in the European Union by promising to hold a vote on the UK's future membership if he keeps his position after the 2015 elections. Cameron, who campaigned to keep Scotland within the UK, also oversaw the Scottish referendum on independence in September 2014. The Scottish National Party, which won the majority in the 2011 Scottish Parliament elections, called the referendum and campaigned for Scottish independence. However, the independence referendum was defeated by a majority of Scotland's voters.

Political Parties

The following parties have significant representation in the House of Commons:

The Labour Party came to power in May 1997, ending the Conservative Party's 18-year rule. It gains most of its support from organized labor, and on the political spectrum, it is a center-left party. Although it traditionally advocated gradual socialization of the economy and a reduction of the nation's nuclear arsenal, the party has gradually adopted a more moderate stance. In recent years there have been several changes to the party's statutes that have reduced the voting power of the labor unions that founded the party. In the past, the unions voted as huge blocs, making the votes of individual members virtually insignificant. The Labour Party favors increasing the United Kingdom's role in the European Union (EU).

The Conservative Party dominated British politics through most of the twentieth century until its defeat in 1997. The right-leaning Conservatives, also known as the Tories, receive most of their support from the business community and the middle class. The party has been skeptical of the EU and opposes replacing the British pound monetary system with the euro. Conservatives also favor lessening EU authority in the United Kingdom. The party favors greater privatization of nationalized industries.

The Liberal Democratic Party was formed in 1988 and advocates an increase in income-tax levels. Although the Liberal Democrats often support the policies of the Labour Party, they also were outspoken critics of the Labour government's decision to enter the Iraq War.

The UK Independence Party (UKIP) was formed in 1993 and is a right-wing libertarian party. In the 2014 elections to decide who would represent the UK in the European Union, UKIP became the first party other than the Conservative or Labour parties to win a majority in a nationwide popular vote since 1906. The party favors broad tax cuts and advocates the UK leaving the EU.

Northern Ireland's largest political party, the Democratic Unionist Party (DUP) favors continued union with Great Britain. However, it opposed the 1998 Good Friday Agreement, which brought peace to Northern Ireland after decades in which militants in Northern Ireland fought against British rule.

We Ourselves, commonly known by its Irish name, *Sinn Fein*, wants Britain out of Northern Ireland and favors reuniting the two Irelands. It supported the Good Friday Agreement and has been linked to the militant Irish Republican Army, which was widely believed responsible for violence during the fight for Northern Ireland's independence from the UK.

Less popular parties in Northern Ireland include the Ulster Unionist Party (UUP), a moderate unionist party whose members are committed to Northern Ireland having governmental authority but still being part of the UK; and the Social Democratic and Labour Party (SDLP), a left-of-center group advocating eventual reunion with the Republic of Ireland.

Other regional parties include the Scottish National Party (SNP), which seeks independence for Scotland; and the Welsh National Party (Plaid Cymru), which advocates greater autonomy for Wales.

ECONOMY

The United Kingdom's gross domestic product is one of the largest in the world and the third-largest in Europe. The nation is also known as a major international banking and insurance center, and such services drive the country's economic growth. Manufacturing accounts for 10% the nation's economy, especially in pharmaceuticals, defense, machinery, and transportation equipment. The agricultural sector is small but efficient and diverse in both crop and livestock production. British agricultural products include grain, vegetables, and fruit. The energy sector is quite large, and the nation has large coal, gas, and oil reserves. In fact, the United Kingdom is the European Union's largest producer of oil and second-largest producer of natural gas. It is also one of the world's largest energy consumers, with ever-increasing consumption levels; the nation became a net importer of fossil fuels in 2013. The United Kingdom's main trade partners include the United States, Germany, the Netherlands, and France, as well as countries that were formerly territories of the British Empire. The UK is a key member of the European Union but has not adopted the euro as its currency. While many favor the UK leaving the European Union, others maintain that could hurt the nation's economy because most of the UK's trade is with fellow EU countries.

SOCIETY

Most citizens of the United Kingdom are English; the Scottish make up 10% of the country's population and are the nation's largest minority group. In 1534, English King Henry VIII made himself the head of the Church of England and denied the authority of the pope, a move that resulted in a break with Roman Catholicism and the establishment of Protestant Anglicanism as the state religion. This break dramatically reduced the number of Catholics in the kingdom dramatically. In Scotland and Wales, other Protestant groups—including Presbyterians and Methodists—thrive today. As the United Kingdom has become more multicultural, religions have diversified from the traditional Christian branches: the nation's Jewish community is the second-largest in Europe, and its Hindu and Sikh communities are also growing.

Linguistically, English is spoken throughout the country, and the prevalence of English around the globe can be credited to the spread of the British Empire in the eighteenth and nineteenth centuries. Regional languages have struggled to compete with English; the Welsh have been the strongest in preserving their ancient language, *Cymraeg*. Scottish Gaelic (*Gàidhlig*) is spoken only in the islands and the northwestern sections of the country. In Northern Ireland, Irish (*Gaeilge*) has experienced a resurgence in the wake of the Good Friday Agreement's call for greater cooperation between the Republic of Ireland and the United Kingdom.

Ethnic Composition

White/White British – 87.2%; Black/African/Caribbean/Black British – 3%; Asian/Asian British: Indian – 2.3%; Asian/Asian British: Pakistani – 1.9%; mixed – 2%; other – 3.7%

Language

English is the primary language. About 20% of the population of Wales speaks Welsh, while some 60,000 Scots speak Scottish Gaelic.

Religion

Christian (includes Anglican, Roman Catholic, Presbyterian, and Methodist) – 59.5%; Muslim – 4.4%; Hindu – 1.3%; other – 2%; none – 25.7%

CONTEMPORARY ISSUES

The Balkanization of Britain?

While the United Kingdom still ruled a globe-spanning empire, national differences between the Scots, Welsh, Irish, and English took a backseat to an overarching British identity. More recently, though, it has become increasingly common for many British people to identify with the historical and cultural heritage of their region more than with a unifying British nationalism. In the early twentieth century, serious unrest emerged among the Irish—the most reluctant British subjects, by far—that eventually culminated in the Easter Rebellion of 1916 and the Irish war for independence. While no armed rebellion has occurred in Scotland or Wales, a rise in Scottish nationalism in the 1990s led the British government to grant Scotland and Wales some autonomous home rule. There now exists a Scottish parliament, a Welsh assembly, and, in 2014, the Scottish people voted on independence from the United Kingdom. One in every five people in Wales speaks the Welsh language, and since 1993 Welsh has had equal status with English in the region. Partly in response to such movements and partly due to the historical distance of the United Kingdom's imperialist past, distinctly English nationalism has also become more prevalent. In addition, a nationalist movement and calls for some autonomy are rising in the Cornwall region of southwest England. If the United Kingdom aligns itself more closely with the European Union (EU), being European may eventually become more important than being British, and there may be fewer reasons to uphold the unity of the kingdom. On the other hand, the competing nationalist feelings could erupt into conflict.

Terrorism and Civil Unrest

Terrorism has been a danger in the United Kingdom for decades. For most of the twentieth century, attacks in the United Kingdom were the work of Irish and Northern Irish separatist groups. Bomb attacks, particularly car bombs, were the most common form of terrorism by these groups. Belfast, Northern Ireland, was usually the location of such bombings (as well as many kidnappings and murders), but many attacks were also carried out in England during the 1970s, 1980s, and 1990s. No terrorist attacks have been attributed to Irish groups since August 2001, likely a result of power-sharing arrangements with Northern Ireland. The most recent terrorist threat comes from Islamic extremists, angered by British assistance in the U.S.-led wars in Afghanistan and Iraq. On July 7, 2005, the London public transportation system was rocked by a series of bomb attacks that left 56 people dead and 700 more seriously injured. Two weeks later, another series of nearly identical attacks almost occurred, but detonators on the bombs proved faulty and the main explosives never went off. The Islamic terrorist organization Al Qaeda claimed responsibility for all the attacks. Just one year before the attacks, British intelligence had broken up an Al Qaeda cell in the city of Luton. British intelligence is now tasked with preventing future attacks, and its foreign policy decisions have been called into question.

Although civil unrest has erupted in the United Kingdom in past years, usually sparked by racial or economic conflict, observers said they had never witnessed anything quite like the widespread, anarchic destruction of the August 2011 riots, looting, and fires. The riots exploded first in lower-income districts of London, leaving police undermanned and thus unable to cope with the chaos, which some said did not seem traceable to any one cause, but rather to a general, pent-up anger among British poor and minorities, and others pinpointed to a controversial police shooting of a mixed-race teenager. The rioting then spread to other cities, confronting the nation with what has been described as a moral crisis. In the wake of the events, Prime Minister David Cameron announced stringent anti-riot measures, and in 2014 a government inquest declared the shooting lawful.

Relations with the United States

Although the United States fought against Britain in two major wars early in its existence, the two countries have had a close—if not always cordial—relationship for more than two centuries. In the twentieth century, two World Wars left the once-dominant British Empire reeling, and the United States took a leadership role among democratic and capitalist western nations. The United States and the United Kingdom, along with France, became the dominant western powers and cooperated militarily, economically, and often politically, and the close alliance between the Americans and the British has remained. Militarily and diplomatically, the two countries have been particularly close since the 1990s, when U.S. President Bill Clinton and British Prime Minister Tony Blair developed a close partnership. After Clinton was succeeded by George W. Bush, the United Kingdom was the most steadfast ally of the United States as it went to war in Afghanistan in 2001 and Iraq in 2003. Though much of the world disagreed with the invasion of Iraq, the United Kingdom pledged troops and diplomatic backing to the operation. Support for that war had dwindled among the British public by 2007, however, and most British troops were withdrawn from Iraq by 2009, calling into question the future of the alliance as many people harshly criticized the United Kingdom for blindly following the United States.

The United Kingdom and the European Union

Though many British people and officials support strong European Union participation, others feel the EU infringes upon British sovereignty. The United Kingdom has largely not aligned its foreign and economic policies with the union, even though it was one of the original members. British involvement in the U.S. invasion of Iraq in 2003 made this rift obvious, as most of the EU condemned the war. The United Kingdom is one of only three original EU member states that have not adopted the euro as their currency (Sweden and Denmark are the other two). The United Kingdom also has not entirely converted to the metric system, using the imperial measurement system instead, and in September 2007 the EU simply gave up trying to force metrics on the British after years of extended deadlines. The conflict between the independent behavior of the British and European cooperation continues, and with many calling for a clean break from the EU, Prime Minister David Cameron has pledged there will be a referendum on EU membership by 2017.

In 2013, U.S. whistleblower and former National Security Agency (NSA) contractor Edward Snowden revealed secret programs used to collect online data from millions of Internet users. That year, it was revealed that UK authorities had given NSA permission to store and analyze personal data of millions of UK citizens, and that the Government Communications Headquarters (GCHQ) was allegedly conducting its own electronic surveillance of at least 1.8 million Internet users around the world, including the collection of digital images and information connected to citizens who were not suspected of involvement with terrorist organizations. Although the GCHQ has claimed that its operations are legal, both the Labour Party and private citizens groups have urged the UK government to investigate the matter. In May 2014, the first legal challenge was brought against the GCHQ, with a UK-based privacy charity organization claiming that the agency violated articles of the European Convention on Human Rights with its "unrestrained, unregulated government spying."

Excerpt from the United Kingdom's Human Rights Act 1998

In contrast to most other countries throughout the contemporary world, the United Kingdom does not have a single written constitution. Rather, governing authority is maintained via numerous documents and proclamations. The United Kingdom's governance is based on the concept of Parliamentary authority, implying that statutes and legal procedures are the responsibility of Parliament and can be amended or changed by future Parliaments.

The most recent statement of human rights in the United Kingdom was enacted by Parliament in 1998. This Human Rights Act 1998 is based on "rights and freedoms guaranteed under the European Convention on Human Rights." Several of these involve the rights of persons accused of criminal activities, including the right to a public, fair trial and the presumption of innocence until guilt is proven. Torture, involuntary servitude, and unlawful detention are prohibited. The Act guarantees the right to freedom of speech, freedom of religion, freedom of assembly, and freedom of the press, along with the right to vote in free and fair elections by secret ballot. The Act makes specific reference to the right to education and proclaims equal rights under the law for all citizens of the United Kingdom. Its provisions also include the abolition of capital punishment.

1998 CHAPTER 42

An Act to give further effect to rights and freedoms guaranteed under the European Convention on Human Rights . . . [9th November 1998]

Be it enacted by the Queen's most Excellent Majesty, by and with the advice and consent of the Lords Spiritual and Temporal, and Commons, in this present Parliament assembled, and by the authority of the same, as follows:—

PART I

Article 2

Everyone's right to life shall be protected by law.

Deprivation of life shall not be regarded as inflicted in contravention of this Article when it results from the use of force which is no more than absolutely necessary:

in defence of any person from unlawful violence;

in order to effect a lawful arrest or to prevent the escape of a person lawfully detained;

in action lawfully taken for the purpose of quelling a riot or insurrection.

Article 3

No one shall be subjected to torture . . .

Article 4

No one shall be held in slavery or servitude.

No one shall be required to perform forced or compulsory labour.

For the purpose of this Article the term "forced or compulsory labour" shall not include:

any work required to be done in the ordinary course of detention . . .

any service of a military character . . .

any service exacted in case of an emergency or calamity threatening the life or well-being of the community;

any work or service which forms part of normal civic obligations.

Article 5

Everyone has the right to liberty and security of person. No one shall be deprived of his liberty save in the following cases . . . :

the lawful detention of a person after conviction . . .;

the lawful arrest or detention of a person for non-compliance with the lawful order of a court . . .

the lawful arrest or detention . . . on reasonable suspicion of having committed an offence . . .

the detention of a minor . . . for the purpose of educational supervision . . .

the lawful detention of persons for the prevention of the spreading of infectious diseases, of persons of unsound mind, alcoholics or drug addicts or vagrants;

the lawful arrest or detention of a person to prevent his effecting an unauthorised entry into the country . . .

Everyone who is arrested shall be informed promptly, in a language which he understands, of the reasons for his arrest . . .

Everyone arrested or detained . . . shall be brought promptly before a judge or other officer . . . and shall be entitled to trial within a reasonable time . . .

Everyone who is . . . arrest[ed] shall be entitled to proceedings by which the lawfulness of his detention shall be decided speedily by a court . . .

Article 6

. . . everyone is entitled to a fair and public hearing within a reasonable time by an independent and impartial tribunal . . .

Judgment shall be pronounced publicly but the press and public may be excluded from all or part of the trial in the interest of morals, public order or national security in a democratic society, where the interests of juveniles or the protection of the private life of the parties so require . . .

Everyone charged with a criminal offence shall be presumed innocent until proved guilty . . .

Everyone charged with a criminal offence has the . . . .rights:

to be informed promptly, in a language which he understands . . . of the . . . accusation against him;

to have adequate time and facilities for the preparation of his defence;

to defend himself in person or through legal assistance . . . if he has not sufficient means to pay for legal assistance, to be given it free . . .

to examine or have examined witnesses against him . . .

to have the free assistance of an interpreter if he cannot understand or speak the language used in court.

Article 7

No one shall be held guilty of any criminal offence on account of any act or omission which did not constitute a criminal offence . . . at the time when it was committed.

Article 8

Everyone has the right to respect for his private and family life, his home and his correspondence.

There shall be no interference . . . except such as is . . . necessary in a democratic society in the interests of national security, public safety or the economic well-being of or for the protection of the rights and freedoms of others.

Article 9

Everyone has the right to freedom of thought, conscience and religion . . . freedom to change his religion or belief and freedom . . . to manifest his religion or belief in worship, teaching, practice and observance.

Freedom to manifest one's religion or beliefs shall be subject only to such limitations as are . . . in the interests of public safety . . . public order, health or morals, or for the protection of the rights and freedoms of others.

Article 10

Everyone has the right to freedom of expression . . . to hold opinions and to receive and impart information and ideas . . . This Article shall not prevent States from requiring the licensing of broadcasting, television or cinema enterprises.

Article 11

Everyone has the right to freedom of peaceful assembly and to freedom of association with others, including the right to form and to join trade unions . . .

No restrictions shall be placed on the exercise of these rights other than . . . in the interests of national security or public safety . . . or for the protection of the rights and freedoms of others . . .

Article 12

Men and women . . . have the right to marry . . .

Article 14

The enjoyment of the rights and freedoms . . . shall be secured without discrimination on any ground such as sex, race, colour, language, religion, political or other opinion, national or social origin, association with a national minority, property, birth . . .

PART II

Article 1

. . . No one shall be deprived of his possessions except in the public interest and subject to the conditions provided for by law . . .

Article 2

No person shall be denied the right to education . . . the State shall respect the right of parents to ensure such education and teaching in conformity with their . . . convictions.

Article 3

The High Contracting Parties undertake to hold free elections at reasonable intervals by secret ballot . . .

ABOLITION OF THE DEATH PENALTY

The death penalty shall be abolished.

Source: "The British Constitution." History Learning Site. http://www.historylearn-ingsite.co.uk/british_constitution1.htm

CHAPTER 4

TRANSITIONAL STATES

A transitional state is one that is undergoing change from one type of government to another. The transition process is sometimes abrupt and can cause significant political and economic turmoil. In many cases, the transition process is successful; in other cases, the transition process does not work and the state reverts to its previous form of government, or a third form of government emerges. Transitions have occurred throughout history. Today, however, the term is used generally to refer to efforts to implement democracy.

The term "regime change" has been used frequently to describe the transition process. In many countries, transition is the result of political independence. Throughout Africa and Asia, former European colonies have achieved independence since World War II. Many newly independent former colonies attempted to establish themselves as democracies. Some of these efforts have been successful, as in the case of India and Botswana. In other cases—for example, Zimbabwe and Uganda—newly established democratic governments were overthrown and replaced by autocratic governments at least on a temporary basis.

Regime change also occurs within already-independent states. In some states, regime change follows a coup d'etat. The coup d'etat sometimes ushers in a period of uncertainty, as various factions compete for control of the state until one side emerges victorious and implements its preferred system of government. An early example of this process was the Russian Revolution, which began with the ouster of Tsar Nicholas II in 1917. After the monarchy was overthrown, several years of civil war took place until the Bolsheviks prevailed and established the Communist government of what became the Soviet Union. The Communists controlled the Soviet Union until they themselves were ousted in 1991.

Foreign intervention can result in regime change, as in the case of Afghanistan, where United States intervention helped to topple the Taliban regime in 2001. Throughout history, powerful countries have worked overtly or covertly to promote regime change. During the Cold War, the United States and the Soviet Union accused each other of promoting regime change in less-developed countries, with the idea of implementing regimes that would support themselves. For example, the Soviets provided financial aid and military assistance to revolutionary movements whose goal was to topple existing regimes and replace them with Communist governments. Meanwhile, the United States provided support for rebel factions attempting to replace Communist regimes and/or dictatorships in countries such as Nicaragua and Angola.

The collapse of Communism in the Soviet Union and Eastern Europe in the late 1980s and early 1990s also resulted in regime change. The former Soviet Union broke apart into fifteen independent countries. Similarly, the former Yugoslavia split into six independent countries, along with Kosovo, whose independence from Serbia is not recognized universally by the international community. The processes and outcomes of regime change varied across newly independent countries in the former Soviet Union and the former Yugoslavia. Several, including Estonia, Latvia, Lithuania, and Slovenia, transitioned quickly to democracy. Others, including Uzbekistan, became autocratic regimes. Transition to democracy was also generally free of conflict in the former Soviet satellites of Eastern Europe.

As a general rule, transition has occurred more rapidly and successfully in states with higher per-capita incomes and levels of economic development. For example, Estonia, Latvia, and Lithuania are the wealthiest former Soviet republics, and all three transitioned to democratic regimes with very little discord. Similarly, Slovenia is the wealthiest of the republics of the former Yugoslavia. On the other hand, transition was slower and more conflict-ridden in Bosnia and Herzegovina, which is poorer and has a longer history of religious and ethnic division. Citizens of Bosnia and Herzegovina were divided along ethnic lines about the desirability of independence, with ethnic Bosnians favoring independence and ethnic Serbs favoring continued union with Serbia as the successor state to Yugoslavia. Bosnia's declaration of independence led to nearly four years of civil war.

Elsewhere, the creation of new states has also resulted in regime change. For example, Eritrea developed its new regime following its separation from Ethiopia in 1993. The transition process has often been violent. The independence of Eritrea, for example, was followed by the Eritrean–Ethiopian War, which lasted two years between 1998 and 2000 and which resulted in thousands of military and civilian casualties. Each country accused the other of initiating the war, but an international commission investigating the situation ruled in 2005 that Eritrea triggered the war by invading Ethiopia. A similar situation has prevailed in South Sudan, which split from Sudan in 2011 following years of discord and civil war. The transition to independence in South Sudan was primarily peaceful, although armed skirmishes have arisen, especially within and near territories claimed by both of these countries.

While some regime changes have been spurred on by the efforts of foreign governments, other regime changes have occurred following large-scale public protests within states. The independence of some former Soviet and Yugoslav republics occurred following popular uprisings. More recently, the autocratic governments of several Middle Eastern countries were overthrown following massive public protests in late 2010 and early 2011. Collectively, these protests came to be known as the "Arab Spring." During this time, the autocratic regimes of Hosni Mubarak in Egypt, Muammar Gaddafi in Libya, and Zine El Abidine Ben Ali in Tunisia were overthrown.

Following the ouster of these autocrats and following transition periods, democratic elections were held in each country. In Egypt, the first nationwide election resulted in the election of Mohammed Morsi as Egypt's new President. However, Morsi attempted to grant himself broad powers and to impose Islamic fundamentalism on the country. As a result, a second wave of protests broke out in 2013. Morsi was ousted in a military coup, and the Islamic constitution that he had promulgated was suspended. The transition in Libya has been more successful, with a democratic government elected in 2012 still in power as of 2014.

Transitions may be gradual or abrupt. In many cases, a regime change begins with a transition period within which the new government is implemented. For example, the ouster of Mubarak in Egypt in 2011 was followed by several months of military rule during which the transition to democracy was planned and put into effect. In Libya, a National Transitional Council took power temporarily after the ouster of Gaddafi and before national elections were held, after which the Transitional Council handed over authority to the newly elected civilian government. The term "provisional government" has been used to describe a temporary government that is in charge of administration of the state while the new government is being implemented. The Palestine National Authority represents the de-facto government of Palestine, which it has administered since 1994.

—Fred M. Shelley

Further Reading

Bassam Haddad, Rosie Bsheer, and Ziad Abu-Rish (eds.), *The dawn of the Arab uprisings: End of an old order?* London: Pluto Press, 2012.

Christian W. Haerpfer, Patrick Bernhagen, Ronald F. Inglehart, and Christian Welzel (eds.), *Democratization*. Oxford: Oxford University Press, 2009.

Jan Teorell, *Determinants of democratization: Explaining regime change in the world, 1972–2006.* New York: Cambridge University Press, 2010.

BOSNIA AND HERZEGOVINA

BOSNIA AND HERZEGOVINA

Communications	Primary School–age Children Enrolled in Primary School
Facebook Users	
1,420,000 (estimate) (2013)	166,620 (2012)
Internet Users	**Primary School–age Females Enrolled in Primary School**
1,422,000 (2009)	
Internet Users (% of Population)	81,029 (2012)
67.9% (2013)	**Secondary School–age Children Enrolled in Secondary School**
Television	
28 sets per 100 population (2005)	313,321 (2012)
Land-based Telephones in Use	**Secondary School–age Males Enrolled in Secondary School**
878,000 (2012)	159,750 (2012)
Mobile Telephone Subscribers	**Secondary School–age Females Enrolled in Secondary School**
3,350,000 (2012)	
Major Daily Newspapers	153,571 (2012)
7 (2004)	**Students Per Teacher, Primary School**
Average Circulation of Daily Newspapers	Not Available
Not Available	**Students Per Teacher, Secondary School**
Education	Not Available
School System	**Enrollment in Tertiary Education**
Bosnia and Herzegovina's public education begins at the age of seven, with nine years of primary school. After completing primary studies, students may attend four years of technical school or four years of general secondary school.	107,083 (2012)
	Enrollment in Tertiary Education, Male
	47,672 (2012)
	Enrollment in Tertiary Education, Female
Mandatory Education	59,411 (2012)
9 years, from ages 6 to 15.	**Literacy**
Average Years Spent in School for Current Students	98% (2012)
	Energy and Natural Resources
	Electric Power Generation
Not Available	12,930,000,000 kilowatt hours per year (estimate) (2012)
Average Years Spent in School for Current Students, Male	
	Electric Power Consumption
Not Available	12,620,000,000 kilowatt hours per year (estimate) (2012)
Average Years Spent in School for Current Students, Female	
	Nuclear Power Plants
Not Available	0 (2014)

Crude Oil Production	**Climate**
59 barrels per day (2010)	Bosnia & Herzegovina is subject to cold winters and hot summers. Summer is shorter in elevated regions, which encounter longer, colder winters.
Crude Oil Consumption	
29,000 barrels per day (2012)	
Natural Gas Production	**Land Use**
0 cubic meters per year (estimate) (2013)	20.0% arable land; 10.9% temporary crops; 1.9% permanent crops; 20.2% permanent meadows and pastures; 42.7% forest land; 15.4% other.
Natural Gas Consumption	
256,900,000 cubic meters per year (estimate) (2013)	
Natural Resources	**Arable Land**
Coal, iron ore, bauxite, copper, lead, zinc, chromite, cobalt, manganese, nickel, clay, gypsum, salt, sand, timber, hydropower	20% (2007)
	Arable Land Per Capita
	1 acres per person (2007)
Environment	**Health**
CO2 Emissions	**Average Life Expectancy**
8.0 metric tons per capita (2009)	76.3 years (2014)
Alternative and Nuclear Energy	**Average Life Expectancy, Male**
10.8% of total energy use (2010)	73.3 years (2014)
Threatened Species	**Average Life Expectancy, Female**
67 (2010)	79.6 years (2014)
Protected Areas	**Crude Birth Rate**
297 (estimate) (2010)	8.9 (estimate) (2015)
Geography	**Crude Death Rate**
Location	9.8 (estimate) (2015)
Bosnia & Herzegovina is located in southern Europe. It is bordered by Croatia to the north and west, by Serbia to the east, and by Montenegro to the southeast. Bosnia & Herzegovina has a short expanse of coast along the Adriatic Sea.	**Maternal Mortality**
	31 per 100,000 live births (2005–2012 projection)
	Infant Mortality
	6 per 1,000 live births (2012)
Time Zone	**Doctors**
6 hours ahead of U.S. Eastern Standard	1.7 per 1,000 people (2010)
Land Borders	**Industry and Labor**
907 miles	**Gross Domestic Product (GDP) - official exchange rate**
Coastline	
12 miles	$20,554,000,000 (estimate) (2015)
Capital	**GDP per Capita**
Sarajevo	$5,320 (estimate) (2015)
Area	**GDP - Purchasing Power Parity (PPP)**
19,775 sq. miles	$32,596,000,000 (estimate) (2013)

GDP (PPP) per Capita	**Economic Aid Received**
$8,406 (estimate) (2013)	$425,000,000 (2011)
Industry Products	**Population**
Steel, minerals, motor vehicles, wooden furniture, tobacco products, textiles.	**Population**
	3,867,055 (estimate) (2015)
Agriculture Products	**World Population Rank**
Wheat, corn, oats, barley, potatoes, grapes, strawberries, raspberries, walnuts, livestock.	118 th (2010)
	Population Density
Unemployment	233.7 people per square mile (estimate) (2011)
28.2% (2012)	
Labor Profile	**Population Distribution**
agriculture: 20.5% industry: 32.6% services: 47% (2008)	49% urban (2011)
	Age Distribution
Military	0-14: 14.2%
Total Active Armed Forces	15-64: 70.9%
11,099 (2010)	65+: 14.9%
Active Armed Forces	(2009)
0% (2010)	**Median Age**
Annual Military Expenditures	40.8 years (estimate) (2014)
$281,000,000 (2009)	**Population Growth Rate**
Military Service	-0.1% per year (estimate) (2015)
(not available)	**Net Migration Rate**
National Finances	-0.4 (estimate) (2015)
Currency	**Trade**
Marka	**Imported Goods**
Total Government Revenues	Fuels and lubricants, transportation equipment, machinery, manufactured goods.
$7,691,000,000 (estimate) (2013)	
Total Government Expenditures	**Total Value of Imports**
$7,497,000,000 (estimate) (2013)	$3,960,900,000 (estimate) (2009)
Budget Deficit	**Exported Goods**
1.0 (estimate) (2013)	Manufactured goods, machinery, transportation equipment, raw materials.
GDP Contribution by Sector	
agriculture: 8.2% industry: 26.2% services: 65.6% (2012 est.)	**Total Value of Exports**
	$5,427,000,000 (estimate) (2012)
External Debt	**Import Partners**
$11,140,000,000 (estimate) (2013)	Croatia - 37.4%; Germany -23.7%; Slovenia - 22.7%; Italy - 20.0%; Austria -11.2% (2009)
Economic Aid Extended	
$0 (2011)	

Export Partners	Paved Roads		
Croatia - 27.3%; Slovenia - 26.6; Italy - 24.1%; Germany - 19.1%; Austria - 14.7% (2009)	92.1% (2010)		
	Roads, Unpaved		
	6,475 (2006)		
Current Account Balance	**Passenger Cars per 1,000 People**		
$-939,500,000 (estimate) (2013)	119 (2008)		
Weights and Measures	**Railroads**		
The metric system is in use.	621 (2008)		
Transportation	**Ports**		
Airports	Major: 5—Orasje; Inland: Bosanski Brod, Bosanska Gradiska, Bosanski Samac, Brcko.		
25 (2012)			

OVERVIEW

Located in the Balkans of southeastern Europe, Bosnia and Herzegovina is bordered by Croatia to the north and west, Serbia to the east, and Montenegro to the south. Bosnia and Herzegovina is a mountainous country with a short twelve-mile coastline along the Adriatic Sea. Along with its neighbors, it gained independence after the breakup of Yugoslavia in 1992. The nation has a population of about 4 million. Bosnia and Herzegovina has a continental climate and cold winters. The nation's capital is Sarajevo—the site of the 1984 Winter Olympic Games, and of the 1914 assassination of Archduke Franz Ferdinand of Austria-Hungary, an event that triggered World War I.

GOVERNMENT

The Republic of Bosnia and Herzegovina (Republika Bosne i Hercegovine) declared its independence from the Federal Republic of Yugoslavia in April 1992. In 1995, leaders from Bosnia's three main ethnic groups—Christian Orthodox Serbs, Muslim Bosniaks, and Roman Catholic Croats—signed the Dayton Agreement, which ended the country's three-year civil war and created a weak federal government and two semi-autonomous political entities: the Federation of Bosnia and Herzegovina (the Bosniak-Croat federation) and the Bosnian Serb Republic (Republika Srpska). Each entity has its own legislature and executive, but they maintain a loose association through the joint federal government, which is headed by a three-member collective presidency—including one Serbian member from the Republika Srpska and both a Bosniak and a Croat member from the Federation of Bosnia and Herzegovina. Additionally, the United Nations (UN) Office of the High Representative is charged with ensuring the government operates according to the requirements of the Dayton Agreement. The High Representative holds sweeping

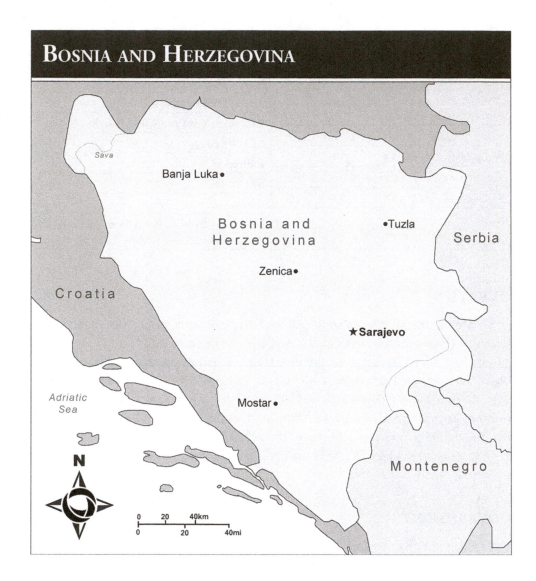

BOSNIA AND HERZEGOVINA

powers, including the authority to fire government officials. As of 2014, the Serbian member of the presidency was Nebojsa Radmanovic, the Bosniak member was Bakir Izetbegovic, and the Croat member was Zeljko Komsic.

Constitution

The Constitution established a multiparty system and guarantees basic civil rights. Efforts to draft a new constitution were initially obstructed by the civil war. A new Bosnian Constitution, however, was successfully adopted in November 1995 as part of the Dayton Agreement and has been amended several times. Each of the entities also has its own separate constitution.

Executive

Executive power is formally vested in a three-member collective presidency consisting of a Bosniak, a Croat, and a Serb. For the initial presidential term from 1996 to 1998, the member who received the highest number of votes served as chairperson of the presidency. Starting in 1998, the chairpersonship began to rotate, with each member serving an eight-month term as chairperson. The chairperson represents the presidency in working with foreign officials on government matters. Decisions are made by consensus, but if agreement cannot be reached, the Constitution allows two of the three presidents to determine the outcome. If the third president objects to the decision, he or she can appeal to parliament of the same ethnicity. Therefore, if the Croat member of the presidency opposes a decision, the appeal would be made to the Croat members of the Federation's legislature. A two-thirds vote from the legislators is necessary to overturn the presidency's decision. The presidents elected in 1996, Bosnia's first presidential election, served only a two-year term. Since the 1998 elections, presidential members serve for four years.

Legislature

The 1995 Dayton Agreement called for the creation of a legislature for the Republic of Bosnia and Herzegovina and for each of its two entities. The bicameral national Parliamentary Assembly comprises a directly elected 42-seat lower chamber (House of Representatives) and a 15-seat indirectly elected upper chamber (House of Peoples). There are also two regional legislative bodies. The unicameral Republika Srpska National Assembly has 83 directly elected seats. The legislature of the Muslim-Croat Federation of Bosnia and Herzegovina comprises a 140-seat directly elected lower chamber (House of Representatives) and a 74-seat indirectly elected upper chamber (House of Peoples).

Judiciary

The 1995 Constitution outlined the creation of a national Constitutional Court that would represent Bosnia and Herzegovina's major ethnic groups. The court comprises four members from the Federation of Bosnia-Herzegovina and two members from the Republika Srpska, as well as three judges from the European Court of Human Rights who are not residents of Bosnia. The Constitutional Court is empowered to resolve any conflicts between the two republics over constitutional issues.

Local Government

Bosnia and Herzegovina is divided into 142 municipalities, 62 of which are in the Republika Srpska and 79 of which are in the Federation of Bosnia and Herzegovina.

Election Qualifications

All citizens 18 years of age and older may vote, as may all working citizens 16 years of age and older.

POLITICS

The new Bosnian government that emerged from the Dayton Agreement got off to a shaky start. However, the decade after the agreement saw most of the nation's tattered infrastructure rebuilt and a slow rise in overall gross domestic product. Nevertheless, corruption continues to be interwoven into Bosnian politics, and unemployment remains high. Nationalist parties have dominated the legislatures of the Federation of Bosnia and Herzegovina and the Republika Srpska and of the national Parliamentary Assembly since 1996, although moderate groups have begun to gain some representation.

In 2004, the North Atlantic Treaty Organization (NATO) relinquished the bulk of its peacekeeping duties to a newly created European Union (EU) force. The High Representative at the time, Paddy Ashdown, fired the Croat member of the nation's presidency, Dragan Covic, in March 2005. Covic had refused to resign after being implicated in a corruption scandal. Later in the year, leaders from each of the three main ethnic groups signed a "Unity Pledge," in which they agreed to overhaul the loose confederation created by the Dayton Agreement in favor of a more centralized state. Steps taken to gradually strengthen the federal government include the adoption of a single defense policy and intelligence service; previously each political entity had its own organizations. Another breakthrough in the effort to unify the country was the creation of a single multiethnic national police force to replace the separate forces controlled by the entities.

Also in 2005, the EU opened talks on a proposed Stabilization and Association Agreement—the first of many steps toward eventual EU membership for Bosnia and Herzegovina. In 2006, Bosnia became the first nation to bring a genocide case before the International Court of Justice, when the court began to hear arguments in Bosnia's case against Serbia. Efforts to strengthen the central government met an obstacle in April 2006, when the Parliamentary Assembly failed to support a series of constitutional amendments that would have replaced the three-member presidency with a single president and changed the nation's voting procedures.

Deep ideological rifts remain between the Federation of Bosnia and Herzegovina and the Republika Srpska, as evidenced by the country's political struggles. The platforms of each of Bosnia and Herzegovina's three presidents reflect the differences—while the Bosniak and Croat members are in favor of creating a more united nation, the Bosnian Serb member favors splitting the country along ethnic lines. In addition, a 15-month deadlock followed the 2010 parliamentary elections, with representatives unable to agree on a prime minister.

Political Parties

The Alliance of Independent Social Democrats (Savez Nezvisnih Socijaldemokrata—SNSD) is a Serbian social democratic party. The party is based on a platform of nonpartisanship and inclusiveness. The Bosnian Serb member of Bosnia's three-person presidency, Nebojsa Radmanovic, is a member of the SNSD.

One of Bosnia and Herzegovina's top parties is the nationalist Party of Democratic Action (Stranka Demokratski Akcije—SDA). The party was organized in 1990 to represent Bosnian Muslims. The SDA has consistently done well in elections. Before the 1998 elections, it formed a coalition with the multiethnic Party for Bosnia and Herzegovina (a former splinter group of the SDA) and other small parties. The group, known as the Coalition for a Single and Democratic Bosnia, won the largest number of seats in the Parliamentary Assembly. Bakir Izetbegovic, the Bosniak president, is a member of SDA.

The Party for Bosnia and Herzegovina (Stranka za Bosnu i Hercegovinu—SBiH) is a liberal party established in 1996. It advocates greater national integration and is a member of the Coalition for a Single and Democratic Bosnia electoral alliance.

The Social Democratic Party of Bosnia and Herzegovina (Socijaldemokratska Partija Bosne i Hercegovine—SDP) grew out of the Socialist League of the Working People of Yugoslavia and has since absorbed the League of Communists of Bosnia and Herzegovina-Party of Democratic Change. The SDP is one of the strongest nonnationalist opposition parties. It is a liberal party, and in 2006 and 2010, the party's Zeljko Komsic was elected as the Bosnian Croat member of the nation's three-person federal presidency.

Zeljko Komsic addressing the United Nations General Assembly in New York in 2007. Komsic served as the Croat member of the Presidency of Bosnia and Herzegovina from 2006 to 2014. (MONIKA GRAFF/UPI/Newscom)

Founded in 1990, the Serbian Democratic Party of Bosnia and Herzegovina (Srpska Demokratska Stranka—SDS) is a Serbian nationalist group. It was established by Radovan Karadzic, the former leader of the then-unrecognized breakaway Yugoslav Republic of Bosnia and Herzegovina. The SDS was technically banned in 1992 due to Karadzic's military role in the country's civil war. In 1995, he was officially indicted by a UN war crimes tribunal. However, the party continued to function with Karadzic as its head until 1996, when he finally stepped down under joint Serbian–U.S. pressure. Despite the absence of Karadzic, the party has continued to maintain a strong presence in the Parliamentary Assembly.

The Croatian Democratic Union of Bosnia and Herzegovina (Hrvatska Demokratska Zajednika—HDZ) was founded in 1990 and is linked to Croatia's party of the same name. It draws strong support from nationalist Bosnian Croats. In 1996, then-party leader Kresimir Zubak was elected to the three-member federal presidency, and in 1998, HDZ candidate Ante Jelavic succeeded him with 50% of the Croat vote.

The Party for Democratic Progress is a conservative, Serbian party established in 1999. It advocates equal rights for all ethnic groups and is in favor of greater cooperation between the Republika Srpska and the European Union.

The Serbian Radical Party (Srpska Radikalna Stranka—SRS) is a hard-line party with connections to the Serbian Radical Party in Serbia. While the party lost a significant number of seats in the Parliamentary Assembly in 1998, SRS leader Nikola Poplasen was elected president of the Serb Republic. He was dismissed from the post in March 1999, due to his lack of compliance with the Dayton Agreement. The party failed to win any seats in the 2006 or 2010 federal elections.

ECONOMY

The war during the 1990s devastated Bosnia and Herzegovina's economy, causing soaring unemployment rates and plummeting production levels, and stymied the nation's economic and emotional recovery. The war destroyed most infrastructure in the country, making trade difficult. Rampant corruption has also stalled economic development. Bosnia and Herzegovina is rich in such minerals as bauxite, copper, iron, and zinc, but it has a weak agricultural sector because most of its land is not suited to farming. Croatia, Italy, Germany, and Slovenia are among Bosnia and Herzegovina's principal trade partners.

SOCIETY

Bosnia and Herzegovina's population is composed of three main ethnic groups. Most citizens identify themselves as either Bosniaks, Bosnian Serbs, or Bosnian

Croats. In 1961 Bosniaks (Bosnian Muslims) were counted as a separate ethnic group in Yugoslavia, thus cementing the official link between religious and ethnic identity. Currently in Bosnia and Herzegovina, the country's largest group is Bosniak, with a smaller component of ethnic Serbs, who generally adhere to the Orthodox Christian faith, and a group of ethnic Croats that is smaller still and mainly follows the Roman Catholic Church. The language of Bosnia and Herzegovina was originally known as Serbo-Croatian, but in recent times is also referred to as Bosnian, Croatian, or Serbian, depending on the ethnicity and political affiliation of the speaker.

Ethnic Composition

Bosniak – 48%; Serb – 37.1%; Croat – 14.3%; other – 0.6%

Language

Roughly 99% of the population speaks what was originally known as Serbo-Croatian, which is written in the Roman alphabet by Croats and Bosniaks and the Cyrillic alphabet by Serbs.

Religion

Muslim – 40%; Orthodox – 31%; Roman Catholic – 15%; other – 14%

CONTEMPORARY ISSUES

Ethnic Conflict

Nationalism and ethnic hatreds remain among Bosnia and Herzegovina's Muslims, Serbs, and Croats years after the Dayton Agreement ended the nation's civil war in 1995. The country still is divided into the Bosniak- and Croat-dominated Federation of Bosnia and Herzegovina and the Serb-dominated Republika Srpska, each with its own government. Efforts to strengthen the multiethnic federal government have met strong resistance, and although nationalist political parties have lost ground to more moderate groups, politicians continue to appeal to ethnicity. Many international observers fear that Bosnia and Herzegovina's two halves are again headed toward separate nationhood, and perhaps another civil war. The International Crisis Group think tank reported in 2007 that "Bosnia remains unready for unguided ownership of its own future; ethnic nationalism remains too strong." Today, the government is still plagued with political divisions, at both the state and the federal level, as seen by power struggles in 2012 that left the Bosnian state without stable leadership for almost a full year.

Bosniaks (Bosnian Muslims) make up more than 48% of Bosnia and Herzegovina's population; Serbs make up 37%; and Croats account for more than 14%. Currently the three groups are equally represented in the federal government, but most powers remain concentrated in the two separate republics. Although some areas have become more integrated with the return of refugees from the war, mistrust and anger remain. Serbs fear domination by the more numerous Bosniaks, while Bosniaks and Croats both worry about rising Serb nationalism, which was the driving force in Slobodan Milosevic's ethnic cleansing campaign of the early 1990s. Croats and Bosniaks also have long-standing disputes with one another. Memorials to those killed in the war have recently become a source of hostility, and the 2008 arrest of Bosnian Serb war crimes suspect Radovan Karadzic and the 2011 arrest of Ratko Mladic raised tensions further. That year, as the European Union (EU) prepared to withdraw its peacekeeping forces and begin talks aimed at Bosnia and Herzegovina's entry into the EU, the nation's former international high commissioner, Paddy Ashdown, warned of the "real threat of Bosnia breaking up again" and "the pain that will ensue if Europe, once again, misjudges or misunderstands what is happening in Bosnia."

Recovery from War

Damaged infrastructure, overwhelming government bureaucracy, a thriving black market, and the return of hundreds of thousands of refugees all continue to hinder Bosnia and Herzegovina's postwar recovery. One of the poorest regions of the former Yugoslavia, Bosnia and Herzegovina's economic troubles only increased with its secession from the federation and subsequent three-year civil war. Roads, water, electricity, education, and health care systems all were destroyed in the fighting, especially in the capital, Sarajevo. About 100,000 people died, and 2.2 million people—about half the population—fled their homes.

Today only about half of the refugees have returned, and at least 100,000 remain displaced within the country, afraid or unwilling to go back to their formerly diverse towns and neighborhoods. Overlapping and rival governments—at both the federal and provincial levels—have largely been blamed for the slow pace of economic reform and infrastructure repairs. Major improvements have been made, especially in Sarajevo, but water shortages, damaged roads, and a lack of urban sewage disposal remain chronic problems. Because there are often no law enforcement agreements between the country's various government entities, police have found it difficult to pursue suspects or prosecute crimes across entity borders. The situation has made Bosnia and Herzegovina vulnerable to drug trafficking, money laundering, and corruption. The informal economy, which may compose up to half of gross domestic product (GDP), also has robbed the various governments of badly needed tax revenue. Since the end of the civil war in 1995, the nation has relied heavily on international aid to shore up its economy and improve services to its population. However, that assistance is now decreasing as foreign powers slowly withdraw from the country.

Unemployment

Although Bosnia and Herzegovina's economy has improved greatly in the past decade, unemployment rates remain extremely high—around 40%. If the large informal economy is taken into consideration, rough estimates put the unemployment rate between 18% and 22%, but this still has left many young Bosnians with few job prospects. The situation has led many, especially skilled professionals, to seek work abroad. This has created a significant source of revenue in the form of money sent home by people working in other countries, which equals an estimated 20% or more of GDP. However, it has also robbed the country of its best-educated citizens. Some of the many unemployed Bosnians who remain in

Bosnia was the scene of a bloody civil war between 1992 and 1995, during which time about 200,000 military personnel and civilians lost their lives. The United Nations provided peacekeeping forces and supplied humanitarian aid during victims of this conflict. (Pascal Deloche/GODONG/picture-alliance/Godong/Newscom)

the country have become involved in the drug trade or other aspects of the black market. International economists have praised Bosnia and Herzegovina for its economic progress, but some note that in recent years such advances have slowed, and say that more reforms are needed to attract private investment. World Bank officials maintain that the overwhelming bureaucracy of the country's various governments discourages new businesses. In addition, privatization of more than 80% of state-owned companies failed as the companies were sold to private investors who then liquidated the assets and declared bankruptcy, leaving thousands unemployed.

Excerpt from the Constitution of Bosnia and Herzegovina

The constitution of Bosnia and Herzegovina was drafted and put into operation as part of the Dayton Agreement, which formally ended civil war in the former Yugoslavia in 1995. In effect, Bosnia and Herzegovina's constitution is a treaty among belligerents in the war, along with representatives from the United States, the United Kingdom, Germany, Russia, and the European Union.

As indicated in the Preamble, the Constitution is "guided by the purposes and principles of the Charter of the United Nations" and "inspired by the Universal Declaration of Human Rights. Thus the concept of human rights articulated in the Constitution is based on "internationally recognized human rights and fundamental freedoms," and it provides for the establishment of a Human Rights Commission.

Article 3 enumerates rights granted by the Constitution to citizens of Bosnia and Herzegovina. Some of these are political rights, including the right to a fair trial and rights to freedom of expression, freedom of assembly, and freedom of religion. The latter is especially significant in that religious conflict was a major factor underlying the civil war. The Constitution also outlaws slavery, torture, and forced labor, and it grants citizens "the right to marry and to found a family." Economic and material rights are emphasized less, although citizens are granted the right to an education without specifying how this right is to be exercised. In accordance with the Preamble's link between the Constitution and international human rights declarations and organizations, the Constitution specifies that the government will cooperate fully with these organizations in order to guarantee human rights.

PREAMBLE

Based on respect for human dignity, liberty, and equality,
Dedicated to peace, justice, tolerance, and reconciliation,
Convinced that democratic governmental institutions and fair procedures best produce peaceful relations within a pluralist society,

Desiring to promote the general welfare and economic growth through the protection of private property and the promotion of a market economy,

Guided by the Purposes and Principles of the Charter of the United Nations

Committed to the sovereignty, territorial integrity, and political independence of Bosnia and Herzegovina in accordance with international law,

Determined to ensure full respect for international humanitarian law,

Inspired by the Universal Declaration of Human Rights, the International Covenants on Civil and Political Rights and on Economic, Social and Cultural Rights, and the Declaration on the Rights of Persons Belonging to National or Ethnic, Religious and Linguistic Minorities, as well as other human rights instruments,

Recalling the Basic Principles agreed in Geneva on September 8, 1995, and in New York on September 26, 1995,

Bosniacs, Croats, and Serbs, as constituent peoples (along with Others), and citizens of Bosnia and Herzegovina hereby determine that the Constitution of Bosnia and Herzegovina is as follows:

Bosnia and Herzegovina shall consist of the two Entities, the Federation of Bosnia and Herzegovina and the Republika Srpska (hereinafter "the Entities").

1. Human Rights

Bosnia and Herzegovina and both Entities shall ensure the highest level of internationally recognized human rights and fundamental freedoms. To that end, there shall be a Human Rights Commission for Bosnia and Herzegovina as provided for in Annex 6 to the General Framework Agreement.

2. International Standards

The rights and freedoms set forth in the European Convention for the Protection of Human Rights and Fundamental Freedoms and its Protocols shall apply directly in Bosnia and Herzegovina. These shall have priority over all other law.

3. Enumeration of Rights

All persons within the territory of Bosnia and Herzegovina shall enjoy the human rights and fundamental freedoms referred to in paragraph 2 above; these include:

a) The right to life.
b) The right not to be subjected to torture or to inhuman or degrading treatment or punishment.
c) The right not to be held in slavery or servitude or to perform forced or compulsory labor.

d) The rights to liberty and security of person.
e) The right to a fair hearing in civil and criminal matters, and other rights relating to criminal proceedings.
f) The right to private and family life, home, and correspondence.
g) Freedom of thought, conscience, and religion.
h) Freedom of expression.
i) Freedom of peaceful assembly and freedom of association with others.
j) The right to marry and to found a family.
k) The right to property.
l) The right to education.
m) The right to liberty of movement and residence.

4. Non-Discrimination

The enjoyment of the rights and freedoms provided for in this Article or in the international agreements listed in Annex 1 to this Constitution shall be secured to all persons in Bosnia and Herzegovina without discrimination on any ground such as sex, race, color, language, religion, political or other opinion, national or social origin, association with a national minority, property, birth or other status.

5. Non-Discrimination

All refugees and displaced persons have the right freely to return to their homes of origin. They have the right, in accordance with Annex 7 to the General Framework Agreement, to have restored to them property of which they were deprived in the course of hostilities since 1991 and to be compensated for any such property that cannot be restored to them. Any commitments or statements relating to such property made under duress are null and void.

6. Implementation

Bosnia and Herzegovina, and all courts, agencies, governmental organs, and instrumentalities operated by or within the Entities, shall apply and conform to the human rights and fundamental freedoms referred to in paragraph 2 above.

8. Cooperation

All competent authorities in Bosnia and Herzegovina shall cooperate with and provide unrestricted access to: any international human rights monitoring mechanisms established for Bosnia and Herzegovina; the supervisory bodies established by any of the international agreements listed in Annex 1 to this Constitution; the International Tribunal for the Former Yugoslavia (and in particular shall comply with orders issued pursuant to Article 29 of the Statute of the Tribunal); and any other organization authorized by the United Nations Security Council with a mandate concerning human rights or humanitarian law.

ANNEX 1

Additional Human Rights Agreements To Be Applied In Bosnia And Herzegovina

1. 1948 Convention on the Prevention and Punishment of the Crime of Genocide
2. 1949 Geneva Conventions I–IV on the Protection of the Victims of War, and the 1977 Geneva Protocols I–II thereto
3. 1951 Convention relating to the Status of Refugees and the 1966 Protocol thereto
4. 1957 Convention on the Nationality of Married Women
5. 1961 Convention on the Reduction of Statelessness
6. 1965 International Convention on the Elimination of All Forms of Racial Discrimination
7. 1966 International Covenant on Civil and Political Rights and the 1966 and 1989 Optional Protocols thereto
8. 1966 Covenant on Economic, Social and Cultural Rights
9. 1979 Convention on the Elimination of All Forms of Discrimination against Women
10. 1984 Convention against Torture and Other Cruel, Inhuman or Degrading Treatment or Punishment
11. 1987 European Convention on the Prevention of Torture and Inhuman or Degrading Treatment or Punishment
12. 1989 Convention on the Rights of the Child
13. 1990 International Convention on the Protection of the Rights of All Migrant Workers and Members of Their Families
14. 1992 European Charter for Regional or Minority Languages
15. 1994 Framework Convention for the Protection of National Minorities

Source: "Constitution of Bosnia and Herzegovina." Legislation Online. http://www .legislationline.org/documents/section/constitutions.

ERITREA

ERITREA

Communications		Average Years Spent in School for Current Students, Female
Facebook Users		
20,000 (estimate) (2013)		4 (2010)
Internet Users		Primary School–age Children Enrolled in Primary School
200,000 (2008)		
Internet Users (% of Population)		334,245 (2012)
0.9% (2013)		Primary School–age Males Enrolled in Primary School
Television		
7 sets per 100 population (2007)		184,404 (2012)
Land-based Telephones in Use		Primary School–age Females Enrolled in Primary School
60,000 (2012)		149,841 (2012)
Mobile Telephone Subscribers		Secondary School–age Children Enrolled in Secondary School
305,300 (2012)		
Major Daily Newspapers		265,600 (2012)
Not Available		Secondary School–age Males Enrolled in Secondary School
Average Circulation of Daily Newspapers		
99		149,444 (2012)
Education		Secondary School–age Females Enrolled in Secondary School
School System		116,156 (2012)
Eritrean students begin primary school at the age of seven and attend for five years. Early secondary school lasts for two years, followed by four years of upper secondary school. Students may leave upper secondary school after two years and enroll in a three-year technical training program.		Students Per Teacher, Primary School
		40.9 (2012)
		Students Per Teacher, Secondary School
		37.9 (2012)
Mandatory Education		Enrollment in Tertiary Education
7 years, from ages 7 to 14.		12,039 (2010)
Average Years Spent in School for Current Students		Enrollment in Tertiary Education, Male
		8,739 (2010)
4 (2010)		Enrollment in Tertiary Education, Female
Average Years Spent in School for Current Students, Male		3,300 (2010)
		Literacy
5 (2012)		70% (2012)

Energy and Natural Resources	Land Borders
Electric Power Generation	1,013 miles
292,500,000 kilowatt hours per year (estimate) (2010)	**Coastline**
	1,388 miles
Electric Power Consumption	**Capital**
253,500,000 kilowatt hours per year (estimate) (2010)	Asmara
	Area
Nuclear Power Plants	46,774 sq. miles
0 (2014)	**Climate**
Crude Oil Production	The climate is semiarid in the western lowland areas, where rainfall is less than 20 inches a year, and wetter and cooler in the central highlands, which receive an average 40 inches of rain annually. Temperatures range from an average 63°F in the highlands to 86°F in the lowlands. There is a hot desert strip along the Red Sea coastline, and some of the highest temperatures on Earth—often topping 122°F—have been recorded in the southeastern Danakil Depression.
0 barrels per day (2013)	
Crude Oil Consumption	
4,700 barrels per day (2012)	
Natural Gas Production	
0 cubic meters per year (estimate) (2011)	
Natural Gas Consumption	
0 cubic meters per year (estimate) (2010)	
Natural Resources	
Gold, potash, zinc, copper, salt, possibly oil and natural gas, fish	**Land Use**
Environment	5% cropland; 40% permanent pasture; 5% forests and woodland; 50% other.
CO2 Emissions	**Arable Land**
0.1 metric tons per capita (2009)	6% (2007)
Alternative and Nuclear Energy	**Arable Land Per Capita**
0.0% of total energy use (2010)	0 acres per person (2007)
Threatened Species	Health
97 (2010)	**Average Life Expectancy**
Protected Areas	63.5 years (2014)
6,044 (estimate) (2010)	**Average Life Expectancy, Male**
Geography	61.4 years (2014)
Location	**Average Life Expectancy, Female**
Located in eastern Africa, Eritrea is bounded by Sudan to the northwest, by Djibouti to the southeast, and by Ethiopia to the south and west. Its northeastern coastline along the Red Sea stretches for almost 620 miles. The Dahlak islands are part of Eritrean territory.	65.7 years (2014)
	Crude Birth Rate
	30.0 (estimate) (2015)
	Crude Death Rate
	7.5 (estimate) (2015)
	Maternal Mortality
Time Zone	630 per 100,000 live births (2005–2012 projection)
8 hours ahead of U.S. Eastern Standard	

Infant Mortality	**Total Government Revenues**
37 per 1,000 live births (2012)	$968,800,000 (estimate) (2013)
Doctors	**Total Government Expenditures**
0.1 per 1,000 people (2004)	$1,417,000,000 (estimate) (2013)
Industry and Labor	**Budget Deficit**
Gross Domestic Product (GDP) - official exchange rate	-13.0 (estimate) (2013)
	GDP Contribution by Sector
$4,346,000,000 (estimate) (2015)	agriculture: 12.4% industry: 29.2% services: 58.4% (2012 est.)
GDP per Capita	
$644 (estimate) (2015)	**External Debt**
GDP - Purchasing Power Parity (PPP)	$1,094,000,000 (estimate) (2013)
$4,619,000,000 (estimate) (2013)	**Economic Aid Extended**
GDP (PPP) per Capita	$0 (2011)
$792 (estimate) (2013)	**Economic Aid Received**
Industry Products	$163,000,000 (2011)
Textiles, beverages, foodstuffs, footwear, cement.	**Population**
	Population
Agriculture Products	6,527,689 (estimate) (2015)
Sorghum, lentils, potatoes, maize, vegetables, coffee, millet, maize, barley, wheat, livestock.	**World Population Rank**
	107 th (2010)
Unemployment	**Population Density**
7.9% (2012)	127.0 people per square mile (estimate) (2011)
Labor Profile	**Population Distribution**
agriculture: 80% industry and services: 20% (estimate) (2004)	22% urban (2011)
	Age Distribution
Military	0-14: 42.5%
Total Active Armed Forces	15-64: 53.9%
201,750 (2010)	65+: 3.6%
Active Armed Forces	(2009)
4% (2010)	**Median Age**
Annual Military Expenditures	19.1 years (estimate) (2014)
$65,000,000 (2005)	**Population Growth Rate**
Military Service	2.3% per year (estimate) (2015)
Service in the Eritrean military is by conscription, with terms lasting 18 months.	**Net Migration Rate**
	0.0 (estimate) (2015)
	Trade
National Finances	**Imported Goods**
Currency	Machinery and transportation equipment, food, livestock, chemicals, petroleum products.
Nafka	

Total Value of Imports	Transportation		
$738,000,000 (2010)	**Airports**		
Exported Goods	13 (2012)		
Food, livestock, chemicals, tobacco, beverages, sorghum.	**Paved Roads**		
Total Value of Exports	21.8% (2008)		
$304,500,000 (estimate) (2012)	**Roads, Unpaved**		
Import Partners	1,949 (2000)		
Saudi Arabia - 20.7%; India - 13.6%; Italy - 12.6%; China - 9.9%; United States - 5.1% (2008)	**Passenger Cars per 1,000 People**		
	6 (2007)		
Current Account Balance	**Railroads**		
$-210,100,000 (estimate) (2013)	190 (2008)		
Weights and Measures	**Ports**		
The metric system is in use.	Major: 2—Massawa, Assab.		

OVERVIEW

Located in northeastern Africa, the nation of Eritrea has a 750-mile coastline along the Red Sea and is bordered by Ethiopia—from which it seceded in 1991—to the south and west. The nation also borders Djibouti to the southeast and Sudan to the northwest. Geographically, the majority of Eritrea can be divided into four regions: the central highlands, the eastern lowlands, the western lowlands, and the Danakil Desert in the southwest. The country is relatively mountainous, with the central highlands rising to an average elevation near 6,500 feet in the center, where the Ethiopian Plateau enters Eritrea and gradually slopes downward toward the sea to the east and the deserts of Sudan to the west. The Eritrean climate varies a great deal according to elevation and location. The eastern coastal desert is one of the hottest places on Earth, while temperatures in the highlands are very cool. Eritrea has a population of about 6.4 million, and the capital is Asmara.

GOVERNMENT

Eritrea is a unitary state established officially when it declared its independence from Ethiopia on May 24, 1993. The Eritrean Constitution of 1997 established a presidential regime with a limited form of political pluralism and a transitional legislature; however, as of 2014 the Constitution had yet to be fully implemented, and power remains in the hands of President Issaias Afewerki. The Constitution vests legislative power in the National Assembly, which elects the president but has not yet been formed.

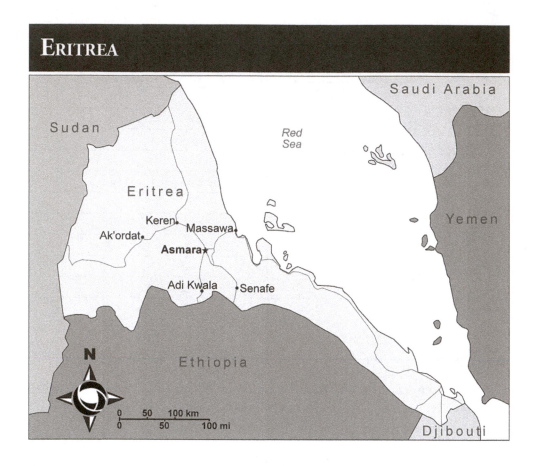

ERITREA

Constitution

A new Eritrean Constitution was adopted in May 1997. The document established the broad executive authority of the president, vested legislative authority in the National Assembly, and created a separate judiciary. No timetable has been established, however, for the complete implementation of the charter.

Executive

The May 1997 Constitution establishes a presidential form of government. The head of state is elected by the legislature to a five-year term, renewable once, and is empowered to appoint a cabinet. The president may be removed from office on a two-thirds vote of the National Assembly. Due to the repeated postponement of popular elections to the National Assembly, however, the transitional legislature has not held a presidential election since June 1993.

Legislature

Supreme legislative authority is vested in a National Assembly, whose members are to be directly elected. Balloting for the new legislature has been postponed indefinitely, however, with the current transitional body made up according to previous guidelines in which People's Front for Democracy and Justice holds no less than 75 of the 150 seats. The National Assembly ratifies changes to the cabinet.

Judiciary

Judicial power is vested in a Supreme Court, to be presided over by a chief justice. Eritrea's legal system is based on customary and Islamic law, along with laws adopted by the Eritrean People's Liberation Front both before and after formal independence in May 1993. The new Constitution provides for independent courts.

Local Government

Eritrea is divided into six provinces.

Election Qualifications

All citizens 18 years of age and older are eligible to vote.

POLITICS

Issaias Afewerki, the leader of the People's Front for Democracy and Justice (PFDJ), has served as Eritrea's first president since 1993. It was the PFDJ, formerly known as the Eritrean People's Liberation Front, that fought for more than 20 years to achieve Eritrean independence from the regime of Ethiopian dictator Mengistu Haile Mariam. Following the adoption of a new constitution in 1997, a transitional legislature was created, comprising PFDJ leaders and other former legislators, and empowered with legislative authority pending new elections initially scheduled for 1998. Elections were postponed when an escalating border conflict with Ethiopia erupted into war in May 1998. For two years the countries fought bloody trench warfare battles, reminiscent of World War I, that left an estimated 100,000 soldiers dead. A peace agreement signed on June 18, 2000, ended the conflict, returned sovereignty of the disputed areas to Ethiopia, and established a 15-mile demilitarized buffer zone in Eritrean territory.

In October 2000, the transitional National Assembly announced that elections would be held in 2001, but the government again postponed them, creating a major rift within the PFDJ. That same month, a group of Eritrean intellectuals met in the German capital of Berlin, where they drafted an open letter to Issaias, criticizing

Eritrea's slow path to democracy and accusing him of abandoning his party's ideals and pursuing authoritarian tactics. Issaias ordered the arrests of numerous editors to prevent the publication of the "Berlin Manifesto" in Eritrea, but it circulated on the Internet, and in May 2001 was followed by an open letter signed by 15 of the PDFJ's most prominent leaders, including top members of Issaias's cabinet and the Eritrean military. The letter's signatories, known as the Group of 15, accused Issaias of failing to implement the 1997 Constitution and began campaigning against his policies in the media. Issaias responded with a swift crackdown, arresting numerous dissenters and banning all privately run newspapers. Eleven members of the Group of 15 remain in prison. Legislative elections have yet to be held.

In the years since, Issaias has grown increasingly heavy-handed in repressing criticism. His actions have brought condemnation from international groups and an investigation of human rights violations by the United Nations.

Political Parties

A limited multiparty political system is provided for in the new Constitution (1997), which has not yet been fully implemented. The government is dominated by the PFDJ, originally formed as the Eritrean People's Liberation Front (EPLF).

Isaias Afwerki, President of Eritrea since the country became independent in 1993. He is also the head of the People's Front for Democracy and Justice, which is the only legal political party in Eritrea. (HANDOUT/MCT/Newscom)

The EPLF was formed in 1970 as a breakaway group of the Eritrean Liberation Front (ELF). It led the fight for Eritrea's independence and formed transitional governments in May 1991 and again in May 1993. It transformed itself into a political party (the PFDJ) in February 1994.

The ELF was formed in 1958 and launched its armed struggle against the Ethiopian government in 1961. It eventually split into a number of factions, including the ELF–Central Leadership (ELF-CL), the ELF–National Council (ELF-NC), the ELF–Revolutionary Council (ELF-RC), and the ELF–United Organization (ELF-UO).

The Eritrean Islamic Jihad, an extremist organization that is largely based in Sudan, reportedly joined with the ELF-NC to form the opposition Eritrean National Alliance in 1996.

ECONOMY

Eritrea once enjoyd some of Africa's most advanced infrastructure as well as a thriving middle class. However, after years of war Eritrea is now one of the poorest countries in Africa. Agricultural production, the mainstay of the economy, was devastated by the bloody border war with Ethiopia. Continuing drought and the government's emphasis on military spending over economic investment have plunged the

An Eritrean soldier stands guard at the Tserona Resettlement Camp, near the border with Ethiopia. Eritrea was merged with Ethiopia during the 1930s and continued as part of Ethiopia until it became independent in 1993 after a protracted conflict. Another major war between Eritrea and Ethiopia was fought from 1998 to 2000, and there remains considerable tension along the boundary between the two countries. (ERIC MENCHER/KRT/Newscom)

nation's residents deeper into famine and poverty. In 2011, the UN estimated that 70% of Eritreans needed outside help to meet their food needs. The government however, insists Eritrea does not need food aid and refuses to accept it.

Despite these difficulties, agricultural production remains the foundation of the economy, with some 80% of Eritreans involved in farming or raising livestock. Principal crops include barley, millet, teff (a local grain), wheat, and sorghum, though cereal output remains well below average. Potential growth areas for the economy include the exploitation of possible oil and gas reserves beneath the Red Sea, as well as known deposits of zinc, magnesium, potash, and marble. In addition, high-grade gold and copper were discovered in the western part of the country in 2004, and the development of fisheries has the potential to yield considerable catches. Eritrea's main trade partners include the United States, Malaysia, Germany, and Italy. Eritrea's currency is the nafka. Widespread government ownership of businesses, along with the nation's poor communications systems, hinder economic progress. The United Nations' International Telecommunications Union has declared Eritrea the least connected country on Earth, with only 1% of its residents going online regularly and only 1% having a landline and 5.6% having a mobile phone.

SOCIETY

The inhabitants of Eritrea comprise nine major ethnic groups, including the Tigrinya, who reside in the south central region, the Tigre, who live in the north, and the Afar, who reside in the southeastern part of Eritrea. The remaining ethnic groups are the Saho, in the south central and southeastern region; the Beni Amir in the west; the Bilien in the central section; the Rashaida, who inhabit the northwest; and the Kunama and Nara, who make their homes in the southwest part of the country. At least 12 languages are spoken in Eritrea. There is no official language of Eritrea, but Tigrinya, Arabic, and English are used extensively for government, business, and commercial affairs. Tigre is also spoken by more than half of the population. Most Eritreans are adherents of the Christian and Muslim religions, with smaller minorities embracing animism.

Ethnic Composition

Eritrea has nine recognized ethnic groups: Tigrinya – 55%; Tigre – 30%; Saho – 4%; Kunama – 2%; Rashaida – 2%; Bilen – 2%; other (Afar, Beni Amir, Nera) – 5%

Language

Eritrea has nine main language groups: Tigrinya, Tigre, Kunama, Hedareb, Afar, Bilien, Saho, Nara, and Rashaida. While Arabic is widely used, English is the language of instruction at secondary school and university levels.

Religion

Sunni Muslims – 50%; Orthodox Christians – 30%; Roman Catholics – 13%; indigenous beliefs – 2%; other (including Protestants, Seventh-day Adventists, Jehovah's Witnesses, and Bahais) – 5%

CONTEMPORARY ISSUES

Crop Failures

Although more than three-quarters of Eritreans are subsistence farmers, droughts and military conflicts have turned famine and malnutrition into common occurrences. With deserts dominating the terrain, less than 5% of Eritrea's land is considered suitable for growing crops, and there are no rivers that provide a constant, reliable source of water. The 1998–2000 border war with Ethiopia contributed to the devastation of what forests Eritrea did have, and resulted in the slaughter of hundreds of thousands of cattle. Following the war, crop production in Eritrea dropped 62% and has never fully recovered, meaning Eritreans are engaged in an ongoing struggle to raise enough food to feed themselves. In addition, Eritrea's large defense force demands large numbers of troops, keeping many farmers away from their fields and siphons off government spending that might have gone to agricultural improvement projects.

In an attempt to cope with crop failures and food shortages at the height of a famine in 2006, the government established a program employing Eritreans in projects to improve food security, including irrigation and road building. The government, which has touted self-reliance in food production, proclaimed this as a long-term solution preferable to the short-term fixes of food aid. However, it gained the ire of donor nations by funding the program through the sale of donated food intended to go to famine-plagued Eritreans. In May 2006, authorities declared that the nation would no longer accept food aid. Although the food security situation worsened in 2011, due to insufficient rains, and remains difficult, the government continues to be committed to self-reliance. Today, the nation produces between 25% and 60% of its food needs, depending on drought and other variables.

Restive Population

The web site run by Eritrea's information ministry describes a young country making rapid gains—one that provides exemplary health care in facilities it has worked tirelessly to upgrade, that offers boundless educational opportunities, including widespread computer training, and whose young people are pitching in to help replant devastated forests and help the families of fallen soldiers. But the estimated 3,000 refugees streaming across the nation's borders in all directions each month tell a different story. In an effort to maintain tight control over the population, Eritrea's leaders have enacted policies that have resulted in international criticism and alienated the country from its neighbors. Many international organizations charge that those policies, combined with ongoing economic struggles, are driving Eritreans from their homeland.

In October 2013, some 400 North Africans died when two boats sank off the coast of Italy. The overloaded vessels were ferrying refugees, including many from Eritrea, trying to enter Europe illegally. Human rights organizations estimated that in the first seven months of 2014, some 63,000 North Africans fled their home countries for Europe. While many were escaping the disintegrating Somalia, a significant portion had left Eritrea. In June of that year, four of the country's Catholic bishops published a letter in which they described Eritrea as "desolate" because so many of its adult males have either fled the country or are away serving in the military. Many observers said the bishops put themselves at risk by writing the letter in a country widely regarded as one of the most repressive in the world. In 2012, four Eritrean athletes, including the 18-year-old runner who was the country's flag bearer in Olympic opening ceremonies, sought asylum in the United Kingdom during the 2012 London Games. At the time, the flag bearer, Weynay Ghebresilasie, said it was Eritrea's "harsh conditions and lack of basic human rights which has compelled me to seek asylum." Three years earlier, the entire Eritrean national soccer team sought refuge in Kenya during a soccer match there. Also in 2014, the government confirmed that its longtime minister of information had fled the country as well.

Freedoms Denied

In addition to poverty, one reason cited for the large numbers of people leaving Eritrea is the requirement of military and national service for nearly all males between the ages of 18 and 40 and most females between 18 and 27. Due to ongoing hostilities with its neighbors, Eritrea has maintained a large fighting force, with 5% of the population actively serving in the military. Although service officially is for 18 months, in reality Eritreans are conscripted indefinitely. The maintenance of such a large military infrastructure has been a tremendous economic burden to this poor country. In 2013, Eritrea's national budget was an estimated $806 million, but more than one-third of that was thought to be spent on defense. Military service has become such a burden that some human rights groups compare it to indentured servitude.

In 2014, the United Nations began a year-long investigation of what it called "systemic" human rights violations in Eritrea, including widespread torture. Eritrean leaders reject the allegations. As the only African nation with no privately owned media, Eritrea has been criticized as having "no freedom of expression" by the international press freedom group Reporters Without Borders. President Issaias Afewerki has all but silenced dissent since his election in 1993, frequently imprisoning journalists for expressing views in conflict with those of the government. In the midst of debate over elections that had been slated for 2001, the government closed all private publications and media outlets for "endangering national security." All of Eritrea's newspapers, radio stations, and television stations are now run by the government, which strictly controls their output.

Territorial Disputes

Border disputes with Ethiopia, Yemen, and Djibouti have left Eritrea with a large and expensive military defense force, as well as tense relations with its neighbors. When the rebel groups claimed independence from Ethiopia in 1993, the border between the two nations was not formally drawn. The resulting disputes over the border led to a 1998 war that ended in a cease-fire two years later. Then, in 2002, a United Nations (UN) panel established an official boundary between the two countries. Ethiopia has disputed the decision (although its appeal was rejected), and UN peacekeepers remained in the border zone until 2008 to prevent further conflict. Several skirmishes have occurred since that time.

In 1995, Eritrea fought Yemen over the Hanish Islands in the Red Sea, which separates the two countries. The islands lie along an important shipping route between Africa and the Middle East and may host significant petroleum reserves in their surrounding waters. Yemen officially won control over the islands in 1998. Also in the 1990s, Eritrea fought twice with Djibouti over its border with that nation. Although that conflict eventually died down, tensions rose once more in 2008, when Djibouti accused Eritrea of amassing troops near the border. In 2010, the two nations decided to resolve their disagreement peacefully.

Excerpt from the Constitution of Eritrea

The Constitution of Eritrea was drafted in 1994, shortly after Eritrea became independent of Ethiopia in 1993. The Constitution, which was adopted formally in 1997, specifies that Eritrea is to be a parliamentary democracy. However, Eritrea has been governed as a one-party dictatorship since independence, and the government has been accused of numerous violations of human rights and has yet to implement the Constitution in practice. National elections have not been held since Eritrea became independent.

Although these clauses are ignored in practice, the Constitution guarantees equality under the law and states that "It is a fundamental principle of the State of Eritrea to guarantee its citizens broad and active participation in all political, economic, social and cultural life of the country." It specifies that those who have been accused of crimes are entitled to the due process of law and the presumption of innocence until guilt is proven. Also, the Constitution guarantees freedom of speech, freedom of the press, the right to vote, and freedom of assembly. Additionally, the Constitution makes reference to various other rights, including the right to "equal access to publicly funded social services." However, these and other rights are subject to limitation when they are deemed to be contrary to "the interests of national security, public safety, or the economic well-being of the country."

Note: This constitution was ratified in 1997 but has not been implemented by the current regime.

Article 7 - Democratic Principles

1. It is a fundamental principle of the State of Eritrea to guarantee its citizens broad and active participation in all political, economic, social and cultural life of the country.
2. Any act that violates the human rights of women or limits or otherwise thwarts their role and participation is prohibited.
3. There shall be established appropriate institutions to encourage and develop people's initiative and participation in their communities.
4. ... all Eritreans, without distinction, are guaranteed equal opportunity to participate in any position of leadership in the country.

Article 8 - Economic and Social Development

1. The State shall strive to create opportunities to ensure the fulfillment of citizens' rights to social justice and economic development and to fulfill their material and spiritual needs.

CHAPTER III: FUNDAMENTAL RIGHTS, FREEDOMS AND DUTIES

Article 14 - Equality under the Law

1. All persons are equal under the law.
2. No person may be discriminated against on account of race, ethnic origin, language, colour, gender, religion, disability, age, political view, or social or economic status or any other improper factors.
3. The National Assembly shall enact laws that can assist in eliminating inequalities existing in the Eritrean society.

Article 15 - Right to Life and Liberty

1. No person shall be deprived of life without due process of law.
2. No person shall be deprived of liberty without due process of law.

Article 16 - Right to Human Dignity

1. The dignity of all persons shall be inviolable.
2. No person shall be subjected to torture or to cruel, inhuman or degrading treatment or punishment.
3. No person shall be held in slavery or servitude nor shall any person be required to perform forced labour not authorised by law

Article 17 - Arrest, Detention and Fair Trial

1. No person may be arrested or detained save pursuant to due process of law.
2. No person shall be tried or convicted for any act or omission which did not constitute a criminal offence at the time when it was committed.
3. Every person arrested or detained shall be informed of the grounds for his arrest or detention and of the rights he has . . . in a language he understands.
4. Every person who is held in detention shall be brought before a court of law within forty-eight (48) hours of his arrest, and if this is not reasonably possible, as soon as possible . . .
5. Every person shall have the right to petition a court of law for a Writ of Habeas Corpus. Where the arresting officer fails to . . . provide the reason for his arrest, the court shall . . . order the release of the prisoner.
6. Every person charged with an offence shall be entitled to a fair, speedy and public hearing by a court of law; provided, however, that such a court may exclude the press and the public from all or any part of the trial for reasons of morals or national security, as may be necessary in a just and democratic society.
7. A person charged with an offence shall be presumed to be innocent . . . unless he is found guilty by a court of law.
8. Where an accused is convicted, he shall have the right to appeal. No person shall be liable to be tried again for any criminal offence on which judgment has been rendered.

Article 18 - Right to Privacy

1. Every person shall have the right to privacy.
2. (a) No person shall be subject to body search, nor shall his premises be entered into or searched or his communications, correspondence, or other property be interfered with, without reasonable cause.
   (b) No search warrant shall issue, save upon probable cause, supported by oath, and particularly describing the place to be searched, and the persons or things to be seized

Article 19 - Freedom of Conscience, Religion, Expression of Opinion, Movement, Assembly and Organisation

1. Every person shall have the right to freedom of thought, conscience and belief.
2. Every person shall have the freedom of speech and expression, including freedom of the press and other media.
3. Every citizen shall have the right of access to information.
4. Every person shall have the freedom to practice any religion . . .
5. All persons shall have the right to assemble and to demonstrate peaceably . . .
6. Every citizen shall have the right to form organisations for political, social, economic and cultural ends.
7. Every citizen shall have the right to practice any lawful profession, or engage in any occupation or trade.

Article 20 - Right to Vote and to be a Candidate to an Elective Office

Every citizen who fulfils the requirements of the electoral law shall have the right to vote and to seek elective office.

Article 21 - Economic, Social and Cultural Rights and Responsibilities

1. Every citizen shall have the right of equal access to publicly funded social services. The State shall endeavor . . . to make available to all citizens health, education, cultural and other social services.
2. The State shall secure, within available means, the social welfare of all citizens and particularly those disadvantaged.
8. Every citizen shall have the right to move freely throughout Eritrea or reside and settle in any part thereof.
9. Every citizen shall have the right to leave and return to Eritrea . . .

Article 22 - Family

1. The family is the natural and fundamental unit of society and is entitled to the protection and special care of the State and society.
2. Men and women of full legal age shall have the right, upon their consent, to marry and to found a family freely, without any discrimination and they shall have equal rights and duties . . .
3. Parents have the right and duty to bring up their children with due care and affection; and, in turn, children have the right and the duty to respect their parents and to sustain them in their old age.

Article 23 - Right to Property

1. . . . any citizen shall have the right, any where in Eritrea, to acquire and dispose property, individually or in association with others, and to bequeath the same to his heirs or legatees.
2. All land and all natural resources . . . belongs to the State.
3. The State may, in the national or public interest, take property, subject to the payment of just compensation and in accordance with due process of law.

Article 26 - Limitation Upon Fundamental Rights and Freedoms

1. The fundamental rights and freedoms guaranteed under this Constitution may be limited only in so far as is in the interests of national security, public safety or the economic well-being of the country, health or morals, for the prevention of public disorder or crime or for the protection of the rights and freedoms of others.

Source: "The Constitution of the State of Eritrea." Embassy of the State of Eritrea. http://www.eritrean-embassy.se/government-agencies/eritrea-constitution/.

LIBYA

LIBYA

Communications	Average Circulation of Daily Newspapers
Facebook Users	Not Available
940,000 (estimate) (2013)	**Education**
Internet Users	**School System**
353,900 (2009)	The Libyan education system begins at the age of four with two years of pre-primary education. Primary school lasts for nine years, followed by four years in an academic or vocational secondary school.
Internet Users (% of Population)	
16.5% (2013)	
Television	
15 sets per 100 population (2004)	**Mandatory Education**
Land-based Telephones in Use	9 years, from ages 6 to 15.
814,000 (2012)	**Average Years Spent in School for Current Students**
Mobile Telephone Subscribers	
9,590,000 (2012)	Not Available

Average Years Spent in School for Current Students, Male	**Electric Power Consumption**
Not Available	25,240,000,000 kilowatt hours per year (estimate) (2010)
Average Years Spent in School for Current Students, Female	**Nuclear Power Plants**
Not Available	0 (2014)
Primary School–age Children Enrolled in Primary School	**Crude Oil Production**
755,338 (2006)	983,600 barrels per day (2013)
Primary School–age Males Enrolled in Primary School	**Crude Oil Consumption**
	170,400 barrels per day (2012)
395,380 (2006)	**Natural Gas Production**
Primary School–age Females Enrolled in Primary School	7,855,000,000 cubic meters per year (estimate) (2011)
359,958 (2006)	**Natural Gas Consumption**
Secondary School–age Children Enrolled in Secondary School	6,844,000,000 cubic meters per year (estimate) (2010)
732,614 (2006)	**Natural Resources**
Secondary School–age Males Enrolled in Secondary School	Natural gas, petroleum, gypsum
	Environment
345,061 (2006)	**CO_2 Emissions**
Secondary School–age Females Enrolled in Secondary School	10.0 metric tons per capita (2009)
	Alternative and Nuclear Energy
387,553 (2006)	0.0% of total energy use (2010)
Students Per Teacher, Primary School	**Threatened Species**
Not Available	44 (2010)
Students Per Teacher, Secondary School	**Protected Areas**
Not Available	1,824 (estimate) (2010)
Enrollment in Tertiary Education	**Geography**
Not Available	**Location**
Enrollment in Tertiary Education, Male	Located in North Africa, Libya is bordered by Egypt to the east, Sudan to the southeast, Chad and Niger to the south, and Algeria and Tunisia to the west. The Mediterranean Sea lies to the north.
Not Available	
Enrollment in Tertiary Education, Female	
Not Available	
Literacy	**Time Zone**
90% (2012)	6 hours ahead of U.S. Eastern Standard
Energy and Natural Resources	**Land Borders**
Electric Power Generation	2,724 miles
29,720,000,000 kilowatt hours per year (estimate) (2010)	**Coastline**
	1,100 miles

Capital	**GDP per Capita**
Tripoli	$13,294 (estimate) (2015)
Area	**GDP - Purchasing Power Parity (PPP)**
685,524 sq. miles	$94,500,000,000 (estimate) (2013)
Climate	**GDP (PPP) per Capita**
Libya's climate is hot and arid, although the coastal areas are cooler than the interior. Temperatures normally range from 55°F to 100°F.	$14,475 (estimate) (2013)
	Industry Products
	Refined petroleum, processed food, textiles, cement, handicrafts, cigarettes, olive oil.
Land Use	**Agriculture Products**
1.0% arable land; 0.2% permanent crops; 7.7% permanent meadows and pastures; 0.1% forest land; 91.0% other.	Tomatoes, barley, wheat, olives, dates, citrus fruit, peanuts, poultry, sheep.
	Unemployment
Arable Land	8.9% (2012)
1% (2007)	**Labor Profile**
Arable Land Per Capita	agriculture: 17% industry: 23% services: 59% (estimate) (2004)
1 acres per person (2007)	
Health	**Military**
Average Life Expectancy	**Total Active Armed Forces**
76.0 years (2014)	76,000 (estimate) (2010)
Average Life Expectancy, Male	**Active Armed Forces**
74.4 years (2014)	1% (2010)
Average Life Expectancy, Female	**Annual Military Expenditures**
77.8 years (2014)	$800,000,000 (estimate) (2008)
Crude Birth Rate	**Military Service**
18.0 (estimate) (2015)	Military service is by selective conscription, with terms lasting one to two years.
Crude Death Rate	
3.6 (estimate) (2015)	**National Finances**
Maternal Mortality	**Currency**
97 per 100,000 live births (2005–2012 projection)	Libyan dinar
	Total Government Revenues
Infant Mortality	$41,540,000,000 (estimate) (2013)
13 per 1,000 live births (2012)	**Total Government Expenditures**
Doctors	$41,870,000,000 (estimate) (2013)
1.9 per 1,000 people (2010)	**Budget Deficit**
Industry and Labor	-0.5 (estimate) (2013)
Gross Domestic Product (GDP) - official exchange rate	**GDP Contribution by Sector**
	agriculture: 1.6% industry: 43.5% services: 54.9% (2012 est.)
$83,825,000,000 (estimate) (2015)	

External Debt	Exported Goods
$6,319,000,000 (estimate) (2013)	Petroleum and petroleum products, natural gas.
Economic Aid Extended	
$0 (2011)	Total Value of Exports
Economic Aid Received	$51,480,000,000 (estimate) (2012)
$642,000,000 (2011)	Import Partners
Population	Italy - 17.4%; China - 10.3%; Turkey - 9.2%; Germany - 9.1%; South Korea - 6.3% (2009 estimate)
Population	
6,411,776 (estimate) (2015)	
World Population Rank	Export Partners
104 th (2009)	Italy - 37.5%; Germany - 10.1%; France - 8.4%; China - 8.4%; United States - 5.3% (2009 estimate).
Population Density	
9.6 people per square mile (estimate) (2011)	Current Account Balance
Population Distribution	$2,727,000,000 (estimate) (2013)
78% urban (2011)	Weights and Measures
Age Distribution	The metric system is used.
0-14: 32.9%	**Transportation**
15-64: 62.6%	Airports
65+: 4.5%	144 (2012)
(2009)	Paved Roads
Median Age	57.2% (2001)
27.5 years (estimate) (2014)	Roads, Unpaved
Population Growth Rate	26,601 (2003)
2.7% per year (estimate) (2015)	Passenger Cars per 1,000 People
Net Migration Rate	225 (2007)
7.8 (estimate) (2015)	Number of Trucks, Buses, and Commercial Vehicles
Trade	195,500 (2001)
Imported Goods	Railroads
Machinery and transportation equipment, basic manufactures, food, beverages, livestock, tobacco, chemicals, animal and vegetable oils.	Not Available
	Ports
Total Value of Imports	Major: 9—including Benghazi, Mersa Brega, Tripoli, Ras Lanouf, Zawiyah.
$21,500,000,000 (estimate) (2009)	

OVERVIEW

Libya lies on North Africa's Mediterranean coast between Tunisia and Egypt, and also borders Algeria, Chad, Niger, and Sudan. With a land area of 679,362 square miles, Libya is the fourth largest country by land area in Africa. The country

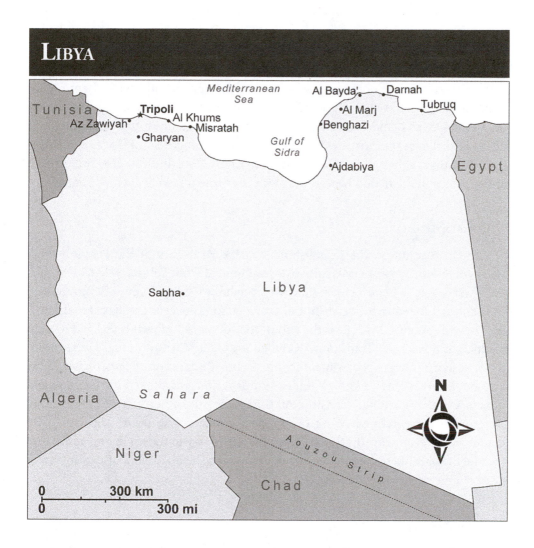

LIBYA

can be divided topographically into four major areas: the Mediterranean coast, the Nafusah Plateau, the Akhdar Mountains, and the Sahara Desert. Of these, the Sahara occupies by far the largest portion of Libya's land, covering some 90% of the country. Two coastal lowland areas are the only agricultural regions: Tripolitania along the northwestern shore and Cyrenaica along the northeastern shore. Libya swelters under an extremely hot, dry climate throughout most of its territory, and it lacks suitable fresh water. Libya has a population of about 6.2 million, and its capital is Tripoli.

GOVERNMENT

Once an Italian colony, Libya became independent on December 24, 1951, following its occupation by French and British forces during World War II. The Libyan government, officially called the Great Socialist People's Libyan Arab Jamahiriya, was a military dictatorship under the regime of Col. Muammar Gaddafi from 1969 until his ouster in August 2011 and death two months later.

After Gaddafi's death, leaders of the revolution crafted a temporary government that included a transitional congress, and called for a prime minister and a president to be chosen by the congress. The transitional government was to be the foundation for a new Libyan democracy. In 2012, Libyan people had their first opportunity in decades to choose their representatives to a national congress in a free and fair election. However, although work continues on a new Constitution, growing turmoil and violence in the nation has left the new government largely dysfunctional.

Constitution

The Declaration on the Establishment of the Authority of the People, which was adopted during a special legislative session held from February 28 to March 2, 1977, served as the country's basic law throughout Gaddafi's reign. It announced the nation's adherence to socialism and provided for a government based on Islamic law. In early August 2011, near the end of the successful Libyan revolt that ousted Gaddafi, the National Transitional Council passed a "Constitutional Declaration" to serve as an interim governing document. This declaration specified civil rights and public freedoms unknown under Gaddafi, and guaranteed an independent judiciary. The transitional Constitution is in place until a permanent Constitution is completed and ratified. Work on the permanent Constitution began in 2014. Under the interim Constitution, Islam is identified as the state religion, and sharia is to be the guiding source for legislation. However, the document also grants freedom of religion to non-Muslims.

Executive

Under the interim government that replaced Gaddafi's regime, a president and a prime minister are elected by the legislature.

Legislature

Under the interim government, political authority is vested in an elected 200-member General National Congress (GNC). In 2014, the GNC changed its name to the House of Representatives. A president and a prime minister are elected by the congress; the latter appoints a Cabinet to be approved by the congress.

Judiciary

Under the interim constitution, the court system consists of a Supreme Court, Courts of Appeals, and Courts of First Instance.

Local Government

Libya is divided into 22 districts.

Election Qualifications

All citizens 18 years of age or older are eligible to vote.

POLITICS

When Col. Muammar Gaddafi seized power in a 1969 military coup against King Idris I, his regime had two main focuses: retaining power and exporting Arab revolution. A failed coup attempt in 1984, led by Libyan exiles with internal support from Gaddafi opponents, was suppressed harshly and led to a reign of terror in which thousands were executed. Gaddafi's support of international terrorism isolated Libya from the Western world and caused the United States, the United Nations, and others, to impose economic sanctions on the country. In 2003, the United Nations Security Council lifted sanctions on Libya after the government took responsibility for the 1988 bombing of an airliner over Scotland that killed 270 people. In addition, Gaddafi agreed to compensate victims' families. That same year, the Libyan government announced it was abandoning efforts to develop weapons of mass destruction. In May 2006, the United States restored diplomatic ties with Libya.

Gaddafi's 42-year authoritarian rule ended in August 2011, when rebel forces that had been fighting for his ouster for months routed his compound in Tripoli. The rebels' organization, the National Transitional Council (NTC) took control of the country. Gaddafi escaped to his hometown of Sirte, where he was killed on October 20, 2011, as NTC forces took the town. The NTC governed until August 2012, when it dissolved after handing over authority to a newly created General National Congress (GNC), whose 200 members had been elected the month before. Following the election, the GNC appointed an interim president, Mohamed Yousef el-Magariaf, and later an interim prime minister, Ali Zeidan.

El-Magariaf, a former ambassador under Gaddafi, was forced to resign in May 2013, after the passage of a law forbidding senior figures from the Gaddafi regime from holding senior positions in the new government. Nouri Abusahmain was chosen as the new interim president. Zeidan was ousted in March 2014 and later fled the country.

On April 21, 2014, members of the newly elected Constitutional Assembly gathered to begin the process of drafting a new constitution. However, turmoil within that group left them widely discredited and dysfunctional. For a month in 2014, disagreement within the assembly led to Libya having two prime ministers, each claiming rights to the office. A court declared Abdullah al-Thani the rightful prime

Muammar Gaddafi was the ruler of Libya for 42 years, until he was deposed and killed in 2011. Gaddafi was the leader of a coup d'etat that deposed Libya's monarchy in 1969. He was condemned widely by the international community for numerous human rights abuses and support for terrorist activities. (Barry Iverson Photography/Newscom)

minster and his rival, Ahmed Maiteeq, stepped down. In the summer of 2014, the GNC was replaced by a new governing body, the House of Representatives. The 200 members of that body were chosen from among nearly 2,000 candidates in a June 2014 election that many hoped would provide a fresh start for Libya's struggling new democracy. Unlike the 2012 election, candidates in 2014 all ran as independents; party affiliations were not included on the ballot. Only 1.5 million people registered to vote in that election, just over half the number for the previous elections.

Nevertheless, the newly elected Libyan House of Representatives replaced the GNC and relocated from Tripoli to the eastern city of Benghazi, where the 2011 revolution began. The move was viewed as an attempt to reunite a country divided along geographic as well as ideological lines. In addition to fighting between extreme Islamist and anti-Islamist groups, there has been discord between eastern Libyans and those in the west. Eastern Libyans, who had felt marginalized since Gaddafi's rule, had been pushing for a federalist Libya that would grant autonomy to two distinct regions, east and west.

Hopes that the 2014 elections would provide a fresh start for Libya's new democracy suffered another blow in August, when al-Thani resigned as prime minister and called for a new government to be formed. By then, violence had forced the Constitutional Assembly out of Benghazi, to a third location in the town of Tobruk.

Political Parties

The only legal political organization from 1971 until Gaddafi's ouster was the Arab Socialist Union (ASU), whose functions were taken over after the 2011 revolution by the General People's Congress. In 2012, the country's first free elections in decades brought masses of people to the polls, where they had dozens of active political parties on the ballot to choose from. In the June 2014 elections, nearly 2,000 candidates were on the ballot, each as independents; party affiliations were excluded from the ballot.

Like the Egyptian party of the same name after which it was modeled, the Arab Socialist Union (ASU) was formed to promote national unity and serve as a link between government and the people. Under Gaddafi, it was less a political party than a vehicle for uniting many elements of Libyan society and providing people with a sense of involvement in local, regional, and national government.

The National Front for the Salvation of Libya (NFSL), formed in Sudan in 1981, was one of many political opposition parties formed by expatriate groups to oppose Gaddafi's government. These groups had little impact on internal Libyan affairs. NFSL was the major organized opposition to Gaddafi's government.

The new National Forces Alliance (NFA), a coalition of moderate political organizations, nongovernmental organizations, and independents, prevailed in the 2012 elections, winning 39 seats of the 80 allotted to party lists. The NFA seeks a democratic civil society, based on a moderate view of Islam.

The Justice and Construction Party, or Justice and Development (Hizb Al-Adala Wal-Bina), founded March 3, 2012, is the Libyan arm of the Muslim Brotherhood. The party advocates a government based on moderate Islam and is widely reported to be a dominant force in Libyan politics. Its showing in the 2012 elections was second only to the NFA.

The National Front Party (Hizb Al-Jabha Al-Wataniyya—NFP) formed in 2012 and is the successor to the NFSL. The NFP claimed three assembly seats in the 2012 elections. It is considered a progressive, liberal party, and one that favors democracy, women's rights, and economic development. It also has made caring for veterans of the 2011 revolution a priority.

ECONOMY

Oil was discovered in Libya in 1959 and was the backbone of the Gaddafi regime's socialist-driven economy. Oil accounted for almost all export earnings and about a quarter of the nation's gross domestic product, which, per capita, has been one of the highest in Africa. Foreign investment in Libya's vital petroleum industry increased after the suspension of UN sanctions in 2006, but little of that wealth trickled down to average Libyans. At the start of the Libyan revolt of 2011, the country was producing 1.7 million barrels a day, to rank it 17th in the world. The revolt inevitably disrupted oil production, but it has rebounded in the wake of the revolt's success and the formation of a government, even as turmoil continues. Unemployment remains high, at an estimated 30%. In addition to oil, food processing and cement production are also important industries. The harsh climate and topography make farming almost impossible, so Libya imports much of its food. However, the Great Manmade River project, the world's largest water redistribution system, is attempting to reclaim some land for cultivation. Libya is a member of the Organization of Petroleum Exporting Countries, and its main trading partners are Italy, Germany, and Spain.

SOCIETY

The vast majority of the population is of mixed Berber and Arab descent, and while virtually everyone speaks Arabic, in certain communities in the mountain regions traditional Berber culture is stronger. Most Libyans, Arab and Berber alike, are Sunni Muslims. The population in the western section is more cosmopolitan with the influences of Berber, Sudanese Africans, and Turks, while the eastern section is more conservative. Before World War II Libya was home to many Italians and Jews, most of whom left during and after the war. Libya had been host to a large number of foreign workers from Africa, Asia, Europe, and the Middle East. The violence and instability during and after the 2011 revolution, however, has driven many of these workers out of the country.

Ethnic Composition

Arab and Berber – 97%; other (including Egyptian, Greek, Indian, Italian, Maltese, Pakistani, Tunisian, and Turkish) – 3%

Language

Arabic is Libya's official language, but English and Italian are widely spoken in the major cities. A number of Berber languages are spoken as well (Nafusi, Ghadamis, Suknah, Awjilah, Tamasheq).

Religion

Muslim (official; virtually all Sunni) – 96.6%; Christian – 2.7%; Buddhist – 0.3%; Hindu – less than .1%; Jewish – less than .1%; folk religion – less than .1%; unaffiliated – 0.2%; other – less than .1%

CONTEMPORARY ISSUES

Transition to Democracy—and Turmoil

Following the ouster and death of Col. Muammar Gaddafi in October 2011, rule in Libya passed to the National Transitional Council (NTC), which had directed the seven-month armed rebellion against Gaddafi, with help from NATO airstrikes against Gaddafi's forces. The NTC formed in Benghazi, where the rebellion began in February 2011, and moved to Tripoli once the capital had been taken. As befits its name, the NTC was intended to be a transitional body as the country prepared for its first democratic election in six decades, held in July 2012. Those elections were deemed to be free and fair by international observers, and a moderate coalition called the National Forces Alliance prevailed in the voting for a new General National Congress. That result, combined with the work that began on a new constitution in early 2014, led many observers to hope that Libya was on the path toward an inclusive civil society after the decades of oppression under Gaddafi.

After the revolution, groups that united to oust Gaddafi found that, once that goal had been reached, they had little in common, and their unity began to fracture. By 2014, those fractures had grown to enormous gulfs, and geographic, tribal, and ideological differences threatened the shaky underpinnings of Libya's new democracy. Many observers feared that civil war was more likely in Libya than was a functioning democratic government. The central government remained in turmoil, unable to control warring militias who unleashed violent attacks throughout the country, including such key facilities as the nation's parliament and its largest airport.

Strong regional tensions emerged as many in the east of the country, where the anti-Gaddafi rebellion first gained momentum, pushed for a federalist Libya that would grant a significant amount of autonomy to separate regions. From its independence in 1951 until Gaddafi seized power in 1969, Libya was a unified kingdom with a federal constitution uniting the traditional provinces of Cyrenaica in the east (with Benghazi as its capital), Tripolitania in the west, and Fezzan to the south. Benghazi held status as the home of the monarchy, even though Tripoli was the capital. Under Gaddafi's ironfisted rule from Tripoli, easterners felt marginalized. In 2014, leaders attempted to ease some of the nation's geographic tensions by relocating the new House of Representatives, which replaced the General National Congress, from Tripoli to Benghazi.

The instability has opened the door for Islamist extremists to gain power. On September 11, 2012—the anniversary of the 2001 World Trade Center and Pentagon attacks in the United States—heavily armed Islamic militants attacked the U.S. Consulate in Benghazi and killed U.S. ambassador to Libya Christopher Stevens and three other American diplomats. In June 2014, U.S. special forces captured the alleged mastermind of the Benghazi attacks, Abu Khatallah, in Libya. Added to the concern was the passage of a 2013 parliamentary resolution declaring Libya a Muslim nation bound by sharia law.

Immigration

Libya hosts an estimated 1 million illegal immigrants, who make up about 12% of the population and more than one-quarter of the work force. The majority came from sub-Saharan African countries to work in Libya's lucrative oil industry, but others are refugees and asylum seekers fleeing violence in Eritrea, Somalia, and elsewhere. Libya also is a major transit point for illegal immigration to Europe. In the late 1990s, Gaddafi helped create the African Union and advocated uniting Africa's nations into a single federation. Seeking much-needed cheap labor, he opened Libya's doors to increased immigration. However, by 2000, the job market was saturated, and by 2004, the unemployment rate hovered around 30%. Anger and resentment toward foreign workers is common.

During Gaddafi's rule, sub-Saharan Africans were subject to harassment, discrimination, and, according to reports by Human Rights Watch (HRW), systematic abuse at the hands of Libyan authorities. Libya continues to deport tens of thousands of immigrants each year, and HRW maintains that European nations hoping to stem illegal immigration themselves have willfully ignored the country's violations of international human rights and immigration procedures. The intensifying migration issue and a perceived lack of aid from the EU has, however, created frustration for Libyan authorities, who in 2014 threatened to help facilitate a "flood" of illegal migration to Europe if the Europeans did not increase financial resources to combat the problem.

That threatened flood had already begun, but the immigrants heading to European shores weren't just those in Libya illegally but Libyans themselves. Driven out by the increasing violence of their country, thousands of Libyans attempted to cross the Mediterranean, many in overloaded, rickety boats. The mass exodus left European governments struggling for a solution to the growing immigrant issue, even as Italian and other European officials rescued hundreds of Libyan migrants from sinking vessels—though they were unable to rescue hundreds of others, who died trying to escape their country.

International Role

During the last years of Muammar Gaddafi's reign, Libya began to end its support of the terrorist attacks that had caused the country to be isolated from much of the world for decades, and sought foreign investment and improved relationships with other countries, including the United States. Gaddafi's foreign policy had long included eliminating Western influence in the Middle East and Africa. When he seized power in 1969, one of his first moves was to close U.S. and British military bases in Libya, and to grab partial control of foreign business ventures in the country, especially the oil industry.

During the 1980s Libya financed and supported numerous attacks on Western interests, including the bombings of a Pan Am passenger flight, which exploded over Lockerbie, Scotland, in 1988, killing all 259 people on board and 11 people on the ground. Libya was also behind the bombing of a French UTA plane and a Berlin disco. In response, the United States imposed economic sanctions against Libya in the 1980s; European countries and the United Nations followed suit. Losing foreign aid seriously hindered the development of Libya's massive oil reserves. In 2003, Gaddafi acknowledged responsibility for both the Lockerbie bombing and the 1989 French Airline attack. That same year, he announced that Libya would abandon its weapons-production program. Those moves, along with monetary compensation for the victims' families, led to improvement of Libya's relationships with other countries. By 2004, sanctions had been lifted, and Libya's diplomatic ties with the United States and Great Britain were restored. Foreign investment in Libya's oil industry created a major economic boost for the country.

Human Rights

The authoritarian regime under Col. Muammar Gaddafi was accused of countless human rights abuses, including the suppression of political freedom, and torture. Steps toward reforming human rights practices toward the end of Gaddafi's tenure were largely attributed to his attempts to gain acceptance in the international community and attract foreign investment. However, the nation's judicial system continues largely unchanged even after the fall of his government, and numerous human rights violations continue, as regional militias operate with little legal restriction.

Some 35,000 Libyans from the northeastern region of Tawergha remain displaced and forcibly barred from their homes due to accusations that they supported Gaddafi and committed serious crimes against their neighbors in 2011. Thousands of the displaced have suffered from harassment, torture, and arbitrary imprisonment at the hands of local militia. Militia fundamentalists have also threatened the lives of journalists and media personnel for publishing information considered anti-Islamic.

Thousands of those alleged to have helped Gaddafi in the 2011 rebellion are still in detention. Many have no access to lawyers or judicial review and are subject to forced labor and widespread abuses. The judicial system is plagued by unfair trials, corruption, and slow-paced investigations. Additionally, many judges, lawyers, and trial witnesses have been victims of documented threats and violence by militias, with authorities refusing to investigate or prosecute those responsible.

A Tawergha refugee camp in the outskirts of Bani Wallid, Libya. The city of Tawergha in northwestern Libya contained many residents who supported the regime of Muammar Gaddafi prior to Gaddafi's ouster in 2011, but after Gaddafi was killed, anti-Gaddafi forces stormed Tawergha, forcing residents to flee. (Marcilhacy Cyril/ABACA/Newscom)

Excerpt from the Libyan Interim Constitution

The supreme law of Libya is based on the Constitutional Declaration, which was written in 2011 following the overthrow of the dictatorship of Muammar al-Gaddafi. The Constitutional Declaration calls for the writing and implementation of a permanent constitution for Libya, but as of late 2014 such a constitution has yet to be drafted.

The Constitutional Declaration specifies that Libya is an Islamic state, "and the principal source of legislation is Islamic Jurisprudence (Shari'a)." Within these stipulations, the Declaration guarantees equality under the law, prohibiting discrimination on the basis of race, religion, social status, or tribal affiliation. It guarantees to each Libyan citizen the right to a fair trial, including the presumption of innocence until guilt has been proven.

Several clauses in the Constitutional Declaration deal with the State's responsibility to provide for social welfare. For example, "The State shall also guarantee the right of work, education, medical care, and social security, the right of intellectual and private property." The Declaration also specifies the State's responsibility to ensure a fair distribution of "national wealth" among its citizens. As is the case with other constitutions, the Declaration makes clear that Libyan citizens have the responsibility to defend the Libyan motherland, promote democracy, and eliminate long-standing tribal biases and discrimination.

In the Name of God, the Merciful, the Compassionate
The Interim Transitional National Council

In view of our belief in the Revolution of the 7th day of February, 2011 AD corresponding to the 14th day of Rabi' al-awwal, 1432 (Islamic calendar) which has been led by the Libyan people in different districts of their country and due to our faithfulness to the martyrs of this blessed Revolution who sacrificed their lives for the sake of freedom, living with dignity on the land of home as well as retrieving all the rights looted by Al-Gaddafi and his collapsed regime.

Based on the legitimacy of this Revolution, and in response to the desire of the Libyan people and their hopes to achieve democracy, establish the political multitude and the estate of institutions, to create a society wherein all of us can live in stability, tranquility and justice; a society that can raise by science, culture, welfare and health, and that can bring up the new generations according to the Islamic spirit and love of goodness and home.

In the hope of seeking a society of citizenship, justice, equality, booming, progress and prosperity wherein there is no place for injustice, tyranny, despotism, exploitation and dictatorship. The interim Transitional National Council has decided to promulgate this Constitutional Declaration in order to be the basis of rule in the transitional stage until a permanent Constitution is ratified in a plebiscite.

PART ONE

General Provisions

Article (1)

Libya is an independent Democratic State wherein the people are the source of powers. The city of Tripoli shall be the capital of the State. Islam is the Religion of the State and the principal source of legislation is Islamic Jurisprudence (Shari'a). The State shall guarantee for non-Muslims the freedom of practicing religious rituals. Arabic is its official language. The State shall guarantee the cultural rights for all components of the Libyan society and its languages shall be deemed national ones.

Article (4)

The State shall seek to establish a political democratic regime to be based upon the political multitude and multi party system in a view of achieving peaceful and democratic circulation of power.

Article (5)

The family is the basis of society and shall be entitled to protection by the State. The State shall also protect and encourage marriage. The State shall guarantee the protection of motherhood, childhood and the elderly. The State shall take care of children, youth and the handicapped.

Article (6)

Libyans shall be equal before the law. They shall enjoy equal civil and political rights, shall have the same opportunities, and be subject to the same public duties and obligations, without discrimination due to religion, doctrine, language, wealth, race, kinship, political opinions, and social status, tribal or eminent or familial loyalty.

PART TWO

Rights and Public Freedoms

Article (7)

Human rights and basic freedoms shall be respected by the State. The state shall commit itself to join the international and regional declarations and charters which protect such rights and freedoms. The State shall endeavor to promulgate new charters which shall honor the human being as being God's successor on Earth.

Article (8)

The State shall guarantee for every citizen equal opportunities and shall provide an appropriate standard of living. The State shall also guarantee the right of work, education, medical care, and social security, the right of intellectual and private property. The State shall further guarantee the fair distribution of national wealth among citizens, and among the different cities and districts thereof.

Article (9)

Defense of the motherland, safeguarding national unity, keeping the civil, constitutional and democratic system, abiding by civil values, combating tribal, kindred and eminent bias shall be the duty of each and every citizen.

Article (10)

The State shall guarantee the right of asylum by virtue of the law. The extradition of political refugees shall be prohibited.

Article (11)

Dwelling houses and homes shall have their sanctity and they may not be entered or inspected except in cases prescribed by the law and according to the manner set forth therein. Caring for the public and private funds shall be duty of each and every citizen.

Article (12)

The law shall protect the inviolability of the private life of citizens and the State shall not spy on the same except by a causal judicial warrant in accordance with the provisions of the law.

Article (13)

Correspondence, telephone calls and other means of communication shall have their own sanctity and their secrecy shall be guaranteed. They may not be confiscated or monitored except by a causal judicial warrant and for a definite period in accordance with the provisions of the law.

Article (14)

Freedom of opinion for individuals and groups, freedom of scientific research, freedom of communication, liberty of the press, printing, publication and mass media, freedom of movement, freedom of assembly, freedom of demonstration and freedom of peaceful strike shall be guaranteed by the State in accordance with the law.

Article (15)

The State shall guarantee the freedom of forming political parties, societies and other civil societies, and a law shall be promulgated to regulate same. The establishment of clandestine or armed societies, or societies in violation of public system or of public morals and others which may be detrimental to the State or the unity of the State shall be prohibited.

Article (16)

Property shall be inviolable. No owner may be prevented from disposing of his property except within the limits of the law.

PART FOUR

Judicial Guarantees

Article (31)

There shall be no crime or penalty except by virtue of the text of the law. Any defendant shall be innocent until he is proved guilty by a fair trial wherein he shall be granted the guarantees necessary to defend himself. Each and every citizen shall have the right to recourse to the judiciary authority in accordance with the law.

Article (32)

The Judiciary Authority shall be independent. It shall be exercised by courts of justice of different sorts and competences. They shall issue their judgments in accordance with the law. Judges shall be independent, subject to no other authority but the law and conscience.

Article (33)

Right of resorting to judiciary shall be preserved and guaranteed for all people. Each and every citizen shall have the right to resort to his natural judge. The State shall guarantee to bring the judiciary authorities near the litigants and shall guarantee the swift determination on lawsuits. Laws shall not provide for the prohibition of judiciary authority to control any administrative decree.

The Interim Transitional National Council

Benghazi on the 3rd day of Ramadan, 1432 AH corresponding to 03/ 08/ 2011 AD.

Source: "Draft Constitutional Charter for the Transitional Stage." World Intellectual Property Organization. http://www.wipo.int/edocs/lexdocs/laws/en/ly/ly005en.pdf

THEOCRACIES

Theocracy is a form of governance in which the divinity is regarded as the head of state, and the state is governed in accordance with principles associated with religious belief. In theocracies, the government is believed to derive its power from God or gods. Although many ancient states were theocracies, only a very few countries in the world today can be regarded as theocracies.

Examination of theocracy as a form of governance can be placed within the context of relationships between secular or civic authority and religious authority. Historically, many cultures regarded both secular authority and religious authority as derived from the divine. The head of state was also the head of that state's religious institution and believed to have been inspired divinely. For example, the Hebrew patriarch Moses was the leader of the Israelite community, and he was seen as having derived his authority from God. Rulers of ancient Egypt were regarded as divinities, and the Emperor of Japan was regarded as a divinity until after World War II. Today, rulers are no longer regarded as incarnations of divinities, although law in theocracies continues to be based on religious principles.

As the modern state system as we know it today began to develop in the seventeenth and eighteenth centuries in the Western world, secular authority and religious authority began to become separated from each other. This separation underlay the Peace of Westphalia, which formed the basis of international law governing relationships among sovereign states. The Peace of Westphalia was based on the principle that a ruler in central Europe could choose the official religion of his or her kingdom or principality from among Roman Catholicism, Lutheranism, or Calvinism. However, the ruler could not claim divine authority. Thus the Peace of Westphalia codified the idea that religion and civic authority were to be separated.

By granting a ruler the right to select an official religion, the Peace of Westphalia also established the principle that the state could identify a state religion. States could and usually did privilege the state religion in a variety of ways. Tax revenues were used to subsidize the state church, for example by constructing religious buildings and training members of the clergy. Religious leaders had a formal say in the government. For example, 26 seats in the House of Lords in the United Kingdom are reserved for leaders of the Church of England. Historically, in some states citizens were required to belong to the state church, but this practice has disappeared in the Western world today.

The history of these relationships is illustrated by the example of Sweden. The Church of Sweden, whose theology is based on that of the Evangelical Lutheran Church, broke with the Roman Catholic Church in the early sixteenth century and became the official religion of Sweden in 1593. During the eighteenth century, all Swedes were required to belong to the Church of Sweden, and religious gatherings and services without a Lutheran clergyman present were forbidden by law. At that time it was illegal for a Swedish citizen to convert to another religion. These provisions were repealed in 1860. Swedes could convert to other recognized religions between 1860 and 1951, after which they could leave the church without giving a reason. In 2000, the Church of Sweden was formally disestablished as that country's state church, and the current constitution of Sweden guarantees freedom of religion.

Today, many countries continue to identify state religions, although others, including the United States, eschew a state church and specifically call for the separation of church and state. In countries with state religions, authority is divided formally between secular authorities and religious authorities. The specifics of this division vary from country to country. Some countries grant religious authorities control over matters directly involving religion, including marriage, divorce, and management of church property. However, a country with a state religion can be regarded as a theocracy only if secular authority is subordinate to religious authority.

Vatican City is a Roman Catholic theocracy. The pope, who is elected by leaders of the Roman Catholic hierarchy, is the head of the Roman Catholic Church worldwide. The pope is the head of state of the Vatican and appoints all government officials. Thus the pope can be viewed as an absolute monarch of the Vatican theocracy.

Theocracy is much more commonplace, however, in predominantly Islamic states, including many Middle Eastern countries. The prevalence of theocracy in the Islamic world relative to the Western world is due to a fundamental difference between Christian and Islamic theology. Under Christian doctrine, religious and secular spheres of authority are distinct from each other, as indicated in the Bible verse, "Render unto Caesar the things that are Caesar's, and unto God the things that are God's" (Matthew 22:21). This verse implies the Church has a sphere of influence separate from that of the state, although the two are closely connected in Vatican City. Close connections between church and state also existed in Utah under the leadership of the Church of Jesus Christ of Latter-Day Saints (Mormon Church) in the nineteenth century, in Puritan New England, and in John Calvin's city-state of Geneva in present-day Switzerland during the Protestant Reformation. These governments can also be regarded as theocratic.

Under Islam, however, religion is not separated from the state. Rather, states derive their legitimacy from religion, and the laws of the state are to be based on Islamic principles. Sharia law, which is based directly on Islamic theology, governs religious matters, as well as matters such as the economy and prosecution of criminal acts, that are regarded as secular administrative matters in the Western legal and religious tradition.

Several countries, including Iran, Saudi Arabia, Sudan, and Yemen, can be considered theocracies, in that their legal systems are based officially on Sharia law. Under Sharia law, as interpreted in some Islamic countries, public criticism of Islam or statements that can be interpreted as insulting to the Prophet Muhammad are regarded as crimes of blasphemy. It is also illegal in many Islamic countries for persons to convert to other religions, and some people have been executed for public conversion to other faiths. Religious courts issue judgments on matters involving both religious and secular matters. In some countries, Sharia law applies only in certain places. For example, Nigeria allows individual states to use Sharia law, while the country as a whole is a secular democracy. In such countries, Sharia law applies only to Muslims and is not applied to non-Muslims.

Although Sharia law forms the basis of civil law in Islamic theocracies, the specific form of government differs among these countries. Saudi Arabia is an absolute monarchy, while others, such as Iran, are republics whose leaders are elected by the people.

The United States Central Intelligence Agency regards Iran as a "theocratic republic." The theocratic principles under which Iran is governed are codified in Iran's constitution, which was adopted in 1979. Article 2 outlines the "foundational principles" of the Iranian Islamic state. It reads, in part, "The Islamic Republic is a system based on belief in the One God (as stated in the phrase *There is no god except Allah*), His exclusive sovereignty and right to legislate, and the necessity of submission to His commands; Divine revelation and its fundamental role in setting forth the laws." This Islamic principle underlying Iran's government is reiterated in Article 4, which reads "All civil, penal financial, economic, administrative, cultural, military, political, and other laws and regulations must be based on Islamic criteria."

Under principles outlined in the Constitution, Iran's president is elected by popular vote. However, the power of the president is subordinate to that of the supreme leader, who, in accordance with the Iranian constitution, must be a high-ranking religious leader recognized as an authority on Islamic law and scholarship. The supreme leader is the head of state and commander in chief of the Iranian armed forces, and has the authority to declare war. He also appoints the Guardian Council, whose twelve members include six high-ranking Islamic clerics and six additional jurists with expertise in Islamic law. Thus the supreme leader has considerably more power than does the president.

—Fred M. Shelley

Further Reading
Thomas C. Berg, *The state and religion*. Saint Paul, MN: West Academic Publishing, 2004.
Lila Perl, *Theocracy*. London: Cavendish Square Press, 2007.

IRAN: Theocratic Republic

IRAN

Communications	Primary School-age Children Enrolled in Primary School
Facebook Users	5,746,859 (2012)
Not Available	**Primary School-age Males Enrolled in Primary School**
Internet Users	
8,214,000 (2009)	2,960,140 (2012)
Internet Users (% of Population)	**Primary School-age Females Enrolled in Primary School**
31.4% (2013)	
Television	2,786,719 (2012)
17 sets per 100 population (2003)	**Secondary School-age Children Enrolled in Secondary School**
Land-based Telephones in Use	
28,760,000 (2012)	7,118,357 (2012)
Mobile Telephone Subscribers	**Secondary School-age Males Enrolled in Secondary School**
58,160,000 (2012)	
Major Daily Newspapers	3,733,482 (2012)
172 (2004)	**Secondary School-age Females Enrolled in Secondary School**
Education	
School System	3,384,875 (2012)
Primary school in Iran begins at the age of six and lasts for five years. Lower secondary school lasts for three years, followed by three years of upper secondary or vocational education. Students may then continue for a year of pre-university studies.	**Students Per Teacher, Primary School**
	20.5 (2009)
	Students Per Teacher, Secondary School
	Not Available
	Enrollment in Tertiary Education
	4,404,614 (2012)
Mandatory Education	**Enrollment in Tertiary Education, Male**
8 years, from ages 6 to 14.	2,213,205 (2012)
Average Years Spent in School for Current Students	**Enrollment in Tertiary Education, Female**
15 (estimate) (2012)	2,191,409 (2012)
Average Years Spent in School for Current Students, Male	Literacy
15 (estimate) (2012)	84% (2012)
Average Years Spent in School for Current Students, Female	Energy and Natural Resources
	Electric Power Generation
15 (estimate) (2012)	239,700,000,000 kilowatt hours per year (estimate) (2011)

Electric Power Consumption	**Land Borders**
199,800,000,000 kilowatt hours per year (estimate) (2011)	3,380 miles
	Coastline
Nuclear Power Plants	1,976 miles
1 (2014)	**Capital**
Crude Oil Production	Teheran
3,192,400 barrels per day (2013)	**Area**
Crude Oil Consumption	636,296 sq. miles
1,709,400 barrels per day (2012)	**Climate**
Natural Gas Production	Iran has a mostly desert climate that undergoes unusual extremes. Temperatures exceeding 131°F occasionally occur in the summer, while in the winter the high elevation of most of the country often results in temperatures of 0°F and lower.
162,600,000,000 cubic meters per year (estimate) (2012)	
Natural Gas Consumption	
144,600,000,000 cubic meters per year (estimate) (2010)	
Natural Resources	**Land Use**
Petroleum, natural gas, coal, chromium, copper, iron ore, lead, manganese, zinc, sulfur	10.4% arable land; 7.6% temporary crops; 1.0% permanent crops; 18.1% permanent meadows and pastures; 6.8% forest land; 63.7% other.
Environment	
CO2 Emissions	**Arable Land**
8.2 metric tons per capita (2009)	10% (2007)
Alternative and Nuclear Energy	**Arable Land Per Capita**
0.4% of total energy use (2010)	1 acres per person (2007)
Threatened Species	**Health**
102 (2010)	**Average Life Expectancy**
Protected Areas	70.9 years (2014)
116,334 (estimate) (2010)	**Average Life Expectancy, Male**
Geography	69.3 years (2014)
Location	**Average Life Expectancy, Female**
Iran is located on the Persian Gulf between the Middle East and South Asia. It is bordered to the north by Turkmenistan and Azerbaijan, to the east by Afghanistan and Pakistan, to the south by the Persian Gulf and the Gulf of Oman, and to the west by Iraq and Turkey.	72.5 years (2014)
	Crude Birth Rate
	18.0 (estimate) (2015)
	Crude Death Rate
	5.9 (estimate) (2015)
	Maternal Mortality
Time Zone	76 per 100,000 live births (2005–2012 projection)
8.5 hours ahead of U.S. Eastern Standard	

Infant Mortality	**National Finances**
15 per 1,000 live births (2012)	**Currency**
Doctors	Iranian rial
0.9 per 1,000 people (2010)	**Total Government Revenues**
Industry and Labor	$47,840,000,000 (estimate) (2013)
Gross Domestic Product (GDP) - official exchange rate	**Total Government Expenditures**
$419,643,000,000 (estimate) (2015)	$66,380,000,000 (estimate) (2013)
GDP per Capita	**Budget Deficit**
$5,306 (estimate) (2015)	-4.5 (estimate) (2013)
GDP - Purchasing Power Parity (PPP)	**GDP Contribution by Sector**
$1,002,900,000,000 (estimate) (2013)	agriculture: 11.3% industry: 37.6% services: 51% (2012 est.)
GDP (PPP) per Capita	**External Debt**
$13,008 (estimate) (2013)	$15,640,000,000 (estimate) (2013)
Industry Products	**Economic Aid Extended**
Petroleum products, steel, cement, textiles, refined sugar, cigarettes, rugs, vegetable oil.	$0 (2011)
	Economic Aid Received
Agriculture Products	$102,000,000 (2011)
	Population
Wheat, rice, sugar beets, barley, potatoes, nuts, fruit, cotton, dairy products, caviar, wool, sheep, cattle, opium poppies (illicit).	**Population**
	81,824,270 (estimate) (2015)
Unemployment	**World Population Rank**
13.1% (2012)	19 th (2009)
Labor Profile	**Population Density**
agriculture: 25% industry: 31% services: 45% (2007)	122.4 people per square mile (estimate) (2011)
Military	**Population Distribution**
Total Active Armed Forces	71% urban (2011)
523,000 (estimate) (2010)	**Age Distribution**
Active Armed Forces	0-14: 21.3%
1% (2010)	15-64: 73.2%
Annual Military Expenditures	65+: 5.4%
$9,590,000,000 (2008)	(2009)
Military Service	**Median Age**
Iran has a selective conscription system, with terms of service lasting 18 months.	28.3 years (estimate) (2014)
	Population Growth Rate
	1.2% per year (estimate) (2015)

Net Migration Rate	Current Account Balance
-0.1 (estimate) (2015)	$-8,659,000,000 (estimate) (2013)
Trade	**Weights and Measures**
Imported Goods	The metric system is officially used but some traditional weights and measures are also widely employed.
Machinery and transportation equipment, foodstuffs, livestock, paper, chemicals, pharmaceuticals, metals, textiles.	
	Transportation
Total Value of Imports	**Airports**
$59,778,000,000 (estimate) (2009)	324 (2012)
Exported Goods	**Paved Roads**
Petroleum, rugs, fruit, nuts, animal hides, caviar.	80.6% (2010)
	Roads, Unpaved
Total Value of Exports	29,126 (2006)
$66,370,000,000 (estimate) (2012)	**Passenger Cars per 1,000 People**
Import Partners	113 (2008)
United Arab Emirates - 15.0%; China - 14.8%; Germany -9.6%; South Korea - 7.3%; Italy - 5.2% (2009 estimate)	**Railroads**
	5,246 (2008)
Export Partners	**Ports**
China - 16.5%; India - 13.0%; Japan - 11.5%; Turkey- 4.2%; South Africa - 3.6% (2009 estimate).	Major: 9 (including Bandar Shahid Rajai, Bandar Khomeini, Bushehr, Bandar Abbas, Kharg Island, Bandar Anzali).

OVERVIEW

Iran, formerly called Persia, is located in the Middle East between the Persian Gulf and the Caspian Sea, bordering on Afghanistan, Armenia, Azerbaijan, Iraq, Pakistan, Turkey, and Turkmenistan. Its terrain is mostly desert, consisting of a high central plateau rimmed by rugged mountains, with a few subtropical areas in the coastal plains. The population of 80.8 million is extremely diverse, reflecting the distinct waves of migration into the country, which was one of the most important empires of the ancient world, as well as its conquest by numerous powers through the ages. The capital of Iran is Tehran.

GOVERNMENT

Iran is an Islamic theocratic republic—meaning it is ruled by religious leaders—that was established on April 1, 1979, following a turbulent one-year Islamic Revolution. The revolution deposed the previous ruler, an ally of the United States, Shah Muhammad Reza Pahlavi. The Islamic Republic of Iran is governed by a supreme spiritual leader (*wali faqih*), who serves as the head of state and ultimate decision

Iran

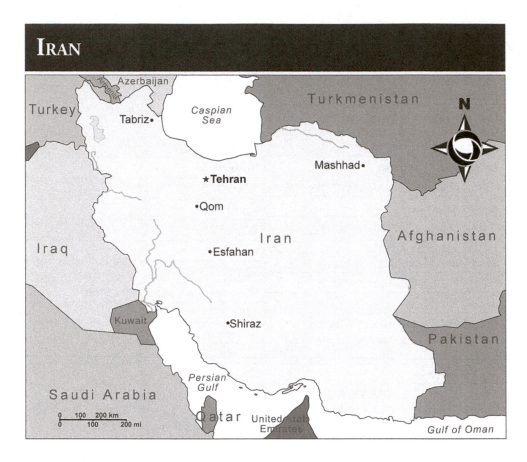

maker. An elected president, who answers to the supreme leader, serves as the head of government. The president appoints a cabinet, which must be approved by the legislature. The current *wali faqih* is Ayatollah Ali Khamenai. Hassan Rouhani, elected in June 2013, is the president.

Constitution

Adopted by national referendum in December 1979, the Iranian Constitution establishes an Islamic republic in which Islam is the basis of all social, political, and economic relations. The Council for the Protection of the Constitution ensures that all legislation is in accordance with the Constitution and Islamic law. The Constitution guarantees basic human rights for ethnic minorities and women. A July 1989 referendum approved 45 amendments, including the abolition of the office of prime minister and increased powers for the president.

Executive

The supreme spiritual leader (*wali faqih*), serves for life after being chosen by the Council of Experts, a publicly elected body of 83 religious clerics. The *wali faqih* appoints and is assisted by a supreme Council of Guardians, composed of six Islamic intellectuals and six Muslim lawyers. The council reviews all legislation to make sure it is faithful to Islamic law. The Council of Guardians also must approve the eligibility of all candidates for president and for the legislative assembly. A publicly elected president holds administrative power and serves a four-year term, but the supreme leader has the power to overrule the president's decisions. The Council of Ministers (cabinet) is selected by the president, subject to approval by the legislature. A 13-member Committee to Determine the Expediency of the Public Order arbitrates all policy disputes between the Council of Guardians and the legislature.

Ayatollah Ali Khamenei, the Supreme Leader of Iran. Under Iran's theocratic government, Khamenei is also the head of state. The Supreme Leader must be a prominent Shi'ite cleric and wields more power than does the President. (Morteza Nikoubazl/ZUMA Press/Newscom)

Legislature

Legislative power is vested in a unicameral Islamic Consultative Assembly (Majlis al-Shura al-Islami). The 290 members of the assembly are popularly elected on a nonpartisan basis to four-year terms.

Judiciary

All courts in existence prior to the 1979 Islamic Revolution were abolished in October 1982. In 1983, Islamic codes of correction were introduced, including the dismemberment of a hand for theft, flogging for fornication and dress code violations (for women), and stoning for adultery (for men). Islamic revolutionary courts were established to dispense speedy justice in the interest of keeping imprisonment to a minimum. A system of retribution (*qisas*) was also introduced, in which more than 1,000 traveling justices were appointed to tour the country and punish offenders, although investigative teams exist to ensure that they do not exceed their legal authority. In 1987, Supreme Leader Ayatollah Khomeini ordered the creation of clerical courts to try members of the clergy opposed to government policy. There are 109 offenses punishable by death, including saying, writing, or doing anything that encourages disobeying the government, and homosexuality, as well as adultery and prostitution (for women). Despite the constitutional right to legal counsel, summary trials and executions are common. A Supreme Court oversees the judicial system and has 16 branches.

Local Government

For administrative purposes, Iran is divided into 31 provinces (*ostan*), which are further divided into 472 counties (*shahrestan*) and 499 municipalities (*bakhsh*).

Election Qualifications

All citizens 18 years of age and older may vote.

POLITICS

Following the 1979 Islamic Revolution, politics in Iran have featured conflicts between fundamentalists and reformers. Ayatollah Ruhollah Khomeini rose to power during the Islamic Revolution and established an anti-Western, single-party, Shiite Muslim government marked by severe political repression. After Khomeini's death in June 1989, Ayatollah Ali Khamenai, then Iran's president, became the country's supreme religious leader. The next two popularly elected presidents, Hashemi Rafsanjani (1989–1997) and Mohammed Khatami (1997–2005) pursued economic reforms, an easing of repression, and an end to the country's international isolation, but both had very limited success in facing down opposition from religious conservatives. In February 2004, the limit of Iranian democracy was demonstrated when the Guardian Council of the Constitution, a powerful panel of fundamentalist clerics appointed by supreme leader Khamenai, disqualified 2,500 reformist candidates for legislative elections. The unsurprising result was a landslide for conservative candidates.

The conservative tide continued in June 2005, when hardline Tehran mayor Mahmoud Ahmadinejad was elected to the presidency. Over the next eight years, Ahmadinejad was a highly controversial figure who aimed incendiary rhetoric at Israel and the United States and defiantly pursued a uranium enrichment program that the international community believed was a step toward creating nuclear weapons. Following Ahmadinejad's reelection in 2009, mass protests throughout Iran were put down by violent force.

Much of the world was then surprised by the election in June 2013 of a relative moderate, Hassan Rouhani, to replace Ahmadinejad. On taking office in August, Rouhani called for talks with the West. Since Rouhani could not have run without at least tacit approval from Khamenai and the approval of the Guardian Council, many observers said that the election may signal a wish on the part of the ruling religious leaders for some improvement in relations with Western countries. Ongoing negotiations between Iran and the United States and European Union countries have resulted in tentative agreements for Iran to scale back its uranium enrichment program. In July 2014, United Nations weapons experts announced that Iran had dialed back its uranium processing so that the country's uranium could no longer be used for nuclear weapons. In response, Western countries, including the United States, began a temporary halt to sanctions, including a ban on buying Iran's oil, that have crippled the country's economy.

President Hassan Rouhani of Iran was elected in 2013. Regarded as a moderate in Iranian politics, Rouhani has promoted increased political freedom within Iran's theocratic structure of governance. (Mikhail Metzel/ZUMA Press/Newscom)

Political Parties

After 1979, the Islamic Republican Party was the nation's sole ruling party, until it was disbanded in 1987 on the grounds that it encouraged political "discord and factionalism." Since October 1988, political parties have been allowed to function, but only if they demonstrate "commitment to the Islamic system." Candidates put forward by the parties for elected office must be approved by the government before they are allowed to run. Iranian parties today can be generally grouped into two camps: the conservatives and the reformists.

The Moderation and Development Party (Hizb-i Ettedal va Toseh) is a centrist, comparatively moderate party founded in 1999. It is the party of Hassan Rouhani, the moderate cleric elected president in 2013.

The Alliance of Builders of Islamic Iran (Etelaf-e Abadgaran-e Iran-e Eslami—Abadgaran) is Iran's dominant conservative party. The party's first showing was in February 2003, when it successfully competed in local elections in Tehran. Since 2004, it has formed part of the conservative majority in the Iranian Majlis. Past and present party leaders include Gholam Ali Haddad-Adel (who is related by marriage to Iran's supreme spiritual leader, Ayatollah Ali Khamenai); Ahmad Tavakoli, a former presidential candidate; and Ahmadinejad. Mojtaba Khamenai, the son of the supreme leader, also has great influence with members of the party.

The Combatant Clergy Association (Jamee Rohaniat Mobarez—JRM) is a hard-line conservative party, founded in 1977 by supporters of Khomeini who sought to overthrow the shah, among them Khamenai and Rafsanjani. The party was particularly influential during the mid-1990s, but its importance has been waning since 2003 as Abadgaran has risen to become the dominant conservative party in Iran.

The Islamic Coalition Society (Jamiat-e Motalefeh-e Eslami—Motalefeh) is a conservative party that was founded in 1963 as one of the first groups supporting Khomeini's resistance against the shah's reforms. The party has strong ties to many economically and politically influential charities that finance popular services and government activities.

The Association of Combatant Clerics (Majma-e Rowhaniyun-e Mobarez—MRM) is a reformist party established in 1988. The party was instrumental during the rise of the reformist movement in the late 1990s. The MRM is now part of the Green Path of Hope movement.

The Islamic Iran Participation Front (Jebhe-ye Mosharekat-e Iran-e Eslami—IIPF) was formed in December 1998 to oppose the hard-line religious faction in government. Upon its formation, its stated goal was to revitalize the reform movement and promote democracy and political pluralism through civic participation and the rule of law.

The National Trust (Etemad-e Melli—NT) is a reformist party that supports greater international dialogue and strongly supports the rights of women and minorities. The party also publishes a newspaper and pushes for greater press freedom in Iran. It was banned in 2009.

The Organization of the Mojahedin of the Islamic Revolution (Sazeman-e Mojahedin-e Enqelab-e Eslami—OMIR) is a reformist party that was originally formed by former revolutionary groups in 1979. It is now a party in exile and advocates an end to Iran's current government.

ECONOMY

Until the 1979 revolution, Iran's economy was one of the Middle East's healthiest, enjoying rapid growth thanks largely to oil revenues (Iran possesses the world's fourth-largest petroleum reserves). Following the Islamic takeover, however, the economy suffered due to several factors, including a steep drop in oil prices, the debilitating effects of a costly war with Iraq that lasted from 1980 to 1988, and mismanagement of industries including petroleum, transportation, and mining, that had been taken over by the Islamic government. In addition, most Western countries drastically reduced their purchases of Iranian oil—the lifeblood of the country's economy—as punishment for what they believed were Iran's efforts to create nuclear weapons. In 2012, the European Union countries banned Iranian oil completely. The United States has banned all trade with Iran for years. Altogether, effects of the most recent round of economic sanctions cost Iran an estimated $7 billion. Compounding the country's problems, an influx of an estimated 2 million refugees from Afghanistan and Iraq put a huge strain on domestic resources. After a few years of modest growth, the Iranian economy shrank sharply in 2013, while inflation hovered around 20 percent. Soon after Rouhani took office in 2013, he revealed that the country's economy was in such a mess—due to sanctions and mismanagement—that the government was struggling to pay its workers. Many observers believe a desire to revive the country's comatose economy was one reason Rouhani agreed to limit Iran's nuclear production. While Iran has been shunned by Western countries, its main trading partners have been China, India, and the United Arab Emirates.

SOCIETY

The population of Iran is very diverse. Persians make up most of the population. Such minorities as the Kurds, Azeris, Baluchis, Turkmen, and Arabs may feel greater loyalty to homelands than to the government in Tehran. The Kurds of the western mountains have put up particularly fierce resistance to assimilation. Half of the people speak the official Farsi (Persian), and another fourth speak Turkic languages. The vast majority of Iranians are Shiite Muslim; only 5–10 percent are Sunni (including the Kurd, Baluchi, and Turkmen populations). Small numbers of Jews, and of Christians among Armenian and Assyrian populations, continue to live in Iran and practice their faith openly. Both religions have special status within Islam because they are also Abrahamic faiths.

Ethnic Composition

Persian – 61%; Azeri – 16%; Kurd – 10%; Lur – 6%; Baloch – 2%; Arab – 2%; Turkmen and Turkic tribes – 2%; other – 1%

Language

Farsi (also known as Persian) is the official language. While only about half of Iran's population speaks Farsi as their primary language, it is the common language of business. Other languages spoken include Azeri Turkic, other Turkic dialects, Kurdish, Gilaki and Mazandarani, Luri, Balochi, and Arabic.

Religion

Muslim (official) – 99.4% (Shia – 90–95%, Sunni – 5–10%); other (includes Zoroastrian, Jewish, and Christian) – 0.3%; unspecified – 0.4%

CONTEMPORARY ISSUES

The Green Movement

The June 2009 Iranian presidential election was followed and participated in by a record number of Iranian citizens. On election day, it appeared that reformist candidate Mir-Hossein Mousavi was in position to win the election, unseating controversial incumbent Mahmoud Ahmadinejad. However, official results gave Ahmadinejad an exceptionally improbable majority (more than 62% of votes cast), which was celebrated by the government as a clear mandate for Ahmadinejad's policies. Irregularities and questionable actions surrounding the election led large numbers of reformist supporters to declare the election results fraudulent. Many of these reformists took to the streets in the days following the election, demanding that the election be overturned. The protesters identified with the color green, which had been associated with Mousavi during the campaign, and the demonstrations came to be known as the Green Movement. Ayatollah Ali Khamenai, Iran's supreme leader, backed Ahmadinejad, and the issue was officially dropped following a summary investigation that many considered insufficient. The government eventually used force to halt the growing protests, which garnered international attention despite government efforts to prevent news from leaking. Numerous arrests and violent incidents, some leading to death and injury, stoked the fires of popular discontent and brought condemnation from many around the world.

In the wake of the initial demonstrations, the Green Movement used social networking Web sites and other Internet outlets to coordinate and disseminate information. Protests have continued sporadically—often on holidays, when large gatherings of people are common and difficult to prevent—and government crackdowns during Ahmadinejad's tenure were severe. Despite government efforts to arrest and intimidate members of the movement, including placing Mousavi and other leaders under house arrest in 2011, resistance has been ongoing. With a more moderate government led by Hassan Rouhani in office since August 2013, there have been new calls to end the attack against the Green Movement and release Mousavi from confinement.

Nuclear program

Iranian research into nuclear power dates back to U.S.-sponsored initiatives during the late 1950s, and Shah Muhammad Reza Pahlavi actively pursued nuclear power during the 1970s, with U.S. and European assistance. The first nuclear power plant in the country was to be built near the southwestern coastal city of Bushehr, but construction stopped in 1978 due to the Islamic Revolution. (The incomplete Bushehr facilities later sustained major damage during the Iran–Iraq War.) Following the revolution, Western governments pressured companies not to become involved with the Iranian nuclear program. The International Atomic Energy Agency (IAEA) agreed in 1983 to provide technical assistance to Iran for peaceful nuclear energy research; soon, however, pressure from the United States led the IAEA to abandon the program. U.S. diplomatic efforts similarly curtailed a nuclear assistance relationship between Iran and Argentina in the late 1980s and early 1990s.

Russia began to take an interest in Iran's ongoing nuclear activities during the 1990s, but Iranian financial problems derailed early agreements. In 1995, the two countries agreed to a contract to finally complete the Bushehr plant, and although U.S. efforts led Russia to scale back its involvement in 1998, the project continued. China also began to assist Iran in the mid-1990s, providing expertise and planning construction of a nuclear plant at Darkhovin, the site of an ill-fated French project in the 1970s; again, though, U.S. pressure (coupled with the Iranians' inability to pay) brought an end to the agreement.

In 2003, the IAEA revealed that Iran had been secretly participating in nuclear research and development. The European Union (EU) engaged in diplomatic efforts that led Iran to agree to suspend activities that could lead to nuclear weapon development, in return for assurances that it would be allowed to pursue civilian nuclear power. However, some uranium enrichment—necessary for nuclear weapons but also useful for nuclear energy production—continued. EU negotiators continued to engage Iran in 2004 and 2005, and Iran agreed to temporarily stop enriching uranium. Following the election of Mahmoud Ahmadinejad to the presidency in August 2005, Iran resumed uranium enrichment. In 2006, Ahmadinejad declared that Iran had developed a significant enrichment capacity and was committed to further development, though he maintained that the country was not developing nuclear weapons.

United Nations (UN) Security Council resolutions in 2006, 2007, 2008, and 2010 called for Iran to halt its program, but Iran continued to insist that the sole purpose of its nuclear program was generating nuclear power and that it had a right to continue the program. The discovery of a previously secret nuclear facility near the Iranian city of Qom in September 2009 heightened tensions and led to admonishment by the IAEA. The Bushehr plant, for which Russia provides the nuclear materials, finally opened in August 2010, but Iran continued its own nuclear development efforts as well.

In 2012, the United States and the EU increased economic sanctions against Iran, effectively crippling the country's economy, but it was not until the election of moderate leader Hassan Rouhani that Iran began to come around. In November 2013, the UN negotiated an interim deal to ease sanctions in return for a halt in enriched uranium production and a dilution of the stockpile Iran had already collected. Talks on a longer-term deal opened in early 2014.

Unemployment

Due to a baby boom during the Iran–Iraq War, a large percentage of Iran's population falls between the ages of 15 and 29, and the country has had difficulty providing employment for its young job applicants. Although the unemployment rate is reported as 10 percent, many believe it to be much higher. Unemployment is twice as high among women, despite the fact that increasing numbers of women are attending universities. College graduates often end up working in retail or as taxi drivers, and it is believed that many students are simply enrolling in higher education to put off the job search, which could further overwhelm the job market in a few years. The government, with international assistance, is working to create more jobs.

Relations with the United States

Iran and the United States have had troubled relations since the ousting of the shah, a close ally of the United States, and subsequent Islamic Revolution. The taking of 52 American hostages by Iranian students in 1979 confirmed U.S. government suspicions that the new theocracy had extremist intentions. The two countries have had very little direct contact since and conduct all legal matters concerning U.S. nationals in Iran or Iranian nationals in the United States through a third party. Iranian politicians use strong anti-U.S. rhetoric, and the George W. Bush administration labeled Iran part of the "axis of evil." The United States opposes Iran's nuclear program, stance on Israel, alleged support of Hezbollah in Lebanon and Shiite militants in Iraq, and Iran's political conditions, and has stated that relations cannot be normalized until these issues are resolved. However, with the emergence of the ruthless organization known as the Islamic State in Iraq and Syria (ISIS) has come speculation that the United States and its longtime foe might work together—possibly with the United Kingdom, Russia, and even Syria—to stop the radical Islamist terror group's violent push to dominate the Middle East.

Stance on Israel

Iran and Israel do not have any diplomatic relations. Since its Islamic Revolution, Iranian leaders have called Israel an illegal state and have called for its removal. Israel has accused Iran of supporting Hezbollah militants in Lebanon in their ongoing battle against the Jewish state. Some perceive Iran and Israel to be engaged in a cold war of sorts, with each nation reportedly developing weaponry to use against the other.

Human Rights Violations

Although the Iranian Constitution pledges to protect civil, political, economic, and social rights, the nation is plagued with human rights violations. While millions of Iranians participated in the 2013 elections, voter discrimination, election monitoring, and limits on freedom of press continued to hamper the freedom and fairness of the nation's electoral system. In the months leading up to the election, the supreme leader Ayatollah Ali Khamenai warned journalists not to judge the freedom and fairness of the election, and during the election period some 40 journalists and bloggers were imprisoned for violating such decrees. Also, the majority of the registered presidential candidates were disqualified on vague grounds, and dozens of key opposition figures remained imprisoned during the election.

The death penalty is widely used for a multitude of crimes, with international experts claiming that official execution tallies are far lower than the actual number of executions committed. Crimes punishable by death include murder, rape, drug possession and trafficking, and armed robbery. In 2013, at least 16 people were executed for committing crimes against God or for having alleged connections to armed opposition groups. Under Iranian law, capital punishment can be legally sought for anyone over puberty—age 9 for girls and 15 for boys. It is believed that dozens of child offenders are currently awaiting execution in Iranian prisons.

Excerpt from the Constitution of the Islamic Republic of Iran

The Constitution of the Islamic Republic of Iran was adopted in 1979, shortly after the Iranian Revolution toppled the regime of Shah Mohammad Reva Pahlavi and instituted Iran's current theocratic government. It was amended in 1989.

The Constitution specifies that Iran is a theocratic republic. Its Preamble calls for the establishment of a "universal holy government and the downfall of all others." Throughout the Constitution, reference is made to Islamic principles underlying state organization, and many rights are constrained or limited by religious considerations.

The Constitution also makes reference to colonialism and oppression. For example, Article 3 calls for "the complete elimination of imperialism and the prevention of foreign influence."

Various types of rights are identified in the Constitution. The Constitution guarantees equal rights for all citizens regardless of ethnic background or gender, with the proviso that equal protection under the law is "in conformity with Islamic criteria." Likewise, freedom of the press is guaranteed "except when [publication] is detrimental to the fundamental principles of Islam or the rights of the public." Freedom of assembly and the freedom to form political parties are also allowed when not contradictory to the principles of Islam. The Constitution makes reference to various social and economic rights such as the right to free public education, welfare, and social security as fundamental rights in Iran.

Article 3

. . . the government . . . has the duty of directing all its resources to the following goals:

free education and physical training for everyone . . . and the facilitation and expansion of higher education;

strengthening the spirit of inquiry, investigation, and innovation in all areas of science, technology, and culture, as well as Islamic studies, by establishing research centers . . .

the complete elimination of imperialism and the prevention of foreign influence;

ensuring political and social freedoms within the framework of the law;

the participation of the entire people in determining their political, economic, social, and cultural destiny;

the abolition of all forms of undesirable discrimination . . .

the planning of a correct and just economic system, in accordance with Islamic criteria in order to create welfare, eliminate poverty . . . abolish all forms of deprivation . . . and the provision of social insurance for all;

securing the multifarious rights of all citizens, both women and men, and providing legal protection for all, as well as the equality of all before the law;

the expansion and strengthening of Islamic brotherhood and public cooperation among all the people;

Article 9

. . . No individual, group, or authority, has the right to infringe . . . upon the political, cultural, economic, and military independence or the territorial integrity of Iran under the pretext of exercising freedom. Similarly, no authority has the right to abrogate legitimate freedoms, not even by enacting laws and regulations for that purpose, under the pretext of preserving the independence and territorial integrity of the country.

Article 10

Since the family is the fundamental unit of Islamic society, all laws, regulations, and pertinent programmes must tend to facilitate the formation of a family . . . and to safeguard its sanctity and the stability of family relations on the basis of the law and the ethics of Islam.

Article 13

Zoroastrian, Jewish, and Christian Iranians are the only recognized religious minorities, who, within the limits of the law, are free to perform their religious rites and ceremonies, and to act according to their own canon in matters of personal affairs and religious education.

Article 19

All people of Iran, whatever the ethnic group or tribe to which they belong, enjoy equal rights; and color, race, language, and the like, do not bestow any privilege.

Article 20

All citizens of the country, both men and women, equally enjoy the protection of the law and enjoy all human, political, economic, social, and cultural rights, in conformity with Islamic criteria.

Article 21

The government must ensure the rights of women in all respects, in conformity with Islamic criteria, and accomplish the following goals:

1. create a favorable environment for the growth of woman's personality and the restoration of her rights, both the material and intellectual;
2. the protection of mothers, particularly during pregnancy and childbearing, and the protection of children without guardians;
3. establishing competent courts to protect and preserve the family;
4. the provision of special insurance for widows, and aged women and women without support;
5. the awarding of guardianship of children to worthy mothers, in order to protect the interests of the children, in the absence of a legal guardian.

Article 22

The dignity, life, property, rights, residence, and occupation of the individual are inviolate, except in cases sanctioned by law.

Article 23

The investigation of individuals' beliefs is forbidden, and no one may be molested or taken to task simply for holding a certain belief.

Article 24

Publications and the press have freedom of expression except when it is detrimental to the fundamental principles of Islam or the rights of the public.

Article 25

The inspection of letters and the failure to deliver them, the recording and disclosure of telephone conversations, the disclosure of telegraphic and telex communications, censorship, or the willful failure to transmit them, eavesdropping, and all forms of covert investigation are forbidden, except as provided by law.

Article 26

The formation of parties, societies, political or professional associations, as well as religious societies, whether Islamic or pertaining to one of the recognized religious minorities, is permitted provided they do not violate the principles of independence, freedom, national unity, the criteria of Islam, or the basis of the Islamic republic. No one may be prevented from participating in the aforementioned groups, or be compelled to participate in them.

Article 27

Public gatherings and marches may be freely held, provided arms are not carried and that they are not detrimental to the fundamental principles of Islam.

Article 28

Everyone has the right to choose any occupation he wishes, if it is not contrary to Islam and the public interests, and does not infringe the rights of others. The government has the duty, with due consideration of the need of society for different kinds of work, to provide every citizen with the opportunity to work, and to create equal conditions for obtaining it.

Article 29

To benefit from social security with respect to retirement, unemployment, old age, disability, absence of a guardian, and benefits relating to being stranded, accidents, health services, and medical care and treatment . . . is accepted as a universal right

Article 30

The government is responsible for providing the means for public education for everyone up to the end of high school.

Article 31

Every Iranian . . . has the right to have a dwelling that meets their needs. The government is required to provide the means for the execution of this principle by giving priority to those who are in greater need . . .

Article 32

No one can be arrested except in accordance with the rule and the procedures that are set by the law. In the case of arrest, the charge and the reason for the arrest must be immediately . . . communicated to the defendant in writing. The preliminary file must be submitted to qualified judicial authorities within twenty-four hours and the preliminaries for the trial must be set as quickly as possible.

Article 33

Seeking justice is the indisputable right of every individual. Anyone may have access to the qualified courts for this purpose.

Article 35

In all courts of law, the opposing parties to a dispute have the right to choose an attorney . . . If they cannot afford to hire an attorney, they should be provided with the means to do so.

Article 37

Innocence is presumed.

Article 38

Torture . . . to obtain confession or information is forbidden. It is not permissible to force someone to testify, confess, or swear an oath.

Article 41

Citizenship of Iran is the indisputable right of every Iranian, and the government cannot take this right away . . .

Source: "Constitution of the Islamic Republic of Iran, 1979." World Intellectual Property Organization. http://www.wipo.int/wipolex/en/text.jsp?file_id=332330

VATICAN CITY: Ecclesiastical

Vatican City is the world's smallest state by land area and population. It has a land area of about 110 acres (0.17 square miles) and is surrounded entirely by the city of Rome, Italy. Its permanent population is about 800. Vatican City is the headquarters of the Roman Catholic Church. It includes St. Peter's Basilica and the Sistine Chapel. It also includes the Apostolic Palace, which is the official residence of the pope, who serves as head of state of Vatican City as well as the head of the Church. Official documents are written in Latin, but Italian is used in the conduct

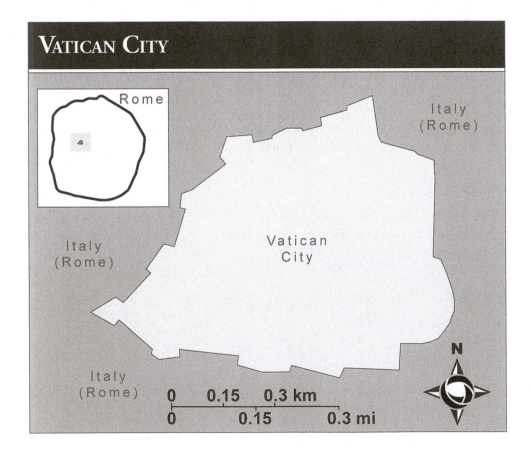

of day-to-day business. As of July 2014, the pope is Francis I, who was born Jorge Mario Bergoglio in Buenos Aires, Argentina. Before being elected in March, 2013, Pope Francis was the Archbishop of Buenos Aires.

GOVERNMENT

The Catholic Church held temporal sovereignty over the Papal States—a large portion of present-day central Italy, including the city of Rome—since the eighth century A.D. However, present-day Italy was unified as a single sovereign state during the middle of the nineteenth century. In 1870, Italian unification forces took control of the Papal States, forcing the Church to give up temporal control of Rome and the Papal States. In 1929, Italy recognized Vatican City as an independent state. Today, Vatican City is intertwined closely with the Holy See, or the formal institution governing the Church.

Constitution

Vatican City has no formal constitution, but it is governed under the auspices of the Fundamental Law of Vatican City State. The Fundamental Law was established by Pope St. John Paul II in 2000. It confirms the role of the pope, who is known also as the Supreme Pontiff, as the head of state. The first article of the Fundamental Law states that "The Supreme Pontiff, Sovereign of Vatican City State, has the fullness of legislative, executive and judicial powers."

Executive

The pope is the head of state. Executive authority is delegated to the Governorate of Vatican City. The Governorate is headed by the president of the Pontifical Commission for Vatican City State, who is appointed by the pope for a five-year term. Normally, the president is a cardinal of the Roman Catholic Church. The president is assisted by a general secretary and a vice general secretary, who are also appointed by the pope for five-year terms. The Governorate oversees various departments in charge of transportation, finances, security, and other administrative functions. The heads of these departments are appointed by the pope. Foreign policy is conducted through the office of the Secretary of State, who is also a cardinal appointed by the pope.

Legislature

The Pontifical Commission for Vatican City State serves as the legislative body for Vatican City. The seven members of the Commission, including its president, who serves as the de-facto executive of Vatican City, are cardinals of the Roman Catholic Church who are appointed by the pope for five-year terms.

Pope Francis, the Supreme Pontiff of the Roman Catholic Church, is also the head of state and the head of government of Vatican City. Francis was elected Pope in 2013 following the resignation of his predecessor, Pope Benedict XVI. (Vatican/Pool/Galazka/SIPA/Newscom)

Judiciary

The Supreme Court of Vatican City consists of three members, all of whom are cardinals of the Roman Catholic Church. The president is the Cardinal Prefect of the Apostolic Signatura. The other members of the Supreme Court are cardinals who are appointed by the pope for one-year terms. The Supreme Court hears appeals from trial judges, lower tribunals and a Court of Appeals. Trial judges and members of the lower tribunals are lay jurists, and members of the Court of Appeals include both laypersons and members of the Church hierarchy. The pope is the final arbiter of any decisions made by the Supreme Court and the lower courts.

Local Government

Vatican City has no local governments.

Election Qualifications

The only elective office in Vatican City is the office of the Supreme Pontiff. The pope is chosen for life. In the event of the death or resignation of the pope, a new pope is elected by the College of Cardinals. All members of the College of Cardinals who are less than eighty years of age may participate in the conclave that elects the new pope. Election to the papacy requires a two-thirds majority of members of the conclave.

POLITICS

In effect, Vatican City is an absolute monarchy within which the Supreme Pontiff holds all legislative, executive, and judicial power. Thus there are no politics and no political parties. Elections for the papacy are conducted in secret, although election results as well as policies implemented by Vatican authorities are often interpreted as signals over the eventual direction of the Church.

ECONOMY

Revenues to support Vatican City are generated by the sale of stamps and coins, admission fees to the Vatican museums, including the Sistine Chapel, and the sale of publications issued by the Church.

PEOPLE

The permanent population of Vatican City consists of members of the Roman Catholic clergy, along with the Pontifical Swiss Guard, which is responsible for the personal security of the pope and for security within the Apostolic Palace. Members of the Swiss Pontifical Guard are unmarried, Roman Catholic Swiss citizens between

Vatican City is the world's smallest sovereign state, which consists of approximately 110 acres surrounded completely by the city of Rome, Italy. The Pope of the Roman Catholic Church is simultaneously the head of state of Vatican City and wields complete authority over the state. (Gavin Hellier/Robert Harding/Newscom)

19 and 30 years of age. About 2,000 laypersons are employed by the Church and work in Vatican City, but they reside outside Vatican City and are citizens of Italy.

Religion

All residents and citizens of Vatican City are Roman Catholics.

CONTEMPORARY ISSUES

The issues faced by Vatican City are those faced by the Roman Catholic Church in general. The overriding issue is the role of the Church in a rapidly changing contemporary world. Some have argued that the Church should relax its traditional stances against abortion, birth control, same-sex marriage, and the ordination of women in order to appear more relevant to the contemporary world. Others argue that the Church should uphold its long-standing traditions.

Church officials have also dealt with evidence of sexual abuse of children on the part of priests. During the first decade of the twenty-first century, more than 3,000 priests from throughout the world were accused of sexual abuse. In some countries, priests suspected of sexual abuse were transferred to other positions rather than being subject to discipline or prosecution. Thus the Church leadership has been accused of covering up the scandal, as opposed to protecting abused children and prosecuting the priests accused of these crimes. In response, the Vatican has endeavored to improve and speed up the process of removing and defrocking priests who commit sexual abuse.

As the head of state of Vatican City, the pope often participates in debates over questions involving war, peace, and international relations. Although the pope's views on these questions have no legal force, as the spiritual leader of the world's 1.2 billion Roman Catholics—about one-sixth of the world's population—his ideas can carry considerable moral authority. The pope's positions on international questions are usually linked closely to the Church's theology, which emphasizes peace and service to the poor and dispossessed. For example, recent popes have called for nuclear disarmament, spoken in opposition to war and militarism, and promoted social justice and a reduction in inequality.

Excerpt from Fundamental Law of Vatican City State

The Fundamental Law of Vatican City, which was adopted in 2000, is the de-facto constitution of the Vatican state. The Fundamental Law specifies explicitly that Vatican City is a theocracy ruled by the pope, or the Supreme Pontiff. The first clause of the Fundamental Law states that "The Supreme Pontiff, Sovereign of Vatican City State, has the fullness of legislative, executive and judicial powers." Legislative power is granted to a Commission that consists of members of the College of Cardinals.

However, the pope appoints members of the Commission and has the right to reserve legislative powers to himself. The pope must also approve any proposed legislation before it becomes law within Vatican City.

Most of the remaining clauses of the Fundamental Law specify the processes by which the Commission proposes legislation. The Fundamental Law does not address any questions of human rights, except to state that someone who "claims that a proper right or legitimate interest has been damaged by an administrative act" has the right to appeal this violation to specified judicial authorities. However, the Fundamental Law makes clear that any rights granted to Vatican City's citizens are subject to the direct control of the pope.

26 November 2000

Art. 1

1. The Supreme Pontiff, Sovereign of Vatican City State, has the fullness of legislative, executive and judicial powers.
2. During the vacancy of the See, the same powers belong to the College of Cardinals which, however, can issue legislative dispositions only in a case of urgency and with efficacy limited to the time of the vacancy, unless they are confirmed by the Supreme Pontiff subsequently elected in conformity with Canon Law.

Art. 2

The representation of the State in relations with foreign states and with other subjects of international law, for the purpose of diplomatic relations and the conclusion of treaties, is reserved to the Supreme Pontiff, who exercises it by means of the Secretariat of State.

Art. 3

1. Legislative power, except for those cases which the Supreme Pontiff intends to reserve to himself or to other subjects (*istanze*), is exercised by a Commission composed of a Cardinal President and other Cardinals, all named by the Supreme Pontiff for a five-year term.
2. In case of the absence or impedance of the President, the Commission is presided over by the first of the Cardinal Members.
3. The meetings of the Commission are convoked and presided over by the President; the Secretary General and the Vice Secretary General participate in them with a consultative vote.

Art. 4

1. The Commission exercises its power within the limits of the Law concerning the sources of law, according to the indications to be given below and its proper Regulations (*Regolamento*).
2. In the drawing up of draft laws, the Commission makes use of the collaboration of the Councillors of the State, of other experts and of the Organizations of the Holy See and of the State which could be affected by them.
3. The draft laws are submitted in advance, through the Secretariat of State, for the consideration of the Supreme Pontiff.

Art. 5

1. Executive power is exercised by the President of the Commission, in conformity with the present Law and with the other normative dispositions in force.
2. In the exercise of such power, the President is assisted by the General Secretary and by the Vice General Secretary.
3. Questions of greater importance are submitted by the President to the Commission for its study.

Art. 6

Matters of greater importance are dealt with together with the Secretariat of State.

Art. 7

1. The President of the Commission can issue Ordinances, putting into effect legislative and regulatory norms.
2. In cases of urgent necessity, he can issue dispositions having the force of law, which however lose their force if they are not confirmed by the Commission within ninety days.
3. The power to issue general Regulations remains reserved to the Commission.

Art. 8

1. Without prejudice to what is established in articles 1 and 2, the President of the Commission represents the State.
2. He can delegate legal representation to the General Secretary for ordinary administrative activity.

Art. 9

1. The Secretary General assists the President of the Commission in his functions. According to the modalities indicated in the Laws and under the directives of the President of the Commission, he:

    a) oversees the application of the Laws and of the other normative dispositions and the putting into effect of the decisions and directives of the President of the Commission;
    b) oversees the administrative activity of the Governorate and coordinates the functions of the various Directorates.

2. He takes the place of the President of the Commission when the latter is absent or impeded, except in what is determined in art. 7, n. 2.

Art. 10

1. The Vice Secretary General, in accord with the General Secretary, oversees the activity of the preparation and drafting of the various proceedings and of the correspondence and carries out the other activities attributed to him.
2. He takes the place of the General Secretary when the latter is absent or impeded.

Art. 11

1. In the preparation and the study of accounts and for other affairs of a general order concerning the personnel and activity of the State, the President of the Commission is assisted by the Council of Directors, which he periodically convenes and leads.
2. The Secretary General and the Vice Secretary General also take part in the Council.

Art. 12

The financial budgets and reports of the State, after their approval by the Commission, are submitted to the Supreme Pontiff through the Secretariat of State.

3. The financial

Art. 13

1. The Councillor General and the Councillors of the State, named by the Supreme Pontiff for a five-year term, offer their assistance in the drafting of Laws and in other matters of particular importance.
2. The Councillors can be consulted both individually and collegially.

3. The Councillor General presides over the meetings of the Councillors; he also exercises functions of coordination and representation of the State, according to the indications of the President of the Commission.

Art. 14

The President of the Commission, in addition to using the Corps of Vigilance, can request, for the purpose of security and policing, the assistance of the Pontifical Swiss Guard.

2. The Secretary

Art. 15

1. Judicial power is exercised, in the name of the Supreme Pontiff, by the organs constituted according to the judicial structure of the State.
2. The competence of the individual organs is regulated by the law.
3. Acts of jurisdiction must be carried out within the territory of the State.

Art. 16

In any civil or penal case and in any stage of the same, the Supreme Pontiff can defer the instruction and the decision to a particular subject (*istanza*), even with the faculty of pronouncing a decision according to equity and with the exclusion of any further recourse (*gravamen*).

Art. 17

1. Without prejudice to what is determined in the following article, whoever claims that a proper right or legitimate interest has been damaged by an administrative act can propose hierarchical recourse or approach the competent judicial authority.
2. Hierarchical recourse precludes a judicial action in the same matter, unless the Supreme Pontiff authorizes it in the individual case.

Art. 18

1. Controversies concerning labour relations between the employees (*dipendenti*) of the State and the Administration are within the competence of the Labour Office of the Apostolic See, according to its own Statute.
2. Recourses against disciplinary provisions taken in regard to the employees of the State can be proposed before the Court of Appeal, according to its own norms.

Art. 19

The faculty to grant amnesties, indults, remissions and favours is reserved to the Supreme Pontiff.

Art. 20

1. The flag of Vatican City State is constituted by two fields divided vertically, a yellow one next to the staff and a white one, and bears in the latter the tiara with the keys, all according to the model which forms attachment A of the present Law.
2. The coat of arms is constituted by the tiara and keys, according to the model which forms attachment B of the present Law.
3. The seal of the State bears in the centre the tiara with the keys and around it the words "Stato della Città del Vaticano", according to the model which forms attachment C to the present Law.

The present Fundamental Law replaces in its entirety the Fundamental Law of Vatican City, 7 June 1929, n. I. Likewise all the norms in force in the State which are not in agreement with the present Law are abrogated.

The Law will enter into force on 22 February 2001, Feast of the Chair of Saint Peter Apostle.

We order that the original of the present Law, bearing the seal of the State, be deposited in the Archive of the Laws of Vatican City State, and that the corresponding text be published in the Supplement to the Acta Apostolicae Sedis, enjoining upon all those concerned to observe it and to have it observed.

Given from Our Apostolic Vatican Palace on the Twenty-Sixth of November, Two Thousand, Solemnity of Our Lord Jesus Christ, King of the Universe, in the Twenty-Third year of Our Pontificate.

—Pope John Paul II

Source: "Fundamental Law of Vatican City State." Legislation Online. http://www.legislationline.org/documents/section/constitutions

CHAPTER 6

OTHER GOVERNMENT TYPES

Many states throughout the world have governments that cannot easily be categorized as democracies, Communist regimes, autocracies, monarchies, or theocracies. In this chapter, several examples illustrating these various governmental types are described.

In general, governments can be distinguished between authoritarian and democratic regimes. In authoritarian regimes, power is held by a single individual or a ruling faction or party, whereas in democracies leadership is determined by vote of the people. Communist regimes and absolute monarchies are authoritarian regimes, while republics and most constitutional monarchies operate as democracies.

In addition to Communist regimes and absolute monarchies, several other states are governed by other types of autocratic regimes. Dictatorships are autocratic regimes in which power is held by a single individual or a small group of leaders. Generally speaking, the activities of a dictatorship are not governed by a constitution. Thus the dictator can govern without being answerable to any internal authority. Some dictatorships are totalitarian regimes, in which the dictator has complete authority over the economy and all day-to-day activities within their states. Other authoritarian regimes maintain control of the government but do not attempt to control their countries' economies.

Although dictatorial regimes are not answerable to constitutional authority, their control of the countries over which they rule may be threatened by other political forces. Especially in recent years, dictatorial regimes have been overthrown following popular protests. For example, authoritarian regimes were ousted in the Middle Eastern countries of Tunisia, Libya, Egypt, and Yemen following widespread public protests during "Arab Spring" in 2011. Social media, the Internet, and cell phones have played instrumental roles in publicizing and intensifying protests that may result in the removal of dictatorships and other authoritarian regimes.

Some autocratic regimes are military dictatorships. Military leaders have seized power in coups d'etat in many less-developed countries, often replacing civilian-led democracies. Frequently, military leaders justify their actions by citing the need to restore order, to guarantee political stability, or to prevent the accession of autocratic regimes. Often, military leaders who seize control of governments have imposed martial law, at least temporarily.

In some cases, the military leaders who seize control of a government are top-ranking officers in their countries' armed forces. However, in other cases lower-ranking officers have seized power, in part because their superior officers remain loyal to the government in control of the country. Many military officers who take over a country's government have promised to return that country to civilian rule once order has been restored. For example, after Hosni Mubarak was ousted from power in Egypt following the Arab Spring protests, military officers seized power. Elections were held the following year, but the military took over the government again following another wave of protests against the Islamist-oriented government of elected president Mohammed Morsi.

In other cases, military leaders who seized power in coups d'etat became dictators themselves. In Libya, for example, military officers led by then-Colonel Muammar Gaddafi ousted the Libyan monarchy in 1960. However, Gaddafi seized power himself, ruling Libya as a dictator for more than 40 years until he himself was deposed in the wake of Arab Spring.

The situation in Mauritania illustrates the process of initiating and maintaining military rule. High-ranking military officers under the leadership of General Mohamed Ould Abdel Aziz took over the government of Mauritania in 2008. During the following year, Abdel Aziz dissolved the military government and called for democracy. He was elected president of Mauritania, although his opponents regarded his election as fraudulent. As of 2014, Abdel Aziz remains in power.

Not all autocratic governments are military dictatorships. In other countries, civilian leaders who were initially elected via democratic voting procedure have consolidated their power and begun to function as dictators. In Uzbekistan, for example, Islam Karimov was elected President in 1991 following the collapse of the Soviet Union. Karimov's party was accused of harassing its opposition in order to assure that Karimov would be elected. After taking office, Karimov began to govern as an authoritarian ruler. In 1995, he engineered passage of a referendum extending his term of office until 2000. The international community, including the United States, regarded this referendum as fixed and maintained that the election was not a "free and fair" one under principles of democratic governance. Karimov was reelected in 2000, in another election regarded as biased in accordance with international law. Ignoring Uzbekistan's constitutional provision that a president can serve only two terms, Karimov ran for and was elected to a third term in 2007.

Some countries have lacked effective governance—in some cases, for many years. Such countries are known as failed states or anocracies. Within these failed states, various factions compete for control of the government, and in many cases some regions attempt to declare independence, while others function autonomously in the absence of national governmental control.

Somalia is a case in point. Military leaders led by General Mohamed Siad Barre, the head of Somalia's armed forces, removed Somalia's civilian government in 1969. Siad Barre became the head of state, ruling as a dictator with a socialist ideology until 1991, when his government was ousted from power. Since that time, control of Somalia has been contested by various political factions and warlords. The northern part of Somalia, a former British colony, has declared its independence, although Somaliland has not been recognized by the international community as an independent sovereign state. Meanwhile, the Puntland region along the Arabian Sea and Indian Ocean coasts in the northeast operates as a de facto state, with much of its income derived from piracy at sea. Yemen and Afghanistan have also been recognized as failed states.

Most of the world's states are recognized by the international community as having the right to govern, or sovereignty over, their territories. However, some states are recognized by only a portion of the international community. They maintain de facto control over their territories, although their right to govern these territories is not recognized or accepted by other states. Palestine and Kosovo, which have declared their independence from Israel and Serbia respectively, are examples. The Palestine National Authority serves as the effective government of Palestine, although Israel does not recognize Palestine as a state and does not view the National Authority as Palestine's legitimate government. Many, but not all, other states throughout the world recognize Palestine, but some, including the United States, do not. Similarly, Kosovo declared its independence from Serbia in 2008. Serbia has not recognized Kosovo's independence and continues to regard Kosovo as a "special region" within Serbia. However, as of early 2014, 107 members of the United Nations, including the United States and 23 of the 28 members of the European Union, have recognized Kosovo formally.

Puerto Rico is an example of a commonwealth, or a self-governing territory under the sovereignty of another country. Puerto Rico is under the sovereignty of the United States but is not one of the 50 states. Commonwealth status is often held by current or former Western colonies. For example, newly independent British colonies throughout the world were invited to become members of the British Commonwealth, with continued British influence in their governments along with special trade privileges. The British monarch is regarded as the head of state in some of these countries, which are known as Commonwealth realms.

Although the entire inhabited surface of Earth is under the control of sovereign states, there are large areas of the earth's surface that are not under the sovereign control of any state. Antarctica, with a land area considerably larger than that of the United States, is uninhabited and is not part of any state, although various countries claimed portions of Antarctica during the early twentieth century. Antarctica is governed under the Antarctic Treaty. Similarly, the world's oceans cover more than two-thirds of the earth's surface. The oceans are governed by the Law of the Sea agreements, which—like the Antarctic Treaty—was established following international negotiations and the eventual drafting and ratification of international treaties.

—Fred M. Shelley

Further Reading

Natasha M. Ezrow and Erica Frantz, *Failed states and institutional decay: Understanding instability and poverty in the developing world.* London: Bloomsbury Publishing, 2013.

Carl Schmitt, *Dictatorship.* London: Polity Press, 2014.

Gabrielle Walker, *Antarctica: An intimate portrait of a mysterious continent.* New York: Houghton Mifflin, 2013.

ANTARCTICA: Antarctic Treaty System

The Antarctic Treaty system is a series of international treaties that govern the management of the continent of Antarctica. The original treaty went into effect in 1961 for a period of 30 years. The treaty was renewed and revised in 1989, and the updated treaty went into effect in 1991 for an additional 50 years.

The continent of Antarctica occupies the southernmost part of the world, including the South Pole. It has a land area of about 5.4 million square miles, nearly twice that of the 48 contiguous United States. About 98 percent of Antarctica is covered with ice. The first documented landing on the Antarctic coast was by a U.S. sealing ship in 1821. By about 1840, it had become clear to mariners that Antarctica was a continent, separated by the Southern Ocean from the continents of Australia, Africa, and South America.

European explorers began to penetrate the interior of Antarctica in the late nineteenth century. The South Pole was first reached by Norwegian explorer Roald Amundsen in 1911. After the South Pole had been reached, several countries claimed portions of the Antarctic continent. However, these claims are not recognized internationally today.

GOVERNMENT

Lacking a permanent population, Antarctica has no formal government, and it does not have legislative, executive, or judicial systems. However, Antarctica is governed by the current Antarctic Treaty. In effect, the Antarctic Treaty can be regarded as Antarctica's constitution.

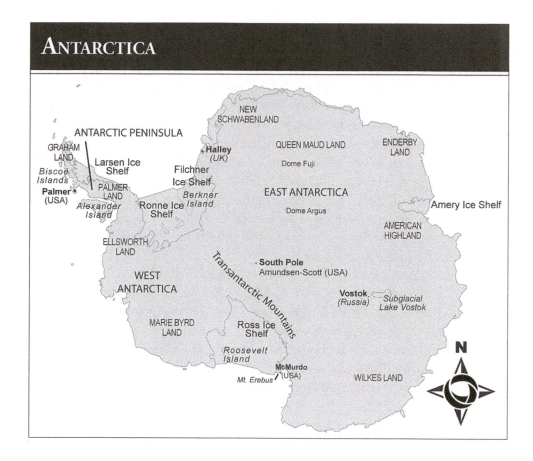

The Antarctic Treaties

During the twentieth century, several countries established territorial claims, some of which overlapped, in Antarctica. In 1957 and 1958, scientists from these and other countries, including the United States and the Soviet Union, worked on a variety of research projects in Antarctica associated with the International Geophysical Year (which actually lasted for 18 months). Important scientific discoveries associated with the International Geophysical Year included the discovery of the ozone hole in the atmosphere over Antarctica and the discovery of the Van Allen radiation belts. These and other scientific breakthroughs helped to convince the scientific community of the value of international cooperation despite the fact that the 1950s were a decade in which the Cold War was in full swing.

The success of the International Geophysical Year encouraged scientists and government leaders to consider the international management of Antarctica and its resources. In 1959, delegates from 12 countries met in Washington, DC to discuss these questions. Participating countries included the nine that had made territorial claims on the Antarctic continent (Britain, France, West Germany, Norway, Chile, Argentina, Australia, New Zealand, and South Africa) along with the United States, the Soviet Union, and Japan.

The Antarctic Treaty was drafted at this conference. The purpose of the Treaty was that "Antarctica shall continue for ever to be used exclusively for peaceful purposes and shall not become the scene or object of international discord." The Treaty had several key provisions. It stipulated that Antarctica (which, for purposes of the treaty, is defined as everywhere south of 60 degrees South latitude) would be reserved for peaceful purposes. It could not be used for military purposes. Territorial claims to Antarctica would not be recognized. Scientists from all countries had the freedom to conduct research in Antarctica, and Antarctica could not be used for nuclear testing. The Treaty went into effect in 1961 for a 30-year period, during which time 30 additional countries signed it.

The impending expiration of the Antarctic Treaty in 1991 led to the convening of a second international conference in Madrid to discuss revisions. The Madrid Protocol, which emerged from this conference, renewed the treaty for an additional 50 years, until 2041. In addition, exploitation of Antarctica for commercial purposes was prohibited. Mining is also prohibited, and nonscientific tourist access was limited strictly. The Environmental Protocol, which is part of the 1991 treaty, is based on the premise that "Antarctica has been designated as 'a natural reserve, devoted to peace and science'. Activities are subject to regulations concerning environmental impact assessments, protection of fauna and flora, waste management and others. All activities relating to Antarctic mineral resources, except for scientific research, are forbidden."

The treaty is managed by the Secretariat of the Antarctic Treaty, which was established in 2004 and is headquartered in Buenos Aires. The mission of the Secretariat is "Supporting the annual Antarctic Treaty Consultative Meeting (ATCM) and the meeting of the Committee for Environmental Protection (CEP), facilitating the exchange of information between the Parties required in the Treaty and the Environment Protocol, collecting, storing, archiving and making available the documents of the ATCM, and providing and disseminating information about the Antarctic Treaty system and Antarctic activities."

PEOPLE

Antarctica is uninhabited and has no permanent population, although at any given time several thousand scientists and support personnel live temporarily at research stations on the Antarctic continent and on nearby islands south of the 60th parallel of South latitude, in order to conduct scientific research and investigation. These temporary residents of Antarctica are citizens of their countries of origin.

An Argentinian research station located on Half Moon Island off the coast of Antarctica. Under the terms of the Antarctic Treaty, research stations such as this one are used for scientific investigation but are off limits for military and commercial purposes. (PASIEKA/ SCIENCE PHOTO LIBRARY/Alfred Pasieka/SPL/Newscom)

CONTEMPORARY ISSUES

Antarctica's status as a continent free from permanent human habitation and commercial exploitation remains paramount. The underlying purpose of the Antarctic Treaty has been to preserve this status. The Treaty guarantees maintenance of Antarctica's pristine environment as much as possible. Hence, large numbers of valuable scientific research projects have been conducted in and about Antarctica and the nearby waters south of the 60th parallel. This research has had global implications for understanding the Earth's physical systems dating back to the International Geophysical Year in 1957–58.

Current research in Antarctica involves measurement of actual and potential increases in global sea levels. In recent years, several very large ice sheets and glaciers along the Antarctic coast have collapsed and entered the ocean, increasing worldwide sea levels. Sea-level rise can affect low-lying coastal countries dramatically in the years ahead. However, investigations during the early twenty-first century have confirmed that while the overall surface temperature of the Earth has been increasing, temperatures in some parts of the Antarctic region have decreased, and ice cover has increased. Investigations as to why this is so are ongoing, and the results

An iceburg in the Weddell Sea in Antarctica. About 98 percent of Antarctica's land surface is covered with ice, but with increased global surface temperatures, large sheets of ice have been melting and collapsing into the ocean. (Walter Huber/picture alliance/moodboard/Newscom)

of this analysis will have major implications for understanding climate change and its potential impacts on societies throughout the world.

Scientists continue to monitor the ozone hole over Antarctica. The discovery of the ozone hole during the International Geophysical Year led to research that determined that the emission of chlorofluorocarbons from such products as aerosols, Freon, and various refrigerants and coolants, were a major cause of ozone depletion. As a result, many countries banned the use of these products. However, there remains evidence that the ozone hole continues to increase in size despite this ban, and research about why the ozone hole may be expanding at least temporarily is ongoing. In general, the international community is recognizing the value of Antarctica as a place in which scientific research with global implications must continue.

Excerpt from the Antarctic Treaty

The Antarctic Treaty was drafted in 1959 and ratified originally by twelve countries, including seven that had established territorial claims in Antarctica. The original treaty went into effect in 1961 for a period of thirty years and was updated in 1991. Because the original treaty has been supplemented by other international agreements, the Treaty and these agreements are known collectivity as the Antarctic Treaty System. Today, 50 countries are signatory to the Antarctic Treaty System.

For purposes of the Treaty, the Antarctic region is defined as all land areas located south of the 60th parallel South latitude, including the continent of Antarctica and offshore islands. The Antarctic Treaty is unique among international treaties, in that its provisions govern an area of the world that has no permanent population. Thus the Treaty does not deal directly with human rights issues. Among its original purposes was to provide for the renunciation of individual countries' territorial claims in Antarctica. Rather, the Treaty stipulates that the Antarctic region is to be managed by the international community.

The guiding principle of the Treaty is that "it is in the interest of all mankind that Antarctica shall continue forever to be used exclusively for peaceful purposes and shall not become the scene or object of international discord." Thus military activities, including the testing and use of nuclear weapons, are prohibited. The treaty also encourages scientific research, including cooperation among countries that maintain research stations in the Antarctic region.

The Governments of Argentina, Australia, Belgium, Chile, the French Republic, Japan, New Zealand, Norway, the Union of South Africa, The Union of Soviet Socialist Republics, the United Kingdom of Great Britain and Northern Ireland, and the United States of America,

Recognizing that it is in the interest of all mankind that Antarctica shall continue forever to be used exclusively for peaceful purposes and shall not become the scene or object of international discord;

Acknowledging the substantial contributions to scientific knowledge resulting from international cooperation in scientific investigation in Antarctica;

Convinced that the establishment of a firm foundation for the continuation and development of such cooperation on the basis of freedom of scientific investigation in Antarctica as applied during the International Geophysical Year accords with the interests of science and the progress of all mankind;

Convinced also that a treaty ensuring the use of Antarctica for peaceful purposes only and the continuance of international harmony in Antarctica will further the purposes and principles embodied in the Charter of the United Nations;

Have agreed as follows:

Article I

1. Antarctica shall be used for peaceful purposes only. There shall be prohibited, inter alia, any measures of a military nature, such as the establishment of military bases and fortifications, the carrying out of military maneuvers, as well as the testing of any type of weapons.
2. The present Treaty shall not prevent the use of military personnel or equipment for scientific research or for any other peaceful purposes.

Article II

Freedom of scientific investigation in Antarctica and cooperation toward that end, as applied during the International Geophysical Year, shall continue, subject to the provisions of the present Treaty.

Article III

1. In order to promote international cooperation in scientific investigation in Antarctica, as provided for in Article II of the present Treaty, the Contracting Parties agree that, to the greatest extent feasible and practicable:
   (a) information regarding plans for scientific programs in Antarctica shall be exchanged to permit maximum economy and efficiency of operations;
   (b) scientific personnel shall be exchanged in Antarctica between expeditions and stations;
   (c) scientific observations and results from Antarctica shall be exchanged and made freely available.

Article V

1. Any nuclear explosions in Antarctica and the disposal there of radioactive waste material shall be prohibited.

Article VI

The provisions of the present Treaty shall apply to the area south of 60° South latitude, including all ice shelves, but nothing in the present Treaty shall prejudice or in any way affect the rights, or the exercise of the rights, of any State under international law with regard to the high seas within that area.

Article VII

3. All areas of Antarctica, including all stations, installations and equipment within those areas, and all ships and aircraft at points of discharging or embarking cargoes or personnel in Antarctica, shall be open at all times to inspection by any observers . . .
4. Aerial observation may be carried out at any time over any or all areas of Antarctica by any of the Contracting Parties . . .
5. Each Contracting Party shall . . . inform the other Contracting Parties, and give them notice of
   (a) all expeditions to and within Antarctica. . .
   (b) all stations in Antarctica occupied by its nationals; and
   (c) any military personnel or equipment intended to be introduced by it into Antarctica . . .

Article IX

1. Representatives of the Contracting Parties . . . shall meet . . . at suitable intervals and places, for the purpose of exchanging information, consulting together on matters of common interest pertaining to Antarctica, and formulating and considering, and recommending to their Governments, measures in furtherance of the principles and objectives of the Treaty including measures regarding:
   (a) use of Antarctica for peaceful purposes only;
   (b) facilitation of scientific research in Antarctica;
   (c) facilitation of international scientific cooperation in Antarctica;
   (d) facilitation of the exercise of the rights of inspection provided for in Article VII of the Treaty;
   (e) questions relating to the exercise of jurisdiction in Antarctica;
   (f) preservation and conservation of living resources in Antarctica.

Article X

Each of the Contracting Parties undertakes to exert appropriate efforts, consistent with the Charter of the United Nations, to the end that no one engages in any activity in Antarctica contrary to the principles or purposes of the present Treaty.

Article XI

1. If any dispute arises between two or more of the Contracting Parties . . . those Contracting Parties shall consult among themselves with a view to having the dispute resolved by negotiation, inquiry, mediation, conciliation, arbitration, judicial settlement or other peaceful means of their own choice.
2. Any dispute of this character not so resolved shall, with the consent, in each case, of all parties to the dispute, be referred to the International Court of Justice for settlement . . .

Article XII

1. (a) The present Treaty may be modified or amended at any time by unanimous agreement of the Contracting Parties . . .
   Done at Washington the first day of December, one thousand nine hundred and fifty-nine.

Source: "The Antarctic Treaty." Secretariat of the Antarctic Treaty. http://www .ats.aq/index_e.htm

MAURITANIA: Military Junta

MAURITANIA

Communications	Primary School–age Children Enrolled in Primary School
Facebook Users	
132,000 (estimate) (2013)	553,584 (2012)
Internet Users	**Primary School–age Males Enrolled in Primary School**
75,000 (2009)	
Internet Users (% of Population)	273,834 (2012)
6.2% (2013)	**Primary School–age Females Enrolled in Primary School**
Television	
5 sets per 100 population (2006)	279,750 (2012)
Land-based Telephones in Use	**Secondary School–age Children Enrolled in Secondary School**
65,100 (2012)	
Mobile Telephone Subscribers	152,011 (estimate) (2012)
4,024,000 (2012)	**Secondary School–age Males Enrolled in Secondary School**
Major Daily Newspapers	
3 (2004)	83,501 (estimate) (2012)
Average Circulation of Daily Newspapers	**Secondary School–age Females Enrolled in Secondary School**
Not Available	
Education	68,510 (estimate) (2012)
School System	**Students Per Teacher, Primary School**
Mauritania's educational system begins at the age of six with six years of primary school. Early secondary school lasts for three years, followed by three to five years in a technical school or three years in an academic upper secondary school.	40.1 (2012)
	Students Per Teacher, Secondary School
	26.6 (2007)
	Enrollment in Tertiary Education
	17,878 (2012)
Mandatory Education	**Enrollment in Tertiary Education, Male**
9 years, from ages 6 to 15.	12,634 (2012)
Average Years Spent in School for Current Students	**Enrollment in Tertiary Education, Female**
	5,244 (2012)
8 (estimate) (2012)	**Literacy**
Average Years Spent in School for Current Students, Male	58% (2010)
	Energy and Natural Resources
8 (estimate) (2012)	**Electric Power Generation**
Average Years Spent in School for Current Students, Female	701,000,000 kilowatt hours per year (estimate) (2010)
8 (2012)	

Electric Power Consumption	**Area**
651,900,000 kilowatt hours per year (estimate) (2010)	397,950 sq. miles
	Climate
Nuclear Power Plants	The climate is dry and hot, especially in the north, which is mainly desert. The temperature in winter can reach 85°F, while in summer it is usually around 100°F. Sandstorms are common and sometimes violent.
0 (2014)	
Crude Oil Production	
6,800 barrels per day (2013)	
Crude Oil Consumption	
18,000 barrels per day (2012)	**Land Use**
Natural Gas Production	0.4% arable land; 0.0% permanent crops; 38.1% permanent meadows and pastures; 0.2% forest land; 61.2% other.
0 cubic meters per year (estimate) (2011)	
Natural Gas Consumption	
0 cubic meters per year (estimate) (2010)	**Arable Land**
Natural Resources	0% (2007)
Iron ore, gypsum, copper, phosphate, diamonds, gold, oil, fish	**Arable Land Per Capita**
	0 acres per person (2007)
Environment	**Health**
CO2 Emissions	**Average Life Expectancy**
0.6 metric tons per capita (2009)	62.3 years (2014)
Alternative and Nuclear Energy	**Average Life Expectancy, Male**
Not Available	60.0 years (2014)
Threatened Species	**Average Life Expectancy, Female**
58 (2010)	64.6 years (2014)
Protected Areas	**Crude Birth Rate**
12,073 (estimate) (2010)	31.3 (estimate) (2015)
Geography	**Crude Death Rate**
Location	8.2 (estimate) (2015)
Mauritania, situated in northwestern Africa, is bordered by Algeria and Western Sahara to the north, Mali to the southeast, and Senegal to the south. The Atlantic Ocean lies to the west.	**Maternal Mortality**
	1,000 per 100,000 live births (2005–2012 projection)
	Infant Mortality
	65 per 1,000 live births (2012)
Time Zone	**Doctors**
5 hours ahead of U.S. Eastern Standard	0.1 per 1,000 people (2010)
Land Borders	**Industry and Labor**
3,153 miles	**Gross Domestic Product (GDP) - official exchange rate**
Coastline	
469 miles	$4,662,000,000 (estimate) (2015)
Capital	**GDP per Capita**
Nouakchott	$1,197 (estimate) (2015)

GDP - Purchasing Power Parity (PPP)	**Economic Aid Extended**
$8,286,000,000 (estimate) (2013)	$0 (2011)
GDP (PPP) per Capita	**Economic Aid Received**
$2,230 (estimate) (2013)	$370,000,000 (2011)
Industry Products	**Population**
Processed fish, iron ore, gypsum.	**Population**
Agriculture Products	3,596,702 (estimate) (2015)
Millet, sorghum, rice, pulses, dates, roots, sheep, cattle, goats, milk.	**World Population Rank**
	134 th (2009)
Unemployment	**Population Density**
31.0% (2012)	8.2 people per square mile (estimate) (2011)
Labor Profile	**Population Distribution**
agriculture: 50% industry: 10% services: 40% (estimate) (2001)	41% urban (2011)
Military	**Age Distribution**
Total Active Armed Forces	0-14: 40.7%
15,870 (2010)	15-64: 55.9%
Active Armed Forces	65+: 3.4%
1% (2010)	(2009)
Annual Military Expenditures	**Median Age**
$20,000,000 (estimate) (2008)	19.9 years (estimate) (2014)
Military Service	**Population Growth Rate**
The Mauritanian military uses a conscription system, with terms lasting two years.	2.3% per year (estimate) (2015)
	Net Migration Rate
National Finances	-0.8 (estimate) (2015)
Currency	**Trade**
Ouguiya	**Imported Goods**
Total Government Revenues	Foodstuffs, petroleum and petroleum products, capital goods.
$1,677,000,000 (estimate) (2013)	**Total Value of Imports**
Total Government Expenditures	$2,108,300,000 (estimate) (2009)
$1,702,000,000 (estimate) (2013)	**Exported Goods**
Budget Deficit	Iron ore, fish and fish products, gypsum, cattle.
-0.6 (estimate) (2013)	**Total Value of Exports**
GDP Contribution by Sector	$2,878,000,000 (estimate) (2012)
agriculture: 14.9% industry: 48% services: 37.1% (2012 est.)	**Import Partners**
External Debt	France -13.7%; China - 13.0%; Netherlands - 9.9%; Brazil - 5.3%; Belgium - 4.7% (2009 estimate)
$3,233,000,000 (estimate) (2013)	

Export Partners	Paved Roads
China - 43.9%; Italy - 9.6%; Japan - 7.5%; Cote d'Ivoire - 6.1%; Spain - 5.5% (2009 estimate).	29.7% (2010)
	Roads, Unpaved
Current Account Balance	5,033 (2006)
	Passenger Cars per 1,000 People
$-1,240,000,000 (estimate) (2013)	Not Available
Weights and Measures	**Railroads**
The metric system is in use.	452 (2008)
Transportation	**Ports**
Airports	Major: 3—Nouadhibou, Nouakchott, Point-Central.
28 (2012)	

OVERVIEW

Mauritania is a hot, dry desert nation located in northwestern Africa. Two-thirds of the country lies within the Sahara Desert. Sand dunes cover most of the northern and central regions of the country, and violent sandstorms and droughts

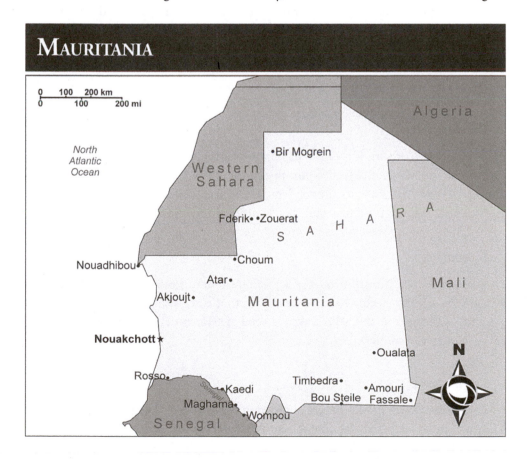

are frequent. Mauritania is mostly flat, with its vast, forbidding plains occasionally broken by ridges and sandstone plateaus. In some areas, isolated peaks rise above the plateaus. A long coastline on the Atlantic Ocean marks the western extent of Mauritanian land, running from the Senegal River in the south to the Ras Nouadhibou Peninsula in the north. The country can be divided into five major geographic regions: the coastal areas, the central plateaus, the Taoudeni Basin, the northern and eastern plains, and the Senegal River Valley. Most of the country's more than 3 million people are Muslim. Nouakchott is Mauritania's capital. A substantial portion of the population—including several traditionally nomadic groups—live in the cities, forced there by devastating droughts and plagues of locusts.

GOVERNMENT

Mauritania is an Islamic republic established on November 28, 1960, when it gained independence from France. Under the 2006 Constitution, the country is governed under a multiparty system by a president with broad executive powers. Legislative authority resides with the bicameral Parliament, but the judicial system integrates Islamic sharia law and elements borrowed from the French penal code. The country's current leader, Gen. Mohamed Ould Abdelaziz, seized power in an August 2008 military coup, overthrowing the country's first freely elected president, Sidi Ould Cheikh Abdallahi. After 11 months of military rule, Abdelaziz was elected to a five-year term as president on July 18, 2009. He was reelected with an overwhelming majority in 2014.

Constitution

The current constitution of Mauritania was adopted following a national referendum in June 2006 and built upon the earlier 1991 Constitution that embraced multipartyism. The 2006 document, which was amended in 2012, established strict presidential term limits and established multiparty elections.

Executive

Under the 2006 Constitution, the president of Mauritania, who is required to be Muslim, is directly elected to a five-year term that is renewable once. The president appoints a prime minister, who serves as head of government and appoints a Council of Ministers (cabinet).

Legislature

Legislative power in Mauritania is vested in the bicameral Parliament, which contains a popularly elected National Assembly (lower house) and an indirectly elected

Senate (upper house). The members of the 146-seat National Assembly serve for five years. Municipal leaders elect 53 of the Senate's 56 members, while the remaining three senatorial seats are voted on by Mauritanian nationals abroad. One-third of the Senate is renewed every two years, and its members serve six-year terms.

Judiciary

Sharia law, which is based on Islam's Koran, was introduced in March 1980 and is integrated with modern law. The highest courts are the Supreme Court (Cour Supreme), which is divided into one criminal and two civil chambers, each with a president and five counselors, and the Constitutional Council, which consists of six members. The Constitution provides for an independent court system; however, the Supreme Court President and three of the members of the Constitutional Council are appointed by the nation's president. Regional Courts (Wilaya) are located in each of the country's 13 regions. Other subordinate courts include commercial and labor courts; criminal courts and district (moughataa) courts.

Local Government

There are 12 administrative regions and the capital district of Nouakchott, each ruled by an appointed governor. The regions are subdivided into a total of 208 districts. Elections for rural councils were established in 1989.

Election Qualifications

All citizens 18 years of age and older may vote.

POLITICS

Maaouya Ould Sid Ahmed Taya seized control of the government in 1984 and ruled Mauritania for the next two decades. Though Taya introduced a new Mauritanian constitution that called for a multiparty system in 1991, his Democratic and Social Republican Party maintained a virtual monopoly on power, and successive elections were widely condemned as fraudulent by international observers. In August 2005, while Taya was out of the country, his government was ousted by a military junta led by Col. Ely Ould Mohamed Vall. After another constitution passed in a June 2006 national referendum, Vall, a former adviser to Taya, steered the country to legislative elections in November and December 2006 and its first-ever free and fair presidential elections in March 2007.

Former government minister, exile, and political prisoner Sidi Ould Cheikh Abdallahi narrowly won the presidency in a second-round runoff against Ahmed Ould Daddah, the leader of the Rally of Democratic Forces and brother of the nation's founding president, Moktar Ould Daddah. In a nation ruled almost exclusively by men of the country's fair-skinned Arab-Berber (*Beydane*) population since independence in 1960, April 2007 signaled a major shift in the makeup of Mauritania's government. Abdallahi's prime minister Zein Ould Zeidane appointed a cabinet on April 30 that included several female ministers and four ministers from the Progressive Popular Alliance (Alliance Populaire et Progressive—APP), a party representing slaves and former slaves. In addition, the party's leader, Messaoud Ould Boulkheir, was elected president of the National Assembly, the second-highest office in the country.

Abdallahi's term in office, however, ended prematurely, as legislators began accusing him of cronyism and blaming him for the skyrocketing cost of living in Mauritania. In July 2008, Parliament passed a no-confidence motion against Abdallahi's government, leading to its dismissal. In response, Abdallahi threatened to dissolve Parliament and also began a military shake-up, dismissing several top officials. Only days later, Gen. Mohamed Ould Abdelaziz led a coup against Abdallahi, installing himself as leader. In the years since, Abdelaziz has been widely credited with helping the country achieve major economic growth, and he has been given credit for successfully preventing terrorist groups like Al Qaeda's regional operation in North and West Africa from moving into Mauritania. Opponents charge that he is authoritarian, and many boycotted the 2014 elections. Abdelaziz won the election, which many observers considered unfairly rigged in his favor, with 81 percent of the vote.

Political Parties

Opposition parties were legalized in July 1991, leading to the official recognition of 16 parties in time for 1992 legislative elections. By the time of the 2014 presidential elections, at least 26 political parties were recognized—roughly one party for every 50,000 registered voters in that election. Following are some of the more important parties.

The National Forum for Democracy and Unity is a coalition of nearly a dozen parties that united to boycott the 2013 elections, which they charged were being conducted unfairly.

The ruling Union for the Republic Party, which is a centrist group, was formed by President Mohamed Abdelaziz in 2009, months after he led a coup that overthrew the previous government.

The Democratic and Social Republican Party (Parti Républicain Démocratique et Social—PRDS) was launched in early 1991 to lobby for Taya's presidential candidacy. It secured a majority of seats in the March 1992 and October 2001 National Assembly elections, and held virtually unchallenged political control in the legislature until April 2007.

President Mohamed Ould Abdelaziz of the Islamic Republic of Mauritania is a career military officer who led a coup d'etat to overthrow Mauritania's previous regime in 2005. He was elected as a civilian president in 2009 and re-elected in 2014. (Pascal Potier/Visual Press Age/ ZUMAPRESS/Newscom)

The Action for Change (AC), formed in 1995 and led by Messaoud Ould Boulkheir, advocated greater rights for dark-skinned citizens and former slaves and their descendants, who still face discrimination in Mauritania. It was the only opposition group to win a seat in 1996 elections to the National Assembly, and it won an additional three seats in 2001 elections. However, the government banned the party in January 2002, and none of its members were allowed to take their Assembly seats.

The Rally of Democratic Forces (Rassemblement des Forces Démocratiques—RFD), formerly known as the Union of Democratic Forces–New Era, was considered the country's main opposition group under the rule of Maaouya Ould Sid Ahmed Taya and was legalized in October 1991.

The Rally of Democratic Patriots (RPD) makes special appeals to Mauritania's darker-skinned citizens and exiles and is committed to "an equal, united Mauritania," the return of Mauritania's dark-skinned refugees and exiles in Senegal and Mali, the end of slave practices in the country, and the practice and protection of a vigorous free press.

ECONOMY

Mauritania is one of the world's poorest countries, and although its desert terrain makes farming difficult, half the workforce is still employed in agriculture and raising livestock. The main agricultural products are dates, millet, sorghum, and rice, though supplies of these foods are not enough to meet the country's food needs. In 2004, widespread drought coupled with a locust invasion devastated crops and livestock, leaving some 400,000 people without enough food. In addition, the nomadic, cattle-raising people who traditionally lived in the north of the country have largely been forced into the cities as a result of the spread of drought-stricken desert across more and more of the region over the past quarter-century.

However, in recent years fishing has become an increasingly lucrative industry, bolstering the nation's domestic food supply and export earnings. Still, though Mauritania has 469 miles of coast along the east of the Atlantic Ocean, its rich stocks are potentially endangered by foreign overfishing. The nation is forced to import much of its food and has a massive foreign debt. Mining, especially of iron ore, is a major industry. Mauritania recently joined the exclusive club of North African oil-producers, and is pinning hopes for economic growth on oil and natural gas reserves that lie beneath the Atlantic off the country's coastline. Other natural resources include gypsum, copper, and salt. Recent discoveries of rare blue granite could also have a substantial impact on the economy. In addition, a number of road-building projects—particularly one linking the capital city to a key commercial port—are expected to increase trade and tourism. The nation's main trading partners are France, Japan, Italy, and Spain.

Mauritania is located in northwestern Africa along the coast of the Atlantic Ocean, but much of the country is situated in the Sahara Desert, where many Mauritanians live in nomadic dwellings. (Michel Gounot/GODONG/picture-alliance/Godong/Newscom)

SOCIETY

The majority of Mauritania's population is of Moorish descent, which refers to Arab and Berber ethnicity. Of the Hassaniya-speaking Moorish population, less than half is considered to belong to the *Beydane* caste, meaning that in the eyes of society, they have no slave ancestry. The *Haratin* caste is viewed as the descendants of slaves. Frequently, the *Haratin* have a larger proportion of dark-skinned African ancestry and are darker skinned than their *Beydane* counterparts. The education acquired by the *Haratin* under the French colonial administration made them vital to the formation of a modern bureaucracy in the cities of Mauritania. The non-Hassaniya-speaking population is composed of several peoples, including the Tukulor, Fulani, Soninke, and Wolof. Most have retained their ethnic languages, and resisted the recent move that made Arabic the country's official language. Nearly all inhabitants of Mauritania are Sunni Muslims.

Ethnic Composition

Haratin Moor – 40%; *Beydane* Moor – 30%; black African – 30%

Language

Arabic is the official and national language. Hassaniya is the particular Arabic dialect spoken in Mauritania. Pulaar, Soninke, and Wolof are also spoken widely. French is used in schools and in business transactions as well.

Religion

Muslim – 100%

CONTEMPORARY ISSUES

Slavery

Despite the official abolition of slavery four times in Mauritania—first by the French colonial administration, again at independence, and twice more through legislation in 1981 and 2007—the United Nations has estimated that between 10 percent and 20 percent of the population is still enslaved. This statistic is higher among members of the "freed slaves" (*Haratin*) caste, many of whom today are free in name only. While some *Haratins* have been socially mobile, with a few even managing to hold government positions, the local antislavery organization SOS-Slaves estimates that several hundred thousand *Haratins* remain in bondage in Mauritania.

Chattel slavery—the outright ownership of one human by another—has a history at least several centuries long in the area encompassed by modern Mauritania. The practice became a region-wide institution with the arrival of Arab-Berber raiders from the north beginning in the seventh century CE, and eventually developed into the vast trans-Saharan slave trade. Some 40 percent of Mauritania's population today belongs to the *Haratin* caste, which consists of slaves and their descendants. Having lived for centuries under the thumb of the elite, slave-owning *Beydane* caste, the *Haratin* are now nearly identical culturally and linguistically with their former masters. Long a taboo subject in Mauritanian politics, slavery finally entered the sphere of public debate during the country's first free and fair presidential elections in 2006–2007. Former slave and antislavery activist Messaoud Ould Boulkheir received 10 percent of the vote in first-round elections contested by 19 candidates. That April, he went on to become president of Parliament, the second-highest office in the country.

Repatriating Deportees

Prior to independence from France in 1960, the Wolof, Soninke, and other dark-skinned African groups dominated Mauritania's colonial bureaucracy, largely because dark-skinned Africans attended French colonial schools more frequently than did members of the lighter-skinned Arab-Berber *Beydane* caste, many of whom saw the educational system as a tool of the Roman Catholic Church for converting Muslims. Beginning in the 1960s, however, the government launched an aggressive Arabization campaign that involved the gradual purge of darker-skinned people from positions in the government and the enforcement of Arabic-language-only education. When dark-skinned Africans rose against these policies, with several leaders signing a document of protest called the "Manifesto of the 19" in 1966, the government responded with a series of violent attacks. Discriminatory policies against dark-skinned Africans only multiplied under successive regimes, peaking with an ethnic cleansing campaign in 1989–1991 under the rule of Maaouya Ould Sid Ahmed Taya. During that period, some 100,000 dark-skinned Mauritanians were deported to neighboring Senegal and Mali. Those who risked reentering Mauritania—often to reconnect with lost family members—were placed in detention camps if caught and were routinely tortured. The government of former president Sidi Ould Cheikh Abdallahi, who served from April 2007 to August 2008, officially welcomed the refugees back into Mauritania and requested assistance in repatriating them from the United Nations High Commissioner for Refugees (UNHCR). Between January 2008 and the end of 2010, almost 20,000 refugees returned to Mauritania with the help of the UNHCR. By mid-2013, some 38,000 refugees remained displaced.

Relations with Israel

In 1996, Mauritania began normalizing its relations with Israel by opening offices for trade. Three years later, it established full diplomatic relations with Israel, becoming only the third Arab League nation to do so, after Egypt and Jordan. Despite the government's warm reception of Israeli officials, popular opposition to the normalization of relations remained strong, and protests occurred sporadically. Some regarded the establishment of relations with Israel as a public relations stunt meant to encourage foreign states to overlook the government's human rights violations; the United States had excluded Mauritania from trade benefits over the slavery issue in 1996 but reversed its policy following the creation of diplomatic ties. In 2009, authorities expelled Israeli diplomats and closed the Israeli embassy in the capital in response to Israeli attacks on Palestinian enclaves in Gaza. A year later, Mauritania officially severed diplomatic ties with Israel.

Fighting Terrorism

In the years since the global war on terror began in 2001, Mauritania has emerged as a key partner for Western counterterrorism efforts. Several major international terrorist organizations, including the Movement for the Unity of Jihad in West

Africa and Al Qaeda, are thought to have strongholds in the country, and concerns over the threat of terrorism have been high since a 2005 attack on a national military installation left 15 soldiers dead. Between 2005 and 2013, there were more than a dozen major attacks on both military and civilian targets. In 2010, Mauritania adopted new counterterrorism legislation, giving security forces expanded power in the fight against Al Qaeda and other terrorist groups. In 2013, the United States began a specialized training program in Mauritania to develop an elite counterterrorism force. Funded by the Pentagon, the program will provide more than $29 million in surveillance equipment and combat training to help take down local terrorist cells.

Excerpt from the Constitution of Mauritania

The current constitution of Mauritania was adopted in 1991. It identifies Mauritania specifically as an Islamic state. Its intent is to "create the durable conditions for a harmonious social development respectful of the precepts of Islam, the sole source of law, but responsive as well to the exigencies of the modern world." Islam is the state religion of Mauritania, and the Constitution requires that the President of Mauritania be a Muslim.

Mauritania identifies itself not only with Islam, but also with Africa and the Arab world. A goal of the state is to "[proclaim] that it will work for the achievement of the unity of the Greater Mahgreb of the Arab Nation and of Africa" (the Maghreb referring to the Arab-majority countries of North Africa including also Morocco, Algeria, Tunisia, and Libya). Within the constraints of Islam, the Constitution specifies equality under the law, the right to vote, freedom of expression, and freedom of assembly. Innocence is presumed unless and until guilt is proven. As is the case with other Islamic-majority states, the Constitution identifies the family as the basic unit of society. However, the Constitution does not address questions of economic rights, including the rights to education, health care, welfare, or social security.

PREAMBLE

Trusting in the omnipotence of Allah, the Mauritanian people proclaims its will to guarantee the integrity of its territory, its independence, and its national unity and to take upon itself its free political economic and social development. Believing strongly in its spiritual values and in the spreading of its civilization, it also solemnly proclaims its attachment to Islam and to the principles of democracy as they have been defined by the Universal Declaration of Human Rights of 10 Dec 1948. . .

Judging that liberty, equality, and the dignity of Man may be assured only in a society which establishes the primacy of law, taking care to create the durable conditions for a harmonious social development respectful of the precepts of Islam, the sole source of law, but responsive as well to the exigencies of the modern world, the Mauritanian people proclaims in particular the inalienable guarantee of the following rights and principles: the right to equality; the fundamental freedoms and rights of human beings; the right of property; political freedom and freedom of labor unions; economic and social rights; and the rights attached to the family, the basic unit of Islamic society. Conscious of the necessity of strengthening its ties with brother peoples, the Mauritanian people, a Muslim, African, and Arab people, proclaims that it will work for the achievement of the unity of the Greater Mahgreb of the Arab Nation and of Africa and for the consolidation of peace in the world.

TITLE I

GENERAL PROVISIONS, FUNDAMENTAL PRINCIPLES

Article 1

(1) Mauritania is an indivisible, democratic, and social Islamic Republic.
(2) The Republic guarantees equality before the law to all of its citizens without distinction as to origin, race, sex, or social condition.
(3) All particularist propaganda of racial or ethnic character shall be punished by the law.

Article 2

(1) The people shall be the source of all power.

Article 3

(1) Suffrage may be either direct or indirect according to the provisions of the law. It shall always be universal, equal, and secret.
(2) All the citizens of the Republic of both sexes, who are adults and possess their civil and political rights, may vote.

Article 4

The law is the supreme expression of the will of the people. All are required to submit to it.

Article 5

Islam shall be the religion of the people and of the State . . .

Article 10

(1) The State shall guarantee to all its citizens public and individual freedoms: the freedom to travel and to settle in all parts of the territory of the Republic; the

freedom of entry to and of exit from the national territory; the freedom of opinion and of thought; the freedom of expression; the freedom of assembly; the freedom of association and the freedom to belong to any political or labor organization of one's choice; the freedom of commerce and of industry; and the freedom of intellectual, artistic, and scientific creative effort.

(2) Freedom may be limited only by the law . . .

Article 13

(1) All persons shall be presumed innocent until the establishment of their guilt by a regularly constituted court.

(2) No one may be prosecuted, arrested, detained, or punished except in cases determined by the law and according to the formalities which it prescribes.

(3) The honor and the private life of the citizen and the inviolability of his person his domicile and his correspondence shall be protected by the State.

(4) All forms of moral or physical violence shall be proscribed.

Article 14

(1) The right to strike is recognized. It may be exercised within the framework of the laws which regulate it.

(2) Strikes may he forbidden by law for all public services or activities of vital interest to the Nation.

(3) It is forbidden in the areas of national defense and security.

Source: "Mauritania Index." International Constitutional Law Project. http://www.servat.unibe.ch/icl/mr__indx.html

PALESTINE: De Facto State

PALESTINE

Communications	Land-based Telephones in Use
Facebook Users	406,000 (2012)
1,180,000 (estimate) (2011)	Mobile Telephone Subscribers
Internet Users	3,041,000 (2012)
1,379,000 (2009)	Major Daily Newspapers
Internet Users (% of Population)	3 (2004)
46.6% (2013)	
Television	Average Circulation of Daily Newspapers
15 sets per 100 population (2004)	35,000 (2004)

Education	Nuclear Power Plants
Average Years Spent in School for Current Students, Male	0 (2014)
	Crude Oil Production
13 (2012)	0 (2013)
Average Years Spent in School for Current Students, Female	Crude Oil Consumption
	23,300 barrels per day (2012)
14 (2012)	Natural Gas Production
Primary School–age Children Enrolled in Primary School	0 cubic meters per year (estimate) (2011)
	Natural Gas Consumption
424,095 (2012)	0 cubic meters per year (estimate) (2011)
Primary School–age Males Enrolled in Primary School	Natural Resources
	Arable land, natural gas
218,299 (2012)	Environment
Primary School–age Females Enrolled in Primary School	CO2 Emissions
205,796 (2012)	0.6 metric tons per capita (2009)
Secondary School–age Children Enrolled in Secondary School	Alternative and Nuclear Energy
	Not Available
705,443 (2012)	Threatened Species
Secondary School–age Males Enrolled in Secondary School	18 (2010)
	Protected Areas
343,863 (2012)	40 (estimate) (2010)
Secondary School–age Females Enrolled in Secondary School	Geography
	Capital
361,580 (2012)	NA
Students Per Teacher, Primary School	Area
24.4 (2012)	2,402 sq. miles
Students Per Teacher, Secondary School	Health
20.2 (2012)	Average Life Expectancy
Enrollment in Tertiary Education	75.2 years (2014)
217,502 (2012)	Average Life Expectancy, Male
Enrollment in Tertiary Education, Male	72.6 years (2014)
92,182 (2012)	Average Life Expectancy, Female
Enrollment in Tertiary Education, Female	77.2 years (2014)
125,320 (2012)	Crude Birth Rate
Literacy	27.1 (estimate) (2015)
95% (2010)	Crude Death Rate
Energy and Natural Resources	3.3 (estimate) (2015)
Electric Power Consumption	Infant Mortality
550,000,000 kilowatt hours per year (estimate) (2011)	Not Available

Doctors	**External Debt**
0.8 per 1,000 people (2001)	$1,040,000,000 (estimate) (2010)
Industry and Labor	**Economic Aid Extended**
Gross Domestic Product (GDP) - official exchange rate	$0 (2011)
	Economic Aid Received
Not Available	$2,444,000,000 (2011)
GDP per Capita	**Population**
Not Available	**Population**
GDP - Purchasing Power Parity (PPP)	7,716,592 (estimate) (2015)
Not Available	**World Population Rank**
GDP (PPP) per Capita	126 th
Not Available	**Population Density**
Unemployment	1,671 (estimate) (2009)
23.0 (West Bank only) (2012)	**Population Distribution**
Labor Profile	72 urban (2008)
agriculture: 16.1% industry: 28.4% services: 55.5% (estimate) (2010)	**Age Distribution**
Military	0-14: 39.5%
Total Active Armed Forces	15-64: 57.2%
0 (2010)	65+: 3.3%
Active Armed Forces	**Median Age**
0% (2010)	20.3 years (estimate) (2014)
Annual Military Expenditures	**Population Growth Rate**
$0 (2009)	2.4% per year (estimate) (2015)
Military Service	**Net Migration Rate**
Not available.	0.0 (estimate) (2015)
National Finances	**Trade**
Currency	**Current Account Balance**
NA	$-2,100,000,000 (estimate, West Bank only) (2011)
Total Government Revenues	**Transportation**
$2,100,000,000 (estimate) (2011)	**Airports**
Total Government Expenditures	3 (2012)
$3,200,000,000 (estimate) (2011)	**Paved Roads**
Budget Deficit	100.0% (2010)
-16.6 (estimate) (2011)	**Passenger Cars per 1,000 People**
GDP Contribution by Sector	33 (2010)
agriculture: 5.3% industry: 12.4% services: 82.2% (2012 est.)	

Palestine, sometimes known as the Palestine Occupied Territories, is a de facto state located in southwest Asia. Its territory has been under the control of the Palestine National Authority (PNA) since 1994, although only some countries recognize the PNA as Palestine's official government. It is not a member of the United Nations but was granted official observer status in 2012. In July 2014, Mahmoud Abbas was the President of Palestine, and Rami Hamdallah was its Prime Minister.

Palestine includes two distinct and separate regions, the West Bank and the Gaza Strip. The West Bank, named for its location on the western side of the Jordan River, has a land area of 2,263 square miles and a population of about 3.1 million. The Gaza Strip is located on the coast of the Mediterranean Sea northeast of the Sinai Peninsula. It has a land area of 141 square miles and a population of about 1.7 million. The two regions are separated by territory belonging to the state of Israel, with Jordan located across the Jordan River east of the West Bank and the Gaza Strip sharing a short border with Egypt northeast of the Sinai Peninsula.

Palestine is located near the eastern end of the Mediterranean Sea near where Europe, Asia, and Africa converge. Its strategic location accounts for the fact that the area has been contested by various civilizations for thousands of years. At various times, present-day Palestine was controlled by ancient Egypt, Israel, Babylon, Assyria, Greece, Rome, the Islamic caliphates, and European Crusaders. The present-day Palestinian state was part of the Ottoman Empire from 1516 until the collapse of the Empire shortly before World War I.

After the war ended, the League of Nations granted Britain a mandate over the territories of Palestine and Transjordan, which became the states of Israel and Jordan, respectively, after World War II. Thousands of Jewish settlers, primarily from Europe, moved to the territory of Palestine before and after World War II. By 1948, when Israel became an independent country, more than a million Jewish settlers were living in the former Ottoman territory of Palestine. The present-day Palestine Occupied Territories became part of Israel upon Israel's independence.

The West Bank became part of Jordan after independence, but Israeli forces captured and occupied the region in 1967. Although Israel did not annex the West Bank formally, its government encouraged Israeli farmers and other settlers to move into the region, although Arabs continued to comprise a majority of the region's population. The Gaza Strip was also occupied by Israel in 1967. A peace treaty signed by Israel and Egypt recognized Israeli sovereignty over the region.

Meanwhile, Palestinian Arabs living in the West Bank and in the Gaza Strip began to demand independence. In both regions, Palestinians—including refugees from other parts of Israel—formed a majority of the population. The Palestinian Liberation Organization (PLO) was founded in 1964 by Yasser Arafat (1929–2004),

PALESTINE OCCUPIED TERRITORIES

who was an early leader of Palestinian resistance to Israeli governance. The goal of the PLO was the creation of an independent Palestinian state. In 1988, the PLO issued a declaration of independence from Israel and established the PNA as its governing body. However, the Israeli government did not recognize the PNA as Palestine's government. In 1993, PNA and Israeli government leaders worked to negotiate the Oslo Accords. Under terms of the Oslo Accords, administration of the West Bank was divided between Israel and the PNA, which administers Palestinian-majority areas of the territory.

GOVERNMENT

The PNA remains in charge of administration of the Gaza Strip and portions of the West Bank. It is accountable to the PLO. Article 5 of the Basic Law of Palestine states that "The governing system in Palestine shall be a democratic parliamentary system, based upon political and party pluralism. The President of the National Authority shall be directly elected by the people. The government shall be accountable to the President and to the Palestinian Legislative Council."

Constitution

The PNA operates under the auspices of the Palestinian National Charter, which is in effect the constitution of the PLO. The Charter was drafted in 1964, in conjunction with the founding of the PLO. The original Charter denied Israel's right to exist, but this provision has been amended. The formal institutions of government are set forth by the Basic Law of Palestine, which was drafted in 1997 and went into effect in 2002. An eventual goal of the Palestinian state is to draft a permanent constitution for an independent Palestine.

Executive

The chief executive of Palestine is the president, who is the head of state and is elected by popular vote for a four-year term. The president must be at least 40 years of age and must be a Palestinian who is descended from Palestinian parents. A president's tenure in office is limited to two terms. The president appoints the prime minister, who is the head of government, whereas the president is the head of state.

However, disputes have arisen over the length of the president's term. In 2005, the Legislative Council passed a law that calls for the president and the Legislative Council to be elected simultaneously. This dispute was a component of the disputes between the Fatah and Hamas political factions that led to the temporary separation of Palestine's government between the West Bank and the Gaza Strip.

Legislative

Palestine has a unicameral legislature or Legislative Council. Following the Oslo Accords, the Legislative Council had 88 members. After the Basic Law took effect, the size of the Legislative Council was increased to 132 members, half of whom are elected from single-member districts and half of whom are elected nationwide via proportional representation. Members of the Legislative Council must be at least 28 years of age. Article IV of the Basic Law stipulates in part that "The principles of Islamic Shari'a shall be a principal source of legislation."

The Prime Minister heads the Legislative Council and is chosen by the political party that holds a majority of the seats in the Legislative Council. The Legislative Council remains in office for up to five years. It can be dissolved upon a vote of no confidence, which requires a majority vote of the Council. It is also dissolved upon the death or resignation of the prime minister. Elections are then held to elect a new Legislative Council.

Judiciary

The Basic Law calls for an independent judiciary. Judicial power is invested in a High Constitutional Court, which is charged with interpreting the constitutionality of legislation. The High Court of Justice resolves administrative disputes, while the Court of Cassation is charged with decisions regarding criminal cases. However, the Basic Law states that religious matters are to be adjudicated by religious courts in accordance with Sharia law, and military courts are to be established to deal with judicial issues involving Palestine's armed forces.

Local governments

Palestine is divided into 16 administrative units of local government, each of which is headed by an elected governor. Of these, 11 are located in the West Bank and 5 are located in the Gaza Strip.

Within each governorate, municipalities are created to administer local areas. Municipalities are divided into four classes based on the populations of their principal cities and towns. A-level municipalities include the seats of administration of most governorates. B-level municipalities include cities and towns of over 8,000 population. C-level municipalities include towns with populations between 4,000 and 8,000, and D-level municipalities are centered on villages with between 1,000 and 4,000 people. As of 2014, there were 14 A-level, 41 B-level, 47 C-level, and 220 D-level municipalities.

Election qualifications

All Palestinians over the age of 18 years are eligible to vote.

POLITICS

Palestine is a multiparty democracy whose elections have been contested by numerous political parties. Since the PNA assumed administration of the Palestine Occupied Territory in 1994, the two major political parties have been the Palestinian National Liberation Movement, which is known as Fatah, and the Islamic Resistance Movement, which is known as Hamas.

Yasser Arafat was the leader of the Palestinian Liberation Organization and served as President of the Palestinian National Authority from 1994 until his death in 2004. He was a founder of the Fatah party, which dominates the current government of Palestine. (Newpress/Ropi/ ZUMA Press/Newscom)

Fatah is associated with the PLO and its founder, Yasser Arafat (1929–2004). Its organization predates the formal establishment of the PNA, and many of its current leaders were active in opposing Israeli domination of present-day Palestine. Fatah is a secular party and espouses generally a center-left political ideology, although the party has become more factionalized since Arafat's death and since the PNA assumed de facto control of Palestine.

Hamas, as its name implies, is an Islamist party that is linked with the Muslim Brotherhood in Egypt. Hamas' goal is to turn Palestine into an Islamic state, and thus it takes a harder line on questions of Islamic principles and Sharia law than does Fatah. The party's charter calls for the "destruction or obliteration" of Israel. Although both parties strongly oppose Israel, in practice Fatah is more oriented to peaceful coexistence with Israel.

The first elections for the Legislative Council after the Oslo Accords were held in 1996. Fatah won 55 of the 88 contested seats, with the rest won by independent candidates or members of small parties. The first presidential election after implementation of the Basic Law was held in 2005 shortly after Arafat, who was the original president of the PNA, died in November 2004. Fatah's candidate, Mahmoud Abbas, was elected to a four-year term with 62 percent of the vote, as Hamas boycotted the election. In 2006, however, Hamas obtained a majority of seats in the Legislative Council. Hamas won 74 of the 132 seats, with 45 for Fatah and the other 13 won by small parties or independent candidates.

Hamas' victory in the 2006 legislative elections meant that it controlled the Legislative Council, while Fatah continued to control the presidency. Conflict arose, and both parties claimed succession from the pre-independence PLO. In 2007, fighters associated with Hamas seized the Gaza Strip in a brief civil war. Abbas declared a state of emergency and attempted to dismiss the Hamas-backed prime minister, Ismail Haniyeh. However, Haniyeh's dismissal was not recognized by the Hamas-controlled Legislative Council. Hamas retained control of the Gaza Strip, while Fatah remained in control of the West Bank. Abbas' term was to expire in 2009, but he remained in power in the West Bank over Hamas' opposition. Elections for the presidency and for the Legislative Council have not been held since 2006; elections were scheduled for 2014 but have been delayed indefinitely.

ECONOMY

The economy of Palestine is based on a combination of agriculture, manufacturing, and services. As of 2008, about 23 percent of Palestine's labor force was employed in manufacturing, with about 12 percent engaged in agriculture. The economy has been affected by ongoing conflict with Israel over Palestine's eventual status. After Hamas seized control of the Gaza Strip in 2007, Israel imposed an economic blockade, citing security concerns. However, Israeli and Palestinian officials have begun implementing cooperative efforts to develop Palestine's economy, including the development of a cross-border industrial park and promoting efforts to hire Palestinian scientists and engineers to work for Israeli high-tech firms. Trade between Israel and Palestine continues to increase, reaching a total value of more than 20 billion U.S. dollars by 2013.

PEOPLE

The majority of Palestine's people are Palestinian Arabs, although there is a significant Jewish minority in the West Bank. According to the Basic Law, Palestine identifies itself as an Arab state. Article I of the Basic Law reads "Palestine is part of the larger Arab world, and the Palestinian people are part of the Arab nation. Arab unity is an objective that the Palestinian people shall work to achieve."

Ethnic Composition

Currently, about 83 percent of Palestine's residents are ethnic Palestinians, and about 17 percent are Jewish. Many Jewish residents of Palestine live in areas of the West Bank outside the de facto control of the PNA.

Language

According to the Basic Law, Arabic is the official language of Palestine. Jewish residents and many Palestinian Arabs speak Hebrew. English is also spoken widely, and study of the English language is compulsory in schools.

Religion

According to the Basic Law, Islam is the official religion of Palestine, and legislation is to be enacted in accordance with the principles of Sharia law. However, "Respect for the sanctity of all other divine religions shall be maintained." About 75 percent of Palestinians are Muslims, 17 percent are Jews, and 8 percent are Christians.

CONTEMPORARY ISSUES

Two major issues currently facing Palestine include the eventual status of Palestine as an independent state and the potential resolution of conflict between Fatah and Hamas over control of Palestine's government.

The United Nations recognizes Palestine as an independent state, as do a majority of its members. However, Palestinian sovereignty is not recognized by the United States, the European Union, Canada, or Australia. Palestine applied for UN membership in 2011. Because UN procedures require that potential members must be approved by the Security Council, Palestinian leaders became concerned about the possibility that the United States would veto its application.

In 2012, Palestine requested non-member observer status, which requires only a majority vote in the UN General Assembly. A resolution granting Palestine non-member observer state status was passed in the General Assembly by a vote of 138–9, with 41 abstentions, on November 27. The United States and Israel were among the nine UN members who voted against this resolution. Observer status allows Palestine to sign international treaties and to participate in the International Criminal Court. Its official status is known as "The Permanent Observer Mission of the State of Palestine to the United Nations." In 2013, U.S. President Barack Obama reiterated that the United States would not recognize Palestinian statehood and would veto any resolution within the Security Council to grant Palestine UN membership as a state.

Hamas celebrating its 27th anniversary in 2014. Palestine is a de facto state that includes two components: the West Bank along the Jordan River and the Gaza Strip along the Mediterranean Sea. Hamas is an Islamist party that dominates the Gaza Strip portion of Palestine. (Mohammed Asad/Apaimages/Ropi/ZUMA Press/Newscom)

Efforts to resolve the split between Fatah and Hamas are ongoing. The two factions negotiated to resolve their differences on several occasions, beginning in 2011. In 2014, PLO officials sent by Abbas signed an agreement with Haniyeh, as the head of Hamas, to implement a unity government and to hold elections for President and the Legislative Council later in the year.

Excerpt from the Palestinian Authority's Basic Law

Palestine is governed by the Basic Law, which was adopted originally in 2002 and modified in 2003. Implementation of the Basic Law is undertaken by the Palestine National Authority and applied to the West Bank and the Gaza Strip, the two territories administered by the Palestine National Authority.

The Basic Law identifies Palestine as an Islamic state, establishes Islam as Palestine's official religion, and specifies that the principles of Sharia law "shall be the main source of legislation." Within the context of Islamic principles, the Basic Law calls for freedom of speech, freedom of religion, freedom of the press, and the right to fair trial. However, these rights are constrained by the larger scope of the law. For example, the clause involving freedom of religion states that "Freedom of belief, worship, and performance of religious rituals are guaranteed, provided that they do not violate public order or public morals." The Basic Law identifies education, welfare, and housing as fundamental rights of the Palestinian people.

The Basic Law also identifies Palestine as a part of a larger, united Arab community. Moreover, it identifies the city of Jerusalem as the capital of the Palestinian state, although this claim is not recognized by the international community.

The Palestinian Authority

TITLE ONE

Article 1

Palestine is part of the large Arab World, and the Palestinian people are part of the Arab Nation. Arab Unity is an objective which the Palestinian People shall work to achieve.

Article 2

The People is the source of power, which shall be exercised through the legislative, executive, and judicial authorities, based on the principle of separation of powers, and in the manner set forth in this Basic Law.

Article 3

Jerusalem is the capital of Palestine.

Article 4

- Islam is the official religion in Palestine. Respect and sanctity of all other heavenly religions shall be maintained.
- The principles of Islamic Shari'a [sharia] shall be the main Source of legislation.
- Arabic shall be the official language.

TITLE TWO: PUBLIC RIGHTS & FREEDOMS

Article 9

All Palestinians are equal under the law and judiciary, without discrimination because of race, sex, color, religion, political views, or disability.

Article 10

- Basic human rights and freedoms shall be binding and respected.
- The Palestinian National Authority shall work without delay to join regional and international declarations and covenants which protect human rights.

Article 11

- Personal freedom is a natural right, and shall be guaranteed and protected.
- It is unlawful to arrest, search, imprison, restrict the freedom, or prevent the movement of, any person, except by judicial order in accordance with the provisions of law. The law shall specify the period of pre-arrest detention. Imprisonment or detention shall only be permitted in places that are subject to laws related to the organization of prisons.

Article 12

Every arrested person shall be informed of the reasons for his arrest or detention. He shall be promptly informed, in a language he understands, of the nature of the charges brought against him. He shall have the right to contact a lawyer and to be tried without delay . . .

Article 14

The accused is innocent until proven guilty in a court of law that guarantees the right to defend himself. Any person accused in a criminal case shall have a lawyer to defend him . . .

Article 17

Homes shall be inviolable; thus, they shall not be subject to surveillance, entrance, or search, except in accordance with a valid judicial order, and in accordance with the provisions of law. Any consequences resulting from violations of this article shall be considered invalid.

Article 18

Freedom of belief, worship, and performance of religious rituals are guaranteed, provided that they do not violate public order or public morals.

Article 19

Every person shall have the right to freedom of thought, conscience, and expression, and shall have the right to publish his opinion orally, in writing, or in any form of art, or through any other form of expression, provided that it does not contradict with the provisions of law.

Article 20

Freedom of residence and movement shall be guaranteed within the limits of law.

Article 22

- Social, health, disability, and retirement insurance shall be regulated by law.
- The welfare of families of martyrs, prisoners of war, the injured, and the disabled is a duty that shall be regulated by law. The National Authority shall guarantee them education, health services, and social insurance.

Article 23

Proper housing is a right for every citizen. The Palestinian National Authority shall secure housing for those without shelter.

Article 24

Every citizen shall have the right to education. It shall be compulsory until at least the end of basic grades, and shall be free in public schools and institutes . . . Private schools and educational institutions shall comply with the curriculum approved by the Palestinian National Authority, and shall be subject to its supervision.

Article 25

- Work is a right, duty, and honor. The Palestinian National Authority shall strive to provide it to any individual capable of performing it.
- Work relations shall be organized in a manner which guarantees justice to all workers, and provides security, health, and social insurance.
- Organization of unions and guilds is a right which shall be regulated by law.
- The right to conduct a strike shall be exercised within the limits of law.

Article 26

Palestinians shall have the right to participate in the political life individually and in groups. They shall have the following rights in particular:

- To form, establish, and join political parties in accordance with the law.
- To form and establish unions, guilds, associations, societies, clubs, and popular institutions in accordance with the law.
- To vote and nominate for election representatives among them by ballot in accordance with the law.
- To hold public office and positions in accordance with the principle of equal opportunities.
- To conduct special meetings without the presence of police members, and to conduct public meetings, processions, and assemblies within the limits of law.

Article 27

- Establishment of newspapers and all media means is a right for all, guaranteed by this Basic Law. However, their financing resources shall be subject to law.
- Freedom of audio, visual, and written media, as well as freedom to print, publish, distribute, transmit, together with the freedom of individuals working in this field, is guaranteed by this Basic Law, and other related laws.
- Censorship on media shall be prohibited. No warning, suspension, confiscation, cancellation, or restrictions shall be imposed on media except by law, and in accordance with a judicial ruling.

Article 28

No Palestinian may be deported from the homeland, prevented or prohibited from returning to or leaving it, deprived of his [citizenship], or surrendered to any foreign entity.

Article 29

Maternity and childhood welfare is a national duty. Children shall have the right to:

- Comprehensive protection and welfare.
- Not to be exploited in any purpose whatsoever, and shall not be allowed to perform works which might damage their safety, health, or education.
- Protection from harm and cruel treatment . . .

Article 31

An independent commission for human rights shall be established by law, which will specify its formation, duties, jurisdiction. The commission shall submit its reports to the President of the National Authority, and to the Palestinian Legislative Council [PLC] . . .

Article 33

A balanced and clean environment is one of the human rights. The preservation and protection of the Palestinian environment from pollution, for the sake of present and future generation, is a national duty.

Source: "Declaration of Principles on Interim Self-Government Arrangements." United Nations Information System. http://unispal.un.org/unispal.nsf/0/71DC8C 9D96D2F0FF85256117007CB6CA

PUERTO RICO: Commonwealth

The Commonwealth of Puerto Rico is located in the Caribbean Sea. It is under the sovereignty of the United States. Whether Puerto Rico will retain its current commonwealth status, become a state of the United States, or become an independent country has been a matter of concern among Puerto Ricans for many years.

Most of the Commonwealth consists of the island of Puerto Rico itself. The island is the smallest of the Greater Antilles, following Cuba, Hispaniola, and Jamaica. In addition to the main island, the Commonwealth includes several nearby islands. The total land area of the Commonwealth of Puerto Rico is 3,515 square miles, somewhat smaller that the state of Connecticut. Its population is about 3.7 million. As of July 2014, the Governor of Puerto Rico is Alejandro Garcia Padilla.

The island of Puerto Rico was inhabited by indigenous Taino people when it was first sighted by Christopher Columbus during his second voyage to the Western Hemisphere in 1493. The Spanish began to establish colonies on the island in the early sixteenth century and began to enslave the Taino. By 1525, most of the indigenous Taino had died from overwork and exposure to European diseases to which they lacked immunity. African slaves were brought in to provide labor, but most of the economic activity in colonial Puerto Rico was concentrated in the port cities and on sugar plantations near the coast. While mainland Spanish colonies in Mexico, Central America, and South America became independent in the early nineteenth century, Spain worked actively to maintain control of Puerto Rico and nearby Cuba because of their ports' importance in maritime trade.

In 1898, the United States invaded Puerto Rico during the Spanish-American War. At the end of the war, Spain ceded Puerto Rico to the United States. At first,

PUERTO RICO

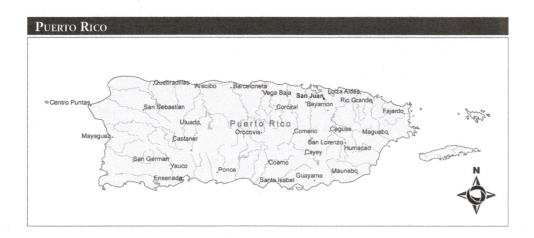

Puerto Rico was governed by military governors from the United States. During the early twentieth century, the current system of government was put in place. Puerto Ricans were granted U.S. citizenship in 1917, and they were given the right to elect their own governor in 1947.

GOVERNMENT

Puerto Rico is governed by the Constitution of the Commonwealth of Puerto Rico. However, the Constitution of the Commonwealth is subordinate to the Constitution of the United States, given Puerto Rico's status as a United States commonwealth. The president of the United States is Puerto Rico's head of state. Puerto Ricans are U.S. citizens, subject to the qualifications for citizenship established in the United States as a whole. They may not vote for the president of the United States or for members of the U.S. Senate and House of Representatives. However, Puerto Rico elects a non-voting delegate to the House of Representatives, who is known as the resident commissioner. The resident commissioner may not vote on legislation but otherwise has the same rights and privileges as other members of the House.

Constitution

In 1950, the United States Congress authorized the creation of a Constitutional Assembly, within which delegates would draft a constitution for the Commonwealth. The Congressional act authorizing the creation of the Constitutional Assembly stipulated that the constitution must include a bill of rights and must establish a republican form of government. On March 3, 1952, the voters of Puerto Rico approved the draft constitution in a referendum, with 82 percent supporting the draft. The draft was approved by Congress with minor modifications, and the Constitution of the Commonwealth went into effect on July 25.

The Constitution of the Commonwealth includes nine articles. Article I establishes Puerto Rico's republican form of government with legislative, executive, and judicial branches. These branches are dealt with in Articles III, IV, and V respectively. Article II includes the Bill of Rights. Article VI authorizes the government to collect taxes and deals with the establishment and operation of local governance. Article VII describes the procedure by which the Constitution can be amended, although it has not been amended since 1962. Article VIII deals with the creation of districts to elect members of the Puerto Rican legislature, and the final article addresses the processes by which the Constitution would be implemented once it went into effect.

The Constitution makes frequent reference to the relationship between Puerto Rico and the United States. The Preamble reads in part, "We consider as determining factors in our life our citizenship of the United States of America and our aspiration continually to enrich our democratic heritage in the individual and collective enjoyment of its rights and privileges; our loyalty to the principles of the Federal Constitution; the co-existence in Puerto Rico of the two great cultures of the American Hemisphere; our fervor for education; our faith in justice; our devotion to the courageous, industrious, and peaceful way of life; our fidelity to individual human values above and beyond social position, racial differences, and economic interests; and our hope for a better world based on these principles." This relationship is reiterated in Section 1 of Article I, which reads, "The Commonwealth of Puerto Rico is hereby constituted. Its political power emanates from the people and shall be exercised in accordance with their will, within the terms of the compact agreed upon between the people of Puerto Rico and the United States of America."

Executive

Article IV of the Constitution of the Commonwealth grants executive power to the governor of Puerto Rico. The governor is elected by popular vote to a four-year term. He or she must be at least 35 years of age, a citizen of the United States, and a resident of Puerto Rico. The powers of the governor include the right to appoint secretaries of executive departments with the advice and consent of the Senate. These secretaries serve collectively as the Council of Secretaries, which serves a role analogous to the Cabinet of the United States. The Secretary of State, who is also a member of the Council of Secretaries, becomes governor upon the death, resignation, removal, or incapacity of the governor, and serves for the remainder of the previous governor's term of office. The governor may veto bills passed by the Legislative Assembly, but the Assembly can override the governor's veto by a two-thirds majority vote of each house.

Legislature

The powers and duties of the Legislative Assembly are spelled out in Article III of the Constitution of the Commonwealth. The Legislative Assembly is a bicameral legislature and includes the Senate, with 27 members, and the House of Representatives, with 51 members. The Commonwealth is divided into 40 representative districts, with each electing one Representative. The 40 representative districts are combined in groups of five into eight senatorial districts, with each electing two Senators. The remaining 11 Senators and 11 Representatives are elected at large. All members of the Senate and the House of Representatives are elected for four-year terms, with no limits on the number of terms that they can serve. According to the Constitution of the Commonwealth, all members of the Legislative Assembly must be able to read and write both Spanish and English.

Judiciary

Judicial power in Puerto Rico rests with the Supreme Court, which includes a Chief Justice and four Associate Justices. The justices are appointed by the governor, subject to the approval of the Senate. The justices remain in office subject to "good behavior," but must retire at the age of 70. Each justice must be a citizen of the United States and of Puerto Rico, and must have been admitted to the Puerto Rican bar at least ten years before being appointed to the Supreme Court. The Supreme Court is the final arbiter of justice within Puerto Rico, but is subject to the legal jurisdiction of the United States.

Local Government

Puerto Rico is divided into 78 municipalities, each of which can be regarded as equivalent to a county within a U.S. state. Each municipality is governed by a mayor and a municipal legislature. The mayor and members of the municipal legislature are elected by the municipality's population. Most municipalities are divided into two or more *barrios,* each of which has administrative authority over its territory within the municipality.

Election Qualifications

All residents of Puerto Rico who are citizens of the United States and are at least eighteen years of age may vote in Puerto Rican elections, including elections for governor, seats in the Legislative Assembly, and for the mayor and the municipal legislature in the municipality of residence.

POLITICS

The future status of Puerto Rico is a major issue in Puerto Rican politics, as it has been since Puerto Rico became an American colony following the Spanish-American War. Puerto Ricans continue to consider four possibilities. These include maintaining the current commonwealth status, free association with the United States outside the commonwealth structure, statehood within the United States, and outright independence.

Periodically, the voters of Puerto Rico have been asked to vote on the future status of the Commonwealth. Referenda on this question were held in 1967, 1993, 1998, and 2012. In each case, a majority of votes was cast for maintaining commonwealth status. The 2012 referendum, which was held on the same day as elections for governor, resident commissioner, and the Legislative Assembly, posed the question in two parts. First, voters were asked whether they preferred to maintain current

A Puerto Rican man holding a sign expressing his opposition to statehood prior to a non-binding referendum in 2012. Many Puerto Ricans support statehood for Puerto Rico, while others support outright independence, and others are in favor of maintaining the current commonwealth status. (Jack Kurtz UPI Photo Service/Newscom)

commonwealth status. Second, they were asked, regardless of how they voted on the first question, to identify their preferences among the alternatives of statehood, independence, or sovereign association. The final alternative was worded, "Puerto Rico should adopt a status outside of the Territory Clause of the Constitution of the United States that recognizes the sovereignty of the People of Puerto Rico. The Sovereign Free Associated State would be based on a free and voluntary political association, the specific terms of which shall be agreed upon between the United States and Puerto Rico as sovereign nations. Such agreement would provide the scope of the jurisdictional powers that the People of Puerto Rico agree to confer to the United States and retain all other jurisdictional powers and authorities."

The results of this referendum showed that a majority of voters preferred not to maintain the status quo. Fifty-four percent voted that Puerto Rico's status should be changed, whereas 46 percent supported maintaining commonwealth society. On the second question, 61 percent preferred statehood, 33 percent supported sovereign association, and 6 percent supported independence. The results of these referenda were presented to the U.S. federal government. However, concerns about ambiguity in the presentation of alternatives have called the validity of these results into question.

Political Parties

In elections, Puerto Rican voters may vote a straight party ticket, in which their vote for a particular party is registered for all of that party's candidates for contested offices. Alternatively, they may split their tickets and vote for candidates from various parties for different contested offices. Under Puerto Rican election law, a political party is considered a "registered" political party if it receives at least 3 percent of straight party ticket votes in the previous election. Any party whose candidate for governor receives 5 percent or more of the vote in the previous election is also registered. As well, any party whose candidates for governor and resident commissioner receive 7 percent or more of the votes for these offices combined is registered. Parties may also be registered by petition. Registration by petition requires that the petition be signed by the number of voters that is equivalent to at least 3 percent of the total votes cast for governor in the most recent election.

As of 2014, six political parties were registered under these qualifications. These parties include the Partido Nueva Progresista (New Progressive Party—PNP), the Partido Popular Democratico (Popular Democratic Party—PPD), the Partido Puertorriquenos por Puerto Rico (Puerto Ricans for Puerto Rico Party—PPR), the Partido del Pueblo Trabajador (Working People's Party—PPT), the Partido Independentista Puertorriquenos (Puerto Rican Independence Party—PIP), and the Movimiento Union Soberanista (Sovereign Union Movement—MUS). Several other smaller parties were unregistered but compete for public offices, although as of the 2012 election none have been successful in winning legislative seats.

The parties differ with respect to their views on the question of Puerto Rico's long-term status. The PNP supports statehood for Puerto Rico, while the PPD advocates retaining Puerto Rico's current commonwealth status. The PIP, as its name implies, supports independence for Puerto Rico. The PPR, which is an outgrowth of Green Parties in the United States and Europe, supports programs of social and economic reform and environmental quality. PPT is a left-wing socialist movement, and MUS supports greater sovereignty for Puerto Rico.

The two largest of these six parties are PPD and PNP. In the 2012 gubernatorial election, PPD candidate Alejandro Garcia Padilla narrowly defeated PNP's candidate, incumbent Governor Luis Fortuno, by a popular vote margin of 47.7 percent to 47.1 percent. Thus these two parties got nearly 95 percent of the popular vote. However, PNP candidate Pedro Pierluisi defeated PPD candidate Rafael Cox Alomar for the office of Resident Commissioner by a margin of 48.4 percent to 47.2 percent. PPD won a majority of seats in the Legislative Assembly, with 18 Senate seats, as opposed to 8 for PNP and one for PIP. In the House, PPD won 28 seats to 23 for PNP. PPD candidates won 47 elections for mayors of municipalities, with 31 for PNP. The partisan division of these offices reflects roughly the division of opinion within Puerto Rico with respect to views on the future status of the Commonwealth.

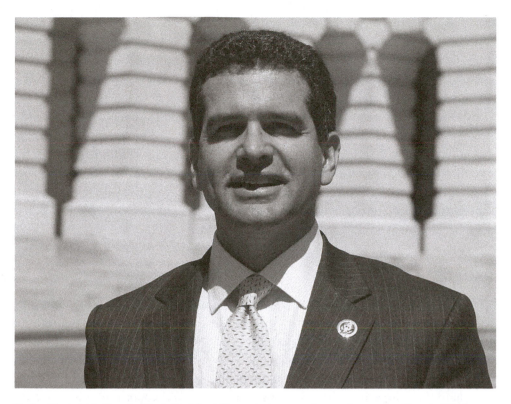

Pedro Pierluisi is Puerto Rico's Resident Commissioner and as such serves as Puerto Rico's non-voting member of the U.S. House of Representatives. A member of the New Progressive Party, he was elected to a four-year term as Resident Commissioner in 2009 and re-elected in 2013. (Bill Clark/Roll Call Photos/Newscom)

In order to reduce the impacts of potential gerrymandering, the Constitution of the Commonwealth stipulates that additional seats in the Legislative Assembly will be created temporarily in the event that one party wins more than two-thirds of the Assembly seats in a given election but wins less than two-thirds of the Commonwealth-wide popular vote in that election. In 2012, PPD won exactly two-thirds of the seats in the Senate, and hence these provisions in the Constitution did not take effect in the 2012–2016 election cycle.

ECONOMY

Historically, agriculture has been the mainstay of Puerto Rico's economy. Tropical crops, including sugar cane, coffee, fruits, vegetables, and tobacco, were grown, primarily for exports. Export agriculture first developed in the sixteenth century under the Spanish and continued into the twentieth century. Beginning after World War II, the United States encouraged the development of manufacturing, with many manufactured goods sold in the United States. Petrochemicals and pharmaceuticals became the largest manufacturing industries in Puerto Rico. Today manufacturing contributes nearly half of Puerto Rico's gross domestic product, as opposed to less than one percent for agricultural production. Tourism has become an increasing component of Puerto Rico's economy.

Some Puerto Rican officials believe that Puerto Rico's economy has suffered because it is subject to U.S. minimum-wage laws. As a result, some manufacturing enterprises in Puerto Rico have moved to Mexico, the Dominican Republic, or other Latin American countries with lower minimum wages. Per-capita gross domestic product has been estimated at about $34,000, or roughly 65 percent of that of the United States as a whole. However, Puerto Rico's gross domestic product is higher than that of any country in Latin America.

PEOPLE

Most Puerto Ricans are of Spanish or mixed-race ancestry, with a small minority of people of African ancestry. As U.S. citizens, Puerto Ricans have the right to move freely to all parts of the United States, and vice versa. Many Puerto Ricans have moved to the mainland, especially to New York, New Jersey, Massachusetts, and Florida. It has been estimated that there are more native Puerto Ricans on the mainland than there are Puerto Ricans living in Puerto Rico itself. Because of emigration, Puerto Rico's population has declined slightly since the 1990s.

Ethnic Composition

According to the United States Census of 2010, 75.8 percent of Puerto Rico's people identified themselves as white, and the remaining 24.2 percent identified themselves as nonwhite. Of these, about half identified themselves as black. Nearly 99 percent of Puerto Ricans identified themselves as Hispanic. Most Puerto Ricans are native-born U.S. citizens, although as of 2010 about 100,000 people, or about 2.5 percent of the population, were legal immigrants from other countries in Latin America.

Language

Spanish is the predominant language of Puerto Rico. It is spoken by more than 95 percent of the population and is the main language of business and government. Public schooling is conducted in Spanish. English is taught as a compulsory second language in elementary and high schools throughout the Commonwealth, although only a minority of Puerto Ricans claim to be fluent in English. Spanish and English are both official languages of Puerto Rico, and both are used by the executive branch of the government.

Religion

Ninety-seven percent of Puerto Ricans identify themselves as Christians. In 2006, about 1.6 million Puerto Ricans, or nearly half of the population, were Roman Catholics. About 400,000 identified themselves as members of various Pentecostal denominations.

CONTEMPORARY ISSUES

Political Future

The major political issue in Puerto Rico continues to be Puerto Rico's future status in association with the United States, given that only a small percentage of Puerto Ricans support outright independence. As recent referenda indicate, a very large majority of Puerto Rico's people favor either statehood or maintaining Puerto Rico's status as a commonwealth. Disputes on these questions have often centered on which alternative would be better for Puerto Rico's economy. Those who support maintaining commonwealth status have predicted that statehood would mean a loss of U.S. federal government support for Puerto Rico's economy, including tax incentives currently given to corporations that locate manufacturing enterprises on the island. Hence, they predict that statehood would increase unemployment and otherwise have a negative impact on the economy.

Economy

Puerto Rico's economic status relative to the rest of the United States is also an ongoing issue. As of 2012, per-person gross domestic product in Puerto Rico was approximately $34,000, or less than two-thirds of that of the U.S. as a whole. In part because of this relative poverty, immigration and emigration has also been an important issue in Puerto Rico in recent years. As American citizens, Puerto Ricans are free to move to and from the 50 U.S. states. Large numbers of Puerto Ricans have left the island for the U.S. mainland, with the majority of these migrants moving to New York, New Jersey, Massachusetts, or Florida. Many of these migrants are young men and women in their 20s, 30s, and 40s who earn incomes on the mainland rather than on the island. Hence Puerto Rico contains a disproportionate share of elderly persons and children who are not in a position to generate income that can be used to promote Puerto Rico's economic development.

Excerpt from the Constitution of the Commonwealth of Puerto Rico

The Constitution of the Commonwealth of Puerto Rico took effect in 1952, after being approved by a majority of Puerto Rico's voters in a referendum. Puerto Rico remains formally a commonwealth of the United States rather than an independent country, and thus Puerto Rico's constitution operates within the context of the Constitution of the United States.

The Constitution of the Commonwealth contains a Bill of Rights, which contains several clauses analogous to those included within the Bill of Rights of the United States. The Puerto Rican Bill of Rights calls for freedom of speech, freedom of assembly, and freedom of religion. It also grants Puerto Ricans the right to fair trial, including prohibition of double jeopardy and of self-incrimination. However, the Puerto Rican Bill of Rights expands beyond the U.S. Bill of Rights in two important respects. First, it calls specifically for equality under the law, stating that "All men are equal before the law. No discrimination shall be made on account of race, color, sex, birth, social origin or condition, or political or religious ideas." In contrast, equality under the law did not become part of the Constitution of the United States until the enactment of the Fourteenth Amendment after the Civil War. Second, the Puerto Rican Bill of Rights identifies education as a fundamental right, including the provision of free and compulsory public education to all Puerto Ricans.

> We, the people of Puerto Rico, in order to organize ourselves politically on a fully democratic basis, to promote the general welfare, and to secure for ourselves and our posterity the complete enjoyment of human rights, placing our trust in Almighty God, do ordain and establish this Constitution for the commonwealth which, in the exercise of our natural rights, we now create within our union with the United States of America.
>
> In so doing, we declare:
> The democratic system is fundamental to the life of the Puerto Rican community;
> We understand that the democratic system of government is one in which the will of the people is the source of public power, the political order is subordinate to the rights of man, and the free participation of the citizen in collective decisions is assured . . .

ARTICLE II: BILL OF RIGHTS

Section 1. The dignity of the human being is inviolable. All men are equal before the law. No discrimination shall be made on account of race, color, sex, birth, social origin or condition, or political or religious ideas. Both the laws and the system of public education shall embody these principles of essential human equality.

Section 3. No law shall be made respecting an establishment of religion or prohibiting the free exercise thereof. There shall be complete separation of church and state.

Section 4. No law shall be made abridging the freedom of speech or of the press, or the right of the people peaceably to assemble and to petition the government for a redress of grievances.

Section 5. Every person has the right to an education which shall be directed to the full development of the human personality and to the strengthening of respect for human rights and fundamental freedoms. There shall be a system of free and wholly non-sectarian public education. Instruction in the elementary and secondary schools shall be free and shall be compulsory in the elementary schools to the extent permitted by the facilities of the state. No public property or public funds shall be used for the support of schools or educational institutions other than those of the state. Nothing contained in this provision shall prevent the state from furnishing to any child non-educational services established by law for the protection or welfare of children.

Compulsory attendance at elementary public schools to the extent permitted by the facilities of the state as herein provided shall not be construed as applicable to those who receive elementary education in schools established under nongovernmental auspices.

Section 6. Persons may join with each other and organize freely for any lawful purpose, except in military or quasi-military organizations.

Section 7. The right to life, liberty and the enjoyment of property is recognized as a fundamental right of man. The death penalty shall not exist. No person shall be deprived of his liberty or property without due process of law. No person in Puerto Rico shall be denied the equal protection of the laws

Section 8. Every person has the right to the protection of law against abusive attacks on his honor, reputation and private or family life.

Section 10. The right of the people to be secure in their persons, houses, papers and effects against unreasonable searches and seizures shall not be violated.

Wire-tapping is prohibited.

No warrant for arrest or search and seizure shall issue except by judicial authority and only upon probable cause supported by oath or affirmation, and particularly describing the place to be searched and the persons to be arrested or the things to be seized.

Evidence obtained in violation of this section shall be inadmissible in the courts.

Section 11. In all criminal prosecutions, the accused shall enjoy the right to have a speedy and public trial, to be informed of the nature and cause of the accusation and to have a copy thereof, to be confronted with the witnesses against him, to have assistance of counsel, and to be presumed innocent.

In all prosecutions for a felony the accused shall have the right of trial by an impartial jury composed of twelve residents of the district, who may render their verdict by a majority vote which in no case may be less than nine.

No person shall be compelled in any criminal case to be a witness against himself . . .

No person shall be twice put in jeopardy of punishment for the same offense.

Before conviction every accused shall be entitled to be admitted to bail.

Incarceration prior to trial shall not exceed six months nor shall bail or fines be excessive. No person shall be imprisoned for debt.

Section 12. Neither slavery nor involuntary servitude shall exist except in the latter case as a punishment for crime after the accused has been duly convicted. Cruel and unusual punishments shall not be inflicted. Suspension of civil rights including the right to vote shall cease upon service of the term of imprisonment imposed.

Section 13. The writ of habeas corpus shall be granted without delay and free of costs. The privilege of the writ of habeas corpus shall not be suspended, unless the public safety requires it in case of rebellion, insurrection or invasion

Section 15. The employment of children less than fourteen years of age in any occupation which is prejudicial to their health or morals or which places them in jeopardy of life or limb is prohibited.

No child less than sixteen years of age shall be kept in custody in a jail or penitentiary.

Section 16. The right of every employee to choose his occupation freely and to resign therefrom is recognized, as is his right to equal pay for equal work, to a reasonable minimum salary, to protection against risks to his health or person in his work or employment, and to an ordinary-workday which shall not exceed eight hours. An employee may work in excess of this daily limit only if he is paid extra compensation as provided by law, at a rate never less than one and one-half times the regular rate at which he is employed.

Section 17. Persons employed . . . shall have the right to organize and to bargain collectively with their employers through representatives of their own free choosing in order to promote their welfare.

Section 18. In order to assure their right to organize and to bargain collectively, persons employed . . . shall have the right to strike, to picket and to engage in other legal concerted activities.

Source: "Constitution of the Commonwealth of Puerto Rico." Welcome to Puerto Rico. http://www.topuertorico.org/constitu.shtml

SOMALIA: Failed State

SOMALIA

Communications	Television
Facebook Users	55 sets per 100 population (2004)
17,000,000 (estimate) (2013)	**Land-based Telephones in Use**
Internet Users	19,220,000 (2012)
28,119,000 (2009)	
Internet Users (% of Population)	**Mobile Telephone Subscribers**
71.6% (2013)	50,663,000 (2012)

Major Daily Newspapers	**Students Per Teacher, Primary School**
151 (2004)	12.6 (2012)
Average Circulation of Daily Newspapers	**Students Per Teacher, Secondary School**
6,183,000 (2004)	11.4 (2012)
Education	**Enrollment in Tertiary Education**
School System	1,965,829 (estimate) (2012)
Spanish students begin their primary education at the age of six. After six years, they continue to four years of early secondary education, followed by two years of academic or technical upper secondary school.	**Enrollment in Tertiary Education, Male**
	911,887 (estimate) (2012)
	Enrollment in Tertiary Education, Female
	1,053,942 (estimate) (2012)
	Literacy
Mandatory Education	98% (2012)
10 years, from ages 6 to 16.	**Energy and Natural Resources**
Average Years Spent in School for Current Students	**Electric Power Generation**
17 (estimate) (2012)	276,800,000,000 kilowatt hours per year (estimate) (2011)
Average Years Spent in School for Current Students, Male	**Electric Power Consumption**
17 (estimate) (2012)	249,700,000,000 kilowatt hours per year (estimate) (2011)
Average Years Spent in School for Current Students, Female	**Nuclear Power Plants**
	7 (2014)
18 (2012)	**Crude Oil Production**
Primary School–age Children Enrolled in Primary School	33,600 barrels per day (2013)
	Crude Oil Consumption
2,816,584 (2012)	1,204,100 barrels per day (2013)
Primary School–age Males Enrolled in Primary School	**Natural Gas Production**
1,452,603 (2012)	61,000,000 cubic meters per year (estimate) (2012)
Primary School–age Females Enrolled in Primary School	**Natural Gas Consumption**
1,363,981 (2012)	35,820,000,000 cubic meters per year (estimate) (2010)
Secondary School–age Children Enrolled in Secondary School	**Natural Resources**
3,296,129 (2012)	Coal, lignite, iron ore, copper, lead, zinc, uranium, tungsten, mercury, pyrites, magnesite, fluorspar, gypsum, sepiolite, kaolin, potash, hydropower, arable land
Secondary School–age Males Enrolled in Secondary School	
1,686,545 (2012)	
Secondary School–age Females Enrolled in Secondary School	**Environment**
	CO2 Emissions
1,609,584 (2012)	6.3 metric tons per capita (2009)

Alternative and Nuclear Energy	**Health**
17.7% of total energy use (2011)	**Average Life Expectancy**
Threatened Species	81.5 years (2014)
240 (2010)	**Average Life Expectancy, Male**
Protected Areas	78.5 years (2014)
47,661 (estimate) (2010)	**Average Life Expectancy, Female**
Geography	84.7 years (2014)
Location	**Crude Birth Rate**
Spain occupies 80% of the Iberian Peninsula in southwestern Europe. It is bordered by France to the north and Portugal to the west, and has coastlines on the Bay of Biscay to the north, the Atlantic Ocean to the west and southwest, and the Mediterranean Sea to the southeast. The nation also encompasses the Canary Isles, situated in the Atlantic Ocean, the Balearic Islands, located in the Mediterranean Sea, and some enclaves within Morocco.	9.6 (estimate) (2015)
	Crude Death Rate
	9.0 (estimate) (2015)
	Maternal Mortality
	92 per 100,000 live births (2005–2012 projection)
	Infant Mortality
	4 per 1,000 live births (2012)
Time Zone	**Doctors**
6 hours ahead of U.S. Eastern Standard	3.7 per 1,000 people (2012)
Land Borders	**Industry and Labor**
1,183 miles	**Gross Domestic Product (GDP) - official exchange rate**
Coastline	
3,084 miles	$1,466,357,000,000 (estimate) (2015)
Capital	**GDP per Capita**
Madrid	$31,601 (estimate) (2015)
Area	**GDP - Purchasing Power Parity (PPP)**
194,834 sq. miles	$1,411,493,000,000 (estimate) (2013)
Climate	**GDP (PPP) per Capita**
Less temperate than most areas of western Europe, Spain has hot summers in most regions, with temperatures averaging about 95°F. The mountainous areas of the interior have cold winters.	$30,620 (estimate) (2013)
	Industry Products
	Wine, cement, iron, steel, sulfuric and nitric acids, automobiles, metals, chemicals, machine tools, textiles, clothing and footwear, food and beverages. Shipbuilding and tourism are also major industries.
Land Use	
25.5% arable land; 9.7% permanent crops; 22.2% permanent meadows and pastures; 37.1% forest land; 5.5% other.	
Arable Land	**Agriculture Products**
26% (2007)	Wine grapes, olives, vegetables, sugar beets, citrus fruit, potatoes, barley, wheat, poultry, sheep, pigs, cows' milk and other dairy products, fish.
Arable Land Per Capita	
1 acres per person (2007)	

Unemployment	**Population Distribution**
25.2% (2012)	77% urban (2011)
Labor Profile	**Age Distribution**
agriculture: 4.2% industry: 24% services: 71.7% (estimate) (2009)	0-14: 14.5%
	15-64: 67.1%
Military	65+: 18.4%
Total Active Armed Forces	(2009)
128,013 (2010)	**Median Age**
Active Armed Forces	41.6 years (estimate) (2014)
0% (2010)	**Population Growth Rate**
Annual Military Expenditures	0.9% per year (estimate) (2015)
$11,700,000,000 (2009)	**Net Migration Rate**
Military Service	8.3 (estimate) (2015)
Service in the Spanish military is voluntary.	**Trade**
National Finances	**Imported Goods**
Currency	Machinery and transportation equipment, electrical equipment, textiles, plastics, chemicals, rubber, wood and wood products, base metals, fish, mineral fuels and products, cinematographic equipment.
Euro	
Total Government Revenues	
$505,100,000,000 (estimate) (2013)	
Total Government Expenditures	**Total Value of Imports**
$597,300,000,000 (estimate) (2013)	$287,775,000,000 (2009)
Budget Deficit	**Exported Goods**
-6.8 (estimate) (2013)	Machinery, motor vehicles, base metals, chemicals, vegetable products, alcoholic beverages, textiles, footwear and accessories.
GDP Contribution by Sector	
agriculture: 3.3% industry: 26.4% services: 70.3% (2012 est.)	
External Debt	**Total Value of Exports**
$2,278,000,000,000 (estimate) (2012)	$303,800,000,000 (estimate) (2012)
Economic Aid Extended	**Import Partners**
$2,281,710,000 (2011)	Germany - 15.0%; France - 12.8%; Italy - 7.2%; China - 5.9%; Netherlands - 5.2% (2009)
Economic Aid Received	
$0 (2011)	
Population	**Export Partners**
Population	France - 19.3%; Germany - 11.1%; Portugal - 9.2%; Italy - 8.2%; United Kingdom - 6.2% (2009).
48,146,134 (estimate) (2015)	
World Population Rank	
32 nd (2009)	**Current Account Balance**
Population Density	$2,100,000,000 (estimate) (2013)
240.0 people per square mile (estimate) (2011)	**Weights and Measures**
	The metric system is in use.

Transportation	Number of Trucks, Buses, and Commercial Vehicles
Airports	
152 (2012)	4,908,000 (2005)
Paved Roads	**Railroads**
99.0% (2003)	9,500 (2008)
Roads, Unpaved	**Ports**
0 (2006)	Major: 19 (including Barcelona, Bilbao, Santa Cruz de Tenerife, Cartegena, Las Palmas, Cadiz, Valencia.
Passenger Cars per 1,000 People	
481 (2010)	

OVERVIEW

Somalia occupies the eastern portion of the Horn of Africa, so named because of its resemblance on a map to a rhinoceros horn. The country contains two distinct regions, one in the north that runs east–west along the Gulf of Aden and another larger territory that runs roughly southwest–northeast along the Indian Ocean. The two coastlines meet at a sharp angle in the northeast at Cape Gwardafuy. The nearby Peninsula of Xaafuun, which juts out into the Indian Ocean, is the easternmost point on the African mainland. Somalia's climate is mostly hot and dry, especially in the interior, but temperatures drop a bit along the coastline, and the southern region is more fertile than the semiarid north. Somalia has a population of about 10.4 million. Its capital, Mogadishu, is located in the south.

GOVERNMENT

Somalia is considered a failed state, having been without a functioning central government since 1991, although in 2012 a new parliament and president have provided the best hope yet for future stability. However, the government is weak, kept in place largely thanks to security provided by African Union troops, and controls only small parts of the country. Somalia formed on July 1, 1960, with the merger of the former colonies of British Somaliland and Italian Somaliland. The existing charter provides for the eventual creation of multiple Somali states united by a national government. A sizeable area of northern Somalia has broken away to form the self-governing republic of Somaliland. The central Somali region of Puntland also is currently self-governing but favors eventual reunification with Somalia. In 2012 Hassan Sheikh Mohamud was elected president of Somalia. In December 2013, Mohamud chose Abdiweli Sheikh Ahmed as prime minister. Somaliland's longtime leader is Ahmed M. Mahamoud Silanyo.

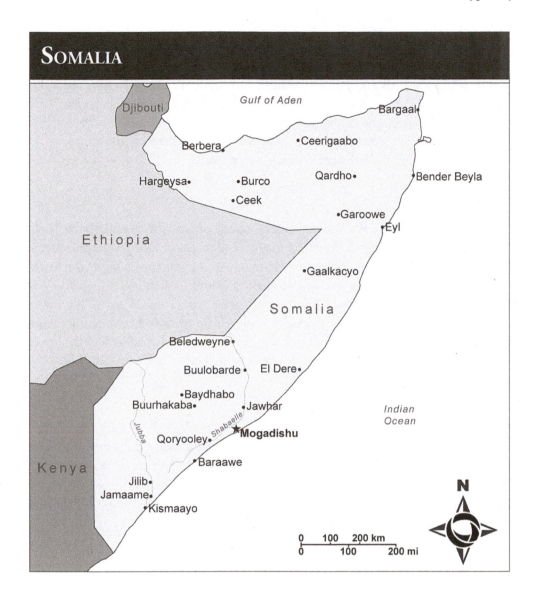

Constitution

Following the 1991 overthrow of President Siad Barre, the 1979 Constitution was suspended, and the United Somali Congress (USC) and five other political groups announced plans to draft a new democratic constitution. In August 2012, Somali elders wrote and approved a new constitution, which provides women and children with greater rights and paves the way for the creation of a new functioning central government.

Executive

In 2004, after years of negotiations to end a catastrophic, decade-long civil war, feuding warlords and politicians agreed to set up a new parliament. In 2012, the newly elected parliament chose Hassan Sheikh Mohamud as president. The president names a prime minister who, in turn, selects a cabinet, which must be approved by the National Parliament. The cabinet is formed by allotting seats to each of the members of Somalia's major warring clans.

Legislature

During 2004 peace talks, the parliament agreed for seats in the legislative body to be divided up among all Somalia's major groups, clans, and geographic areas. The arrangement calls for a bicameral National Parliament consisting of the lower house, called the House of the People of the Federal Parliament, which has 275 seats, and the Upper House of the Federal Parliament, with 54 seats. The lower house members are to be elected directly, while the upper house members are to be elected by the federal member states. Clan elders appointed members to the lower house in 2012; the upper house had not been formed as of late summer 2014.

Judiciary

The 2004 Transitional National Charter (TNC) called for a Supreme Court, based in Mogadishu, and an Appeal Court. The document established a system in which judges would be appointed by the president upon recommendation of a Judicial Service Commission. However, the country does not yet have a working national judicial system. Most regions use local forms of conflict resolution, either secular, traditional practices or Sharia Islamic law.

Local Government

Somalia is divided into 18 administrative regions, including those in the autonomous Somaliland and Puntland areas. Regions are further divided into 90 districts and the capital of Mogadishu.

Election Qualifications

All citizens 18 years of age and older are eligible to vote.

POLITICS

Since the 1991 violent overthrow of Mohamed Siad Barre's socialist regime in 1991, various rival groups have fought to control Somalia. In October 2002, peace talks began in neighboring Kenya, culminating in January 2004, when rival factions agreed to create a new government. The agreement united representatives from each of four major clans and a coalition of several smaller clans in an interim parliament. Members were selected by clan leaders and politicians. Militia leaders controlling much of Mogadishu also signed the agreement. In August 2004, the new parliament was inaugurated, and on October 10, 2004, its members elected career military officer Abdullahi Yusuf Ahmed as the country's president. The northern region of Somaliland, however, announced that it would not accept the new government and worked to form its own self-governing state.

Several militias, however, particularly Islamic groups, opposed the transitional government, and widespread violence continued, forcing the government to operate from Kenya for a time. When the government again faced exile at the hands of militias loyal to a militant Islamic group in 2006, it sought help from the Ethiopian military to regain control of the country. However, Ethiopia and Somalia have a history of conflict, and inviting that country's troops into Somalia angered many Somalis and increased support for the Islamists. With fighting intensifying, national leaders negotiated with the then-powerful Islamist group the Alliance for the Re-Liberation of Somalia (ARS). The government reached a peace agreement in late 2008 that mandated removal of Ethiopian troops and allowed ARS leaders to join the government. President Yusuf Ahmed resigned in protest over the negotiations and was replaced by Islamist leader Sharif Ahmed in 2009. ARS members also joined a newly expanded legislature that year.

Abdiweli Sheikh Ahmed served as Prime Minister of Somalia from December 2013 until his resignation following a vote of no confidence by Somalia's Parliament in December 2014. The post of Prime Minister was created with the establishment of the Federal Government of Somalia in 2012. (DFSA/ZDS WENN Photos/Newscom)

With the mandate of the transitional government expired, in mid-2012 Somali elders created a new 275-member parliament, which, in October, elected Hassan Sheikh Mohamud as president. The president in turn appointed Abdiweli Sheikh Ahmed as prime minister. There is hope that these developments will lead to a return of stable governance to Somalia, though political infighting and corruption have slowed the process. In addition, although the Al Qaeda–linked al-Shabab has lost control over Mogadishu and urban centers, it continues to hold central and southern areas, and to target political leaders who don't share their extremist interpretation of Islam. As of mid-2014, four members of parliament had been killed. In taking responsibility for the July 2014 murder of popular singer and legislator Saado Ali Warsame, al-Shabab leaders said she was killed because of her politics.

Political Parties

Since the 1991 revolution, dozens of political parties have formed, split, disbanded, and been replaced. Many of these formed to reflect allegiance to one clan or another, or to one of the many militias fighting for dominance of the country. The following are some of the more recent parties.

The United Somali Congress (USC) was founded in 1989 by intellectuals. They led the January 1991 coup against President Siad Barre and formed a three-party rebel coalition. The USC split in mid-1991 along clan lines.

The Peace and Development Party, (Xisbiga Nabadda Iyo Horumarka—PDP) is a moderate Islamic democratic party that was formed in 2011. It held a majority in the 2012 parliament and is the party of President Hassan Sheikh Mohamud.

The Tayo party was formed in 2012 by former Prime Minister Mohamed Abdullahi Mohamed and focuses on social issues.

The Justice & Peace Network (Maandeeq—JPN) is a movement that brings together academics, youth activists, and Somalis who have left the country due to violence. With a focus on peace, reconciliation, and a long-term plan for Somali stability, JPN is widely expected to become a political force in the next round of elections.

ECONOMY

A combination of drought and civil war devastated Somalia's economy, which was once based on agriculture. From late 2010 to early 2012, a famine in south and central Somalia killed some 260,000 people, more than half of them children, according to the United Nations. The worst drought in 60 years triggered the famine, but it grew more deadly because other countries were slow to offer aid and, when they did, the militant Islamic group al-Shabab refused to let workers deliver donated food.

Drought and crop failures have decimated the livestock herds that had been among the country's most lucrative exports. Industry in Somalia was looted and reduced to scrap metal, but such foreign investors as the Coca-Cola Company recently have put down roots. International groups have called for a boycott of Somalia's charcoal exports, saying the proceeds of charcoal sales go to al-Shabab's coffers. With increasing stability in recent years, international groups and other countries have been more willing to aid Somalia. From 2009 to early 2013, the United States gave $1.5 billion in aid according to the U.S. State Department. However, unemployment remains extremely high, prompting many Somalis to turn to piracy to make a living.

SOCIETY

The country's internal strife occurs in spite of the fact that Somalia has one of the more homogeneous populations in Africa. The majority are ethnic Somali, which is subdivided into six clans: Daarood, Isaaq, Hawiye, Dir, Reewin, and Digil. Ten percent of the population is non-Somali and includes Bantu-speaking Africans, Arabs, Pakistani, Indians, and Europeans. The majority of Somalis are pastoral or semi-pastoral peoples whose movement with their animal herds takes them regularly into areas officially part of neighboring countries. Somali became the official language in 1972, when its written form was established. Many also speak Arabic, Italian, and English. Sunni Islam is shared by virtually all Somalis. Sufism, or mystical Islam, is also practiced. Many pre-Islamic customs linger in the rural areas.

Ethnic Composition

Somali – 85%; Bantu and other non-Somali – 15% (includes Arabs)

Language

More than a dozen languages are spoken in Somalia. Somali is the official language and is spoken by about 90 percent of the population. Arabic and English are also considered national languages. Italian, Swahili, Garre, Oromo, and Mushungulu are also spoken.

Religion

Muslim – 100%

CONTEMPORARY ISSUES

Political Instability

When Somali dictator Mohamed Siad Barre fled into exile in 1991, the resulting power vacuum prompted a civil war in which political factions, most of them organized along traditional clan lines, vied for control of the country. While Siad Barre's government of so-called scientific socialism—a blend of Marxist theories and Islamic religious values—had not succeeded in bringing prosperity to Somalia, it had helped temporarily to contain the interclan strife that characterized the region's history. No functioning central government existed between 2004 and 2012, when the first internationally backed leadership was installed finally after more than a dozen conferences on national reconciliation. While the international community recognized a transitional government established in exile during the tumultuous period, many Somalis, including some influential political leaders, did not. The government-in-exile did receive a dose of credibility in 2009, when one of its former opponents, Sharif Ahmed—leader of the Alliance for the Re-Liberation of Somalia (ARS)—was named president by a newly expanded legislature that included 149 ARS members. In addition, the expulsion of al-Shabab militants from the capital, Mogadishu, in August 2011 and the creation of a new constitution by Somali elders, which provides women and children with more rights, brought some much-needed stability and structure to the troubled country. Then, in August 2012, more progress toward national stability was made with the creation of a new 275-member parliament by Somali elders. In October 2012 the parliament elected a new president, following the end of eight years of the UN-backed transitional government. Formally recognized by the United States and other Western powers in 2013, the fledgling government installed at the end of 2012 continues to face a daunting task in uniting a nation torn by clan and religious violence.

Religious Fundamentalism

Somalis are predominantly Sunni Muslims and have long adhered to a moderate form of clan-based Islam, blended with a wealth of local traditional practices. However, the growing influence of Islamic fundamentalists and radical Islamist terrorist groups threatens Somalia's efforts to become a stable country. During the 2006 takeover of Somalia by the Union of Islamic Courts (UIC), the United States government alleged that the organization harbored Al Qaeda agents responsible for several terrorist bombings and that it received funds from radical Islamist organizations in Saudi Arabia and Eritrea. These connections served as a basis for U.S. and Ethiopian intervention in Somalia's power struggle. Many Somalis who subscribe to fundamentalist interpretations of Islam also advocate the creation of a "Greater Somalia" that includes portions of Djibouti, Ethiopia, and Kenya.

Kenyans fleeing from an attack by Al Shabab at a shopping mall in Nairobi. Somalia is a failed state, and various factions have contested control of the country since dictator Mohamed Siad Barre was deposed in 1991. The militant Islamist group Al Shabab, which has been designated as a terrorist organization by the United States, controls parts of southern Somalia near the Kenyan border. (George Mulala/Polaris/Newscom)

A serious challenge comes from the militant, radical Islamic group al-Shabab, which hopes to overthrow the existing Somali government. In 2011, African Union troops, with support from the United States, drove al-Shabab from the capital, Mogadishu, and other major urban centers. In retaliation, al-Shabab attacked a shopping mall in Nairobi, Kenya, in September 2013, resulting in at least 67 deaths. In February 2014, al-Shabab attacked the presidential compound in Mogadishu, killing at least 16 people. Then, in May, it struck the parliamentary complex, a multi-pronged assault that resulted in at least 10 deaths. In September 2014, the United States launched air strikes in southern Somalia that reportedly targeted an al-Shabab leader. However, the group continued to control large portions of central and southern Somalia.

Piracy

Somalia's lawlessness and its location on the Horn of Africa and the Gulf of Aden—near shipping lanes connecting the Red Sea and Indian Ocean—have combined to create a lucrative source of income for Somali pirate gangs that prey on international cargo ships. The piracy has had a substantial effect on global shipping costs, as companies must pay ransoms for ships and crews and also for increased security measures. Piracy began in the early 1990s, after former dictator Mohamed Siad Barre went into exile. Initially, gangs sought to protect Somali territorial waters, in the absence of a national coast guard, from foreign ships entering to fish illegally or dump pollutants. Pirate gangs later began to work for their own profit and became more brazen as ransom income allowed them to purchase better equipment and arms.

Several countries have sent warships to patrol shipping lanes off of Somali territorial waters, though the lack of an international legal structure for prosecuting pirates in international waters complicates enforcement. Some have called for an international court backed by the United Nations. Islamic insurgent groups trying to wrest control of the country from the weak central government once condemned the practice of piracy, but in mid-2010 media reported that both sides of the civil war were aligning with pirate groups. The number of attacks on ships peaked in 2011 and has fallen since, but ongoing piracy still exacts a high toll. In early 2013, the World Bank issued a report estimating that Somali piracy costs the global economy $18 billion a year, including increased security, higher fuel costs as shippers alter routes to avoid pirates, and decreases in fish export earnings and tourism revenue in neighboring countries, among other impacts. The report said that 1,068 attacks by Somali pirates were carried out between January 2005 and early 2013, resulting in 218 successful hijackings and an average of $53 million in ransoms paid per year.

The Status of Somaliland

Somaliland is a de facto independent republic in northwestern Somalia that borders Djibouti, Ethiopia, and the autonomous Somali state of Puntland. It was administered by the United Kingdom until it gained independence on June 26, 1960, and then unified with Italian Somaliland when that colony gained independence only days later, forming the Republic of Somalia. Somaliland declared its secession from Somalia in 1991; however, neither the current Somali transitional authority nor any foreign government officially recognizes the republic's right to self-determination. With the transitional government of Somalia still struggling to control the capital city of Mogadishu, the ultimate status of Somaliland remains unknown, and a possible confrontation over the region's claim to independence continues to loom.

Internal Displacement

A September 2003 United Nations report estimated that 370,000 Somalis lived in camps for the internally displaced at that time, practically all of them living without such basic services as clean water and health facilities—though they are still charged rent for their shelters. Drawn northward by the prosperity at such boom towns on the Gulf of Aden as Bosaso and by the relative freedom from violence that the functioning autonomous governments there have ensured, the internally displaced people and other refugees living in northern Somalia now find themselves trapped in a life of abject poverty. For many of these refugees, the Gulf of Aden represents their only hope to escape. In October 2006 alone, the UN High Commissioner for Refugees (UNHCR) registered some 47,000 Somali immigrants who had made the dangerous 24-hour crossing across the gulf to Yemen. The smugglers who transport these migrants in the bottoms of their boats are notorious for torturing and even murdering their passengers, sometimes throwing passengers overboard as they near the port to avoid being caught. In spite of this treatment, smugglers will typically charge the equivalent of $50 to $100 for passage—a sum that takes years for most refugees to save. The surge of violence in Mogadishu in early 2007 that followed the ouster of the Union of Islamic Courts exacerbated the displacement crisis, leading some 124,000 of the capital city's residents to flee. As of early 2014, there were still an estimated 1.1 million internally displaced people in Somalia, according to the UNHCR.

Drought and Famine

Many seasons of failed rain and subsequent drought, combined with political insecurity and conflict, led to a national food crisis in 2010. With thousands of Somali dying of malnutrition and starvation, the UN declared a famine in the Southern Bakool and Lower Shabelle regions of the country in mid-2011. The famine later spread across Somalia, taking the lives of nearly 260,000 people before it ended in February 2012. While several Western aid organizations attempted to provide food aid, clashes between rival clans and al-Shabab's tight control over certain territories made it difficult to bring food to much of the population. In the south and central regions, 10 percent of children under the age of five died, along with 17 percent of young children in Mogadishu. In the hardest-hit areas, thousands of residents abandoned their homes in search of food. All told, approximately 4 million people do not have enough to eat.

Although conditions have improved, data from the UN World Food Programme's Food Security and Nutrition Analysis Unit–Somalia shows that some 860,000 Somali remain in food crisis situations, and about one-third of the nation's population still has difficulty meeting their daily food needs. In April 2014, the agency warned that delayed rains and higher food prices may soon worsen the nation's food security issues once more.

Excerpt from the Provisional Constitution of Somalia

The current Constitution of Somalia went into effect in 2012. However, control of Somalia has been contested among various factions since the early 1990s, and thus the

Constitution conveys no de facto authority outside those areas of the country that are controlled by its legitimate government.

The Constitution identifies Somalia as an Islamic state, and it makes several references to Islam. For example, it bans the "propagation" of any religion other than Islam and requires that Islam be taught in all government-provided schools. It also calls for the establishment of a Human Rights Commission that is charged with "the promotion of knowledge of human rights, and specifically Shari'ah."

Within this context, many of the rights guaranteed in the Constitution are consistent with those guaranteed elsewhere, both within Islamic republics and in other countries. These include political rights such as the right to free speech, rights to freedom of expression and assembly, and the right to a fair trial. It also specifies the state's responsibility to provide for public education and to health care and social security. Other rights and responsibilities guaranteed by the Constitution address problems more specific to Somalia and neighboring countries in the Middle East and Africa. For example, it guarantees the right to "clean potable water." It also forbids female circumcision, forced marriage, slavery, human trafficking, and forced labor, and guarantees the right of Somali citizens to travel freely throughout the country.

Article 10

Human dignity is given by God to every human being, and this is the basis for all human rights.

Human dignity is inviolable and must be protected . . .

State power must not be exercised in a manner that violates human dignity.

Article 11

All citizens, regardless of sex, religion, social or economic status, political opinion, clan, disability, occupation, birth or dialect shall have equal rights . . .

The State must not discriminate against any person on the basis of age, race, colour, tribe, ethnicity, culture, dialect, gender, birth, disability, religion, political opinion, occupation, or wealth.

Article 14

A person may not be subjected to slavery, servitude, trafficking, or forced labour . . .

Article 15

Every person has the right to personal liberty and security.

. . . this includes: the prohibition of illegal detention, . . . violence, including any form of violence against women, torture, or inhumane treatment.

Every person has the right to physical integrity . . . No one may be subjected to medical or scientific experiments without their consent . . .

Female circumcision is a cruel . . . practice, and is tantamount to torture. The circumcision of girls is prohibited.

Abortion is contrary to Shari'ah and is prohibited except in cases of necessity, especially to save the life of the mother.

Article 16

Every person has the right to associate with other individuals and groups. This includes the right to form and belong to organizations, including trade unions and political parties.

Article 17

Every person is free to practice his or her religion.
No religion other than Islam can be propagated in . . . Somalia.

Article 18

Every person has the right to . . . express their opinions . . .

Freedom of expression includes . . . speech . . . the media, including all forms of electronic and web-based media.

Every person has the right to freely express their artistic creativity, knowledge, and information . . .

Article 19

The home . . . shall be inviolable, and their entry, search or surveillance shall not be allowed without a reasoned order from a judge.

Article 20

Every person has the right to organize and . . . to demonstrate and protest peacefully . . .

Article 21

Every person . . . has the right to freedom of movement, freedom to choose their residence, and freedom to leave the country.

Article 22

Every citizen has the right to take part in public affairs. This right includes:

The right to form political parties and to participate in the activities of political parties;

Every citizen . . . has the right to elect and to be elected.

Article 27

Every person has the right to clean potable water.

. . . to healthcare, and no one may be denied emergency healthcare for any reason, including lack of economic capability.

. . . to full social security,

It shall be ensured that women, the aged, the disabled and minorities who have long suffered discrimination get the necessary support to realize their socio-economic rights.

Article 28

Marriage is the basis of the family, which is the foundation of society. Its protection is a legal duty of the State.

Mother and child care is a legal duty of the State.

Every child has the right to care from their parents, including education and instruction . . .where this care is not available from the family, it must be provided by others. This right applies to street children and children of unknown parents, the rights of whom the state has a particular duty to fulfill and protect.

Adults have a duty to support their parents if the parents are unable to care for themselves.

No marriage shall be legal without the free consent of both the man and the woman, or if one or both of them have not reached the age of maturity

Article 29

Every child has the right to a good and righteous name and a nationality from birth.

. . . to be protected from mistreatment, neglect, abuse, or degradation.

No child may perform work or provide services that . . . create a risk to the child's health . . .

Every child may be detained only as a last resort, for a limited time, in appropriate conditions, and . . . separately from adults with the exception of the child's immediate family. The child's immediate family must be informed of the child's detention . . .

Every child shall have the right to legal aid paid for by the State . . .

Every child has the right to be protected from armed conflict, and not to be used in armed conflict.

Article 30

Education is a basic right for all . . .

Every citizen shall have the right to free education up to secondary school.

The teaching of Islam shall be compulsory . . . Schools owned by non-Muslims shall be exempted . . .

Article 31

The state shall promote the positive traditions and cultural practices of the Somali people, whilst striving to eliminate . . . customs and emerging practices which negatively impact the unity, civilization and wellbeing of society.

Article 32

Every person has the right of access to information held by the state.

Article 33

Every person has the right to a fair public hearing . . .

Every person is entitled to defend him or herself.

The state shall provide free legal defence to the people who do not have the means of doing so.

Article 35

The accused is presumed innocent until proven guilty . . .

Every person arrested . . . has the right to be informed promptly of the reason for their arrest

Every person may not be compelled to self-incriminate, and a verdict may not be based on evidence acquired by means of coercion.

Every person who is arrested has the right to be brought before a competent court within 48 hours . . .

Every person who is arrested or detained has the right to . . . a legal practitioner and if he or she cannot afford one, the State must appoint (one) . . .

Every person brought before a court of law for an alleged criminal offence is entitled to a fair trial.

The accused has the right to be present at their trial.

The accused has the right to challenge the evidence presented . . .

The accused has the right to an interpreter if the accused person does not understand the language being used in the court.

The accused cannot be kept in an illegal detention centre, and must be granted visits by . . . family, doctor or lawyer.

Article 41

The Federal Parliament shall establish a Human Rights Commission that is independent of State control, and has adequate resources. . .

The functions of the Human Rights Commission shall include the promotion of knowledge of human rights, and specifically Shari'ah . . .

Source: "The Federal Republic of Somalia Provisional Constitution." United Nations Political Office for Somalia. http://unpos.unmissions.org/LinkClick. aspx?fileticket=RkJTOSpoMME=

UZBEKISTAN: Authoritarian

UZBEKISTAN

Communications	Mandatory Education
Facebook Users	9 years, from ages 6 to 15.
160,000 (estimate) (2013)	Average Years Spent in School for Current Students
Internet Users	
4,689,000 (2009)	12 (estimate) (2011)
Internet Users (% of Population)	Average Years Spent in School for Current Students, Male
38.2% (2013)	
Television	12 (estimate) (2011)
23 sets per 100 population (2006)	Average Years Spent in School for Current Students, Female
Land-based Telephones in Use	
1,963,000 (2012)	11 (estimate) (2011)
Mobile Telephone Subscribers	Primary School–age Children Enrolled in Primary School
20,274,000 (2012)	
Major Daily Newspapers	1,948,128 (2011)
5 (2004)	Primary School–age Males Enrolled in Primary School
Average Circulation of Daily Newspapers	
Not Available	1006293
Education	Primary School–age Females Enrolled in Primary School
School System	
Primary schooling in Uzbekistan begins at the age of six and lasts for four years. Early secondary education lasts for an additional five years. Upper secondary education lasts for two years and can be academically or technically focused. Students can then go on to three years of specialized academic or vocational training.	941835
	Secondary School–age Children Enrolled in Secondary School
	4,370,300 (2011)
	Secondary School–age Males Enrolled in Secondary School
	2,246,233 (2011)

Secondary School–age Females Enrolled in Secondary School	**Environment**
	CO2 Emissions
2,124,067 (2011)	4.2 metric tons per capita (2009)
Students Per Teacher, Primary School	**Alternative and Nuclear Energy**
15.6 (2011)	2.1% of total energy use (2010)
Students Per Teacher, Secondary School	**Threatened Species**
13.3 (2011)	50 (2010)
Enrollment in Tertiary Education	**Protected Areas**
277,437 (2011)	9,549 (estimate) (2010)
Enrollment in Tertiary Education, Male	**Geography**
170,483 (2011)	**Location**
Enrollment in Tertiary Education, Female	Located in Central Asia, Uzbekistan is bordered by Turkmenistan to the southwest, Afghanistan to the south, Tajikistan and Kyrgyzstan to the east, and Kazakhstan to the north and west. Part of the country's northern border crosses the Aral Sea.
106,954 (2011)	
Literacy	
99% (2011)	
Energy and Natural Resources	
Electric Power Generation	**Time Zone**
52,530,000,000 kilowatt hours per year (estimate) (2012)	10 hours ahead of U.S. Eastern Standard
	Land Borders
Electric Power Consumption	3,866 miles
44,510,000,000 kilowatt hours per year (estimate) (2010)	**Coastline**
	261 miles
Nuclear Power Plants	**Capital**
0 (2014)	Tashkent
Crude Oil Production	**Area**
101,800 barrels per day (2013)	172,740 sq. miles
Crude Oil Consumption	**Climate**
106,000 barrels per day (2012)	Temperatures in Uzbekistan can reach extremes at both the upper and lower levels, depending on region. Summer temperatures average 90°F and can reach as high as 104°F. Winter temperatures may fall as low as -36°F.
Natural Gas Production	
62,900,000,000 cubic meters per year (estimate) (2012)	
Natural Gas Consumption	
46,800,000,000 cubic meters per year (estimate) (2012)	**Land Use**
	10.1% arable land; 0.8% permanent crops; 51.7% permanent meadows and pastures; 7.8% forest land; 29.6% other.
Natural Resources	
Natural gas, petroleum, coal, gold, uranium, silver, copper, lead and zinc, tungsten, molybdenum	**Arable Land**
	10% (2007)

Arable Land Per Capita	**Labor Profile**
0 acres per person (2007)	agriculture: 25.9% industry: 13.2% services: 60.9% (estimate) (2012)
Health	
Average Life Expectancy	**Military**
73.3 years (2014)	**Total Active Armed Forces**
Average Life Expectancy, Male	67,000 (estimate) (2010)
70.3 years (2014)	**Active Armed Forces**
Average Life Expectancy, Female	0% (2010)
76.5 years (2014)	**Annual Military Expenditures**
Crude Birth Rate	$94,000,000 (2007)
17.0 (estimate) (2015)	**Military Service**
Crude Death Rate	Service in the Uzbek military is by conscription, with terms lasting 12 months.
5.3 (estimate) (2015)	
Maternal Mortality	**National Finances**
24 per 100,000 live births (2005–2012 projection)	**Currency**
	Uzbekistani som
Infant Mortality	**Total Government Revenues**
34 per 1,000 live births (2012)	$17,840,000,000 (estimate) (2013)
Doctors	**Total Government Expenditures**
2.4 per 1,000 people (2012)	$18,050,000,000 (estimate) (2013)
Industry and Labor	**Budget Deficit**
Gross Domestic Product (GDP) - official exchange rate	-0.4 (estimate) (2013)
	GDP Contribution by Sector
$67,330,000,000 (estimate) (2015)	agriculture: 18.5% industry: 36.4% services: 45.1% (2012 est.)
GDP per Capita	
$2,174 (estimate) (2015)	**External Debt**
GDP - Purchasing Power Parity (PPP)	$8,773,000,000 (estimate) (2013)
$113,865,000,000 (estimate) (2013)	**Economic Aid Extended**
GDP (PPP) per Capita	$0 (2011)
$3,821 (estimate) (2013)	**Economic Aid Received**
Industry Products	$216,000,000 (2011)
Cement, metal products, fertilizers, plastics, paper and paper products, textiles, vegetable oil.	**Population**
	Population
Agriculture Products	29,199,942 (estimate) (2015)
Cotton, vegetables, grains, fruit, potatoes, cattle, sheep, goats, milk, eggs, cannabis (illicit), opium (illicit).	**World Population Rank**
	44 th (2009)
	Population Density
Unemployment	162.8 people per square mile (estimate) (2011)
11.3% (2012)	

Population Distribution	Import Partners		
36% urban (2011)	Russia - 22.1%; China - 20.5%; South Korea - 15.0%; Germany -6.0%; Ukraine - 5.3% (2009 estimate)		
Age Distribution			
0-14: 27.3%	**Export Partners**		
15-64: 68%	Ukraine - 30.5%; Russia - 15.8%; Turkey- 7.7%; Kazakhstan - 7.4%; Bangladesh - 7.0% (2009 estimate).		
65+: 4.7%			
(2009)			
Median Age	**Current Account Balance**		
27.1 years (estimate) (2014)	$1,801,000,000 (estimate) (2013)		
Population Growth Rate	**Weights and Measures**		
0.9% per year (estimate) (2015)	The metric system is in use.		
Net Migration Rate			
-2.4 (estimate) (2015)	**Transportation**		
Trade	**Airports**		
Imported Goods	53 (2012)		
Machinery, agricultural goods, chemicals, petroleum and petroleum products, metals, wood, paper products, building materials, consumer durables, foodstuffs.	**Paved Roads**		
	87.3% (2001)		
	Roads, Unpaved		
Total Value of Imports	6,826 (2000)		
$8,439,900,000 (estimate) (2009)	**Passenger Cars per 1,000 People**		
Exported Goods	Not Available		
Machinery, gold, cotton, textiles, fertilizers, vegetable oil.	**Railroads**		
	2,265 (2008)		
Total Value of Exports	**Ports**		
$12,800,000,000 (estimate) (2012)	Major: 1—Termiz.		

OVERVIEW

Uzbekistan is located in Central Asia, completely landlocked between the mountainous countries to its east and the deserts of Kazakhstan and Turkmenistan to its west. It also lies between the two major rivers of Central Asia, the Syr Darya and the Amu Darya, which run through its eastern and western regions respectively. Roughly 80 percent of Uzbekistan is covered in desert, with high mountains rising in the eastern part of the country and the saline Aral Sea lying on the northwest border. Only in the lowlands areas of the southeast and where the county's eastern borders jut between Kazakhstan, Kyrgyzstan and Tajikistan is the land particularly well-suited to agriculture and habitation. The mostly desert state has an extreme continental climate, with hot summers and very cold winters. Of a population of

UZBEKISTAN

about 29 million, ethnic Uzbeks make up about 80 percent. The capital of Uzbekistan is Tashkent. Uzbekistan, home to several ancient cities that served as market places on the legendary Silk Road trade route, is a land of colorful bazaars, dramatic mosques, and drab Soviet-era architecture.

GOVERNMENT

Uzbekistan is a republic that declared its independence from the Soviet Union on August 31, 1991. It has a severely restricted multiparty political system and a presidential form of government in which a highly centralized executive dominates the other branches of government. The country's current president is Islam Karimov, who has led the country since March 1990, when he served as executive president of the Supreme Soviet of the Uzbek Soviet Socialist Republic. Legislative authority resides with the Supreme Assembly, known as the Oliy Majlis.

Constitution

The Uzbek Constitution was adopted on December 8, 1992, guaranteeing freedom of thought, conscience, and religion. The Constitution also bars the imposition of a state ideology or religion.

Executive

The office of the president, a directly elected post, was created in 1990. The president, who is head of state, may serve a maximum of two consecutive five-year terms. However, Karimov has held referendums and altered the constitution to extend his term in office. The executive also includes a cabinet headed by a prime minister, who is appointed by the president. The appointments of the prime minister and cabinet are subject to legislative approval.

Legislature

As a result of a national referendum on January 27, 2002, the Supreme Assembly (Oliy Majlis) became a bicameral, 250-member legislative body, with an upper chamber, or Senate, and a lower chamber, or Legislative Chamber. (Prior to this, the Constitution had created a 250-member unicameral legislature, which came into existence after elections were held on December 25, 1994.) The Senate consists of 100 seats, with governing councils responsible for electing 84 members and the other 16 appointed by the president. All 120 seats in the Legislative Chamber are elected by popular vote. Legislators serve five-year terms. The president is empowered to dissolve the Supreme Assembly but must first seek the approval of the Constitutional Court.

Judiciary

The judiciary is headed by a Supreme Court. There are also a Constitutional Court and a procurator-general.

Local Government

For administrative purposes, Uzbekistan is divided into 12 provinces (*oblasts*); the capital, Tashkent; and one sovereign republic.

Election Qualifications

All citizens 18 years of age and older are eligible to vote.

POLITICS

Uzbekistan declared independence from the Soviet Union on August 31, 1991. Since independence, Uzbekistan has been governed by its Soviet-era leader Islam Karimov, who was elected president of the republic on December 29, 1991, with the

Islam Karimov became President of Uzbekistan when the country became independent of the Soviet Union in 1991, and has remained in power ever since then. Karimov is known as an authoritarian ruler who has imposed harsh measures to suppress dissent and opposition to his government. (Mikhail Metzel/ZUMA Press/Newscom)

backing of the Uzbek Communist Party's successor group, the People's Democratic Party (PDP). Under Karimov, all political parties must be approved by the government; consequently only parties that support Karimov qualify as legal.

In a 1995 referendum, Karimov's term was extended until 2000. The legislature subsequently agreed that the extension would be considered part of Karimov's first term, making him eligible to stand for election again in 2000. He was reelected to another term in 2000 and again in 2007, amid allegations of government-sponsored election fraud.

Political Parties

Although most communist parties across the former Soviet Union were outlawed following its collapse, the Uzbek Communist Party held onto power in the republic and changed its name to the People's Democratic Party (PDP). The party has 340,000 members and is led by President Islam Karimov. The president has endured international criticism from human rights groups for the repression of opposition parties, including Erk and Birlik, both of which were banned in October 1993. Prominent current and banned parties include the following.

Ecological Movement of Uzbekistan (O'zbekiston Ekologik Harakati) is an environmentally focused party that formed in 2008.

National Rebirth Democratic Party of Uzbekistan (Milliy Tiklanish) was formed in 1995 and advocates a strong sense of Uzbek culture, wants to build closer ties with other Central Asian nations, and opposes Russian influence in the region.

The Justice (Adolat) Social Democratic Party of Uzbekistan was formed in February 1995 as a progovernment, left-of-center party of former Muslim dissidents.

The Freedom Democratic Party (Erk) was founded in 1990 by supporters of an independent Uzbekistan within a federation of former Soviet states. Prominent poet Muhammad Solikh chaired the party and placed second in 1991 presidential balloting, behind Islam Karimov. The party was banned in 1993 but remains active.

The Islamic Renaissance Party was a fundamentalist group that sought the creation of an Islamic state before it was banned in 1991. The party was led by Abdullah Utayev until 1993, when he was reported to have "disappeared."

The Liberal Democratic Party of Uzbekistan (LDPU) was founded in November 2003, by 300 delegates from across the country. By mid-2004, the party had 40,000 registered members. Members are mostly business owners, managers, entrepreneurs, and industrial workers.

In April 2005, human rights activists and prominent outspoken opposition members formed the Coalition of Democratic Forces, also known as My Sunny Uzbekistan (Serquyosh Uzbekistonim—SU). Created to unite the opposition, SU stresses economic reforms—including mass privatization of industries and greater antimonopoly measures. As an opposition party, it is not recognized officially.

ECONOMY

Uzbekistan has done little to transform its economy since the Soviet era, although Karimov has started to privatize the state-owned mining, coal, and energy industries. Uzbekistan's considerable resources include gold (including the world's largest mine), cotton, oil, and natural gas. Karimov is courting international investors to exploit untapped energy reserves. Uzbekistan is the world's fifth-largest exporter of cotton, although cotton production has fallen an estimated 35 percent since Uzbekistan became an independent nation in 1991. Some western clothing companies have pledged not to knowingly use Uzbek cotton because of widespread allegations that it is harvested with child labor and forced labor. Uzbekistan depends on imports for its grain. As of 2011, 16 percent of Uzbeks lived below the national poverty line, according to the World Bank, and population growth remains relatively high. An Uzbek currency, the som, entered circulation in 1994. The country's main trading partners are Russia, China, the United States, and South Korea.

SOCIETY

Eighty percent of the population is descended from ethnic Uzbeks. The nation's Russian population has steadily declined since the late twentieth century because many people of Russian ancestry have been emigrating out of the country—mostly to Russia. Uzbekistan is also home to Tajik, Kazakh, Karakalpak, and Tatar populations. During the Soviet era, Islam was severely repressed in Uzbekistan, but since the collapse of the Soviet Union, Islam has made a revival. Nearly 90 percent of Uzbeks are Muslims. Most of them are Sunnis, but there are some that practice Sufism, Islamic mysticism. The country's Russian population mostly affiliates with the Eastern Orthodox Church. Uzbek, the official language, belongs to the southeastern, or Chagadai branch of the Turkic language group. Russian is spoken by some 14 percent of the population.

Ethnic Composition

Uzbek – 80%; Russian – 5.5%; Tajik – 5%; Kazakh – 3%; Karakalpak – 2.5%; Tatar – 1.5%; other – 2.5%

Language

Uzbek is the country's official language, although there are many dialects spoken. Because of the many years that Uzbekistan was part of the Soviet Union, Russian is also spoken. Many residents of Samarkand and Bukhara speak Tajik as their first language.

Religion

Muslim (mostly Sunni) – 88%; Eastern Orthodox – 9%; other – 3%

CONTEMPORARY ISSUES

Human Rights

Suppression of political and press freedom, arrest and torture of opposition leaders, and religious persecution characterize what international watchdog groups call the systematic violation of human rights in Uzbekistan. The Uzbek Constitution requires freedom of speech; a representative government; and the separation of executive, legislative, and judicial powers. However, authoritarian president Islam Karimov has repeatedly flouted such provisions since he was installed as the nation's leader by the Soviet Union in 1990. Karimov has banned all political parties that do not support him and may dissolve the Oliy Majlis at will, creating a rubber-stamp legislature; he also appoints all judges, the prime minister, cabinet ministers, and provincial governors. In 2009, the independent bar association was dissolved by law, and since that time defense lawyers who have attempted to take on politically sensitive cases have routinely been disbarred. Government control and censorship of the media is nearly absolute, and journalists who fail to comply have been arrested, tortured, and, in at least one case, killed.

Karimov portrays his tight rein on dissent as necessary to thwart Islamic extremist elements, including the Islamic Movement of Uzbekistan (IMU), which has launched sporadic terrorist bombings and allied itself with Afghanistan's former Taliban government. However, according to human rights groups, many moderate Muslims with no ties to IMU have been subject to harassment, arrests, torture, and convictions on false charges of terrorism. Many prisoners have died in custody, not only from abuse, but also from poor conditions and rampant disease in the prison system. Opposition leaders say the government's heavy-handed tactics, along with widespread poverty and the suppression of basic rights, have in fact fueled Islamic extremism in the country. In May 2005, protests against the detainment of Muslims on charges of Islamic extremism in the eastern city of Andijan ended with government troops opening fire on demonstrators. While Uzbek officials put the death toll at less than 190, witnesses maintain that several hundred civilians were killed, and Human Rights Watch has labeled the event a massacre. Since the protest, the government has cracked down further, suppressing all accounts of the incident that contradict the government version, arresting and torturing protestors, and harassing the families of protestors who fled to other countries. Several international human rights groups have been banned from or forced out of the country.

Lack of Water

Intensive irrigation of farmland in the mostly desert nation of Uzbekistan has severely depleted water resources, including the Aral Sea and several major rivers. Virtually all farmland—10 percent of the total land area—is irrigated, mainly from the waters of the Amu Darya, Syr Darya, and Zarafshon rivers. Cotton, which is the nation's biggest crop, requires large amounts of water. Altogether, Uzbekistan withdraws more than 80 percent of its total renewable water resources each year, drying out the Amu Darya River before it reaches the Aral Sea and shrinking the Aral to less than 30 percent of its size before 1960. Agricultural production is responsible for 93 percent of all water consumption, while many rural households have no access to clean drinking water. Much of the nation's fresh water supplies have been polluted by pesticides, fertilizers, and other agricultural runoff. Overuse of the Amu Darya, which forms Uzbekistan's border with Turkmenistan, has also created tensions between the neighboring nations, as disputes grow over water sharing, and years of severe drought in the region continue to add to the water crisis.

A boat in the dry part of the Aral Sea, located along the border between Uzbekistan and neighboring Kazakhstan. The shrinking of the Aral Sea was caused by the Soviets, who dammed its two main tributaries in order to divert water for irrigation. (Europics/Newscom)

Migration

Growing unemployment and a surplus of highly skilled workers is increasing the number of Uzbeks leaving the country. An estimated 5 percent of Uzbeks are unemployed, but another 20 percent are believed to be underemployed; underemployment is most severe in the agricultural sector, which employs most of the rural population. Literacy is nearly universal, and the nation's workforce is well trained, yet the number of skilled jobs has shrunk significantly in recent years, partly due to government restrictions on foreign investment. Several foreign companies also have closed or downsized their Uzbek operations, and those that are left face government-enforced salary caps, which have kept pay rates stagnant, further encouraging skilled workers to find work abroad. The number of Uzbeks seeking employment in Russia, Kazakhstan, Southeast Asia, and the Middle East has increased significantly, and current estimates put the number of working-age Uzbeks living outside the country at between 3 million and 5 million. Because approximately half of the population is currently under 25 years old, economic experts believe that there will not be enough jobs to accommodate the growing workforce. In addition, educational funding has declined since the collapse of the Soviet Union, leaving many schools lacking in supplies and qualified instructors, and the percentage of school-age children enrolled in classes has dropped. As a result, skill levels among those entering the workforce today are not as high, leading to fears of a further deterioration of the economy in the future.

Excerpt from the Constitution of Uzbekistan

The Constitution of Uzbekistan was adopted in 1992, shortly after Uzbekistan became an independent country following the breakup of the former Union of Soviet Socialist Republics. It states that "Democratic rights and freedoms shall be protected by the Constitution and the laws."

The Constitution recognizes equality under the law as fundamental and forbids discrimination on the basis of gender, language, ethnicity, or religion. It guarantees political and legal rights, including the right to freedom of speech and the freedom to join political parties or labor unions. Although the large majority of Uzbekistan's citizens are Muslim, the Constitution states that "Any compulsory imposition of religion shall be impermissible." The Constitution also regards various welfare-related rights as fundamental, including the right to "skilled medical care," education, and social security. The rights of children, elderly persons, and disabled persons are identified specifically.

In addition, the Constitution specifies that parents have the responsibility to care for their minor children, with the state being responsible for the care of orphans and "children deprived of parental guardianship." Adult children are responsible for the welfare of their elderly parents. Recognizing conditions more specific to Central Asia, the Constitution bans forced labor and also requires that "Marriage shall be based on the willing consent and equality of both parties."

PREAMBLE

The people of Uzbekistan,

solemnly declaring their adherence to human rights and principles of state sovereignty, aware of their ultimate responsibility to the present and the future generations, relying on historical experience in the development of Uzbek statehood, affirming their commitment to the ideals of democracy and social justice, recognizing priority of the generally accepted norms of the international law, aspiring to a worthy life for the citizens of the Republic, setting forth the task of creating a humane and democratic rule of law, aiming to ensure civil peace and national accord . . . adopt the present Constitution of the Republic of Uzbekistan.

FUNDAMENTAL PRINCIPLES

Article 7

The people are the sole source of state power.

Article 8

All citizens of the Republic of Uzbekistan, regardless of their nationality, constitute the people of Uzbekistan.

Article 13

Democracy in the Republic of Uzbekistan shall rest on the principles common to all mankind, according to which the ultimate value is the human being, his life, freedom, honor, dignity and other inalienable rights. Democratic rights and freedoms shall be protected by the Constitution and the laws.

Article 14

The state shall function on the principles of social justice and legality in the interests of the people and society.

BASIC HUMAN AND CIVIL RIGHTS, FREEDOMS AND DUTIES

Article 18

All citizens of the Republic of Uzbekistan shall have equal rights and freedoms, and shall be equal before the law, without discrimination by sex, race, nationality, language, religion, social origin, convictions, individual and social status.

Article 24

The right to exist is the inalienable right of every human being. Attempts on anyone's life shall be regarded as the gravest crime.

Article 25

Everyone shall have the right to freedom . . . No one may be arrested or taken into custody except on lawful grounds.

Article 26

No one may be adjudged guilty of a crime except by the sentence of a court . . . Such a person shall be guaranteed the right to legal defense during open court proceedings.

No one may be subject to torture, violence or any other cruel or humiliating treatment.

No one may be subject to any medical or scientific experiments without his consent.

Article 27

No one may enter a home, carry out a search or an examination, or violate the privacy of correspondence and telephone conversations, except on lawful grounds . . .

Article 28

Any citizen . . . shall have the right to freedom of movement on the territory of the Republic, as well as a free entry to and exit from it, except in the events specified by law.

Article 29

Everyone shall be guaranteed freedom of thought, speech and convictions. Everyone shall have the right to seek, obtain and disseminate any information, except that which is directed against the existing constitutional system and in some other instances specified by law.

Freedom of opinion and its expression may be restricted by law if any state or other secret is involved.

Article 30

All state bodies, public associations and officials in the Republic of Uzbekistan shall allow any citizen access to documents, resolutions and other materials, relating to their rights and interests.

Article 31

Freedom of conscience is guaranteed to all. Everyone shall have the right to profess or not to profess any religion. Any compulsory imposition of religion shall be impermissible.

Article 33

All citizens shall have the right to engage in public life by holding rallies, meetings and demonstrations in accordance with the legislation of the Republic of Uzbekistan. The bodies of authority shall have the right to suspend or ban such undertakings exclusively on the grounds of security.

Article 34

All citizens of the republic of Uzbekistan shall have the right to form trade unions, political parties and any other public associations, and to participate in mass movements.

Article 35

Everyone shall have the right, both individually and collectively, to submit applications and proposals, and to lodge complaints with competent state bodies, institutions and public representatives.

Article 37

Everyone shall have the right to work, including the right to choose their occupation. Every citizen shall be entitled to fair conditions of labor and protection against unemployment in accordance with the procedure prescribed by law.

Any forced labor shall be prohibited, except as punishment under the sentence of a court, or in some other Instances specified by law.

Article 38

Citizens working on hire shall be entitled to a paid rest. The number of working hours and the duration of paid leave shall be specified by law.

Article 39

Everyone shall have the right to social security in old age, in the event of disability and loss of the breadwinner as well as in some other cases specified by law.

Pensions, allowances and other kinds of welfare may not be lower than the officially fixed minimum subsistence wage.

Article 40

Everyone shall have the right to receive skilled medical care.

Article 41

Everyone shall have the right to education. The state shall guarantee free secondary education. Schooling shall be under state supervision.

Article 42

Everyone shall be guaranteed the freedom of scientific research and engineering work, as well as the right to enjoy cultural benefits. The state shall promote the cultural, scientific and technical development of society.

Article 45

The rights of minors, the disabled, and the elderly shall be protected by the state.

Article 46

Women and men shall have equal rights.

Article 57

The formation and functioning of political parties and public associations aiming to do the following shall be prohibited: changing the existing constitutional system by force; coming out against the sovereignty, territorial integrity and security of the Republic, as well as the constitutional rights and freedoms of its citizens; advocating war and social, national, racial and religious hostility, and encroaching on the health and morality of the people, as well as of any armed associations and political parties based on the national or religious principles.

All secret societies and associations shall be banned.

Article 61

Religious organizations and associations shall be separated from the state and equal before law. The state shall not interfere with the activity of religious associations.

Article 62

Public associations may be dissolved or banned, or subject to restricted activity solely by the sentence of a court.

Article 63

Marriage shall be based on the willing consent and equality of both parties.

Article 64

Parents shall be obliged to support and care for their children until the latter are of age.

The state and society shall support, care for and educate orphaned children, as well as children deprived of parental guardianship, and encourage charity in their favor.

Article 65

All children shall be equal before the law regardless of their origin and the civic status of their parents.

Motherhood and childhood shall be protected by the state.

Article 66

Able-bodied children who are of age shall be obliged to care for their parents.

Article 67

The mass media shall be free and act in accordance with the law. It shall bear responsibility for trustworthiness of information in a prescribed manner. Censorship is impermissible.

Source: "The Constitution of the Republic of Uzbekistan." Legislation Online. http://www.legislationline.org/documents/section/constitutions

CHAPTER 7

TRANSNATIONAL ORGANIZATIONS

Transnational organizations, which are sometimes known as international organizations or intergovernmental organization, are formal associations of sovereign states. These states hold formal membership in transnational organizations, which have procedures in place to make collective decisions on behalf of the entire membership. Transnational organizations can thus be distinguished from formal organizations such as the Red Cross, which operate across international boundaries but are not governed by sovereign states as members.

Transnational organizations can be categorized in several ways, including by location and by purpose. Some transnational organizations operate worldwide. The largest such organization is the United Nations (UN), whose members include nearly all of the world's sovereign states and which has more members than any other transnational organization. The World Trade Organization (WTO) and the International Monetary Fund (IMF) also operate on a global basis. Others operate on a regional basis. Examples include the European Union (EU), the Association of Southeast Asian Nations (ASEAN), the African Union, and the Arab League. Membership in these organizations is restricted to countries located in their respective regions.

Transnational organizations can also be categorized on the basis of purpose. The UN, the EU, and ASEAN are multipurpose transnational organizations. Their functions include economic development, trade, political integration, human rights, and cultural activities. Other transnational organizations address specific purposes. For example, the North Atlantic Treaty Organization (NATO) focuses on defense and security issues. The World Trade Organization (WTO), as its name implies, and the North American Free Trade Agreement (NAFTA) address issues associated with international trade. Other organizations focus on cultural issues and activities. Aside from the United Nations, the three transnational organizations with the most states as members are the International Olympic Committee, the Fédération Internationale de Football Association (FIFA), which governs international soccer competition, and the Fédération Internationale des Échecs (FIDE), which governs international chess competition.

Most international organizations are governed by treaties and/or charters that specify criteria for membership and decision-making procedures. In some cases, these charters arise from treaties or agreements among founding members. For example, the United Nations grew out of an international conference held in San Francisco in April 1945. Attendees at this conference drafted the United Nations Charter, which took effect after it was ratified by all five members of the Security Council (the United States, the United Kingdom, France, the Soviet Union, and China) and by a majority of the other states that had participated in the conference. The EU began as the European Coal and Steel Community, which was established per agreement among its six original members. Over time, the UN, the EU, and other transnational organizations have expanded their memberships. The EU, for example, has expanded from its original six members in the 1950s to 28 members as of 2014. Similarly, the UN consisted of 51 members in 1945, and has grown to nearly 200 members today.

Although membership in many transnational organizations tends to increase over time, most transnational organizations maintain criteria associated with eligibility for membership. For example, the EU requires potential new members to adhere to the Copenhagen criteria, including democracy, respect for human rights, and a market economy. Some states have declined invitations to join transnational organizations despite the fact that they meet membership criteria. Norway, for example, declined to join the EU in 1972 and again in 1994. Countries that fail to adhere to membership criteria may be suspended or expelled from transnational organizations. This is illustrated by the example of South Africa, which was suspended from participating in the United Nations General Assembly and from the British Commonwealth of Nations, in response to that country's apartheid policy, which institutionalized racial segregation and white supremacy. After apartheid was eliminated and South Africa became a multiracial democracy, it was readmitted to both organizations.

Charters of international organizations establish policies by which decisions are made. The United Nations, for example, is governed by the Security Council, with five permanent and ten temporary members, and by the General Assembly, within which each member country has one vote. Allocating one vote to each member is a common practice. For example, the International Olympic Committee has established a procedure for selecting sites of the Olympic Games. Each member country has one vote, and voting continues over several rounds until one of the candidate sites gets a majority of the votes and is selected.

Kingdoms and other governments have maintained temporary or permanent alliances such ancient times. However, transnational organizations as we know them today were not established until the nineteenth century, after the concept of sovereignty became accepted universally. Sovereignty gave independent countries the authority to sign treaties, and therefore to join transnational organizations on the basis of agreement to adhere to their missions and their membership criteria. The oldest formal transnational organization in the world is believed to be the Central Commission for Navigation on the Rhine (CCNR), which is still in existence and operation today. CCNR was founded in 1815, at the end of the Napoleonic Wars. Its purpose is to guarantee freedom of navigation on the Rhine River. CCNR was established by the countries through which the Rhine flows. Its original members were Switzerland, Germany, France, and the Netherlands. Belgium joined CCNR after it became independent from the Netherlands in 1830. These countries remain the five members of CCNR today.

The operation of transnational organizations can be controversial. Leaders in some countries have sometimes argued that the decision-making processes are biased. Some in the United States and other wealthy, developed countries argue that decisions by the UN General Assembly are biased in favor of the interests of less-developed countries, which make up a majority of the UN's membership. Critics of the UN argue that this bias is especially inappropriate given that much of the funding used to operate the UN comes from the developed countries. The larger question becomes the extent to which wealthier and more developed states should have power and influence in transnational organizations proportional to their size and economic strength, as opposed to equal levels of influence. However, critics of the UN argue also that the five permanent members of the Security Council have disproportionate influence, in that any of them can veto any proposed Security Council action.

The question of the extent to which a member state gives up its own sovereignty as a member of a transnational organization also arises frequently. In signing a treaty or a charter that governs a transnational organization, a country may be agreeing to cooperate with other members of that organization, regardless of whether this cooperation serves the interests of the signatory state. Members of the EU must abide by EU policies regarding trade, economic development, and other activities. For example, EU policy regarding migration guarantees the rights of citizens of EU countries to move freely among these countries, although the migration process can place stress on countries that receive large numbers of migrants. Similarly, the EU's policies regarding immigration from outside the EU have been opposed in countries receiving large numbers of international migrants. On the other hand, membership in transnational organizations can provide member countries with resources to address common problems, and can help to coordinate efforts to address issues such as climate change and environmental degradation, that extend across state boundaries.

Other transnational organizations include the African Union and the League of Arab States. The African Union was established in 2002. It replaced the Organization of African Unity (OAU), which had been formed in 1963, a time when many former European colonies throughout Africa were becoming independent.

According to its charter, the aims of the Organization of African Unity included "to promote the unity and solidarity of the African States; to co-ordinate and intensify their cooperation and efforts to achieve a better life for the peoples of Africa; to defend their sovereignty, their territorial integrity and independence; to eradicate all forms of colonialism from Africa; and to promote international cooperation, having due regard to the Charter of the United Nations and the Universal Declaration of Human Rights." Thus a major goal of the OAU was to enable its members to maintain their independent status in a world characterized by conflict between East and West, and at a time when some European countries continued to hold on to their African colonies. Although most of the boundaries between Africa's newly independent countries had been drawn by European colonial powers without regard for local conditions and interests, the OAU tended to oppose any efforts on the part of its members to redraw international boundaries.

The OAU was dissolved and replaced by the African Union in 2002. Although maintaining territorial integrity and independence was a goal of the African Union, its mission was expanded to include "To accelerate the political and social-economic integration of the continent. To promote and defend African common positions on issues of interest to the continent and its peoples . . . [and to] promote sustainable development at the economic, social and cultural levels as well as the integration of African economies." Thus the African Union's role included a focus on economic development, as opposed to only political independence.

Today, the African Union has 54 members, and every country on the African continent, with the exception of Morocco, is a member. At various times, the African Union has suspended member countries whose actions have been inconsistent with the Union's charter. For example, the Central African Republic was suspended in 2013 during its civil war, when its warring factions were accused of murdering and torturing their political opponents. The African Union's headquarters are located in Addis Ababa, the capital of Ethiopia.

The Arab League, which is known formally as the League of Arab States, plays a similar role in Southwest Asia and North Africa. It was founded in 1945. According to its charter, "The purpose of the League is to draw closer the relations between member States and co-ordinate their political activities with the aim of realizing a close collaboration between them, to safeguard their independence and sovereignty, and to consider in a general way the affairs and interests of the Arab countries." Thus the Arab League recognizes the cultural unity of the Arab people, although its charter recognizes the territorial integrity and sovereignty. The Arab League has 22 members, although Syria was suspended in 2011 following political turmoil and repression in that country. Its permanent headquarters are located in Cairo, the capital of Egypt.

—Fred M. Shelley

Further Reading

Paul F. Diehl and Brian Frederking (eds.), *The politics of global governance: International organizations in an interdependent world*. Boulder, CO: Lynne Rienner Publishers, 2010.

Margaret P. Karns and Karen A. Mingst, *International organizations: The politics and processes of global governance* (2nd edition). Boulder, Colorado: Lynne Rienner Publishers, 2009.

Kelly-Kate S. Pease, *International organizations* (6th edition). New York: Pearson, 2011.

THE AFRICAN UNION

The African Union (AU) was formed in July 2002 with a stated mission of uniting the African countries in order to create "an integrated, prosperous and peaceful Africa driven by its own citizens and representing a dynamic force in the global arena." The 54-member organization works to promote economic development, fight poverty and corruption, and end the continent's many conflicts.

The AU replaced the Organization of African Unity (OAU). The OAU formed in 1963, at a time when African countries were shaking off the colonial rule of European countries and achieving independence, in some cases for the first time in more than a century, and in other cases for the first time ever. Recognizing that the new countries faced numerous challenges, and that cooperation would benefit them all, they decided to organize in order to foster cooperation. However, throughout its existence, the OAU proved incapable of effectively uniting African nations, or of helping them improve their economies.

By 1999 it was clear the organization as it was structured was not effective. Leaders of the OAU issued what is now known as the Sirte Declaration, in which they called for the establishment of a new organization to unify and promote Africa. Touted by leaders as more people-oriented than the OAU, the AU was the brainchild of a group led by former Libyan dictator Muammar Gaddafi. Throughout the last decade of his life, Gaddafi argued for a continent-wide federal system, much like that of the United States, that would bind African countries together in a single state, to be called the United States of Africa. Just 12 years after he shepherded the creation of the AU and the Sirte Declaration, Gaddafi was killed on the outskirts of Sirte, trying to flee rebels who had forced him from power.

A key difference between the OAU (which some regarded as a club for dictators) and the new African Union is that the AU has authority to intervene in other countries' domestic affairs in cases of war crimes, unconstitutional changes of government, genocide, and other human-rights violations. According to observers, the AU is the only multinational organization to give its members that authority. In addition, the AU actively works to "promote democratic principles and institutions," while the OAU was less explicitly enthusiastic about democracy.

The new organization and its constitution were adopted, and the African Union officially debuted in 2002. It is headquartered in Addis Ababa, the capital of

Ethiopia. Modeled after the European Union, the AU aims to build economic and political stability. AU membership includes every country on the continent except Morocco, which quit the OAU in 1985 after the group admitted the disputed territory of Western Sahara as a member. (Morocco considers the territory part of its domain.) The AU's constitution lists 16 principles, or areas of focus, which can be separated into three main categories: peace and security; socioeconomic development; and governance and social justice.

The main organizations within the AU include:

The Assembly

The Assembly consists of the heads of state of member countries, who meet at least once a year. It is the AU's main decision-making body. Members of the assembly elect an AU chairperson, who serves for one year. The assembly determines AU policies, establishes its priorities, and adopts its annual program.

Nkosazana Dlamini Zuma, Chairperson of The African Union Commission, attending a press conference at the AU headquarters in Addis Ababa, Ethiopia, in July 2013. She was elected to this position in 2012 and became the first women to serve in this capacity. Prior to her election, she was a leading anti-apartheid activist in South Africa and served as a member of South Africa's cabinet as Minister of Health and Minister of Foreign Affairs. (imago stock&people/Newscom)

Executive Council

The council is made up of foreign ministers of member states, who advise the assembly. It also monitors the implementation of policies adopted by the assembly.

Commission

The commission's 10 members implement AU policies and coordinate the organization's meetings. Within the commission are subgroups dedicated to Peace and Security; Political Affairs; Trade and Industry; Infrastructure and Energy; Social Affairs; Rural Economy and Agriculture; Human Resources, Science and Technology; and Economic Affairs.

The Pan-African Parliament

Set up in 2004, the Parliament (PAP) was created as a vehicle to give individuals and grassroots organizations a voice within the union. Currently, the 230 members are nonvoting advisors, although the union officially hopes the PAP will evolve into an institution with voting power.

The Economic, Social, and Cultural Council

Established in 2005 to encourage partnerships between African governments and other aspects of society, the council includes cultural groups, professional organizations, and social groups.

African Court on Human and Peoples' Rights

The Union also has established the Court, which technically has existed since 2006. The court, established in part because African leaders have long felt that other international human rights courts, including the International Criminal Court, have unfairly targeted the continent's government officials for prosecution, adopted its official rules in 2010. The court's effectiveness may be hampered, however, because only 15 of the AU's members have so far adopted the court rules. In July 2014, African leaders further jeopardized the court's credibility by voting to give immunity from war crimes prosecution to Africa's sitting leaders and senior officials.

Peace and Security Council

The 15-member Peace and Security Council (PSC) is the main decision-making body for preventing, managing, and resolving conflicts. The PSC has the authority to recommend AU intervention when member states experience war crimes, genocide, and other critical situations.

In 2003, the first AU chairman, South African president Thabo Mbeki, told leaders at the second AU summit that their top priority must be ending the violence and conflict that have torn the continent apart for decades. Led by the PSC, the AU has indeed orchestrated numerous peace-keeping operations in such trouble spots as Burundi, the Comoros, Sudan, and Somalia. Together, those operations have involved some 20,000 uniformed troops and produced mixed success, partly because many impoverished AU countries have not provided the necessary troops or other resources.

In its first peace-keeping mission, undertaken in 2003 when the AU was just a year old, the organization sent nearly 3,000 troops to help end the decade-long civil war dividing Burundi. That same year, rebel groups began fighting the Sudanese government in a conflict that would eventually kill more than 300,000 and drive 2.5 million from their homes in the Darfur region of that country. By 2005, the African Union had 2,300 troops in the Darfur region of Sudan, in an attempt to bring peace. But the force was ill-equipped, outmanned, and lacked a clear mandate. In 2005, the AU asked the United Nations for $460 million to help it increase its forces and their effectiveness in Darfur. Because the government of Sudan would not allow United Nations troops into the country, AU soldiers alone carried the burden of trying to bring peace in Darfur. By 2006, there were 7,000 AU troops there, although many African countries were reluctant to send forces because Sudan is a powerful member of the AU, and they feared retribution. Ultimately, the troops could not protect humanitarian organizations trying to deliver aid to refugees, so many of those assistance efforts had to stop. The AU did craft an 85-page peace agreement between the warring parties, but the rebels ultimately refused to sign. In 2007, AU troops left Darfur, hoping that UN forces could take over, but the government of Sudan continued to refuse them access to the country.

Starting in 2007, the presence of several thousand troops in Somalia initially proved effective in stabilizing that collapsed state. However, those troops were unable to prevent extremists from uniting with al-Shabab and other Islamic terrorist groups that have gained power in what remains a lawless country.

Whatever the level of its success, the AU has made consistent efforts toward peace in warring countries. Its record of holding the leaders of member states accountable for their actions is less consistent. In 2007 for example, the AU denied Sudanese president Omar Hassan Ahmed al-Bashir his turn as AU chairman, citing the violence in his country. But in 2005, the AU refused international requests to help stop Zimbabwean president Robert Mugabe's demolition of homes in urban areas. The Mugabe-ordered destruction left hundreds of thousands homeless, and at least three children were crushed to death. Mugabe maintained he was just "cleaning up" cities in his country and ridding them of criminals. His critics charged that Mugabe was punishing urban voters who opposed him in the recent election. Whatever the truth, AU leaders refused to intervene, saying they had more urgent matters to deal with.

For most of its existence, wars and humanitarian crises have required so much of the AU's resources and attention that its efforts at economic development and addressing human rights issues have taken a back seat. However, the organization has taken some notable first steps in those directions. In 2002, the AU proposed to stamp out corruption by requiring all public officials to declare their assets when they take office, allowing governments to seize bank documents when necessary, and requiring that those convicted of fraud or corruption have their assets confiscated. The action came after an AU-commissioned report showed that corruption costs Africa nearly $150 billion a year. The report found that bribery at lower levels of most governments is rampant, as is fraud at higher levels, allowing national leaders to become wealthy while their people live in poverty. The report concluded that corruption increases the cost of African goods by up to 20 percent, deters foreign investment, and holds back development. By 2006, 34 nations had signed onto the anti-corruption agreement, and in 2011, the AU unveiled a comprehensive program for implementing the goals of the agreement.

In 2003, the AU crafted the Maputo Protocol on the Rights of Women in Africa. The far-reaching protocol calls for a number of steps considered radical in many parts of Africa. The document has been signed and ratified by only 28 countries—far short of the two-thirds needed for implementation. Another 18 countries have signed but not ratified the agreement. It would ban female genital mutilation, outlaw violence against women, promote education among women and girls, guarantee women the right to family planning information, end forced marriages, and set the minimum age for a girl to marry at 18.

With so many members, the AU's decision-making progress can be slow. Achieving a two-thirds majority on controversial major issues can be especially difficult. The AU walks a difficult road as it tries to bring together a continent plagued by poverty, economic trade barriers, soaring debt, poor infrastructure, and widespread violence. All those, and many more, factors contribute to what is a mixed record of achievement for the AU as it assesses its first decades.

Excerpt from the Constitutive Act of the African Union

The Constitutive Act of the African Union was signed in 2000 and went into effect after having been ratified by two-thirds of its 53 members. The African Union replaced the Organization of African Unity, which had been founded in 1963 and was disbanded in 2002. Today, every country on the African continent except for Morocco is a member of the African Union.

The Constitutive Act is "guided by our common vision of a united and strong Africa" and is "determined to promote and protect human and people's rights." Within this context, the Constitutive Act identifies the African Union's guiding principles. These include the achievement of "greater unity and solidarity between the African countries" and respect for democracy and democratic institutions, although not all African countries currently operate as democracies. Other goals include sustainable social and economic development, social justice, and the peaceful resolution of conflicts.

At several points, the Constitutive Act makes reference to human rights, although these rights are not generally spelled out in detail. For example, the Executive Council of the African Union is empowered to make decisions and promote international cooperation and coordination on policies involving education, environmental protection, health, and social security. However, it does not specifically identify these as human rights, although the constitutions of many African Union members do so.

INSPIRED by the noble ideals which guided the founding fathers of our Continental Organization . . . in their determination to promote unity, solidarity, cohesion and cooperation among the peoples of Africa . . . ;

CONSIDERING the principles and objectives stated in the Charter of the Organization of African Unity . . . ;

RECALLING the heroic struggles waged by our peoples and our countries for political independence, human dignity and economic emancipation;

CONSIDERING . . . the Organization of African Unity has played a determining and invaluable role in the liberation of the continent, the affirmation of a common identity and . . . has provided a unique framework for our collective action . . .

DETERMINED to take up the multifaceted challenges that confront our continent . . .

CONVINCED of the need to accelerate the process of implementing the Treaty establishing the African Economic Community in order to promote the socio-economic development of Africa . . . ;

GUIDED by our common vision of a united and strong Africa . . . ;

CONSCIOUS of the fact that the scourge of conflicts in Africa constitutes a major impediment to the socio-economic development . . . ;

DETERMINED to promote and protect human and peoples' rights . . . and to ensure good governance . . . ;

FURTHER DETERMINED to take all necessary measures to strengthen our common institutions . . . ;

HAVE AGREED AS FOLLOWS:

Article 2

The African Union is hereby established in accordance with the provisions of this Act.

Article 3

The objectives of the Union shall be to:

(a) achieve greater unity and solidarity between the African countries . . . ;
(b) defend the sovereignty, territorial integrity and independence of its Member
States;
(c) accelerate the political and socio-economic integration of the continent;
(d) promote and defend African common positions . . . ;
(e) encourage international cooperation . . . ;
(f) promote peace, security, and stability. . . ;
(g) promote democratic principles and institutions . . . ;
(h) promote and protect human rights . . . ;
(i) . . . enable the continent to play its rightful role in the global economy and in
international negotiations;
(j) promote sustainable development at the economic, social and cultural levels
as well as the integration of African economies;
(k) promote co-operation in all fields of human activity to raise the living
standards of African peoples;
(l) coordinate and harmonize the policies between . . . Regional Economic
Communities . . .
(m) advance the development of the continent by promoting research in all fields,
in particular in science and technology;
(n) work with relevant international partners in the eradication of preventable
diseases . . . on the continent.

Article 4

The Union shall function in accordance with the following principles:

(a) sovereign equality and interdependence . . . ;
(b) respect of borders . . . ;
(c) participation of the African peoples . . . ;
(d) establishment of a common defence policy for the African Continent;
(e) peaceful resolution of conflicts . . . ;
(f) prohibition of the use of force or threat [of] force among Member States of
the Union;
(g) non-interference by any Member State in the internal affairs of another;
(h) the right of the Union to intervene . . . in grave circumstances, namely: war
crimes, genocide and crimes against humanity;

(i) peaceful co-existence of Member States . . .
(j) the right of Member States to request intervention . . . to restore peace and security;
(k) promotion of self-reliance . . . ;
(l) promotion of gender equality;
(m) respect for democratic principles, human rights . . . ;
(n) promotion of social justice to ensure balanced economic development;
(o) respect for the sanctity of human life, condemnation and rejection of . . . terrorism;
(p) condemnation and rejection of unconstitutional changes of governments.

Article 6

1. The Assembly shall be composed of Heads of States and Government . . .
2. The Assembly shall be the supreme organ of the Union.
3. The Assembly shall meet at least once a year in ordinary session. At the request of any Member State and on approval by a two-thirds majority . . . the Assembly shall meet in extraordinary session.
4. The Office of the Chairman of the Assembly shall be held for a period of one year by a Head of State or Government . . .

Article 7

The Assembly shall take its decisions by consensus or . . . a two-thirds majority . . .

Article 9

The functions of the Assembly shall be to:

(a) determine the common policies of the Union;
(b) receive, consider and take decisions on reports and recommendations . . . ;
(c) consider requests for Membership . . . ;
(d) establish any organ of the Union;
(e) monitor the implementation of policies and decisions of the Union . . . ;
(f) adopt the budget of the Union;
(g) give directives to the Executive Council on the management of conflicts . . . and the restoration of peace;
(h) appoint and terminate . . . judges of the Court of Justice;
(i) appoint the Chairman of the Commission . . .

Article 10

The Executive Council shall be composed of the Ministers of Foreign Affairs . . .

Article 11

The Executive Council shall take its decisions by consensus or . . . a two-thirds majority . . . procedural matters . . . shall be decided by a simple majority.

Article 13

1. The Executive Council shall coordinate and take decisions on policies . . . including:
   (a) foreign trade;
   (b) energy, industry and mineral resources;
   (c) food, agricultural and animal resources;
   (d) water resources and irrigation;
   (e) environmental protection, humanitarian action and disaster response and relief;
   (f) transport and communications;
   (g) insurance;
   (h) education, culture, health and human resources development;
   (i) science and technology;
   (j) nationality, residency and immigration matters;
   (k) social security . . . mother and child care policies [and] policies relating to the disabled and the handicapped;
   (l) establishment of a system of African awards, medals and prizes.

Article 14

. . . Specialized Technical Committees shall be responsible to the Executive Council:

Article 15

Each Committee shall . . . :

(a) prepare projects and programmes . . . ;
(b) ensure the supervision, follow-up and evaluation of . . . decisions taken by . . . the Union.

The Pan-African Parliament

In order to ensure the full participation of African peoples . . . a Pan-African Parliament shall be established.

Article 18

A Court of Justice of the Union shall be established.

Article 19

The Union shall have the following financial institutions . . . :

(a) The African Central Bank;
(b) The African Monetary Fund;
(c) The African Investment Bank.

Article 20

There shall be established a Commission of the Union, which shall be the Secretariat of the Union.

Article 21

1. There shall be established a Permanent Representatives Committee.
2. The Permanent Representatives Committee shall be charged with the responsibility of preparing the work of the Executive Council . . .

Article 22

The Economic, Social and Cultural Council shall be an advisory organ composed of different social and professional groups . . .

Article 23

The Assembly shall determine the appropriate sanctions . . . on any Member State that defaults in . . . contributions to the budget . . . : [including] denial of the right to speak at meetings, to vote, to present candidates for any position . . . or to benefit from any activity or commitments . . . ;

Any Member State that fails to comply with the decisions and policies of the Union may be subjected to other sanctions . . .

Article 24

The Headquarters of the Union shall be in Addis Ababa, . . . Ethiopia.

Article 25

The working languages of the Union . . . shall be, African languages, Arabic, English, French and Portuguese.

Article 29

Any African State may . . . notify the Chairman of the Commission of its intention to accede to this Act and to be admitted as a member of the Union.

Article 30

Governments which shall come to power through unconstitutional means shall not be allowed to participate in the activities of the Union.

Article 32

Amendments or revisions shall be adopted by the Assembly by consensus or, failing which, by a two-thirds majority and submitted for ratification by all Member States . . .

Article 33

This Act shall replace the Charter of the Organization of African Unity . . .
Done at Lome, Togo, this 11th day of July, 2000.

Source: "Constitutive Act." African Union. http://www.au.int/en/about/constitutive_act

THE ARAB LEAGUE

The Arab League, officially known as the League of Arab States, is an association of Arab nations. When it formed in 1945, the league had two main goals: to help secure independence for Arab lands that were then other nations' colonies; and to prevent the creation of a Jewish state. Today, with those goals no longer relevant, the league's mission has shifted to one of strengthening ties among members, attempting to settle disputes among Arab nations, ensuring their collective security, promoting their economic integration, and supporting development.

Officially the Arab League has 22 members: Algeria, Bahrain, the Comoros islands, Djibouti, Egypt, Iraq, Jordan, Kuwait, Lebanon, Libya, Mauritania, Morocco, Oman, the Palestinian Autonomous Region, Qatar, Saudi Arabia, Somalia, Sudan, Syria, Tunisia, the United Arab Emirates, and Yemen. The league considers the Palestinian Autonomous Region an independent state and grants it full membership. However, the league suspended Syria in 2011 because of what it termed the "brutal" tactics the Syrian government used to fight rebels trying to overthrow the government. Of the 22 member states, eight are monarchies. Of the 22 current members, only the seven founding countries—Egypt, Iraq, Lebanon, Saudi Arabia, Syria, Yemen, and Transjordan, as the Kingdom of Jordan was known then—were independent nations when the League was created. The remaining 15 were then colonies or protectorates ruled by other countries.

Arab unity and independence became an important goal during the late nineteenth and early twentieth centuries. At that time, Arab territories in North Africa and the Arabian Peninsula had been consolidated under the rule of the Islamic-led Ottoman Empire for centuries. By the beginning of World War I in 1914, the Ottoman Empire was in decline. When the empire entered the war on the side of Germany and the other Central Powers, many Arab nationalists saw a chance to rid themselves of Ottoman rule and gain independence by siding with the Allies against the Turks. When the war ended, however, instead of granting independence to territories in North Africa and the Arabian Peninsula, the victorious United Kingdom, France, and Italy divided up the region, creating colonies. Though the outsiders' control over the Arab world weakened its power, it also promoted the spread of Arab nationalism.

During World War II, many Arab politicians felt that the time was right to begin unification of the Arab world, or at least parts of it. However, world events, along with disagreements among Arab states and leaders over which countries to include, prevented the creation of any official Arab organization. By the end of World War II, the growing communist threat persuaded the United Kingdom to champion Arab unity, in hopes that the Arab countries would form a block to oppose communism. A conference to settle differences among Arab leaders was convened September 28, 1944. It concluded October 7 with the proclamation of the creation of the League of Arab States. The league was formally established on March 22, 1945, and Cairo was chosen as the site of its headquarters.

Azzam Pasha was the first Secretary General of the League of Arab States, and served in this capacity from 1945 to 1952. The League of Arab States, founded in 1945, includes 22 predominantly Arabic-speaking, primarily Muslim states in southwest Asia and North Africa. (akg-images/Paul Almasy/Newscom)

As more and more North African colonies gained independence, they were welcomed into the Arab League. The unified opposition to communism that Western Europe hoped for did not materialize, however. Some Arab states—namely Saudi Arabia, Kuwait, Qatar, Bahrain, Oman, the United Arab Emirates, Tunisia, Morocco, and at times Lebanon and Iraq—sided with Western countries, while others, such as Syria, Egypt, and Libya, embedded themselves further into the communist camp during most of the Cold War. These states also supported dissidents within each other's borders and attempted to destabilize one another.

Structure of the Arab League

The supreme organ of the Arab League is the Council, which consists of representatives of all member states and meets twice a year. Extra sessions may be held at the request of any two members. On all decisions, each member has one vote; unanimous decisions are binding upon all states. There are 16 committees attached to the Council: the Administrative and Financial Affairs Permanent Committee, the Arab Oil Experts Committee, the Arab Women's Committee, the Committee of Arab Experts on Cooperation, the Communications Committee, the Conference of Liaison Officers for Trade and Commercial Activities, the Cultural Committee, the Economic Committee, the Health Committee, the Human Rights Committee, the Information Committee, the Legal Committee, the Meteorology Permanent Committee, the Organization of Youth Welfare, the Political Committee (usually composed of foreign ministers of member states), and the Social Committee.

The administrative and financial organ is the Secretariat. There are also 11 councils of Arab ministers, including ministers of interior, culture, education, health, higher education, housing, information, science, social affairs, youth and sports, and transport. The organization includes an Economic and Social Council, set up in 1950, designed to coordinate Arab economic policies. The Arab Unified Military Command coordinates military strategies to liberate Palestine. Through the Joint Defense Council, foreign and defense ministers implement joint defense agreements. These agreements are drawn up by representatives of the military general staffs of the member states on the Permanent Military Council. There is also a Standing Commission for Afro-Arab Cooperation and an Arab Fund for Technical Assistance to African and Arab Countries.

Throughout much of its existence, internal disputes have kept the league from becoming a more potent voice for the Middle East. However, league members have consistently agreed on two major issues: advocating the creation of a Palestinian state and opposing the existence of Israel. According to its protocol:

The Committee declares its support of the cause of the Arabs of Palestine and its willingness to work for the achievement of their legitimate aim and the safeguarding of their just rights. The Committee also declares that it is second to none in regretting the woes which have been inflicted upon the Jews of Europe by European dictatorial states. But the question of these Jews should not be confused with Zionism, for there can be no greater injustice and aggression than solving the problem of the Jews of Europe by another injustice, i.e., by inflicting injustice on the Arabs of Palestine of various religions and denominations.

Although the League has been involved in the resolution of many crises between member states, unity has remained out of reach. After it signed the Camp David Accords, which brought peace between Egypt and Israel, Egypt was expelled from the league from 1979 to 1989, and during that time league headquarters moved to Tunisia. The Iraqi invasion of Kuwait in 1991 also caused deep divisions in the organization. A majority of states endorsed sending troops to protect Saudi Arabia from a potential Iraqi attack, while the minority was divided between supporters of Iraqi leader Saddam Hussein and those who, while critical of Iraq, were opposed to the presence of U.S. troops in the region.

Arab Spring

Many observers believe that events of the so-called Arab Spring that began in late 2010 and toppled several Arab governments, has transformed the Arab League, galvanizing its membership into unprecedented decisive and unified action. In March 2011, after suspending Libya's membership, the league voted to support NATO intervention that aided the rebels who ultimately toppled Libyan dictator Muammar Gaddafi. That same year, the league's Arab Human Rights Committee, which had formed in 2009, issued its first statement, in which it condemned Libya for violating human rights. Also in 2011, the league condemned Syrian leader Bashar al-Assad for his repression of uprisings in his country and called for an end to the violence. Later that year, the league suspended Syria for failing to stick to a deal that was supposed to halt military action and start talks with the opposition. In 2012, the League hosted Syrian opposition groups at a conference in Cairo. The league surprised many when it later called on the Syrian president to leave office and even offered its help in securing a safe exit for him and his family. al-Assad declined.

Others, however, maintain that League members took decisive action in these situations only because they perceived that the popular uprisings of the Arab Spring potentially threatened their own power, and felt that standing with those leading the uprisings would benefit them. In early 2014, member nations Bahrain, Saudi Arabia, and the United Arab Emirates withdrew their ambassadors from Qatar, charging that country was interfering in their domestic affairs. Regardless, there is little doubt that upheaval in the Arab world is shaking up the Arab League. Egypt, a founding member that, for much of the League's existence, had provided both official and unofficial leadership, has lost much of its influence as that nation struggles to create a strong government. In its place, leaders of rising nations like Qatar have emerged to begin guiding the Arab League in what many believe will be new directions that will take it into the future.

Excerpt from the Charter of the Arab League

The Charter of the League of Arab States was written in 1945 and signed by six countries: Egypt, Iraq, Lebanon, Saudi Arabia, Syria, and Transjordan (now Jordan). Today, the League includes 22 members, located in Southwest Asia and in northern and eastern Africa. An underlying principle of the League is to "achieve co-operation between [the member states] and to safeguard their independence and sovereignty." This principle implies that the League has the authority to settle disputes among its members, and that members do not have the right to interfere in one another's affairs. This includes respect for each country's system of government, which vary widely among the League's member states.

The Charter specifies that the League will promote "close co-operations" among its members in the areas of economic activities and development, social and cultural affairs, and health. However, the Charter does not identify specific human rights among its objectives, nor does it deal with legal systems or political rights in member countries. That it does not do so reflects the wide differences in the member states' own constitutions and legal institutions. For example, some member states, such as Saudi Arabia, are governed under Sharia law, which does not imply gender equality in the sense that this is recognized in Western democracies. Specifics about human rights are left to the constitutions of the League's individual members.

Article I

The League of Arab States is composed of the independent Arab states which have signed this Charter.

Any independent Arab state has the right to become a member of the League. If it desires to do so, it shall submit a request . . .

Article II

The League has as its purpose the strengthening of the relations between the member-states, the coordination of their policies in order to achieve co-operation between them and to safeguard their independence and sovereignty; and a general concern with the affairs and interests of the Arab countries. It has also as its purpose the close co-operation of the member-states . . . in the following:

A. Economic and financial affairs, including commercial relations, customs, currency and questions of agriculture and industry.
B. Communications; this includes railroads, roads, aviation, navigation, telegraphs and posts.
C. Cultural affairs;
D. Nationality, passports, visas, execution of judgments and extradition of criminals;
E. Social affairs;
F. Health affairs;

Article III

The League shall possess a Council composed of the representatives of the member-states of the League; each state shall have a single vote . . .

It shall be the task of the Council to achieve the realisation of the objectives of the League and to supervise the execution of agreements which. the member-states have concluded . . .

It likewise shall be the Council task to decide upon the means by which the League is to co-operate with the international bodies to be created in the future . . .

Article IV

For each of the questions listed in Article II there shall be set up a special committee . . . These committees shall be charged with the task of laying down the principles and extent of co-operation.

Article V

Any resort to force . . . between . . . member-states . . . is prohibited. If there should arise among them a difference which does not concern a state's independence, sovereignty, or territorial integrity, and if the parties to the dispute have recourse to the Council for the settlement of this difference, the decision of the Council shall then be enforceable and obligatory.

In such case, the states between whom the difference has arisen shall not participate in the deliberations and decisions of the Council.

Decisions of arbitration and mediation shall be taken by majority vote.

Article VI

In case of aggression or threat of aggression by one state against a member-state, the state which has been attacked or threatened with aggression may demand the immediate convocation of the Council.

The Council shall by unanimous decision determine the measures necessary to repulse the aggression. If the aggressor is a member-state, his vote shall not be counted in determining unanimity.

Article VII

Unanimous decisions of the Council shall be binding . . . majority decisions shall be binding only upon those states which have accepted them.

Article VIII

Each member-state shall respect the systems of government established in the other member-states. . .

Article IX

Treaties and agreements already concluded or to be concluded in the future between a member-state and another state shall not be binding or restrictive upon other members.

Article X

The permanent seat of the League of Arab States is established in Cairo. The Council may, however, assemble at any other place it may designate.

Article XI

The Council of the League shall convene in ordinary session twice a year . . . It shall convene in extraordinary session upon the request of two member-states. . .

Article XII

The League shall have a permanent Secretariat-General which shall consist of a Secretary-General, Assistant Secretaries and an appropriate number of officials.

The Council of the League shall appoint the Secretary-General by a majority of two thirds of the states of the League. The Secretary-General, with the approval of the Council, shall appoint the Assistant Secretaries and the principal officials of the League.

The Secretary-General shall have the rank of Ambassador . . .

Article XIII

The Secretary-General shall prepare the draft of the budget of the League . . .

Article XIV

The members of the Council of the League as well as the members of the committees . . . shall enjoy diplomatic privileges . . .

Article XV

The representatives of the member-states of the League shall alternately assume the presidency. . .

Article XVI

. . . a majority vote of the Council shall be sufficient to make enforceable decisions on the following:

A. . . . personnel.
B. Adoption of the budget . . .
C. Establishment of the administrative regulations for the Council, the committees and the Secretariat General.
D. Decisions to adjourn . . .

Article XVII

Each member-state of the League shall deposit with the Secretariat-General one copy of treaty or agreement concluded or to be concluded in the future between itself and another member-state of the League or a third state.

Article XVIII

If a member state contemplates withdrawal from the League, it shall inform the Council of its intention one year before such withdrawal is to go into effect.

The Council of the League may consider any state which fails to fulfill its obligations under the Charter as separated from the League. . .

Article XIX

This Charter may be amended with the consent of two thirds of the states belonging to the League. . .

Article XX

This Charter and its annexes shall be ratified according to the basic laws in force among the High Contracting parties.

This Charter has been drawn up in Cairo in the Arabic language on this 8th day of Rabi' II, thirteen hundred and sixty four H. (March 22, 1945), in one copy which shall be deposited in the safe keeping of the Secretariat-General.

An identical copy shall be delivered to each state of the League.

(1) Annex Regarding Palestine

Since the termination of the last great war the rule of the Ottoman Empire over the Arab countries, among them Palestine . . . has come to an end. She has come to be autonomous. . .

However, even though she was as yet unable to control her own affairs, the Covenant of the League (of Nations) in 1919 made provision for a regime based upon recognition of her independence.

Her international existence and independence in the legal sense cannot, therefore, be questioned. . .

Although the outward manifestations of this independence have remained obscured for reasons beyond her control, this should not be allowed to interfere with her participation in the work of the Council of the League.

The states signatory to the Pact of the Arab League are therefore . . . considering the special circumstances of Palestine and until that country can effectively exercise its independence, the Council of the League should take charge of the selection of an Arab representative from Palestine to take part in its work.

(2) Annex Regarding Cooperation with Countries Which Are Not Members of the Council of the League

Whereas the member states of the League will have to deal . . . with matters which will benefit and affect the Arab world at large;

And whereas the Council has to take into account the aspirations of the Arab countries which are not members of the Council and has to work toward their realization;

Now, therefore, it particularly behooves the states . . . to enjoin the Council of the League, when considering the admission of those countries to participation . . . that it should spare no effort to learn their needs and understand their aspirations and hopes; and that it should work thenceforth for their best interests . . .

Source: "Charter of Arab League." The Arab League Online. http://www.arableague-online.org/charter-arab-league/

THE ASSOCIATION OF SOUTHEAST ASIAN NATIONS (ASEAN)

The Association of Southeast Asian Nations (ASEAN) is an organization of countries in Southeast Asia. Its mission is to promote economic development, unrestricted trade, international understanding, and peaceful relationships among its member countries. ASEAN's members are Brunei, Cambodia, Indonesia, Laos, Malaysia, Myanmar, the Philippines, Singapore, Thailand, and Vietnam. East Timor (Timor-Leste) and Papua New Guinea hold observer status. ASEAN's headquarters are in Jakarta, Indonesia.

Bangkok Declaration

With the exception of Thailand, all ASEAN members are former European colonies that were granted independence between the 1940s and the 1970s. Regional international cooperation among the member countries began in 1961, when the Philippines, Thailand, and Malaysia (which then included Singapore) established

Leaders of the ten ASEAN member countries gather at ASEAN's 25th summit meeting in Nay Pyi Taw, Myanmar, in 2014. The Association of Southeast Asian Nations (ASEAN) was founded in 1967, and its membership currently includes ten mainland and island countries in Southeast Asia. Headquartered in Jakarta, Indonesia, ASEAN's mission is to promote peace, political stability, and economic development. (imago stock&people/imago/Xinhua/Newscom)

the Association of Southeast Asia. In 1967, the foreign ministers of those countries, along with Indonesia and newly independent Singapore, met in Bangkok and established ASEAN formally by drafting and signing the Bangkok Declaration, officially known as the ASEAN Declaration. At that time, one of ASEAN's goals was to resist the spread of communism at a time when Communists controlled northern Vietnam, were expanding their influence into what was then South Vietnam, and were actively opposing the legitimate governments of the member countries. The Bangkok Declaration also called for international cooperation to promote economic development and to resist domination by the major powers then engaged in the Cold War. Specifically, the principles of the Bangkok Declaration included:

1. Mutual respect for the independence, sovereignty, equality, territorial integrity, and national identity of all nations;
2. The right of every state to a national existence free from external interference, subversion or coercion;
3. Non-interference in the internal affairs of one another;
4. Settlement of differences or disputes peacefully;
5. Renunciation of the threat or use of force; and
6. Effective cooperation among themselves.

ASEAN began to expand in 1984, when Brunei became independent and joined the organization. Vietnam was accepted as a member in 1995, despite the fact that it continued to be ruled by a Communist government. Laos and Myanmar joined ASEAN in 1997, and Cambodia followed in 1999.

Beginning in the 1990s, ASEAN's activities also expanded. In 1992, ASEAN's members established the ASEAN Free Trade Area (AFTA). AFTA called for the elimination of trade barriers among member states, as well as the promotion of economic development and the encouragement of foreign direct investment. Vietnam, Laos, Myanmar, and Cambodia, which had not yet joined ASEAN, were required to sign AFTA as a condition of membership.

At the same time, ASEAN's member countries began to discuss environmental issues and to draft and sign individual agreements such as the ASEAN Agreement on Transboundary Haze Pollution, which was signed in 2002. The agreement's intent was to initiate member cooperation in addressing problems associated with air pollution, which intensifies as ASEAN's members industrialize and increase manufacturing. To promote economic development, ASEAN initiated the East Asia Summit, which includes ASEAN's 10 members, along with Japan, South Korea, China, India, Australia, New Zealand, Russia, and the United States. The East Asia Summit meets annually, and the heads of states of the member countries or their representatives discuss common problems involving the region's economy and environment. ASEAN also sponsors a variety of educational and cultural activities, including the Southeast Asian Games and educational exchange programs.

ASEAN Charter

In early 2007, a task force of representatives from each ASEAN member state was charged with drafting a formal constitution for the association. The task force worked throughout 2007, completing the ASEAN Charter, which was signed by representatives of each member country, on November 20. The charter was to go into effect upon ratification by each of the 10 member states. Ratification occurred during 2008, and the charter went into effect December 15, 2008. The charter provides ASEAN with a formal legal status and institutional framework, building upon the principles already established through the Bangkok Declaration.

The ASEAN Charter reinforced many of ASEAN's founding principles. These include: respect for the territorial integrity and sovereignty of member states, commitment to peacefully resolving disputes between member countries, collective responsibility to promote peace and stability in the region, and respect for cultural, linguistic, and religious diversity.

ASEAN Community

The implementation of the ASEAN Charter led to the creation of the ASEAN Community, whose goal is to promote regional integration and cooperation along the lines already established by the European Union. The ASEAN Community includes the Political-Security Committee, the Economic Community, and the Socio-Cultural Community. Each of these communities is guided by a blueprint that states that community's goals and targets.

The purpose of the Political-Security Community is to "ensure that countries in the region live at peace with one another and with the world in a just, democratic and harmonious environment." In accordance with this purpose, the Political-Security Community manages the ASEAN Intergovernmental Commission on Human Rights. It also sponsors regular meetings of member states' foreign ministers and defense ministers, to discuss collective security and dispute resolution.

The Economic Community blueprint calls for achieving regional economic integration. To achieve this goal, the ASEAN Economic Community "envisages the following key characteristics: (a) a single market and production base, (b) a highly competitive economic region, (c) a region of equitable economic development, and (d) a region fully integrated into the global economy." Achieving this goal would create a unified economic bloc in Southeast Asia like that of the European Union. The Economic Community sponsors annual meetings of the member states' economic and finance ministers, and it also oversees the ASEAN Free Trade Agreement.

The Socio-Cultural Community "aims to contribute to realising an ASEAN Community that is people-oriented and socially responsible with a view to achieving enduring solidarity and unity among the peoples and Member States of ASEAN. It seeks to forge a common identity and build a caring and sharing society which is inclusive and where the well-being, livelihood, and welfare of the peoples are enhanced." Its activities include promoting culture and the arts, sports, and education. Common actions involving the management of natural resources and the region's physical environment also are overseen by the Socio-Cultural Community.

Southeast Asia is a highly diverse region. ASEAN member countries differ widely in culture and religion, and residents of those countries speak hundreds of languages. Buddhism is the predominant religion of Myanmar, Thailand, Laos, Cambodia, and Vietnam. However, the predominant religion of Brunei, Indonesia, and Malaysia is Islam. In the Philippines, the majority are Christians. Forms of government also vary. Brunei is an absolute monarchy, and Vietnam is a communist state, whereas Singapore, Malaysia, Indonesia, and the Philippines are democracies. Cambodia and Thailand are constitutional monarchies, although Thailand is also a democracy. In combination, however, ASEAN's members form a significant and growing presence within the global economy. The overall land area of ASEAN's member countries is nearly 2.8 million square miles, or nearly 80 percent of the land area of the United States. Their combined population is more than 600 million, or almost twice as many people as in the United States and more than 8.5 percent of the world's population. The combined gross national product of the region was estimated at $2.3 trillion, or more than $3,500 per capita, in 2012.

Throughout ASEAN's history, representatives of member states, as well as international observers, have recognized the organization's success in preventing and resolving conflicts and in promoting regional economic development. Its leaders' commitment to collective agreement is one commonly cited reason for the organization's success. However, changes within ASEAN's member countries themselves, as well as in its relationships with other states, are likely to affect ASEAN's future actions. In particular, the continued rapid economic growth of China and India, both of which adjoin ASEAN members, is likely to have a significant impact on Southeast Asia and therefore on ASEAN as an institution in the years ahead.

Excerpt from the Charter of the Association of Southeast Asian Nations (ASEAN)

The Association of Southeast Asian Nations (ASEAN) was established in 1967 by agreement among Indonesia, Malaysia, the Philippines, Singapore, and Thailand. Since then, five additional countries have joined ASEAN. The Charter of the

Association was drafted in 2007 and went into effect following ratification by ASE-AN's ten member countries in 2008.

As articulated in the Charter, the purposes of ASEAN include cooperation among member states, economic development, the alleviation of poverty, and the peaceful resolution of disputes between members. These purposes include "adherence to the rule of law, good governance, [and] the principles of democracy." In practice, not all of ASEAN's members are actually democracies; for example, Vietnam and Laos are governed by Communist one-party regimes.

As is the case with the charters governing other regional organizations, ASEAN's Charter makes few specific references to human rights. The Charter identifies promotion of "fundamental freedoms," human rights, and social justice among its purposes. It states also that ASEAN is to uphold the principles of the Charter of the United Nations. However, as elsewhere, specifics concerning human rights are detailed in the constitutions of ASEAN's individual member states, as opposed to being articulated in the Charter itself.

PREAMBLE

WE, THE PEOPLES of the Member States of the Association of Southeast Asian Nations (ASEAN)...

MINDFUL of the existence of mutual interests and interdependence among the peoples and Member States of ASEAN which are bound by geography, common objectives and shared destiny;

INSPIRED by and united under One Vision, One Identity and One Caring and Sharing Community;

UNITED by a common desire . . . to live in a region of lasting peace, security and stability, sustained economic growth, shared prosperity and social progress . . . ;

RESPECTING the fundamental importance of amity and cooperation, and the principles of sovereignty, equality . . . and unity in diversity;

ADHERING to the principles of democracy, the rule of law and good governance . . . ;

RESOLVED to ensure sustainable development . . .

CONVINCED of the need to strengthen existing bonds of regional solidarity to . . . effectively respond to current and future challenges and opportunities;

COMMITTED to intensifying community building . . .

HEREBY DECIDE to establish, through this Charter, the legal and institutional framework for ASEAN,

Article 1

The Purposes of ASEAN are:

1. To maintain and enhance peace, security and stability . . . ;
2. To enhance regional resilience by promoting greater political, security, economic and socio-cultural cooperation;
3. To preserve Southeast Asia as a Nuclear Weapon-Free Zone . . . ;
5. To create a single market and production base which is stable, prosperous, highly competitive and economically integrated . . .
6. To alleviate poverty and narrow the development gap within ASEAN . . . ;
7. To strengthen democracy . . . and to promote and protect human rights and fundamental freedoms . . . ;
8. To respond effectively . . . to all forms of threats . . . ;
9. To promote sustainable development . . . ;
10. To develop human resources through closer cooperation in education and life-long learning, and in science and technology . . . ;
11. . . . providing the [people of ASEAN] with equitable access to opportunities for human development, social welfare and justice;
12. . . . building a safe, secure and drug-free environment . . . ;
13. To promote a people-oriented ASEAN . . . ;
14. To . . . foster greater awareness of the diverse culture and heritage of the region; and
15. To maintain the centrality and proactive role of ASEAN as the primary driving force in . . . a regional architecture that is open, transparent and inclusive.

Article 2

ASEAN and its Member States shall [pursue]:

(a) respect the independence, sovereignty, equality, territorial integrity and national identity of all ASEAN Member States;
(b) shared commitment and collective responsibility in enhancing regional peace, security and prosperity;
(c) renunciation of aggression . . . ;
(d) reliance on peaceful settlement of disputes;
(e) non-interference in the internal affairs of ASEAN Member States;
(f) respect for the right of every Member State to [be] free from external interference;
(g) enhanced consultations . . . ;
(h) adherence to the rule of law, good governance, the principles of democracy . . . ;
(i) respect for fundamental freedoms, . . . human rights, and . . . social justice;
(j) upholding the United Nations Charter . . . ;
(k) abstention from participation in any policy or activity . . . which threatens the sovereignty, territorial integrity or political and economic stability of ASEAN Member States;

(l) respect for the different cultures . . . of ASEAN, while emphasising their common values . . . ;

(m) adherence to multilateral trade rules . . .

Article 4

The Member States of ASEAN are Brunei Darussalam, the Kingdom of Cambodia, the Republic of Indonesia, the Lao People's Democratic Republic, Malaysia, the Union of Myanmar, the Republic of the Philippines, the Republic of Singapore, the Kingdom of Thailand and the Socialist Republic of Viet Nam.

Article 5

Member States shall have equal rights and obligations. . .

Article 6

Admission shall be based on . . . :

(a) location in . . . Southeast Asia;
(b) recognition by all ASEAN Member States;
(c) agreement to . . . abide by the Charter;
(d) ability and willingness to carry out the obligations of Membership.

Admission shall be decided by consensus by the ASEAN Summit . . .
The ASEAN Summit shall comprise the Heads of State or Government of the Member States.
The ASEAN Summit shall:

(a) be the supreme policy-making body of ASEAN;
(b) . . . take decisions on key issues pertaining to the realization of the objectives of ASEAN . . . ;
(d) address emergency situations affecting ASEAN . . . ;
(g) appoint the Secretary-General of ASEAN, with the rank and status of Minister . . .

Article 8

1. The ASEAN Coordinating Council shall comprise the ASEAN Foreign Ministers and meet at least twice a year.
2. The ASEAN Coordinating Council shall:
   (a) prepare the meetings of the ASEAN Summit;
   (b) coordinate the implementation of agreements and decisions of the ASEAN Summit;

Article 9

The ASEAN Community Councils shall comprise the ASEAN Political-Security Community Council, ASEAN Economic Community Council, and ASEAN Socio-Cultural Community Council.

Article 11

The Secretary-General of ASEAN shall be appointed by the ASEAN Summit for . . . five years, selected . . . based on alphabetical rotation . . .

2. The Secretary-General shall: . . .
   (b) facilitate and monitor progress in the implementation of ASEAN agreements . . . submit an annual report on the work of ASEAN . . . ;
   (d) present the views of ASEAN and participate in meetings with external parties . . .
3. . . . be the Chief Administrative Officer of ASEAN.
4. . . . be assisted by four Deputy Secretaries-General . . .

Article 12

1. Each ASEAN Member State shall appoint a Permanent Representative to ASEAN with the rank of Ambassador . . .
5. The four Deputy Secretaries-General shall be of different nationalities from the Secretary-General . . .

Each ASEAN Member State shall establish an ASEAN National Secretariat which shall: . . .

(c) coordinate the implementation of ASEAN decisions at the national level;
(e) promote ASEAN identity and awareness at the national level;

Article 14

. . . ASEAN shall establish an ASEAN human rights body.

Article 15

The ASEAN Foundation shall support the Secretary-General of ASEAN and collaborate . . . to support ASEAN community building by promoting greater awareness of the ASEAN identity . . .

Article 20

1. ... decision-making in ASEAN shall be based on consultation and consensus.
2. Where consensus cannot be achieved, the ASEAN Summit may decide how a specific decision can be made.

CHAPTER VIII

Member States shall endeavour to resolve peacefully all disputes . . .

Article 25

. . . appropriate dispute settlement mechanisms, including arbitration, shall be established . . .

Article 27

The Secretary-General of ASEAN . . . shall monitor the compliance with the findings, recommendations or decisions resulting from an ASEAN dispute settlement . . .

Article 30

1. The ASEAN Secretariat shall be provided with the necessary financial resources . . .
2. The operational budget of the ASEAN Secretariat shall be met by ASEAN Member States through equal annual contributions . . .
3. The Secretary-General shall prepare the annual operational budget . . . for approval by the ASEAN Coordinating Council . . .

Article 31

The Chairmanship of ASEAN shall rotate annually . . .

Article 32

The Member State holding the Chairmanship of ASEAN shall:

(a) actively promote and enhance the interests and wellbeing of ASEAN . . .
(c) ensure an effective and timely response to urgent issues or crisis . . .

Article 34

The working language of ASEAN shall be English.

Article 36

The ASEAN motto shall be: *"One Vision, One Identity, One Community."*

CHAPTER XII

1. ASEAN shall develop friendly relations . . . with countries . . . and international organizations . . .
7. ASEAN may conclude agreements with countries or . . . international organizations and institutions.

Article 44

External parties may be invited to ASEAN meetings or cooperative activities without being conferred any formal status, in accordance with the rules of procedure.

Article 48

1. Any Member State may propose amendments . . .
3. Amendments to the Charter agreed to by consensus by the ASEAN Summit shall be ratified by all Member States . . .

Done in Singapore on the Twentieth Day of November in the Year Two Thousand and Seven

Source: "Charter of the Association of Southeast Asian Nations." Association of Southeast Asian Nations. http://www.asean.org/asean/asean-charter/asean-charter

THE EUROPEAN UNION

The European Union (EU) is an organization of 28 European nations that have relinquished some national sovereignty in return for collective representation on certain continental and global issues. The EU is the world's largest single economic market, within which people and goods can move freely across national borders.

What is now the EU began in 1951 with the goal of eliminating the rivalries and warfare that had plagued Europe for centuries. The original coalition of countries, known as the European Coal and Steel Community (ECSC), brought together former enemies France and Germany as well as Belgium, the Netherlands, Italy, and Luxembourg. In the six decades since, EU membership has grown nearly fivefold, with the addition of Austria, Bulgaria, Cyprus, the Czech Republic, Denmark,

Estonia, Finland, Greece, Hungary, Ireland, Latvia, Lithuania, Malta, Poland, Portugal, Romania, Slovakia, Slovenia, Spain, Sweden, the United Kingdom, and most recently Croatia. Serbia, Montenegro, and the former Yugoslav Republic of Macedonia, which, like Croatia, formed after the Balkan wars of the 1990s, are in the process of qualifying to join the EU. Iceland and Turkey have also begun the process of gaining admission. Twenty-three official languages are used to conduct EU business: Bulgarian, Czech, Danish, Dutch, English, Estonian, Finnish, French, German, Greek, Hungarian, Italian, Irish, Latvian, Lithuanian, Maltese, Polish, Portuguese, Romanian, Slovak, Slovenian, Spanish, and Swedish.

There are three main criteria for becoming an EU member. Politically, a prospective member must have a stable government to guarantee democracy, the rule of law, human rights, and the protection of minority populations. Economically, candidate countries must have market economies equipped to deal with competitive outside pressure and EU market forces. In addition, a candidate for membership must adhere to the aims of the EU and adopt the entire body of EU law into its national law. The European Commission provides new EU members and candidate countries with financial aid to help their economies catch up to EU standards. The funds are designated for structural projects, farming, rural development, domestic policies, and administrative costs.

The role of the European Coal and Steel Community was to eliminate trade barriers associated with coal and production. By 1957, the group expanded its scope and transformed itself into the European Economic Communities (EEC). The EEC created a common economic market with no customs duties between member nations, and adopted common trade and agriculture policies for all members. Denmark, Ireland, and the United Kingdom joined the EEC in 1973, and the enlarged group adopted further common policies on social, regional, and environmental issues. With the admission of Greece in 1981 and Spain and Portugal in 1986, the EEC adopted structural programs aimed at reducing economic gaps between individual members. The Single European Act of 1987 set the goal of creating a single common economic market by 1993.

That goal was met with the ratification of the Maastricht Treaty on European Union, which created the EU by increasing cooperation on economic, foreign, immigration, and crime and drug policies. The treaty set further development goals calling for the implementation of a monetary union by 1999, as well as cross-border European citizenship for residents of all EU countries, common foreign and security policies, and greater internal security cooperation. By 2002, the EU's common currency, the euro, had replaced the national currencies of 12 EU members.

Starting in 2002, EU leaders began work on a single treaty that would incorporate all the various treaties that governed EU operations into one document. However, the document needed to be ratified by all member nations to take effect. After years of work and the rejection of proposed treaties by voters in several countries, members in 2007 drafted a document that they expected would be supported by all EU members. The Treaty of Lisbon, agreed upon in October 2007 and signed by the heads of government of all EU states in December 2007, would reduce the number of commissioners from 27 to 18, create a nonrotating presidency of the European Council, allow for a more cohesive foreign and security policy, and establish various EU-wide human rights laws. Every member state except Ireland vowed to ratify the treaty solely by parliamentary vote, but Irish voters narrowly rejected the treaty in June 2008. With EU leaders very much against scrapping yet another reform treaty, a second Irish referendum was held in October 2009. The second time, a more effective informational strategy won voters over, and Ireland ratified the treaty. The other EU countries ratified the treaty as well between December 2007 and November 2009, and it went into effect December 1, 2009.

The EU's main organizational units are the Council of the European Union, the European Council, the European Parliament, the European Commission, the Court of Justice of the European Union, the European Central Bank, and the Court of Auditors.

European Commission

The European Commission (EC) is the EU's executive branch, charged with upholding EU interests. Although each EU nation is represented on the EC, the commissioners do not represent the governments of their countries. The treaties that form the basis of the EU structure forbid EC members from taking instructions from member states. Commissioners serve five-year renewable terms. The EC applies the provisions of the EU and has the power to refer cases of noncompliance to the Court of Justice. The EC is the only EU institution entitled to propose new legislation and is responsible for managing the EU's policies, including development aid, research, and agriculture. The EC also proposes and manages the EU budget. Although it is politically independent, the EC answers to the European Parliament, and members must resign if the parliament votes to censure. Among the issues the commission and its 33,000 employees work on are rights and security of member nations, climate change, strengthening Europe's role in the world, and, since roughly 2008, developing strategies to steer numerous member nations out of their ongoing economic crises.

Council of the European Union

Previously known as the Council of Ministers, the Council of the European Union (often referred to simply as "the Council") is the EU's main decision-making body. Each EU member holds the presidency of the Council for six months;

Jean-Claude Juncker, President of the European Union, meeting with France's President Fran-cois Hollande. (Gilles ROLLE/REA/SIPA/Newscom)

however, every three consecutive presidencies share a coordinated eighteen-month program. Based in Brussels, Belgium, the Council meets in public, and each EU member sends a cabinet member qualified to discuss the theme of the meeting (i.e., agriculture, foreign policy, trade, etc.).

The Council approves international agreements negotiated by the European Commission and is empowered to amend the treaties that are the EU's legal foundation. The Council also implements EU policies and allows new members to join. Many decisions previously required unanimous approval by all Council members, but since 2009 supermajorities based on the total number of member states and total population representation (that is, the larger a country's population, the more votes it gets) are required for most. Taxation, defense, foreign policy, and adoption of treaties still require unanimous votes. The Council shares legislative power with the European Parliament, and the two bodies are also responsible for approving the EU budget.

European Council

The European Council is the EU's highest policy-making body, consisting of the presidents or prime ministers of each member nation, who meet four times per year. A non-voting president serves a term of two-and-a-half years. At their meetings, the heads of state discuss major European and world issues and initiate EU policies.

European Parliament

The European Parliament is an elected legislature representing EU citizens. The parliament holds its full sessions in Strasbourg, France, and smaller meetings in Brussels, while the secretariat-general is based in Luxembourg. There are 20 parliamentary committees and a number of political groups representing cross-national coalitions of political parties. The European Parliament issues opinions on draft directives and proposed regulations from the European Commission, approves international agreements negotiated by the European Commission, and also approves any proposed enlargement of the EU and changes to election rules. The parliament and the Council of the European Union must agree on most legislation before it is adopted. The European Parliament shares budget approval power with the Council of the European Union, though the parliament has the ultimate authority to pass a budget that the Council does not agree to.

Members of the European Parliament (MEPs) are directly elected for five-year terms. Since adoption of the Treaty of Lisbon in 2009, the European Parliament has been limited to 750 MEPs plus the parliamentary president (for a total of 751 members). An MEP's representation is based on population, and the most MEPs that can represent one member state is 96; the fewest is six. The president of the Parliament is elected by the parliament and presides over its sessions, enforces procedure, signs parliamentary acts, and officially represents the parliament.

Court of Justice

Based in Luxembourg, the Court of Justice of the European Union upholds the rule of EU law and ensures that treaties are correctly interpreted and applied in all member states. Each EU member names one judge, and there are 11 advocates-general to assist the justices. The judges and advocates-general serve renewable six-year terms. The judges elect one of their own to serve as president for a renewable three-year term.

Court of Auditors

The Court of Auditors comprises one member from each EU nation. It monitors EU revenue and spending. It also determines whether the EC is soundly managing the EU budget, and can audit any organization using EU funds.

European Central Bank

Based in Frankfurt, Germany, the European Central Bank is responsible for managing the euro (the common currency of thirteen EU nations) and for setting EU monetary policy. The bank is politically and financially independent of other

EU institutions; its funds come from the central banks of EU member states, not from the EU budget.

Committees

The European Economic and Social Committee is made up of nongovernmental interest groups and must be consulted on decisions involving employment, social welfare, vocational training, and other labor issues. It is also authorized to provide opinions on other EU matters. The Committee of the Regions is composed of representatives from regional and local governments. The Committee of the Regions must be consulted on matters of regional importance.

Charter of Fundamental Rights

The Charter of Fundamental Rights of the European Union, approved in 2000, lists the various rights that must be granted to citizens of EU member states. The Charter was modeled after the United Nations' Universal Declaration of Human Rights (1948) and the European Convention on Human Rights (1950). Notably, however, the United Kingdom, Poland, and the Czech Republic officially opted not to be bound by the Charter.

Excerpt from the Maastricht Treaty (Treaty on the European Union)

What is now the European Union (EU) was founded as the European Coal and Steel Community by Belgium, France, Italy, Luxembourg, the Netherlands, and West Germany in 1951. The purpose of the Community was to eliminate trade barriers associated with the production of steel and manufactured products made from steel, including machinery and automobiles. The Community became the European Economic Community in 1957 and soon became known informally as the European Community. Today, 28 European countries are members of the European Union.

The European Union, as the successor to the European Economic Community, was officially launched with the implementation of the Treaty on European Union in 1993. The Treaty is known unofficially as the Maastricht Treaty, after the Dutch city in which it was negotiated and drafted. An important purpose of the Treaty was the creation of the euro as the EU's common currency, although several member states do not use the euro as their currencies.

The Treaty differs from the charters of several other regional international organizations in two important respects. First, it calls specifically for EU citizenship. This concept allows citizens of all EU members to move freely among EU countries. Second, the Treaty makes specific reference to human rights by invoking the European Convention for the Protection of Human Rights and Fundamental Freedoms, which had been written in 1950. The European Convention identifies the rights of free speech, freedom of conscience, and freedom of association, along with the right to a fair trial. It also provides that Europeans may not be denied education. Other rights, including social and economic rights, are spelled out in more detail in the constitutions of the EU's member states.

COMMON PROVISIONS

Article A

By this Treaty, the High Contracting Parties establish among themselves a European Union, hereinafter called 'the Union.'

The Union shall be founded on the European Communities, supplemented by the policies and forms of cooperation established by this Treaty. Its task shall be to organize, in a manner demonstrating consistency and solidarity, relations between the Member states and between their peoples.

Article B

The Union shall set itself the following objectives:

to promote economic and social progress which is balanced and sustainable, in particular through the creation of an area without internal frontiers, through the strengthening of economic and social cohesion and through the establishment of economic and monetary union, ultimately including a single currency in accordance with the provisions of this Treaty;

to assert its identity on the international scene, in particular through the implementation of a common foreign and security policy including the eventual framing of a common defense policy, which might in time lead to a common defense;

to strengthen the protection of the rights and interests of the nationals of its Member States through the introduction of a citizenship of the Union;

to develop close cooperation on justice and home affairs;

to maintain in full the *acquis communautaire* and build on it with a view to considering, through the procedure referred to in Article N (2), to what extent the policies and forms of cooperation introduced by this Treaty may need to be revised with the aim of ensuring the effectiveness of the mechanisms and the institutions of the Community.

Article C

The Union shall be served by a single institutional framework which shall ensure the consistency and the continuity of the activities carried out in order to attain its objectives while respecting and building upon the *acquis communautaire*.

The Union shall in particular ensure the consistency of its external activities as a whole in the context of its external relations, security, economic and development policies. The Council and the Commission shall be responsible for ensuring such consistency. They shall ensure the implementation of these policies, each in accordance with its respective powers.

Article D

The European Council shall provide the Union with the necessary impetus for its development and shall define the general political guidelines thereof.

The European Council shall bring together the Heads of State or Government of the Member States and the President of the Commission. They shall be assisted by the Ministers for Foreign Affairs of the Member States and by a Member of the Commission. The European Council shall meet at least twice a year under the chairmanship of the Head of State or Government of the Member State which holds the Presidency of the Council.

Article F

(1) The Union shall respect the national identities of its Member States, whose systems of government are founded on the principles of democracy.
(2) The Union shall respect fundamental rights, as guaranteed by the European Convention for the Protection of Human Rights and Fundamental Freedoms signed in Rome on 4 November 1950 and as they result from the constitutional traditions common to the Member States, as general principles of Community law.
(3) The Union shall provide itself with the means necessary to attain its objectives and carry through its policies."

TITLE V   PROVISIONS ON A COMMON FOREIGN AND SECURITY POLICY

Article J.1

1. The Union and its Member States shall define and implement a common foreign and security policy . . .
2. The objectives of the common foreign and security policy shall be:
   - to safeguard the common values, fundamental interests and independence of the Union;
   - to strengthen the security of the Union and its Member States in all ways;
   - to preserve peace and strengthen international security . . . ;

- to promote international co-operation;
- to develop and consolidate democracy and the rule of law, and respect for human rights and fundamental freedoms.
3. The Union shall pursue these objectives:
- by establishing systematic co-operation between Member States . . .
- by gradually implementing . . . joint action in the areas in which the Member States have important interests in common.

Article J.2

1. Member States shall inform and consult one another within the Council on any matter of foreign and security policy of general interest in order to ensure that their combined influence is exerted as effectively as possible by means of concerted and convergent action.
2. Whenever it deems it necessary, the Council shall define a common position. Member States shall ensure that their national policies conform to the common positions.
3. Member States shall co-ordinate their action in international organizations and at international conferences. They shall uphold the common positions in such forums.

Article J.3

1. The Council shall decide, on the basis of general guidelines from the European Council, that a matter should be the subject of joint action.

Whenever the Council decides on the principle of joint action, it shall lay down the specific scope, the Union's general and specific objectives . . . and conditions for its implementation.

Article J.4

1. The common foreign and security policy shall include all questions related to the security of the Union, including the eventual framing of a common defence policy . . .

Article J.5

1. The Presidency shall represent the Union in matters coming within the common foreign and security policy.

2. The Presidency shall be responsible for the implementation of common measures; in that capacity it shall in principle express the position of the Union in international organizations and international conferences.

Article J.8

1. The European Council shall define the principles of and general guidelines for the common foreign and security policy.
2. The Council shall take the decisions necessary for defining and implementing the common foreign and security policy on the basis of the general guidelines adopted by the European Council. It shall ensure the unity, consistency and effectiveness of action by the Union.

   The Council shall act unanimously, except for procedural questions

PROVISIONS ON CO-OPERATION IN THE FIELDS OF JUSTICE AND HOME AFFAIRS

Article K-1

For the purposes of achieving . . . the free movement of persons . . . Member States shall regard the following areas as matters of common interest:

(1) asylum policy;
(2) rules governing the crossing by persons of the external borders of the Member States . . . ;
(3) immigration policy and policy regarding nationals of third countries:

   (a) conditions of entry and movement by nationals of third countries on the territory of Member States;
   (b) conditions of residence by nationals of third countries on the territory of Member States, including family reunion and access to employment;
   (c) combating unauthorized immigration, residence and work by nationals of third countries on the territory of Member States;

(4) combating drug addiction . . . ;
(5) combating fraud on an international scale . . . ;
(6) judicial co-operation in civil matters;
(7) judicial co-operation in criminal matters;
(8) customs co-operation;
(9) police co-operation for the purposes of preventing and combating terrorism, unlawful drug trafficking and other serious forms of international crime . . .

ARTICLE O

Any European State may apply to become a Member of the Union. It shall address its application to the Council, which shall act unanimously after consulting the Commission and after receiving the assent of the European Parliament, which shall act by an absolute majority of its component members.

Done at Maastricht on the seventh day of February in the year one thousand nine hundred and ninety-two.

Source: "Charter of Fundamental Rights of the European Union." European Commission. http://eur-lex.europa.eu/LexUriServ/LexUriServ.do?uri=OJ:C:2010:083:0389:0403:en:PDF

THE NORTH ATLANTIC TREATY ORGANIZATION (NATO)

The North Atlantic Treaty Organization (NATO) is an alliance of 28 European and North American countries, including the United States, that have agreed to provide mutual defense, support, and cooperation. NATO's mission is to "safeguard the freedom and security of its members through political and military means," as well as to promote democratic values and peace. The alliance promotes stability and tries to foster economic partnership among its members.

One of NATO's core principles, as outlined in its founding treaty, is that "an attack against one or several members is considered as an attack against all." According to the North Atlantic Treaty, ratified by the 10 founding nations in 1949, if such an attack occurred, each ally would take "such action as it deems necessary, including the use of armed force" in response. In more than six decades of NATO's existence, that principle has triggered action only once, in response to the Sept. 11, 2001, terror attacks against the United States.

NATO was launched in the aftermath of World War II, when devastation across Europe threw many governments into turmoil and forced millions who were left homeless to fend for themselves in the rubble of bombed-out cities or seek shelter in refugee camps. As European nations struggled to rebuild after the war, many western European countries feared that the communist Soviet Union would take advantage of power vacuums and try to extend its influence beyond the eastern European states that it was absorbing quickly. To counteract that threat, western European countries, along with the United States and Canada, saw wisdom in uniting to protect their collective interests. In addition to safeguarding themselves against communist expansion, the founding NATO countries sought also to head off the kind of militant nationalism that had fueled the Nazi party's rise and ignited the war in Europe.

To promote unity among the allies, the new organization established procedures to assure that all members have an equal voice and that no action is taken without the consensus of the entire membership. The leader of that membership is the secretary general. The secretary general guides consultation and decision-making within the alliance and ensures that decisions are implemented. The secretary general is also NATO's chief spokesperson and heads the organization's international staff, which provides advice, guidance, and administrative support to the national delegations.

Each member country has a permanent delegation at NATO's political headquarters in Brussels, Belgium. Each delegation is headed by an "ambassador," who represents his or her government. Today, NATO has a staff of around 4,000 people who work at its headquarters, including some 2,000 who are members of national delegations, along with supporting staff members of national military representatives. Another 300 people work at the missions of NATO's partner countries. NATO is funded from the military budgets of member nations. NATO's North Atlantic Council meets weekly, and the alliance oversees committees that deal with policy and planning areas. These include the European Quality Alliance (a political consultation forum meeting in Brussels), the Defense Planning Committee, and the Nuclear Planning Committee. There are also committees on economics, armaments, science, infrastructure, logistics, and communications.

The North Atlantic Treaty Organization (NATO) is headquartered in this building in Brussels, Belgium. Flags of NATO's member countries are flown outside the building. (Delmi Alvarez/ ZUMAPRESS/Newscom)

The military structure of NATO is coordinated by the Military Committee, which consists of the chiefs of staff, or their representatives, of all member nations except Iceland, which has no military and is represented by a civilian official. The committee is led by a chairperson, who is elected for a term of two to three years. The chiefs of staff meet at least twice a year, with permanent military representatives meeting in Brussels between these sessions. The Military Committee makes recommendations on military matters to the North Atlantic Council and to the Defense Planning Committee. It also gives directions to the three NATO supreme commands. These are the Supreme Headquarters Allied Powers Europe (SHAPE), located in Belgium; the NATO Allied Command Transformation in the United States; and the NATO Allied Maritime Component Command in the United Kingdom.

Mission

During the Cold War era, which extended into the 1980s, NATO's primary focus was defense of the member allies. But with the demise of the Soviet Union and the diminished communist threat, NATO's role began to evolve in the late 1980s and early 1990s. As the former Yugoslavia splintered and ethnic tensions escalated into violence, NATO carried out a nine-day air campaign in September 1995. In

The North Atlantic Treaty Organization (NATO) was founded in 1949 by countries in Western Europe, the United States, and Canada to promote collective security against possible Communist expansion in Europe. Today, many former Soviet satellites and Soviet republics are members of NATO, whose headquarters are in Brussels, Belgium. (State Department/Sipa USA/Newscom)

December of that year, NATO deployed a United Nations–mandated, multinational force of 60,000 soldiers to help implement the Dayton Peace Agreement. Three years later, the Alliance again directed air strikes in the Balkans, this time with the goal of allowing multinational troops to enter Kosovo and to stop ethnic cleansing. NATO–led peacekeeping forces remain in Kosovo.

At the same time it was flexing its military muscle trying to halt ethnic violence in Eastern Europe, the alliance was building links with former Eastern European rivals through the establishment of the North Atlantic Cooperation Council. In March 1999, Hungary, Poland, and the Czech Republic became the first former Communist-bloc countries to join NATO, expanding the group's membership to 19. Five years later, in April 2004, seven former communist states—Estonia, Latvia, Lithuania, Bulgaria, Romania, Slovakia, and Slovenia—joined the alliance.

In recent decades, NATO missions have ranged from combat and peacekeeping to humanitarian relief. After Hurricane Katrina in 2005, nine NATO-member countries helped the United States by providing 189 tons of needed material. From October 2005 to February 2006, NATO airlifted some 3,500 tons of relief supplies to Pakistan, where an October 8, 2005, earthquake had left millions without food or shelter.

In 2010, the alliance adopted a Strategic Concept that outlined strategies for dealing comprehensively with crises. According to the concept, instability around the world demands complex remedies that rely not just on military might but which employ diplomacy and post-conflict stabilization as well. To achieve the concept's goals, NATO is developing partnerships with countries across the Mediterranean, the Persian Gulf region, and Pacific island nations. In addition, it is forming alliances with other international organizations.

As terrorist organizations have overshadowed hostile nations as the greatest threat to member nations' peace and stability, NATO has expanded its focus to include anti-terrorist strategies and operations. From 2003 to 2014, NATO led approximately 87,000 troops from 49 countries on a United Nations mission in Afghanistan designed to prevent terrorists from regaining a foothold there. In addition to anti-terrorism efforts, in 2012 NATO launched a program aimed at thwarting cyber attacks that could disrupt or threaten member countries' communication systems.

After decades of redefining itself in a post-Cold War world, NATO now has described a new mission for itself: extending peace through the strategic projection of security.

Excerpt from the North Atlantic Treaty

The North Atlantic Treaty Organization (NATO) was founded by twelve Western democracies in 1949. The twelve original members comprised ten Western

European states, along with the United States and Canada. Its original purpose was collective security against the threat of Soviet expansion following World War II. Representatives of these twelve states signed the North Atlantic Treaty, which governs NATO, at an international conference in Washington, DC. Today, NATO has 28 members.

According to the North Atlantic Treaty, member states are "determined to safeguard the freedom, common heritage and civilization of their peoples, founded on the principles of democracy, individual liberty and the rule of law." An important principle underlying this statement was that member states were concerned about possible expansion of Communist influence, including the elimination of democracy and the establishment of one-party dictatorship, into central and Western Europe. At that time, Greece and Turkey were seen as especially vulnerable to Communist influence, and both joined NATO in 1952.

Much of the Treaty is associated with issues of collective security, by which NATO members would work together in the event that one or more were to be attacked externally. However, the Treaty makes specific reference to the Charter of the United Nations as a guide to the peaceful settlement of potential disputes among its member countries. The Treaty makes no specific reference to human rights other than its expression of commitment to liberty, democracy, and the rule of law.

THE NORTH ATLANTIC TREATY

The Parties to this Treaty reaffirm their faith in the purposes and principles of the Charter of the United Nations and their desire to live in peace with all peoples and all governments.

They are determined to safeguard the freedom, common heritage and civilization of their peoples, founded on the principles of democracy, individual liberty and the rule of law.

They seek to promote stability and well-being in the North Atlantic area.

They are resolved to unite their efforts for collective defense and for the preservation of peace and security.

They therefore agree to this North Atlantic Treaty:

Article 1

The Parties undertake, as set forth in the Charter of the United Nations, to settle any international dispute in which they may be involved by peaceful means in such a manner that international peace and security and justice are not endangered, and to refrain in their international relations from the threat or use of force in any manner inconsistent with the purposes of the United Nations.

Article 2

The Parties will contribute toward the further development of peaceful and friendly international relations by strengthening their free institutions, by bringing about a better understanding of the principles upon which these institutions are founded, and by promoting conditions of stability and well-being. They will seek to eliminate conflict in their international economic policies and will encourage economic collaboration between any or all of them.

Article 3

In order more effectively to achieve the objectives of this Treaty, the Parties, separately and jointly, by means of continuous and effective self-help and mutual aid, will maintain and develop their individual and collective capacity to resist armed attack.

Article 4

The Parties will consult together whenever, in the opinion of any of them, the territorial integrity, political independence or security of any of the Parties is threatened.

Article 5

The Parties agree that an armed attack against one or more of them in Europe or North America shall be considered an attack against them all, and consequently they agree that, if such an armed attack occurs, each of them, in exercise of the right of individual or collective self-defense recognized by Article 51 of the Charter of the United Nations, will assist the Party or Parties so attacked by taking forthwith, individually, and in concert with the other Parties, such action as it deems necessary, including the use of armed force, to restore and maintain the security of the North Atlantic area.

Any such armed attack and all measures taken as a result thereof shall immediately be reported to the [United Nations] Security Council. Such measures shall be terminated when the Security Council has taken the measures necessary to restore and maintain international peace and security.

Article 6

For the purpose of Article 5, an armed attack on one or more of the Parties is deemed to include an armed attack:

(a) on the territory of any of the Parties in Europe or North America, . . . on the territory of Turkey or on the islands under the jurisdiction of any of the Parties in the North Atlantic area north of the Tropic of Cancer;

(b) on the forces, vessels, or aircraft of any of the Parties, when in or over these territories or any area in Europe in which occupation forces of any of the Parties were stationed on the date when the Treaty entered into force or the Mediterranean Sea or the North Atlantic area north of the Tropic of Cancer.

Article 7

The Treaty does not affect, and shall not be interpreted as affecting, in any way the rights and obligations under the Charter of the Parties which are members of the United Nations, or the primary responsibility of the Security Council for the maintenance of international peace and security.

Article 8

Each Party declares that none of the international engagements now in force between it and any other of the Parties or any third State is in conflict with the provisions of this Treaty, and undertakes not to enter into any international engagement in conflict with this Treaty.

Article 9

The Parties hereby establish a Council, on which each of them shall be represented, to consider matters concerning the implementation of this Treaty. The Council shall be so organized as to be able to meet promptly at any time. The Council shall set up such subsidiary bodies as may be necessary; in particular it shall establish immediately a defense committee which shall recommend measures for the implementation of Articles 3 and 5.

Article 10

The Parties may, by unanimous agreement, invite any other European State in a position to further the principles of this Treaty and to contribute to the security of the North Atlantic area to accede to this Treaty. Any State so invited may become a party to the Treaty by depositing its instrument of accession with the Government of the United States of America. The Government of the United States of America will inform each of the Parties of the deposit of each such instrument of accession.

Article 11

This Treaty shall be ratified and its provisions carried out by the Parties in accordance with their respective constitutional processes. The instruments of ratification shall be deposited as soon as possible with the Government of the United States of America, which will notify all the other signatories of each deposit . . .

Article 12

After the Treaty has been in force for ten years, or at any time thereafter, the Parties shall, if any of them so request, consult together for the purpose of reviewing the Treaty, having regard for the factors then affecting peace and security in the North Atlantic area including the development of universal as well as regional arrangements under the Charter of the United Nations for the maintenance of international peace and security.

Article 13

After the Treaty has been in force for twenty years, any Party may cease to be a Party one year after its notice of denunciation has been given to the Government of the United States of America, which will inform the Governments of the other Parties of the deposit of each notice of denunciation.

Article 14

This Treaty, of which the English and French texts are equally authentic, shall be deposited in the archives of the Government of the United States of America.

Source: "North Atlantic Treaty." The North Atlantic Treaty Organization. http://www.nato.int/cps/en/natolive/official_texts_17120.htm

THE UNITED NATIONS

The United Nations (UN) is an association of independent and sovereign countries established "to maintain international peace and security" and promote social progress, better living standards, and human rights. The UN currently has 193 member countries. The United Nations charter, which sets forth the organization's mission, purpose, and operating rules, was drafted in San Francisco in 1945. The UN formally came into existence on October 25 of that year, when the necessary number of countries ratified the charter.

The UN's charter calls for all member states "to settle their international disputes by peaceful means, . . . refrain in their international relations from the threat or use of force against any other State, . . . [and] give the United Nations every assistance in any action it takes in accordance with the Charter." The charter forbids UN intervention in any nation's domestic matters.

While its main missions are keeping peace and providing humanitarian aid, the United Nations works on a broad range of issues, including sustainable development, protection of the environment, aid to refugees, disaster relief, counterterrorism efforts, and the reduction of military forces and weapons, as well as promoting democracy, human rights, gender equality, economic and social development, and international health. The UN is also involved in clearing landmines and expanding food production. Member states contribute to the UN budget based on each nation's ability to pay. The maximum contribution for any nation is 25 percent of the regular budget (which is the approximate contribution of the United States), while the minimum contribution is 0.01 percent. The main organizational units of the UN are the Secretariat, the International Court of Justice, the Economic and Social Council, the Security Council, and the General Assembly. Until it suspended operations in 1994, the Trusteeship Council also played a major role.

The General Assembly

The main decision-making body of the UN is the General Assembly. Much of the UN's work is based on the decisions and mandates of the General Assembly. Each member state sends a delegation of up to five members to the General Assembly, and each delegation has one vote. The General Assembly meets in regular session every year for three months, although additional special sessions are sometimes

China's representative Liu Jieyi addressing the United Nations General Assembly in New York City in 2014. Each member of the UN has one vote in the General Assembly. (Niu Xiaolei Xinhua News Agency/Newscom)

called. At the beginning of every regular session, each delegation makes a statement on behalf of its nation regarding the major issues facing the UN. The Assembly then reviews agenda items and makes recommendations for the six Main Committees to study.

The committees study and debate matters referred to them and issue reports to the Assembly, which votes on recommendations on the issues. The Main Committees are as follows:

First Committee—Disarmament and international security
Second Committee—Economics and finance
Third Committee—Social, humanitarian, and cultural issues
Fourth Committee—Special politics and decolonization
Fifth Committee—Administration and budget
Sixth Committee—Legal

There are also various special, advisory, and non-permanent committees and commissions on such matters as peacekeeping operations, disarmament, science and technology, the environment, international law, and administrative matters. Any topic or issue within the UN Charter can be decided upon by the General Assembly, except matters being reviewed in the Security Council. On these matters, the Assembly may make nonbinding recommendations to the Security Council. In addition the General Assembly typically crafts the UN budget, chooses a General Assembly president who serves a one-year term, and votes on the Secretariat's recommendation for the secretary-general.

The Secretariat

The Secretariat administers the policies and programs of the other five principal UN organs. Its head is the secretary-general, who is elected by the General Assembly, after a recommendation by the Security Council, for a five-year term. The secretary-general is both the CEO of the UN and its representative to the world. He or she attends meetings of many of the organization's bodies, including the General Assembly. At the same time, the secretary-general acts as a diplomat, meeting with world leaders, issuing statements on behalf of the UN, and representing the interests of the world's people, especially the poor and the vulnerable. The secretary-general may recommend that the Security Council address any issue that might threaten international peace. The secretary-general and the Secretariat staff take orders from no government or authority outside the UN, but are required to remain neutral in their dealings with member countries.

The secretary-general's team includes the deputy secretary-general. The deputy assists with management of the Secretariat and strengthens UN leadership. The

Senior Management Group (SMG), composed of senior UN officials, acts as the secretary-general's cabinet and is the UN's central policy-planning body. The secretary-general is also assisted by special representatives and envoys who act as diplomats and mediators in conflicts and crises around the world. In addition, the secretary-general appoints Messengers of Peace—individuals "who possess widely recognized talents in the fields of arts, literature, music, and sports and who help focus world-wide attention on the work of the United Nations." Messengers of Peace have included conservationist Jane Goodall and actor George Clooney.

A number of departments and offices exist within the Secretariat. These include the Department of Peacekeeping Operations (DPKO), the United Nations Office for the Coordination of Humanitarian Affairs (OCHA), the Department of Economic and Social Affairs (DESA), the Office of the UN Security Coordinator (UNSECOORD), and the UN Office on Drugs and Crime (UNODC). In addition to UN headquarters in New York City, the Secretariat also operates out of Geneva, Switzerland; Nairobi, Kenya; Rome, Italy; and Vienna, Austria.

International Court of Justice

Also known as the World Court, the International Court of Justice (ICJ) was established in 1946. The ICJ holds sessions in the Peace Palace, in The Hague, the Netherlands. It replaced the Permanent Court of International Justice established by the League of Nations in 1919. The ICJ settles international legal issues, such as border disputes, between member states. It also advises other main UN organs on legal issues. The court consists of 15 judges, each from a different nation, who are nominated by national panels of jurists and elected for nine-year terms by the General Assembly and the Security Council. The ICJ president and vice president serve three-year terms.

Economic and Social Council (ECOSOC)

As the coordinating organ between the UN and its specialized agencies, ECOSOC is the central forum for the discussion of all economic, social, cultural, and humanitarian issues. The council is made up of representatives from 54 member states, who, during their three-year terms, coordinate the work of some of the UN's most recognizable agencies and projects, including the World Bank, the International Monetary Fund, and the UN Educational, Scientific, and Cultural Organization (UNESCO).

Among the 14 agencies, 5 regional and 9 functional commissions that provide reports and implement the mission of the ECOSOC are those charged with achieving an ambitious set of objectives the council set in 2000. The eight Millennium Development Goals include eradicating extreme poverty; providing primary education for all children; reducing child mortality; promoting gender equality; improving maternal health; combating HIV, malaria, and other diseases; ensuring environmental sustainability; and fostering global partnerships for economic development.

Security Council

The Security Council is charged with one of the UN's primary missions: maintaining international peace. The council consists of 15 member states, including 5 permanent members: China, France, Russia, the United Kingdom, and the United States. Of the 10 nonpermanent members, 3 must be from Africa; 2 each must be from Asia, Latin America, and Western Europe; and 1 must be from Eastern Europe. The council also includes a presidency, which is occupied in month-long terms. On procedural matters, decisions require the votes of nine council members. On all other matters, all voting permanent members must agree. A veto by any permanent member defeats the vote. Any Security Council member that is party to a dispute before the council must abstain from voting on that issue.

The Security Council can investigate international disputes that threaten peace, and make recommendations for a resolution. The council can ask UN members to institute nonmilitary enforcement measures, including partial or complete suspension of economic relations or communications (sanctions) and severing diplomatic ties. If these actions don't resolve the issue, the Security Council may call on UN members to provide military forces or facilities to help maintain the peace. The Security Council also regulates weapons, recommends new UN members, nominates a secretary-general for General Assembly approval, and, along with the General Assembly, elects judges to the ICJ.

Many bodies report to the Security Council, including peacekeeping operations and missions, two international criminal tribunals (for war crimes committed in Rwanda and the former Yugoslavia), and the UN Military Staff Committee—which helps plan the deployment of forces under Security Council resolutions and is responsible for the strategic direction of UN forces. The International Atomic Energy Agency (IAEA), which promotes the safe and secure use of atomic energy, also reports to the Security Council and the General Assembly.

Trusteeship Council

The Trusteeship Council suspended operation on November 1, 1994. This organ of the UN had been charged with encouraging independence or self-government among colonial territories. With the independence of the last UN trust territory, Palau, in 1994, the Trusteeship Council stopped holding regular meetings. It still exists, but now only meets by special request.

Excerpt from the United Nations Charter

The United Nations was established in 1945 at the end of World War II. From a practical standpoint, the UN can be seen as a successor to the League of Nations, which had proven unsuccessful in promoting international peace and cooperation between World Wars I and II, and was dissolved formally in 1946. The UN had 51 members at the time of its founding, and today includes 193 member states.

The UN is governed by the United Nations Charter, which was written in 1945 and took effect after being ratified by the five permanent members of the UN Security Council (China, France, the Union of Soviet Socialist Republics, the United Kingdom, and the United States) along with a majority of the other 46 original members.

A major purpose of the UN has been the promotion of peace and security. On numerous occasions since the Charter was drafted and ratified, the UN has intervened in efforts to resolve international wars and conflicts. To that effect, the UN recognizes the "sovereign equality" of each member country and expects that disputes among these member countries will be resolved peacefully. However, the promotion of human rights is also an important purpose of the UN. The Preamble to the Charter states specifically that the UN is committed to "reaffirm[ing] faith in fundamental human rights, in the dignity and worth of the human person, in the equal rights of men and women and of nations large and small."

Specifics of these human rights are spelled out in the Universal Declaration of Human Rights, which was adopted by vote of the UN General Assembly in 1948. The Universal Declaration states that all persons "are born free and equal in dignity and rights." Its clauses include legal rights, the prohibition of slavery and torture, and the rights to free speech, freedom of religion, and freedom of assembly. The Universal Declaration also identifies education and health as fundamental rights of all persons, including "[a] standard of living adequate for the health and well-being of himself and of his family, including food, clothing, housing and medical care and necessary social services." The Universal Declaration, along with the Charter of the United Nations itself, has informed the constitutions of numerous countries throughout the world since its original adoption.

WE THE PEOPLES OF THE UNITED NATIONS DETERMINED

- to save succeeding generations from the scourge of war, which twice in our lifetime has brought untold sorrow to mankind, and
- to reaffirm faith in fundamental human rights, in the dignity and worth of the human person, in the equal rights of men and women and of nations large and small, and
- to establish conditions under which justice and respect for the obligations arising from treaties and other sources of international law can be maintained, and
- to promote social progress and better standards of life in larger freedom,

AND FOR THESE ENDS

- to practice tolerance and live together in peace with one another as good neighbours, and
- to unite our strength to maintain international peace and security, and
- to ensure, by the acceptance of principles and the institution of methods, that armed force shall not be used, save in the common interest, and
- to employ international machinery for the promotion of the economic and social advancement of all peoples,

HAVE RESOLVED TO COMBINE OUR EFFORTS TO ACCOMPLISH THESE AIMS

Accordingly, our respective Governments, through representatives assembled in the city of San Francisco, who have exhibited their full powers found to be in good and due form, have agreed to the present Charter of the United Nations and do hereby establish an international organization to be known as the United Nations.

CHAPTER I: PURPOSES AND PRINCIPLES

Article 1

The Purposes of the United Nations are:

1. To maintain international peace and security, and to that end: to take effective collective measures for the prevention and removal of threats to the peace, and for the suppression of acts of aggression or other breaches of the peace, and to bring about by peaceful means, and in conformity with the principles of justice and international law, adjustment or settlement of international disputes or situations which might lead to a breach of the peace;
2. To develop friendly relations among nations based on respect for the principle of equal rights and self-determination of peoples . . . ;
3. To achieve international co-operation in solving international problems of an economic, social, cultural, or humanitarian character, and in promoting and encouraging respect for human rights and for fundamental freedoms for all without distinction as to race, sex, language, or religion; and
4. To be a centre for harmonizing the actions of nations in the attainment of these common ends.

Article 2

The Organization and its Members, in pursuit of the Purposes stated in Article 1, shall act in accordance with the following Principles.

1. The Organization is based on the principle of the sovereign equality of all its Members.
2. All Members . . . shall fulfill in good faith the obligations assumed by them in accordance with the present Charter.
3. All Members shall settle their international disputes by peaceful means in such a manner that international peace and security, and justice, are not endangered.
4. All Members shall refrain in their international relations from the threat or use of force against the territorial integrity or political independence of any state, or in any other manner inconsistent with the Purposes of the United Nations.
5. All Members shall give the United Nations every assistance in any action it takes in accordance with the present Charter, and shall refrain from giving assistance to any state against which the United Nations is taking preventive or enforcement action.
6. The Organization shall ensure that states which are not Members of the United Nations act in accordance with these Principles so far as may be necessary for the maintenance of international peace and security.
7. Nothing contained in the present Charter shall authorize the United Nations to intervene in matters which are essentially within the domestic jurisdiction of any state or shall require the Members to submit such matters to settlement under the present Charter . . .

Article 4

1. Membership in the United Nations is open to all other peace-loving states which . . . in the judgment of the Organization, are able and willing to carry out these obligations.
2. The admission of any such state to membership in the United Nations will be effected by a decision of the General Assembly upon the recommendation of the Security Council.

Article 5

1. A member of the United Nations against which preventive or enforcement action has been taken . . . may be suspended . . . The exercise of these rights and privileges may be restored by the Security Council.

Article 6

1. A Member of the United Nations which has persistently violated the Principles contained in the present Charter may be expelled from the Organization by the General Assembly upon the recommendation of the Security Council.

CHAPTER VI: PACIFIC SETTLEMENT OF DISPUTES

Article 33

The parties to any dispute, the continuance of which is likely to endanger the maintenance of international peace and security, shall, first of all, seek a solution by negotiation, enquiry, mediation, conciliation, arbitration, judicial settlement, resort to regional agencies or arrangements, or other peaceful means of their own choice.

Article 35

1. Any Member of the United Nations may bring any dispute . . . to the attention of the Security Council or of the General Assembly.
2. A state which is not a Member of the United Nations may bring to the attention of the Security Council or of the General Assembly any dispute to which it is a party . . .

VII: ACTION WITH RESPECT TO THREATS TO THE PEACE, BREACHES OF THE PEACE, AND ACTS OF AGGRESSION

Article 39

The Security Council shall determine the existence of any threat to the peace, breach of the peace, or act of aggression and shall make recommendations, or decide what measures shall be taken . . . to maintain or restore international peace and security.

Article 40

. . . the Security Council may, before making the recommendations . . . call upon the parties concerned to comply with such provisional measures as it deems necessary or desirable

Article 41

The Security Council may decide what measures not involving the use of armed force are to be employed . . . and it may call upon the Members of the United Nations to apply such measures. These may include complete or partial interruption of economic relations and of rail, sea, air, postal, telegraphic, radio, and other means of communication, and the severance of diplomatic relations.

Article 42

Should the Security Council consider that measures provided for in Article 41 would be inadequate or have proved to be inadequate, it may take such action by air, sea, or land forces as may be necessary to maintain or restore international peace and security. Such action may include demonstrations, blockade, and other operations by air, sea, or land forces of Members of the United Nations.

Article 43

1. All Members of the United Nations, in order to contribute to the maintenance of international peace and security, undertake to make available to the Security Council, on its call . . . armed forces, assistance, and facilities, including rights of passage, necessary for the purpose of maintaining international peace and security.
2. Such agreement or agreements shall govern the numbers and types of forces, their degree of readiness and general location, and the nature of the facilities and assistance to be provided.

Source: "Charter of the United Nations." United Nations. http://www.un.org/en/documents/charter/

OPPOSING VIEWPOINTS

WHAT WILL CUBA BE LIKE IN 2022?

Perhaps against all odds, Cuba has managed to maintain the socialist regime that Fidel Castro put in place in 1959. Among other travails, the regime has survived more than fifty years of a total trade embargo from the United States, and the collapse of its major benefactor, the Soviet Union, from 1989 to 1991. It has even, to the surprise of some observers, survived the resignation of Fidel Castro himself. In 2006 Castro ceded his position as leader to his younger brother Raúl (both are in their eighties), though it is believed that major decisions are still cleared with Fidel. Cuba's is one of the last remaining communist regimes, along with China, Vietnam, and North Korea, though like those countries it has had to implement reforms over the years, including modest steps toward allowing some private enterprise and private property.

Recent economic reforms and the advancing age of the Castro brothers have naturally provoked much speculation on Cuba's future. Will a tightly controlled communist regime on the island nation outlive the Castro brothers? How much longer will the U.S. embargo—which many critics say hurts the Cuban people worse than the government—be in place? Cuba is a land of rich resources, and before the 1959 revolution that brought Fidel Castro to power, it was a favored vacation spot for Americans and had much investment from U.S. corporations (as well, notoriously, from U.S. organized crime). There is a well-organized and politically powerful Cuban exile community based in southern Florida that is hoping for an end to the current regime. Cuban Studies is an area of considerable academic interest, and many experts on the island nation's history, culture, politics, and economic life are considering the question: What will Cuba be like in the coming years?

VIEWPOINT 1: "SIN PRISA PERO SIN PAUSA": CUBA WILL CHANGE, BUT SLOWLY

Two decades after the collapse of the Soviet Union, Cuban communism survives. But for how much longer? What will Cuba be like in 2022?

By that year, I believe that Cuba will have become a more open and dynamic society, characterized by a mixed market economy and relatively broader political freedoms. However, the process of change will be incremental and evolutionary, rather than sudden and revolutionary. Moreover, the island will still be a one-party state under Communist Party rule. In short, I predict Cuba will undergo a limited transition like the one that took place in China during the 1980s, when the nation embarked on a journey towards state-sponsored capitalism without undergoing a corresponding process of democratization.

Here is why I believe Cuba will follow this path.

First, the transition to capitalism has already begun. When Fidel Castro retired from public life in 2006 after ruling single-handedly since 1959, his younger brother Raúl assumed leadership of the island's Communist Party and of the Cuban state. Raúl has since undertaken to reform the island's painfully unproductive economy. Agriculture is being successfully transitioned into the hands of private cultivators, and during the Communist Party's Sixth Congress in April 2011, the decision was taken to further reduce the sectors of the economy remaining under state control. As a result, as many as one-third of the nation's workers are expected to move to private-sector jobs by 2014. Recent legislation has also authorized Cubans to buy and sell real estate and automobiles, and even to employ others in their own small businesses. As part of this trend toward economic liberalization, new laws also permit Cubans to own cellular phones and to have greater access to computers and the Internet.

However, economic change does not necessarily mean political change, at least not in the short term. Cuba has already proven itself capable of overcoming enormous economic challenges, adapting the way it does business without allowing for a corresponding political opening. After the fall of the Soviet Union in 1991, the loss of Soviet subsidies caused the Cuban economy to contract suddenly and by as much as 40%. Fuel shortages, blackouts, and hunger characterized much of the rest of the decade, known as the "Special Period." It was also, albeit briefly, a time of economic opening, as Fidel Castro allowed massive foreign investment in tourism, legalized the U.S. dollar, and authorized private farmers' markets. Many of these policies were reversed after Castro established an alliance with Venezuela's Hugo Chávez, who provided the island with the hard currency and subsidized petroleum that prompted a modest economic recovery.

Just as Fidel did in the 1990s, Raúl is now moving the island toward a freer economy. However, in both cases, the Castro brothers have taken these steps reluctantly, and only in order to ensure the survival of the socialist Revolution. Thus, even though Raúl is considered to be more pragmatic than his elder sibling, and in spite of the fact that the changes he has introduced are much broader and more firmly entrenched, he should not be misunderstood as a political reformer. Along with the rest of the aging and ideologically stalwart senior leadership of the Cuban Communist Party, he remains a committed Marxist and is willing to punish dissent severely, as demonstrated by the arrest of dozens of the regime's opponents before Pope Benedict XVI's visit to the island in April 2012.

There are other obstacles to democratization. Bureaucrats and lower-level party members are also opposed to political change, for reasons that combine ideology and opportunism—they fear the loss of power and special benefits available to them as members of the ruling apparatus. Furthermore, the island lacks a credible political opposition. The few dissent groups, known or perceived to be funded by the U.S. government, enjoy little legitimacy with the majority of the population; after fifty years of resisting outside attempts to destroy or destabilize the Revolution, most Cubans remain suspicious of American efforts to interfere with the island's destiny. Finally, the powerful specter of Fidel Castro, the quasi-mythical revolutionary leader who ousted control from the despised dictator Fulgencio Batista in 1959 and defied repeated U.S. efforts to topple his regime, continues to confer legitimacy on the government.

Fidel's eventual passing may open a space for further change, but it will most likely do so without threatening the stability of the government, which is now firmly in his younger brother's hands. Nonetheless, in the unlikely event that his passing produces turmoil, the island's formidable military and security forces are ready to quash any incipient threats to the regime. And they remain steadfastly loyal to the Party—Raúl Castro was, after all, Minister of the Cuban Armed Forces from 1959 to 2008, when he was officially designated Fidel's successor. Even after Raúl's death, the very real possibility of police or military repression will ensure that radical political transformation remains unlikely.

Strict one-party rule, as enshrined in Cuba's socialist constitution, will thus almost certainly continue to define the nation in 2022. But it will not continue indefinitely. History has shown that economic liberalization usually leads over time to political change. This was the case in the Soviet Union, where Gorbachev's economic reforms led inexorably to political opening that resulted finally in the breakup of the communist superpower, and it will hold true in Cuba as well. Cubans today are restless, unhappy with the deterioration of the island's once-exemplary public health care system and schools, and resentful of the growing socioeconomic inequality that has been produced by the circulation of U.S. dollars and the legalization of small business. The social contract which the Revolution made with the Cuban citizenry in 1959—that political unfreedom would be compensated for by economic equality—is being tested increasingly. As long as the Castro brothers remain in power, however, the contract will hold. The question, then, is not what will happen when Fidel and Raúl die, but rather, who will replace them.

Since the party has failed to prepare a new generation of well-known leaders, the next leader of Cuba will likely be a relatively obscure party member who lacks the revolutionary legitimacy that still clings to the elderly Castro brothers. He or she will thus have to earn Cubans' loyalty by providing for their material needs and desire for continued social equality. If this person proves unable to do so, demands for political change will increase, and continued Communist Party rule of the island will be threatened.

Much remains uncertain. One thing, however, is clear: if the U.S. government wants to support democratization in Cuba, it must end the fifty-year economic embargo of the island. This misguided policy has been the single most important factor in keeping the Castro regime in power, providing it with a convenient means of explaining the island's longstanding economic hardships, and justifying continued repression as necessary to maintaining unity in the face of ongoing U.S. aggression. If Americans want to see real change in Cuba, they must pressure their leaders to rethink U.S.–Cuban relations in light of post–Cold War realities. We have already accepted that re-establishing relations with communist China and Vietnam serves American interests; it is time now for a similarly pragmatic relationship with our island neighbor.

Dr. Anita Casavantes Bradford earned her PhD in U.S. Latina/o History at the University of California-San Diego. She is a President's Postdoctoral Fellow in the Department of Chicano/Latino Studies at University of California-Irvine. Her book, *For the Children? The Politics of Childhood in Havana and Miami, 1959–1962*, is forthcoming from the University of North Carolina Press.

VIEWPOINT 2: A FREE AND PROSPEROUS SOCIETY WILL EMERGE

Since January 1, 1959, Fidel Castro and now his brother Raúl have ruled Cuba. The Revolution welcomed with enthusiasm by the majority of the Cuban people and the world slowly became a centralized, communist, totalitarian regime. With the fall of the Soviet Union and the loss of subsidies, Cuba suffered a deep economic depression. Presently, in spite of Venezuela's aid, the state is bankrupt. It has started modest economic reforms in an effort to retain power and maintain the now almost defunct education and health systems that were once hailed as the Revolution's main accomplishments. The Cuban government's frequent overtures to the United States to solve the longtime feud between the two nations have failed. The Cuban Revolution has aged, and so have the Castro brothers, 89 and 84 years old respectively in 2015. It is safe to predict that by 2022, Fidel, Raúl, and their cadre will have passed away. Cuba will be very different from what it is today.

Exactly how and when real changes will begin in Cuba is hard to predict, but the examples of Eastern Europe tell us that once they start, they will develop rapidly. By 2022 Cuba will have reformed its constitution and much of its legal and electoral systems. It will have eliminated restrictions to freedom of speech, religion, and affiliation. Property rights will have been redefined. Politically, the Communist Party will not be dissolved, but a substantive portion will have transformed itself into a Social Democratic Party. A Christian Democratic Party will have emerged. The political arena will be pluralistic. Coalitions will be formed. The road to democracy will be very visible. Whether a transitional or a freely elected government is in power, it will have mended the strained relationship with the United States and, very importantly, with Cuba's growing diaspora.

Cuba's population is aging rapidly, the birth rate is low, and about 35,000 people emigrate from Cuba every year. According to Cuban government projections, by 2021 more Cubans will be leaving the workforce than entering it. To reverse this trend, the country will have encouraged circular migration. Many now living abroad, whether in the United States or other countries, will have returned. Either as retirees, investors, or visiting professors, doctors, attorneys, and teachers, they will be contributing to the island's transformation.

By 2022 tourism to Cuba will have increased from about 2 million visitors a year to 15 million. It will be an ideal place for many Cuban-Americans and Americans to retire or have a second home. The country will offer excellent medical care at low cost. Medical tourism will proliferate. Mainly, Cuba will have a service economy to satisfy the needs of tourists and retirees. There will be a continuous flow of people between Havana and Miami. With only a forty-minute flight separating the cities, many will go for the day on business or for the weekend to enjoy the country's beaches and flourishing nightlife.

In the same manner that the United States offered Cuba very favorable conditions for the exportation of sugar during the first half of the twentieth century, in 2022 the U.S. will be purchasing ethanol under preferential provisions from the island's resurrected sugar industry.

As the country stabilizes politically and creates a new legal framework, confidence in the future of the country will ensue. Foreign investment will grow. Because of its geographic location, as in centuries past, Cuba will be a hub for both cruise ships and commercial vessels.

Cuba's nationalism will still be a factor and will not allow the country to be controlled by foreign capital. With support from their relatives living abroad and a system of microcredits, small businesses will proliferate and create a healthy, strong middle class of entrepreneurs.

Free education has been important to Cubans for half a century, but the deterioration of the system has made younger generations lose faith in it. Private schools will return to the island. Curricula will be modernized. New emphasis will be given to learning English and service careers in tourism and the medical field, as well as in marketing, advertising, public relations, and business administration.

A new pragmatism in the educational field will not diminish but encourage Cuba's rich cultural life. Ballet, visual arts, theater, and literature will thrive. The creative works of Cubans in the diaspora will be incorporated to the island's rich heritage.

The Roman Catholic Church will play an important role in the transition of Cuba from a socialist, vertical structure to a democratic society. It will serve as mediator in difficult situations, and will educate a generation of men and women with Christian ethical values that will influence society. Without the control of the state, the media will flourish. Most importantly, Cubans will have access to the Internet, and the void in information they now suffer will cease. Cuba will have caught up with the technology of the twenty-first century. All major international networks and press agencies will have offices in Havana and other cities on the island. Cubans will produce their own versions of *Dancing with the Stars* and *American Idol*, but will also watch TV shows from the United States live on cable channels.Slowly, the relationship between the government and its citizens will change. While for half a century Cubans have worked for the government, and the government has been vigilant of their actions, Cubans will begin to understand that in a democracy the government is the employee of the citizens, and it is the citizens who have the right and duty to ensure that the government does its job right. When this happens, the transition toward democracy will be secured.

Uva de Aragón, a native of Havana, Cuba, obtained a PhD in Latin American studies from the University of Miami. Until her retirement in 2011, she was associate director of the Cuban Research Institute at Florida International University, where she also taught in the Modern Languages Department. Dr. de Aragón served for six years as associate editor of *Cuban Studies*, the most important academic journal on Cuba. She writes a weekly column for *Diario Los Américas* and has published twelve books, including poems, essays, short stories, a novel, and a play. Some of her works appear in anthologies, both in Spanish and translated into English. She has lived in the United States since 1959, and since 1999 has visited Cuba frequently.

Further Reading

Carlos Frías, *Take me with you: A secret search for family in a forbidden Cuba.* New York: Atria Books, 2009

Ted A. Henken, *Cuba: A global studies handbook.* Santa Barbara, CA: ABC-CLIO, 2007. Louis A Pérez Jr., *To die in Cuba: Suicide and society.* Chapel Hill, NC: The University of North Carolina Press, 2007.

Louis A Pérez Jr., *Cuba: Between reform and revolution.* New York: Oxford University Press USA, 2010.

Marifeli Pérez-Stable, *Intimate enemies: The United States and Cuba.* New York: Routledge, 2011.

Yoani Sanchez, *Havana real: One woman fights to tell the truth about Cuba today.* New York: Melville House, 2011.

Julia E. Sweig, *Cuba: What everyone needs to know.* New York: Oxford University Press USA, 2009.

WHAT WILL NORTH KOREA LOOK LIKE IN 2024?

After World War II, the Allies divided Korea, then a Japanese colony, in two. The northern half of the peninsula was occupied by the Soviet Union, and the southern half was occupied by the United States. As a result, a communist regime was established in North Korea, and a democratic regime was installed in the South. However, both sides claimed sovereignty over the entire peninsula. From 1950 to 1953, the two sides fought a war that accomplished little. Tensions between the two countries, which refuse to recognize each other as sovereign states, continue today.

North Korea continues to hobble along under a repressive, dictatorial regime. The country suffers from food shortages and relies on foreign aid to feed its population. North Korea has a reputation for human rights abuses, and reports of prison camps, tortures, and executions are commonplace. It pursues nuclear development despite international sanction and vacillates between halting the development to receive foreign aid, and restarting its nuclear program and receiving international sanctions. The country's largest ally is China, although in recent years, its giant neighbor has avoided condoning and has even cautioned North Korea about its provocative foreign policy. Despite North Korea's problems, the country continues to survive, although many analysts believe its reckless path is unsustainable.

VIEWPOINT 1: REUNIFICATION IS A DISTANT DREAM

Unfortunately, in 2024 the Korean peninsula will still be split along the 38th parallel. The Democratic People's Republic of Korea (DPRK, or North Korea), the master of muddling through turmoil and isolation, will have continued to do so, allowing the Kim family regime to survive. Kim Jong Un, the grandson of Kim Il Sung, North Korea's first leader, will have had over ten years of experience as the head of the country. North Korea in 2024 will still be a threat to South Korea and the United States, and will still be supported by China to prevent instability. The possibility of reunification of the Korean Peninsula will remain in the distant future.

North Korea has time on its side and will likely use the opportunity to enhance its missile technology. In 2011, U.S. secretary of defense Robert Gates predicted that North Korea could develop the capability for its missiles to hit the continental United States within five years. That prediction will have come true by 2024. General Charles Jacoby, head of the Northern Command and North American Aerospace Defense Command (NORAD), testified to Congress in 2014 that North Korea's "limited ballistic missile threat to the homeland has matured from a theoretical to a practical consideration" for the United States. Thus, U.S. assets in Asia and in its own territory are now and will continue to be at risk. The main question today and in the future will be: Is North Korea capable of miniaturizing a nuclear warhead and mounting it on a missile?

North Korea will still be armed dangerously with some nuclear weapons capabilities. There will be some effort between 2014 and 2024 to persuade North Korea to give access to or place a moratorium on the Yongbyon nuclear facility. Those agreements, however, will probably not be permanent. Hence, North Korea will likely have been able to keep some or all of its nuclear weapons capabilities. Despite the likelihood of many sincere efforts, the major players in the region—China, North Korea, South Korea, Japan, Russia, and the United States—will not have been able to meet for the official six-party talks on the denuclearization of the Korean Peninsula. The further development of an agreement issued at the 2005 six-party gathering in Beijing that called for the denuclearization of the Korean Peninsula in exchange for energy assistance is still possible, but all sides are likely to be willing to come to the table if a different framework for the talks can be agreed upon.

North Korea will continue to build weapons through Chinese economic support and by circumventing sanctions. China is North Korea's largest trading partner and, despite provocations from North Korea, consistently increases trade to its neighbor. China's foreign minister in 2014 stated that China "would not allow war or instability on the Korean peninsula," suggesting that Chinese support would continue. North Korea has also been able to stay afloat by evading sanctions that have been issued by a number of countries. A 2014 United Nations panel of experts report illustrated how North Korean leadership uses "multiple and tiered circumvention techniques" to obtain luxury goods and materials despite the sanctions.

With its sanction-eluding skills and help from China, North Korea's economy can survive with little connection to the globalized economy. The Bank of Korea in South Korea indicated that North Korea's economy likely grew approximately 1% in 2011 and 2012. North Korea's gross domestic product per capita likely increased 4.8% in 2013. Thus, it is possible that North Korea can muddle through economically and still be present as a separate country in 2024.

In that time, it is possible that North Korea will have only dealt with two U.S. presidents. Granted, a U.S. president who serves two terms often has more flexibility and time to deal with foreign policy issues like North Korea; however, even that stretch of time is not enough to dramatically shift U.S. policy toward North Korea. Therefore, the impetus for a dramatic or forceful change in the current trajectory of North Korea is unlikely to come in this amount of time from the United States.

A similar political timeframe issue occurs with South Korea. Even if South Korea has successive presidents from the more progressive side of their political spectrum, which advocates greater engagement with North Korea, ten years may still not be enough time. South Korea already had almost ten years of "Sunshine Policy" toward North Korea under presidents Kim Dae Jung and Roh Moo-hyun. The best attempts from these two presidents to get North Korea to open up through engagement were mired in South Korean politics and North Korean intransigence. Moreover, polls indicate that many South Koreans would rather see reunification delayed to the future rather than an immediate joining of the two countries. The year 2024 may seem like the distant future, but more time is likely needed politically for better relations to develop between the two Koreas.

It is hard to forecast how North Korea will look in 2024. Predictions of North Korea's collapse have abounded since the 1990s and continue each year. Yet the unpleasant reality of North Korea's ability to muddle though and survive strongly suggests that North Korea in 2024 will continue to be a major problem for the United States and South Korea. It is likely that by 2024 North Korea will still have nuclear weapons and will have improved its ballistic missile capabilities. North Korea will also still have a benefactor in China, providing aid, development, and diplomatic support to prevent instability and collapse. Furthermore, reunification will still be a distant dream. As much as people and governments around the world hope for a brighter future on the Korean peninsula, the trends and arguments enumerated in this essay suggest that North Korea will still exist as a separate country, one that is more armed and dangerous to South Korea and the United States.

Nicholas Hamisevicz is the director of research and academic affairs at the Korea Economic Institute of America (KEI). He is responsible for issues affecting the U.S.–South Korea alliance, especially issues related to North Korea. He also comments on inter-Korea relations and South Korea–India relations. In addition, Mr. Hamisevicz is tasked with leading KEI's outreach efforts to connect the policy and academic communities. Mr. Hamisevicz has visited Asia numerous times, including a trip to North Korea in August 2011.

VIEWPOINT 2: CHINA WILL ANNEX NORTH KOREA

North Korea remains a remarkably resilient country, illustrated by its survival of and since the Cold War, despite the famine of the 1990s that claimed the lives of millions of its citizens, and despite sanctions from the United States and the United Nations for its nuclear weapons program. By 2024, however, I predict that the Kim family will have lost control of the government and China will have annexed North Korea.

The key problem that faces North Korea's supreme leader Kim Jong Un is how to initiate needed reforms without losing control over the elites and the government. China has spent decades trying to convince North Korea to undertake steps toward limited economic reforms similar to the reforms Chinese leader Deng Xiaoping undertook in the 1980s. The North Korean government opposes such reforms because of fears that once reforms are initiated the government will lose control over the country.

Western North Korea analysts did not expect Kim Jong Il's hereditary succession in 1994 to succeed in the long term, because of North Korea's steady economic downturn, as well as growing international suspicions of the country's nuclear weapons program. Kim Jong Il, however, maintained control despite the growing poverty and famine in his country and began a pattern of leveraging the country's nuclear program for foreign aid.

On the death of Kim Jong Il in 2011, his youngest son, Kim Jong Un, took the reins in a much more uncertain transfer of power. Kim Jong Un had never been seen in public until 2009, when his father began grooming him to take his place. When Kim Jong Il died, his son's succession had not been formalized. This, in addition to

Kim Jong Un's youth and inexperience, lent uncertainty to the succession.Between 2011 and 2013, Kim Jong Un undertook numerous purges of his father's supporters within the Korean Worker's Party and the Korean People's Army. Some of these officials and generals were the hardline supporters of his father's military-first policy, which had put the emphasis on North Korea developing a strong military over the economy. After the removal of Kim Jong Il's old-guard supporters, Western analysts believed that Kim Jong Un would begin to initiate economic reforms throughout the country. The purge of his key advisor and uncle, Jang Song Thaek, in 2013 was seen by some as the initial sign of the North Korean regime unraveling.

I predict that by 2024, North Korea will have been annexed by China. Leading up to this absorption, the North Korean government will be torn apart by various factions attempting to claim true legitimacy as heirs to Kim Il Sung, the founder of North Korea; Kim Jong Un will be unable to keep the elites unified under his leadership. Without the guiding hands of the Kim elder family, a coup will be attempted by the military and North Korean political officials, but it will fail keep the country together.

To stop the collapse from spreading across the region, China will annex North Korea as a safety measure. (China has had plans for this contingency for decades.) The collapse of the North Korean government is China's biggest security issue: Not only would China need to secure North Korea's nuclear weapons program and chemical and biological weapons from U.S. intervention, it must stop North Korean refugees from flooding the northeast provinces of China. The official rationale to be used by the Chinese government for annexing North Korea will be historical: the territory of North Korea was once part of the Chinese empire and will remain part of China, similar to China's claims on the province of Tibet and the Republic of Taiwan.

North Korea will accept China's offer of annexation because it would still keep the foundations of the North Korean political system in place and provide security for the elites who want protection from execution by the North Korean masses. The annexation would stabilize the balance of power in the region. It would prevent South Korea from acquiring North Korean nuclear technology and becoming a nuclear power itself. China will keep North Korea as a buffer state. The unification of North and South Korea under South Korean rule will be prevented, an outcome undesirable to China because of South Korea's alliance with the United States. This will avoid any U.S. and U.S.–allied activities near the Chinese border that could constrain China's influence in Asia.

After North Korea is annexed, China will install North Korean officials supportive of Chinese-style reforms. China will also develop North Korea's natural resources for export, as well as improve North Korea's sea ports to provide advantageous infrastructure to move China's exports across Asia. The Chinese government will treat the new North Korean government similarly to Hong Kong, allowing it to keep its own governance system but pledge its loyalty to Beijing.

North Korea of 2024 will be a survivor, dependent upon its last remaining ally for a lifeline. Absorption into China will serve both countries' purposes by ensuring

North Korea's safety from southern invasion and by continuing China's strategy of keeping North Korea as a buffer zone against the U.S.–allied South Korea. North Korea will be transformed into a province that provides China extensive mineral resources and access to new seaports for its goods. With North Korea under China's domain, China will achieve its foreign policy goal of bringing stability to Northeast Asia without the expense of a unified Korean state.

Nicholas Miller is an independent North Korean analyst/East Asian researcher based in Dallas, Texas. He received his BA from Guilford College in political science and MA in international relations from Flinders University. He also received graduate certificates in Asian governance at Flinders University and advanced international affairs, with a focus on intelligence, from the Bush School of Government and Public Service at Texas A&M University. He is the resident Chinese geo-strategic and border security analyst for the North Korean research site Sino-NK.com. His work has appeared on numerous international affairs sites including *The Diplomat*, *Real Clear News*, and *NK News*. He authored the monograph *China–North Korea Dossier No. 4: Focus on Chinese Ambassador Liu Hongcai* for Sino-NK.com.

Further Reading

"China draws 'Red Line' on North Korea, says won't allow war on peninsula," *Reuters*, March 8, 2014.

"N. Korea's per-capita GDP grows 4.8 PCT in 2013: Report," *Yonhap*, March 16, 2014.

Tania Branigan, "Korean unification: Dreams of unity fade into past for young South Koreans," *The Guardian*, May 26, 2013.

Elisabeth Bumiller and David E. Sanger, "Gates warns of North Korea missile threat to U.S.," *New York Times*, January 11, 2011.

Nicholas Hamisevicz, "No illusions on North Korea," The National Bureau of Asian Research, February 12, 2013.

Chico Harlan, "South Korea's young people are wary of unification," *Washington Post*, October 17, 2011.

Jiyoon Kim and Karl Friedhoff, "South Korean public opinion on North Korea & the nations of the Six-Party Talks," The Asan Institute for Policy Studies, October 2011.

"North Korea ably evades its sanctions, panel says," *New York Times*, March 11, 2014.

Troy Stangarone and Nicholas Hamisevicz, "The prospects of economic reform in North Korea after Kim Jong-il and the China factor," *International Journal for Korea Unification Studies*, Vol. 20, No. 2, 2011, pages 175–197.

WHAT SHOULD BE THE POLITICAL STATUS OF PUERTO RICO?

When Puerto Rico was annexed by the United States in the wake of the Spanish-American War, it was not clear what the status of the island and its numerous inhabitants would be. Like other newly acquired territorial possessions, Puerto Rico was not considered an integral part of the United States, but rather a dependency of sorts. Unlike such territories as Cuba and the Philippines, however, Puerto Rico was never granted independence; and unlike such territories as Hawaii and Alaska, it was never granted full statehood. Instead, the U.S. government extended to the Puerto Rican people certain rights and privileges and allowed the island a certain degree of autonomy while still retaining control.

Puerto Rico has had its own local government since 1900, and Puerto Ricans were made full U.S. citizens by Congress in 1917. Puerto Ricans can serve in (and be drafted into) the U.S. military, travel with U.S. passports, and freely trade with or move to the United States. Yet Puerto Ricans are not subject to federal income taxes, have no voting representation in Congress, cannot vote for the U.S. president, and are not fully protected by the entirety of the U.S. Constitution. Since 1952, Puerto Rico has had its own constitution, determined and collected its own income taxes, had its own political parties, and has largely been responsible for its local affairs. However, the Puerto Rican government has very little control over anything other than practical administration of the island. Perhaps most importantly, it cannot determine its own political status— that power lies with the U.S. Congress. Though several attempts have been made to gauge popular opinion among Puerto Ricans, there has been no change in the island's status in more than fifty years. Some want Puerto Rico to become a full state, others hope for eventual independence, and still others believe that continuation of the status quo is the most beneficial arrangement for Puerto Rico. With opinion divided among the populace and politicians in both Puerto Rico and the mainland United States, it is important to consider the question: What should be the political status of Puerto Rico?

VIEWPOINT 1: PUERTO RICO SHOULD BECOME THE FIFTY-FIRST STATE

Puerto Rico became a territory of the United States in 1900, and the sovereign power and authority of the U.S. Congress over the territory has remained unchanged ever since. Though afforded partial enfranchisement with limited local self-government in 1952, some 4 million Puerto Ricans remain subordinate to laws enacted by Congress without their participation, rendering them powerless, in a state of inequality without sovereignty. The current, unequal "Commonwealth" status, translated by island-based supporters as *Estado Libre Asociado* (Free Associated State), is neither free, nor associated, nor a state, and does not—indeed cannot—provide citizenship equality. Puerto Rico can only accomplish equality within the prescriptions of the U.S. Constitution and federation of states through the attainment of statehood, which brings proportionate voting representation in both chambers of the U.S. Congress. There can be no political or citizenship equality within the Union without statehood, and until then, 4 million people will remain condemned perpetually to second-class citizenship.

Myths and mistruths abound about Puerto Rico's status, all of which are put forward with the purpose of denying equality to Puerto Rico. Although they are U.S. citizens, Puerto Ricans are linked routinely to immigration and assimilation debates to which they should not be subject. Puerto Ricans are Americans residing on American soil. Puerto Ricans have been American citizens since 1917 and have fought in the service of their country ever since. Though U.S. citizenship is currently statutory and without constitutional guarantee, Puerto Rican allegiance to the United States and its values and principles is unquestionable. Only the smallest of minorities in Puerto Rico would readily discard U.S. citizenship for political independence, but island-based supporters of inequality seek to protect the status quo for narrow political and economic ends, and a majority of these would never discard their U.S. citizenship.

Puerto Ricans have contributed significantly to U.S. national life in the areas of business, the arts, music, education, medicine, politics, science, and sports, and have served in all branches of the armed forces. Puerto Rico's per-capita participation in the U.S. military is rivaled by only one state, yet hundreds of thousands of veterans residing in Puerto Rico do not share the equal democratic and civil rights enjoyed by their mainland counterparts. Unequal citizenship is the direct result of continued territorial status and the absence of equal representation in Congress. Puerto Ricans elect a sole delegate with no voting rights to the House of Representatives, instead of a full voting delegation. Puerto Ricans remain voiceless in the U.S. Senate. Without voting representation, Puerto Ricans do not have a say as to whether their sons and daughters will fight in wars approved by Congress; similarly, they are not allowed to vote for their commander-in-chief.

Arguments offered by opponents mislead the uninformed, lack foundation, and are often intellectually superficial. Equality opponents cite language use as an obstacle to statehood, a position for which there is no precedent. Some states are officially bilingual, namely New Mexico and Hawaii. Puerto Rico has been officially bilingual since 1902, and its constitution is written in English and Spanish. Many states have adopted English as their official language, and others have chosen not to adopt official languages. Louisiana officially recognizes English and French. As such, choice of official language, or the choice not to have one, is a firmly established state right. French is the second-most widely spoken language in several northern states, and Spanish is widely spoken throughout the southwestern states, California, and Florida. Many communities throughout the country speak languages other than English without detriment to the national or state social identity.

Opposition to Puerto Rican equality centered on the island's sociological cohesion and identity conveniently overlooks the fact that Puerto Rican identity is as strong today as it was in 1898, and that culture is not a static phenomenon. Opponents suggest that social and cultural identity should be barriers to statehood and offer them as reasons why Puerto Rico could never integrate successfully into the

Union, ignoring the fact that Texas and Hawaii were both independent countries before their admission as states. To pretend that their identity, culture, and nationhood have been impediments to their successful integration belie the facts. Neither language nor social identity has ever been a prerequisite for statehood, but population size has, and Puerto Rico more than meets that requirement with a population that is larger than half of the current states.

Statehood and admission to the Union does not require extraordinary constitutional measures; neither constitutional amendment nor convention is required. Statehood for Puerto Rico merely requires simple majorities in the Congress, followed by the president's signature.

While process is integral to ending the territorial status, the promise and benefits of statehood for all Americans cannot be understated. Annual subsidies and preferential corporate tax treatment for Puerto Rico cost U.S. taxpayers over $22 billion each year. Though economic advances have been made in Puerto Rico since the 1950s, growth has been flat since the 1980s, and blame must be directed at the uncertainty of the island's territorial status. Puerto Rico's growth potential as a state, however, is unquestionable. Many argue that federal taxes in Puerto Rico would sink the local economy, but they do not mention the disproportionately high local taxes, their effects on the economy, and the income thresholds for paying federal taxes. Once the federal income tax system is in place, local taxes will necessarily require adjustment to rebalance the island taxpayer burden.

Puerto Ricans already participate in the federal payroll tax system with mainland taxpayers, through the Federal Insurance Contributions Act (FICA), which funds Social Security and Medicare. Island residents pay more in local income taxes, proportionate to income, than most of their mainland counterparts. Statehood will alleviate the public costs of inequality with an infusion of federal funding. For example, the federal Medicaid health care program provides 80% of the funding to states, with the states responsible for the remaining 20%. In contrast, because of its territorial status and consequent congressional funding caps, Puerto Rico receives only 13% and is responsible for the remaining 87%. Puerto Ricans are ineligible for supplemental security income (SSI) funds by virtue of the territorial relationship. Federal transportation and infrastructure funding are other examples. Simultaneously, Puerto Rico operates quasi-independently of the federal tax structure with a patchwork of preferential federal tax treatments for various industries, interests, and commercial enterprises that cost mainland taxpayers billions of dollars in annual subsidies and lost federal revenue. With parity, Puerto Rico will be able to manage its economic future with a soundness and consistency not afforded by the uncertain future of a territory, which imposes artificial constraints on the island's market economy. Statehood will reduce the unbalanced fiscal burdens that the current status forces all Americans to endure.

Affording equal rights to 4 million unenfranchised citizens is a moral imperative made starker when we are reminded of the words of General Nelson A. Miles, upon the U.S. invasion of Puerto Rico on July 25, 1898: "We have not come to make war upon the people of a country that for centuries has been oppressed, but . . . to bring you protection . . . to promote your prosperity, and to bestow upon you the immunities and blessings of the liberal institutions of our Government."

That Puerto Ricans have demonstrated their commitment to the Republic during this longest of territorial relationships is undeniable. To suggest that second-class citizenship is acceptable by virtue of limited self-governance must be anathema to the just. That suggestion belongs to times in our history when paternalism and bigotry once held that minorities desired to be led by others and had neither capacity nor yearning for political rights and empowerment. Such beliefs are unacceptable, opposed to America's values and principles.

Justice dictates that equal rights and citizenship should not be usurped by intellectual dishonesty. Language, culture, and geography have never been prerequisites for the admission of states to the Union; rather, commitments to republicanism, democratic principles, patriotism, population size, and economic considerations have. Puerto Rico meets all those necessary requirements to become the fifty-first state. Only narrow political interests and allied xenophobic posturing obscure these truths. Absent statehood, Puerto Rico can never be equal under the Constitution. Puerto Ricans deserve equal citizenship, democratic and civil rights, and a sovereign voice in their political and economic futures.

Javier Arvelo-Cruz-Santana is a research associate at the U.S. Council for Puerto Rico Statehood, a non-profit, non-partisan education and advocacy organization dedicated to promoting statehood for Puerto Rico. He is a graduate of Western Carolina University (WCU), where he earned a bachelor's degree in English and a master's degree in public administration. Mr. Arvelo-Cruz-Santana was a founding member and president of the Student Congress for the Advancement of Humanitarian Work at WCU, an organization dedicated to providing assistance to victims of natural disasters in the state and was also involved in numerous community outreach and cultural activities. A longstanding resident of North Carolina, he is a native of Santa Isabel, Puerto Rico, having relocated with his family to the U.S. mainland as a teenager.

VIEWPOINT 2: ONLY INDEPENDENCE WOULD MAKE PUERTO RICO A FREELY ASSOCIATED STATE

In 1998, Puerto Rico's pro-statehood governor, Pedro Juan Rosselló González, held a plebiscite (referendum) on statehood, the island's third since 1967. Pro-statehood leaders expected a landslide in their favor. Instead, the results were ambiguous: 46.5% voted for statehood, 2.5% for independence, 0.1% for "territorial" commonwealth status (the current form of government), 0.3% for free association, and 50.3% percent for "None of the Above."

If one considers the wording on the ballot—"*ninguna de las anteriores*," most accurately translated as "none of the preceding"—it can been argued that the Puerto Rican electorate was attempting to communicate to their leaders that they no longer wanted to approach the status question as it had been approached for the last fifty years, during which a succession of pro-statehood and pro-commonwealth leaders have run the insular government, while the independence movement has been all but silenced.

From the 1920s through the 1950s, a series of laws and governors' decrees classified pro-independence speech as sedition, expression advocating the overthrow of the U.S. government. Under the 1948 Gag Law, for example, even displaying the Puerto Rican flag was considered prohibited political expression punishable by imprisonment. Today, the Puerto Rican flag flies freely throughout the island. However, many voters can remember a time not so long ago when even to speak of independence was grounds for imprisonment. Some of Puerto Rico's most famous uprisings, from the 1868 Grito de Lares to the Nationalist Insurrection of 1950, were partially planned and/or carried out in the United States. Perhaps this is because the only place Puerto Ricans feel safe enough to consider independence is off-island.

If Puerto Rico were to opt for independence, many voters fear that the United States would make the island pay dearly for its freedom. This fear is also grounded in history. In the 1930s, angered by a series of confrontations between U.S. officials and Puerto Rican nationalists, the Tydings Bill was drafted. The Bill would have granted Puerto Rico its independence, along with punishing economic provisions designed to crush the island's nascent industrial economy.

Some voters say independence would leave Puerto Rican workers open to the kind of labor exploitation perpetuated by transnational corporations in other developing regions. It could no longer entice investment with the tax incentives it enjoys due to its special relationship with the United States. These fears are understandable, but there is another way. The island is not as dependent on U.S. trade as it once was, as just over a half of its GDP is reliant on exports to the United States. Further, an independent Puerto Rico could dictate its own worker-safety provisions and its own trading terms.

The insular government refers to itself officially as the Freely Associated State of Puerto Rico. According to U.S. law, as clarified by the President's Task Force on Puerto Rico's Status in 2007, Puerto Rico is in fact an "unincorporated territory of the United States." The U.S. Congress can choose to modify this status at any time, while Puerto Rico has no legal basis for making changes in the relationship. In other words, the governing principle that guides Puerto Rico's relationship with the United States is not free, Puerto Rico is not a state, and its association does not represent a compact of consent, as pro-commonwealth leaders often insist that it does. In all but name, Puerto Rico is a colony of the United States.

The Jones Act (1917) effectively decoupled U.S. citizenship from the right to political participation through democratically elected representation; that is, it established that Puerto Ricans are U.S. citizens without full voting and representation rights. Since its passage, Puerto Ricans have been afraid to speak out in favor of independence for fear that they might lose their U.S. citizenship. With as many Puerto Ricans living in the United States as live on the island, loss of U.S. citizenship and the ease of travel that goes with it would end the complex cross-migration patterns that exist between the island and the mainland, potentially severing family relationships and limiting economic and professional opportunities for some 8 million people. However, commonwealth status provides no guarantee of continued U.S. citizenship for Puerto Rican voters because, according to the U.S. Constitution, Congress can simply enact legislation that trumps the Jones Act, revoking citizenship and the perks that go with it, at any time.

The steps to amend this situation were clearly laid out in the President's Task Force report. Either Puerto Rico can become a state and risk losing the cultural autonomy it holds so dear, or it can become a freely associated state in fact and not just in name. Freely associated states, such as Micronesia or the Marshall Islands, are independent countries whose residents enjoy many of the privileges of U.S. citizens, including the right to live, work, and study in the United States as non-immigrants, or "habitual residents." The United States can amend its relationship with these countries at any time, as it can legally amend its relationship with Puerto Rico at will. However, Micronesia and the Marshall Islands, as freely associated states and independent nations, have the reciprocal power to change the nature of their association with the United States as they and their voters see fit. This is a right Puerto Rico has not had since 1898.

It is time for Puerto Ricans to consider what living in a true freely associated state, an independent Puerto Rico, might be like. How might the Puerto Rican people choose to tackle issues of economic stability and social justice on their own terms without the veto power of the U.S. Congress and U.S. courts looming over their decisions? The President's Task Force recommended that plebiscites be held periodically until one of two choices—statehood or independence—gains a clear majority of votes. The nature of the task force's report indicates that the political will exists for Puerto Rico to be granted either of these political futures. Puerto Rico is, and always has been, a separate geographic, social, cultural, and historical entity. It can stand on its own.

Lisa Pierce Flores is an editor and freelance writer, and the author of *The History of Puerto Rico* (2009), part of ABC-CLIO's Histories of Modern Nations series. She began her journalism career at the newspaper *El Nuevo Pais* in Caracas, Venezuela. As founding editor of *The American Mosaic*, she launched a suite of Web sites and blogs exploring multicultural America. Her journalism, fiction, and poetry have appeared in *The New York Times*, *The Charlotte Observer*, *West Wind Review*, *Poem*, *Inkwell*, and Leeds University's *Stand Magazine*.

VIEWPOINT 3: EXISTING COMMONWEALTH STATUS IS STILL THE BEST OPTION FOR PUERTO RICO

Puerto Ricans have been discussing the same political issue for more than one hundred years: their political relationship with the United States. Boricuas (the self-designation for Puerto Ricans) are a population united culturally but divided politically. Their three political options usually include becoming the fifty-first state, complete independence, or the current commonwealth status. Nowadays, the best option for most Puerto Ricans is still the commonwealth relationship with the United States. Currently, the island enjoys almost complete administrative autonomy while benefitting from U.S. federal funding. The two main reasons to advocate for the existing commonwealth relationship are economic and cultural.

Recent attempts, like the 2009 Puerto Rican Democracy Act, have tried to force a final and permanent resolution to this political dilemma. Puerto Ricans have already held three plebiscites (in 1967, 1993, and 1998) to decide their political future, and support for retaining the current commonwealth status has always obtained the majority of votes. However, all plebiscites and referendums provide only the illusion of local political empowerment. They are only suggestions to the U.S. Congress, which has complete discretion over the island. These voting exercises actually provide a distraction from dealing with current social problems on the island, such as violent crime, soaring unemployment rates, and increasing drug addiction and trafficking rates.

Puerto Rico has never been an independent nation. Consequently, a certain level of interest in independence is understandable. However, the independence option has never received more than 4% of the votes on previous plebiscites. The people have already spoken loudly and clearly, but a few loud politicians will apparently not let this moribund option die out. Proof of their ineffectiveness is that the Independence Party has never elected anyone to an important political position on the island. Only two political parties have ever elected governors since the 1952 Puerto Rican constitution was adopted: the Popular Democratic Party (PDP) and the New Progressive Party (NPP).

The average Puerto Rican usually rejects the independence option, based on economic terms. Boricuas often cite practical reasons for maintaining the current political status and benefits. The current commonwealth status offers tangible advantages: (a) U.S. citizenship, which gives them the right to work, travel, and study legally anywhere in the United States; (b) federal funding of at least $5.4 billion a year; and (c) the continuation of the Nutritional Assistance Program—similar to food stamps in the United States—at an annual cost of $1.6 billion a year. If independence were implemented, all these benefits would disappear. Unemployment could become even higher than the current 16%, because many U.S.-based companies might pull out of the island without the federal subsidies. In addition, the island would also incur tremendous expenses associated with maintaining a full diplomatic corps, an efficient Coast Guard, a military, and a customs and immigration force. Currently, all these expenditures are covered by the U.S. federal government. Recent proposals for independence have emerged, suggesting some type of association with the United States, which has not yet been defined or adequately explained to the island's population. This ambiguity pretends to offer speculative benefits, but it does not inspire a lot of confidence.

Statehood has been also proposed as an alternative solution to the current political status. Becoming the fifty-first state includes both advantages and perils. However, the U.S. Congress has the only legal authority to grant statehood to any territory. Becoming a state would provide Puerto Ricans with the right to vote in federal elections and have voting representation in the U.S. House of Representatives and Senate. Despite the political benefits, however, the statehood option faces considerable economic objections. For example, Americans living on the mainland worry about allowing another state to join the Union when it would bring a high level of poverty. In fact, Puerto Rico would replace Mississippi as the poorest state in the Union.

Accepting Puerto Rico as the fifty-first state would also incur a tremendous cost to the federal government, and this may not be palatable for many U.S. politicians. In 2010, the United States is paying for two separate wars, dealing with a rising foreign debt, and spending billions to rescue financial firms and stimulate the economy. Consequently, the prospect of infusing large amounts of money to create a new state is not very appealing. Further, if Puerto Rico were to become a state, Puerto Ricans living on the island would have to pay federal and state income taxes, which represent an additional financial burden, especially for economically disadvantaged families. Boricuas also question the statehood option for cultural reasons. They are deeply concerned that their vibrant culture would be diluted as future generations would be assimilated into U.S. traditions and lifestyles. However, one cultural trait that is not negotiable with Puerto Ricans is the threat of losing Spanish as their main language. If Puerto Rico were to become a state, Puerto Ricans would be required to accept English as their only official language. Language is a powerful part of culture, and Puerto Ricans certainly treasure their linguistic background.

Since the independence and statehood options represent serious economic and cultural challenges to average Puerto Ricans, the best political option is still the current commonwealth status. Though there is perhaps room to negotiate better benefits, this option provides Puerto Rico with local autonomy while benefiting from the political and economic connection to the United States.

Javier A. Galván is a professor of History, Spanish, and English as a Second Language (ESL) at Santa Ana College. He holds a BA in Spanish from California State University, Los Angeles; MAs in History and Spanish Linguistics from the University of Southern California (USC) and California Polytechnic University, Pomona; an MS in Teaching ESL from the USC; and a PhD in History from USC. Galván is the author several books, including the *Culture and Customs of Puerto Rico* and *Inglés Esencial*, as well as scholarly articles and conference papers on many topics relevant to Latin America and the Caribbean.

Further Reading

César J. Ayala and Rafael Bernabe, *Puerto Rico in the American century: A history since 1898*. Chapel Hill, NC: The University of North Carolina Press, 2007.

Lisa Pierce Flores, *The history of Puerto Rico*. Santa Barbara, CA: Greenwood Press, 2009.

Javier A. Galván, *Culture and customs of Puerto Rico*. Westport, CT: Greenwood Press, 2009.

Let Puerto Rico Decide (http://www.letpuertoricodecide.com/index.php)

Frances Negron-Muntaner, ed., *None of the Above: Puerto Ricans in the global era*. New York: Palgrave MacMillan, 2007.

Report by the President's Task Force on Puerto Rico Status (http://www.usdoj.gov/opa/documents/2007-report-by-the-president-task-force-on-puerto-rico-status.pdf)

Efren Rivera Ramos, *American colonialism in Puerto Rico: The judicial and social legacy*. Princeton, NJ: Markus Wiener Publishers, 2007.

Dick Thornburgh, *Puerto Rico's future: A time to decide*. Washington DC: Center for Strategic and International Studies, 2007.

WHAT CAN THE EUROZONE CRISIS TEACH US ABOUT ECONOMIC INTERDEPENDENCE?

With the signing of the Maastricht Treaty in 1992, members of the European Union (EU) set in motion the creation of a common currency, the euro. What is called the eurozone came into full force a decade later for twelve countries that met the economic criteria, including strict limits on government deficit spending and overall debt. More countries joined later, and in early 2014, the addition of Latvia brought the total to eighteen. With a common currency these countries hoped to create a stronger unified economic market for the benefit of all, including the elimination of currency-exchange costs and greater price stability across the countries. For a few years, the euro was strong, Germany remained an economic powerhouse despite giving up its iconic deutschmark, and countries like Spain and Ireland continued the surprising economic growth that they had begun in the 1990s.

However, cracks were forming from the beginning, and those cracks became fissures in the wake of the global recession that began in 2008. The crisis is often thought of as having three related parts: a government debt crisis, a banking crisis, and a political crisis. Some countries had been underreporting debt to qualify for Eurozone membership—most disastrously Greece, which found its credit rating slashed once the real size of its massive debt was revealed in 2009. This contributed to a crisis of confidence in the euro generally. Ireland and then Spain were hit hard with the crash of "housing bubbles" that left banks reeling with defaulted mortgages (mirroring a crisis in the United States that had played a large part in setting off the global crisis to begin with).

The eurozone's interrelated economies all suffered amid political fighting over how to respond—for example, Germany's insistence on government austerity measures set off rioting in Greece. Many said that the EU's political structures were not strong enough to enforce policies across sovereign countries with differing social and economic cultures. The eurozone's recovery has lagged behind that of the United States and many other countries that had been hit by the global crisis. Economies across the world increasingly influence each other in the age of globalization. It is therefore no mere academic exercise to consider what the eurozone crisis can teach us about economic interrelatedness.

VIEWPOINT 1: THE EUROZONE WAS DOOMED TO FAIL

The eurozone has shown us that a group of various-sized economies arbitrarily joined together cannot financially work together.

The eurozone was doomed to fail since day one. Combining the currencies of twelve (now eighteen) European countries into one single currency was a lot like putting students from every level of math into a single class. Obviously the students who were originally taking a more advanced math class, like calculus, before the switch would do much better than those students who were taking basic math. In the case of the eurozone, Germany is by far one of the most competitive economies, while countries like Greece and Italy are struggling to stay afloat.

To continue using the math class analogy, stronger economies like Germany gain very little from being a part of the class. Countries like Greece struggle (and bend the rules) to stay in the class, while continuously relying on Germany's high grade to keep the class average artificially high.

Understanding the economy of a single country is hard work. Central banks tinker constantly with monetary policy in an attempt to create an environment for economic prosperity. They will buy or sell government bonds (a type of loan) to banks within the country, which affects the interest on loans either negatively or positively. Buying bonds from banks increases the amount of money banks hold, which allows banks to increase their number of loans. Increasing the number of loans can also be done by lowering interest rates, making it attractive for individuals and businesses to borrow.

Loans can vary for each country depending on that country's credit rating, a score system that reflects whether a country can pay back its loans in full and on time. Northern countries in the eurozone, such as Norway and Germany, tend to have better credit ratings than southern countries, such as Spain, Italy, and Greece.

The eurozone has combined the complex banking systems of these countries into a single entity, to be administered by a single central bank, the European Central Bank (ECB). Under this single banking system and common currency, countries with lower credit ratings borrow more while leveraging their debts against higher-rated countries in the eurozone. This is like cheating on the test. This allows these countries to borrow more, and allows their countries' governments to push themselves further into debt.

Originally the formation of the eurozone was based on a strict set of rules that were supposed to deter countries from amassing large amounts of debt, but as international agreements tend to go, not all countries play by the rules. Now Greece has to cheat off Germany's math test in order to pass the class, and if Germany does not allow Greece to cheat, then the whole class average will diminish.

Right now only a few countries are keeping the euro afloat compared to internationally competing currencies like the U.S. dollar and Japanese yen. While many may view this highly valued euro as a good thing for the eurozone as a whole, it is actually hurting the weaker economies within the eurozone. These weaker black-hole economies are hesitant to leave the safe haven of the euro and return to their own currencies. Meanwhile competing economies, such as Germany, see no need to leave when they are being graded on a class average well below their own. It is only when failing countries in the eurozone come calling for a financial bailout that countries like Germany begin to wonder whether entering into the euro was ever the right choice: It wasn't.

A single currency tends to work only when either individual countries, or all parties to that currency, are similar on all economic levels. This means similar in societal, financial, and governmental structures. But even then, some parties can still be dragged down by the single-currency system. There are many today who say that even the United States should break up its single-currency system of the dollar and allow different regions, and/or states, in the U.S. to develop their own currencies. These new currencies would better reflect their region's economies, allowing the financial institutes of each region to compete their currencies against one another in an attempt to maximize the value of their currencies.

What the eurozone has shown us is that when these economies are combined under a single currency system, competition is taken out of the financial sector, and when the competition is taken out of the financial sector, all economies begin to feel the financial burden of supporting each other. Hopefully other countries will see the eurozone as an example and realize that they should avoid the combining of their economies under the single authoritarian rule.

Riley Walters is a research assistant for The Heritage Foundation's Japan Fellows Program in their Asian Studies Center. He received his BA from George Mason University in economics with a minor in Japanese studies. He also served as a research associate for the Competitive Enterprise Institute.

VIEWPOINT 2: EUROZONE COUNTRIES MUST WORK TOGETHER TO CREATE STRONGER RULES

The eurozone debt crisis can teach us that creating a shared currency for a variety of nations, without requiring those nations to follow specific economic policies and responsibilities, will result in economic imbalance. Politics, national habits, cultural assumptions, and failure to follow agreed-upon policies must be addressed so that the eurozone countries can come to a consensus on the nature of the crisis and then implement and enforce appropriate policies.

Analysis reveals that some nations (including Italy, Spain, Portugal, Ireland, and Greece) sharing a common currency were unable to control deflation or inflation to protect themselves. In the past each of these nations devalued currency or printed additional currency to protect their single national interests. It became clear that each nation continued to work with its own economies as if still economically independent, but depended on the European union for a bailout, revealing major cracks in the eurozone unification plan. Weak economic strategies included a continuing dependence on their own politicians and unreasonable labor union protections even in the shadow of financial doom. For example, before Italy adopted the euro, its central bank could draw foreign income to help prop up the economy by reducing the exchange-rate value of the Italian lira. Taking that step would mean that such Italian-made products as Fiat cars would be available more cheaply in other countries, and so more would be sold, bringing in more export income. This would help keep workers on the job at those Italian companies making goods for export. Now, such countries are unable to devalue the euro because it has the same value throughout the eurozone. Result: exports have plummeted, and the old economic strategies can no longer help them.

What happened is not a consequence of government alone. It also involves poor private-sector choices, especially in finance. Before 2008, banks and mortgage companies contributed to the crisis with unwise decisions that helped create the housing bubble and trade imbalances. When Germany's exports far exceeded imports, the resulting cash surplus was loaned to southern Europe (a profitable investment for Germany). This fueled an unsustainable increase in southern European wages, although Germany's unions did not increase their own wage base. The end result: increased human hourly costs in southern Europe drove production prices too high for southern European exports (bad for southern Europe) that ended in a market of less employment and the inability to afford purchase of German exports: a circle of economic ruin (bad for both Germany and the south).

Eurozone nations joined the economic union to maintain one currency, but failed to adopt one economic policy. For example, the German work ethic is very strong, and Germany proudly maintains minimal welfare programs. But Spain, Italy, Greece, Ireland, and France have large social welfare programs, and government is a major employer for each, with expanded social benefits. In Italy an employee is hired "for life." It is almost impossible to downsize or discharge employees for cause, a policy which deters business growth and expansion. Some eurozone countries had laws supporting traditions of paid August vacations, with an added extra month's bonus. When faced with a need to change such traditions, workers balked. In good times business can afford such laws, but now such laws further weaken the entire economic structure. Historically, when economies have lost spending power, the result is recession. Caught in a cycle of no jobs, no exports, and no power to purchase imports, recession deepens. Europe's major concern is that countries like Greece, Portugal, Ireland, Spain, and Italy will default on their debts. The banks that own their debts are balancing on the edge of ruin, and if they fail, that will plunge Europe into a further impasse. Can anything be done to save the euro?

In principle, yes. The European Central Bank can buy its members' debts to protect the value of the euro, and maintain economic stability for the future. But so far, it has not embraced that concept, preferring to register dismay, assign guilt, and avoid responsibility for any part of the dilemma.

Eurozone members, although distinctly different countries, are in essence one, economically. Their future as an economic union and political entity looks into the abyss. The internal disagreement over how to rescue the situation is based on differing viewpoints as to what the crisis actually is and what each nation needs to do to cure it.

Deep-set cultural, social, traditional, and historical national differences make a unified solution challenging. Cultural perspectives unify nations and also separate them from other cultures. For instance, it is a telling detail that *schulden*, the German word for "debt" is the singular form of the word *shuld*, which means "guilt or fault." Germany, with a strong economy, sincerely believes it should not be victimized by paying for the irresponsible *shuld* of other nations—this is no doubt at least partly reflected in the ECB's refusal to buy its members' debts.

France, after decades of deficit spending, high unemployment, increased taxes, and swelling welfare rolls, has reached a point that many economists think of as "no return." French workers consider it their right to kidnap employers who do not accede to their demands. In January 2013, workers at Goodyear in France held two executives captive while they "negotiated" for severance pay, finally agreeing to settle for 120,000 to 130,000 euros ($163,000 to $176,000) for each of 1,173 workers. Goodyear noted that French workers only worked a 3-hour day, and were told: "It's the French way."

The European Union can still solve the challenges of its situation. Member nations must come to consensus about what the crisis actually is, and agree to work together. Collective action by all members is a first step. An amended approach, perhaps adapting something similar to the U.S. system that requires each state to have a balanced budget, is a second one. Each EU nation must agree to produce and live within a balanced budget, or the European Union will never work. The solution is within the European Union's grasp if it can, at the least, agree that differences are less important than a unified solution.

Lynn Galvin, BA (history), JD (law), is a board member and past president of the Arizona Council for the Social Studies, a National Consortium for Teaching Asia Master Teacher, curricula writer for the Japanese American Museum's Enduring Communities Project, and a teacher consultant with the Arizona Geographic Alliance. She taught middle and high school social studies, college, and university classes over thirty years. She is an adjunct faculty member at Arizona State University.

Further Reading

European Central Bank's euro site: https://www.ecb.europa.eu/euro/html/index.en.html European Commission's euro site: http://ec.europa.eu/economy_finance/euro/index_en.htmThe Eurozone Portal: http://www.eurozone.europa.eu/home/

Costas Lapavitsas, *Crisis in the eurozone.* New York: Verso, 2012.

Jens Nordvig, *The fall of the euro: Reinventing the eurozone and the future of global investing.* New York: McGraw-Hill, 2013.

Heikki Patomäki, *The great eurozone disaster.* London: Zed Books, 2013.Manuel Sanchis i Marco, *The economics of the monetary union and the eurozone crisis.* New York: Springer, 2013.TEAM Europe: http://www.teameurope.info/

Euclid Tsakalotos and Christos Laskos, *Crucible of resistance: Greece, the eurozone and the world economy.* London: Pluto Press, 2013.Kaarlo Tuori, *The eurozone crisis: A constitutional analysis* (Cambridge Studies in European Law and Policy). Cambridge, UK: Cambridge University Press, 2014.

ARE FREE TRADE AGREEMENTS SUCH AS NAFTA STILL RELEVANT TO NATIONAL INTERESTS?

With the growing pace of economic globalization has come ever-greater interconnectedness among world economies. This process is aided by regional multinational groupings like the European Union (EU) and the Association of South East Asian Nations (ASEAN), as well as such global agencies as the World Trade Organization (WTO) and the International Monetary Fund (IMF). A key way these organizations promote world trade is by working toward the removal of barriers to free trade imposed by individual countries, such as import tariffs. In addition, countries often negotiate bilateral free trade agreements (FTA), such as those between the United States and Colombia, and the United States and Panama—both implemented in 2011 after many years of contentious debate in the U.S. Congress.

There are many heated controversies surrounding global free trade. Some political interests from within developed countries are concerned that the removal of barriers to trade result in losing jobs to poorer countries with lax labor and environmental standards, while developing countries often find that cheap, subsidized imports from richer countries undercut and thus outcompete local goods and produce. Such fears have stalled negotiations for WTO treaties, and they were expressed with the implementation of the North American Free Trade Agreement (NAFTA) in 1994, a pact that specifies free trade terms for the United States, Canada, and Mexico. Proponents of free trade believe that the economic benefits gained by all countries participating in free trade agreements far outweigh the costs. Since NAFTA now has a working track record of more than 18 years, this pact can provide a meaningful case study in determining, for the twenty-first century, whether free trade agreements are still relevant to individual national interests.

VIEWPOINT 1: TRADE AGREEMENTS FACILITATE NATIONAL ECONOMIC GROWTH AND POLITICAL REFORM

The steady expansion of global trade since the end of the Second World War has fueled economic growth and political freedom around the world. In 1970, global gross domestic product (GDP) was about US$2 trillion, and world trade represented only 4% of that total. By 2010, global GDP had risen to almost US$60 trillion, and world trade represented 18% of that total. This expansion of trade could only occur through the negotiation of free trade agreements (FTAs) among the world's countries. These trade agreements have been global, such as the General Agreement on Tariffs and Trade (GATT) and World Trade Organization (WTO), and regional, such as the European Union (EU) and the North American Free Trade Agreement (NAFTA).

In the absence of trade agreements, many states would respond to political pressure from certain special interest groups, such as businesses and labor unions from inefficient industries that were unable to compete against foreign competition. This political pressure would result in the institution of trade protectionist policies. Trade protectionism can take the form of a tax such as duties and tariffs, or through nontariff trade barriers such as regulations favoring domestic producers. Trade protection increases costs to domestic consumers by artificially raising the prices of imports. This also hurts downstream industries because they now face higher costs for inputs. For example, when President George W. Bush instituted a steel tariff in 2002 to protect steelworker jobs in Pennsylvania and Ohio, it led to increased costs for all products that rely on steel, such as automobiles. The result was a loss of American-made automobile jobs in Michigan. Finally, when one country adopts trade protectionism, it often leads to other states retaliating, which further restricts trade. When Bush applied his steel tariff on Germany, the Germans retaliated by slapping duties on frozen orange juice from Florida. In these types of trade wars, nobody wins.

The general benefits of all trade agreements come into focus more clearly when we turn our attention to NAFTA. NAFTA, which came into force in 1994, resulted in the gradual and comprehensive elimination of trade barriers among the United States, Mexico, and Canada over fifteen years. This included the full, phased elimination of import tariffs, the elimination of most non-tariff trade barriers, the protection of intellectual property rights, and the creation of dispute-settlement procedures. NAFTA created the largest trade pact in the world based on population, territory, and gross domestic product. It is even larger than the Europe Union, despite the EU having 28 member states. Another unique feature of NAFTA is that it brought together developed and developing countries into the same trade agreement.

The biggest impact of NAFTA has been the vast increase in trilateral trade. Canada's exports to its NAFTA partners increased by 87% in value; U.S. exports to Canada and Mexico increased by 50%; and Mexican exports to Canada and the United States increased by more than an astounding 200%. Overall, trilateral trade now exceeds $1 trillion. Investment flows among the three countries also quintupled. This level of growth was most magnified in the case of Mexico, where foreign direct investment increased tenfold. Overall, direct foreign investment among Canada, Mexico, and the United States has increased by over $600 billion since 1994.

There were fears at the time of ratification that there would be massive job losses in Canada and the United States, as corporations moved operations to Mexico in search of lower wages and weaker environmental standards. Ross Perot, a U.S. presidential candidate in 1992, said famously that there would be a "large sucking sound" as companies moved south. That prediction has not held. Any trade deal creates winners and losers, but in the aggregate there are more winners than losers. That is exactly what has happened with NAFTA. It is true that some Canadian and American manufacturing moved to northern Mexico (*maquiladoras*), but these numbers pale in comparison to the job creation that came with new market opportunities becoming available. For example, between 1993 and 2006 the U.S. economy gained 26 million jobs, and the Canadian economy gained 3 million jobs. This job growth was not due solely to NAFTA, but it does put to bed the view that NAFTA would export jobs to Mexico. Similarly, the fears of an environmental "race to the bottom" have not been supported by empirical evidence. In fact, the opposite has occurred, with Mexico increasing its environmental regulations.

The Mexican peso crisis of 1994, which saw the peso become devalued by 50% almost overnight, also showed the utility of NAFTA. Contrary to more critical views, the Mexican peso crisis was not caused by NAFTA. Rather, NAFTA facilitated the American-led multibillion-dollar bailout. In a very strong sense, the economic ties forged through NAFTA forced the Americans to intervene in the currency crisis and prevented a larger economic meltdown that would have encompassed the entire region.

The closer economic ties forged among Canada, the United States, and Mexico were maintained even in the face of some domestic groups (labor, environmental, and nationalist) in each country that remain opposed to trade agreements. They even refrained from building new trade barriers during recessions, especially the great global recession of 2008–2011. While candidate Barack Obama promised to re-negotiate NAFTA during the Democratic presidential primaries in 2008, as president Obama has been a steadfast supporter of NAFTA.

At the same time, analysts such as Robert Pastor have argued for a "NAFTA+" category of arrangements, to expand North American cooperation in new policy areas and create better governance structures. Some of Pastor's ideas include creating a North American investment fund to close the development gap with Mexico; deepening economic integration by adding a customs union; and establishing a high-level advisory committee for issues like transportation, infrastructure, energy, the environment, and labor standards. In fact, there have been a number of initiatives among the three countries to further enhance integration among the three NAFTA countries. For example, negotiations on a Security and Prosperity Partnership of North America (SPP) were launched in 2005. Already there are preliminary agreements on intellectual property, cooperation in energy science and technology, pandemic cooperation, safe foods, and standardization of nutritional information labeling requirements. The fact that NAFTA is being maintained and even expanded shows that its benefits are well recognized and entrenched.

NAFTA's primary goals were all about increasing economic integration leading to economic growth. However, it is obvious that a number of political benefits have emerged from NAFTA. Most importantly, NAFTA was a critical driver in the democratization process in Mexico. This was best symbolized by the peaceful transition of power following the free and fair election of Vicente Fox in 2000. The election ended seventy years of the Institutional Revolutionary Party's (PRI's) single-party rule. A second political benefit has been the increase in political ties among the three countries. Although the bureaucratic infrastructure of NAFTA is nowhere near as elaborate as that of the EU, there are now regular summits among the Mexican and American presidents and the Canadian prime minister. There has also been a proliferation of trilateral working groups that include cabinet ministers and bureaucrats.

More than 17 years after its ratification, it is clear that NAFTA has achieved much of what was expected in the pursuit of economic growth through an expansion of trade and investment. In addition, it has had some important political repercussions, seen through the democratization of Mexico and closer political relations between the three North American countries. Just as importantly, it has avoided many of the fears concerning job losses, corporatization, and environmental destruction that were circulated in the early and mid-1990s. There remain disputes between the three countries—illegal immigration, drugs, a development gap—but NAFTA provides the political framework to address them.

Dr. Duane Bratt is chair and associate professor in the Department of Policy Studies at Mount Royal University in Calgary, Alberta. He was educated at the universities of Windsor (BA 1991, MA 1992) and Alberta (PhD 1996). He teaches in the area of international relations and Canadian public policy, with a specialty in the subfield of Canadian foreign policy. His primary research interest is in the area of Canadian nuclear policy.

VIEWPOINT 2: THE COSTS OF NAFTA TO CIVIL SOCIETY

From a purely quantitative perspective, the answer to whether free trade agreements remain relevant to national interests would be yes. I will, however argue, that when one takes a more qualitative perspective, focusing on social and political factors as well as the economics of who actually benefits, the answer is not as positive as free trade proponents would have us believe.

In 1817 David Ricardo penned *Principles of Political Economy and Taxation*; a treatise extolling the virtues of free trade and the benefits to all places that maximize their comparative advantages. Ever since, economists and policy makers in support of unfettered capitalism have endeavored to both deregulate markets and construct as many regional free trade associations as possible. The simple argument is that competition, efficiency, and lower costs to consumers are the inevitable results of free trade, and to resist it or erect barriers is anathema to human progress and against collective national interests. However, critics of the free trade logic maintain that in a globalizing market system, only the largest and strongest corporations are able to survive and prosper, while those in the periphery of the world economy are forced into dependency and comparative disadvantage. There are additional issues of environmental and labor exploitation, and disempowerment of local government in the face of global free market institutions. In assessing the specific effects and relevancy to national interests of the 1994 North American Free Trade Agreement (NAFTA), the question is: has it promoted and facilitated economic development, social justice, and political stability, or has it promoted the privileged position of capitalist elites, facilitated neocolonial economic exploitation, and expanded U.S. regional political hegemony? To address this question, this essay is structured into the following categories: NAFTA basics; issues and debates; and member perspectives. I argue that free trade agreements between countries can be either beneficial or harmful to national interests; it depends on how the agreements are structured.

NAFTA Basics

In comparison to other trade associations and regional political economic alliances, NAFTA has three discernible characteristics that deserve careful scrutiny. The first characteristic is the goal of the agreement, to promote regional economic integration, which, despite its name, was not merely focused on free trade but on internal restructuring around common rules and regulations. Indeed, by 1990, barriers to trade were already quite low, especially between Canada and the United States under the guidelines of the CUSFTA (Canada–United States Free Trade Agreement) signed in 1988. Along with the promotion of economic integration, NAFTA was also concerned with foreign direct investment (FDI). Producers in the United States were seeking unadulterated access to extremely low-wage, semi-skilled Mexican labor in order to create an export platform for manufactured goods for both its own domestic consumers as well as international markets. Consequently, the treaty includes extensive chapters involving investment, competition, telecommunications, and financial services.

A second characteristic is that NAFTA is decidedly not a supranational institution with political powers delegated to a level above the nation-state, such as the European Union; rather it is designed as an intergovernmental accord. Arguably, this has served to protect each member's sovereignty in the face of de-territorialized global economic regimes such as the World Trade Organization. By decision, there is not supposed to be pooling or sharing of political sovereignty, and there are not to be any specific NAFTA institutions outside the purview of the member governments.

The third characteristic involves the underlying political rationale and expectations of each member in support of the agreement. The United States has long sought to stabilize its border and relations with its southern neighbor. By stimulating and coordinating economic growth in Mexico, NAFTA is viewed as a structural mechanism to ease social stresses and legitimize the existing institutional power arrangements within Mexico. Also, the United States' trade position vis-a-vis Europe, Japan, and China would be strengthened by the larger market and, concomitantly, the United States would gain easier access to both Mexico's and Canada's oil resources. Lastly, the United States could consolidate its diplomatic position by both extending and officially deepening its regional geopolitical hegemony—call it a late twentieth-century version of the Monroe Doctrine, which calls for regional focus rather than global. To a degree, each of these objectives has been met, proving to U.S. NAFTA critics that the free trade agreement can and has been beneficial to national interests in broad terms.

Similarly, Mexico's objective was primarily to preserve its fragile internal social peace and stability by attracting investment, stimulating employment, and alleviating poverty. Ironically, on January 1, 1994, the day NAFTA went into effect, Subcommandante Marcos announced that the revolution of national liberation in Chiapas had begun—hardly an auspicious beginning. Among other pressing issues behind the revolution, Marcos stated quite baldly that NAFTA was a death sentence to indigenous communities. For Mexican ruling elites the trade association would serve as the primary manifestation and reification of President Carlos Salinas de Gortari's neoliberal economic agenda. Similar to the United States, Mexico also viewed NAFTA as an opportunity to strengthen its diplomatic position in Latin America and the developing world as a whole.

The objectives for Canada were initially quite modest; Canada had already entered a free trade association with the United States in 1988. Indeed, the perception was that Canada had much to lose in an expanded free trade association. Yet, Canada has used NAFTA as a source of regional leadership and a vehicle to both crystallize and project its national interests.

NAFTA—Issues and Debates

NAFTA, in both theory and practice, has generated a sizable amount of controversy. Yet, one thing is clear: trade among the members increased substantially since the agreement went into effect—from just $300 billion in 1993, to $500 billion in 1998, to more than $600 billion in 2000. The debate is whether this increase is the result of NAFTA or just the result of globalization in general, especially as Mexico concomitantly entered the General Agreement on Trade and Tariffs (GATT) and the World Trade Organization (WTO) in the early 1990s. Related to this is the regional effect, and whether NAFTA has operated to divert trade rather than generate new trade. For instance, studies have revealed that Caribbean nations, Jamaica in particular, have seen their market positions weakened in comparison to Mexico. Thus, the effects of NAFTA on national interests must also be viewed from the perspective of neighboring, non-NAFTA participants.

Vocal criticisms have focused on NAFTA's impact on employment. The issue for each of the three countries is whether NAFTA has created more jobs or seen jobs eliminated in the face of expanded competition and efforts to locate production in places with the cheapest labor force. Related to employment questions are the associated effects on wages, working conditions, and the movement, both documented and undocumented, of workers between the three countries. The Chapter 11 provisions, and what they have meant for governance, are another strongly criticized feature of NAFTA. The intentions of the provisions were to protect the interests of foreign investors from unlawful government seizure of their assets and to create an independent board to settle disputes between aggrieved parties and the member government in question. In practice, according to critics, it lacks legitimacy, is disruptive to ordinary lawmaking, places the interests of investors ahead of the public, and provides an elaborate ruse to avoid checks on corporate activity. How the Chapter 11 tribunals exercise authority over public decisions is viewed as being wildly inconsistent with the expectations of legitimate political and judicial processes. In short, Chapter 11 is seen as having the potential to: 1) undermine efforts to enact laws and regulations in the public interest, especially those associated with the environment and human health; and 2) require governments to compensate polluters for making them literally stop polluting. The irony is that during the initial development of NAFTA

Chapter 11 attracted little attention; but as Atik observes: "it is now viewed as having been something of a Trojan horse; seemingly benign upon first delivery, but later understood to have brought destruction to national democratic institutions."

Conclusion

In terms of broad economic statistics and trade data, NAFTA has been beneficial to national interests—at least the interests of corporations and their business and cultural elites. However, benefits have not been equally shared. Further, NAFTA has failed to create a truly trilateral economic partnership. Rather, it has resulted in two bilateral regimes—one between Mexico and the United States, and the other between Canada and the United States. The Canada–Mexico integration has been conspicuously underdeveloped. Perhaps this is just a developmental stage in the maturation of NAFTA, but effectively the United States is the dominant economic partner, with the other two serving as dependents.

NAFTA must be reconstructed if it is going to benefit its members' national interests beyond mere GDP/capita growth data. It must include provisions to protect the environment and public health, as well as promote the interests of labor across the full economic spectrum. But national interests are not the logic behind free trade agreements. The logic of these agreements is the efficiency of the capitalist system and profit—the majority of which, as the Occupy Wall Street movement so aptly describes, trickles up to the 1%.

Dr. Troy Burnett is currently an associate professor of geography and geography program coordinator at Mount Royal University in Calgary, Alberta. He earned a doctorate in geography in 2005 from UCLA, where he also earned a master's degree in geography in 2000. He has bachelor's degrees from the University of California–Santa Barbara, in economics and environmental studies. His areas of academic interest are political, economic, environmental, and cultural geography. His research focuses on the post-Socialist transformation of East Central Europe. Dr. Burnett is an active member of both the American Association of Geographers (AAG) and Canadian Association of Geographers (CAG).

Further Reading

Bruce Campbell, *Viva la historieta! Mexican comics, NAFTA, and the politics of globalization*. Jackson: University Press of Mississippi, 2009.Norman Caulfield, *NAFTA and labor in North America*. Urbana: University of Illinois Press, 2010.

Duke Law Library & Technology. Research Guides: NAFTA. http://www.law.duke.edu/lib/researchguides/nafta.htmlTexas A&M International University's Western Hemispheric Trade Information Center. http://freetrade.tamiu.edu/

LIST OF ALL COUNTRIES AND GOVERNMENTS

Country	Government Type
Afghanistan	Islamic republic
Albania	Parliamentary democracy
Algeria	Republic
Andorra	Parliamentary democracy
Angola	Republic; multiparty presidential regime
Antarctica	Antarctic Treaty System
Antigua & Barbuda	Constitutional monarchy with a parliamentary system of government and a Commonwealth realm
Argentina	Republic
Armenia	Republic
Australia	Federal parliamentary democracy and a Commonwealth realm
Austria	Federal republic
Azerbaijan	Republic
Bahamas	Constitutional parliamentary democracy and a Commonwealth realm
Bahrain	Constitutional monarchy
Bangladesh	Parliamentary democracy
Barbados	Parliamentary democracy and a Commonwealth realm
Belarus	Republic in name
Belgium	Federal parliamentary democracy under a constitutional monarchy
Belize	Parliamentary democracy and a Commonwealth realm
Benin	Republic
Bhutan	Constitutional monarchy
Bolivia	Republic
Bosnia & Herzegovina	Transitional (emerging federal democratic republic)

Country	Government Type
Botswana	Parliamentary republic
Brazil	Federal republic
Brunei	Constitutional sultanate
Bulgaria	Parliamentary democracy
Burkina Faso	Parliamentary republic
Burundi	Republic
Cambodia	Multiparty democracy under a constitutional monarchy
Cameroon	Republic
Canada	Parliamentary democracy with a constitutional monarchy
Cape Verde	Republic
Central African Republic	Republic
Chad	Republic
Chile	Republic
China	Communist state
Colombia	Republic
Comoro Islands	Republic
Congo Republic	Republic
Costa Rica	Democratic republic
Cote d'Ivoire	Republic
Croatia	Parliamentary democracy
Cuba	Communist state
Cyprus	Republic
Czech Republic	Parliamentary democracy
Democratic Republic of Congo	Republic
Denmark	Constitutional monarchy
Djibouti	Republic
Dominica	Parliamentary democracy
Dominican Republic	Democratic republic
Ecuador	Republic
East Timor	Republic
Egypt	Republic
El Salvador	Republic
Equatorial Guinea	Republic
Eritrea	Transitional
Estonia	Parliamentary republic
Ethiopia	Federal republic

Country	Government Type
Fiji	Republic
Finland	Republic
France	Republic
Gabon	Republic
Gambia	Republic
Georgia	Republic
Germany	Federal republic
Ghana	Constitutional democracy
Greece	Parliamentary republic
Grenada	Parliamentary democracy and a Commonwealth realm
Guatemala	Constitutional democratic republic
Guinea	Republic
Guinea-Bissau	Republic
Guyana	Republic
Haiti	Republic
Honduras	Democratic constitutional republic
Hungary	Parliamentary democracy
Iceland	Constitutional republic
India	Federal republic
Indonesia	Republic
Iran	Theocratic republic
Iraq	Parliamentary democracy
Ireland	Republic, parliamentary democracy
Israel	Parliamentary democracy
Italy	Republic
Jamaica	Constitutional parliamentary democracy and a Commonwealth realm
Japan	Parliamentary government with a constitutional monarchy
Jordan	Constitutional monarchy
Kazakhstan	Republic
Kenya	Republic
Kiribati	Republic
Kosovo	Republic
Kuwait	Constitutional emirate
Kyrgyzstan	Republic
Laos	Communist state
Latvia	Parliamentary democracy

Country	Government Type
Lebanon	Republic
Lesotho	Parliamentary constitutional monarchy
Liberia	Republic
Libya	Transitional
Liechtenstein	Hereditary constitutional monarchy
Lithuania	Parliamentary democracy
Luxembourg	Constitutional monarchy
Macedonia	Parliamentary democracy
Madagascar	Republic
Malawi	Multiparty democracy
Malaysia	Constitutional monarchy
Maldives	Republic
Mali	Republic
Malta	Republic
Marshall Islands	Constitutional government in free association with the US
Mauritania	Military junta
Mauritius	Parliamentary democracy
Mexico	Federal republic
Micronesia	Constitutional government in free association with the US
Moldova	Republic
Monaco	Constitutional monarchy
Mongolia	Parliamentary
Montenegro	Republic
Morocco	Constitutional monarchy
Mozambique	Republic
Myanmar	Parliamentary
Namibia	Republic
Nauru	Republic
Nepal	Federal democratic republic
Netherlands	Constitutional monarchy
New Zealand	Parliamentary democracy and a Commonwealth realm
Nicaragua	Republic
Niger	Republic
Nigeria	Federal republic
North Korea	Communist state with dictator leader
Norway	Constitutional monarchy

Country	Government Type
Oman	Monarchy
Pakistan	Federal republic
Palestinian Autonomous Region	De facto state
Panama	Constitutional democracy
Papua New Guinea	Constitutional parliamentary democracy and a Commonwealth realm
Paraguay	Constitutional republic
Peru	Constitutional republic
Philippines	Republic
Poland	Republic
Portugal	Republic; parliamentary democracy
Qatar	Emirate
Romania	Republic
Russia	Federation
Rwanda	Republic; presidential, multiparty system
Samoa	Parliamentary democracy
San Marino	Republic
Sao Tome & Principe	Republic
Saudi Arabia	Absolute monarchy
Senegal	Republic
Serbia	Republic
Seychelles	Republic
Sierra Leone	Constitutional democracy
Singapore	Parliamentary republic
Slovakia	Parliamentary democracy
Slovenia	Parliamentary republic
Solomon Islands	Parliamentary democracy and a Commonwealth realm
Somalia	Failed state
South Africa	Republic
South Korea	Republic
South Sudan	Republic
Spain	Parliamentary monarchy
Sri Lanka	Republic
St. Kitts & Nevis	Parliamentary democracy and a Commonwealth realm
St. Lucia	Parliamentary democracy and a Commonwealth realm

Country	Government Type
St. Vincent & the Grenadines	Parliamentary democracy and a Commonwealth realm
Sudan	Federal republic ruled by the National Congress Party (NCP)
Suriname	Constitutional democracy
Swaziland	Monarchy
Sweden	Constitutional monarchy
Switzerland	Formally a confederation but similar in structure to a federal republic
Syria	Republic under an authoritarian regime
Taiwan	Multiparty democracy
Tajikistan	Republic
Tanzania	Republic
Thailand	Constitutional monarchy
Togo	Republic under transition to multiparty democratic rule
Tonga	Constitutional monarchy
Trinidad & Tobago	Parliamentary democracy
Tunisia	Republic
Turkey	Republican parliamentary democracy
Turkmenistan	Secular democracy and a presidential republic
Tuvalu	Parliamentary democracy and a Commonwealth realm
Uganda	Republic
Ukraine	Republic
United Arab Emirates	Federation
United Kingdom	Constitutional monarchy and Commonwealth realm
United States	Federal republic
Uruguay	Constitutional republic
Uzbekistan	Authoritarian
Vanuatu	Parliamentary republic
Venezuela	Federal republic
Vietnam	Communist state
Yemen	Republic
Zambia	Republic
Zimbabwe	Parliamentary democracy

Source: CIA World Factbook. https://www.cia.gov/library/publications/the-world-factbook/fields/2128.html

FACTS AND FIGURES SOURCES

Active Armed Forces (% of Population)
This statistic shows the percent of population from each country that is in the active armed forces.

Source: Military Balance

Agricultural Products
This statistic shows each country's major crops, livestock, and associated products.

Source: CIA World Factbook. http://www.cia.gov

Airports
This statistic shows the number of airports and airfields in each country. It includes paved, unpaved, and abandoned runways as long as they are visible from the air.

Source: CIA World Factbook. http://www.cia.gov

Alternative and Nuclear Energy
This statistic shows the percentage of each country' s total energy use from Sources that do not produce carbon dioxide, such as wind, nuclear, and geothermal power.

Source: World Bank. http://www.worldbank.org

Annual Military Expenditure
This statistic shows how much money each country spends every year on its military, expressed in U.S. dollars.

Source: Military Balance

Arable Land
This statistic shows the percentage of each country's total land area that is suitable for cultivation.

Source: World Bank. http://www.worldbank.org

Arable Land per Capita
This statistic shows how many hectares per person in each country are suitable for cultivation. One hectare is about 2.5 acres, or the size of two American football fields (including the endzones).

Source: World Bank. http://www.worldbank.org

Area
This statistic shows the physical area of each country in square miles.

Source: CIA World Factbook. http://www.cia.gov

Average Life Expectancy
This statistic shows the average number of years a person lives in each country.

Source: U.S. Census Bureau (International Data Base). http://www.census.gov

Average Life Expectancy (Female)
This statistic shows the average number of years lived by women in each country.

Source: U.S. Census Bureau (International Data Base). http://www.census.gov

Average Life Expectancy (Male)
This statistic shows the average number of years lived by men in each country.

Source: U.S. Census Bureau (International Data Base). http://www.census.gov

Budget Deficit
This statistic shows the net difference between a country's income and expenditures, expressed as a percent of total GDP. A positive number represents a budget surplus, while a negative number represents a deficit.

Source: CIA World Factbook. http://www.cia.gov

Capital
This category shows the capital city for each country.

Source: CIA World Factbook. http://www.cia.gov

Coastline
This statistic shows how many miles of coastline each country has.

Source: CIA World Factbook. www.cia.gov

CO_2 Emissions
This statistic lists amount of carbon dioxide (in metric tons per capita) produced in each country through the burning of fossil fuels and manufacturing.

Source: World Bank. http://www.worldbank.org

Crude Birth Rate
This statistic shows the number of births per 1,000 people in each country per year.

Source: U.S. Census Bureau (International Data Base). http://www.census.gov

Crude Death Rate
This statistics shows the number of deaths per 1,000 people in each country per year.

Source: U.S. Census Bureau (International Data Base). http://www.census.gov

Crude Oil Consumption

This statistic shows the amount of crude oil consumed (in barrels) in each country per year. One barrel of oil is 42 gallons, and in the United States a barrel can be used to produce about 19 gallons of gasoline.

Source: U.S. Energy Information Administration. http://www.eia.gov

Crude Oil Production

This statistic shows the amount of crude oil produced (in barrels) in each country per year. One barrel of oil is 42 gallons, and in the United States a barrel can be used to produce about 19 gallons of gasoline.

Source: U.S. Energy Information Administration. http://www.eia.gov

Currency

This statistic shows the name of the currency that is in general use in each country.

Source: CIA World Factbook. http://www.cia.gov

Current Account Balance

This statistic shows the net balance of all international monetary transactions for each country during one year. A positive number reflects a surplus of money coming into a country. A negative number reflects more money flowing out of the country.

Source: CIA World Factbook. http://www.cia.gov

Doctors

This statistic shows the number of doctors per 1,000 people in each country.

Source: World Bank. http://www.worldbank.org

Economic Aid Extended

This statistic shows the amount (in US$) of Official Development Assistance (ODA) donated by each country. ODA is defined as the money provided by official agencies, which is administered with the goal of promoting economic development and welfare, and having a gift element of at least 25 percent.

Source: OECD (Organization for Economic Cooperation and Development). http://www.oecd.org/dac/stats/idsonline.htm

Economic Aid Received

This statistic shows the amount (in US$) of Official Development Assistance (ODA) received by each country. ODA must be administered with the goal of promoting economic development and welfare and have a gift element of at least 25 percent.

Source: OECD (Organization for Economic Cooperation and Development). http://www.oecd.org/dac/stats/idsonline.htm

Electric Power Consumption

This statistic shows electricity consumed in kilowatt-hours by each country in a given year.

Source: CIA World Factbook. http://www.cia.gov

Electric Power Generation

This statistic shows electricity generated in kilowatt-hours by each country in a given year.

Source: CIA World Factbook. http://www.cia.gov

Enrollment in Tertiary Education

This statistic shows the number of people enrolled in post-secondary education in each country in a given year.

Source: UNESCO. http://www.unesco.org

Export Partners

This list shows the main countries to which each country exports goods, along with the percentage of total export volume they receive.

Source: IMF Direction of Trade Statistics

Exported Goods

This list shows each country's main export products.

Source: IMF Direction of Trade Statistics

External Debt

This statistic shows the amount of public and private debt, expressed in U.S. dollars, owed to foreign creditors by each country.

Source: CIA World Factbook. http://www.cia.gov

Facebook Users

This statistic shows the number of registered Facebook users within each country.

Source: Facebook. https://www.facebook.com/

Government Type

This statistic shows the type of government each country has, such as republic, monarchy, communist, etc.

Source: CIA World Factbook. http://www.cia.gov

Gross Domestic Product

This statistic shows the total value of goods and services produced within each country in a given year, expressed in U.S. dollars, according to the current official exchange rate. As a measure of a country's productivity, this statistic is a commonly used measure of the health of the country's economy. If a country's GDP figure does not grow from year to year, its economy is in recession.

Source: IMF (World Economic Outlook). http://www.imf.org

GDP per Capita

This statistic shows the value of goods and services produced in each country in a given year, or gross domestic product (GDP), divided by the population, resulting in a per-person value.

Source: IMF (World Economic Outlook). http://www.imf.org

GDP—Purchasing Power Parity (PPP)

This statistic shows the value of goods and services produced in each country in a given year, or gross domestic product (GDP), adjusted to reflect differences in purchasing power between countries. The new value is based on a common international dollar.

Source: IMF (World Economic Outlook). http://www.imf.org

GDP (PPP) per Capita

This statistic shows the value of goods and services produced in each country in a given year, adjusted for purchasing power parity and divided by the population, resulting in a per-person value.

Source: IMF (World Economic Outlook). http://www.imf.org

Import Partners

This list shows the main countries from which each nation imports goods.

Source: IMF Direction of Trade Statistics

Imported Goods

This list shows the main goods that each country imports.

Source: IMF Direction of Trade Statistics

Industry Products

This list shows the main industrial products each country produces.

Source: ILO (LABORSTA database). http://www.ilo.org

Infant Mortality

This statistic shows the number of children per 1,000 live births that do not survive to the age of 5 in each country.

Source: World Health Organization. http://www.who.int

Internet Users

This statistic shows the number of users in each country who access the Internet in a given year.

Source: CIA World Factbook. http://www.cia.gov

Internet Users (% of Population)

This statistic shows the number of users in each country that access the internet as a percent of the total population.

Source: World Bank. http://www.worldbank.org

Land Borders

This statistic shows the total length of all land borders of each country, in miles.

Source: CIA World Factbook. http://www.cia.gov

Land Use

This statistic shows the percentage of a country's total land used for several purposes: arable land, temporary crops, permanent crops, permanent meadows and pastures, forest land, and other.

Source: FAO (FAOSTAT database). http://www.fao.org

Land-Based Telephones in Use

This statistic shows the number of land-based telephones used in each country.

Source: CIA World Factbook. http://www.cia.gov

Literacy

This statistic shows the percentage of each country's total population, age 15 and over, that can read and write.

Source: World Bank. http://www.worldbank.org

Mandatory Education

This statistic shows the number of years children are required to attend school and at what ages they are required to attend. Actual enforcement of these laws may vary.

Source: Country government

Maternal Mortality

This statistic shows the number of women who die from causes related to pregnancy and childbirth per 100,000 live births in each country.

Source: World Health Organization. http://www.who.int

Median Age

This statistic shows the age distribution of each country's population—half of the population is older than the median age, and the other half is younger than the median age.

Source: CIA World Factbook. http://www.cia.gov

Mobile Telephone Subscribers

This statistic gives the number of people in each country who subscribe to a mobile telephone service.

Source: CIA World Factbook. http://www.cia.gov

Natural Gas Consumption

This statistic shows how much natural gas each country consumes, in cubic meters, in a given year.

Source: CIA World Factbook. http://www.cia.gov

Natural Gas Production

This statistic shows how much natural gas each country produces, in cubic meters, in a given year.

Source: CIA World Factbook. http://www.cia.gov

Natural ReSources

This statistic lists each country's mineral, petroleum, hydropower, and other reSources of commercial importance; in general, products appear only if they make a significant contribution to the economy, or are likely to do so in the future.

Source: CIA World Factbook. http://www.cia.gov

Net Migration Rate

This statistic shows the difference between in-migration and out-migration in each country per 1,000 people in a given year.

Source: U.S. Census Bureau (International Data Base). http://www.census.gov

Nuclear Power Plants

This statistic shows the number of nuclear power plants there are in each country.

Source: International Atomic Energy Agency (PRIS database). http://www.iaea.org

Passenger Cars per 1,000 People

This statistic shows the number of passenger cars that exist for each 1,000 people in a country.

Source: World Bank. http://www.worldbank.org

Paved Roads

This statistic shows the amount of paved roads in a country, as a percentage of the total.

Source: CIA World Factbook. http://www.cia.gov

Population

This statistic shows the total estimated population for each country.

Source: U.S. Census Bureau (International Data Base). http://www.census.gov

Population Density

This statistic shows how many people there are per square kilometer in each country. There are about 2.6 square kilometers to 1 square mile.

Source: U.S. Census Bureau (International Data Base). http://www.census.gov

Population Distribution

This statistic shows the percentage of each country's population that lives in an urban environment.

Source: CIA World Factbook. http://www.cia.gov

Population Growth Rate

This statistic shows how much each country's population grows by percentage per year. This increase or decrease is a combination of migration and the natural rate of growth.

Source: U.S. Census Bureau (International Data Base). http://www.census.gov

Protected Areas (Marine and Terrestrial)

This statistic shows the square kilometers of land and water that are protected by each country.

Source: UN Statistical Database. http://unstats.un.org/unsd/databases.htm

Railroads

This statistic shows the total route length of each country's rail system, in miles.

Source: CIA World Factbook. http://www.cia.gov

Threatened Species

This statistic shows the total number of threatened plant and animal species in each country.

Source: United Nations Statistical Yearbook http://unstats.un.org/unsd/syb/

Time Zone

This statistic lists the number of hours the time zone of each country's capital is ahead of U.S. Eastern Standard Time

Source: CIA World Factbook. http://www.cia.gov

Total Active Armed Forces

This statistic shows the number of people there are in each country's active armed forces.

Source: Military Balance

Total Government Expenditures

This statistic shows the amount of money (expressed in U.S. dollars at official exchange rates) the government of each country spent in a given year.

Source: CIA World Factbook. http://www.cia.gov

Total Government Revenues

This statistic shows the amount of money (expressed in U.S. dollars at official exchange rates) the government of each country took in in a given year.

Source: CIA World Factbook. http://www.cia.gov

Total Renewable H$_2$O ReSources

This statistic shows the annual amount of water (in cubic meters) available for renewable use per person in each country.

Source: Food and Agriculture Organization of the UN. http://www.fao.org/home/en/

Total Value of Exports

This statistic shows the total amount of money (expressed in U.S. dollars at official exchange rates) each country earned from total merchandise exports in a given year.

Source: CIA World Factbook. http://www.cia.gov

Total Value of Imports

This statistic shows the total amount of money (expressed in U.S. dollars at official exchange rates) each country spent on total merchandise imports in a given year.

Source: CIA World Factbook. http://www.cia.gov

Unemployment

This statistic shows the percent of each country's total labor force that is unemployed, averaged over a given calendar year.

Source: World Bank. http://www.worldbank.org

Weights and Measures

This statistic lists the standard system of weights and measures in use, typically metric, imperial, or traditional.

Source: Europa World Year Book

World Population Rank

This statistic lists the rank of each country by population.

Source: Calculated secondary statistic using population data from U.S. Census Bureau (International Data Base). http://www.census.gov.

INDEX

Page references to photos are in *italics*.

509

ABOUT THE EDITOR

Fred M. Shelley is professor of geography in the Department of Geography and Environmental Sustainability at the University of Oklahoma, Norman, Oklahoma. His research interests include political geography, the global political economy, and the political, economic, and cultural geography of the United States. His published works include *Nation Shapes: The Story behind the World's Borders* (ABC-CLIO, 2013); *The World's Population: An Encyclopedia of Critical Issues, Crises, and Ever-Growing Countries* (ABC-CLIO, 2014); *Atlas of the Great Plains* (coauthor); *Atlas of the 2008 Presidential Election*; and *Engaging Geopolitics*, as well as numerous articles, book chapters, and other publications.